THE HAMLYN ILLUSTRATED HISTORY OF MANCHESTER UNITED

THE HAMLYN ILLUSTRATED HISTORY OF MANCHESTER UNITED

TOM TYRRELL AND **DAVID MEEK**

TED SMART

This edition published in 1996 for The Book People,
Guardian House, Borough Road, Godalming, Surrey GU7 2AE
by Hamlyn, an imprint of Reed Consumer Books Limited,
Michelin House, 81 Fulham Road, London SW3 6RB
and Auckland, Melbourne, Singapore and Toronto

First published in Great Britain in 1988
under the title
Manchester United, the Official History
by Hamlyn,
an imprint of Reed Consumer Books Limited,
Michelin House, 81 Fulham Road, London SW3 6RB
and Auckland, Melbourne, Singapore and Toronto

Revised and reprinted 1992. Revised, enlarged and reprinted 1994, 1995. Revised and updated 1996

ISBN 1 85613 315 X

A catalogue record for this book is available at the British Library

Printed in Great Britain

Photographic acknowledgments

The Publishers should like to thank the following individuals and organisations for their kind permission to reproduce the photographs in this book;

Allsport 6 insert, 125, 126, 127 bottom, 128, 130, 132, 156, 157 bottom, /Clive Brunskill 91 bottom and top, 181 top left, /Shaun Botterill 186 top, 186 bottom, 189,/Simon Bruty 89 bottom left, 158,177, /David Cannon 143, 144, 145, 147, 148 bottom, 149 top left, top right, 150 top, bottom, 152 top, bottom, 155, 166 left, 175 bottom, /Mike Cooper 169, / Mike Hewitt 160, 177 bottom, /Trevor Jones 148 top, /Michael King 159 centre, /Ross Kinnaird 184 top,/Simon Miles 151, /Steve Morton 171 bottom, /Ben Radford 162-163, /Dave Rogers 173 bottom, / Mark Thompson 183;
Cheshire Press Photos 140;
Graham Collin 56-7, 57 bottom, 66 top, 66-7, 67, 69, 70 right, 80 top;
Colorsport 86 top and bottom, 86-7 centre, 89 bottom right, 157 top, 161, 162, 164, 166-7 top, 167, 168, 170, 172, 173 top, 174, 179, 180 centre middle, 181 bottom right, 182 bottom, top, 184 bottom, 185 bottom, top, 187, 188;
Clive Cooksey 62;
Daily Mirror 11 bottom, 12 bottom, 13, 15 left and right, 17, 24-5, 26 top, 29 right, 36 centre,
64 right, 92, 97, 101, 102, 105, 107, 108, 116;
Empics/Steve Etherington 88 top left /Neal Simpson 178 /Barry Coombs 180 centre top/ Laurence Griffiths 180 centre bottom;
Express Newspapers 36 bottom;
Harry Godwin 12 top;
Dick Green 50-1, 60 top, 61, 122, 129, 136;
Hulton Picture Company 29 top and bottom left7 31, 42 top, 75;
The Illustrated London News Picture Library 106;
International News Photos 71;
Mark Leech 90 top;
Manchester Evening News endpapers, 2, 8 bottom, 11 top, 18, 20 bottom, 23, 28 bottom, 53 bottom, 55, 87 top, 99 top, 118, 137, 138, 142, /David Meek 45 bottom, 46, /Tom Tyrrell 42 bottom inset;
David Meek 10 left, 20 top, 24, 25, 30 top, 112, 113, 131;
Oldham Evening Chronicle 8 top, 68 top and bottom, 73, 80 bottom, 83 right;
Harry Ormesker 76;
Popperforto 6 main, 40 bottom;
The Press Association 120, 134;
Press Association/Topham 180 right;
Provincial Press Agency 21;
Reed International Books Ltd/(Frank Power) 41;
Peter Robinson 84 left, 146, 154 top and bottom;
David Smith Sports Photography 158-9 bottom;
Sport and General Picture Library 51 top and bottom;
Syndication International 10 right, 26 bottom, 36 top, 38 top, 42 bottom, 45 top, 58, 60 centre, 120-1, 124, 127 top, 139, /Tom Tyrell 47;
Bob Thomas Sports Photography/ Thomas 171 top, 175 top, 176 bottom, /Monte Fresco 176 top left and top right;
Tom Tyrrell 1, 30 bottom, 33 right, 35, 38 bottom, 40 top, 50 centre and bottom, 60 bottom, 64 top, 66 bottom, 70 left, 81, 83 left, 88 top right, 98 top and bottom, 104, 110, 111 left and right, 114, 123, 126, 130 131 144 top, 156 top, 175, 192 top, 206 top left.

Contents

Foreword

by Bobby Charlton CBE

Manchester United seems to have been the focus of my sporting life for almost as long as I can remember.

When I think about it, I suppose it is really not so surprising considering that my association with the club now goes back some 35 years, even longer if you take into account my schooldays back home in Ashington in the north-east when Joe Armstrong, the United scout, first came round to our house. I shall always remember little Joe with the beaming smile because he was the first to take an interest, and later when there were a few more on the scene and I had to choose a club to go to, I thought I couldn't do better than stay with Joe. The fact that he represented Manchester United and Matt Busby came into it as well of course, but I think my first instincts were right.

I have had a most exciting and rewarding lifetime associated with Manchester United and the fact that I am now honoured to serve the club as a director has been the ultimate satisfaction. Outside my home and family, the club has been my life, and I guess there have even been times when Norma, my wife, has wondered whether football hasn't taken over at home as well. I have got to admit that the game fascinates me as much as ever, especially Manchester United, the club which gave me much of my education and most of my inspiration.

I was privileged to know and play alongside the Busby Babes, lucky to escape with my life when so many of those fine young players failed to survive that terrible crash at Munich. The experience perhaps left me a little more appreciative of the many good things which have happened to me since then, the successes and even the disappointments that make up a career.

Sir Matt Busby and Jimmy Murphy I hold in great affection and respect as the men who did so much to fashion me as a footballer and who led us to those achievements in Europe, to the League Championship and the FA Cup. I have so many memories of matches, friends and team-mates, not to mention opponents and the people I have met in my football travels. Now as I read this latest book on Manchester United my mind is refreshed as the events leap to life again, partly because I was there for 20 years as a player, but also because of the detailed touch of authority brought to a formidable task by Tom Tyrrell and David Meek.

For they were there as well! Tom reports for Piccadilly Radio and was writing about Old Trafford nearly 20 years ago. David has been the *Manchester Evening News* representative covering the club for more than 30 years.

There have been other fine books written about Manchester United, but not with quite the same insight and feel for the club and its many famous players. Even when they are writing about the early days I feel they have captured the essence and spirit of a club which so many of us hold so dear.

So it is with particular pleasure that I write this foreword to a book which I know will stand the test of time as a history of Manchester United.

Matt Busby: Birth of the Babes

Matt Busby in Naples during the Second World War with some other famous faces from professional soccer.
Back row: Jack Martin, Willie Watson, Tommy Lawton, Bert Sproston, Frank Swift, Danny Winter and Joe Mercer.
Front row: Billy Elliott, Matt Busby, George Smith, Douglas Howe.
Matt Busby was playing for Liverpool when war broke out in 1939. Like most of the other players at Anfield he joined the army, serving in the 9th Battalion of the King's Liverpool. Later he was transferred to the Army Physical Training Corps and towards the end of the war toured Italy with a football team playing matches to entertain the troops

Soon after he took over as Manchester United's manager, Matt Busby had a few trophies to show for his leadership with replicas of the FA Cup, Championship, Central League and FA Youth Cup among the pots on show in 1955. With Matt are his management partners Jimmy Murphy on the left and Bert Whalley on the right

Sir Matt Busby lent his name to the most romantic and tragic experiences of football. The 'Busby Babes' of Manchester United fired the imagination of the public as they came bounding onto the scene a few years after the Second World War. They were the creation of a remarkable manager, a man of genius and vision who was to change the face of English football.

Tragically, the Busby Babes were destroyed in the Munich air disaster of 1958 before they had reached their prime, and their manager came close to perishing with them. But he survived and Manchester United rose again from the ashes of their despair. Busby started all over again and produced more splendid teams so, as Bobby Charlton once put it, Old Trafford became a theatre of dreams.

United blazed a trail for English football in Europe. Winning the European Cup in 1968 just ten years after the tragedy at Munich was an incredible achievement and, of course, a testament to the life and work of Matthew Busby, born in 1909 in a two-roomed pitman's cottage in Orbiston, a small Lanarkshire mining village some miles from Glasgow.

The young Busby was no stranger to loss. His father and all his uncles were killed in the First World War. The result was that the remainder of the family, one by one, emigrated to America, looking for a better life than coal mining. Matt's mother was due to join her sister, and Matt himself was only waiting for a visa quota number. Then, just before he was 17, came the invitation to join Manchester City after he had played a few games for Denny Hibs, a local side.

Plans to go to the United States were scrapped, though Matt probably wished at times that he had gone, because life at Maine Road was not easy. He was homesick and he struggled to get into the first team. A switch of position to take the place of an injured player at wing half in the reserves finally launched him on a distinguished career with City and won him Scottish international honours.

He won a Cup-winners' medal in 1934 and by 1936 he was captain of City, but he decided he wanted a change and he signed for Liverpool. Like most of the Liverpool team he joined the army when the Second World War started and served in the 9th Battalion of the King's Liverpool Regiment, and eventually in the Army Physical Training Corps. After the war Liverpool wanted him back as a player and as assistant to manager George Kay. But, as Matt says: 'I got this opportunity to go as manager of Manchester United. I had a soft spot for Manchester after my City days and it attracted me.'

So began a 25-year reign in which he produced three great teams, all different in character but reflecting his desire to create and entertain. In his time with United they won five League Championships, the FA Cup twice (from four finals), the FA Youth Cup six times, five of them on the trot as he fashioned the Busby Babes, and achieved crowning glory in 1968 with the winning of the European Cup. He was never naive in pursuit of honours, either on the field or in the transfer jungle, but he always set responsible standards. Busby took the appalling tragedy of Munich at both personal and club level with a quiet fortitude. The heady delights of football victory and the gloomy setbacks were alike treated with an admirable calm and sense of proportion.

His great gift was as a leader and manager of men. Obviously, he was a perceptive judge of players and a shrewd tactician, but he always had the additional advantage of being able to inspire. He enjoyed the respect of players, rather like the old type of headmaster. Some say Busby failed to handle George Best; but he did get nearly 500 first-team games from him – and some priceless performances – and it's quite possible that without Busby in the background Best might have burnt out in half the time he did.

Honours have been heaped upon him. He was awarded the CBE in 1958, he was given the Freedom of Manchester in 1967 and he was knighted the following year. Pope Paul conferred one of the highest civil awards in the Roman Catholic Church on him in 1972 by making him a Knight Commander of St Gregory

the Great. When he retired as manager of Manchester United in 1970 he was made a director and then the club's first president, a position he still holds. Over the years he has changed little; certainly success never swayed him. As Geoffrey Green, then a distinguished reporter for *The Times*, so admirably expressed it: 'Now he is a legendary eminence who has always been approachable and modest, with time to spare for everybody. It is a humility born of early struggle and given only to those who found the answer when the way ahead looked bleak and life itself seemed an insuperable mountain.'

Even after retirement, life posed great tests for Sir Matt and he again was not found wanting. For some years now he has supported his invalid wife with daily visits although Lady Busby has been unable to recognise him. Few outside his family guessed at the strength he needed, but then it took a strong man to wake the slumbering giant that was Manchester United when he was appointed manager in 1945. It must have been a daunting prospect as he looked at a bombed ground and examined the books.

United were £15,000 overdrawn at the bank, and it was impossible to play at Old Trafford. The dressing rooms were derelict and there were no facilities for training. The club offices were lodged at the nearby premises of the chairman. Matches had to be played at Maine Road, the ground of neighbouring Manchester City. Of the players on the books, some were still away in the services.

The first great team

The new manager wasted little time, and right from the start showed the character and judgement that eventually became legendary. To start with, he insisted on a five-year contract when the chairman, James Gibson, offered him one of three years. Gibson was a man used to having his own way, but he gave Busby what he wanted . . . time to create a team using the ideas that had been simmering in his mind during his days as a player with Manchester City and as a Scottish international.

His next move was to don a tracksuit and go out on the field with his players. In those days this was revolutionary. As Johnny Carey, the captain when Busby was demobbed as a company sergeant-major, and later a manager himself, explains: 'When I joined United, Scott Duncan, with spats and a red rose in his buttonhole, typified a soccer manager. But here was the new boss playing with his team in training, showing what he wanted and how to do it. He was ahead of his time.'

Players on the books included Carey, Henry Cockburn, Jack Rowley, Johnny Morris, Stan Pearson, Allenby Chilton, Joe Walton, Charlie Mitten, John Aston and goalkeeper Jack Crompton. Some say Busby was lucky to start with such a promising nucleus of established players, but many a manager has taken over as good a squad and not made anything of it. He also soon showed the shrewdness in the transfer market that stood him in good stead over the years. He paid £4,000 to Glasgow Celtic in February 1946 for Jimmy 'Brittle Bones' Delaney, a fast right-winger. Delaney was no youngster and with a history of injuries he was regarded as past his best. But Busby saw something that others had missed, and as Carey says: 'It was like fitting the last piece in a jig-saw to complete the picture.'

Behind the scenes he had also made a good signing. Jimmy Murphy, a player in his day with West Bromwich and Wales, was brought to Old Trafford as assistant manager after a friendship formed during the war abroad, and he became

Above left: Matt Busby, his wife Jean and son Sandy at Buckingham Palace for the CBE award ceremony in 1958. The honour came in the Birthday Honours in June shortly after the manager's return home from hospital in Munich

Above: Matt Busby and his wife Jean arrive at Manchester Town Hall for the ceremony which granted the Manchester United manager the Freedom of the City in 1967 . . . a fitting recognition of his 21 years' service to football

Right: Matt Busby (right) gets in a header in a training session with Johnny Carey (number 3) and Henry Cockburn. Busby, home from the war, put his old playing gear back on and worked out on the pitch with his men as a coach as well as their manager. He moved soccer management into an entirely different era. The old style manager was mostly chairborne and wore suit and spats

Above: Old Trafford was blitzed on 11 March 1941, the main stand destroyed along with the dressing rooms and offices. By the end of the war there was even a small tree growing on the terraces. The club made a claim to the War Damage Commission for reconstruction, but it was not until August 1949 that they were able to play football again at Old Trafford. In the meantime they made an arrangement with Manchester City, hiring their neighbours' ground for around £5,000 a year with a percentage of the gate money also going to the Maine Road club

Busby's able lieutenant, the hard man to complement his own more fatherly role in an outstanding football partnership. Busby also showed an early appreciation of tactics, making international full-backs from modest inside-forwards John Aston and Johnny Carey.

When he took over the job in October 1945 United were 16th in the table but by the end of the season they had risen to fourth with a team which read:

Crompton, Hamlett, Chilton, Aston, Whalley, Cockburn, Delaney, Pearson, Rowley, Buckle, Wrigglesworth.

United were on their way, and the following season, 1946-47, as football returned to a national league instead of being divided into northern and southern leagues, they finished second, one point behind Liverpool, in the Championship. Busby's talented collection of experienced players, many of them seasoned by life in the services, were runners-up for two more years.

That was impressive consistency, even if they did miss out on the Championship itself. They were not to be denied a deserved honour, though, giving Busby his first trophy by winning the FA Cup in 1947-48. The 4–2 victory over Blackpool at Wembley was regarded as a classic final. United dominated the competition right from the start and reached Wembley by scoring 18 goals in five ties, indicating their great attacking strength.

They had a magnificent forward line. Jimmy Delaney played on the right wing with Charlie Mitten, one of the sweetest strikers of the ball in the game, operating on the left wing to give the Reds a two-winged attack that was normal in those days and is only just back in fashion. The dashing Jack Rowley was a traditional centre-forward with a fierce shot. He was flanked by the delightfully skilful Stan Pearson at inside-left and the clever Johnny Morris at inside-right. The most commanding figure of all featured further back in the team at right-back – the captain, Johnny Carey, an influential man both on and off the field.

In the third round of the Cup United played at Villa Park and found themselves a goal down without touching the ball. Scoring after only 13

Left: Sir Matt Busby and Jimmy Murphy (seen here shortly before their retirement) formed one of the most effective partnerships in football management. Busby, a Scot, and Murphy, a Welshman, were quite different characters, but they shared a common ideal in football and the sum of their work roused the slumbering giant that was Manchester United. They worked together from just after the Second World War until they retired, still a partnership, in 1971

Below: One of Matt Busby's early teams. Back row: Walter Crickmer (secretary), John Aston, Tom Curry (trainer), Jack Warner, Joe Walton, Jack Crompton, Allenby Chilton, Jimmy Murphy (assistant manager), Billy McGlen, Matt Busby (manager). Sitting: Jack Rowley, Ronnie Burke, Johnny Morris, Johnny Carey, Johnny Hanlon, Stan Pearson, Charlie Mitten

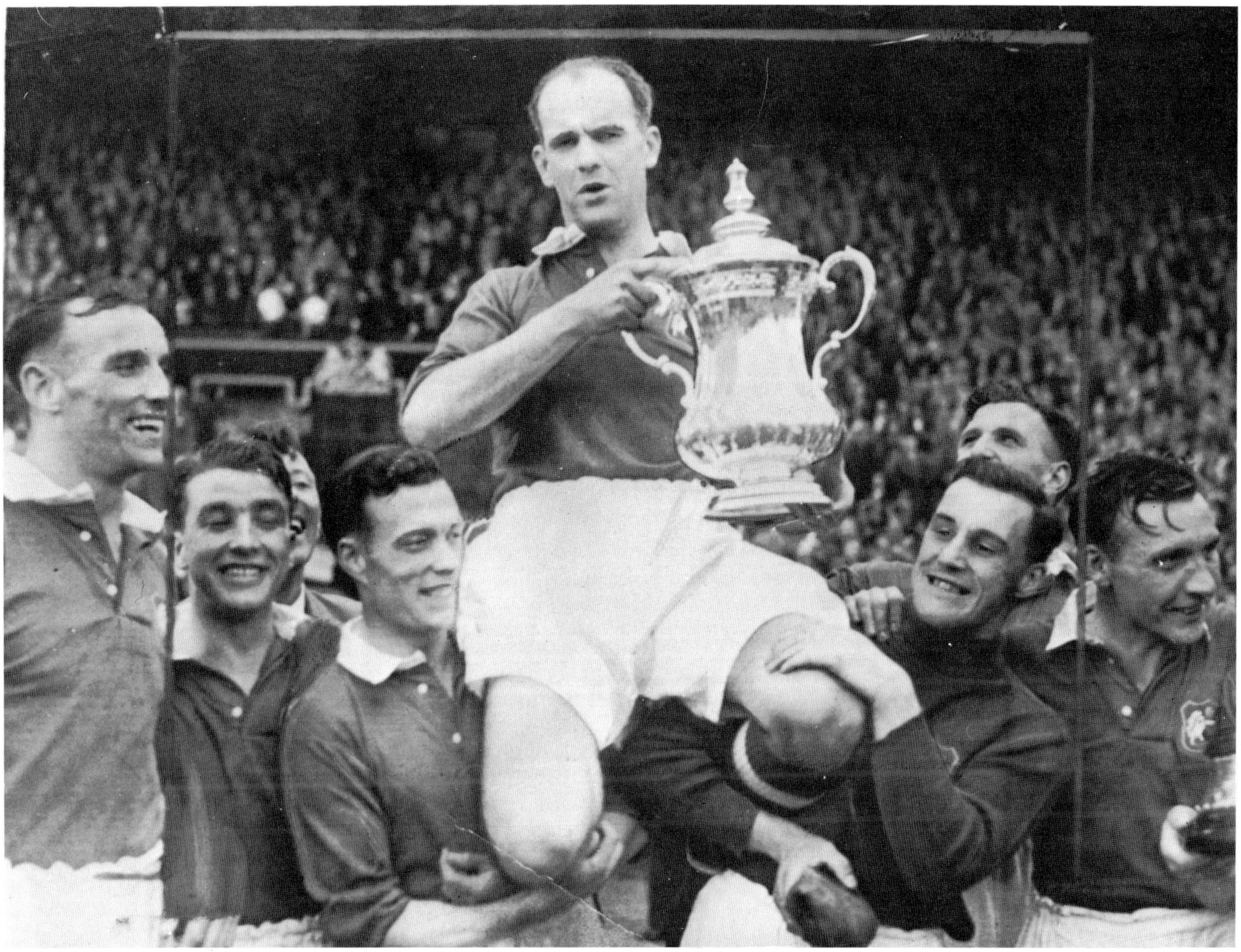

Above: Johnny Carey is hoisted shoulder high by his team-mates after leading United to victory in the FA Cup competition of 1948. The genial Irishman enjoyed many successes, including the captaincy of the Rest of the World when they played against Great Britain in 1947. He was voted Footballer of the Year in 1949, the season he skippered the Republic of Ireland to a notable 2–0 win against England at Goodison Park

seconds was, perhaps, the worst thing Villa could have done, for United's reply was to produce such devastating football that they were leading 5–1 by the interval. Villa creditably fought back in the rain and mud to cut United's lead to 5–4, but United still had the last word, with a goal from Pearson giving them a dramatic 6–4 victory.

United beat Liverpool 3–0, Charlton 2–0, Preston 4–1 and Derby County in the semi-final 3–1, with a hat-trick from Pearson. They arrived at Wembley for the final against Blackpool full of confidence but respecting an opposition that included players like Stanley Matthews, Stan Mortensen and Harry Johnston.

Blackpool gave early notice of their intentions. After only 12 minutes Mortensen broke clean through and was heading for goal when he was brought down by centre-half Allenby Chilton. He fell into the penalty area and Eddie Shimwell beat Jack Crompton with his spot kick. United were a shade lucky with their equaliser in the 28th minute, despite their pressure. For it was a misunderstanding between Blackpool goalkeeper Joe Robinson and centre-half Eric Hayward that let Rowley step in to walk the ball over the line. It was an evenly contested match with Blackpool taking the lead again in the 35th minute with a goal hammered home by Mortensen.

Blackpool led 2–1 until the 69th minute, soaking up a whole stream of punishing United raids. Then their defence cracked under the pressure with Rowley heading a free-kick from Morris into the roof of the net. The game was now 2–2 with both teams redoubling their attacking efforts. Crompton saved brilliantly from Mortensen and then within seconds the ball was in the other net to put United in front. Crompton's clearance was switched by Anderson to Pearson who scored off the post from 25 yards.

It was the 'killer' goal and three minutes later United clinched victory. Anderson shot from a long way out and with the help of a deflection Robinson was wrong-footed to give United a memorable 4–2 win. The team was:

Crompton, Carey, Aston, Anderson, Chilton, Cockburn, Delaney, Morris, Rowley, Pearson, Mitten.

The old sweats still had another shot in their locker, and after finishing runners-up in the League three years on the trot, then fourth followed by another second, the 'nearly men' finally cracked it. They won the Championship in 1951-52, four points ahead of Spurs. They were mean at the back and prolific up front, with 30 goals from Jack Rowley and 22 from Stan Pearson. The team which clinched the title read:

Allen, McNulty, Aston, Carey, Chilton, Cockburn, Berry, Downie, Rowley, Pearson, Byrne.

Rowley opened the Championship season in spanking form, scoring hat-tricks in the first two games for a 3–3 draw at West Bromwich and a 4–2 win at home against Middlesbrough. United weren't invincible, as they showed with a 1–0 defeat at Bolton in September. Then they lost successive games at the end of the month at Tottenham and at home against Preston.

Portsmouth were the early pace-setters, but they fell away to leave United, Spurs and Arsenal looking the strongest teams. Arsenal were, in fact, chasing a League and FA Cup double. They went all the way to Wembley, where they lost 1–0 to Newcastle after an early injury to their right-back Wally Barnes. In the League they hit Championship form with an unbeaten run from just after Christmas until the end of April. United matched them except for another double defeat in successive matches, losing at Huddersfield and again to Portsmouth.

United, Spurs and Arsenal were almost neck and neck on the last lap, with United having their noses just in front. The destiny of the title was decided on the last game of the season, with a grand finale between two of the top three teams. Arsenal came to Old Trafford on 26 April as outsiders because, thanks to the scoring prowess of Rowley and Pearson, they had an inferior goal average. In fact they needed to win 7–0 to become champions, which of course was asking a lot. In the event United established themselves as worthy champions by running rampant for a 6–1 victory.

What a shoot-out! Naturally, the scorers were led by a hat-trick from Rowley, with two goals coming from Pearson and one from Roger Byrne.

So United finished on 57 points, with Spurs and Arsenal level on points, four behind. Tottenham took second place on goal average. The big difference was in the scoring. United had notched a magnificent 95 as opposed to 76 from Spurs and 80 by Arsenal. It was a worthy climax for what was still largely the first post-war team. It was a fitting peak for them after coming so close for five years. And the first League Championship for Manchester United for 41 years established Matt Busby in the record books as a manager of style and perception.

Jack Rowley

Busby's team was packed with men not just of ability but also of character . . . people like Jack Rowley who was not nicknamed 'The Gunner' for nothing. For this man gunned his shots on the football field with the kind of ferocity and accuracy he had used as an anti-tank gunner with the South Staffordshire infantry. Perhaps for the fans of those days his two occupations as a gunner on and off the field made an obvious nickname. We don't know how many tanks he hit as part of the invasion force in France during his six-and-a-half years in the army, but he certainly made a habit of hitting the net as a footballer.

Until Dennis Viollet came along a few years later Rowley held the United League scoring record for a season with his 30 goals in 1951-52. Overall, he scored 175 goals in 359 League appearances, which is a remarkable record when you consider that the war deprived him of six of his peak years as a player. Not that he stopped scoring during the war. He played as a 'guest' for Spurs, Wolves and Distillery in Ireland among other clubs, and it's war-time football that provides him with one of his most cherished memories. He recalls: 'I played for Spurs one week and scored seven, and then a few days later I got eight out of eight for Wolves.'

Jack dominated the scoring in the post-war years. He hit two in the 1948 FA Cup Final win against Blackpool and he was in fact the team's top marksman in each of the first four seasons after the war. His record season helped win the Championship and he thrilled the supporters from the time he scored those hat-tricks in the first two games.

Rowley won six caps, playing in four different positions for England, with his highspot the scoring of four goals against Northern Ireland in 1949. His shot was reckoned to be the hardest of his day, a finish in keeping with the strong, aggressive style of the traditional centre-forward of the time.

Perhaps it is because of this physical nature of his game that if he is watching a match these days it is likely to be just down the road from his home in Shaw, Oldham, on the touchline at the local Rugby Union ground, or as a guest at Swinton Rugby League ground.

'I am still interested in soccer, but it's convenient to go three minutes down the road to watch the rugby. I like the way they take the knocks and shake them off and later are the best of pals in the bar,' he explains. 'I was always hard, but fair, as a player, and I see that these days more in rugby.'

Born in Wolverhampton, he was a junior at his local club under the legendary Major Frank Buckley, but made his League debut playing for Bournemouth. United signed him for £3,000 in 1937. He was soon among the goals, scoring four out of five against Swansea to help United win promotion to the First Division on the eve of the war.

Jack played for ten years after the war and then joined Plymouth as player-manager for a couple of seasons. His management career saw him twice at Oldham and with Ajax in Amsterdam, Wrexham and Bradford. During his second spell with Oldham he took a local post office and newsagency which became his job when he left the soccer scene until his retirement in the 1980s.

Stan Pearson

Stan Pearson, the other half of the high-scoring partnership, was the perfect foil for Rowley. They often say strikers are born in pairs, and these two players certainly complemented each other.

Stan Pearson was one of the most gifted inside forwards to play for United in post 1945 football. He struck a particularly effective partnership with Jack Rowley, and together they formed one of the highest scoring strike forces in football. Salford born, Jack joined the club before the war and returned with a number of his colleagues to provide Matt Busby with his first successful team

Pearson was the more subtle, and created a great many of Rowley's goals, while at the same time he himself profited from the big man's more forceful style. He was a lethal finisher as well as the traditional inside-forward of that period, good on the ball and skilful, with a deceptive body swerve. He made 345 League and FA Cup appearances, scoring 149 goals, a tremendous scoring rate. As with Rowley, the war took six years out of his United career.

Pearson was a Salford schoolboy who joined the club at the age of 15 in 1936. He made his debut at the age of 17 in a 7–1 win at Chesterfield, and he scored in each of the next two games. But he had only two seasons before the war interrupted normal football. He served in the Second/Fourth South Lancashires, ending up in India where he played in a British Army touring team with Dennis Compton to entertain the troops after the Japanese had been pushed back in Burma. Incidentally, Johnny Morris, another of United's post-war stars at inside forward, was touring India in another 'Select' side around the same time. One by one, United's soldier footballers came home after the war to play for Sergeant-Major Busby, and Stan Pearson remembers it well.

'For two or three seasons leading up to the Championship, the forward line picked itself. We all got to know each other so well that instinctively we knew what was going to happen next. For instance, if Johnny Aston had the ball at left-back I would come towards him, and I knew without looking that if I slipped it straight, Jack Rowley would be moving for it. He would then push it out to Charlie Mitten on the left wing and in seconds we had the ball in front of goal. They talk about one-touch football these days as if it is something new, but we were doing it in 1948, and in my view no team has done it better.'

Stan signed for Bury in 1954 after a 17-year association with United. He later played for Chester and managed them. Finally, he settled at Prestbury in Cheshire, running the local post office and newsagent's shop.

Johnny Carey

United were a star-studded team in that era, but they had one major, influential character, the captain, Johnny Carey. Carey took Busby's philosophy of attacking football out to the pitch. He had joined United in 1936 from the Dublin club, St James' Gate, for the modest sum of £250 after being spotted by Louis Rocca, a scout who was one of the founding fathers of the latter-day United.

Rocca had gone to Dublin to watch an entirely different player. It is said that Carey was playing only his third real game of soccer, but his natural ability shone through and Rocca quickly made arrangements for him to come to Old Trafford.

United played Johnny Carey in every position except on the wing. This included one game in goal after the usual goalkeeper had been taken ill on an away trip. He started as an inside-forward, made his name at right-back and then became a commanding wing-half. Louis Rocca brought him over from Dublin in 1936 for £250 and he didn't retire until 1953, when he was given a special vote of appreciation by the Old Trafford directors

Carey was 17 at the time and made his League debut the following year. He started as an inside-left, became an outstanding right-back, played centre-half, and finished his career as a polished wing-half. In fact he played in every position except wing for United, including a game in goal when Jack Crompton was taken ill on the day of a match. In all he played 344 League and FA Cup games spanning 17 years with the club. He would have made many more appearances for the club but for army service in Italy during the war. A fine international, he had the distinction of playing for both Northern Ireland and the Republic. Perhaps his greatest honour was captaining the Rest of Europe against Great Britain in 1947. Two years later he was voted Footballer of the Year by the Football Writers' Association.

Carey retired from playing in 1953 and started in management as coach at Blackburn. He was promoted to manager there before managing Everton, Leyton Orient, Nottingham Forest and Blackburn again. A genial, pipe-smoking man, he was known as 'Gentleman John' and as a manager the gist of his team talks would be to urge his players to 'fizz it around'.

He ended his managerial days by returning to Old Trafford as a part-time scout while working in the borough treasurer's office at Sale, Cheshire. Later golf took over from football to fill his sporting interests, though he says: 'I still think football is a terrific game. I perhaps wish people would accept defeat with a little more grace sometimes, and I would like to see players allowed to express themselves more, but soccer is super, the best game in the world.'

Jack Crompton

Another of the stalwarts in the post-war period was Jack Crompton, who joined the club in 1944 from the local works side, Goslings, having played for Oldham as an amateur. He was in Busby's first team and was prominent in the 1948 FA Cup win. His highlight was stopping a piledriver from Stan Mortensen when the score was 2–2 and then making the long clearance which saw Stan Pearson streak away to score.

Jack was born in 1921 and United was his only club as a professional. He made about 200 League appearances before joining Luton Town as their trainer in 1956. Just over a year later he returned to Old Trafford as trainer to help Jimmy Murphy in the crisis of Munich.

He served Matt Busby well as both player and staff man, and admits that in the early days he did not appreciate the impact Busby was going to make on the soccer world.

'He was such a quiet, unassuming and modest man that at first you didn't know the strength,' says Jack. 'The first thing I remember he did was to change the them and us of management and players to we, and he kept it that way. Naturally, when he first took charge he had to fight to make his presence felt and he had still to win the great respect he enjoyed later.

'I think he had the sympathy of the players as someone fresh from our ranks in his first job as a manager and I am sure he would agree that the players were patient and understanding. But, of course, a manager must command more than that from his players and though his outstanding ability was apparent after only a few months, I think he was still feeling his way up to the 1948 Cup final win. Ironically, it was this first major trophy success, evidence to all and sundry that he was a man destined to do big things in football, that brought the one and only crisis between players and club that I can remember.

'We went on strike a few months after the final for something we thought we should have. Details don't matter now and I only mention the incident to show that he did not win his place as a master manager without his share of problems. It was finally sorted out though it took a little while before the trouble was forgotten. It was a big test for a comparatively new boss and it was probably only due to his ability as a manager of men that the problem was finally compromised.

'No doubt he had many a struggle to get his way at the board meetings, though as a player I could feel his presence becoming more widely felt all the time. I realised that he had really won his battle when another challenging problem arose in 1949 as we were heading for the Cup final again.

'Johnny Morris, our talented inside-forward was giving the Boss some headaches and after dropping him for one Cup-tie he had him transferred to Derby. To my mind, if Johnny had played we would have reached the final again. Naturally, the players thought the club should have kept him. I thought so, too, at the time. But this is where you live and learn and time proved that the manager was right to stick to his beliefs. Johnny Morris was transferred on a matter of principle. Matt must have had a tremendous fight with his own conscience and with other people before taking such a drastic step. I can appreciate now that he was right and it is this almost uncanny foresight and judgement, even if it involved an unpopular decision, that kept Manchester United at the front in post-war football.

'He was accurate in his assessment of players and always thoughtful. I remember our first flight to the Continent after the Munich disaster. After we had landed at Amsterdam, Bill Foulkes telephoned his wife to let her know we had arrived safely. Teresa Foulkes already knew. Busby had been on the phone to tell her. You can perhaps appreciate the concern behind this phone message when you stop to think about the aftermath of Munich.

'As a manager he had a tremendous memory for players' strengths and failings. He never lost the common touch, the knack of understanding, and being in touch with players. He never forgot a player, past or present, and his memory for

Manchester at the start of the 1952–53 season complete with the League trophy and FA Charity Shield which they won by beating Newcastle United 4–2. Jack Rowley scored twice with the other goals from Johnny Downie and a young Roger Byrne.
Back row: Tom Curry (trainer), Walter Crickmer (secretary), Alan Gibson (director), Dr W McLean (director), George Whittaker (director), Bill Petherbridge (director), Matt Busby (manager).
Middle: Johnny Downie, Jack Rowley, John Aston, Reg Allen, Allenby Chilton, Roger Byrne, Stan Pearson. Front: Johnny Berry, Johnny Carey, Henry Cockburn, Tommy McNulty. They were champions for the first time under Matt Busby in 1951–52

people's names is uncanny. There are many facets to the character of Matt Busby.'

Jack Crompton later tried management himself at Barrow and Preston. A keen YMCA member in his youth, he was always fitness minded, and in the mid-1980s he was still coaching youngsters at Manchester's splendid Platt Lane sports complex used by Manchester City. To prove how young at heart he remains, his big present on his retirement birthday was a course of flying lessons to help him achieve his lifelong ambition to be a pilot.

The 1951-52 Championship side

Jack played only a handful of games in the Championship year after losing his place to Reg Allen, the first goalkeeper to attract a five-figure transfer fee. Busby paid Queen's Park Rangers £11,000 for him and he held the first-team job down for two seasons, including the Championship year, before he was overtaken by illness which finished his career.

John Anderson had gone from wing-half to prompt the masterly switch of Carey to form the dominating half-back line of Carey on the right, Allenby Chilton at centre-half and Henry Cockburn on the left. Tom McNulty took Carey's place at right-back with John Aston still on the left, though starting to concede that place to Roger Byrne.

It was the balance and blend of the half-back line which was the key to the way the team took charge in so many games and managed to supply their marvellous front runners and wingers with quality service.

Henry Cockburn, recruited like Crompton from the local works team Goslings, which had become something of a United nursery, was the typical little guy who made up for lack of inches with fire and determination. He also had class and timing, which meant he often outjumped taller men for the ball.

He made his first-team debut in war-time football and he was there for the first League game after the war in a 2–1 win against Grimsby at Maine Road. He was still working in an Oldham mill and had played only a handful of League games when he was selected for the first of his 13 England caps. At international level he was part of another famous half-back line, featuring with Neil Franklin and Billy Wright. For United he played in the 1948 Cup-winning team and in the 1951-52 Championship side. In all he spent ten years at Old Trafford before moving in 1954 to Bury. Later he worked as a coach for Ian Greaves, the former United full-back, at Huddersfield.

The pillar of the team and the kind of player Matt Busby always preferred at centre-half was the remarkable Allenby Chilton, a man who played before the war yet lasted to see the Busby Babes settling in around him. After being signed from Seaham Colliery in the north-east, he made his League debut against Charlton in September 1939. War was declared the following day and sliced out seven years of his United career.

Chilton fought in France and was wounded at Normandy, and he was nearly 28 before he was able to resume his life with United. But he played in the first team for another ten seasons, with Busby always claiming that he played his best football in his later years. In all, he played nearly 400 League and Cup games and he was the only player ever-present in the Championship side, not that that was anything special to Chilton, who was as durable as he was big and strong. Towards the end he took over the captaincy from Johnny Carey, and when he lost his place to Mark Jones in 1955 he had achieved a club record of 166 consecutive League appearances.

Chilton played twice for England; he would have played more often if Busby had been manager of the national side. After Old Trafford, he led Grimsby to the Third Division North Championship as player-manager and then had spells in management with Wigan and Hartlepool.

Johnny Carey has been discussed already. His switch to right-half with Tommy McNulty coming in at right-back was a masterly move in the second half of the Championship season.

Up front, Rowley and Pearson were still the scoring stars but Busby had brought in new wingers and changed one of the inside-forwards.

After sacrificing Johnny Morris from the 1948 team on a point of principle, selling him for a British record fee of £24,500 to Derby County, Busby bought Johnny Downie for a club record £18,000 from Bradford Park Avenue in 1949. Downie had established himself in the team the season before the Championship, and he is perhaps not so well remembered as some of the other players of that era. He simply wasn't there as long as most of the others, but he certainly played his part in bringing the title to Old Trafford after such a long absence, and he scored 35 goals in the 110 League appearances he made in his five seasons with the Reds. Later he played for Luton, Hull City, Mansfield and Darlington, yet another Scotsman with a good career in English football.

The 1948 wingers had also gone by 1951-52. Jimmy Delaney had been given something of an Indian summer when Matt Busby made him his first signing in 1946, and he played a total of 164 League games plus 19 in the FA Cup spread over five seasons. But there was still a lot more football left in him, despite his spate of injuries before coming down from Scotland. At the end of 1950 he went back home to Scotland to join Aberdeen. Later he played for Derry City to win an Irish FA Cup medal and complete a unique

Jimmy Delaney shooting for goal against Weymouth in the third round of the FA Cup in January 1950, when he scored in a 4–0 home win. Delaney was Matt Busby's first signing after becoming manager at the end of the Second World War. He was tagged Brittle Bones because of a number of broken limbs and he was generally regarded as being past his best, but he proved a brilliant buy at £5,000 from Glasgow Celtic. He was a speedy winger who played a key role in helping to win the FA Cup in 1948, United's first post-war success

hat-trick of winners' medals. In 1937, when he was with Glasgow Celtic, he had been in their Scottish Cup-winning team, and while with United he collected a medal with the 1948 team. Derry in 1954 gave him his third medal, and a couple of years later, at the age of 40, he was close to picking up a fourth. He was player-manager of Cork Athletic when they reached the final of the FA of Ireland Cup in the Republic, but this time he was on the losing side against Shamrock Rovers, despite Cork leading 2–0 at one point.

Delaney finally hung up his boots back home in Scotland with Highland League club Elgin City after 23 years as a player. Martin Edwards, the current chairman of Manchester United, went to Scotland in 1987 to talk to Delaney, the one remaining member of the 1948 Cup team he hadn't met. He was introduced by the United manager, Alex Ferguson, who had played football in his early days with Jimmy's son Pat. One of the happy outcomes of the meeting was a sportsmen's dinner at Old Trafford later in the year with 'Brittlebones', turned 70, the guest of honour among a reunion of virtually every member of Matt Busby's first honours team.

The transfer of Delaney came soon after the departure of his fellow winger, Charlie Mitten, though he left for a quite different reason. Charlie, one of the great characters of all time at the club, joined straight from school locally in 1936 and was just about ready for his League debut when war broke out. He made war-time appearances for the Reds as well as playing for Tranmere, Aston Villa and Chelsea. His debut proper came in the first League fixture after hostilities and he was one of the 'famous five' forwards who helped win the 1948 Cup. Always a speedy winger, he gave superb service from the left and he scored a lot of goals himself as well.

Then, in the summer of 1950, he became one of the 'rebels' of English football who rocked the boat to try for fame and fortune, especially fortune, in Colombia. United were on an end-of-season tour in South America when Charlie was approached by a representative of the Bogota club, Sante Fe, to play in Colombia. There was talk of a £5,000 signing-on fee, a lot of money in those days, plus wages of £60 a week, four times as much as the maximum pay at home. Neil Franklin, the England and Stoke centre-half, threw in his lot with the South American adventure, perhaps influencing men like Mitten.

Busby counselled caution, pointing out that playing outside FIFA jurisdiction would mean suspension at home. Charlie gave it a year, and with a lot of the promises unfulfilled returned to England. He was duly banned and had to be transfer-listed by United. After completing his suspension, he joined Fulham for five years, subsequently becoming player-manager of Mansfield.

The whole affair was a sad blow for United fans, who saw Charlie in their colours for only four seasons. His tally of 50 goals in 142 League appearances reflected his ability as a high-scoring winger. In all, he played nearly 400 League games. After Mansfield he became manager of Newcastle United where it seems he indulged his passion for dog racing. There are colourful stories of him at St James's Park, such as his having a hot line from his office to the dog track, and occasionally bringing in his dogs for medical treatment at the football ground!

Mitten later worked as a manager at Manchester's White City dog track. In more recent years he turned to sports promotion and, holding a UEFA licence, he arranged soccer tours, with Manchester United among his customers. His two sons, John and Charles, both played junior football for United.

So with both Delaney and Mitten gone, Busby had need of new wingers. He bought Harry McShane, a player who later became the club announcer and then a scout, from Bolton, and he also played Ernie Bond. But four games into the Championship season he was still casting around, when he recalled a match the previous season against Birmingham City. He remembered the performance of a little winger who had scored an outstanding goal against them at Old Trafford.

Busby swooped for Johnny Berry at a cost of £25,000 and was delighted with his capture. Berry's debut against Bolton ended in defeat, but he soon settled down to solve the right-wing position with his tricky, ball-playing ability, which also saw him net half-a-dozen goals. Berry made the position his own for the next seven seasons, making nearly 300 League and Cup appearances for 43 goals until he was severely injured in the Munich crash. He was critically ill with head injuries for some weeks and made only a slow recovery. There was never any chance of him playing again. He returned to his native Aldershot where he opened a sports shop with his brother Peter, a former Crystal Palace and Peterborough player. After that he worked in the parts warehouse of a television company.

By the end of the Championship season the new outside-left was Roger Byrne. He had made his League debut midway through the campaign at left-back but was switched to the left-wing with devastating effect, playing in the last six games and scoring seven times. Roger, later to become a distinguished captain, was the first of the home-grown kids to come pushing through the ranks as the Busby Babes concept gathered force behind the scenes and at junior level.

The season after the Championship Roger Byrne returned after a few games to left-back, where he played with great distinction using his instinct as a winger to attack down his flank. His flair took him into the England team at left-back in 1954 and he won 33 successive caps until he was a victim of the Munich disaster. He was only 28 when he died. His wife, Joy, gave birth to their son, Roger, eight months after his death.

In all Byrne made nearly 300 League and

Cup appearances involving three Championships. Few who were there at the time will forget, though, his dramatic impact on the wing to help clinch that first vital title in 1952.

Manchester United's achievement, perhaps because of its then rarity, was considered worthy of a tribute from the *Manchester Guardian* in their esteemed leader column, usually reserved for weightier matters. The leader writer eulogised:

'After an interval of forty-one years, Manchester United have regained the Championship of the Football League. The title has never been better earned.

'Not only has the team, in the five seasons before this one, finished second four times and fourth once in the League and won the FA Cup; it has been captained, managed and directed in a way that is a lesson to many others. J. Carey, the captain in this period, has been a model footballer – technically efficient, thanks to hard work; a fighter to the last, without ever forgetting that he is a sportsman; a steadier of the younger and inexperienced, an inspirer of the older and tiring, and at all times the most modest of men, though he has won every football honour open to him.

'M. Busby, the manager, has shown himself as great a coach as he was a player, with an uncannily brilliant eye for young local players' possibilities, whether in their usual or in other positions; a believer in the certainty of good football's eventual reward, and a kindly, yet, when necessary, firm father of his family of players.

'Between them they have built up a club spirit which is too rare in these days, a spirit which enables men to bear cheerfully personal and team disappointments and to ignore personal opportunities to shine for the good of the whole.

'Moreover, by eschewing the dangerous policy of going into the transfer market whenever a weakness develops and giving their chances instead to the many local citizens on the club's books they have made it likely that this club will persist, since the club today is a Manchester one not in name only but in fact as far as most of its players are concerned.

'Manager and captain could never have brought about this happy state of affairs had they not had through these years such full authority and support from the Board of Directors as must be the envy of many other officials in all parts of the country.'

The emergence of the Babes

After winning the Championship in 1951-52, Busby naturally kicked off the following season with his winning team, but it was soon obvious that the first great post-war side had passed its peak. Six of the first 11 matches were lost, and Busby realised he had to start drafting in new players, and making changes. The situation did not take him altogether by surprise because he had already laid the foundations for the future.

Always in his mind had been the creation of a team based on youngsters he had taken from school and brought up in his ways. Right from the start he had paid a lot of attention to this aspect of the club and he had taken great care to appoint the right kind of men to make a success of his plan. The result was that in addition to having Jimmy Murphy as his right-hand man, he had Joe Armstrong busy signing the best schoolboy players he could find, with Northern Ireland and the Republic of Ireland proving rich recruiting areas.

Bob Bishop and Bob Harper in Belfast and Billy Behan in Dublin, three grand football men, didn't miss much. And when it came to persuading anxious parents to let their sons come to Old Trafford, Joe Armstrong was a charmer but honest and sincere with it.

Left: Roger Byrne clutching the cherished championship trophy after leading the Reds to success. He won three championship medals in his seven seasons of first-team football with Manchester United. He made his League debut in the November of season 1951–52 to share in the club's first post-war success as champions. Then he went on to become an integral part of the Busby Babes as their captain, leading the youngsters to the championship in two successive seasons before his tragic and untimely death at Munich. He won 33 consecutive caps for England

Below: Bill Foulkes, one of United's longest serving players, flanked on the right by his mentor, Bert Whalley (right), and assistant manager Jimmy Murphy (left), another of the highly influential figures bringing on the reserves at United. Foulkes had to play for two years as an amateur before he was invited to join the professional ranks in 1951. But he was always made to feel part of the club, and in his early days when he was away in the army on national service coach Bert Whalley used to write to him regularly commenting on his performances

Then Busby had Bert Whalley as a dedicated, gifted coach and Tom Curry as the kindly trainer. Helped by enthusiastic part-timers like Jack Pauline, they put great emphasis on grooming the youngsters. They had good material to work with, and they made sure the finished product had excellence. United dominated the game in this area, as can be seen in their FA Youth Cup record. They won the competition for five successive seasons, starting from its inception in the 1952-53 season, the year the first team started to come apart.

The result was that towards the end of that rather troubled season players such as David Pegg, Jeff Whitefoot, John Doherty, Jackie Blanchflower, Bill Foulkes, Dennis Viollet and Duncan Edwards started to get the occasional game.

Busby also went into the transfer market to pay £29,999 to Barnsley for Tommy Taylor. The team finished a modest eighth, but Busby knew he had talent in the making. He made his decisive move in October the following season. Busby explained: 'We played a friendly at Kilmarnock and I played half-a-dozen of the youngsters. They did well and we won 3–0. Then, as I walked the golf course in the next few days, I pondered whether this was the moment to play them all in the League team. One or two had already come into the side, and I decided that I would go the whole way with the youngsters.'

This meant that Edwards, Viollet and Blanchflower squeezed out three more of the veterans to give the team a more youthful look. Most things in football have to be worked for, and the Busby Babes didn't find overnight success. They finished only fourth in that 1953-54 season, and then, with more youngsters like Albert Scanlon, Mark Jones and Billy Whelan occasionally drafted in, the best they could do in 1954-55 was fifth place.

But then everything began to click and the Busby Babes hit the headlines. They took the First Division by storm in 1955-56, winning the Championship by a devastating 11 points from Blackpool and with an average age of barely 22. By this time precociously talented youngsters were rolling out of the Busby academy. Eddie Colman, whose shimmy of the hips was said to send even the crowd the wrong way, had forced his way into the team while top-class reserves like Ian Greaves and Geoff Bent were ready in case there were any injuries.

The team which played most for the 1955-56 title lined up:

Wood, Foulkes, Byrne, Whitefoot then Colman, Jones, Edwards, Berry, Blanchflower or Doherty or Whelan, Taylor, Viollet, Pegg. Ian Greaves, Albert Scanlon and Colin Webster also played.

John Aston, who later became a chief scout at Old Trafford, was in both the 1948 Cup and 1952 League-winning teams, and was one of the men who had had to make way for youth.

'It was very disappointing for the players who had brought the Championship to Old Trafford for the first time in 40 years to have to give way to new men,' he says. 'But we were not blind to the fact that the Boss had also been busy creating a tremendously successful youth team, winning the FA Youth Cup five times off the reel when it was started.

'Matt Busby had also been at the club long enough to have established himself as a very far-seeing and shrewd manager. He had won the respect of all of us which meant that it was easier for him to put over these new ideas. We just

Left to right: Duncan Edwards, Ian Greaves, Ray Wood, Dennis Viollet, Mark Jones, David Pegg and Eddie Colman celebrate the victory against Blackpool which gave them the League championship in 1956. The achievement was remarkable in that it had come so soon after winning the title in 1952 with an almost entirely rebuilt team. This was the first trophy for the sensational Busby Babes who had nearly all graduated through the junior teams at Old Trafford to fulfil Matt Busby's dream of fashioning a team in his own image from schoolboys

accepted the changes because when he said it was for the good of the club we knew that it was. For Matt Busby is an amazing man. He is kind, he is gentle, but he can also be very strong and firm. He treats everyone with respect and he in turn is greatly respected. It is this quality which enabled him to move from one successful era to another with a team that became the great Busby Babes.'

Only right-winger Johnny Berry and left-back Roger Byrne bridged the four-year transition from the 1951-52 Championship side to the 1955-56 Championship.

Ray Wood had taken over in goal from Allen by this time. United had signed him as a teenager from Darlington in 1949 and he gradually worked his way through to the first team after providing cover for Allen and Crompton. He played in all but one of the 1955-56 Championship games. He collected a second Championship medal the following season and was the central figure in the controversy with Peter McParland in the 1957 FA Cup final.

Just before the air crash Ray lost his place to new signing Harry Gregg. He recovered from the relatively minor injuries he suffered to play again, but he was forced to move on, playing for Huddersfield Town, Bradford City and Barnsley. Later he turned to coaching with great success in Cyprus, the Middle East and Africa. He won three caps for England.

Roger Byrne was at left-back, but with a new partner. Bill Foulkes had dug in at right-back with the kind of dour tenacity associated with his coalmining background. His father was a miner at St Helens, and Bill was also working at the pit when he was picked up by United as an amateur with Whiston Boys Club. He became a full-time professional and won a regular place in 1953, going on to become one of the club's greatest ever servants.

Foulkes lasted a long course, playing First Division football for 18 years, involving some 600 games for the club. He won just about everything in the course of his career: four Championship medals, an FA Cup winner's medal and he went on to win a 1968 European Cup medal. As a survivor of Munich he played an important part in bridging the gap between the Babes and later teams, at one point captaining the club. He was never regarded as one of the more skilful stars, but he had them all licked for staying power, as Allenby Chilton had before him, and like Chilton he played at centre-half later in his career.

After retiring as a player in 1970 Bill became a youth coach at Old Trafford. Then he played and managed in the United States and more recently in Norway. Such is the esteem of his old team-mates that they elected him the first chairman of the association of former Manchester United players.

Jeff Whitefoot started the season at right-half, and indeed won a Championship medal, but such was the competition for places that he was forced to concede to Eddie Colman. Whitefoot was a schoolboy international and he was only 16 when he was given his League debut in 1950. He was a brilliant, cultured wing-half, yet he played only 95 League and Cup games for United before being squeezed out by the stream of starlets coming through. He underlined his great ability by going on to play nearly 300 games for Nottingham Forest, and win an FA Cup medal with them.

There was no holding back Colman, though. 'Snake Hips' played the second half of the season at right-half, striking up an uncanny understanding with Duncan Edwards at left-half. They both loved to attack, which is probably why Busby went for the rocklike steadiness of Mark Jones between them at centre-half.

Mark was a traditional 'stopper', arriving as a schoolboy from Barnsley and fitting perfectly into the mould established by Allenby Chilton. Together Colman, Jones and Edwards formed one of the finest half-back lines ever assembled. All three were to die tragically young at Munich.

Duncan Edwards is probably the player mentioned most often as the best-ever footballer to wear a Manchester United shirt. Certainly Jimmy Murphy, assistant to Sir Matt Busby until the day they both retired, has not the slightest doubt in his mind.

'When I used to hear Muhammad Ali proclaim to the world that he was the greatest, I used to smile,' he says. 'You see, the greatest of them all was an English footballer named Duncan Edwards.

'If I shut my eyes I can see him now. Those pants hitched up, the wild leaps of boyish enthusiasm as he came running out of the tunnel, the tremendous power of his tackle – always fair but fearsome – the immense power on the ball. In fact the number of times he was robbed of the ball once he had it at his feet could be counted on one hand. He was a players' player. The greatest . . . there was only one and that was Duncan Edwards.'

Jimmy tells the story of when he was manager of Wales and preparing a team to play against Duncan Edwards and England. He carefully went through all the England players, detailing their strengths and weaknesses. Then, at the end of his team talk, Reg Davies, the Newcastle and Welsh inside-forward, said to Jimmy that he hadn't mentioned Edwards, the player probably marking him. Replied Murphy: 'There is nothing to say that would help us. Just keep out of his way, son.'

Duncan Edwards played his first League game for United at the age of 15 and 285 days, against Cardiff City at Old Trafford on Easter Monday 1953. During the next five years he became the youngest England international, making his debut at the age of 17 and 8 months in a 7–2 victory against Scotland at Wembley.

Tom Curry, the much loved trainer who helped the Busby Babes along their road to success, chatting to Tommy Taylor, Ray Wood and Mark Jones as they prepare to hit the FA Cup trail to Wembley in January 1957

He won two Championship medals and played 19 times for England. He would have been a natural successor as captain to Billy Wright.

'From the first time I saw him as a boy of 14,' says Jimmy Murphy, 'he looked like and played with the assurance of a man, with legs like tree trunks, a deep and powerful chest and an unforgettable zest for the game. He played wing-half, centre-forward, inside-forward and centre-half with the consummate ease of a great player. He was never bothered where he played. He was quite simply a soccer Colossus.'

By 1955-56 the attack had also taken on a new look, and not every player had come from the youth ranks. The gap at centre-forward caused by the absence of Jack Rowley was filled by a man they found at Barnsley, Tommy Taylor.

United were not his only admirers. Jimmy Murphy says that the last time he saw him play at Barnsley there were so many managers and club chairmen there that he thought it was an extraordinary general meeting of the Football League. Altogether 20 clubs were chasing the 21-year-old forward, and Murphy says that the biggest problem was trying to persuade him he was good enough to play for Manchester United in the First Division.

'He had this mop of black hair and a perpetual smile on his face which prompted one sportswriter of the time, George Follows, to christen him "the smiling executioner",' says Murphy. 'He didn't really want to leave Barnsley where everyone knew him. Eventually Matt Busby's charm won him over, and convinced him that if he came to Old Trafford to link up with the youngsters we had produced ourselves, the sky was the limit to his future in football.'

Taylor was signed for the odd-sounding fee of £29,999 so as not to burden him with a £30,000 tag, and he was an immediate success with his penetrating stride, fierce shot and powerful heading. He crossed the Pennines in 1953 and two months after signing he won the first of 19 England caps. He played 163 League games for United, scoring 112 goals. He scored 25 of them from 33 appearances to help win the 1956 Championship.

The inside-right berth was causing something of a problem, with first Jackie Blanchflower, then John Doherty and finally another exciting youngster, Billy Whelan, all sharing in the Championship race. Inside-left was more settled with Dennis Viollet now a regular, but more of him later as a Munich survivor who hit the scoring headlines in 1960.

Johnny Berry was still at outside-right, while the youthful David Pegg occupied the left wing for most of the title season. David was another of the successful youth team, a Busby Babe recruited at Doncaster. He was able to make only 127 League appearances in his five seasons before losing his life at Munich. He played just once for the full England team, joining team-mates Roger Byrne, Tommy Taylor and Duncan Edwards against the Republic of Ireland. Munich was England's loss as well as Manchester United's.

United were at the forefront of the 1955-56 Championship race right from the start, though it wasn't until around Christmas that the rest of the First Division felt their real power. They went to the top of the table in early December when they beat Sunderland 2–1 at Old Trafford. They lost only twice in the second half of the season. They clinched the title with two games to spare by beating their closest rivals, Blackpool, 2–1. They were a goal down at half-time and it looked possible that they would suffer their first home defeat of the season, but goals from Johnny Berry, representing the old guard, and Tommy Taylor, the comparative newcomer, saw them home.

Taylor's 25 goals were backed by 20 from Viollet and nine from Pegg. United's 11-point margin from Blackpool at the top of the table equalled the record shared in the previous century by Preston, Sunderland and Aston Villa.

All but three of the team had been nurtured as home-produced players. As Jimmy Murphy would say: 'As ye sow . . . so shall ye reap.'

Busby summed up: 'From the very start I had envisaged making my own players, having a kind of nursery so that they could be trained in the kind of pattern I was trying to create for Manchester United.'

The League champions were now in peak form and they won the title again the following season, this time romping home eight points in front of Spurs. The team had settled down to read:

Wood, Foulkes, Byrne, Colman, Jones, Edwards, Berry, Whelan, Taylor, Viollet, Pegg.

There was one other notable player who began to crop up in this season, playing whenever Taylor or Viollet was injured, another home-produced starlet, Bobby Charlton. Making his debut at Charlton Athletic in October, he scored twice in a 4–2 win. Altogether that season he made 14 League appearances, scoring ten goals. Clearly he was a youngster with a great future, as events subsequently bore out.

It was a high-scoring season, with United's goals topping the ton thanks to Charlton's youthful contribution, plus 16 from Dennis Viollet, 22 from Tommy Taylor and an outstanding 26 from Billy Whelan.

Billy, or back home in Dublin, Liam, was a ball-playing inside-forward, very gifted and a surprisingly good marksman for one whose main job was to create for others. But then most of this talented team were good all-rounders and Whelan was at the peak of his powers. He had joined the club as a youngster from Home Farm, the Irish team which served United well over the

Matt Busby leads out Manchester United for the final of the 1957 FA Cup at Wembley against Aston Villa. Roger Byrne follows him as captain of the team labelled the Busby Babes in tribute to their youth and precocious talent which had already earned them the championship. It was a team which had already taken Europe by storm, reaching the semi-finals of the European Cup in the first season in the competition

Below left: Manchester United's goalkeeper Ray Wood lies clutching his broken face watched by anxious team-mates. Jackie Blanchflower took over in goal, but though United fought bravely they couldn't prevent Aston Villa emerging 2–1 winners with the villain of the piece, Peter McParland, scoring Villa's two goals

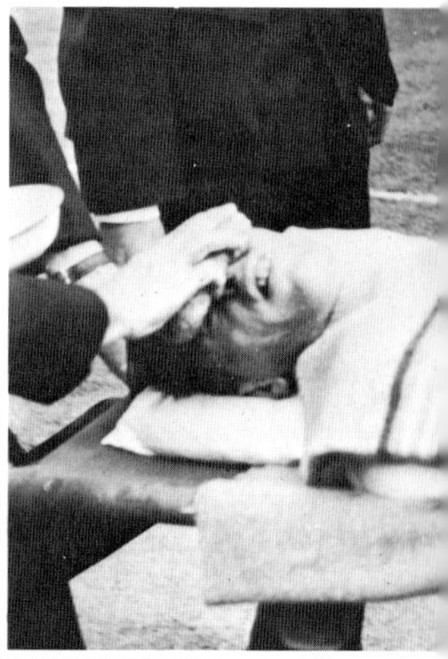

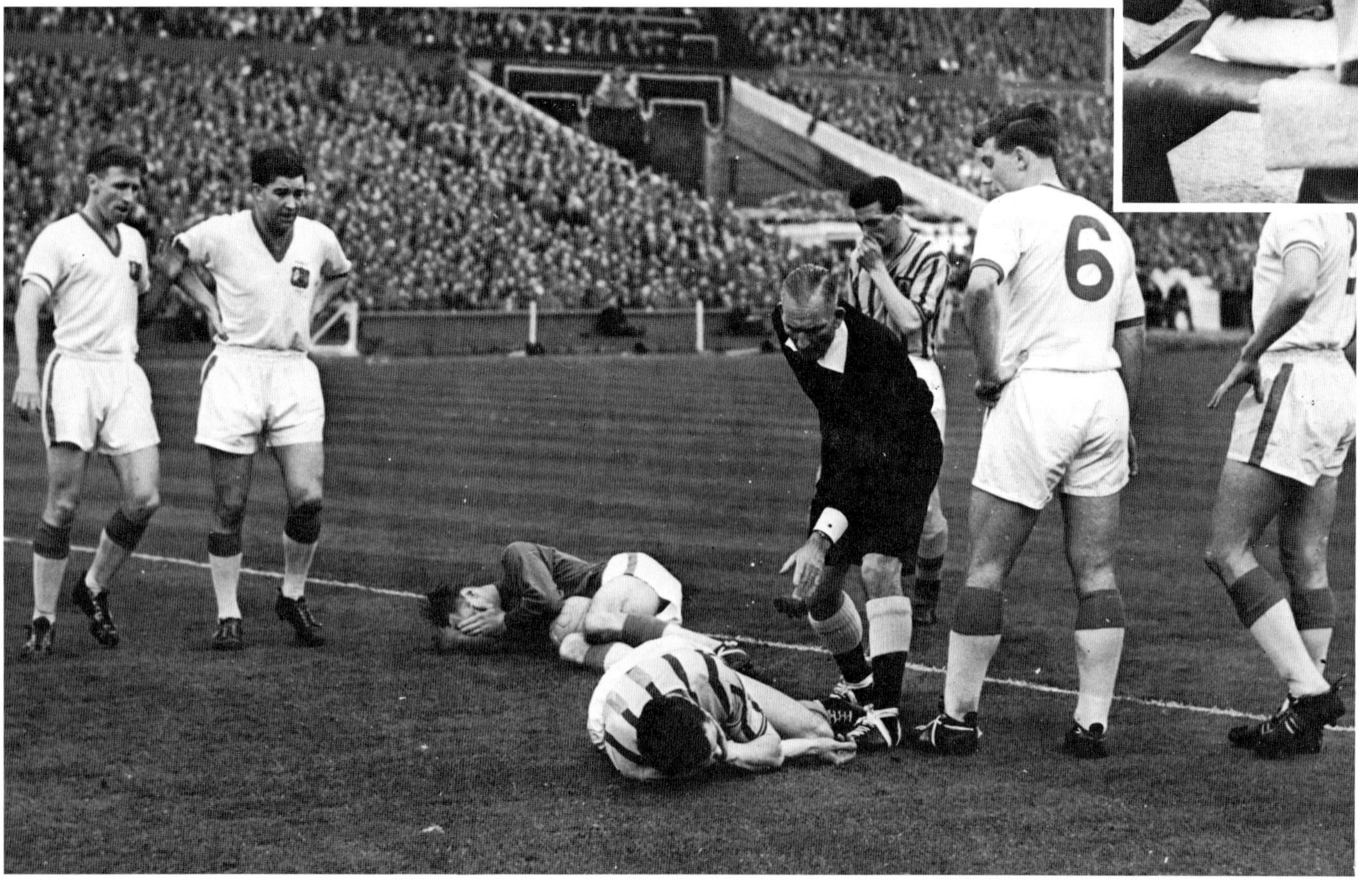

Above: Ray Wood, his cheekbone shattered by Peter McParland, is taken off on a stretcher at Wembley. The injury also shattered Matt Busby's dreams of a League and FA Cup double. The manager, with the 1957 championship already won, said later that on the morning of the Cup final against Aston Villa he had come downstairs at the team hotel never more certain of anything in football than that Manchester United would complete the double . . . but that of course had not taken into account the injury to his goalkeeper in the days before substitutes were allowed

years. In four seasons at Old Trafford before the crash he played 96 League and Cup games for a total of 52 goals. He won four Republic of Ireland caps, and was a player with immaculate control.

United were named as League champions by Easter. Busby rang the changes for the following match because of Cup commitments and he played seven reserves. The Football League could hardly complain because United won 2–0 with a goal from Alex Dawson on his debut and another from Colin Webster. To illustrate the club's great strength in depth, the 'reserve' side made up mostly of youth team players won 3–1 at Burnley on the same day.

United's final points total of 64 was the highest for 26 years.

The 1956-57 season was notable not only for winning the Championship for the second successive season. The Busby Babes were also flying high in the FA Cup as well as storming along in the European Cup. In the FA Cup they went to Wembley and came within an ace of achieving the elusive League and FA Cup double. Matt Busby says now that when he came downstairs on the morning of the final against Aston Villa he had never been more sure of victory before in his football life. The Championship was already in the bag, and the form book pointed only one way for the winner at Wembley. But just six minutes into the match goalkeeper Ray Wood was carried off the field suffering from a smashed cheekbone. Peter McParland had headed the ball into Wood's arms and it seemed a routine matter for the goalkeeper to kick it clear. But McParland, perhaps fired up for the final, kept on coming to crash into the United man. Even allowing for the fact that in those days goalkeepers did not enjoy the kind of protection they get now from referees, it was an outrageous charge, and in 1957 there were no substitutes.

Jackie Blanchflower took over in goal and, with the rest of the defence, performed heroically to keep the game goalless at the interval. Ray Wood bravely returned to the field for spells at outside-right, but could not do much and the team's pattern had been destroyed, even though Tommy Taylor managed to score with a fine header.

At half-time physiotherapist Ted Dalton took Wood to the back of the stadium and tested him with a few shots and throwing the ball at him, but, as Busby reports: 'Poor Ray saw no more than a couple out of every six balls sent to him.'

McParland the villain then became Villa's hero by scoring two second-half goals for a 2–1 victory. Towards the end Busby sent the dazed Wood back into goal in a desperate gamble to pull the game out of the fire. The players responded by giving a tantalising glimpse of what might have been but for the injury to their goalkeeper, but Wood was really in no condition to play. It was rough, tough luck for United, and the incident helped bring in the substitute rule, but that was little consolation at the time as the dream of the double collapsed.

There was no denying that Manchester United in 1957 were the outstanding team in the country, playing some majestic football and so young that they were only on the threshold of their full potential. At home and in Europe they had covered themselves in glory and there was a tremendous expectation and excitement as they readied themselves for another treble bid in season 1957-58. But all these hopes were to come crashing to the ground in the February snow and ice in what was to be one of the saddest seasons in English football history.

BEA
BEA

Munich: End of a dream

Players, officials and journalists prepare to board the BEA Elizabethan which was to crash at Munich. The aircraft stopped at the snowbound German airport to refuel as the party made its way back to England from Yugoslavia.

Friday, 7 February 1958 and the cold light of dawn reveals the horror of Munich. In the foreground the shredded tail of the aircraft is almost unrecognisable. This part of the Elizabethan had struck a house, setting it on fire. The occupant, Anna Winkler, rescued her children by throwing them out of a window into the deep snow. In the centre background is the main body of the aircraft

The team Matt Busby had built from the club's successful youth policy seemed destined to dominate football for many years. Such was the power of the Babes that they seemed invincible. The average age of the side which won the Championship in 1955-56 was just 22, the youngest ever to achieve such a feat. A year later, when they were Champions again, nothing, it seemed, would prevent the young braves of Manchester United from reigning supreme for the next decade.

United had taken their first steps into European football in defiance of the football authorities and it was on foreign soil that the final chapter in the story of the Babes was to be written. The aircraft carrying the United party back from a victorious visit to Yugoslavia crashed in the snow of Munich airport and the Babes were no more.

The young Champions flew out of Manchester to face Red Star Belgrade remembering the cheers of 63,000 intoxicated football fans. Five days before Munich, United had played Arsenal at Highbury and thrilled all those who witnessed that game with a display of the attacking football that they had made their trademark. Nine goals were scored . . . four by Arsenal, five by United.

That game, on Saturday, 1 February 1958, had typified the Busby Babes. They played with such flair and enthusiasm that they thought nothing of conceding four goals in their efforts to score five. United were trying to win the League Championship for the third successive season and by then had already reached the fifth round of the FA Cup.

To set the scene for the tragedy which was to shock football, let us consider how the 1957-58 season led up to a symbolic game with Arsenal and the fateful journey to Yugoslavia. For United, the season had started well, victories over Leicester at Filbert Street, then Everton and Manchester City at Old Trafford being the perfect launch towards the title. Their scoring record was remarkable with 22 goals coming in the opening six games. Yet when they lost for the first time it was not by just an odd goal, but by 4–0 at Burnden Park, where Bolton Wanderers ran rampant in front of a crowd of 48,003.

As 1957 drew to an end the Babes lost 1–0 to Chelsea at Old Trafford, then picked themselves up to beat luckless Leicester 4–0. On Christmas Day goals from Charlton, Edwards and Taylor secured two points against Luton in Manchester. On Boxing Day they met Luton again at Kenilworth Road and drew 2–2 and two days later the 'derby' game with Manchester City ended in the same scoreline at Maine Road. A crowd of 70,483 watched that game as the old rivals battled for pride as well as points.

As the European Cup-tie with Red Star approached, the side also made progress in the FA Cup with a 3–1 win at Workington and a 2–0 victory over Ipswich at Old Trafford to see them through to the fifth round, where they were to meet Sheffield Wednesday.

But the third target for Matt Busby, success in Europe, was perhaps the greatest. In 1956 United had become the first English club to compete in the European Champions' Cup, falling at the semi-final to the might of Real Madrid, winners of the trophy in the competition's first five years.

That year, the European seed had been sown. Manchester had witnessed the skills of di Stefano, Kopa and Gento, had seen United score ten times against Belgian club Anderlecht, then hang on against Borussia Dortmund before a remarkable quarter-final against Atletico Bilbao. In this match the Babes defied the odds by turning a 5–3 deficit from the first leg into a 6–5 victory, with goals from Taylor, Viollet and Johnny Berry, to win the right to challenge Real Madrid in the penultimate round.

That was where the run ended, but when United qualified to enter the European competition again in the 1957–58 season it was clear where the club's priorities lay. Matt Busby wanted a side which was good enough to win everything. The FA Cup had been snatched out of his grasp because of an injury to goalkeeper Ray Wood in the 1957 final, but his Babes were capable of reaching Wembley once again, and having secured the League Championship in

1956 and 1957 they could certainly emulate the great sides of pre-war Huddersfield Town and Arsenal and win it for a third successive time.

United's second European campaign saw them stride over Shamrock Rovers before beating Dukla Prague 3–1 on aggregate to reach the quarter-final against Red Star.

The Yugoslavs came to Manchester on 14 January 1958, and played a United side which was smarting from a 1–1 draw at Elland Road against Leeds United, who had been beaten 5–0 at Old Trafford earlier in the season.

Bobby Charlton and Eddie Colman scored the goals which gave United the edge in a 2–1 first-leg victory over Red Star, but it would be close in Belgrade. The run-up to the second leg was encouraging. A 7–2 win over Bolton, with goals from Bobby Charlton (3), Dennis Viollet (2), Duncan Edwards and Albert Scanlon, was just the result United needed before visiting Highbury, then leaving on the tiring journey behind the Iron Curtain.

The great match at Highbury

The United side which faced Arsenal was the eleven which was to line up against Red Star four days later. With Irish international Harry Gregg, a new signing, in goal, United were without some of their regulars. Jackie Blanchflower, the centre-half who had replaced Ray Wood in goal in the FA Cup final, was missing from the side along with wingers David Pegg and Johnny Berry and the creative inside-forward Liam Whelan, all of whom were being rested by Busby.

The two full-backs were Bill Foulkes and captain Roger Byrne, with the half-back line of Eddie Colman, Mark Jones and Duncan Edwards supporting the forward line of Ken Morgans, Bobby Charlton, Tommy Taylor, Dennis Viollet and Albert Scanlon.

Jack Kelsey was in goal for the Gunners and he was first to feel the power of United. Only ten minutes had gone when Dennis Viollet laid off a pass to an advancing Duncan Edwards who struck the ball with such ferocity that it was past Kelsey and in the net despite the efforts of the Welsh international. The goal was typical of Edwards. His power and strength had become a hallmark of his game despite his youth. Duncan was just 21, yet had played for England 18 times and represented his country at every level. In his short career with United he played 151 games and that first goal on that February afternoon was his 19th and final League strike.

Arsenal fought back, urged on by the huge crowd, and it took a superb save by Gregg to prevent them from equalising. He somehow kept out a certain scoring chance by grabbing the ball just under the crossbar and his clearance led to United's second. The ball was pushed out to Albert Scanlon on the left wing and he ran virtually the full length of the field before crossing. Two Arsenal defenders had been drawn into the corner by the United winger and his centre found Bobby Charlton running into the penalty area from the right. Charlton's shot was unstoppable and all Kelsey could do was throw up both arms in a token gesture as he dived to his right, but the shot was past him and the young Charlton was turning to celebrate the Babes' 2–0 lead.

By half-time it was 3–0, and again Scanlon's speed had played its part. The winger broke down the left, rounded Arsenal right-back Stan Charlton and crossed to the far side of the pitch where right-winger Kenny Morgans met the cross and chipped the ball back into the penalty area. England centre-forward Tommy Taylor scored his 111th goal in the First Division after five seasons with United.

United seemed to be on their way to a comfortable victory, ready to take four points away from the London club following a 4–2 win in Manchester earlier in the season. High-scoring clashes between the two seemed commonplace, United having beaten Arsenal 6–2 on their way to the 1956-57 Championship. Was this to be another massive victory for the Babes?

For 15 minutes of the second half there was no further score, then Arsenal took heart when David Herd, later to be a United player, broke through and hit a fierce shot at Gregg's goal. The big Irishman tried to keep the ball out but Herd's power and accuracy beat him. It was 3–1 with half an hour remaining.

Within two minutes the scores were level as Arsenal staged a sensational fight back. Wing-half Dave Bowen was the man driving Arsenal forward. It was from his cross that Herd had got the first of the home side's goals and he was involved in the move which led to the second

Above: Action from the Babes' last game as Dennis Viollet (left) and Tommy Taylor attack the Arsenal goal. Jack Kelsey in the Gunners' goal runs to his left to cover as Dennis Evans, his full-back, glances the ball towards Jim Fotheringham his centre half. On the far left of the picture is United winger Ken Morgans, and in the background referee G. W. Pullin from Bristol

Above right: The flying Albert Scanlon, the speedy winger who had just begun to establish himself in the side when he was injured in the air crash. He returned to play in every League game the following season in the position previously filled by his uncle Charlie Mitten. In 1960 he was transferred to Newcastle, and ended his career at Mansfield in 1965 after a spell with Lincoln City

Left: A gymnasium training session for wingers Johnny Berry (left) and David Pegg as they prepare for a cup-tie. Berry suffered serious head injuries in the air crash which ended his career and Pegg was killed

Above: Duncan Edwards spreads his arms to appeal for a goal-kick as 'keeper Harry Gregg goes down to cover this Arsenal scoring attempt. Racing back to cover are Bill Foulkes and Mark Jones while on the far left captain Roger Byrne looks on

Arsenal strike. Vic Groves jumped above the United defence to head down a cross from Gordon Nutt which fell to Jimmy Bloomfield, who scored. It was Nutt again who made the pass to Bloomfield some 60 seconds later for the London-born striker to dive full length and head home a magnificent goal which turned Highbury into a deafening stage for the final drama.

No scriptwriter could have dreamt up the plot for the last chapter of the Babes' challenge for Football League supremacy. No-one in that arena knew that they were witnessing the last magnificent demonstration of sheer genius which had taken English – and to a certain extent European – football apart in that decade. Under Busby the Babes had created a new style, a game that was refreshing, flowing, entertaining, and a game which was putting England back on the map after falling to the skills of the Hungarians and the Brazilians in the early and mid-1950s.

Would United collapse under the Arsenal onslaught? Lesser teams would have been forgiven if they had defended in depth to hold out for a draw, having seen a three-goal lead disintegrate, but Manchester United went all out in search of more goals, and got them.

The speed of Scanlon and the skill of young Charlton combined to give Dennis Viollet a goal. The Manchester supporters screamed their delight, and were in raptures a few minutes later when Kelsey had to retrieve the ball from his goal for a fifth time, after Eddie Colman had found Morgans with a precise pass and Tommy Taylor had scored his last goal.

Yet even then this magnificent game had not ended. Derek Tapscott ran through the centre of United's near exhausted defence to put Arsenal within one goal of United again. But it was the final goal of the afternoon. The referee blew for time and the players collapsed into one another's arms. United, their white shirts mud-spattered and clinging to their breathless bodies, shook hands with the opposition and each other. Supporters on the terraces embraced one another as a reaction to the sheer enjoyment of the game, and the massive crowd left the stadium with a feeling that they had witnessed something unique in football.

Fate had decided that for fans at home this game would be the epitaph to those young heroes of Manchester. In the weeks which were to follow many words would be written about the greatness of Busby's Babes and in the years which have passed since the Munich air disaster they have become legendary characters, but that

5–4 scoreline, in a game played with all the passion and creative expression those tens of thousands had watched, said all that needed to be said as far as the ordinary football fans were concerned. They knew they had seen something special in Busby's young cavaliers.

The fatal European Cup trip

After that symbolic game, all thoughts were now on Europe. Could United hold on to that slender lead from the first leg? For the supporters left behind it seemed a narrow margin, but they had faith in those young players – after all had they not proved themselves time and again in similar circumstances?

For the players the damp, grey smog of Manchester's winter was replaced by the fresh crispness of mid-Europe. They had seen snow on their journey to the Yugoslav capital yet they had been welcomed with warmth by the people of Belgrade who understood the greatness of Manchester United in the common language of football.

It was time for the game and as the two sides lined up in the stadium the roar of thousands of Yugoslav voices rang in the ears of the Babes. Cameras clicked as last-minute photographs were taken, and above the players in the press area British journalists filed stories which were to be read in England the following morning.

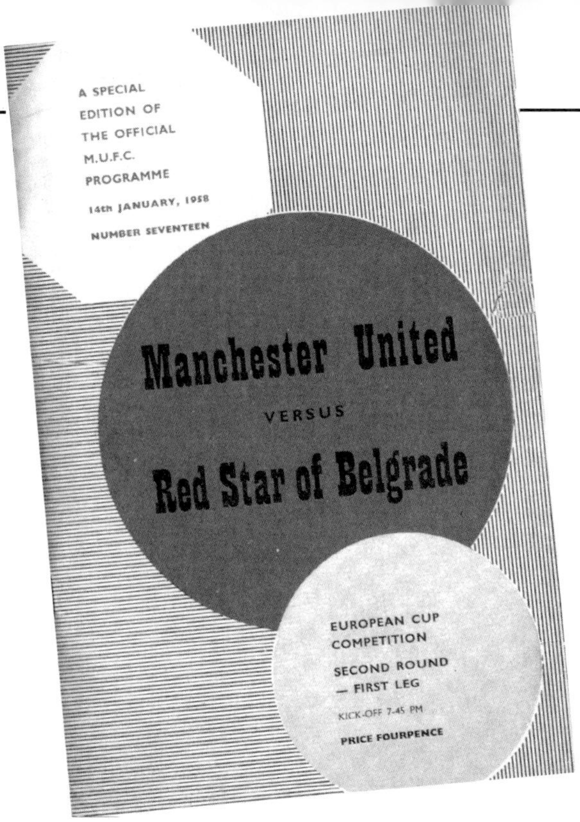
A SPECIAL
EDITION OF
THE OFFICIAL
M.U.F.C.
PROGRAMME
14th JANUARY, 1958
NUMBER SEVENTEEN
Manchester United
VERSUS
Red Star of Belgrade
EUROPEAN CUP
COMPETITION
SECOND ROUND
— FIRST LEG
KICK-OFF 7-45 PM
PRICE FOURPENCE

Above: Over 60,000 copies of this programme were sold as Red Star of Belgrade came to Old Trafford for the first leg of the European Cup quarter-final in 1958. United won the game 2–1 thanks to goals from Bobby Charlton and Eddie Colman

Among them was Frank Swift, a giant of a man who had kept goal for Manchester City and England, and who had a reputation of being **the** gentle giant. Big 'Swifty' had retired from the game and taken a job as a sportswriter with the *News of the World*, and his role in Belgrade was to write a column for the following Sunday edition.

The final team talk. Matt Busby chats to his players following their pre-match meal in Belgrade, shortly before the Red Star game. Listening to his words Bert Whalley rests an arm on the shoulder of Tommy Taylor as next to him stand Jackie Blanchflower and Duncan Edwards. Seated right is Dennis Viollet and in the foreground Bobby Charlton (right) and Ken Morgans

The last line-up in Belgrade. 5 February, 1958 and the Busby Babes are ready for their final game. Left to right: Duncan Edwards, Eddie Colman, Mark Jones, Ken Morgans, Bobby Charlton, Dennis Viollet, Tommy Taylor, Bill Foulkes, Harry Gregg, Albert Scanlon, and captain Roger Byrne who leans forward to shout encouragement to his colleagues before the European cup tie

Frank had played in the same Manchester City side as Matt Busby and was a team-mate of the United manager when City won the FA Cup in 1934. The big goalkeeper had made headline news in that game when, aged just 19, he had fainted as the final whistle was blown, overcome with the emotion of such an occasion. Perhaps he, more than any other spectator, understood the feelings of the young players as they stood together for the last moments before the start of the game.

Also looking out from that crowded press box were journalists who had travelled to Europe for each of United's previous games: Tom Jackson of the *Manchester Evening News* and his close friend and rival Alf Clarke of the now defunct *Manchester Evening Chronicle*. Both men loved Manchester United and lived to see their every game. Alf Clarke had been on United's books as an amateur, and was with the club before Matt Busby arrived to rebuild it after the war.

Because Manchester was a printing centre for the northern editions of the national newspapers, and also because of the tremendous popularity of the United side, most other daily newspapers were represented.

From the *Daily Mirror* was Archie Ledbrooke, who had only just made the trip having been on the point of being replaced by Frank McGhee because he (Ledbrooke) had still to complete an outstanding feature only hours before the flight had left England. Others included Eric Thompson from the *Daily Mail*, George Follows of the *Daily Herald* – the daily newspaper which was succeeded by *The Sun* following its closure – Don Davies of the *Manchester Guardian*, Henry Rose of the *Daily Express* and Frank Taylor from the *News Chronicle*, another publication which has since gone out of existence.

Don Davies wrote under the pen-name of 'Old International' and had been in the England amateur side which played Wales in 1914, having been a member of the famous Northern Nomads side. On 5 February 1958 this is the story Davies filed back to the *Manchester Guardian* office in Cross Street, Manchester:

> Who would be a weather prophet? At Belgrade today in warm sunshine and on a grass pitch where the last remnants of melting snow produced the effect of an English lawn flecked with daisies, Red Star and Manchester United began a battle of wits and courage and rugged tackling in the second leg of their quarter-final of the European Cup competition. It ended in a draw 3–3, but as United had already won the first leg at Old Trafford by 2–1 they thus gained the right to pass into the semi-final round of the competition for the second year in succession on a 5–4 aggregate.
>
> Much to the relief of the English party and to the consternation of the 52,000 home spectators, Viollet had the ball in the net past a dumbfounded Beara in ninety seconds. It was a beautifully taken goal – a characteristic effort by that player – but rather lucky in the way a rebound had run out in United's favour. But, as Jones remarked, 'You need luck at this game'; and he might have added, 'a suit of chain mail also would not have come amiss'. A second goal almost came fourteen minutes later, delightfully taken by Charlton after a corner kick by Scanlon had been headed by Viollet, but this was disallowed, because of offside, by the Austrian referee whose performance on the whistle so far had assumed the proportions of a flute obligato. That was due to the frequency which fouls were being committed by both sides after Sekularac had set the fashion in shabbiness by stabbing Morgans on the knee.
>
> But in spite of many stops and starts events in the first half ran smoothly for United, on whose behalf Taylor led his line like a true Hotspur from centre-forward. Other factors telling strongly in Manchester's favour at this time were the clean hands and sound judgement of Gregg in goal.
>
> Further success for United was impending. Charlton this time was the chosen instrument. Dispossessing Kostic about forty yards from goal, this gifted boy leaned brilliantly into his stride, made ground rapidly for about ten yards, and then beat the finest goalkeeper on the Continent with a shot of tremendous power and superb placing. There, one thought, surely goes England's Bloomer of the future. Further evidence of Charlton's claim to that distinction was to emerge two minutes later. A smartly taken free kick got the Red Star defence into a real tangle. Edwards fastened on the ball and did his best to oblige his colleagues and supporters by bursting it (a feat, by the way, which he was to achieve later), but he muffed his kick this time and the ball rolled to Charlton, apparently lost in a thicket of Red Star defenders. Stalemate

surely. But not with Charlton about. His quick eye detected the one sure route through the circle of legs; his trusty foot drove the ball unerringly along it. 3–0 on the day: 5–1 on the aggregate. Nice going.

As was natural, the Red Star players completely lost their poise for a while. Their forwards flung themselves heatedly against a defence as firm and steady as a rock; even Sekularac, after a bright beginning in which he showed his undoubted skill, lost heart visibly and stumbled repeatedly. Nevertheless there was an upsurge of the old fighting spirit when Kostic scored a fine goal for Red Star two minutes after half time. It ought to have been followed by another one only three minutes later when Sekularac placed the ball perfectly for Cotic. Cotic's terrific shot cleared the bar by a foot – no more. Next, a curious mix-up by Foulkes and Tasic, Red Star's centre-forward, ended in Foulkes falling flat on top of Tasic and blotting him completely out of view. According to Foulkes, Tasic lost his footing, fell over, and pulled Foulkes over with him. But it looked bad and the whistle blew at once with attendant gestures indicating a penalty. Tasic had the satisfaction of converting that one, although his shot only just evaded Gregg's finger tips.

The score was now 3–2 and the crowd broke into an uncontrolled frenzy of jubilation and excitement. So much so that when Cotic failed to walk the ball into a completely unprotected goal – Gregg was lying hurt and helpless on the ground – a miniature repetition of the Bolton disaster seemed to occur at one corner of the arena.

Down the terraces streamed a wild horde of excited spectators who hung limply along the concrete walls with the breath crushed out of their bodies, if indeed nothing else had befallen them.

A quarter of an hour from the end Red Star, with their confidence and self-respect restored, were wheeling and curvetting, passing and shooting in their best style, and the United's defenders had to fight their way out of a regular nightmare of desperate situations. It was significant hereabouts that United's inside forwards were not coming back to chase the ball as they had done so effectively in the first half and this, of course, threw added pressure on the rearguard. As soon as this fault was rectified the Red Star attacks, though frequent enough, lost something of their sting. In fact, United began to pile on the pressure at the other end and once Morgans struck a post with a glorious shot.

The furious pace never slackened, and as England's champions tried to find their flowing, attacking play of the first half, they were pelted by a storm of snowballs. Two minutes from time Harry Gregg came racing out of his goal, and hurled himself full length at Zebec's feet. He grasped it safely, but the impetus of his rush took him outside the penalty area with the ball, and Red Star had a free kick some twenty yards out.

Kostic watched Gregg position himself by the far post, protected by a wall of United players. There was just a narrow ray of light, a gap, by the near post, and precision player Kostic threaded the ball through as Gregg catapulted himself across his goal. Too late. The ball eluded his grasping fingers, and hit the back of the net. The score was 3–3.

It had always been Davies's ambition to be a football writer. For most of his life he had worked as an education officer with a Manchester engineering firm, but after it was suggested that he should try his hand at journalism he had been taken onto the *Guardian* staff when the editor saw a report of a fictitious match. It was the key he needed to open the door to a career of full-time writing. His style was that of the essayist, ideally suited to the *Manchester Guardian*, and contrasting totally with that of Henry Rose, the most popular daily writer of that time – certainly with the Old Trafford supporters.

Rose saw the game from the same vantage point as Davies, yet his description was totally different:

Red Star 3 Manchester United 3
Star Rating ***

Manchester United survived the Battle of Belgrade here this afternoon and added another shining page to their glittering history by drawing 3–3 with Red Star and winning the two-leg tie 5–4.

They had to fight not only eleven desperate footballers and a fiercely partisan 52,000 crowd, but some decisions of Austrian referee Karl Kainer that were double-Dutch to me. I have never witnessed such a one-sided exhibition by any official at home or abroad.

The climax of Herr Kainer's interpretations, which helped inflame the crowd against United, came in the 55th minute when he gave a penalty against Foulkes, United's star defender. Nothing is wrong with my eyesight – and Foulkes confirmed what I saw . . . that a Red Star player slipped and pulled the United man back down with him. A joke of a ruling it would have been had not Tasic scored from the spot.

Later in his report, Rose wrote:

Gregg was hurt, Morgans and Edwards were limping; Byrne was warned for wasting time. United players were penalised for harmless-looking tackles.

I thought Herr Kainer would have given a free-kick against United when one of the ballboys fell on his backside!

He described the United side as:

Heroes all. None greater than Billy Foulkes. None greater than Bobby Charlton, who has now scored twelve goals in the eleven games he has played since he went into the side at inside-right on 21 December. But all eleven played a noble part in this memorable battle.

The game over and the work completed, it was time to relax, and the party of journalists joined the United officials, players and their opposite numbers from the Red Star club at a banquet in the Majestic Hotel in Belgrade. It was a friendly affair, despite the disappointment felt by the host club at losing such an important game. There was a great friendship between the clubs in those early years of the European competition.

Roger Byrne, captain of the Busby Babes. The England full-back would have learned on his return home that he was to be a father. His wife was preparing to break the good news to Roger when she heard about the air-crash. Years later the son Roger never saw was one of the team of ball-boys at Old Trafford

Two young men drink to the future . . . Duncan Edwards (left) survived the air crash but died two weeks later from his injuries. The laughing Tommy Taylor was killed instantly and Manchester United and England had lost two great players

In a moving scene the meal ended when waiters entered the dining room carrying trays of sweetmeats lit by candles set in ice. The United party stood to applaud the skill of the Yugoslav chef, and Roger Byrne led his colleagues in song:

> We'll meet again,
> Don't know where, don't know when,
> But we know we'll meet again
> some sunny day. . . .

That scene was remembered clearly by Yugoslav writer Miro Radojcic in an article for his newspaper *Politika*, which he translated into English 20 years later for Geoffrey Green, and which was published in *There's Only One United* (Hodder and Stoughton, 1978). Part of it read:

> Then followed the simple warm-hearted words of Matt Busby and Walter Crickmer as they said: 'Come and visit us, the doors of Old Trafford will always be open to you' . . . and after that lovely, crazy night as I parted from 'Old International' – Don Davies from the *Manchester Guardian* – he said to me: 'Why didn't you score just one more goal then we could have met for a third time?

Radojcic sat up throughout most of the night musing over a feature article he planned to write for his newspaper. *Politika* was not a sporting publication – in fact he was a political writer – but he had a great love for football and the flair of Manchester United's young side attracted him.

After chatting and drinking with Tommy Taylor and Duncan Edwards in a bar named Skadarija, Radojcic was left alone with his thoughts. He decided that he would arrange to fly back to Manchester with the team, and write his story from the Manchester angle, a look at England's top team seen through the eyes of one of Yugoslavia's most celebrated journalists.

The players had gone off to bed when Radojcic came to his decision so he went back to his flat, packed a bag and made his way to the airport only to discover that he had left his passport at home. He asked the airport authorities to hold the aircraft for as long as possible while he took a return taxi trip back to his hime. By the time he got back with his passport the twin-engined Elizabethan had taken off, bound for England via Munich where it was to stop to re-fuel.

The tragedy at Munich airport

Those on board were in a relaxed mood when the plane landed on German soil. They had played cards, chatted over the latest news, read any books and magazines which were around and passed the time away as best they could. There was the usual air of nervous apprehension about the flight, but card schools and conversation hid any fears of flying and some even managed to catch up on lost sleep rather than gaze out on the snowscape below.

By around 2 pm G-ALZU AS 57 was ready once more for take-off with Captain Kenneth Rayment, the second in command, at the controls. The man in charge, Captain James Thain, had flown the plane out to Belgrade, and his close friend and colleague was now taking the 'Lord Burleigh' home again.

At 2.31 pm the aircraft control tower was told that '609 Zulu Uniform is rolling' and Captain Thain later described what happened:

> Ken opened the throttles which were between us and when they were fully open I tapped his hand and held the throttles in the fully open position. Ken moved his hand and I called for 'full power'. The engines sounded an uneven note as the aircraft accelerated and the needle on the port pressure gauge started to fluctuate. I felt a pain in my hand as Ken pulled the throttles back and said: 'Abandon take-off'. I held the control column fully forward while Ken put on the brakes. Within 40 seconds of the start of its run the aircraft was almost at a halt again.

The cause of the problem had been boost surging – a very rich mixture of fuel causing the engines to over-accelerate – a fault which was quite common in the Elizabethan. As the two men talked over the problem Captain Rayment decided that he would attempt a second take-off, this time opening the throttles gradually before releasing the brakes, and then moving to full power.

At 2.34 pm permission for a second take-off attempt was given by air traffic control and for a second time the plane came to a halt.

During their wait while the aircraft was being refuelled, the passengers had gone into a lounge for coffee. Now, after the two aborted attempts to take off, the party was in the lounge once more. It had begun to snow quite heavily. Full-back Bill Foulkes remembers:

> We'd been playing cards for most of the flight from Belgrade to Munich, and I remember when we left the aircraft thinking how cold it was. We had one attempt at taking off, but didn't leave the ground, so I suppose a few of those on board would start to worry a little bit, and when the second take-off failed we were pretty quiet when we went back into the lounge.

Some of the players must have felt that they would not be flying home that afternoon. Duncan Edwards sent a telegram to his landlady back in Manchester: 'All flights cancelled returning home tomorrow'. The telegram was delivered at around 5 pm.

Bill Foulkes recalls how after a quarter of an hour delay the passengers were asked to board again but it was another five minutes before everyone was back in the aircraft.

> Alf Clarke from the *Evening Chronicle* had put a call through to his office and we had to wait for him to catch up with us. We got back into our seats, but we didn't play cards this time. . . . I slipped the pack into my jacket pocket and sat back waiting for take-off.

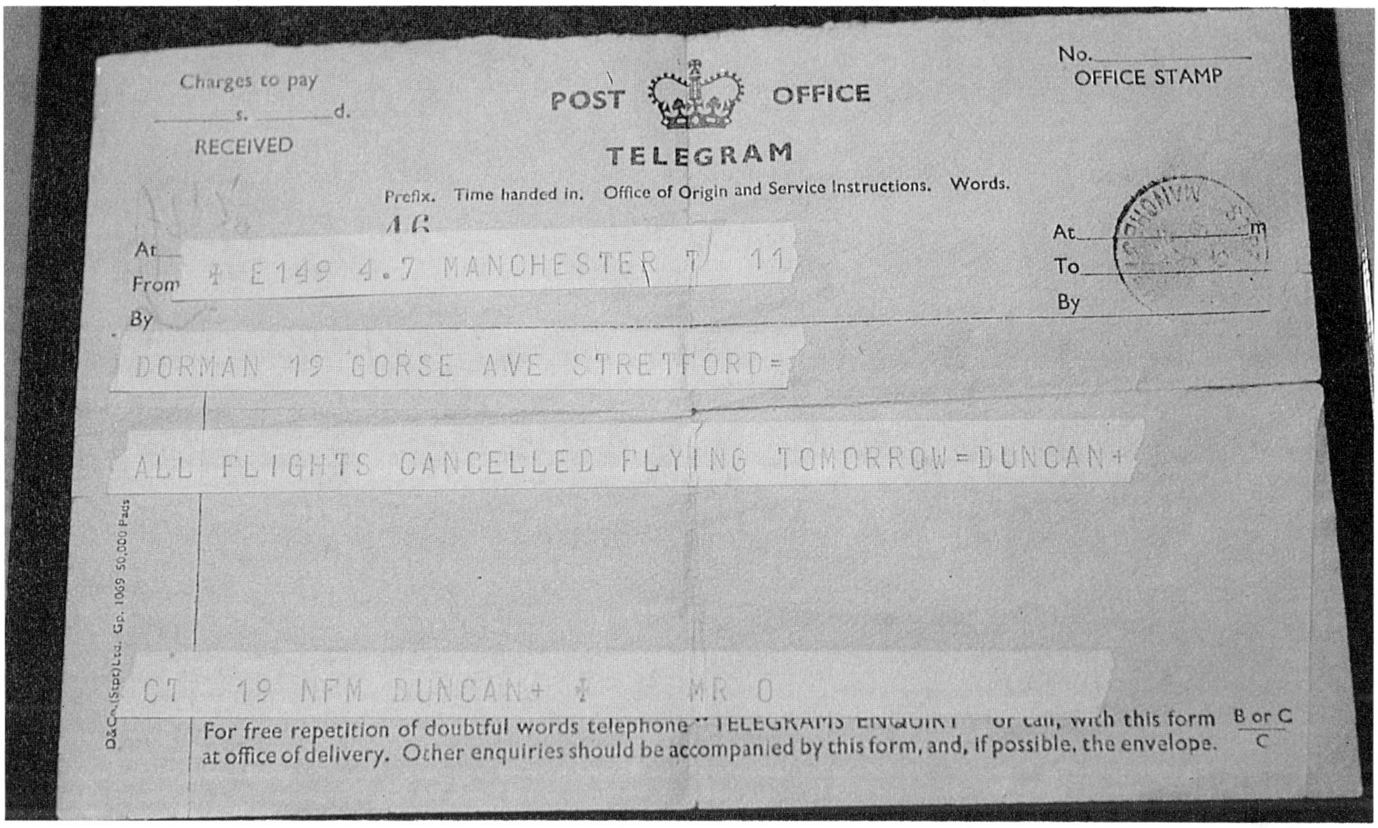

Charges to pay
s. d.
RECEIVED

POST OFFICE
TELEGRAM

No.
OFFICE STAMP

Prefix. Time handed in. Office of Origin and Service Instructions. Words.

At
From E149 4.7 MANCHESTER T 11
By

At
To
By

DORMAN 19 GORSE AVE STRETFORD=

ALL FLIGHTS CANCELLED FLYING TOMORROW=DUNCAN+

CT 19 NFM DUNCAN+ MR O

For free repetition of doubtful words telephone "TELEGRAMS ENQUIRY" or call, with this form at office of delivery. Other enquiries should be accompanied by this form, and, if possible, the envelope. B or C C

After the second unsuccessful take-off the players and journalists decided that it would be impossible to leave Munich until the next day. Duncan Edwards sent this telegram to his landlady back in Manchester telling her of the delay . . . but a third attempt at take-off was made. The telegram was delivered after the crash

I was sitting about half-way down the aircraft next to a window, on the right-hand side of the gangway. Our card school was Ken Morgans, who was on my right, and facing us David Pegg and Albert Scanlon. Matt Busby and Bert Whalley were sitting together on the seat behind us and I remember how Mark Jones, Tommy Taylor, Duncan Edwards and Eddie Colman were all at the back.

David Pegg got up and moved to the back: 'I don't like it here, it's not safe,' he said and went off to sit with the other players. I saw big Frank Swift back there too, he also felt that the rear was the safest place to be.

There was another card school across the gangway from us, Ray Wood and Jackie Blanchflower were sitting on two of the seats, Roger Byrne, Billy Whelan and Dennis Viollet on the others with one empty seat amongst them.

Back on the flight deck Captain Thain and Captain Rayment had discussed the problem they were having with the station engineer William Black, who had told them that the surging they were having was quite common at airports like Munich because of its altitude. At 3.03 pm 609 Zulu Uniform was rolling again. Captain Thain describes the next attempt at take-off:

I told Ken that if we got boost surging again, I would control the throttles. Ken opened them to 28 inches with the brakes on. The engines were both steady so he released the brakes and we moved forward again.

He continued to open the throttles and again I followed with my left hand until the levers were fully open. I tapped his hand and he moved it. He called 'Full power' and I checked the dials and said: 'Full power'.

Captain Thain again noticed that there was a sign of boost surging and called this out to Captain Rayment above the noise of the engines. The surging was controlled and the throttle pushed back until it was fully open:

I glanced at the air speed indicator and saw it registered 105 knots and was flickering. When it reached 117 knots I called out 'V1' [Velocity One, the point on the runway after which it isn't safe to abandon take-off]. Suddenly the needle dropped to about 112 and then 105. Ken shouted, 'Christ, we can't make it' and I looked up from the instruments to see a lot of snow and a house and a tree right in the path of the aircraft.

Inside the passengers' compartment Bill Foulkes had sensed that something was wrong:

There was a lot of slush flying past the windows and there was a terrible noise, like when a car leaves a smooth road and starts to run over rough ground.

The Elizabethan left the runway, went through a fence and crossed a road before the port wing struck a house. The wing and part of the tail were torn off and the house caught fire. The cockpit struck a tree and the starboard side of the fuselage hit a wooden hut containing a truck loaded with fuel and tyres. This exploded.

Bill Foulkes had crouched down in his seat after tightening his safety belt. He remembered afterwards a terrific bang, then after being unconscious for a few moments, seeing a gaping hole in front of him.

The back of the aircraft had just disappeared. I got out as quickly as I could and just ran and ran. Then I turned and realised that the plane wasn't going to explode, and I went back. In the distance I could see the tail part of the aircraft blazing and as I ran back I came across bodies. Roger Byrne still strapped to his seat, Bobby Charlton lying quite still in another seat, and Dennis Viollet. Then Harry Gregg appeared and we tried to see what we could do to help.

The two team-mates helped the injured. Matt Busby, badly hurt, was taken away on a stretcher, Bobby Charlton had walked over to Gregg and Foulkes and was helped into a mini-bus, sitting alongside Dennis Viollet in the front seats as other survivors were picked up. They were taken to the Rechts de Isar Hospital in Munich. It was the following day before the true horror of the air crash became evident to Bill Foulkes and Harry Gregg:

We went in and saw Matt in an oxygen tent, and Duncan Edwards, who seemed to be badly hurt. Bobby Charlton had a bandaged head, Jackie Blanchflower was nursing a badly gashed arm which had been strapped up by Harry Gregg in the snow of the night before. Albert Scanlon lay with his eyes closed, he had a fractured skull, and Dennis Viollet had a gashed head and facial injuries. Ray Wood's face was cut and he had concussion and Ken Morgans and Johnny Berry lay quite still in their beds. I spoke to a nurse and she told me that she thought Duncan had a better chance of making a full recovery than Johnny did. . . .

We came across Frank Taylor in another bed; he was the only journalist around and he asked if we'd like to have a beer with him. Like us, he didn't know the full implications of what had happened the afternoon before.

We were about to leave the hospital when I asked a nurse where we should go to see the other lads. She seemed puzzled so I asked her again: 'Where are the other survivors?' . . . 'Others? There are no others, they are all here.' It was only then that we knew the horror of Munich.

The Busby Babes were no more.

Roger Byrne, Geoff Bent, Mark Jones, David Pegg, Liam Whelan, Eddie Colman and Tommy Taylor had been killed instantly. Club secretary Walter Crickmer had also died, along with the first team trainer, Tom Curry, and coach Bert Whalley.

Duncan Edwards and Johnny Berry were critically injured and fighting for their lives, Matt Busby had suffered extensive injuries and was the only club official to survive the crash.

Eight of the nine sportswriters on board the aircraft had also perished: Alf Clarke, Don Davies, George Follows, Tom Jackson, Archie Ledbrooke, Henry Rose, Eric Thompson and the gentle giant, Frank Swift.

One of the aircrew had been killed, together

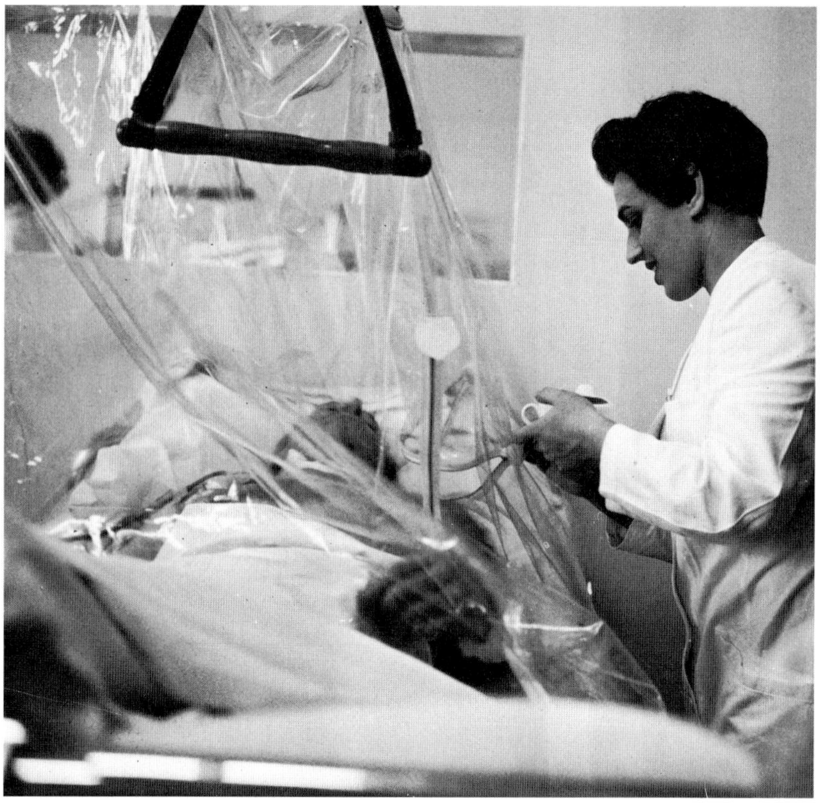

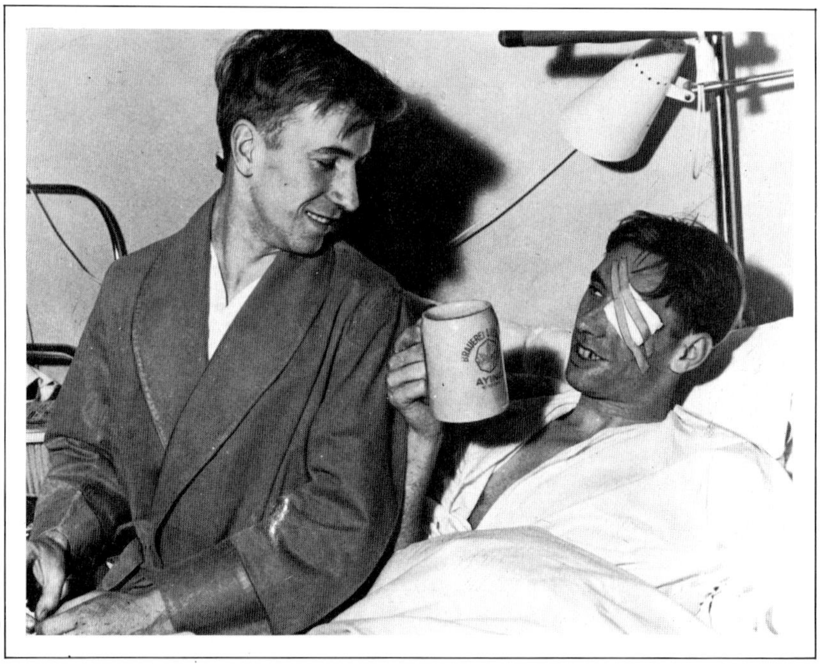

A last photograph of football writer Henry Rose (right), and Tommy Taylor as they share a moment together on the Elizabethan aircraft which crashed at Munich. Eight journalists died in the disaster, among them former England goalkeeper Frank Swift who was working as a correspondent for the *News of the World*

Matt Busby lies in an oxygen tent as he fights for his life in the Rechts der Isar Hospital. The United manager told Jimmy Murphy to keep the flag flying when his assistant visited him the day after the disaster

A youthful Bobby Charlton sits at the bedside of goalkeeper Ray Wood in the Rechts der Isar Hospital in Munich a few days after the crash.
Charlton was able to return home in time to play in the sixth round of the FA Cup on 1 March 1958, but Wood played just one more League game for United following Munich. Six weeks before the disaster he had lost his place to Harry Gregg and although Wood returned to Old Trafford in the weeks following the crash he was unable to win back his position and was transferred to Huddersfield Town

with two other passengers: the travel agent who had arranged the flight details, and a supporter who had flown out to watch the game. Nine players had survived, but two of them, Johnny Berry and Jackie Blanchflower – brother of Tottenham Hotspur's Danny – never played again.

Two photographers, the travel agent's wife, and two Yugoslav passengers, one with a young baby, had survived, together with Frank Taylor. On the afternoon of the crash 21 people had died, 18 had survived, of whom four were close to death.

Of those four, Duncan Edwards, Matt Busby, Johnny Berry and Captain Kenneth Rayment, two would survive. Three weeks after the aircrash which had become known simply as 'Munich', Duncan Edwards and Kenneth Rayment had lost their battle to live.

The news reaches Manchester

On the afternoon of the crash Alf Clarke had telephoned the *Evening Chronicle* sports desk to say that he thought the flight would be held up by the weather and made arrangements to return the following day. By three in the afternoon the paper had more or less 'gone to bed', and the final editions were leaving Withy Grove. In other parts of the city the daily newspaper staffs were beginning their routines. Reporters were heading out on diary jobs, sub-editors were looking through agency stories to see what was to form the backbone of the Friday morning editions.

That weekend United were to play League leaders Wolves at Old Trafford. Despite the long journey home it looked on form as if the Reds would close the four-point gap at the top of the table, putting them just one victory behind Billy Wright's side, and ready to increase their efforts for that third successive Championship. Could United emulate Huddersfield Town and Arsenal? Surely if they did it would be an even greater achievement than in those pre-war days. Saturday was coming round again. United would make the headlines.

Then on the teleprinter came an unbelievable message: 'Manchester United aircraft crashed on take off . . . heavy loss of life feared.'

The BBC interrupted its afternoon programming to broadcast a news flash. The football world listened to the words but few understood their meaning.

Jimmy Murphy, Matt Busby's wartime friend and now his assistant, was manager of the Welsh national side, and a World Cup qualifying game had coincided with the Red Star fixture. Murphy told Matt Busby that he would go to Yugoslavia rather than the game at Ninian Park, Cardiff, but his manager told him that his place was with the Welsh side.

'I always sat next to Matt on our European trips,' Murphy recalls, 'but I did what he said and let him go off to Red Star without me. Mind you, I've got to be honest – my mind was more on our game in Yugoslavia than the match I was watching. When I heard that we were through to the semi-final it was a great load off my mind; I didn't like not being there.'

He had just returned to Old Trafford from Wales when news of the aircrash reached him. Alma George, Matt Busby's secretary, told him that the charter flight had crashed. Murphy failed to react.

'She told me again. It still didn't sink in, then she started to cry. She said many people had been killed, she didn't know how many, but the players had died, some of the players. I couldn't believe it. The words seemed to ring in my head. Alma left me and I went into my office. My head was in a state of confusion and I started to cry.'

The following day Jimmy Murphy flew out to Munich and was stunned by what he saw: 'Matt was in an oxygen tent and he told me to "keep the flag flying". Duncan recognised me and spoke. It was a terrible, terrible time.'

Murphy was given the job of rebuilding. Life would go on despite the tragedy, and Manchester United would play again: 'I had no players, but I had a job to do.'

After the agency newsflash had reached the Manchester evening newspapers, extra editions were published. At first details were printed in the Stop Press. By 6 pm a special edition of the *Manchester Evening Chronicle* was on sale:

> About 28 people, including members of the Manchester United football team, club officials, and journalists are feared to have been killed when a BEA Elizabethan airliner crashed soon after take-off in a snowstorm at Munich airport this afternoon. It is understood there may be about 16 survivors. Four of them are crew members.

The newspaper, which was carrying Alf Clarke's match report and comments from the previous night's game, said on its front page: 'Alf Clarke was talking to the *Evening Chronicle* reporters in Manchester just after 2.30 pm when he said it was unlikely that the plane would be able to take off today.' Even though only three hours had elapsed since the crash the newspaper had a detailed report of how the disaster occurred.

Twenty-four hours later, as the whole of Europe reacted to the news of the tragedy, the *Evening Chronicle* listed the 21 dead on its front page under a headline: 'Matt fights for life: a 50-50 chance now'. There was a picture of Harry Gregg and Bill Foulkes at the bedside of Ken Morgans, and details of how the other injured were responding to treatment. The clouds of confusion had lifted – Munich had claimed 21 lives, 15 were injured and, of these, four players and Matt Busby were in a serious condition.

In the days following, Manchester mourned as the bodies of its famous footballing heroes were flown home to lie overnight in the gymnasium under the main grandstand before being passed on to relatives for the funerals. Today that gymnasium is the place where the players' lounge has been built, where those who succeeded the Babes gather after a game for a chat and a drink with the opposition.

Thousands of supporters turned out to pay their last respects. Where families requested that funerals should be private, the United followers stayed away from gravesides but lined the route to look on in tearful silence as corteges passed.

Cinema newsreels carried reports from Munich, and the game itself responded with memorial services, and silent grounds where supporters of every club stood, heads bowed, as referees indicated a period of silence by a blast on their whistles.

Desmond Hackett wrote a moving epitaph to Henry Rose, whose funeral was the biggest of all. A thousand taxi drivers offered their services free to anyone who was going to the funeral and there was a six-mile queue to Manchester's Southern Cemetery. The cortege halted for a moment outside the *Daily Express* offices in Great Ancoats Street where Hackett wrote in the style of Henry: 'Even the skies wept for Henry Rose today. . .'

Football returns to Old Trafford

Rival clubs offered helping hands to United. Liverpool and Nottingham Forest were first to respond by asking if they could do anything to assist. Football had suffered a terrible blow.

To give United a chance of surviving in football the FA waived its rule which 'cup-ties' a player once he has played in an FA Cup round in any particular season. The rule prevents him from playing for another club in the same competition, so that if he is transferred he is sidelined until the following season. United's need for players was desperate and the change of rules allowed Jimmy Murphy to begin his rebuilding by signing Ernie Taylor from Blackpool.

Manchester United took a deep breath. Football would return to Old Trafford.

Thirteen nights after news of Munich had reached Jimmy Murphy the days of torture ended when United played again. Their postponed FA Cup-tie against Sheffield Wednesday drew a crowd of 60,000 on a cold February evening of immense emotion. Spectators wept openly, many wore red-and-white scarves draped in black – red, white and black were eventually to become United's recognised colours – and the match programme added a poignant final stroke to a tragic canvas.

Under the heading 'Manchester United' there was a blank teamsheet.

Spectators were told to write in the names of the players. Few did, they simply listened in silence as the loudspeaker announcer read out the United team. Harry Gregg in goal and Bill Foulkes at right-back had returned after the traumas of Munich, other names were not so familiar.

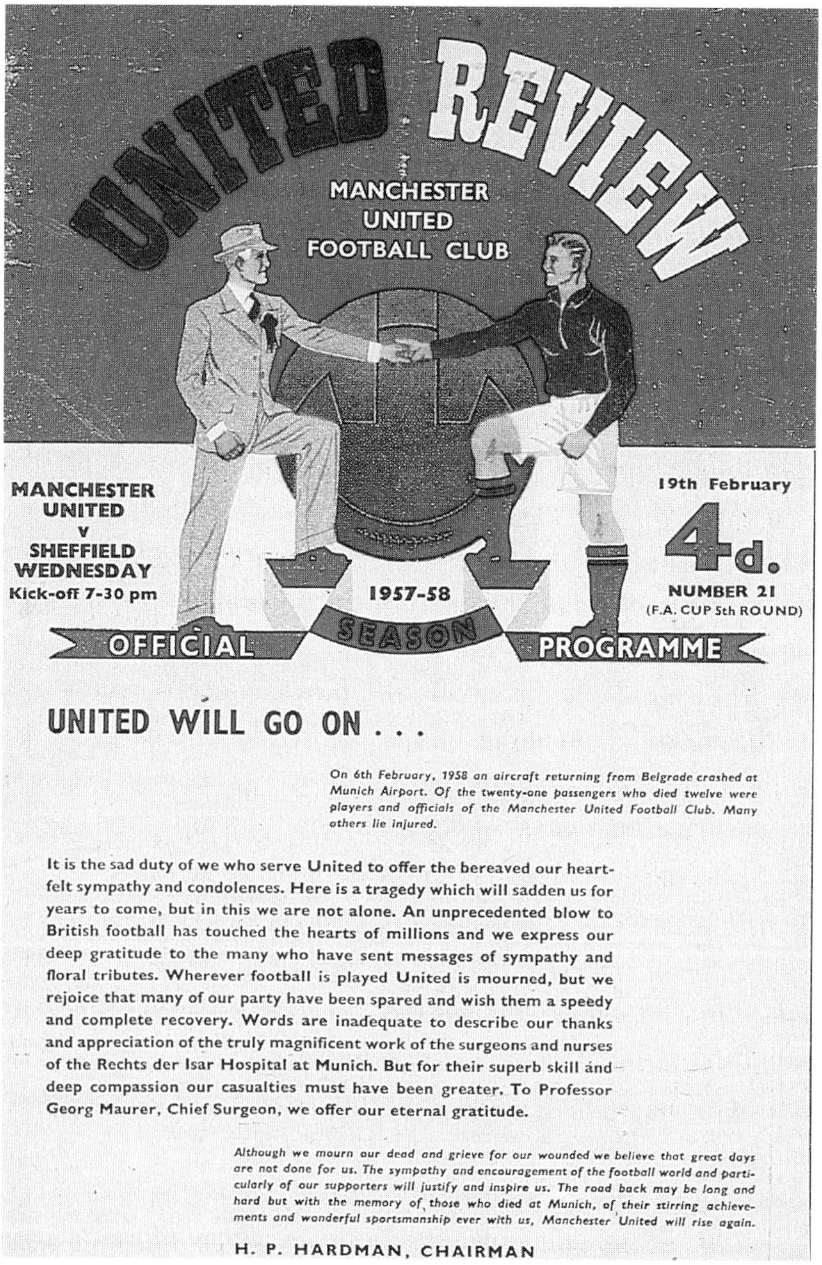

UNITED WILL GO ON . . .

On 6th February, 1958 an aircraft returning from Belgrade crashed at Munich Airport. Of the twenty-one passengers who died twelve were players and officials of the Manchester United Football Club. Many others lie injured.

It is the sad duty of we who serve United to offer the bereaved our heartfelt sympathy and condolences. Here is a tragedy which will sadden us for years to come, but in this we are not alone. An unprecedented blow to British football has touched the hearts of millions and we express our deep gratitude to the many who have sent messages of sympathy and floral tributes. Wherever football is played United is mourned, but we rejoice that many of our party have been spared and wish them a speedy and complete recovery. Words are inadequate to describe our thanks and appreciation of the truly magnificent work of the surgeons and nurses of the Rechts der Isar Hospital at Munich. But for their superb skill and deep compassion our casualties must have been greater. To Professor Georg Maurer, Chief Surgeon, we offer our eternal gratitude.

Although we mourn our dead and grieve for our wounded we believe that great days are not done for us. The sympathy and encouragement of the football world and particularly of our supporters will justify and inspire us. The road back may be long and hard but with the memory of those who died at Munich, of their stirring achievements and wonderful sportsmanship ever with us, Manchester United will rise again.

H. P. HARDMAN, CHAIRMAN

Bare headed workmen pay their respects as a cortege leaves Old Trafford. Immediately after the disaster the bodies of those who died were brought back to Old Trafford where they lay in the club gymnasium until arrangements for the funerals were completed. Supporters kept vigil at the stadium as the football world mourned the passing of the Babes

At left full-back was Ian Greaves who had played his football with United's junior sides and found himself replacing Roger Byrne: 'I can remember the dressing room was very quiet. I couldn't get Roger out of my mind, I was getting changed where he would have sat. I was wearing his shirt. . .'

At right-half was Freddie Goodwin, who had come through from the reserve side after joining United as a 20-year-old. He had played his first League games in the 1954-55 season. Another reserve regular was centre-half Ronnie Cope, who had come from United's juniors after joining the club in 1951. At left-half was Stan Crowther, whose transfer to United was remarkable. He played for Aston Villa, and was not very keen to leave the Midlands club. Jimmy Murphy recalls: 'Eric Houghton was Villa manager at the time and he had told Stan that we were interested in him. He didn't want to leave Villa, but Eric got him to come to Old Trafford to watch the Sheffield Wednesday game. On the way up he told him he thought that he should help us out, but Stan told him he hadn't brought any kit with him. "Don't worry, I've got your boots in my bag," Eric said. We met at about half-past five and an hour before the kick-off he'd signed!'

Colin Webster at outside-right had joined United in 1952 and made his League debut in the 1953-54 season. He had won a League Championship medal in 1956 after 15 appearances, but had since been edged out of the side by Johnny Berry. Ernie Taylor was inside-right, and at centre-forward was Alex Dawson, a brawny Scot who had made his debut as a 16-year-old in April 1957, scoring against Burnley. Inside-left was Mark Pearson, who earned the nickname 'Pancho' because of the Mexican appearance his sideburns gave him. Like the Pearson who preceded him, Stan, and the one who was to follow him almost two decades later, Stuart, Mark was a powerful player and a regular goalscorer with the lower sides. That night he took the first steps of his senior career. The new United outside-left was Shay Brennan, who was a reserve defender. Such was United's plight that the 20-year-old was to begin his League career not as a right-back but as a left-winger.

Sheffield Wednesday had no chance. Murphy's Manchester United were playing for the memory of their friends who had died less than a fortnight earlier. The passion of the crowd urged them on. To say that some played beyond their capabilities would be unfair, but with Wednesday perhaps more affected by the occasion than the young and new players, the final score was United 3 Wednesday 0.

Football returns to Old Trafford 15 days after the air crash. The programme for the fifth round FA Cup tie against Sheffield Wednesday bears the moving words of chairman Harold Hardman who told supporters 'United will go on '. Inside the United teamsheet was blank; even up to kick-off time no-one was certain who would be playing as the club searched for players

Playing in the Sheffield side was Albert Quixall, later to join United in a record transfer deal, who recalls: 'I don't think anyone who played in the game or who watched it will ever forget that night. United ran their hearts out, and no matter how well we had played they would have beaten us. They were playing like men inspired. We were playing more than just eleven players, we were playing 60,000 fans as well.'

United scored in the 27th minute after two errors by Brian Ryalls in the Wednesday goal. Bill Foulkes had taken a free-kick from well outside the penalty area and his shot was going wide when Ryalls palmed it away for a corner. There had seemed no danger from the shot, but Brennan's corner kick brought his first goal for the senior side. Ryalls tried to collect the cross under the bar and could only turn the ball into his own net.

Brennan got a second later in the game when a shot from Mark Pearson rebounded off the 'keeper and straight into the Irishman's path. He made no mistake and United led 2–0. Five minutes from the end of that unforgettable night Alex Dawson scored the third. United had reached the quarter-finals of the FA Cup.

The crowd turned for home, their heads full of memories of that remarkable game, their hearts full of sadness as they realised the full extent of Munich. The new team had carried on where the Babes had left off . . . but they would never see their heroes again.

Two days after that cup-tie Duncan Edwards lost his fight to survive, and the sadness of Munich was rekindled.

Farewell to the flowers of Manchester

Manchester United had to continue and chairman Harold Hardman had made this clear in his message on the front cover of the Sheffield Wednesday programme:

> United will go on . . . the club has a duty to the public and a duty to football. We shall carry on even if it means that we are heavily defeated.
>
> Here is a tragedy which will sadden us for years to come, but in this we are not alone. An unprecedented blow to British football has touched the hearts of millions. Wherever football is played United is mourned.

The weeks following the tragedy revealed moving stories about the players who lost their lives.

Roger Byrne would have learned when he returned to Manchester that his wife Joy was expecting a child. Thirty-eight weeks after his death Roger had a son.

Geoff Bent treasured a picture of himself taking the ball off Tom Finney in one of the 12 First Division games he played, and the newspaper cutting was kept by his young wife Marion. His daughter Karen was a babe in arms when he died.

Eddie Colman, the 'cheekie chappie' from Salford, was just three months past his 21st birthday when he was killed.

Duncan Edwards, the youngest player to appear for England, was planning to get married to his fiancée, Molly. He had been a senior footballer for only four years, and was 22. Today, a stained glass window in St Francis's Church in his home town of Dudley remains as a tribute to a great player.

Mark Jones left a young wife, June, and a baby son, Gary. The ex-bricklayer was just 24 years of age. He doted on his black Labrador retriever, Rick. The dog pined away to its death shortly after the disaster.

David Pegg was only 22 and had edged himself into the England side at a time when Tom Finney and Stan Matthews were ending their international careers. His ambition was to be successful with United, and he had achieved that aim.

Tommy Taylor was also planning to marry and had told his fiancée, Carol, that he was looking forward to getting home from Belgrade for a pint of Guinness and to listen to his records with her.

Liam Whelan was a deeply religious boy, and Harry Gregg remembers clearly his last words as the aircraft accelerated down the runway: 'If the worst happens I am ready for death . . . I hope we all are.'

Eleven years later an official inquiry cleared Captain James Thain of any responsibility for the accident. The official cause was recorded as a build-up of melting snow on the runway which prevented the Elizabethan from reaching the required take-off speed.

Through the Munich Air Disaster a bond between Manchester United and its supporters was welded. Since that day, the club has been one of the best supported in Britain, and even though it never achieved the domination

The original Munich Memorial above the main entrance to Old Trafford. Due to extensive development at the stadium the club had a new memorial made and re-sited at the Warwick Road end of the ground. The tablet bears the names of the officials and players who died in the air crash. A plaque in memory of the journalists who died hangs in the press box

Two of the players who lost their lives in the Munich tragedy. Liam Whelan (left) spoke of the possibility of the worst happening as the plane took off. Duncan Edwards (right), the youngest player to play for England, and already one of the greatest, had his forthcoming marriage on his mind.

The stained glass window at St Francis in the Priory Church in Dudley, Worcestershire in memory of Duncan Edwards. Although only 21 when he died, Duncan played a total of 175 games for United and scored 21 times. He played for his country 18 times.

threatened by the potential of the Babes, since 1972-73 Old Trafford's attendances have been the highest in the Football League. Anyone who was a supporter at the time of Munich has remained loyal to the club. Those who came afterwards perhaps failed to understand the magnitude of the club's loss but have absorbed the meaning of Munich. It was the day a team died, but still plays on.

THE FLOWERS OF MANCHESTER

One cold and bitter Thursday in Munich Germany,
Eight great football stalwarts conceded victory,
Eight men will never play again who met destruction there,
The Flowers of British football, the Flowers of Manchester.

Matt Busby's boys were flying, returning from Belgrade,
This great United family, all masters of their trade,
The pilot of the aircraft, the skipper Captain Thain,
Three times they tried to take off and twice turned back again.

The third time down the runway disaster followed close,
There was slush upon that runway and the aircraft never rose,
It ploughed into the marshy ground, it broke, it overturned
And eight of the team were killed when the blazing wreckage burned.

Roger Byrne and Tommy Taylor who were capped for England's side
And Ireland's Billy Whelan and England's Geoff Bent died,
Mark Jones and Eddie Colman, and David Pegg also,
They lost their lives as it ploughed on through the snow.

Big Duncan he went too, with an injury to his frame,
And Ireland's brave Jack Blanchflower will never play again,
The great Matt Busby lay there, the father of his team,
Three long months passed by before he saw his team again.

The trainer, coach and secretary, and a member of the crew,
Also eight sporting journalists who with United flew,
And one of them Big Swifty, who we will ne'er forget,
The finest English 'keeper that ever graced the net.

Oh, England's finest football team its record truly great,
Its proud successes mocked by a cruel turn of fate.
Eight men will never play again, who met destruction there,
The Flowers of English football, the Flowers of Manchester.

'The Flowers of Manchester', words anon. Recorded by The Spinners on their album 'Black and White', Phillips International 6382 047.

The 1960s: Greatness and glory

The United squad immediately after Munich. Of the 12 only Bobby Harrop (extreme left back row) did not take part in the cup tie against Sheffield Wednesday
Back row: Bobby Harrop, Ian Greaves, Freddie Goodwin, Harry Gregg, Stan Crowther, Ron Cope, Shay Brennan and Bill Inglis. Front row: Jack Crompton, Alex Dawson, Mark Pearson, Bill Foulkes, Ernie Taylor and Colin Webster. Former goalkeeper Crompton had left United two years before Munich and joined Luton Town as their trainer. He came back to Manchester at the request of Jimmy Murphy as the club rebuilt

18 April 1958 and Matt Busby is home again. Seventy one days after the air crash the United manager arrives at his home in Kings Road, Chorlton, to be welcomed by a group of supporters. For the schoolboys of the fifties the effect of the Munich disaster was lasting: those who followed the club at that time would always remain loyal. They had lost their heroes and would find new ones under the leadership of Busby

Inset: Jimmy Murphy brings together two players of contrasting backgrounds who played an important part in the rebuilding of United. On the left is Bobby Charlton, who survived Munich to become one of the game's finest ambassadors With him is Ernie Taylor, signed from Blackpool as he was on the verge of joining Sunderland

The great side of the 1960s

Some men are born great, some achieve greatness and some have greatness thrust upon them. Jimmy Murphy came to appreciate what Shakespeare had in mind when Busby whispered to him: 'Keep the flag flying', and suddenly the responsibility for the survival of Manchester United was laid on his shoulders.

How do you continue playing a game against a background of death and destruction with so much suffering and grief? As Jimmy wrote in his book:

> At first I felt as if I was going out of my mind, not knowing where to start. Previously Old Trafford had worked like a machine with Matt at the top presiding over all our efforts, sound in judgment and experience, with that incredible flair for public relations, always courteous, urbane and seemingly never forgetting anyone's face, so that he was always able to put people at their ease and talk to them.
>
> But now I had to try and keep the club in business, without Matt's guidance and strength to fall back on, without dear Bert Whalley's unflagging energy and zeal for the club, without Tom Curry, the quiet-spoken yet highly professional team trainer, who also had a lifetime of football experience to draw on. On the administrative side we had lost the club secretary, Walter Crickmer, a man with a shrewd brain which worked with a computer-like efficiency.

Murphy's obvious problem was to get a side out for the next match, but he also had to attend to the survivors, help the bereaved and go to the funerals. He did all these things. Cometh the hour, cometh the man, and though he started in management as an assistant and retired in a similar capacity, during his time in command he brought order out of chaos and answered the call like a born leader.

Jimmy Murphy assembled the boys and his new signings to beat Sheffield Wednesday in the rearranged fifth round of the FA Cup. He took away his youngsters to prepare them for men's work in the comparative calm of the Norbreck Hydro Hotel at Blackpool. For the rest of that season he kept taking his squad to the Norbreck, so that many of the accompanying football writers will forever associate the smell of the chlorine from the indoor baths with those emotionally charged weeks in the aftermath of Munich.

Jimmy Murphy had been an integral part of the post-war success and the creation of the Busby Babes, but this was the time when the depth of the club was put to the test and the quality of the youngsters was not found wanting. Working with the reserves and juniors had always been the special preserve of Murphy. It was Jimmy who honed the young reserves ready for the final push into the League team. A great many players owe a lot to his perception and thoroughness, as even the greatest, like Bobby Charlton, will tell you.

Wilf McGuinness, another who graduated through the Murphy academy, simply says: 'Without Jimmy Murphy a lot of us would never have made it as footballers. At times we almost hated him because he drove us so hard. But it was always for our own good and we certainly respected him.'

In 1986 United's association of former players made Jimmy their first honorary life member in appreciation of his work. Despite retiring as assistant manager in 1971 when Sir Matt stepped down, he carried on scouting for the club part-time for many more years.

As a player Murphy, a fiery wing half capped by Wales, was with West Bromwich Albion from 1928 until the outbreak of the Second World War. The son of a Welsh mother and Irish father brought up in Wales, he was naturally musical, and as a young man when he wasn't playing football he played the organ in Treorchy Parish Church. He was the youngest player in the Welsh team when he was 21. In all he was capped 22 times and also captained his country.

Murphy finished the war as an NCO in charge of a Services Sports Centre at Bari in Italy. One day he was talking in his usual Welsh way to a group of soldiers. On the fringe listening and liking what he heard was Sergeant-Major Busby. At the end he came up to shake hands and said that if Jimmy fancied a job when he was demobbed then he should call in at Old Trafford. Jimmy Murphy became Busby's first signing, a shrewd one, too, as he proved in the vital early days and then when the chips were really down and he had to take over.

He fought back the tears after Munich to become the lifeline for the club's survival. Although always well respected at home, the way he coped brought him to the notice of the world and the following year he had offers to manage Brazil and Juventus. He turned them down. He had found his life's work at Old Trafford and he knew it.

Three days after United beat Wednesday in that emotional post-Munich Cup-tie they were plunged back into League football with 66,000 packed into Old Trafford to see a 1–1 draw with Nottingham Forest. The patched-up team won only one of the remaining 14 League fixtures after Munich, but they were never humiliated and they never lost heart. They picked up five draws which with the win at Sunderland saw them hang on for an extremely commendable ninth place.

United's really sterling efforts came in the FA Cup, of course. After beating Sheffield Wednesday – described in the previous chapter – they had to travel to West Bromwich for the sixth round. They ran themselves ragged to lead 2–1 with only four minutes to go, but then Harry Gregg was ruled to have carried a cross over his goal line. It didn't matter, as inspired again by the fervour of the Old Trafford crowd and the return to action of Bobby Charlton for the replay the Reds won 1–0. The winner came from Colin Webster after a last-minute run down the wing by Charlton.

Then it was back to the Midlands for a 2–2 draw in the semi-final at Villa Park with Fulham. The replay at Highbury, with Fulham enjoying almost a home tie, was a momentous match, won by United 5–3 with the help of a hat-trick from Alex Dawson, nicknamed the Black Prince. So United were through to Wembley for a final against Bolton. A telephone call from Munich saying that Matt Busby was no longer on the danger list somehow seemed to set the seal on a truly remarkable achievement.

Nat Lofthouse, the legendary 'Lion of Vienna' after his exploits for England in Austria, and the Bolton captain, recalls the final vividly:

> Some of the fellows who died at Munich were among my pals. Barely a fortnight before the disaster I was having a drink with them at Old Trafford after they had thrashed us 7–2 in the League.
>
> The thousands of neutrals at Wembley wanted United to beat us. Their incredible fight-back from Munich had captured the imagination of the world. We walked out of that tunnel into an incredibly emotional atmosphere. But I would not be honest if I did not say that I was only interested in beating them. I was a professional who played for Bolton Wanderers. All that mattered was for Bolton to win the FA Cup.

The teams for the final were:

Bolton: Hopkinson, Hartle, Banks, Hennin, Higgins, Edwards, Birch, Stevens, Lofthouse, Parry, Holden.

Manchester United: Gregg, Foulkes, Greaves, Goodwin, Cope, Crowther, Dawson, Taylor, Charlton, Viollet, Webster.

Had United scored first, it is more than likely that the wave which had carried them to Wembley would have engulfed Bolton. But Lofthouse saw to it that whatever the Reds wanted they would have to fight for. Inside five minutes the old warhorse struck the first decisive blow. A corner from Holden was only half cleared and fell to the feet of Bryan Edwards. His centre towards the far post was met by Lofthouse, whose low drive gave Gregg no chance. It was as if in that moment the Red bubble had burst – as if the tragic events of the recent past had suddenly caught up with them.

Deflated, they fell apart. A terrific drive from Charlton did crash against the Bolton upright, and had that gone in the magic may have stirred them again. But within minutes Bolton scored again at the other end . . . although it was a goal which to this day the United lads claim should never have been allowed. Dennis Stevens hit a fierce shot from out on the left. Gregg, perhaps deceived by the pace of the shot, could only palm the ball into the air. As he jumped to catch it, the onrushing Lofthouse barged the ball and Gregg into the back of the net. Even Lofthouse could hardly believe his luck when referee Sherlock awarded a goal:

> I am quite convinced that I did foul Gregg, but you could hardly expect me to argue when the referee gave a goal! Even so, I believed that we deserved to win. United never put us under pressure. We always seemed to have something in hand. It was an emotional occasion when the final whistle blew, but what really left me with a lump in my throat was when Matt Busby, supported by walking sticks and by Jimmy Murphy and physiotherapist Ted Dalton, limped into our dressing room after the match to congratulate us. What a magnificent gesture.

Harry Gregg was made of stern stuff. Like Bill Foulkes he escaped the crash without injury, and he stayed on the scene despite warnings to get clear for fear of an explosion. He helped dazed and injured survivors from the wreckage, including a baby.

Signed from Doncaster only a few weeks before the disaster for a then record fee for a goalkeeper of £23,500, Gregg became one of the firm foundations in the rebuilding. He emerged as one of the stars of the 1958 World Cup in Sweden as he helped Northern Ireland through to the quarter-finals.

He was angry about the Lofthouse incident!

Right: Harry Gregg gets the better of this challenge with Nat Lofthouse but couldn't prevent the Lion of Vienna scoring both goals to give Bolton Wanderers a 2–0 victory in the FA Cup final of 1958

Below: Jimmy Murphy and Bill Ridding (left) lead out their teams at Wembley for the 1958 FA Cup final. Matt Busby was there as a spectator on sticks, barely recovered from the Munich accident. United had battled on after the crash, carried on a tide of emotion through ties against Sheffield Wednesday, West Bromwich Albion and Fulham. Though the second goal by Nat Lofthouse when he knocked goalkeeper Harry Gregg into the back of the net was controversial, Bolton were worthy winners

'Nat blatantly barged me over the line,' he said. 'A goal should never have been awarded. I remember sitting seething in the bath at Wembley praying that Lofthouse wouldn't retire before I had had chance to get my own back. I'm happy to tell you that he didn't . . . and I did!'

The heroes of the post-Munich season

The following season might have been expected to come as an anti-climax. Certainly another Wembley trip was soon removed from the possibilities with a third round knock-out at Norwich, but in the League the Reds finished the 1958–59 season as runners-up behind Wolves.

That was really an incredible achievement and it was done without any dramatic rush into the transfer market. Dennis Viollet and Albert Scanlon returned to action after recovering from their injuries.

Warren Bradley, an England amateur international winger from Bishop Auckland was

signed midway through the season and Matt Busby had recovered sufficiently by the end of September to pay a then record £45,000 for Albert Quixall from Sheffield Wednesday. The rest of the team was made up of reserves suddenly given a new responsibility and, of course, the youngsters who had been in the pipeline. The success of the team spoke volumes for the quality of the juniors who had been working in the shadow of the Busby Babes.

The team took a few weeks to settle, but a run of 11 wins out of 12 games between November and February put them in the frame with the Wolverhampton team of Stan Cullis.

United was a team built for attack and they netted more than a hundred League goals with 29 from Charlton, the best scoring season of his career, 21 from Viollet, 16 from Scanlon and 12 from 24 appearances by Bradley. The team had emerged by the end of the season to line up:

Gregg, Greaves, Carolan, Goodwin, Foulkes (Cope), McGuinness, Bradley, Quixall, Viollet, Charlton, Scanlon.

Both inside-forward Ernie Taylor and wing-half Stan Crowther, the emergency signings after Munich, had departed, their brief but vital holding missions accomplished. They had helped give United a breathing space, Crowther bringing vigour to the team while Taylor used his vast experience to put his foot on the ball and direct operations. He had played only 30 League and Cup games for United, but the little general had been priceless. He was 33, with his great years of winning FA Cup medals with Newcastle and Blackpool well behind him. He was only 5ft 4in (1.63m), with tiny feet, but his reading of the game and his passing more than made up for the lack of inches. United let him move on to his home team of Sunderland and he still managed another 70 games before going into non-League football with Altrincham. He emigrated to New Zealand to do some coaching before returning to England to settle in the north-west again. He died in 1985. His short career at Old Trafford had been long enough to see others step forward to pick up the baton.

Bobby Charlton

None stepped forward so effectively as Bobby Charlton, who went into Munich a boy and came out of that season a man. He had of course already given ample notice of his prodigious talent in the youth team and as a young player beginning to nudge the original Busby Babes. His 14 appearances and 10 goals had brought him a championship medal in 1957 and he had won a first-team place again just before the crash.

Matt Busby, back on his feet after grievous injuries at Munich, gathers his forces around him for the start of the 1958–59 season, a mixture of survivors, new signings, a few old hands and youngsters suddenly thrust into the fray.
Front row: Jack Crompton (trainer), Ted Dalton (physiotherapist), Johnny Berry, Jimmy Murphy (assistant manager), Ernie Taylor, Ronnie Cope, Albert Scanlon, Stan Crowther, Matt Busby (manager), Bobby English, Shay Brennan, Bill Foulkes, Dennis Viollet, Ray Wood, Tommy Heron, Freddie Goodwin, Kenny Morgans, Wilf McGuinness, Warren Bradley, Bill Inglish (assistant trainer).
Back: Nobby Lawton, Barry Smith, Jimmy Elms, Reg Holland, Harold Bratt, David Gaskell, Mark Pearson, Alex Dawson, Bobby Harrop, Joe Carolan, Jimmy Shiels, Johnny Giles, Ian Greaves, Gordon Clayton

He says about those early days leading up to his League debut in a 4–2 win at Charlton Athletic in October 1956:

> I thought I was never going to get into the team. I was scoring a lot of goals in the reserves and I kept thinking surely Matt Busby would play me now. Everyone kept telling me I would get a game soon, but it never seemed to happen. Ironically three weeks before my debut I sprained my ankle in a collision with Keith Marsden of Manchester City when playing for the reserves. Then just before the Charlton match, Sir Matt asked me if I was OK. Actually I wasn't, but I wasn't going to let my long awaited chance go by, so I crossed my fingers and said yes.
>
> The Boss said good and that I would be playing the next day. I carried the leg a little, but it went well for me and I managed to score two goals, one from close in and one from outside the box. I was still dropped for the next game, which just shows you how severe the competition was that season. I had played in place of Tommy Taylor who had been injured and he was fit again so had to come back.
>
> I got back into the team for the following match in place of the injured Dennis Viollet, and that's how it went for the rest of the season, in and out whenever Tommy, Dennis or Billy Whelan was injured. I didn't become a regular until the following season, about two months before the Munich accident. Then I was in off my own bat. In those days they didn't put you in until you were really ready. For ages they just seemed to move the more experienced players around.

Bobby Charlton was such an outstanding figure at Old Trafford and played for such a long time that it is difficult to know at what point of the club's history a tribute to his service should be made. He had many fine moments in a distinguished career for both Manchester United and England, spanning 17 seasons of First Division football.

In terms of facts and figures, Charlton made 604 League appearances, scoring 198 goals, a club record on both counts which looks capable of standing for all time. In the FA Cup he played in 78 ties to score 20 goals. In European competition he made 45 appearances for a tally of 22 goals. He collected three championship medals, an FA Cup winner's medal in 1963 and of course the European Cup winner's medal in 1968, as well as helping to win the World Cup for England in 1966 in an international career of 106 appearances, during which he set a scoring record of 49 goals, another achievement likely to stand the test of time.

He was awarded the OBE in 1969, and the CBE in 1974. In 1966 he was voted Footballer of the Year in both England and Europe. But even the stream of honours and medals don't really do justice to his career, because there was both a warmth and a dignity about him which endeared him not just to Manchester United fans, but to followers of football all over the world.

The name of Bobby Charlton is universally known. It's possible to strike a chord of recognition with a foreigner, neither knowing a

Even as a young man Bobby Charlton was the Pied Piper of football. Back home in Beatrice Street, Ashington, Northumberland, he shows the local youngsters how it's done at Old Trafford. He is still teaching aspiring young players 30 years later at his world famous summer schools which now cover many other sports besides football

word of each other's language, based simply on mentioning Manchester and Bobby Charlton. Russian border guards on Checkpoint Charlie in Berlin, not known for their sense of fun, grinned hugely on the day Charlton passed through with United.

There was always a grace about his play which some have thought took football more into the realms of ballet than any other player's. He was loved for his thundering goals: not for him the tap-in, more the zoom of the rocket. His sporting attitude was impeccable. The only time he was booked somehow got lost from the record when everyone realised it had been a mistake of one kind or another. Not that there wasn't passion in his game. His desire to win never flagged, and he had the reputation among his team-mates as something of a moaner who used to nag at them if they were falling short of what he expected.

No-one could doubt Charlton's dedication to his sport, a quality which had him at considerable variance with George Best when the Irishman began to stray from the fold. Bobby brought the old Corinthian spirit into the modern game and served it well. He proved a soccer idol without feet of clay, even moving smoothly into another successful career after a brief and not particularly encouraging essay into management. He found the ideal outlet to follow his playing career. He took up interests in the travel business, but soon concentrated on his summer soccer schools which now embrace nearly all sports. All his courses get the Charlton personal touch as he weaves his sporting magic with new generations of budding stars.

It was certainly a fitting move by the board of Manchester United when they asked him to become a director in 1986, an invitation which keeps alive great traditions of the past while introducing an able man who will contribute to the future.

But this is running on far ahead of our story. Bobby Charlton in 1959 was a fledgling. He had joined Old Trafford as a schoolboy from Ashington in Northumberland. He came from good footballing stock, his mother, Cissie, being from the well-known Milburn soccer family. Two uncles, Jim and George, played for Leeds. Uncle Stan played for Leicester. His cousin Jackie Milburn was Newcastle United's great centre-forward of the 1950s.

Bobby was an outstanding schoolboy prospect, playing in the same England team as

Bobby Charlton is the shoulder-high hero with (left to right) Matt Busby, Harry Gregg, Noel Cantwell, Pat Crerand, David Herd, Shay Brennan, Denis Law, Nobby Stiles and John Connelly

another Babe and future United manager, Wilf McGuinness, and he drew scouts like a magnet, including Joe Armstrong from Old Trafford. Joe, never a professional player himself, spent a lifetime in junior circles and was a scout for Manchester City when Matt Busby had played at Maine Road. Busby invited the man with a twinkling eye and cherubic, smiling face to Old Trafford and when Joe retired from the GPO made him his chief scout. One day in 1953 he was peering through the mist at a schoolboy match in the north-east, and noticed the talents of the young Charlton shining through the fog, and Jimmy Murphy says Joe couldn't get back quickly enough to report that he had seen a boy who he reckoned would become a world-beater.

Later, when he was ready to leave school and a host of clubs were knocking on his door, Bobby remembered that Joe Armstrong had been the first to take a real interest in him. He had liked 'Uncle Joe' and paid tribute to him when he was presented with his Footballer of the Year trophy in London many years later.

Bobby did not have an easy apprenticeship. Murphy reckons they had to work hard on him to improve his short-passing game and curb his tendency to hit speculative long balls all the time. Charlton well remembers the lessons. 'Jimmy used to play with us in practice matches and he used to come up behind me and kick me on the back of the legs. I think he was trying to toughen me up, and also perhaps to encourage me to pass the ball a bit quicker,' he says now.

Certainly Bobby proved a quick learner as he emerged after Munich as one of the key players round whom Manchester United could build. He missed two games immediately after the crash and then resumed playing with a heightened responsibility. By the start of the 1958–59 season he was in full flow. He scored a hat-trick in the opening game of the season at home to Chelsea and he bagged a couple more four days later at Nottingham Forest. He stormed through the season for his total of 29 League goals. When he and Dennis Viollet hit scoring form together, United were unstoppable. They each scored twice to finish with a 6–1 win against Blackburn Rovers, and later in the season Portsmouth also crashed 6–1 at Old Trafford with Charlton and Viollet again sharing four of the goals.

Charlton and Viollet scored a goal apiece to beat Wolves 2–1 at Old Trafford in the February, so that by April the two clubs were level on points at the top of the table. But Wolves had a couple of games in hand and they finished powerfully to take the title by six points. Really United had no right to finish runners-up after the grievous blow suffered at Munich just the previous season. Such a position was really beyond their wildest dreams and even Busby admitted that it had been far better than he had expected.

What made it so startling of course was that the club had been able to find so many players from within. Warren Bradley enjoyed great success after joining as an amateur. He was quickly launched into the England team and in fact won three caps to add to 11 amateur appearances. Born in Hyde, Cheshire, he was a school teacher and soon made himself at home among the professional stars. His intelligence and quiet confidence helped, qualities which later saw him become headmaster of a big Manchester comprehensive school, but he hardly ranked as a major signing, at least not as far as his fee was concerned, a modest donation to Bishop Auckland.

The only real concession United had made to the transfer market following the emergency signings of Taylor and Crowther was in recruiting inside-forward Albert Quixall from Hillsborough. The blond-haired Yorkshireman was bought in keeping with Busby's policy of putting players on to the Old Trafford stage who had personality and entertainment value as well as being able to do a job of work. Albert was the golden boy of his day. In his native Sheffield he had swept everything before him . . . captain of his school, his city, his county, his country and then playing for the full England team by the age of 18.

Quixall helped to maintain the Busby tradition for creative, skilful football in a difficult period. He had charisma, though he didn't make a fortune from football. Looking back he says: 'I suppose I was born 20 years too early. I remember an article on me at the time saying that my record transfer fee made me worth my weight in gold. Perhaps that was true, but it didn't do much for me personally. I don't harp on that though because you can't translate everything into money. I achieved a lot in my teens and had some great times in football. I'm not bitter by any means.'

You could hardly blame him if he was. Working after football for years in a scrap metal yard near Manchester where he settled, he was young enough to see near-contemporaries prosper out of all proportion with a fraction of his talent . . . yet he was too old to have caught the gravy train himself.

Dennis Viollet was another supremely gifted player who hit the heights just a little too soon to catch the explosion in football wages and finances. Dennis, a local youngster who grew up playing ball around Maine Road, was in fact a Manchester City fan like the rest of his family. Joe Armstrong and Jimmy Murphy persuaded him to come to Old Trafford and his career straddled the Munich disaster. He was one of the Busby Babes who survived the crash to play a vital role in the rebuilding period.

Viollet's best season came as United embarked on the 1959–60 season, hoping to build on their runners-up position of the previous season. That they finished only seventh was hardly the fault of Viollet, who broke Jack Rowley's club scoring record by notching 32 League goals.

He was a master craftsman, a sleek ghost of a player who scored his goals with stealth, skill and speed. He was not a typical robust centre-forward, but his rather frail-looking appearance belied his strength. He was resilient, and overall he scored 159 goals in 259 League appearances spread over ten seasons of first-team soccer.

He eventually left Old Trafford in 1962 to play for Stoke, and helped them win the Second Division Championship for Tony Waddington. He played in the States for a spell, then after winning an Irish FA Cup winners' medal with Linfield he settled in America, becoming involved in their football. His next visits to England were to accompany his talented tennis daughter on trips to play at Junior Wimbledon.

Viollet's record scoring season should have brought him more than two caps for England. There was, in fact, a case to be made out around 1960 for playing the entire United forward line at international level.

United again topped 100 League goals in that 1959–60 season, with Dennis's 32 being followed by 18 from Charlton, 13 from Quixall, and eight and seven from wingers Bradley and Scanlon. Alex Dawson, a centre-forward who also played on the wing, was also forcing his way into the team and grabbed a promising 15 from only 22 appearances. Johnny Giles and Mark Pearson, pilloried by Burnley's controversial and outspoken chairman Bob Lord as a Teddy Boy, played occasionally.

United were too erratic to win the title. One week they would score four, the next they would concede four. Things came to a head in January when the team went to Newcastle and lost 7–3. Busby suddenly swooped in the transfer market to pay £30,000 for wing-half Maurice Setters from West Bromwich Albion. He wanted the bandy-legged, tough-tackling Setters to stiffen the midfield. What a contrast he made with Quixall. Their styles were at the opposite ends of the football spectrum and there wasn't much love lost between them.

It was a period of retrenchment for United, with Busby taking the rebuilding in steady fashion. At the end of 1960 he bought again, paying £29,000 for the West Ham and Republic of Ireland left-back Noel Cantwell.

The intelligent and articulate Irishman became a sound influence and a splendid captain. But there was no instant success with United unable to improve on seventh in the League in the 1960–61 season, and making a fourth-round exit in the FA Cup.

The 1961–62 season did bring a run in the Cup, United reaching the semi-finals only to lose 3–1 against Spurs at Hillsborough. The League, however, saw them slip to 15th. Busby knew it was time for action. There were not enough talented youngsters coming through fast enough. Just before the start of the 1961–62 season he had bought centre-forward David Herd, son of his former team-mate Alex, from Arsenal for £32,000. Herd had obliged by scoring 14 goals, but the goal touch had deserted the others and Herd's tally was the best effort.

The arrival of Law and Crerand

So in the summer of 1962 Busby spent again and pulled off his best-ever transfer coup. He brought Denis Law home from Italy's Torino for a record £115,000.

United now had a twin strike force of Law and Herd, backed by Charlton and Quixall and a new youngster, Johnny Giles, with another home product, Nobby Stiles, occasionally forcing his way into the team at half-back.

Still it wasn't quite right. The attack looked full of goals, but they only clicked spasmodically. Busby decided that the service to the men up front wasn't good enough. So he went out to buy a player who could supply the right kind of ammunition for Law and Herd to fire. The result was the arrival, in February 1963 for £43,000 from Glasgow Celtic, of right-half Pat Crerand. Busby now had the right balance in the half-back line, Setters the ball-winner on the left and Crerand the distributor on the right.

It was too late to pull things round in the League and the Reds ended the 1962–63 season in 19th place, their lowest position under Busby's management. But the potential was there, and it showed in the FA Cup as the Reds sailed through every round without a replay, to beat Southampton 1–0 in the semi-final at Villa Park and face Leicester City at Wembley.

For a change, because of their League position, the Reds were the underdogs. Leicester had finished fourth in the First Division and had the reputation of being a side with an iron defence. So the stage was set for a clash between the irresistible force and the immovable object when the following teams took the field at Wembley on 25 May 1963:

Manchester United: Gaskell, Dunne, Cantwell, Crerand, Foulkes, Setters, Giles, Quixall, Herd, Law, Charlton.

Above: Once they were team-mates at Old Trafford but here a confrontation of like characters . . .the fiery Denis Law of United and the aggressive Maurice Setters in the white shirt of Stoke City

Left: Up for the Cup . . . and Manchester United's first success five years after the calamity of the Munich air crash

Below left: Noel Cantwell, captain of Manchester United, shakes hands with Leicester City skipper Colin Appleton under the watchful eye of referee Ken Aston at the start of the 1963 FA Cup final

Above right: Gordon Banks clears from Denis Law at Wembley in 1963, but the Leicester City and England goalkeeper couldn't stop United winning 3–1 to take the FA Cup. It was sweet relief for United who struggled all season in the League, looking relegation candidates at one stage, and finishing in 19th place, the low water mark in Matt Busby's management career

Right: Celebration time for Pat Crerand, Albert Quixall and David Herd after winning the FA Cup in 1963. The Sheffield-born Quixall, crowned with the Cup, was the golden boy of his era, playing international football at every level and costing then a record fee of £45,000 from Sheffield Wednesday

Leicester: Banks, Sjoberg, Norman, McLintock, King, Appleton, Riley, Cross, Keyworth, Gibson, Stringfellow.

From the first whistle it was obvious that the Reds had torn up the form book. Law, in particular, was in one of those moods when it would have taken a Centurion tank to stop him. The famous Leicester 'iron curtain' looked more like a torn curtain, as Law danced through at will.

Crerand, who had taken time to settle into the side, was also having a field day on Wembley's wide-open spaces, and it was one of those inch-perfect passes which enabled Law to swivel and drive home the first goal after 29 minutes. The longer the game went on, the more composed and confident United looked. In the 58th minute, they underlined their superiority when Herd rounded off a sweet move, involving Giles and Charlton, by sweeping the ball past Gordon Banks. The game was as good as won. In a late flurry Keyworth scored for Leicester, but Herd grabbed his second to make the final scoreline 3–1 to United.

The victory more than made up for the Reds' disappointing League form, and finally buried the memory of their two Wembley defeats in 1957 and 1958. More than that, it indicated that from the ashes of Munich, Busby was on the way towards building another side capable of taking English soccer by storm.

United had flexed their muscles and had given notice that they were back in business as a top team again. They looked forward to season 1963–64 in more confident mood, and used their Cup victory as a launching pad to go with more conviction for the big prizes. They didn't do too well in the European Cup Winners' Cup, squandering a first leg win of 4–1 against Sporting Lisbon by losing 5–0 in Portugal. It was United's most embarrassing defeat in their history and the story is told more fully in the chapter on Europe.

However, they reached the semi-finals of the FA Cup to play West Ham and finished runners-up in the League. Denis Law, the matador of Old Trafford, enjoyed his best scoring season in a year which was also significant for the debut in League football of a young, black-haired Irishman with flashing eyes.

Matt Busby gave George Best his first game on 14 September 1963, playing him at outside-right against West Bromwich Albion at Old Trafford. David Sadler, the young bank clerk from Maidstone, Kent, with whom he shared digs at Mrs Fullaway's in Davyhulme, scored in a 1–0 win.

Ian Moir replaced Best for the next League match, but Busby had noted his performance and called up the youngster to play against Burnley at Old Trafford in December. Busby was ringing the changes because two days previously, on Boxing Day, his team had gone down 6–1 at Turf Moor. Best came in for the return and scored in a sweet 5–1 revenge win.

The famous football litany of Charlton, Law and Best had now come together, though at this stage Best was very much the junior partner. The man at the height of his powers was Law, scoring a fantastic total of 46 goals in League and Cup. Thirty of them came from 30 League appearances, helping the Reds finish second to Liverpool, four points adrift. He scored ten in six FA Cup-ties and notched another eight in ten games in the European Cup Winners' Cup. There was the usual 20 from David Herd, while Bobby Charlton weighed in with nine, but Busby was still tinkering with the team.

He changed goalkeepers at one point, replacing Harry Gregg for a spell with David Gaskell. Halfway through he switched Tony Dunne to left-back in place of Noel Cantwell and brought in Shay Brennan at right-back. Inside-right was causing him problems with one of his youngsters, Phil Chisnall, dropped in favour of Graham Moore, the Welsh international. David Sadler was in and out, still searching for his best position, defender, midfield or striker. Nobby Stiles was brought in at left-half to take over from Maurice Setters, and give nothing away in terms of matching fire with fire. Ian Moir played half a season on the wing. There had probably been just a few too many changes to get the better of Liverpool, who proved their right to be champions by winning 1–0 at Old Trafford in November and then beating United 3–0 at Anfield on the run-in for the title. Those four points separated the two teams at the end of the season.

All-in-all, it was a marked improvement on the previous season's 19th position, and they had also fought some sterling battles in the FA Cup especially against Sunderland in the quarter-final. The fans had enjoyed a spectacular 3–3 game at Old Trafford and then admired a stout 2–2 draw after extra time at Roker Park. United proved to be the team with the stamina as Sunderland finally collapsed and went down 5–1 in the second replay at Huddersfield.

The semi-final took United to Hillsborough on an exceedingly wet day to meet West Ham and they didn't play well as they slid to a 3–1 defeat. Geoff Hurst scored the decisive third goal after a splendid run down the wing by Bobby Moore. The Hammers' theme tune of 'Forever Blowing Bubbles' had an appropriate twist as the London fans sang their heads off in the rain while United's followers trekked miserably back home across the Pennines. The Hillsborough hoodoo had struck again. But there was happier news on the Cup front at youth level as the club gathered momentum again. The kids won the FA Youth Cup after a seven-year gap, heralding the arrival of more promising youngsters.

George Best, Willie Anderson and David Sadler had already played in the first team. Other players from the successful youth team who went on to play in the League side were Jimmy Rimmer, the goalkeeper, full-back Bobby Noble, winger John Aston and wing-half John Fitzpatrick.

United were blooming again at all levels accompanied by imaginative development off the field. Plans were announced for the building of a new cantilever stand in readiness for Old Trafford as a venue for the 1966 World Cup in England. The bulk of the finance was to be raised by a football pool run by a Development Association on a scale not previously seen in soccer.

There was a buzz about the place again, though Busby knew he needed a more settled side than the one which had just chased Liverpool home, and despite his many changes he felt he needed a top-class winger. So during the summer of 1964 he bought the experienced John Connelly from Burnley for £60,000. The winger, equally at home on either flank, had already won League and FA Cup medals at Turf Moor and it proved to be an inspired signing.

Champions again

Connelly was the final piece in the jigsaw which turned a team of runners-up into champions. The whole thing fell into place as the Reds swept to success in season 1964–65, pipping Leeds United for the title. In the days when goal average, rather than difference, settled issues, United won by the narrow margin of 0.686 of a goal.

United still had a game in hand when they knew they had won the Championship, so the final game at Villa Park didn't matter all that much and it was duly lost. The significant aspect was that they were champions for the first time

Manchester United were champions for the first time after the Munich disaster in season 1964–65, no mean feat considering that they had virtually had an entire team destroyed.
Their medal-winning squad lined up:
Front Row: John Connelly, Bobby Charlton, David Herd, Denis Law and George Best. Middle: Jack Crompton (trainer), Shay Brennan, David Sadler, Bill Foulkes, John Aston, Noel Cantwell and Matt Busby (manager). Back: Nobby Stiles, Tony Dunne, David Gaskell, Pat Dunne, Pat Crerand and John Fitzpatrick

Denis Law and David Herd in the dark shirts watch eagerly as United storm to a 3–1 victory against Arsenal at Old Trafford, the match which brought them the 1965 championship. Law scored twice while George Best got the other goal

Autographs :

since Munich. Bobby Charlton and Bill Foulkes were the only crash survivors remaining in the team.

Connelly more than played his part, scoring 15 goals from outside-right while Best dazzled on the left to score ten. Charlton, now operating in a midfield role, scored ten as well, while Law led the scoring with 28, supported again by 20 from Herd. But while the forwards attracted the headlines, they owed a great deal to the defence. Bill Foulkes, the centre-half, and the two full-backs, Shay Brennan and Tony Dunne, were ever-presents. They conceded only 39 goals to help provide their personable new goalkeeper, Pat Dunne, with a championship medal. Pat was to flit quickly across the Old Trafford stage. A modest £10,000 signing from Shamrock Rovers, he spent less than three seasons at United. He seemed to come from nowhere and disappear almost as quickly, but he played his part.

The team's championship qualities had not

been immediately apparent when only one win had come in the opening six games, but they picked up thereafter, dropping only one point in their next 14 games. The highlight was a 7–0 thrashing of Aston Villa at Old Trafford with four of the goals down to Law.

They dropped a few points in mid-season, but put in another searing run of ten wins in 11 games to take the title.

United had an all-round strength now that also saw them do well in the other competitions. They were, in fact, chasing a treble for most of the season. They reached the semi-finals of the European Fairs Cup (later to become the UEFA Cup), and at the same time stormed through to the semi-finals of the FA Cup and an appointment with their deadly rivals from Elland Road. Leeds United were coming to the height of their powers under Don Revie, and not everyone admired their methods. Manchester United had more than an abrasive streak as well, so it was a volatile mix when the two teams met at Hillsborough.

League points had been shared, each side winning 1–0 on their own ground, and the atmosphere for the Cup-tie was hostile. The match was fierce and bad-tempered and could have done with stricter refereeing. There were no goals and the replay was staged at Nottingham Forest's ground. Referee Dick Windle, perhaps conscious of his leniency at Sheffield, tightened up considerably, and the players also held themselves in check better, knowing full well that one or two of them had been fortunate to stay on the field for the full 90 minutes in the first game. But it was still a mess of a match which constantly had to be stopped for fouls. It was reckoned that Manchester United had conceded more than 20 free-kicks in the original game, and almost as many in the replay. They finally paid the penalty for trying to play Leeds at their own game. With less than two minutes to go they gave away one free-kick too many and their former inside-forward, Johnny Giles, who had failed to hit it off with Busby after coming through the juniors, punished them. His cleverly flighted kick into the goalmouth was headed home by Billy Bremner, the Leeds ball of fire. So Leeds went to Wembley, leaving the Reds contemplating their third semi-final defeat in four years.

The other leg of the treble collapsed as well with semi-final defeat in the Fairs Cup after a play-off third game against Ferencvaros in Budapest long after the official end to the season. Nevertheless it had been a mighty year with many memorable games on the three fronts, and they had made their mark with the Championship trophy back at Old Trafford to show for their efforts. The team showed few changes with the medals going to:

Pat Dunne, Brennan, Tony Dunne, Crerand, Foulkes, Stiles, Connelly, Charlton, Herd, Law, Best.

It was a well balanced strong side.

Denis Law

Law was at his peak in that Championship season as the attacking star, yet when he had started his career in England with Huddersfield Town in 1955, Bill Shankly had said of him: 'He looked like a skinned rabbit.' But once Shankly had seen him play he knew that here was something special. After only 80 games, and with Huddersfield having slid into the Second Division, he was sold for £56,000 to First Division Manchester City.

City kept Law for a season and then made a handsome profit, selling him to Torino for £110,000, giving him what he describes as the worst 12 months of his life.

'It was like a prison' said Law. 'I am not one for the high life. All I wanted was to be treated like a human being. It wasn't long before I realised I had made a ghastly mistake. It all finally blew up when Torino refused me permission to play for Scotland. That was the end as far as I was concerned. I stormed out so quickly that I left all my clothes behind. I never saw them again.'

Torino threatened Law with all sorts of legal sanctions to try to get him back to Italy, but in the end they gave in. So on 12 July 1962, Denis Law signed for Manchester United for a record fee of £115,000. And what a marvellous deal it turned out to be. For a decade, the 'king' ruled over his Old Trafford empire. The United fans respected the skills of Bobby Charlton, they revelled at the sight of the genius which was George Best, but they worshipped Denis Law, the hero of the Stretford End.

'What I walked into from Italy was the finest football club in the world with the finest manager,' said Law. 'Matt Busby always stuck by me through thick and thin. Your problems at home, your illnesses, any little worries – they were all his business. That's what made him so different. That is why you gave everything for him on the field.'

Not that Law was always the apple of Busby's eye. Three times between 1963 and 1967, his fiery temperament landed him in trouble with referees. Twice he was suspended for 28 days. And that is not the type of record guaranteed to endear you to Matt Busby.

He had a head-on clash with Busby in 1966, when he grandly told the club in a letter that unless he was offered better terms he would ask for a transfer. Busby refused to be blackmailed, even by the jewel in his Old Trafford crown, called his bluff and transfer-listed him. A few days later, a sheepish Law made a public apology.

But the good times outweighed the bad. Law helped the Reds win the League title in 1964–65 and 1966–67, and collected an FA Cup winners' medal in 1963. He was also voted European Footballer of the Year in 1964. Sadly injury forced him to miss United's greatest triumph – the European Cup final victory in 1968. Perhaps because of this his fondest memory at Old Trafford remains the 1963 FA Cup final against

A well earned breather and a glass of refreshment for Denis Law as he relaxes alongside Noel Cantwell after clinching the League championship in 1965

Leicester: 'It was one of the greatest games I played for United. I can see Paddy Crerand now hitting me with a perfect ball from the left wing. I turned quickly and hit the ball into the net past Gordon Banks' right hand. It was the first goal, and one I had always dreamed of scoring at Wembley.'

The Demon King was electric near goal. When he jumped he seemed to have a personal sky hook, so long did he hang in the air above defenders.

His razor reflexes and courage brought him 171 goals from 305 League appearances in his ten years at Old Trafford. In the FA Cup he had an incredible return of 34 goals in 44 appearances, while European competition brought him the even more impressive scoring rate of 28 goals in 33 matches. The Stretford End took him to their heart: they perhaps loved not just his goals but the streak of villainy that also ran through his game.

In July 1973, after battling against a knee injury for two years, United allowed him to join Manchester City on a free transfer in recognition of his services. Perhaps the best way to illustrate the bond which existed between Law and Old Trafford, is to recall an incident in April 1974, when Law's back-heeled goal for Manchester City sent United plunging into the Second Division. This time there was no characteristic punching of the air in celebration. Law, head down, walked slowly back to the centre circle with the look of a man who had just stabbed his best friend in the back.

Law scored 30 goals in 55 international appearances for Scotland. His whole career brought him 217 League goals in 452 games. After retiring in 1974, at the end of his second spell with Manchester City, he virtually hung up his boots. His bravery had left him with a legacy of injuries which wouldn't really permit him to play any more. That was the price he paid for his storming career.

The other Championship winners

Just like Denis Law, there was something of the lost waif about George Best when he arrived at Old Trafford. He was a skinny 15-year-old from Belfast, desperately homesick at being away from home for the first time in his life. Indeed, after 24 hours, he and his young Irish companion from Belfast, Eric McMordie, fled back to Ireland. But Busby was quickly on the phone, and with the help of his father, George was persuaded to give it another go.

Best had been recommended by United's legendary Northern Ireland scout Bob Bishop, who sent this simple note to Busby: 'I think I have found a genius.' It wasn't long before Harry Gregg and his United team-mates found out that Bishop was not exaggerating. Gregg recalls:

> I think the first time I ever saw George in action was when I volunteered to go to our training ground, The Cliff, one afternoon to help with the kids. There was a bit of a practice game planned and I went in goal on one side with George on the other. After a while he got the ball and raced clear of our defence. I had always prided myself on the fact that I could make forwards do what I wanted in these circumstances. But this slip of a boy shook his hips and had me diving at fresh air while the ball went in the other corner of the net.
>
> I thought, right, you won't get away with that again. But blow me, a few minutes later he brought the ball up to me again . . . and did exactly the same thing. I knew in that moment that the club had a very rare talent on their hands.

Best brought his young genius to bear on the left wing, often roaming far for the ball, while the more orthodox Connelly supplied penetration on the right flank. Law and Herd fired in most of the ammunition, scoring nearly 50 goals between them.

Charlton and Crerand generated ideas and movement while the whole pattern was based on solid defence. Centre-half Bill Foulkes was rightly proud of his department's contribution and was the first to point up the increasingly effective role of the fast emerging Nobby Stiles. After winning the Championship he said:

> The forwards are the glamour boys, especially the ones who score goals. But I would say we are stronger in defence now than we have ever been since I joined the club 17 years ago.

The career of Nobby Stiles is perhaps an example of how hard it is for a defender to steal the limelight. He must be one of the most under-rated players in the game. He is regarded by most people as a strong-tackling wing-half, a destroyer if you like, and indeed this is an important role in any team which he does exceptionally well for Manchester United.

But he also has skills which are often overlooked. For instance he is a fine reader of a game. He brings aggression to the team, and let's be honest, without some aggression in your team you might as well stop in the dressing room. Nobby will also supply hard work involving a lot of unselfish running.

He probably didn't help himself in his early days by getting into trouble. He is impetuous, though if you knew him off the field you would find it difficult to imagine. His nickname for instance at the club is 'Happy'.

I must admit that Happy has had his unhappy moments on the field of play, but I think he has improved. Fortunately Alf Ramsey has been able to see his real worth. He at least has a high regard for his skills or he would not be playing him as a link man at wing-half for England.

England need more players like him. It is all very well having a team full of highly skilled individualists, but not all of them are noted for hard work and someone has to supply the steam for the outfit to function.

If you had 11 Nobby Stiles in a team you would not need to worry about losing. He is a player in the real meaning of the world. I think he and I struck up a good understanding in our Championship season.

Our full backs, Tony Dunne and Shay Brennan, also played well together. What a contrast this pair make to the old-time defenders who were invariably big brawny fellows whose aim was to stop the wingers at any cost. Both Tony and Shay are strong and they don't lack courage, but they are not exactly bruisers. They fit into the modern concept which calls for defenders to have the skill of forwards with an eye for going up in attack whenever the situation calls for it.

Both of them rely on skill for getting the ball rather than brute strength, and they can speed along, especially Tony who must be one of the fastest backs in the business.

The tackling of Nobby Stiles improved when he began to wear contact lenses. He had worn glasses from a young age and naturally took them off for football. The situation left him short on visual judgement. As Bobby Charlton once said: 'Nobby doesn't so much tackle people as bump into them.' It's said that his eyesight was so defective that he once left a football banquet in a big hotel, returned, sat down and then realised he was at someone else's dinner.

Certainly there was a marked improvement in Stiles' timing when he started to wear contact

Above: Trouble and George Best went hand in hand towards the end of his career as his name went into referees' notebooks with increasing regularity

Top: Nobby Stiles was a terrier defender for both United and England as he clearly demonstrates here

Left: Alex Stepney, the United goalkeeper, is on the receiving end of a finger-wagging lecture from Nobby Stiles

lenses, and he went on to become one of England's heroes when they beat West Germany to win the World Cup at Wembley in the summer of 1966. Who can forget the merry jig he did round Wembley without his front teeth but with a grin that seemed to spread across his entire face? Stiles and Bobby Charlton reflected great credit on Manchester United with the way they performed for England on the World Cup stage.

Disciplinary problems

What did not reflect so well on Old Trafford around this period was the number of times United players were in trouble with referees.

Although Stiles improved his tackling with the advantage of being able to see, he still let his feelings run away with him with gestures of annoyance at referees.

Denis Law rarely finished a season without being sent off, Pat Crerand had his volatile moments and eventually George Best ran into trouble with referees.

In the 1963–64 season Noel Cantwell, David Herd, Denis Law and Pat Crerand were all sent off. Albert Quixall was dismissed while playing for the reserves and even Bobby Noble was sent off playing for the youth team.

In 1964–65, on the way to the Championship, Law received the second of his four-week bans after clashing at Blackpool with the ego of York referee Peter Rhodes, who was determined to make clear who had the last word in such matters. Cantwell and Harry Gregg were given early baths with the reserves and Stiles was fined £100 for totalling too many cautions.

Gregg and Crerand received marching orders in 1965–66. Another Championship year in 1966–67 saw Stiles sent off and later suspended for three weeks for accumulating too many bookings. Law survived the season but managed to get himself dismissed on a summer tour in Australia.

The European Cup triumph of 1967–68 was accompanied by a six-week ban for Law following a spectacular bust-up and very early bath with Ian Ure against Arsenal. John Fitzpatrick, Brian Kidd and Carlo Sartori were also sent off.

Needless to say, cautions were numerous and revealed an undisciplined trait in the make-up of an otherwise gloriously successful period. The black streak contrasted so vividly with the man at the helm, a manager who throughout his career represented all that was fair and best in the game of football. There is no simple explanation except to say that United were playing more games than most, matches of high tension, in this period, and that many of their offences were in retaliation. Crerand for one couldn't abide cheats, and if he felt an opponent was taking a liberty with him he was more inclined to take an immediate swing at him than wait in the time-honoured way to get his own back with a hard tackle when the chance arose.

Law was a highly strung character who reacted fiercely to provocation and Stiles was another impatient character who couldn't suffer fools, poor referees and poor linesmen gladly.

Busby never went in for the tactics of Don Revie at Leeds, but possibly, after the experience of Munich, he was prepared to turn a blind eye to some of the excesses of his players in his ambition to make Manchester United a power in the game again. As the years went by he was not getting any younger and he was a man in a hurry. In any case how did you control the emotions of a player like Denis Law, so explosive and so often kicked black and blue by opponents seeking to contain him?

The talented trinity of Denis Law, George Best and Bobby Charlton celebrate a goal for Manchester United against Wolves in March 1966. It was because of the entertainment value of players like this famous trio, coupled with success, that attendances at Old Trafford started to boom. An average League crowd of 53,984 watched the team in 1966–67. The following season a record was established with a League average at Old Trafford of 57,759, a figure never likely to be bettered on an English club ground in these days of stricter crowd control and reduced capacities

A second title in 1966–67

United launched into the 1965–66 season as champions determined to make an impression on three fronts and that is exactly what they did, even though they failed to land a trophy.

They were playing in their beloved European Cup again and produced some splendid football until stopped by Partizan Belgrade in the semi-finals. The Reds reached the semi-finals of the FA Cup as well after one or two scares. For instance in the fifth round at Wolves they were two goals down after only nine minutes, both from penalties, but recovered for Law (two), Best and Herd to give them a 4–2 win. They beat Preston in the sixth round after a replay at Old Trafford to reach the semi-finals for the fifth successive season. But a hectic season seemed to catch up with them when they played Everton at Burnden Park just three days after meeting Partizan Belgrade in the second leg of the European semi-final. Best was missing with a knee injury and his colleagues looked jaded in contrast to Everton, who had fielded virtually a reserve team the previous Saturday in order to rest their senior players. They were later fined £2,000, but that was little consolation for United, who fought stubbornly but without any spark on their way to a 1–0 defeat.

It seemed as if the two Cup runs had dissipated United's strength in the League, too. David Herd scored 24 League goals, Charlton got 16 and Law 15, but the Reds never strung more than three wins together on the trot. They were always among the leading group of clubs and put in a great finish, beating Blackburn 4–1 away and whipping Aston Villa 6–1 at Old Trafford, but they had to be content with fourth place while Liverpool took the title six points ahead of Leeds and Burnley and ten ahead of United.

Bobby Charlton and Nobby Stiles went off to play for England in the World Cup triumph and everybody reported back for the start of season 1966–67 determined to learn from the near-misses.

They didn't make a particularly good start, but Busby made a few changes. He had Bobby Noble and Johnny Aston ready after coming through with the team which had won the FA Youth Cup in 1964. Noble took over at left-back and Aston at outside-left, with Best switched to the right to replace the departed Connelly. David Sadler also won a regular place as an attacking midfield player.

Busby bought a new goalkeeper, paying Tommy Docherty at Chelsea £50,000 for Alex Stepney. At the end of the season the manager described the arrival of Stepney as the biggest single factor behind the winning of the 1966–67 Championship four points in front of Nottingham Forest. United were particularly strong in the second half of the season, perhaps helped by the fact that they were not in Europe and that they were knocked out of both the FA Cup and the League Cup in early rounds.

The Reds certainly clinched the title with a flourish, beating West Ham 6–1 in London to take the honours with a match to spare. It was the biggest away win of the season in the First Division. The team went through the season unbeaten at home, where they were watched by a League average crowd of 53,800. They were in relentless mood, even to the end. As Nobby Stiles said afterwards: 'Just after we had scored our sixth goal at West Ham I trotted over to Bill Foulkes and said: "Congratulations, Bill, on your fourth championship medal", but all he did was give me a rollicking and tell me to concentrate on the game.'

It was determination by Stiles that had started the scoring, though. The England wing-half thrust for goal and pressured the West Ham defence into trouble. The ball spun loose across the area for Bobby Charlton to streak through a gap between two players and hammer home a goal after only two minutes. Pat Crerand, Bill Foulkes and George Best added goals to put the Reds four up in the first 25 minutes. Denis Law scored twice in the second half, one from the penalty spot, for a swashbuckling finale.

It was a crashing climax to a season in which the Reds paced the title with a perfect sense of timing and produced a remorseless last lap that was too good for their opponents. For this was a Championship won on the classical formula of winning at home and drawing away. This was the pattern from Christmas as they turned for home into the second half of the season. The sequence started with a 1–0 win at Old Trafford against Spurs on 14 January. The following week at Maine Road the Reds drew 1–1 with Manchester City. And they never looked back as they marched on to a run of eight away draws backed by eight home victories. This was the solid base, consistent and relentless, from which they sprang to tear West Ham to pieces and take the title.

At the turn of the year United had been locked in a three-horse race, jockeying for top place with Liverpool, while Nottingham Forest were the dark horses rising swiftly after a long and powerful winning run. By mid-March United were still level pegging with Liverpool, though ahead on goal average, and Forest had dropped back a little. On 25 March came one of those decisive games, for on that day United, the challengers, took on Liverpool, the reigning champions, in the lion's den at Anfield.

The Reds had feared Liverpool all season, particularly after only drawing with them at Old Trafford in December. In fact Denis Law was having nightmares. He dreamed that he was playing at Anfield, took the ball up to Ron Yeats, beat him, scored a goal . . . and then fell into The Kop! As it turned out, no-one scored, but the point was a great result for United and a bad one for Bill Shankly's men, who slowly slid out of the picture after failing to close the gap that the match had offered.

Forest now turned out to be the greater danger. The Forest fire was spreading and they were breathing down United's neck. They got within a point at one stage, and the game that proved decisive for them was on 11 February when they came to play at Old Trafford.

There was a 62,727 attendance, with the gates locked. It took the Reds until five minutes from the end to crack Forest, but the scoring maestro, Law, then banged in the winner. That was the beginning of the end for the team, managed by old United maestro Johnny Carey, though no-one at Old Trafford will forget the first encounter of the season between the two clubs at Nottingham in October. The Reds crashed to their heaviest defeat of the season, beaten 4–1, and they slipped to eighth in the table, the low water mark of the campaign.

The 'Busby boobies' had been one football writer's description of that performance. Hardly that perhaps, but it was certainly a critical game, and a significant one for Bobby Noble, who along with Noel Cantwell was drafted into the team after the defeat. The choice of Noble meant that Matt Busby had once again turned to his fruitful youth in an hour of need. The youngster took his chance brilliantly until a car accident following his return from Sunderland robbed him of the last few games and his career.

Shay Brennan slipped quietly but effectively back into his place to keep the victory push going. A much more difficult problem was posed when David Herd broke his leg against Leicester City at Old Trafford on 18 March in the act of scoring his 16th League goal. It could easily have been Herd's best scoring season with United and it was with some anxiety that the manager waited to see whether the team could get by without any more goals from him.

No doubt he recalled the injury to George Best at a similar stage of the previous season. For when Best had injured his knee, leading to a cartilage operation, the whole team faded and they lost the FA Cup semi-final and the European Cup semi-final. But this time they stayed steady, and others came forward to help shoulder the scoring burden.

Law, of course, remained the leading spirit in United's sparkling attack. Charlton came back to his best in the second half of the season, and after Herd's injury stepped up his scoring rate, notably with a fine pair against Sheffield Wednesday at Hillsborough. The United manager also helped cover Herd's absence by switching Stiles into the attack to add more fire and bringing David Sadler, a most versatile performer, back from the forward line to form a fine double centre-half pairing with Foulkes.

Stiles, now wearing his dental plate for matches because he considered that his fierce toothless appearance as seen on television during the World Cup frightened referees and got him into trouble, finished the season in fine form. Although the attack dazzled in many games with George Best another brilliant ace in the pack, United's defence paved the way by holding on through some lean scoring spells and hard away games. Foulkes started the season with many people wondering whether the club should have bought a new centre-half; he gave the answer himself with some uncompromising displays.

Every player played his part, including Tony Dunne, brilliant at full-back and Irish Footballer of the Year; Pat Crerand, the architect of so much of United's midfield play; the young left-winger John Aston, who came through a critical spell superbly, and players who came in for brief but vital periods like Noel Cantwell, wing-half John Fitzpatrick and forward Jimmy Ryan.

And what wonderful support there was to urge them to the Championship. The Old Trafford crowd – over a million watched United's home League games, the highest since the war – and the fans who travelled to bring record gates at several away matches, also helped bring European football back to Old Trafford.

Matt Busby gave notice he would be there to lead the next campaign. 'I'm too young to retire,' said the longest serving club manager in the game.

It wasn't just winning the Championship that brought the crowds flocking to watch United home and away in such numbers: it was the quality of their football and the personalities packed into their team.

George Best

George Best had become a cult figure by this time. He took your breath away with his finesse on the field and he was worshipped off it, especially by the girls. He was a new breed of footballer, with a following more like that of a pop star.

It was the age of the Beatles and the swinging sixties and George, with his cute eyes and Beatle haircut was ready to swing with the best of them. Girls sobbed as they stared at him through the windows of the team coach. Writers flocked to his door to examine the magic not just of his play but of his appeal for beauty queens and actresses.

Busby had already declared: 'George has the lot. He's a world-class footballer.' Alf Ramsey was sighing: 'I wish he had been born in England.' Of course it all went wrong at the end, but in 1967 he was simply a brilliant player. His life style off the field was still regarded as a bit of a lark, certainly by the media.

After all, he was different. By early 1966 he had opened a men's boutique with a partner, Malcolm Mooney, in Cheshire. Later he moved

Right: George Best in full flight against Manchester City at Maine Road

Opposite: The bewitching George Best liked at times to taunt opponents, at least those who tried to kick him!

Below: Fame on the football field made George Best into a much sought after figure on the social scene, even meeting Prime Minister Harold Wilson at Downing Street . . . and no doubt hearing a few tales of Huddersfield Town!

Bottom: In the Swinging Sixties George Best, complete with the status symbol of a Jaguar car, set new trends for football by opening his own boutique

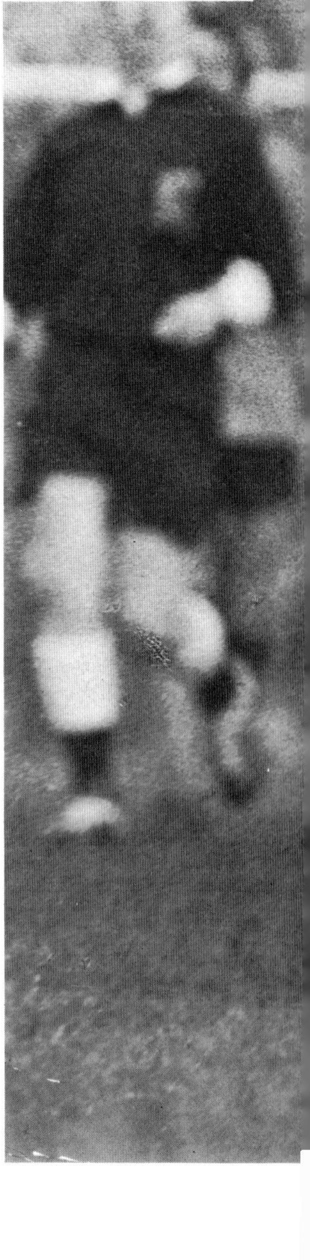

his shop into the centre of Manchester. Later still he had a night club. But at the beginning he simply swept everything before him, a prince of players who also planned to become the first British footballer millionaire.

It was already difficult to appreciate that this was the young boy who had come over from Belfast to join United aged 15 and almost immediately gone back to Ireland because he was homesick and didn't like it. Now he was so cool that he was always the last man into the dressing room to get changed for the match.

Defining what made him such a great player is difficult. Most simply, he could do virtually everything just a little better than almost everybody else. His balance was exquisite, helped by a natural grace of movement. He had a perfectly proportioned physique, and was much stronger than he appeared. He had the ability not only to take the ball past opponents but to get himself past as well, skipping neatly over flying boots and avoiding all the other physical attempts to stop him which his skill provoked.

Few succeeded in nailing him, and he was rarely injured, although often going into areas where players get hurt. He was just so nimble, a quality which also made him a very good ball-winner. He seemed able to go in for the ball and come out with it without even making contact with the man in possession.

He could run with the ball seemingly tied to his proverbial bootlaces. He could play one-twos off an opponent's legs; it would look like a lucky break the first time, and then you realised he was doing it deliberately. On reflection he didn't seem to score many headers, but it didn't matter because he could do so much with his feet; he was a true footballer.

The players all had their own ideas about how the team came to win the 1966–67 Championship. Bobby Charlton said: 'We won it because we believed right from the start that we could do it.'

Pat Crerand said: 'Being knocked out of the FA Cup so early was a blessing in disguise. Also the fact that we weren't competing in Europe. There were no Wednesday matches to worry about, no race against time to get players fit. By Saturday everybody was bursting to play. There was no pressure. In fact it was our easiest season.'

George Best reflected: 'If the Championship were decided on home games we would win it every season. This time our away games made the difference. We got into the right frame of mind.'

Tony Dunne added: 'We realised that teams without as much ability as us were giving more effort. Our great players in particular realised this and came through at just the right time.'

Noel Cantwell, no longer a regular, summed up: 'It's simply that Matt Busby has built another great team.'

So United celebrated the success which had given them another tilt at the European Cup after the disappointment of failing to do justice to themselves in foreign competition against Partizan Belgrade two years previously.

Busby, now in his 21st year as manager at Old Trafford, had only one cloud on his horizon. He needed another forward to take over from David Herd, who had broken his leg the previous season.

Herd knew all about scoring long before Busby had persuaded Arsenal to part with him in the summer of 1961 for £40,000. The previous season he had finished second to Jimmy Greaves as the Football League's top marksman. The United manager had played with his father, Alex Herd, at Manchester City and watched father and son achieve the rare distinction of playing in the same League team together at Stockport County.

The Manchester clubs had let Herd slip through their fingers as a youngster. His father still lived near the Edgeley Park ground when David travelled north to join an exciting era at Old Trafford. Because of players like Charlton, Law and Best, Herd often seemed to get second billing, but his contribution should never be underestimated.

In his first season at Old Trafford, while still settling in, he scored 14 League goals, but then he reeled off a string of 19, 20, 20 and 24 before breaking his leg in March of the 1966–67 Championship season with his tally at 16. He was actually in the process of scoring against Leicester in a 5–2 win when the fracture occurred. It was a bad one and you could see his foot hanging at a broken angle.

'I was watching my shot on its way into goal when Graham Cross came sliding in and that was it,' he recalls now. 'I was getting a bit long in the tooth, and there were a few in the team in a similar position, so the following season I was transferred to Stoke. I had two good seasons there, but the broken leg was the end of the good times for me with Manchester United.'

After Stoke, and two years in management at Lincoln, he retired from football to concentrate on his motor car and garage business in Davyhulme, near Manchester, and play cricket locally at Timperley and Brooklands. He has been a

Matt Busby leads his players round Old Trafford on a lap of honour after United won the championship again in 1966–67. Bill Foulkes holds the trophy aloft followed by Tony Dunne, Pat Crerand, Alex Stepney, Denis Law, George Best, John Aston, Bobby Charlton and Shay Brennan. The manager named Alex Stepney as the biggest single factor behind the title success after buying him from Chelsea for £50,000 early in the campaign. United went through the season unbeaten at home and clinched the title with a flourish, winning 6–1 at West Ham, the best away win of the season in the First Division

United season ticket holder for years and has seen a procession of strikers struggle to achieve what seemed to come so naturally to him and reach the target of 20 League goals in a season.

He says: 'I don't like harking back, but in my day 20 goals was quite commonplace, not just by me but by Denis Law, George Best and Bobby Charlton. When we won the Championship the first time in 1964–65 five of us were in double figures. The second time in 1966–67 there were four of us with at least ten apiece. United have had a lot of good players since those days, but because of the way the game is played now by so many teams it is more difficult to score. Actually I feel sorry for the strikers of today.

United certainly found the right man to follow in David Herd's footsteps in 1967. Brian Kidd, born downtown in Collyhurst, went to St. Patrick's School, a place of soccer learning which had already produced Nobby Stiles and many more. His father was a bus driver on the route which went past Old Trafford; perhaps being held up in traffic jams on match days accounted for dad being a Manchester City fan, though he raised no objections to his son joining United when he left school. Busby took young Brian on tour to Australia in 1967, and deemed him ready.

Kidd was always solidly built and strong on the ball and Busby put him in the FA Charity Shield match against Spurs at the beginning of 1967–68, a match entertainingly drawn 3–3. He made his League debut in the opening match of the season, lost 3–1 at Everton. Still only 18, he stayed in the side for the rest of the season to score 15 goals in 38 appearances. After three months of senior football he was picked for the first of his England Under-23 caps, playing on the wing against Wales with team-mate David Sadler at centre-half.

The season saw yet another youngster from the juniors reach the first team. Francis Burns, who had captained the Scottish schoolboys, had also been on the tour of Australia, and after recovering from a close-season cartilage operation was brought in at left-back, with Tony Dunne switching sides to squeeze Shay Brennan out for lengthy spells. The shaggy haired John Fitzpatrick, a Scottish terrier of a wing-half also from the youth team, played quite a few games, but it was still basically the team of the previous season.

Despite losing the opening game, United went the next 11 without defeat and just after the turn of the year, the reigning champions held a five-point lead at the top of the table. They seemed on course to keep their title, and there were many who saw their FA Cup third-round exit in a replay against Spurs as confirmation that they would see success in the League again.

A poor spell which started in mid-February saw them lose their advantage. Five defeats in a run of eight games let Manchester City into the race. Losing to the Blues 3–1 at Old Trafford at this point didn't exactly help their cause.

The two Manchester clubs were level on points when they went into their final matches. With the second leg of their European Cup semi-final against Real Madrid in Spain only four days distant, United wavered and lost 2–1 at home to lowly Sunderland. Manchester City on the other hand finished with a flourish to beat Newcastle United 4–3 at St James's Park and so take the title by two points.

Blame certainly could not be laid at the feet of George Best, who played 41 League games and scored 28 goals, his best season as a marksman, which coupled with his feats in European competition saw him voted Footballer of the Year. In any case finishing second was not exactly failure, particularly when set against their achievement this season of winning the European Cup. The pursuit of the elusive trophy which had cost them so dearly in 1958 had become something of an obsession by this time, and as the quarter-finals approached in late February, their concentration was focusing more and more on Europe.

Law was missing in the last couple of championship games with a further recurrence of knee trouble which finally put him into hospital for an operation while his team were playing Benfica in the final of the European Cup. The Scot had been troubled for a long time by his knee, and at one point he was told that there was nothing physically wrong with it and that the problem was his imagination. Subsequently after an operation had removed some foreign bodies from the joint, he had them bottled in preservative and labelled: 'They said they were in my mind.'

No-one could really begrudge City their Championship. The partnership of Joe Mercer and Malcolm Allison had produced a fine team featuring players like Francis Lee, Colin Bell, Mike Summerbee, Tony Book, Mike Doyle and Alan Oakes.

The United fans had also seen some splendid matches and had responded to the achievements of the team, their colourful personalities and their entertaining brand of football in unbelievable numbers. The average League attendance at Old Trafford was 57,696, an all-time British record surpassing Newcastle United's crowds of the immediate post-war boom years. United's figures will probably never be beaten following the reduction of ground capacities in keeping with more stringent safety requirements.

The supporters had no time really to feel disappointment at seeing the Championship move across the city. As soon as the Sunderland match was over, the club were packing for Spain and a date with their old friends, the matadors of Madrid. Anticipation was at fever pitch, and after all, it was really a season which belonged to Europe. One only felt sorry for Manchester City, whose Championship achievement after so many long lean years was to be so soon overshadowed by their neighbours' triumph in the European Cup!

EUROPEAN CHAMPION CLUBS' CUP
BENFICA F.C.
MANCHESTER UNITED
MANCHESTER UNITED FOOTBALL CLUB
FINAL
ORGANISED BY THE FOOTBALL ASSOCIATION ON BEHALF OF THE
UNION DES ASSOCIATIONS EUROPÉENNES DE FOOTBALL
WEDNESDAY MAY 29th 1968
Kick-off 7·45 p.m.
ONE SHILLING
OFFICIAL PROGRAMME
WEMBLEY
EMPIRE STADIUM

Europe! Europe! Europe!

Manchester United were the first English club to win the European Cup. The capture of the coveted championship was a journey's end for Matt Busby and a vindication of so much he had striven for in his career.
It was an achievement which represented his patience, planning and philosophy. Some had died along a tragic road involving the air disaster at Munich. The staff and players who had picked up the challenge parade the trophy in this picture taken at the start of season 1968–69. They line up: Front row: Jimmy Ryan, Tony Dunne, Nobby Stiles, Denis Law, Matt Busby (manager), Bobby Charlton, Brian Kidd, George Best, John Fitzpatrick.
Middle: David Sadler, Bill Foulkes, John Aston, Shay Brennan, Jimmy Rimmer, Pat Crerand, Alex Stepney, Alan Gowling, David Herd, Francis Burns, Jack Crompton (trainer).
Back: Ted Dalton (physiotherapist), Denzil Haroun, (director), Bill Young (director), Louis Edwards (chairman), Alan Gibson (director), Jimmy Murphy (assistant manager), Les Olive (secretary)

Manchester United beat Benfica 4–1 in extra time at Wembley to win the European Cup . . . grasped firmly here at long last by Bobby Charlton, the captain

Manchester United travelled through a vale of tears to become the champions of Europe. It must have been a bittersweet moment indeed for Matt Busby when his club finally won the European Cup. How the memories must have flooded back that fine May evening at Wembley in 1968 when the Reds beat Benfica 4–1 in extra time to become the first English team to conquer the Continent.

It had been a long, hard journey, setting out in recriminations with the Football League and enduring the misery and woe of Munich before arriving at that golden triumph. So many Busby Babes had perished on the way.

'For a long time the responsibility of urging us down that road to Europe weighed heavily on my mind, but of course no-one knew the catastrophe that lay ahead. Like the rest of life we just have to do our best and do what seems right at the time,' explained Matt Busby.

Certainly there was sadness as well as joy when Busby and Bobby Charlton fell into each other's arms out on the pitch at Wembley. It was much more than the glow of victory as one of the surviving players of the Munich tragedy turned to the manager who had himself come back from the brink of death. It was the journey's end, the climax to a great adventure, which like life itself had contained sorrows and successes.

As Bill Foulkes, the other crash survivor who also shared a winning hug with Busby, reflects: 'I had come the whole way with the Boss trying to make Manchester United the champions of Europe. I thought the destruction of our team at Munich would have been the end of it, but he patiently put together another side. I'm proud to have been a part of it, and for those of us who lost our friends coming home from a European Cup-tie in 1958, our victory seemed the right tribute to their memory.'

Years of work fashioning a team capable of challenging the best in Europe had been destroyed on that fateful trip home from Belgrade.

Back in 1956, Busby and his chairman, Harold Hardman, had even defied the authority of the League for the right to compete in a championship of champions. Together they had changed the face of English football and Wembley saw Matt Busby fulfil his great dream. It was a triumph against adversity as well as a gladiatorial victory. Little wonder the tears flowed afresh, almost drowning the happiness of winners. You could see the emotion in the faces of the two Munich survivors, Bill Foulkes, who was making his 30th appearance in the European Cup, and Bobby Charlton, who had played in 20 of the ties. Both certainly knew what the occasion meant to Matt Busby.

Even the youngest, Brian Kidd, who celebrated his 19th birthday on the day of the final, was gripped by the significance of the game.

'I want us to win for the Boss', he kept saying.

Foulkes, who had scored the winning goal in the semi-final second leg in Real Madrid, was convinced that if they were good enough to beat their old Spanish rivals, they could account for Benfica. For although Benfica were still a fine side, packed with internationals, United had beaten them 5–1 in Lisbon at the quarter-final stage of the European Cup two years earlier, and with the advantage of playing the final in England at Wembley, defeat was simply never contemplated.

The team that played Benfica reflected the patience, planning and philosophy of Busby. For although money had played its part in rebuilding the club after the shattering tragedy of Munich the fact remained that only two men in the Wembley line-up had come to Old Trafford for big fees. It was basically a team fashioned from boys recruited when they left school and groomed at Old Trafford. With Denis Law watching the final from a hospital bed after a knee operation, only Alex Stepney and Pat Crerand had cost fees among the 12 men named for the big day.

The absence of Law, who had had an injury-haunted season anyway, United took in their stride. By now George Best had arrived in world class. He was at his peak. Matt Busby knew that the spirit of the team was right. During the sunny days at Egham he had described it: 'Their heart is right and this is the important thing.'

Best certainly needed heart as he ran up

against the hard tackling of the Portuguese champions. He was tripped early by Cruz, and when his colleague Humberto joined in the harassing, the Portuguese player had his name taken by the referee. But with Benfica obsessed with the necessity for marking Best – no doubt they had vivid memories of their massacre at his hands two years previously – other players were left with more freedom. David Sadler, for instance, missed more than one opportunity of opening the scoring. Bobby Charlton saved his embarrassment when he leapt into the air to head a centre from Tony Dunne high into the far corner of the net. A Charlton header was a rarity, and this one was beautifully timed.

Perhaps sensing victory, John Aston began the first of many brilliant runs on the left wing and Best contributed a dazzling piece of football to help Sadler to another near-miss. Ten minutes from the end Benfica pulled themselves together and Jaime Graca hit an equaliser after Torres, who up to this point had been well held by Bill Foulkes, had headed the ball down to him.

Below: A serious looking Manchester United walk out for the final of the European Cup in 1968 led by skipper Bobby Charlton followed by Alex Stepney, Brian Kidd and George Best. Italian referee Concetto Lo Bello (left) leads the two teams

Above: John Aston was an unlikely star in the final of the European Cup. He produced a sparkling display of fast, elusive running down the flank capped by threatening crosses. Late in the game he cut Benfica's right side to ribbons and was a key figure in the victory which must have been especially sweet for him

Left: Best was tightly marked right from the start of the Wembley final. Henrique won this challenge, but the Irish imp was to have the last word

Top: Matt Busby said his team had great heart and that it was a quality which filled him with confidence as he prepared the players for the final of the European Cup. They certainly had to draw on something as they sank on to the Wembley turf with the score level 1–1 at the end of normal time. For five precious minutes Busby moved among them to inspire their will to fight and massage their spirit of heart which he knew in the end could be the winning factor . . . and how right he was proved

Now it was United's turn to wilt as Benfica surged forward and Eusebio, for once escaping Nobby Stiles, had victory at his feet. He burst through and hammered a tremendous shot which Stepney saved superbly with a sheer reflex action. Perhaps if Eusebio had been content to try and score modestly, he would have made it easily; but the Portuguese star hit the ball hard and his shot was too close to Stepney, whose reflexes were tested as he parried the ball away. It was the save of the match and Eusebio stayed behind to pat his opponent on the back and contribute his applause.

Stiles reckoned afterwards that if the game had gone on without a break for a few more minutes Benfica would have won.

'For me it was like the World Cup Final with England all over again when Germany pulled level just before the end,' he said. So normal time ended with the score 1–1 and Matt Busby strode on to the field to talk to his tired team for five precious minutes.

'I told them they were throwing the game away with careless passing instead of continuing with their confident football. I told them they must start to hold the ball and play again.' This was the Busby inspiration that roused the players and brought out the 'heart' he had spoken about before the match.

John Aston hit back at the fans who had booed him at Old Trafford earlier in the season with a tremendous display in extra time, cutting Benfica's right flank to pieces. Aston led the offensive, but in the first minute of extra time it was Stepney who kicked a long clearance which Kidd headed forward for Best. Watch-dog Cruz was tiring now and he failed to hold his opponent as Best tore away. Henrique came out of his goal to narrow the angle, but Best swerved to his left on a curve round the Benfica goalkeeper before clipping the ball into the net.

Benfica were on their knees as United came in for the kill. Kidd headed Charlton's corner kick at Henrique. The goalkeeper somehow beat out

the ball but Kidd was there again to head in off the bar for a real birthday celebration. Charlton supplied the final touch as he flicked Kidd's right-wing centre high into the Benfica goal to hammer home a 4–1win.

United's long quest was over, the European Championship was at Old Trafford at last. Best was voted Footballer of the Year by the English soccer writers, and a little later he was elected European Player of the Year, the youngest ever. Soon afterwards Matt Busby was knighted for his services to sport.

John Aston confessed to a great deal of personal satisfaction, to which he was entitled following a trying time in the League. United had worn blue in the final. 'Blue is a good colour for the Astons,' he said. 'My dad wore a blue shirt when he won an FA Cup winners' medal with United in 1948.'

David Sadler was also a relieved man: 'I was ready to shoulder the blame of losing after missing a couple of early chances.' But in any case he underestimated his contribution with spot-on passing and the way he had constantly turned defence into attack.

A lot of people had also underestimated Nobby Stiles after a press build-up suggesting he might try to kick the great Portuguese World Cup star Eusebio out of the game. He explained: 'I was frightened before the game with all the ballyhoo about how I would mark Eusebio. People were suggesting I was a clogger. One newspaper said he had asked the referee for protection. I just don't believe he ever said that.

Left: Bobby Charlton is the first to admit that losing his hair at a relatively early age was not caused by too much heading of the ball. Thunderbolts from either foot were a speciality, but headed goals were rare . . . perhaps reserved for special occasions. Certainly his sense of occasion was immaculate when he headed this goal to open the scoring against Benfica in the final of the European Cup. It was a superb score as he leapt high into the air to flick a centre from full-back Tony Dunne into a corner of the net. The header, perhaps not unnaturally, seemed to take most of the Press photographers by surprise. Graham Collin of the *Oldham Evening Chronicle* was one of the few, perhaps the only, cameraman to catch the United captain in full flight just a fraction of a second after striking the ball

Left: George Best completed a hat-trick of European Players of the Year when he was voted top man by continental soccer writers in 1968. Bobby Charlton and Denis Law were previous holders of the Golden Ball award chosen by football reporters from 24 countries. George's European success followed his election as Footballer of the Year in England and at home in Northern Ireland. His *Le Ballon D'Or* came from 61 votes with Bobby Charlton second on 53 and Dragan Dzajic, the Yugoslav winger from Belgrade, third with 46 votes. Sir Matt Busby made the presentation at Old Trafford with Bobby Charlton and Denis Law out on the pitch to add their congratulations

I respect him and I find him all right. I have never gone out to kick him and I have played against him four times.'

Three of those games were for United and the other was for England and in all those matches the scoring star had managed only one goal, and that was from the penalty spot. That night Stiles again played him fairly with the emphasis on positioning rather than contact. Stiles does hasten to add, though: 'In the European final I have got Alex Stepney to thank for two great saves which kept my personal scoresheet clean.'

It was a good day for Tony Dunne, who not only completed a hat-trick of Cup medals, adding a European medal to those he won in the English FA Cup and the Irish Cup, but backed the Derby winner as well.

Shay Brennan enjoyed a change of fortune: 'I lost my place just before United played in the final of the FA Cup in 1963. This time I came in on the last lap, so naturally it meant even more to me.'

Brennan had taken over from young Francis Burns two games before the end of the season, but Burns was not forgotten by the thoughtful Pat Crerand, already displaying his skills as a television panellist, who told guests at the civic reception: 'We have a squad of first-team players and I would like you to thank from us those who were not on the park against Benfica but who helped us reach the final.'

Bobby Charlton summed up: 'On the morning of the game I can remember thinking that we had come too far and had been through too much for us to fail. When the final whistle had gone I remember feeling it was the ultimate achievement, not just for the individual players but for Matt Busby. It had been our duty. For some of us it had become a family thing. We had

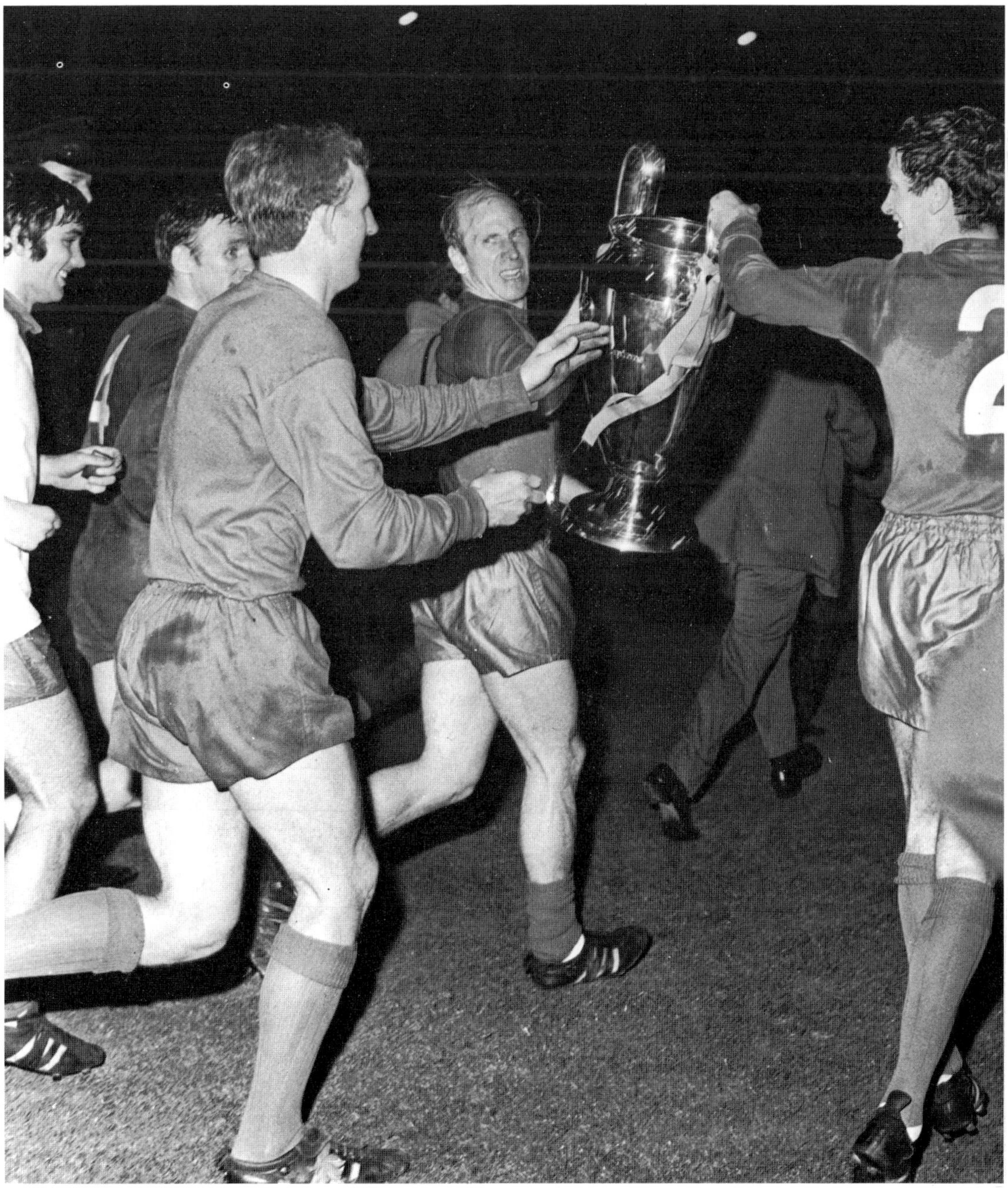

Right: Victory parade as Alex Stepney, Bobby Charlton and Shay Brennan finally get their hands on the European Cup

Above left and above: Home in triumph outside Manchester Town Hall with the European Cup while police link arms to keep huge and enthusiastic crowds at a safe distance

been together for so long, and while people recognised that we had had some great teams, there had been nothing in the European record book until 1968 to show for it.'

The teams for the final of the European Cup at Wembley on 29 May 1968 were:

Manchester United: Stepney, Brennan, A. Dunne, Crerand, Foulkes, Stiles, Best, Kidd, Charlton, Sadler, Aston. Sub: Rimmer.

Benfica: Henrique, Adolfo, Humberto, Jacinto, Cruz, Jaime Graca, Coluna, Jose Augusto, Torres, Eusebio, Simoes. Sub: Nascimento.

Referee: Concetto Lo Bello of Italy. Attendance: 100,000

United enter Europe despite League

Of course the story of Manchester United in Europe began a lot earlier than Wembley 1968, 12 years earlier to be precise, and the first battle was not out on the pitch but in the boardroom.

Modern European club competition began in the season 1955–56, originally the idea of a Frenchman and taken up again by the sporting magazine *L'Equipe*, who urged that the respective League champions of the member nations of the European Football Associations should compete for a European Championship. Representatives of clubs from 16 countries met in Paris in April of 1955 to draw up rules and a format for the new contest. Chelsea had been invited to attend, as champions of the Football League, but under pressure from the League declined. It was argued that they would have difficulty fulfilling their home commitments in League and Cup if they were involved in travelling all over Europe. It's done quite easily now of course, but in 1955 it was an entirely novel concept. Credit is due then to the Scottish authorities who had the imagination to see the possibilities and to allow Hibernian to enter.

FIFA gave its blessing to the idea and the first tournament was a great success, though in the usual insular way it was largely ignored in England. Hibernian reached the semi-finals, where they lost to Rheims, picking up around £20,000 for their trouble. At least England had a man in the final . . . Arthur Ellis refereed in Paris when Real Madrid beat Rheims 4–3.

The following season Manchester United were champions and accordingly were invited to participate. Busby was keen to take part. It seemed to him a logical progression for the best in England to put themselves up against the best from other countries. He had seen the standard of international football in England fail to move with the times. He had watched with alarm the pupils of other countries proving better than their teachers in Britain. He had marvelled as the Hungarians, who had come to Wembley in 1953 and won 6–3, demonstrated that it hadn't been an accident by beating England 7–1 in Budapest six months later. England had even been beaten by the United States of America.

Now here was a chance to show that at club level at any rate England were still powerful. He knew he had a good team backed with enough quality reserves to cope with injuries and a busy fixture programme. The League management committee again advised against entering and a letter duly arrived forbidding United to take part. But of course this was really a Football Association matter beyond the parish of the League competition, and Busby quietly had a word with Stanley Rous, then secretary of the FA, later to become president of FIFA. Rous already had a global view of football and Busby had a similar vision. Besides, it was an opportunity to earn more revenue and stimulate both players and fans.

Rous gave the nod, and Harold Hardman, the chairman of Manchester United, did not need much persuading. 'This is where the future of the game lies,' said Matt, and the chairman, a solicitor and game little man who never lost his enthusiasm for football, carried the board. Hardman had been a full international player while an amateur winger at Everton, and was one of only three amateur players this century to win an FA Cup winners' medal.

So United entered and were drawn in the preliminary round against Anderlecht, the

Johnny Berry was a key link between Matt Busby's first championship team of 1952 and the two title successes with the Busby Babes four years later. Busby signed him from Birmingham City in 1951 to fill the gap left by Jimmy Delaney at outside right. He was a tricky little winger who also won four England caps before the Munich accident ended his career with crippling injuries. He returned to his native Aldershot where he opened a sports shop business with his brother Peter, who also played League football, and later retired to continue living in the area

champions of Belgium. The first leg was played in Brussels on 12 September 1956; it was a step into the unknown for United, who were disappointed that for their first competitive match on foreign soil they were going to be without the powerful Duncan Edwards.

In the event Jackie Blanchflower, who took his place, turned in a star performance. United had an early let-off when Mark Jones handled only for Jef Mermans, the Anderlecht captain, to hit the post. Bill Foulkes hastily cleared the rebound. Then Eddie Colman created a goal for Dennis Viollet and Tommy Taylor scored to give the Manchester men a 2–0 win.

The return leg was played a fortnight later at Maine Road – the Old Trafford floodlights weren't yet ready – and United were in a purposeful mood. No-one realised just how determined they were to make sure there was no slip-up. It turned out that 43,635 spectators that night were privileged to see one of the finest performances from one of the finest sides England has ever produced.

United would have beaten any club side in the world that night. The ball sped from man to man as though it were moved by some magical influence. Ten times in 90 minutes the Anderlecht keeper picked the ball out of his net. It would have made news if an English First Division side had beaten a Fourth Division side by that margin. But this was Anderlecht, one of the top sides in Europe. The poor keeper must have felt he was having a nightmare as the goals poured past him from Viollet (4), Tommy Taylor (3), Billy Whelan (2) and Johnny Berry. Busby, who before that night must have thought he had seen it all, could scarcely believe his eyes.

However, the cocky Busby boys were nearly shot out of the Cup in the next round when they took on West German champions Borrussia Dortmund. Thousands packed into Maine Road expecting another goal glut. It looked possible for 35 minutes as Viollet (2) and David Pegg put United in a commanding position. But the Red Devils took things too easily. Roger Byrne tried to put a ball back to goalkeeper Ray Wood only to hand a goal on a plate to Kapitulski. A few minutes later another silly mistake gave the Germans a second, to cut United's lead to 3–2.

Now United had a real battle on their hands when they travelled to the Ruhr for the return. They were cheered on by 7,000 British servicemen and held the Germans to a goal-less draw with an uncharacteristic backs-to-the-wall defensive performance.

Six weeks later England's new soccer ambassadors took on Spanish champions Bilbao in the first leg of the quarter-finals. Bilbao had not been beaten on their own ground for three years. It looked as if the Babes were to learn their first bitter European lesson when they trooped off at half-time trailing 3–0. Amazingly, within eight minutes of the restart, they had pulled back to 3–2 with goals from Taylor and Viollet. But United slumped and Bilbao were coasting home again at 5–2. With five minutes to go the Reds were as good as out of the European Cup. Then Billy Whelan, the quiet boy from Dublin, picked up the ball in his own half. He started to dribble, dragging the ball through the mud, beating man after man in a wriggling 40-yard run before drawing keeper Carmelo and thumping the ball into the top left-hand corner.

The return at Maine Road was not a masterly display of football. Bilbao came with one thought in mind – they were two goals to the good and from the first whistle they brought everyone back in defence. But United were too fast, too eager. The crowd fell silent as chance after chance was missed. Busby, on the touchline, lost his usual composure. He wriggled and squirmed, smoking one cigarette after the other. As half-time approached he waved big Duncan Edwards upfield to try to break the deadlock. A minute later Edwards struck – a drive which was speeding towards the net until a defender stuck out a foot. The ball flew to the unmarked Viollet and the Reds needed only two goals.

The game restarted even more feverishly. Within minutes the crowd was roaring again. Viollet had scored. No, he hadn't. German referee Albert Deutsch had whistled for offside.

Now it was Tommy Taylor's big moment. He took the game by the scruff of the neck and shook it until victory was won. In the 70th minute he danced around Garay and cracked a left-foot drive against the post. Two minutes later he sailed around Garay again. This time there was no woodwork to help Bilbao.

The scores were level. The fans had screamed themselves hoarse and the Reds were whipped into a frenzy to get the extra goal which would give them absolute victory. Five minutes to go and still Bilbao hung on. Then Taylor again made a breathtaking dash along the right touchline. Little Johnny Berry, anticipating the move, had raced into the centre-forward position. Gently Taylor rolled the ball back. Berry's right foot did the rest.

That gay night in Manchester when Busby and his young braves celebrated a European Cup semi-final appearance, took place on 6 February 1957 . . . just 12 months precisely before the appalling disaster at Munich.

Real Madrid, United's opponents in the semi-final, were the greatest football team in the world. On a spying mission to Nice in the spring of 1957 Busby saw them in action for the first time. He saw the electrifying pace of Gento on the left wing, the class of Riall, the brilliance of Mateos, who goaded his opponents like a matador, Frenchman Kopa, who had the full range of skills, and above all the man who was one of the greatest footballers of all time – Alfredo di Stefano.

The United manager knew that his young team were going to need a slice of luck to win through but he had planned his assault on Real to the last detail when the party flew to Madrid for the first leg in April. The game at Real's magnificent Bernabeu Stadium was watched by a crowd of 120,000, and from the first whistle it was obvious what was Busby's trump card. The man he set to mark maestro di Stefano was not the powerful Duncan Edwards but the little man from Salford, Eddie Colman. Colman stuck to his man as though he was a long-lost brother.

Nevertheless Real's artistic, colourful football opened up a two-goal lead. The Reds pulled one back through Tommy Taylor, but the Spanish champions scored a third through Mateos late in the second half. United flew back to Britain and in the following weeks strode majestically on to win the League title again and reach the Cup Final. In between came the return with Real.

The game at Old Trafford, with floodlights now installed, illustrated once again the gap between top-class Continental soccer and the best in Britain. Real Madrid did not fall into the same defensive trap as Bilbao. For 20 minutes they absorbed everything that the Reds could throw at them and then struck with lightning speed. Gento opened up the United defence for Kopa to put Real ahead. Another burst from the flying left-winger created a goal for di Stefano. The 60,000 crowd were shocked into silence.

Sheer guts brought the Reds back into the game with a goal from Taylor and another from young Bobby Charlton. For once the Real defenders were glad to kick for safety but like true European champions they withstood the assault, and won the tie on a 5–3 aggregate.

Busby gave his verdict on the first season in Europe: 'The performance at the start of the competition when we beat Anderlecht so handsomely was the finest exhibition of teamwork I had ever seen from any side either at club or international level. At the end, when we met Real Madrid in the semi-final it was a contest between two great teams – a mature side and a young one, and of course experience told. But our time will come.'

The United manager had every right to fling out such a confident promise. He had built a team which had made a big impression in Europe as well as winning the First Division for the second year running and looking certain to win the FA Cup at Wembley as well.

The decision to brave the wrath of the insular Football League and enter Europe had been entirely vindicated. There had been a scare though. The team were close to being snowbound in northern Spain after the Bilbao match. The players actually helped to clear snow off the wings of their aircraft so that they could take off. You could see the dangers the League had in mind, but United had coped.

There is no knowing what Manchester United might have achieved in season 1957–58 and thereafter but for the calamity at Munich. They were in the European Cup again as champions, of course, and they opened their campaign in convincing manner with a 6–0 win over Shamrock Rovers in Dublin. Billy Whelan turned on the style for his visit home to score twice, and there were two goals from Tommy Taylor and one apiece from wingers Johnny Berry and David Pegg. United took the return leg at Old Trafford in casual mood, much to the delight of the Irishmen, who scored twice before going down 3–2 as Dennis Viollet struck a couple of times and Pegg scored again.

Dukla Prague presented stiffer oppostion in the first round proper. The Czechs had a half-back line of internationals but they could not prevent the Reds from establishing a 3–0 lead from the first leg at Old Trafford. Colin Webster, Tommy Taylor and David Pegg were the scorers. United were more accustomed now to the niceties of two-legged ties and they adopted a careful approach in Prague. With the help of some sterling play from Eddie Colman at wing-half they restricted Dukla to a 1–0 win to sail through with an aggregate 3–1 victory.

United had another fright on the way back home, though. Their plane back to London couldn't take off from Prague because the airport in England was closed through fog. Busby knew that the League would come down on them like a ton of bricks if they were late for a domestic fixture. Hastily they made other arrangements. They caught a flight to Amsterdam and completed the journey by taking a boat from the Hook of Holland to Harwich and then travelling by train and coach to Manchester.

They arrived home weary on the Friday, a day later than planned. It was the experience in Prague that made the club take the first ill-fated decision to charter a plane for their next foreign trip . . . to play Red Star in Belgrade.

In the first leg at Old Trafford international goalkeeper Beara made a string of super saves to see the Yugoslavs take an interval lead through Tasic. With Duncan Edwards still in dominant mood and winning his battle with the skilled Sekularac, United finally got the goals they deserved through Eddie Colman and Bobby Charlton for a 2–1 win.

They hadn't had such a slender lead to take abroad before and everyone wondered whether it would be enough, but they were an increasingly powerful team as they had demonstrated in their classic 5–4 victory at Arsenal on the eve of departure for Belgrade.

We have dealt in detail with that fateful final match in Belgrade before the disaster. The club were jubilant at the end of the game, of course, because their 3–3 result for an aggregate 5–4 win had put them into the semi-finals of the European Cup for the second season running.

Just as Manchester United had had to carry on in the FA Cup and the League, so they had to face up to their commitments in Europe. By the time the semi-finals came round it was May. This gave the team a breathing space, but by then the pressure of their do-or-die efforts in the FA Cup were beginning to catch up with them. Five days after losing to Bolton at Wembley they were facing up to AC Milan at Old Trafford.

It seemed that sentiment for United had run out in high places. England picked Bobby Charlton for a friendly against Portugal at Wembley, so that the Reds were unnecessarily deprived of one of their quality players, the kind needed for a match against a team like AC Milan. United also lost him to England for the second leg as he was chosen to play against Yugoslavia – in Belgrade of all places. Little wonder he had a poor game. What else could have been expected from a visit so soon to the scene of the last match before the crash? England didn't play Charlton at all during the World Cup in Sweden that summer, adding insult to injury so far as United were concerned.

Manchester United's first campaign in Europe ended with defeat in the semi-finals against Real Madrid. But it was defeat with honour, for the Reds had shocked a few people on their way to the last four in the European Cup and had reminded the Continent that the game in England was still alive and kicking despite disappointing international results. United lost the first leg 3–1 in Spain, but could only draw 2–2 at Old Trafford. Here Tommy Taylor goes for goal and indeed scored along with Bobby Charlton. But as Busby summed up: 'When we met Real Madrid it was a contest between two great teams – a mature side and a young one, and of course experience told.' He added: 'But our time will come,' as indeed it did

So the patched-up Reds had to call up young Mark Pearson to add to the other youngsters who had already struggled manfully to fulfil the obligations of the club following the disaster. Their emergency signings, Ernie Taylor and Stan Crowther, were both in the team, along with Munich survivors Harry Gregg, Bill Foulkes, Dennis Viollet and Kenny Morgans.
They fought bravely in the first leg to win 2–1 with a penalty from Taylor and a goal from Viollet. But it was a slim lead to take to the San Siro Stadium for the second leg six days later. There was no great tide of emotion willing them on in Milan, just the usual massive, noisy crowd of Italians complete with fireworks and flares.

An 80,000 crowd bombarded the English players with cabbages and carrots, a quite new experience for most of the United team who slowly but surely slid to a 4–0 defeat. As Bill Foulkes put it: 'I think we had run out of emotional steam.'

The team which lined up for both legs against the Milanese was:

Gregg, Foulkes, Greaves, Goodwin, Cope, Crowther, Morgans, Taylor, Webster, Viollet, Pearson.

While Manchester United recuperated mentally as well as physically during the summer, the club received an invitation to play in the European Cup the following year, in addition to Wolves, the new English champions. It was a gesture born out of sympathy for the grievous blow they had suffered, and perhaps there was a practical motive in that another run in Europe would help the club survive by boosting their financial resources. The English Football Association initially gave their blessing, but it soon became apparent that the League still harboured resentment at the way United had flouted their authority to enter European competition in the first place. They seized the opportunity to write and say they could not give their consent.

The Old Trafford board were incensed at what they privately considered to be a petty decision. They promptly went to the board of appeal of the Football League who came down on United's side and said they *could* take part. The rules of the League say that decisions by the appeal board are final, but the League weren't finished yet. They referred the matter to the joint FA and League Consultative Committee, which decided that United were ineligible.

They instructed Stanley Rous, secretary of the FA, to write saying: 'The committee is of the opinion that, as by its name this is a competition of champion clubs, Manchester United does not qualify to take part in this season's competition. Consent is therefore refused.'

There was of course no denying the logic of the finding, but where was the spirit? United had no option but to bow out of Europe to concentrate on rebuilding and fighting their way back in the normal way. No more concessions for Munich.

The next European adventure

It took another six years for the club to qualify for a European tournament again. The gateway back to Europe came with the FA Cup success in 1963 to put the Reds into the European Cup Winners' Cup the following season.

Season 1963–64 was a good all-round effort by the Reds in that they reached the semi-finals of the FA Cup and finished runners-up in the League behind Liverpool. They also opened their campaign in Europe convincingly enough, drawing 1–1 with a goal from David Herd against Willem II in Holland and then going to town on the Dutchmen in the second leg at Old Trafford. Denis Law grabbed a hat-trick while Bobby Charlton, Phil Chisnall and Maurice Setters also scored to complete a rousing 6–1 win to go through 7–2 on aggregate.

The next round brought the kind of opposition disliked in European football, a tie against fellow countrymen. On this occasion Spurs, as holders, were their opponents. The first leg was at White Hart Lane where Spurs registered a 2–0 win with goals from Dave Mackay and winger Terry Dyson. The stage was set for another close encounter in the return, with Tottenham confident they could turn their advantage into an aggregate win. But the second leg went sour for the Londoners. Mackay broke his leg in an accidental collision and they went down to a 4–1 defeat. David Herd and Bobby Charlton shared United's four goals.

The Reds were rampaging through everything on three fronts . . . contesting the League, sailing along in the FA Cup and in the next round of the Cup Winners' Cup running up a handsome 4–1 lead against Sporting Lisbon in the first leg at Old Trafford.

Then a few cracks began to appear as Sunderland exhausted them in the FA Cup by taking them to three games in the sixth round on wet, muddy pitches before they were able to finish off the Roker Park club. This was followed by the disappointment of losing their FA Cup semi-final against West Ham.

But no-one expected the collapse that occurred in the second leg of the Cup Winners' Cup against Sporting Lisbon in Portugal. The Reds squandered their three-goal advantage to lose by an incredible 5–0 and go out of their second major competition in five days.

It was the extent of their surrender which was so devastating, and to this day it remains their darkest hour in Europe, their only humiliation.

Lisbon hit United with two early goals and then repeated the punishment straight after the interval. Silva completed a hat-trick and they were never in any trouble. It just seemed as if the Manchester men were a spent force. They weren't though, as they showed on their return home by winning 3–2 at Tottenham with a top-class performance to keep their championship hopes alive.

But they had certainly made a mess of their ambitions in two Cup competitions. United were flabbergasted by the extent of their defeat in Lisbon and Matt Busby was outraged. Bill Foulkes said that for the one and only time in his long career the manager slammed into them for their performance. Pat Crerand describes it by saying: 'Matt raged at us. He was normally dignified in defeat and even when he was angry he didn't lose his temper. But he did that night, and what was going to happen to us when we got back to Manchester was nobody's business. He told us our performance was an insult to the people of Manchester.'

In public Busby was more diplomatic, which of course was his way. He said: 'The boys left so much of themselves at home. The three matches against Sunderland took a lot out of them, and the semi-final at Hillsborough against West Ham on such a muddy pitch finally drained them mentally and physically. I am sure the heavy programme of matches pulled us down.'

The players didn't help themselves when they tried to drown their sorrows after the match. They stayed out late and several of them broke the team curfew. They got themselves off the hook by winning so well at White Hart Lane and Busby scrubbed the fines he had threatened them with for being late back to the team hotel in Lisbon.

The embarrassed team which would like to forget the nightmare in Lisbon lined up:

Gaskell, Brennan, A Dunne, Crerand, Foulkes, Setters, Herd, Chisnall, Charlton, Law, Best.

Full points at Tottenham kept United on the title trail, so all was not lost, though a run of three draws and a couple of defeats in the last nine games saw them lose their grip on the championships to finish second. Nevertheless a runners-up spot was enough to qualify for a place in the Fairs Cup the following season.

It was another exciting season all round in 1964–65, with the Reds once again chasing a treble until the very last stages. They went all the way in the League of course, taking the Championship at the expense of Leeds, and they reached the semi-final of the FA Cup again, this time losing to Leeds in a replay. They were scoring goals galore, with Denis Law mean and magnificent, David Herd on target again, George Best accelerating into magic gear, and new signing John Connelly bringing flair to the right wing. In defence they gave little away as Bill Foulkes and Nobby Stiles struck the perfect partnership, allowing Pat Crerand and Bobby Charlton to create in midfield.

United operated like a well-oiled machine and

Manchester United had just one season in the Inter Cities Fairs Cup before it was taken over to become the UEFA Cup. But they did well in the competition which was originally established as a football extension of trade fairs held around Europe in the big commercial centres. They reached the semi-finals when they went out after three tough games against Ferencvaros, losing 2–1 in the final game in Budapest. The semi-final against Racing Strasbourg produced one of their notable away leg performances, winning 5–0 in France. John Connelly scores one of the goals watched by Denis Law (number 10) who scored twice

nowhere was this more in evidence than in the Fairs Cup. Although they only drew 1–1 in the first leg of their opening round against Djurgaarden in Sweden, they went to town in the return to the tune of 6–1. Law got a hat-trick.

The Germans of Borussia Dortmund in the next round didn't know what had hit them. Charlton scored a hat-trick in another 6–1 win in Dortmund, and narrowly missed repeating his three-goal salvo in the second leg 4–0 victory in Manchester.

The scoring slowed in the third round when United drew English opponents. Everton did well to hold them to a 1–1 draw in the first leg at Old Trafford, Connelly providing the lifeline for the Reds. Everton were favourites at Goodison Park for the return, but United, with goals from Connelly and Herd, won 2–1.

The Reds were quickly back in form in the next round, banging in five against Racing Club in Strasbourg. They conserved their energies at Old Trafford with a goalless game to go through to the semi-finals.

United had been the new League Champions for a month by the time the first leg of the semi-final against Ferencvaros came round on 31 May 1965. This time, because of the competition's complicated format they had had time for a rest, but it didn't do them much good. Law got a penalty and Herd scored twice, but the men at the back didn't have their usual tight grip with the result that United, with a 3–2 win, had only a one-goal lead from the first leg at Old Trafford. The Hungarians' second goal was particularly unfortunate for the Reds, a long lob into the goalmouth from Rakosi so deceiving Pat Dunne that he allowed the ball to bounce in front of him and then sail gently over his head into the net. It was a gift for Ferencvaros, who were top of their League and boasted players like centre-forward Florian Albert.

It was with some misgiving that the Reds set off for the second leg, and their mood was not helped by the difficulties of the journey, with a strike delay at London Airport and a hold-up in Brussels. It was a trip when everything seemed to go wrong and misfortune spilled over into the match. Just before half-time Albert set Varga off running for goal. He was still some way out when he tried a speculative shot which Pat Dunne looked to have well covered. In fact the shot didn't reach him because the ball struck Stiles on the shoulder and he cleared. The referee amazingly awarded a penalty for handball. Even allowing for the referee thinking it had hit him on the arm, the shot had come too quickly for it to be anything but accidental.

Novak scored with the penalty and United lost their cool. Pat Crerand was sent off along with Orosz when they finally turned on each other after a running battle. The goal was the only one of the match, levelling the tie. United were fortunate in that the rule counting away goals double in the event of an aggregate draw was not yet in force. But it still wasn't their lucky day, and Matt Busby returned grimly to the dressing room having lost the toss for choice of venue for the replay. Back to Budapest went United, now a month into the close season with most other British footballers enjoying their summer holidays. It was a difficult trip again, and they even forgot the English sausages the British Embassy had asked them to bring out!

United, this time determined to wrap up the tie, went straight to the attack and dominated the first half hour. Unhappily Denis Law hesitated a fraction too long with a good chance, and Ferencvaros punished them just before the interval. Their right-winger cut inside Tony Dunne for just about the first time in the match and let fly with a swerving shot which dipped into the top corner of the goal. In the second half Ferencvaros' left-winger scored after a series of shots had been blocked. John Connelly pulled a goal back, but other chances went begging.

The team which played unchanged in all three matches against Ferencvaros was:

Pat Dunne, Brennan, Tony Dunne, Crerand, Foulkes, Stiles, Connelly, Charlton, Herd, Law, Best.

The Championship put the Reds back into the top competition, the European Cup, in 1965–66 and they produced another brave campaign on three fronts. They slipped to fourth in the League, but they again reached the semi-finals of the FA Cup and the semi-finals in Europe.

The European season will be remembered for an incredible performance at the quarter-final stage against Benfica in Lisbon which was inspired by George Best, who came home as El Beatle. Best destroyed the Portuguese champions with one of the finest individual displays ever seen in European football, or anywhere else for that matter. He must have had cotton wool in his ears when Matt Busby delivered his pre-match tactics, because the performance bore no relation to the script.

When that season opened Best was just making the English soccer fans sit up and take notice. He had established a regular place in Manchester United's side the season before, in which he only missed one game in helping the Reds pip Leeds United for the First Division title on goal average. However, glimpses of his future life-style were beginning to emerge. A string of late nights took the edge off his form and brought the first of many dressing-downs from Matt Busby. Then, after a miserable performance against Newcastle, he was dropped for three games, including the opening round of the European Cup against HJK Helsinki.

United won 3–2 in Finland without him, but he was restored for the second leg after turning in a brilliant performance for Northern Ireland against Scotland. The shock of losing his place had done the trick and George was back to his impudent best, running the Finns ragged in a 6–0 victory in which he scored twice.

The East Berlin army team Vorwaerts were beaten 2–0 away and 3–1 at home to give United a quarter-final tie against Benfica.

The Portuguese side, managed by the wily Bela Guttman, had taken over from Real Madrid as the masters of European soccer, winning the European Cup in 1961 and 1962 and losing the next final to Milan only after being hit by injuries during the game. Best can still vividly recall the first leg at Old Trafford on 2 February 1966: 'It was one of those nights when you could almost feel the crackle of the atmosphere. I recall best of all the fantastic pace at which the game was played and then thinking during the second half that our lead of 3–1 was ideal. Then Eusebio worked one of his tricks to get his side a valuable goal. He sent our defence the wrong

Matt Busby had the gift of commanding respect from his players without needing to rant and rave. It was a relationship akin to that of pupil and headmaster during schooldays. Yet he was not aloof and loved in his early days to get among his players on the training field. In later years golf was frequently the common meeting ground. Left to right on this occasion in 1966 are Pat Crerand, Bill Foulkes, Matt Busby and Noel Cantwell

way with a quick shuffle of his feet and curled in a centre for a goal which Torres scored with his knee.'

A fantastic victory in Lisbon

So the Reds were going to Lisbon with the slenderest of leads, and with bitter memories of their last visit two years earlier when they had surrendered a three-goal lead to Sporting Lisbon. The second leg was played at the Stadium of Light. This was how the Reds lined up:

Gregg, Brennan, A Dunne, Crerand, Foulkes, Stiles, Best, Law, Charlton, Herd, Connelly.

The atmosphere was electric, with all roads to the stadium jammed solid. Concetto Lo Bello, the Italian referee, was delayed, and Benfica added to the tension by presenting Eusebio with his Footballer of the Year award on the pitch. It worked the crowd up to a fever pitch and the game, scheduled to start at 9.45 pm, did not get under way until after 10 pm.

Busby wanted United to hold Benfica for the first 20 minutes. But Best refused to be held in check. He took the game by the scruff of the neck and didn't let go until victory was assured. He scored the first goal after only six minutes when he soared to head a free-kick from Tony Dunne past Costa Pereira. Then six minutes later he scored one of the finest ever seen when he weaved around three Benfica defenders before stroking the ball into the corner.

Another tremendous burst brought a third goal for John Connelly as Benfica reeled, astounded at the way this brilliant broth-of-a-boy had led an all-out assault when what they had expected was grim defence. Shay Brennan put through his own net to bring Benfica back in the game, but the Reds struck again in the last quarter, Law laying on a goal for Crerand and Charlton waltzing through at the end for a 5–1 win (an incredible 8–3 on aggregate).

Italy's *Corriere dello Sport* declared: 'The myth of Benfica collapsed in fifteen minutes, destroyed by the powerful irresistible Manchester who showed themselves as the great stars of European soccer, worthy rivals to Internazionale of Milan for the European Cup.'

But fate was waiting round the corner for the team now hot favourites to win the European Cup. Just over a fortnight later in the sixth round of the FA Cup Best was brought down from behind. It wasn't a violent tackle but he fell awkwardly for once and twisted his right knee. It was a classic case of a torn cartilage, the occupational hazard of footballers, and it couldn't have occurred at a more critical stage of the season. Best was left out for the next two games. At this stage all the club were admitting was that their Irish star had strained ligaments. Behind the scenes they worked round the clock trying to get him fit for the first leg of the European semi-final against Partizan Belgrade in Yugoslavia. He was put back into the League team for a game against Leicester at Old Trafford as a test for the semi-final which was to follow just four days later. Twice he went down clutching the suspect knee as pain stabbed through it in certain overstretched positions. The rest of the time he moved like the player of old. The fact that the team lost 2–1 at home seemed incidental. The big thing was that George had survived the test and the decision was taken to gamble with him in Belgrade.

Partizan were an ordinary side without much flair, but they did have one redeeming feature which had made them champions at home and brought them to the last four in Europe: they were as hard and unrelenting as the Partizans of the war whom their club was named after.

The Reds started as if capable of carrying on where they had left off in Lisbon. After only five minutes Best had wriggled through only to miss with a fair chance. Then he put Denis Law clear with a centre, but the Scot could only bounce the ball against the bar off his body as he tried to run it into the net. After that United faded. Hasanagic scored for Partizan and soon after Best began to feel the nagging pain in his knee return. Becejac made it a 2–0 win for the home team and Busby admitted: 'We played badly.'

Best had failed to produce his Lisbon fireworks, understandably so in the circumstances of his injury, but the gamble of playing him could hardly be called ill-conceived, because he had still managed to look the most effective player. It was a situation which spoke volumes for the display of the rest of the team! The Belgrade game was the last of the season for Best, who on the return home went straight into hospital for a cartilage operation.

Willie Anderson took Best's place for the second leg a week later but again United were below par. Partizan summoned up all their qualities of resistance and didn't crack until 15 minutes from the end, when an awkward centre from Nobby Stiles was helped into the net by a Yugoslav defender. United attacked all night but Partizan had bolted the door. The Old Trafford cause was not helped when Pat Crerand flared in response to a crunching tackle and was sent off. So Partizan held out, losing 1–0 on the night, but going through on a 2–1 aggregate, leaving Manchester United with the feeling that they had blown a great chance of reaching the final for the first time.

The disappointed men in the second leg were:

Gregg, Brennan, A Dunne, Crerand, Foulkes, Stiles, Anderson, Law, Charlton, Herd, Connelly.

Three days after bowing out of Europe, United lost their FA Cup semi-final against Everton at Burnden Park. Again it was only by the narrow margin of 1–0, but it seemed that when George Best had dropped out of action some of the magic had gone with him. The Championship challenge had also fizzled out with the result that they finished fourth in the League, not good enough for a place in Europe the following season. The big bonus from that was that in 1966–67, free of European commitments and knocked out early in both the FA Cup and the League Cup, United were left to concentrate on winning the League. For a change they had only one target and they made sure they didn't miss it. They emerged Champions of 1966–67 with four points to spare in front of Nottingham Forest to go forward for their big date with destiny in the European Cup.

The 1967–68 European Cup campaign

The 1967–68 campaign opened with an easy tie against the Hibernian part-timers of Malta, coached by a priest, Father Hilary Tagliaferro, who also doubled as a sports writer in a wide-ranging career. The Maltese were a little out of their depth. Indeed Father Hilary even lost one of his flock on the way to Manchester for the first leg. Francis Mifsud went to buy an ice cream in London and got lost. The 17-year-old remembered where he was due to play football though, so caught a train to Manchester to return to the fold and enable Scotland Yard to relax. United made rather hard work of the match until Denis Law and David Sadler scored two goals each for a 4–0 win. The Maltese were pleased to have kept the score so low, and all they wanted back on their George Cross island was an entertaining match.

United have always had an enthusiastic following in Malta with a well-appointed supporters' club and the whole island seemed to be at the airport to welcome the Reds for the return. They escorted the team to the Hilton Hotel in a cavalcade of cars, motor bikes and buses, horns and hooters blaring, so that one wondered who were the home team. The match itself ended in a goalless draw, with United too apprehensive on the rock-hard, sandy pitch to produce anything special.

The next round brought a much tougher draw in all meanings of the word tough. United's opponents were Sarajevo, kinsmen of the Partizan team which had dashed their hopes two years previously. Matt Busby, stifling memories of Munich, ordered a charter plane for the first time since to ease a long, difficult journey. The welcome in Sarajevo was warm, but hardly extended beyond the starting whistle.

George Best was repeatedly chopped down, Brian Kidd was heavily marked and Francis Burns was so violently brought down that Mirsad Fazlagic, the national Yugoslav captain, was booked. Trainer Jack Crompton was on and off the field, treating United players so often that Crerand reckoned that half the crowd probably thought he was playing. But the Reds at least kept their heads and came home with a goalless draw, a good result in the circumstances. Sarajevo were just as hard at Old Trafford, so United were delighted when Best avoided the flying boots to reach Kidd's centre with a header which the goalkeeper could only palm out. John Aston whipped the ball back in for an 11th minute lead.

The Yugoslav tactics rebounded on them when they spotted Best taking a swing at their goalkeeper. The punch missed and was also missed by the referee. So an incensed Fahrudin Prljaca went looking for revenge on behalf of his keeper and kicked Best so blatantly that the referee had no option but to send him off. Down to ten men they had no chance. Best rammed home the fact by scoring in the 65th minute. Outside-right Salih Delalic headed a goal for Sarajevo, but too late to influence the game at three minutes from the end. So the Reds moved on with a 2–1 win to meet Gornik Zabrze in the quarter-finals, and feeling pretty pleased with themselves for winning through while Denis Law served a 28-day suspension.

The Poles themselves had performed well to beat the fancied Dynamo Kiev, who in turn had knocked out Glasgow Celtic, the European Cup holders. They had emerged as the dark horses of the competition.

The first leg in Manchester came as a refresher after the previous round and was a splendidly sporting affair. Henryk Latocha clung closely to Best, but played him very fairly – and well. But around the 60th minute the Irishman escaped to let fly with a rocket of a shot which Florenski could only help into his own goal. Kostka played well in the visitors' goal until Brian Kidd flicked a shot from Jimmy Ryan past him. A 2–0 win was fair especially with Law missing again, this time with the start of his knee problem. Jimmy Ryan had played well in his place, but was replaced by the more defensive John Fitzpatrick for the second leg to help protect the two-goal advantage.

It was bitterly cold and snowing when United arrived in Gornik, so much so that Matt Busby went looking for the referee with a view to seeking a postponement. But the familiar figure of the Italian, Concetto Lo Bello, couldn't be found with the result that the Reds had to go out to play on a snow-covered pitch with snow still falling. United, wilier now in the art of European football, played a mature game. Gornik scored 20 minutes from the end through their danger man, Lubanski, who had played for Poland at the age of 16. His goal gave the Poles a 1–0 victory but it was an aggregate defeat.

So Manchester United were in the semi-finals of the European Cup for the fourth time, and were drawn against their old friends and rivals, Real Madrid. The stage was set for what many fans would have preferred to see as the final. Certainly there couldn't have been a higher hurdle. Although they were not quite the power they had been in their hey-day, when they had won the trophy five times on the trot, Real were still more than capable of beating any club side in the world on their day.

United had the slight disadvantage of being drawn at home for the first leg, but this was balanced by the fact that Real would be without their best forward, Amancio, who was under suspension. Not another person could have been squeezed into Old Trafford when the teams met for the first leg. The teams were:

United: Stepney, A Dunne, Burns, Crerand, Sadler, Stiles, Best, Kidd, Charlton, Law, Aston. Sub: Rimmer.

Real Madrid: Betancort, Gonzales, Sanchis, Pirri, Zunzunegui, Zoco, Peruz, Luis, Grosso, Velazquez, Gento. Sub: Araquistain.

The Spaniards, renowned for their attacking flair, surprisingly adopted an ultra-defensive policy. United, for their part, could never really break down the massed Real defence, due perhaps to the fact that Denis Law was a pale shadow of his usual self because of the knee injury which was to put him in hospital just a few days later. In the end United were thankful to take a one-goal lead to Madrid – scored by George Best – but that was a frighteningly slender advantage against a team like Real in front of their own fanatical supporters.

In between the two ties Busby flew to Lisbon to see the other semi-final between Benfica and Juventus, where he formed the opinion that whoever won the United-Real tie would go on to win the trophy.

Foulkes the hero of Madrid

Twenty-one days after the Old Trafford tie the two teams met again in Madrid. For the most important game in the history of the club Busby decided not to risk Law, but recalled the ageing defender Bill Foulkes for his 29th European Cup tie. David Sadler kept his place as an extra attacker and Shay Brennan came in at full-back in place of Francis Burns.

On the morning of the match the tension was almost unbearable. Nobby Stiles and Pat Crerand decided that a visit to the local Catholic church would help to take their minds off things. When the collection plate was passed round, Nobby found himself stuck for loose change and put a 100 peseta note on the plate. Crerand glanced up in amazement. 'Hey, Nobby, that's bribery,' he whispered.

At first it seemed that even Nobby's little 'bribe' was not going to save United. Real were the exact opposite of the team which had played at Old Trafford. The ball was whisked from man to man as if on an invisible string and with United defenders chasing shadows it came as no surprise when Pirri headed a free-kick past Stepney after half an hour.

An uncharacteristic error by Shay Brennan allowed Gento to make it 2–0 and although Zoco sliced Dunne's centre past his own keeper, Amancio quickly scored again after fooling two defenders to give Real a 3–1 interval lead. United, it seemed, were down and almost out.

Busby then pulled his master-stroke. As the United players slumped down wearily, waiting for the expected dressing-down, he told them: 'Go out there and enjoy yourselves. You have done well to get so far so don't worry. Let's go out and attack.'

Busby's half-time pep-talk helped to change the players' outlook. But what gave them the heart to fight on was the sight of the Real players coming back for the start of the second half. Says Aston:

> We were amazed. Some of them looked like it was an effort to drag one leg after the other. We looked at ourselves, and compared with Real we were as fresh as daisies. Obviously, their players had been told to come out and run us off our legs in the first half. To an extent that had worked. But the score was only 3–2 for them on aggregate and they had shot their bolt. I have never known a game in which the two halves were so different.'

In the second period the Reds ran their opponents ragged. But the vital goal wouldn't come. Then Crerand lobbed the ball forward. A header by Foulkes fell between the Real goalkeeper and his defenders, and before anyone could move, Sadler had stolen in to glance the ball home. Now the scores were level with just under 15 minutes to go and the stage was set for one of the most memorable, emotional moments in United's various European games. Aston picks up the story:

> The last few minutes are something I shall never forget. I can still see Paddy Crerand taking a throw-in on the right and finding George Best. George set off on a run which left two or three of their defenders kicking fresh air. At the same time big Bill Foulkes suddenly began to gallop out of defence. Just what got into him no one will ever know. I remember that people on the trainer's bench were screaming at him to get back but he ploughed on and on. I don't know if George saw him but he pulled the ball back right into his path. I thought, 'Oh, God, this is going to go over the stand,' because, even in training, Bill always blasted the ball. But this time Bill just calmly side-footed the ball into the corner of the net. I don't know who was the more surprised – Bill or the rest of us.

So Foulkes, the most unlikely goal-scoring hero of all time, a survivor of the other semi-final between the two clubs 11 years earlier, had booked a place in the final with his only European Cup goal. Foulkes insists:

> I still don't know what possessed me to go forward and score the goal which won the tie for us. After so many games with no thought of scoring, it seems almost unbelievable as I look back. I was lucky even to be playing. I had missed the first leg against Real with a bad knee and I had played only two League games when the manager picked me for the return in Madrid. I think Matt went for the experience because I wasn't really fit. My knee was strapped up and I was hobbling really.
>
> Leading up to the goal, I had called for the ball when Paddy Crerand took a throw-in. He threw it to George Best instead who shot off

down the field. Perhaps it was with moving slightly forward to call for the throw-in which prompted me to keep running. Anyway I reached the corner of the box and found myself calling for the ball again. I thought George was going to shoot, but instead he cut back a beautiful pass to me. It was perfect and I just had to side-foot it in at the far side.

In the dressing-room after the match Bobby Charlton and Matt Busby were both unashamedly crying. 'I can't help it, I can't help it,' said Busby, over and over again as if the tension and heartache of striving for the trophy over the years had finally been released.

Aston felt very much the same, as though Real Madrid and not the other finalists – Benfica – were all that stood between Busby and the realisation of his dream. 'After that game in Madrid I really believed that we were somehow

Left: The teams walk out here at Old Trafford for the first leg of the European Cup semi-final against Real Madrid; Denis Law is followed by Alex Stepney. United won 1–0 with a goal from George Best, and it didn't seem enough to take to Spain. But then came that marvellous second leg fight-back for a 3–3 draw which this time saw the Reds through at the expense of their friends and rivals from Real Madrid

Right: Manchester United fans, avid collectors of programmes couldn't understand why Real Madrid weren't producing one for the prestigious European Cup semi-final in Spain. They were not left high and dry, though. The people who trade in football programmes promptly filled the gap in the market and produced their own 'away' programme which was flown to Madrid and sold there for 10 pesetas. The programmes also became an item available in the collectors' shops in England

Below: United battle for their all-important 1–0 victory in the first leg of their European Cup semi-final at Old Trafford on the night of 24 April 1968

fated to win the European Cup,' he admits. 'The way Real ran out of steam, the way Bill Foulkes scored his goal . . . it was as if it had all been decided beforehand.'

Perhaps it had. Perhaps the hand which had plucked away those marvellous Busby Babes decided to do something to settle the score. Perhaps Nobby Stiles's little 'bribe' did the trick. Whatever the reasons, Manchester United went on to win the European Cup in a never-to-be-forgotten final at Wembley. But in many respects, the trophy had been won in Madrid 35 days earlier when the Reds conquered the most fabulous club side in the history of soccer.

The shabby matches with Estudiantes

Winning the European Cup brought two tilts in foreign football the following season. The immediate challenge was to play for the World Club Championship against Estudiantes, the South American champions . . . and what a bitter experience this turned out to be.

The series of world games between the northern and southern hemispheres had long been marred by violence, and the match between Glasgow Celtic and Racing Club of the previous year had been a particularly bad example, so the warm, hospitable welcome afforded United as they arrived in Buenos Aires for the first leg was pleasant and encouraging. There were parties, barbecues and even a specially arranged polo match for the entertainment of the visiting Englishmen. The first jarring note came when Matt Busby took his team to an official reception with the object of building goodwill with the opposition, only to find that Estudiantes had pulled out. An angry Busby took his team back to their hotel. The United manager was none too pleased either to read in the press an interview purporting to come from Otto Gloria, the Benfica manager, describing Nobby Stiles as 'an assassin'.

Estudiantes even carried an article in the match programme quoting Otto Gloria saying that Stiles was 'brutal, badly intentioned and a bad sportsman'. The Argentinians were still smarting, of course, from Alf Ramsey's description of their World Cup team in England two years previously as 'animals'. Stiles was in the 1966 tournament, so from the Argentinian point of view it was good retaliatory stuff. However, it was irresponsible of Estudiantes to put such remarks in their programme and it did nothing to cool an already hostile atmosphere.

A bomb releasing a thick cloud of red smoke seemed to be the starting gun for hostilities rather than the referee's whistle. The home team laced into United with Bilardo, the manager of Argentina at the 1986 World Cup in Mexico, one of the most violent players. Busby said later: 'Holding the ball out there put you in danger of your life.'

It was hardly surprising that United never really got going. They fought mainly a rearguard

action which was pierced only once. In the 28th minute the centre forward, Conigliario, headed in a corner from Veron.

It was inevitable that Stiles would get into trouble. Even the officials seemed to be gunning for him. At one point a linesman had called the referee over apparently to complain that he had been standing too close to Bilardo. Then he was sent off for angily waving his arm at a linesman when he was flagged for offside. Considering he had been butted, punched and kicked, yet had walked calmly away without retaliating, it seemed a relatively minor offence. Yet it cost him his place in the return leg in Manchester through automatic suspension as United went out to face the South Americans a goal down.

United were confident they could pull back, but they were hit by Veron breaking through a badly guarded goalmouth to score after only five minutes. From then on they found it difficult to penetrate the well-drilled defence of the visitors. Denis Law had to go off with a badly cut leg, which brought on Carlo Sartori as substitute, and George Best got himself sent off after squaring up to Medina who was dismissed with him. Brian Kidd sent Willie Morgan through to score for a 1–1 draw on the night, but of course the Inter-Continental Cup went to Buenos Aires on the strength of their home victory.

The European Cup defence

United hoped for better things as they began to defend their precious European Cup. They went willingly to work on Waterford in the opening round, winning 3–1 in Ireland with a hat-trick from Denis Law and piling on the agony with a

7–1 win at Old Trafford. This time Law went one better and scored four.

George Best missed both legs against Anderlecht in the next round because of a two-match suspension stemming from his dismissal against Estudiantes. But Law was still in form near goal and scored twice in a 3–0 home win. There was nearly a hiccup in the away leg. United lost 3–1 in Belgium, but survived thanks to the goal scored by newcomer Carlo Sartori, another young lad from Collyhurst.

The Reds were back to their best for the quarter-final against Rapid Vienna, who arrived at Old Trafford for the first leg with the boost of having just knocked Real Madrid out of the tournament. They received short shrift from United in the second half, though, and were sent back home to Austria as 3–0 losers. Best made up for his absence in the previous round with a sparkling performance. He scored the first and third goals, with Willie Morgan, United's £100,000 summer signing from Burnley, marking his European debut by notching the other.

United conformed more now to European tactics and played carefully in Vienna for a 0–0 result. But Rudolf Vytacil, the Rapid manager, still felt moved to say: 'I was astounded at United's ability to attack away from home. United have a very good tactical approach and they are the tops of all Europe.'

With Best in the side the team's performance just could not be predicted; to a large extent it was the secret of their European success, though they more than met their match when they came up against AC Milan in the semi-finals. The San Siro Stadium, scene of their European Cup defeat in the Munich season, was again a bedlam of rockets, smoke bombs and fanatical supporters waving huge banners. It was an atmosphere which called for nerves of steel, and though United had vast experience at this stage, their team had a high proportion of players who had passed their peak and under pressure were showing hairline cracks.

They certainly found Milan a tough nut to crack. Winners of the trophy in 1963, they had a magnificent defence which had conceded only 11 goals in 26 League games. Fabio 'The Spider' Cudicini, the keeper, had men who wove a nearly impenetrable web in front of his goal. The Reds failed to get through it as Best felt the full weight of the Italian marking system. A goal from Angelo Sormani in the 33rd minute and one from Kurt Hamrin just after the interval gave Milan a 2–0 win.

United were not without hope for the second leg. They approached the tie with every confidence, though Crerand had warned: 'Two goals down against any team is bad enough, but against Milan it's like being four down, they are so good at the back.' He proved a good judge. The Reds flung themselves forward but didn't break through until the 70th minute. It was a fine goal, created when Best at last eluded Anquilletti, and was scored fittingly enough by Bobby Charlton. It was United's 100th in European football, But it wasn't enough on the night. The fans thought their team had equalised 13 minutes from the end when Pat Crerand chipped a ball in. The players swore that the ball had crossed the line, but it wasn't given.

The unruly element in the Stretford End couldn't contain their disappointment at this decision. They started hurling all manner of rubbish and missiles on to the pitch with the result that Cudicini was hit by a piece of brick. The Italian goalkeeper might well have overdramatised, but the fact remained that he had been hit and play was held up for some considerable time while the referee sorted out the pandemonium which erupted. As it happened, the behaviour of the hooligans might well have cost their team their last chance of a replay, because when the game was finally resumed the momentum which the Reds had been building up was never picked up again. The team had lost their rhythm, and though they finished 1–0 winners on the night they went out 2–1 on aggregate.

It was a sad end for Matt Busby on his last game in Europe as team manager before going upstairs to become general manager. But he still found the sporting spirit to say: 'I was very proud of the team. They were magnificent. They gave everything and you cannot ask for more.'

An even sadder ending was the sequel to the missile throwing at Old Trafford and the wild scenes in Milan. Both clubs were warned by UEFA about the future conduct of their fans, and United were ordered to erect a screen behind their goals before playing in European competition again. There was no need to start work immediately, though, because their finishing place of 11th in the League and a sixth-round knock-out in the FA Cup meant there was no place for them in any of the Continental tournaments.

It was in fact eight years before United qualified for a European return, a completely different era with a new generation of players and staff.

The return to Europe under Docherty

Tommy Docherty was the manager who led the Reds back to the Continent, and he did not disguise either his excitement or the way he was going to try to uphold the tradition established by Sir Matt Busby. He declared:

> Ever since I came here I've planned for the return of United to the team's natural element of European football. That is why we have played as many games as possible against European teams during my two years. I hang the pennants which are presented to us when we go abroad for friendly matches round my office and I mentally tick off each country visited. The pennants are piling up now and each one represents valuable European experience. Now we are back to try to recreate more of the old glories of Manchester United,

Bobby Charlton in the dark shirt anxiously following the action in the second leg of the World Championship match with Estudiantes at Old Trafford.
The World Championship matches with Estudiantes widened Manchester United's horizons considerably. Although the fixture between the champions of Europe and South America had an unhappy history of violence, it hadn't really prepared United for the naked aggression and general hostility they met in Buenos Aires. As Matt Busby summed up: 'Holding the ball out there put you in danger of your life.'
United lost the first leg 1–0 and then drew 1–1 at Old Trafford in the return, with Willie Morgan their goal scorer. The interesting thing is that Busby's conclusion after the match was that given the chance of competing again he

would still choose to enter. He argued that only by playing more would a better understanding be reached, and that to stay out of the confrontations with the South Americans would only widen the rift still further

and we shall endeavour to do it with style, playing adventurous football true to the traditions of Manchester United and striving to bring a smile back into European football.'

Sir Matt, now a director at Old Trafford, was clearly overjoyed to see the return. 'It is very gratifying to look back and consider what we started 20 years ago,' he said.

So the Doc led the charge back into Europe with a place in the 1976–77 UEFA Cup on the strength of third place in the League the previous season, and true to his promise they opened like the cavalry against Ajax in Holland's Olympic Stadium. They failed to score but went close several times. Indeed the players were convinced they had scored just after the interval when a fierce shot from Stewart Houston was fumbled by the goalkeeper. Piet Schrijvers turned sharply to scoop the ball away, with nearby players like Stuart Pearson convinced it had crossed the line. Lou Macari hit the post with a flick at goal from Gordon Hill's corner, and Ajax were involved in several other scrambles. Yet the Dutchmen survived to emerge 1–0 winners when Rudi Krol, their World Cup star and a survivor from the days when Ajax ruled the European roost, left his sweeper's post to jink through to slip the ball past Alex Stepney just before the interval.

United were disappointed to lose, but as Docherty chortled at the end to the Ajax president: 'Sorry, my friend, one goal won't be enough for you in Manchester.'

That's how it worked out, too, after Docherty had sent on his substitute, Steve Paterson, to allow Brian Greenhoff to move from centre-half into midfield. Greenhoff stepped up the tempo after Lou Macari had scored two minutes before the interval to make it 1–1 on aggregate. He powered down the right and with the help of Steve Coppell crossed for Sammy McIlroy to touch home the winner. United, lacking Stuart Pearson in the second leg through injury, had been short of penetration, but the tactical switch had made all the difference.

But as United celebrated their return to Europe, Tomislav Ivic, the Yugoslav manager of Ajax, pointed out: 'United play beautiful football, but the Germans and the Italians have harder man-to-man marking and a more defensive attitude . . . and that will be the test.'

So it proved with round two bringing United up against Juventus, who had just knocked neighbouring Manchester City out of the competition. United won the first leg at Old Trafford 1–0 with a beautifully struck goal in the 31st minute from Gordon Hill to earn this compliment from the Juventus coach, Giovanni Trapattoni: 'Hill was superb, not just for his goal but for his skills. Sometimes there were three or four of my men on him but still he got through. A very clever player indeed.'

But the Reds had also been stunned by some of the ferocity of the Italians, especially early on. It was clear the Reds were in the big league this time, and if they had any doubts about the class of the opposition, they were soon dispelled in Turin. The Reds were without Martin Buchan again, a defender they needed more than ever in the Stadio Communale. Hill headed a cross from Coppell wide early on, and Alex Stepney made some brave saves, but it was only a matter of time. Roberto Boninsegna struck a brilliant goal after half an hour and another just after the hour. Romeo rubbed in the defeat with a goal five minutes from the end for 3–0 on the night.

Docherty summed up: 'We were babes in Europe, but I was glad that I had been able to

Left: Action in the second leg of the 1969 European Cup semi-final at Olds Trafford

Below: United reached the semi-finals in defence of their European crown in 1969, but found A C Milan too strong for them. The Italians won the tie with a powerful performance in

bring back a taste of European action.'

In the second leg, in fact, it had been men against boys and it was clear United had a lot to learn, but as Sir Matt Busby had discovered 20 years previously, you don't conquer Europe in a season. It takes time, application and patience.

At least the club didn't have to wait long for another crack at Europe. For though dispatched very efficiently by Juventus in their European adventure, they had picked themselves up in splendid style in the FA Cup to beat Liverpool at Wembley and so qualify for the European Cup Winners' Cup in season 1977–78.

Trouble with the fans

By then they were under new management of course with Dave Sexton having replaced the sacked Tommy Docherty, and Sexton could hardly have had a more traumatic baptism when he took his team to France to play at St Etienne. For this was a tie fought on two fronts, on and off the field. Out on the pitch United performed well in a 1–1 draw. Gordon Hill smashed home a right-wing centre from Stuart Pearson in the 76th minute, with Christian Synaeghel scrambling in an equaliser just three minutes later.

But the real drama was happening on the terraces where the French club had ignored all United's appeals for segregation of the fans. Fighting broke out and the riot police swept in to charge at the English fans and lay about them indiscriminately.

The reaction of UEFA's disciplinary committee was simply to toss United out of the competition and award the tie to St Etienne. But United appealed and won the day in front of a tribunal in Zurich, producing a mass of evidence to show that they had warned the French club of the risks they were taking in neglecting segregation. The appeal commission ruled that the original sanction had been too severe and they said that the excellent behaviour of the United players had been taken into consideration as well. They allowed United to stay in the competition, but ordered them to pay a £7,500 fine and play the second leg at a neutral stadium at least 200 kilometres from Manchester.

Although reinstatement was a victory, the ban on playing at Old Trafford was a set-back for Dave Sexton in his first venture into Europe as manager of the Reds. But the club kept cool heads and after deciding to play at Plymouth won 2–0. They gambled with a semi-fit Stuart Pearson and he obliged with a 33rd minute goal before limping off with a recurrence of hamstring trouble. United clinched the tie when Steve Coppell turned inside to beat two men and Curkovic in goal with a firm shot.

Unfortunately for the second year running United came to grief in the next round. FC Porto proved far too good for them. The power, pace and precision of the Portuguese men o' war sank the Reds 4–0 in Portugal. It was like the Juventus away leg all over again, only this time United responded much better at home. In fact they came close to turning the tie upside down with a dazzling 5–2 victory at Old Trafford.

In this match, Steve Coppell led a superb assault all evening. He scored an early goal himself, forced Murca to put through his own goal and then after Jimmy Nicholl had rifled one in, shot the Reds into a 4–1 lead. Seninho broke away to score a second for Porto, so that although Pearson got a fifth for the Reds, it was an aggregate defeat. At least a 5–6 exit was splendid entertainment and it had been a fighting farewell.

United missed a couple of seasons of European competition, but finishing runners-up in

the first leg on their own ground. Milan won 2–0 and then defended with all the expertise the Italians can muster to escape with a 1–0 defeat at Old Trafford. Bobby Charlton scored United's 100th in European football but otherwise it was an unhappy night with missile throwing from the Stretford End

the Championship to Liverpool in 1979–80 saw them return to Europe for season 1980–81 in the UEFA Cup again.

This proved to be their shortest ever European run, as they failed at the first fence against Widzew Lodz. Unusually their undoing was at home in the first leg. Sammy McIlroy scored, but they allowed the Poles to leave with a 1–1 draw and it was simply not good enough. Over in Poland United fought gamely but without inspiration for a goalless draw. Widzew went through on the away goals rule which had been introduced into European matches, having scored at Old Trafford.

It was an undistinguished season all round, with the club finishing eighth in the League and going out of the FA Cup in the fourth round. It wasn't a huge surprise when Dave Sexton was asked to leave, with Europe's early exit one of the factors behind his departure.

Ron Atkinson took over; it was another blank season on the European front but Bryan Robson, Remi Moses, Frank Stapleton and Norman Whiteside were all introduced to help the club finish third in the League. This meant another run in the UEFA Cup 1982–83, though once again it was a short-lived campaign.

Valencia were the first-round opposition and what a stormy tie it proved to be. By the end everyone was calling them the villains of Valencia. Again United let themselves down in a home first leg. The Spaniards were tough and tactical, and the Reds were simply knocked out of their stride to finish with a 0–0 result. Later Valencia were reprimanded and fined for what UEFA described as 'repeated misdemeanours'.

But the punishment was laughable compared with the result the Spanish side had achieved. Over in Spain United made a tremendous fight of it. Their opening was marvellous as Bryan Robson led a fierce assault only to have a goal disallowed for raising his foot too high in the scoring of it. A minute before half-time they scored a good goal, Robson sending Ray Wilkins away and then sprinting to the far post to head home the captain's pin-point cross.

United seemed set for a fine win, but a quarter of an hour from the end Kevin Moran tripped Ribes for Solsona to score with a penalty. Valencia were on the boil again and Roberto soon rammed the winner home.

The tie had really been lost in Manchester where Valencia owed a lot to their strong-arm tactics. Ron Atkinson declared afterwards: 'The time has come for UEFA to put a stop to those teams which seek to win European matches by consistently breaking every rule in the book. The only way is to kick the offenders out of the competition. Reprimands and fines are a small price to pay for ultimate victory.'

There was violence off the field as well, much of it prompted by the Spanish police who were responsible for some indiscriminate baton charges at English supporters. United were so appalled that they announced that they no longer wanted their supporters to travel on to the Continent with them.

After losing to Valencia, United went on to beat Brighton in the final of the FA Cup to earn a return to the European Cup Winners' Cup in season 1983–84. This time they put up a much better show to reach the semi-finals, a run that was more like the old days. The first-round draw against Dukla Prague also sent the minds of older fans racing down memory lane. The Czechs had given the old Busby Babes a good game and they certainly tested Ron Atkinson's men. In fact United only escaped defeat in the first leg at Old Trafford by a few minutes. Ray Wilkins got a late penalty for a 1–1 draw. Even so Dukla were optimistic about the return and things certainly did not look good for the Manchester men when Dukla took a 10th minute lead in Prague.

That seemed to be the signal for United to reveal the best of their character, and they hit back to go in front with goals from Bryan Robson and Norman Whiteside. Dukla pulled level for 2–2 on the night and 3–3 overall, but United went through on the away goals rule.

Spartak Varna were gobbled up without too much trouble. Robson and Arthur Graham scored in a 2–1 win in Bulgaria and then the Reds won 2–0 in Manchester, Frank Stapleton netting both goals.

Then came a mighty tussle with Barcelona in the quarter-final. The first leg in the magnificent Nou Camp Stadium was lost 2–0. Graeme Hogg sliced through his own goal and the Spaniards nicked their second goal just before the end. United missed a lot of chances. In fact Bryan Robson, like a true captain, came home saying don't blame Hogg for the own-goal but himself for the opportunities he had failed to put away.

The great match with Barcelona

Robson seemed to take the second leg as a personal challenge and he led a fight back which belongs in the top drawer of United's European achievements. There was a tremendous rapport from the 58,000 fans as United took the game to their opponents, at the same time keeping a wary eye on Diego Maradona.

They pulled back the first goal after 25 minutes, Hogg touching on a Wilkins corner for Robson to score with a diving header, bravely ignoring the flying boots. Robson smashed in number two after the Spanish goalkeeper had failed to hold a drive from Wilkins. Whiteside headed a ball down for Stapleton to score the winner. It was a nail-biting finish with Mark Hughes lucky to escape being penalised in the area for a foul on Alonso.

Unhappily United were without the injured Robson and Arnold Muhren for the first leg of the semi-final against Juventus at Old Trafford, and to make matters worse Wilkins was serving a suspension. The Reds tried willingly enough but couldn't stop Paolo Rossi scoring with the

Above: After putting Barcelona to flight in the European Cup Winners Cup in 1983–84, the semi-final came as an anti-climax. The Reds drew the first leg 1–1 at Old Trafford against Juventus and then crashed to a 2–1 defeat in Italy

Above left, left and above right: The quarter-final against Barcelona in the European Cup Winners Cup in 1984 produced an epic, with a fight-back by Manchester United. United lost the first leg in Spain 2–0. The second leg at Old Trafford was a personal triumph for the captain who was mobbed and carried off shoulder high by fans at the end of United's inspiring 3–0 victory. The confrontation with Barcelona brought United up against world star Diego Maradona. In this European collision, Maradona was eclipsed by Robson who scored two of the goals

help of a deflection off Hogg after 15 minutes. Substitute Alan Davies made it 1–1, but most fans feared the worst in Turin.

The Reds were still without Robson, and Whiteside was only fit enough to make the substitutes' bench. He came on late in the game to demonstrate his liking for the big occasion by scoring an equaliser after Boniek had given Juventus an early lead. It seemed likely to be enough to take the match into extra time, but with only a minute remaining, Rossi sped away to score a beautiful winner.

United finished fourth in the League that season to give them their final run in Europe before the ban on English clubs which followed the tragedy at the European Cup final at the Heysel Stadium, Brussels, in 1985. They opened season 1984–85 in the UEFA Cup with a home first leg against Raba Gyor of Hungary and won comfortably 3–0 with goals from Robson, Hughes and Muhren. The Hungarians made more of a show in their own country but goals from Alan Brazil and Muhren, a penalty, provided the Reds with a 2–2 draw and safe passage through to meet PSV Eindhoven.

The Dutchmen provided two tight games, goalless in Holland and then 1–0 in United's favour at Old Trafford, the goal coming from a penalty by Gordon Strachan. Dundee United saw the Reds at their best. The Scots came to Old Trafford first and played well for a 2–2 draw. Robson scored and Strachan got another penalty, though he also let his countrymen off the hook by missing one as well. United played a storming game in Dundee with goals from Hughes and Muhren along with an own-goal seeing them safe with a 3–2 win.

Videoton, another Hungarian club, whom United played in the quarter-finals provided a huge anti-climax. United outplayed them over the two legs but couldn't finish them off. In the first leg in Manchester Frank Stapleton had two goals disallowed for offside before netting one that counted for a 1–0 win. It wasn't much of a lead but everyone was confident it would be enough because there had been nothing special about the Hungarians. But the goals wouldn't come in Hungary, either, despite United supplying most of the pressure, and Videoton sneaked a 1–0 win with the help of a deflection from a free kick. So it was all square, and extra time saw the teams still level. So for the first time in Europe United went into a penalty shoot-out . . . and lost 4–5. Frank Stapleton and Mark Hughes, the two strikers of all people, missed their penalties while the luckless Gary Bailey dived the wrong way for every one of Videoton's kicks!

It was 1990 when UEFA decided to lift the ban on English clubs and United were invited to play in the Cupwinners Cup competition of the 1990-91 season.

Football was returning to normal and for a second time Manchester United became Eng-

land's ambassadors in Europe having been first to show the way in the Fifties.

During the ban United had been denied European football three times missing the Cup-winners Cup of 1985-86, and the UEFA competition in 1986-87, and 1988-89 but after winning the FA Cup in 1990 the door re-opened.

The last game before the ban was against a Hungarian side and it was therefore fitting that Hungary provided the opposition for the first game of 1990, the little known Pecsi Munkas. Perhaps it was no surprise that Old Trafford's attendance that night was less than 30,000.

Clayton Blackmore was the man who found his way into the record books with a 25 yard shot which bridged the years from the night when Stapleton had netted the last European goal.

This was Alex Ferguson's first European campaign as United manager and having succeeded in the Cupwinners Cup when in charge at Aberdeen he was determined to repeat that feat. But it was the lack of support which brought this comment from the manager:

> I think one of the problems is that after missing European football for five years a lot of fans have forgotten how exciting it can be and some of the younger ones have never seen a European game at all. You get out of the habit.

Unfamiliarity plus live television coverage saw a drop in attendances for both the game against the Hungarians which was won 2-0, thanks to a second goal by Webb, and for the first leg of the Second Round.

This followed a 1-0 win in Pecs (pronounced Paich) through a McClair header.

The draw for Round Two was greeted with mixed feelings by the players. United faced Wrexham the Welsh Cup holders and their neighbours from less than 50 miles away and the home town of Mark Hughes!

Without being uncomplimentary to their opponents there was some excitement that United would still be in the competition in the New Year because the Third Round was not until March and the optimism proved correct as Wrexham were beaten 5–0 over the two legs.

There was disappointment for Hughes who so dearly wanted to play at The Racecourse in the second leg but missed the game because of a calf strain.

It was Hughes though who made the headlines in Round Three.

United met French club Montpellier in the first game at Old Trafford. Interest in the competition had increased bringing in a crowd of just under 42,000 and United got off to a marvellous start when within a minute McClair rifled home a Sharpe cross after Hughes had found him with a pass wide to the left wing.

Then disaster struck when the player who had put United in Europe scored for the opposition.

It was Lee Martin's FA Cup winning goal which secured the European place and with seven minutes of the game gone he flicked the ball past Les Sealey while trying to control it.

That lifted the French and they held out against everything United could throw at them until the incident which marred the night. Mark Hughes fell to the ground after what appeared to be a head butt from Pascal Baills the full back.

Baills screamed his innocence as he was sent off and television later proved that whilst the player deserved to be punished for violent conduct there appeared to have been little or no contact with the United striker.

Hughes said afterwards:

> I went down as a reaction to the attack and I stayed down until the referee sorted it out.

The incident did little to cement Anglo-French relationships nor did the Montpellier president who made it known that Hughes would not be very welcome in France.

But Hughes strode out at Montpellier ignoring the chants and the obscene banners written in English and had the last laugh.

Almost on half time Clayton Blackmore fired home a free kick from just inside the French half

Above left: Andrei Kanchelskis takes on Red Star Belgrade's Goran Vasilijevic during the European Super Cup final on 19 December 1991. A single Brian McClair goal was enough to secure United's second European trophy in seven months, neither of which had graced the Old Trafford trophy room before. Kanchelskis was one of nine regular first team players in 1991-92 who were classed as foreign under UEFA's new rules for European competition. As a result of the regulations, Alex Ferguson was forced to draft in young players to defend the Cup Winners' Cup, and despite a valiant effort United were knocked out by another powerful Spanish side, Atletico Madrid

Far right: Rotterdam played host to the Red Devils for the climax of United's first European campaign since the 1984-85 season. The choice of a stadium capable of holding only 45,000 for the European Cup Winners' Cup final led to calls for the match to be played at a larger venue. But the fans of two of Europe's best supported clubs had to put up with inadequate arrangements, and it was United's fans who came out smiling. Interest in the final contrasted sharply with United's opening match in the competition against Pecsi Munkas in September 1990, which only attracted 30,000 people to Old Trafford

and then after the same player was brought down, Steve Bruce converted a penalty to put United in the semi-final.

They were drawn against Polish club Legia Warsaw who had beaten the favourites Sampdoria in the previous round.

The first leg was in Warsaw and after being stunned by an early goal from the Poles United hit back within a minute through McClair, and Hughes and Bruce gave them a 3–1 advantage for the home leg.

United's Second European Final

A crowd of 45,000 roared United on and the team of 1991 joined their predecessors of 1968 by reaching a European Final for only the second time.

The game was to be staged in Rotterdam despite efforts to have it moved to a larger stadium and for Mark Hughes the final meant so much ... it was against his former club, Spanish giants Barcelona.

United knew they would be up against it and with goalkeeper Les Sealey protecting a badly gashed knee sustained in the League Cup Final less than a month earlier the odds against an English victory were stacked high.

The first shock of the final was Ferguson's decision to drop Neil Webb to make way for the solid Michael Phelan as United lined up:

Sealey
Irwin Bruce Pallister Blackmore
Phelan Ince Robson Sharpe
McClair Hughes

The second shock was the way United outplayed Barcelona.

After 67 minutes it looked as if Steve Bruce had given United the lead with a powerful header but Hughes ripped in to claim the goal as he pushed the ball over the line, and tied up victory eight minutes later with a splendidly taken goal ... an angled shot from the edge of the penalty area as the team's 100th of the season brought the European Cupwinners Cup to Old Trafford for the first time.

Barcelona punished the struggling Sealey to make it 2-1 from a Ronald Koeman free kick but it was too late.

Rotterdam belonged to Manchester United as Alex Ferguson was hailed as the most successful manager since Sir Matt Busby.

The homecoming in Manchester was sensational as United paraded the trophy before hundreds of thousands lining a route from the airport to the city.

But the following season UEFA made things difficult for the English clubs when restrictions were placed on "foreign" players.

Scots, Irish and Welsh were classed as foreign and with the rule allowing just four "non-natives" United were up against it to retain the trophy.

Nine regular first teamers were non-English although only goalkeeper Peter Schmeichel and Ukranian Andrei Kanchelskis were born outside Britain, and Ferguson had to bring in young players to make up the numbers.

The 1991–92 competition began with a visit to Greece and Athinaikos and after 180 minutes without a goal Hughes and McClair sealed victory in extra-time in the second leg game at Old Trafford.

Then came the toughest test apart from the Barcelona final as United faced Spanish club Atletico Madrid and went out of the competition despite a spirited fight at Old Trafford after losing the Spanish leg 3–0.

There was, however, some European success in the 1991–92 season with United as Cupwinners Cup holders beating European Champions Red Star Belgrade in the Super Cup thanks to a Brian McClair goal in a final reduced to one game and played at Old Trafford because of civil war in Yugoslavia.

Below: Two of United's heroes in Rotterdam, Mark Hughes and Steve Bruce. The final was particularly meaningful to Hughes because it had been Barcelona that prised him away from Old Trafford in 1986. Hughes' spell with the Catalan giants wasn't a success, but his two goals in the final demonstrated that the magic that had commanded the original £1.8 million fee was still working. Bruce's contribution to the Cup run, too, was impressive. In defence, United conceded only three goals, and at the other end the big defender hit four, making him the Reds' joint top scorer with Brian McClair

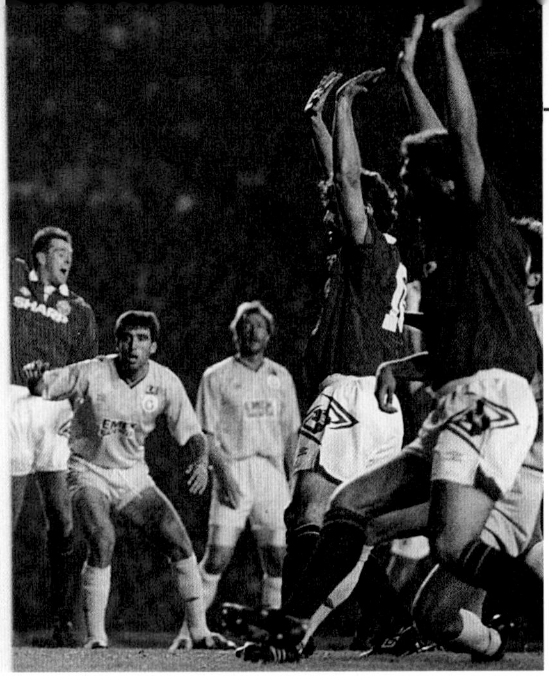

European disappointments

The second-round defeat against Atletico Madrid as Manchester United attempted to defend their European Cupwinners crown in 1991-92 was a firm indication of how difficult it was going to be after the introduction of the rule counting the Scots, Welsh and Irish as non-English players. The problem of being forced to juggle the team around was confirmed the following season in the UEFA Cup, with Alex Ferguson restricted to playing three foreigners and two assimilated players, meaning foreign players who had been affiliated to the English FA as youngsters with six years service.

An indication of how stretched he had become for experienced Englishmen was reflected on the substitutes' bench for the opening round against Torpedo Moscow when his reserves were Russell Beardsmore, Gary Neville, David Beckham, Nicky Butt and Kevin Pilkington, all youngsters of great promise and potential, but hardly ready to play against the giants of Europe!

Injuries to Bryan Robson and Paul Ince had also hit the team which struggled through the first leg 0–0 at Old Trafford. The Reds fought hard in Russia, but it was another goalless game and the Muscovites won 4–3 on penalties.

Season 1993–94 saw them qualify for the European Cup itself, and after sweeping to their first League success for 26 years morale and confidence was understandably better, particularly with the Champions making a good start to the season in the League. Indeed they had won five of their seven fixtures before tackling Honved in Budapest and there was such a confidence sweeping through the side that it was generally felt that Ferguson had a good enough squad to cope with the unsettling effects of the five-foreigner restrictions. United won the first leg 3–2 with two goals from Roy Keane and the other from Eric Cantona. Giving two goals away, careless ones said Ferguson, was disturbing, but it was nevertheless encouraging to score three away from home and the return leg was in fact a formality with two goals by the indomitable Steve Bruce for a 2–1 win.

'No matter who we play in the next round we are capable of scoring a few more goals,' said the manager who was delighted when the draw provided them with the unfancied Turks, Galatasaray.

To be fair, Alex Ferguson got the scoring bit right. His team did in fact score three against Galatasaray in the first leg of Old Trafford; unfortunately the defence had a rare sloppy night and the Reds ended up with egg on their faces and a 3–3 draw.

They opened well enough with Bryan Robson powering through after only three minutes to fire home, and when Gary Pallister challenged to force Sukur Hakan to put through his own goal 10 minutes later it seemed game, set and match.

Unbelievably after taking their two-goal lead United eased up for the Turks to draw level in the next 20 minutes and then just after the hour actually take the lead. Eric Cantona scored a late equaliser to avoid the indignity of a first-ever home defeat in European competition, but it was still a remarkably poor performance, and Alex Ferguson made no bones about it:

> After we had taken our two-goal lead, a few players started to put on one-man shows, running with the ball and treating the match like a carnival. When we play as a team we are very good, but this is more a disappointment than a shock. It was all individual performances rather than team play. We don't stop players being individuals at this club, but when a match becomes a personal show then it has to stop. If we had kept our momentum going after scoring our early goals I wouldn't have to talk like this. Now we have got a hell of a job on our hands.

The manager clearly feared the worst, and events proved he had every right to be worried. United went to Turkey and obviously found themselves up against not only confident opposition, but a whole country in bullish mood. The visit turned out a disaster both on and off the field, and for both the club and the supporters.

The Reds were certainly stiffer in defence and

Above Left: No-one could have asked for a better start to a European Cup tie than for United to find themselves 2–0 up after only thirteen minutes against their virtually unknown Turkish opponents Galatasaray. When Sukur Hakan headed past his own goalkeeper for the second goal (left) it looked as though United would cruise to Round Three. But in front of a stunned Old Trafford the dream rapidly turned into a nightmare as Galatasaray not only drew level, but went into a 3–2 lead. Eric Cantona's 81st minute equaliser saved United's blushes . . . but it was not enough to keep them in the competition

Right: They call the Alisamiyen Stadium in Istanbul 'The Hell' and this picture shows why. Fireworks and flares greeted the players, and at the end of the game the Turkish supporters continued their pyrotechnics earning the club a UEFA fine. The air was filled with choking sulphur fumes throughout the game but it was United's aspirations in the European Cup which went up in smoke.

Below: Time wasting and gamesmanship were part and parcel of the Galatasaray approach to the second leg of the European Cup Second Round tie in Istanbul. Even the ball-boys seemed reluctant to carry out their duties and this proved all too much for Eric Cantona. Late in the second half when the ball went out of play close to the Turkish bench, Cantona went to retrieve it himself. He pushed a member of the Galatasaray backroom staff out of the way and was instantly surrounded by the Turkish players. The incident was seen as the beginning of his clash with the referee which came after the final whistle.

Peter Schmeichel made two excellent saves to keep a clean sheet for a goalless draw; but of course that was not good enough and the Turks went through on scoring away goals.

As Ferguson summed up: 'The nightmare of the first leg haunted us right through the second match.' The game is still haunting the Reds because the frustration saw them lose their tempers, particularly Eric Cantona, who flipped at the end, incensed by the referee failing to stop Galatasaray from wasting time. He went to speak to him at the final whistle and the result was a red card which subsequently saw UEFA give him a four-match suspension for season 1994–95. That was an enormous blow to United after qualifying for the European Cup again.

By the end of October 1995 United had completed three European fixtures in the UEFA Champions League (the European Cup) and although unbeaten, were finding it difficult to field a strong side because of injuries and the non-English player restrictions.

The rules of qualification for the League section of the European Cup had been adjusted from the previous season, giving former winners or clubs which had been successful in recent European competitions free passage beyond the preliminary round. United were grouped with Barcelona, Swedish Champions Gothenburg and Galatasaray, their Turkish rivals from 1993.

Gothenburg were beaten 4–2 at Old Trafford.

The return to the Alisamiyen Stadium in Istanbul saw United dominate Galatasaray but neither side scored, although the game passed without any of the unpleasantness of the previous meeting. Then Barcelona came to Old Trafford and stunned United.

Facing his former club once again, Mark Hughes scored the opening goal. United were on top, but Hughes missed a chance to increase the lead and the Spaniards fought back. They drew level through Brazilian World Cup star Romario and went ahead when Bakero scored. Before the game Alex Ferguson had sprung a surprise by dropping Steve Bruce to substitute but he came into the game in time to see Lee Sharpe salvage a 2–2 draw, before making an heroic clearance himself to prevent disaster.

The record of never losing a European game at Old Trafford remained, but eventually United bowed out of the competition following a 4–0 defeat in Barcelona, and a 3–1 upset in Gothenburg, where Paul Ince was sent off.

1995–96 saw United in the UEFA Cup, drawn against the Russian club, Rotor Volgograd. They seemed mediocre opponents and after a 0–0 first leg in Stalingrad, the return at Old Trafford appeared a formality. It turned out to be anything but. By half-time the Russians led 2–0 and it looked as if a 40-year-old unbeaten European run at Old Trafford would end. With two minutes remaining the Russians lead 2–1. But Schmeichel joined his forwards in the Volgograd penalty area and sensationally headed in a corner for the equaliser. It brought consolation but United went out of the competition under the away goals rule.

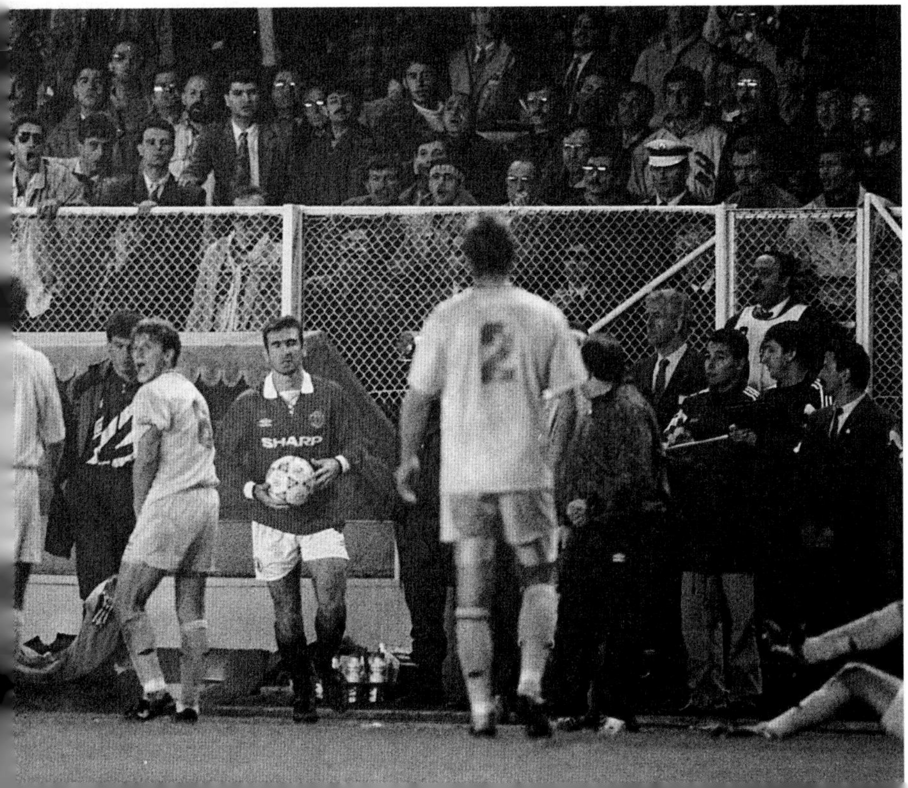

No. 13.—THE NEWTON HEATH TEAM.
TIMMONS (Trainer),
COUPAR.
HENRYS.
CLEMENTS.
FARMAN.
HOOD.
PERRINS.
STEWART.
ERRENIZ.
DONALDSON.
FITZIMMONS.

Birth of a legend

The men of Newton Heath who played in the club's first season in the Football League. Goalkeepers Warner and Davies are missing, otherwise the players are those who appeared regularly throughout the season. Some records show that on 7 January 1893 Newton Heath played with only ten men, with Stewart (third from right, centre row) in goal. Could this be the day when the photographer called?

To give George Stephenson, the railway engineer, a part to play in the Manchester United story might seem the work of an overstretched imagination, but the man who had a leading role in the development of rail transport did indeed make a contribution. He came to Manchester in the late 1820s to build the first passenger railway from the city, to Liverpool. He chose for the Manchester terminal the site of Castlefield, the flat area on the outskirts of the city where the Roman legions had settled on their way north to combat the Picts and Scots and where they had built a fortress named Mancunium, which developed into the city of Manchester. It was the perfect spot for Stephenson, offering no unmanageable gradients to his famous 'Rocket' when it began its journeys to and from Liverpool Road Station, the first railway station in the world.

Stephenson's first passenger railway was the Manchester and Liverpool Railway, and as time passed and it became clear that the project was a success, other lines opened. One of these was a line operating in the opposite direction, the Manchester and Leeds Railway, setting off from Oldham Road, Newton Heath, and terminating in the Leeds area where its lines met with those of the North Midland Railway. Eventually the two companies combined, and formed the Lancashire and Yorkshire Railway Company, which had a branch at one end of its line, in Newton Heath.

This was in 1847 when the game of football was still going through a complicated phase of its progress towards becoming a major part of the lives of British working people. There were plenty of centres where the game was played, but no uniformity in its rules. Schools, colleges and universities had football as part of their recreational activities, but the game played at Cambridge, for example, differed from that of Eton.

It was not until 1863 that a group of football enthusiasts from the London area met in the Freemason's Tavern in Great Queen Street, London, and formed the Football Association, and eventually after much arguing and a walk-out by certain representatives, drew up the first rules of association football.

In 1872 the Football Association introduced its first national competition. A trophy was bought for £20 and named the Football Association Cup, attracting entries from as far apart as the Queen's Park Club in Glasgow and Donnington in Lincolnshire, although the majority of teams were from the London area. Wanderers beat the Royal Engineers 1–0 at Kennington Oval in the first Cup final. Football had arrived as a public sport, with 2,000 having watched the game.

Six years later, when the railways of the country had grown into a gigantic network from the tiny acorn George Stephenson had planted in Manchester, the Dining Room Committee of the Lancashire and Yorkshire Railway Company responded to a request from men of the Carriage and Wagon Works for permission, and funds, to start their own football team.

The men chose the title 'Newton Heath LYR' for the team, (the LYR being Lancashire and Yorkshire Railway) their nearest rivals being the men from the company's Motive Power Division (the engine drivers and maintenance men) whose team was 'Newton Heath Loco'(motive). Newton Heath LYR were given a pitch on a stretch of land in North Road, close to the railway yard. It was a bumpy, stony patch in summer, a muddy, heavy swamp in the rainy months. But the men of Newton Heath LYR didn't really care – football was a means of enjoyment and the mud would wash off. At first games were mostly inter-departmental, or against other railway workers carried in along the lines from Middleton, Oldham, Earlestown and St Helens. The team grew in stature and reputation, and eventually found that it dominated most of the domestic competitions.

There were many other clubs in the area and a Manchester Cup competition had been launched, so Newton Heath LYR entered in 1885 and reached the final. The following year they again competed, and this time won. The game was attracting a great deal of interest, and the success of the side was looked upon as bringing prestige to the Lancashire and Yorkshire Railway Company by the executives, who were quite prepared to make allowances for men to take time off work in order to prepare for important fixtures.

In 1887 Newton Heath LYR again reached the final of the Manchester Cup, only to lose, but the club was now ready for a major step in its history, as football itself took a massive stride forward. Meetings had taken place several times amongst representatives of many of the northern clubs to discuss the formation of a combination of teams who would take part in a new competition. Small leagues were in existence in various parts of the country, but the plans under consideration were for a league of a much grander nature. In 1888 the Football League was formed, its twelve members having a strong northern domination, but with others from the Midlands also involved.

The original twelve were Preston North End, Aston Villa, Wolverhampton Wanderers, Blackburn Rovers, Bolton Wanderers, West Bromwich Albion, Accrington Stanley, Everton, Burnley, Derby County, Notts County and Stoke City. All were based in industrial towns or cities, and each linked to the other by the railways.

Familiar names? All but Accrington Stanley survived the first 100 years of the Football League, but by 1988 there were rumblings that the super-clubs, including United, Liverpool, Tottenham and Everton might form their own breakaway league.

In the first season Preston North End dominated the League, going through their 22 games without a single defeat, and for good measure they won the FA Cup as well, beating Wolves 3–0 at the Oval.

Newton Heath did not consider themselves strong enough to compete with the elite of the game, but they were growing in stature and it became obvious that the opposition being provided locally was not enough to test the mettle of the 'Heathens'. In 1888 they had the proud record of not losing a game at home until October, when a team of touring Canadians came to Manchester and beat them before 3,000 spectators in what was the first 'international' game played at North Road.

The programme for that game has survived the passage of time and reveals the Newton Heath line up for the game, even though two places are not filled:

Goal: T Hay; right-back, J Powell; left-back, A N Other; half-backs, T Bourke, J Davies, J Owen; right-wing, A N Other, R Doughty; centre, J Doughty; left-wing, J Gotheridge, J Gale

The missing players were most likely Mitchell and Tait, for added to the nine names printed in the programme, they formed the eleven who started the following season for the club. The referee that afternoon was Mr J J Bentley from Bolton who, a quarter of a century later, would become secretary-manager of Manchester United, the club not yet created.

The club join the Football Alliance

By that time the idea of League football played between towns rather than within local boundaries, was catching on and in 1889, Newton Heath joined other clubs on the verge of the Football League to form the Football Alliance.

In their first season Newton Heath finished eighth, having played the eleven companions in their new league: Sunderland, Darwen, Crewe Alexandra, Bootle, Grimsby Town, Birmingham St George's, Walsall Town Swifts, Sheffield Wednesday, Small Heath, Nottingham Forest and Long Eaton.

They also played in the first round of the FA Cup, and had the misfortune to be drawn against Preston North End, the holders, who beat them 6–1 at Deepdale, the only consolation for Newton Heath being that they had scored against the 'Invincibles', which is more than many of their Football League 'superiors' had done the previous season.

In 1890 another major step came for Newton Heath. They began to sever their links with the railway company. The letters 'LYR' were dropped from their title. The club appointed its first full-time official, the secretary A H Albut, who arrived from Aston Villa and set up office in a terraced cottage close to North Road, at 33 Oldham Road, Newton Heath.

There was still a strong connection with the railways, even though the club was no longer supported by the social committee of the Lancashire and Yorkshire Railway. Most of the players worked for the railways, and it was this which had made the club successful in the first place. A job on the railways was considered a job for life, and being able to offer a talented footballer work in the Manchester area allowed the club to attract men from all parts of the country. Also, because they were 'staff' the players had concessionary travel, and the team was able to get from game to game without the added burden of transport to pay for.

Professionalism in football had started three years before the formation of the Football League and some of Newton Heath's players earned money by playing for the club. But their reward was small, helping only to boost their wages from their normal employment, and hardly putting them with high wage-earners.

Newton Heath had attracted some players who were highly rated in the game, Welshmen like the Doughty brothers, Jack and Roger, who found work in the railway depot and whose football skills earned them international honours. There were others in the side who had sound reputations, like goalkeeper Tom Hay, who moved to the area from Staveley close to the railway town of Crewe, and Pat McDonnell, a craggy Scot whose search for work led to him walking from Glasgow to Manchester, where he was given a job at Newton Heath and won his place in the side.

Jack Powell, the full-back, had a remarkable rise to fame. He was new to the game when the Welsh club Druids, in Ruabon, signed him but it was obvious that he had a bright future. After just three games he was selected to play for his country against England in 1879. In 1887 he registered as a professional with Newton Heath. Mitchell, Davies, Owen, Tait and Sam Black, skipper before Powell's arrival, had all played a part in the growth of the club from a works team to one good enough to represent the city of Manchester against clubs from other areas.

Sam Black always remained an amateur. He refused payment while those around him accepted the few shillings a week they could earn from their football. Black played with Newton Heath for most of the 1880s before returning to his native Burton on Trent and turning to refereeing.

It was as a referee that Sam Black found his way into football history. During a game between Woolwich Arsenal and Burnley he refused to award the Londoners a goal, because the Burnley 'keeper had pointed out to him that the bladder inside the ball had burst out through the stitching on one of the panels, and its erratic flight had made it impossible to catch. Black's verdict was that he could not award a goal because the game has to be played with a 'ball', and as the object which had ended in the Burnley net did not constitute a ball in the true sense of the word, because it was not round, then it could not constitute a goal either!

At the end of the 1889–90 season Stoke City had finished bottom of the Football League, having won just three games in the entire season, and found life a struggle both on and off the field. They asked if they might stand down, and were replaced by Sunderland from the Alliance, who were highly successful. A link between the two leagues had been forged.

In their second season of Alliance football, Newton Heath did no better than in their first. They won seven games once again, five of them at North Road, their biggest victory being against Crewe, 6–3. Their biggest defeat was 8–2 at Nottingham Forest.

New players had been introduced as some of the older, long serving members retired or moved to other clubs. Slater had taken over in goal, Mitchell and McMillan were full-backs and the half-back line was Roger Doughty, Ramsey and Owen. Farman played right-wing, with Jack Doughty inside him and at centre-forward Evans. Milarvie and Sharpe played on the left for virtually the whole season, but there were changes in other positions. Stewart edged out Jack Doughty, who was in his last season with the club, and Clements arrived on the scene as a left full-back.

That summer Stoke City were allowed to re-enter the Football League, having proved too strong for the Alliance. The move was possible because the League's members decided that they would enlarge their numbers by two, and they also accepted Darwen. Now there were fourteen clubs, and Sunderland had proved their worth by finishing in seventh place, only six points away from the Champions, Everton.

Sunderland's strength was further illustrated the following season when they won the title, and it was also a season of great significance for Newton Heath. With Darwen now out of the Alliance and Stoke back in the higher reaches, two new clubs filled their places, Ardwick FC from Manchester, and Lincoln City.

Ardwick eventually became Manchester City, and the first time the two great Manchester rivals met under senior league conditions was on Saturday, 10 October 1891, when Newton Heath won 3–1 at North Road, thanks to goals from Farman (2) and Donaldson. Strangely, the two sides had met the previous week in an FA Cup qualifying round, when Newton Heath won 5–1, so they had started favourites for that first league 'derby' clash.

The Newton Heath team for the Alliance game was:

Slater, McFarlane, Clements, Sharpe, Stewart, Owen, Farman, Edge, Donaldson, Sneddon, Henrys.

The win marked another milestone for the club, as it was the first time since joining the Alliance that the team had celebrated three successive victories.

By the end of the season they were undefeated at North Road, and had lost just three times: at Burton on Trent to the Swifts, at Muntz Street in Birmingham where Small Heath beat them 3–2, and at the Town Ground in Nottingham, where Forest showed their strength in a 3–0 victory. Forest won the Alliance, Newton Heath were runners up.

Newton Heath became a First Division side

Then in 1892 the Football League again decided to enlarge. It divided into two divisions, the League becoming the First Division, and growing to 16 clubs, whilst a Second Division was formed by others from the Alliance and clubs such as Northwich Victoria, Rotherham and London's first professional club, Woolwich Arsenal.

Nottingham Forest and Newton Heath were invited to join the First Division. So the club which had struggled for those first two seasons had reached a pinnacle just at the right moment, and was now one of football's elite.

Elite by status, but not one of the rich clubs by a long way. Newton Heath seemed to stagger from financial problem to financial problem. Harry Renshaw, the first Newton Heath correspondent from the *Manchester Evening News*, wrote of the club's plight, and its operations from 33 Oldham Road:

> The rent of the cottage was just six shillings a week [30 pence] and to increase the social side the club rented a schoolroom in Miles Platting

as a place where supporters and players might meet. It was a place where they might spend time together in a common cause, and to add to the facilities a billiards table was purchased. But, sad to relate, the venture was not a success. Indeed at one meeting of directors the only light available was from three candles fixed in ginger beer bottles. The reason? The Corporation had cut off the gas supply, and served a summons on the club!

However, according to Renshaw's story, the summons was put to good use by the crafty Albut. He had his eye on a player with another club and knew that the man was unsettled and having problems getting his wages. So he met the player, lent him the summons and let him use it to threaten his club, telling them that he would 'serve it' if they didn't let him join Newton Heath. They did and his presence increased gate receipts by £10 for the next game.

The Heathens first season in the Football League was one of direct comparison with their performance off the field. They struggled, and yet survived.

The first game Newton Heath played in the First Division was against Blackburn Rovers, a formidable force from northern Lancashire. The town of Blackburn had provided football with its first 'super club'. In 1884 Rovers won the FA Cup, beating Queen's Park from Glasgow in the final. The following year they repeated the feat against the same final opponents and then in 1886 beat West Bromwich Albion in a replayed final and were awarded a special trophy for winning the Cup in three successive seasons. In 1890 Blackburn beat Sheffield Wednesday 6–1 in the final, and the next season won the cup for the fifth time in eight years by beating Notts County 3–1.

When the 1892–93 season began Newton Heath approached their first fixture against three-times Cup winners Rovers with some trepidation. The match was at Rovers' ground, and despite goals from Coupar, Donaldson and Farman, ended in a 4–3 defeat.

The men who carried the banner of Newton Heath into football's top section were:

Warner, Clements, Brown, Perrins, Stewart, Erentz, Farman, Coupar, Donaldson, Carson, Matthieson.

Seven days later Manchester witnessed its first Football League game with one change to that original line-up, Mitchell replacing Clements at right full-back and remaining in that position until the end of the season. The first home game ended in a 1–1 draw with Burnley, the Scot Robert Donaldson again scoring as he would do with regularity throughout that first season.

Newton Heath made a poor start, losing their next two games at Burnley and Everton, then followed this with a draw at West Bromich and defeat by the Throstles at North Road. The Heathens had played six games in the first Division without a win, but when victory did arrive it came in true style. The club's first League win was in a game against Wolverhampton Wanderers, a club which would continue to be a rival until the days of the Busby Babes, and on Saturday 15 October 1892 Newton Heath won 10–1!

Nevertheless, the season was a long difficult road for the club, with victories few and far between, and when Blackburn knocked them out of the FA Cup in January 1893 it seemed a bleak journey for the 'Railwaymen'. When April came and the season ended with a 3–3 draw against Accrington Stanley, Newton Heath were 16th in the First Division, bottom of the table.

It is interesting to note here that in the 1986–87 season the League Management Committee caused a minor sensation when they introduced their proposals for end of season play-offs in an effort to trim down the First Division to twenty clubs. The bottom three clubs in the First Division were relegated, the top two from the Second Division promoted. The remaining place (in the first year the number of clubs was cut to 21, the final reduction being made in season 1987–88) was contested by a play-off series between the First Division club finishing fourth from the bottom, and the Second Division clubs in third, fourth and fifth places.

This 'new' method of securing or winning a position in the top division was a cause of great controversy. But it was not a new scheme – far from it.

The Football League in 1892 had decided that at the end of the season, the three bottom clubs in the new First Division would meet the first three of the Second Division for the right to play in the top section the following year.

	P		D	L	F	A	Pts
Sunderland	30	22	4	4	100	36	48
Preston North End	30	17	3	10	57	39	37
Everton	30	16	4	10	74	51	36
Aston Villa	30	16	3	11	73	62	35
Bolton Wanderers	30	13	6	11	56	55	32
Burnley	30	13	4	13	51	44	30
Stoke City	30	12	5	13	58	48	29
West Bromwich Albion	30	12	5	13	58	69	29
Blackburn Rovers	30	8	13	9	47	56	29
Nottingham Forest	30	10	8	12	48	52	28
Wolverhampton Wdrs.	30	12	4	14	47	68	28
Sheffield Wednesday	30	12	3	15	55	65	27
Derby County	30	9	9	12	52	64	27
Notts County	30	10	4	16	53	61	24
Accrington Stanley	30	6	11	13	57	81	23
Newton Heath	30	6	6	18	50	85	18

Small Heath – later to become Birmingham City – were top of the Second Division, so on 22 April 1893, two weeks after the season officially ended, the clubs met at Stoke for the deciding 'Test Match'. It ended 1–1, with Farman's goal earning Newton Heath the right to fight once again in a replay. A crowd of over 6,000, many of them railway workers from Manchester, crossed the Pennines to see Newton Heath win

Take your partners for a game of football! A lighthearted moment during a training session at Bank Street. In the background stands the club's 'twelfth man', the chimneys which were said to belch out acrid fumes if United were losing. This picture was taken about a year before the move to Old Trafford

the replay at Bramall Lane, Sheffield, 5–2. Three goals from Farman, plus one each from Cassidy and Coupar were enough to secure their place in the First Division for the 1893–94 season.

The club's ground at North Road had come in for heavy criticism during the season not only from defeated opponents but from the local supporters and Newton Heath's own players. Secretary Albut had a mission: to find a new playing area. In 1893 the club left the cloying mud of North Road, where on dry days stones and flints made life difficult for the players and on wet afternoons spectators had to squelch their way to and from the ground through ankle deep slime.

The new ground was in Bank Street, Clayton. Here the mud of North Road was replaced by the toxic fumes of a chemical works which ran alongside the pitch. There were those who claimed that if the Heathens were losing, the factory would belch out heavy smoke, on the premise that home players were accustomed to it, while it made life difficult for the visiting side. The registered office moved from Oldham Road to Bank Street, secretary Albut being quite prepared to share the wooden hut with the local newspaper which provided the telephone.

The move from North Road was partly because of the mud, and partly because of the cost of playing there. When Newton Heath was a railway team the Lancashire and Yorkshire Railway had been prepared to pay the rent for the use of the ground to the Manchester Cathedral authorities who owned the land. When Newton Heath broke their connections with the railway company, this arrangement ceased and the rent increased. While the move to Clayton meant a good walk for many of Newton Heath's supporters, the club at least had a ground to call its own, and paid rent directly to the Bradford (a district of Manchester) and Clayton Recreative Committee, instead of being forced to hand over 'a very handsome rent' to the Lancashire and Yorkshire Railway, who were only paying a nominal amount to the church authorities.

So the second season of League Football began and this was to have a significant effect on the future of the club. They won their first game at the new ground, beating Burnley 3–2, and by 23 September 1893 could look back on four games which had seen them winning twice, drawing once and losing 3–1 at West Bromwich.

It was the return fixture against the Midlands club which was to lead to a strange turn of events, and seriously affect Newton Heath's financial position. Football had now become very popular and newspapers assigned correspondents to cover games – readers pored over their words as the only means of following their favourites' progress. The newspaper was the bearer of facts, the bringer of truth, and when West Bromwich were beaten 4–1 on 14 October, readers of the *Birmingham Daily Gazette*, published on the Monday after the game, were stunned to read the words of 'Observer':

> It wasn't football, it was simply brutality and if these are the tactics Newton Heath are compelled to adopt to win their matches, the sooner the Football Association deal severely with them the better it will be for the game generally.

Newton Heath's officials were sent a cutting of the story, and were furious. This was criticism which they felt was unwarranted and decided to take the newspaper and its writer – William Jephcott – to court. They got the referee to back their claim, and he gave them ample support by writing to the *Manchester Guardian* that the game had not been the rough-house described in the Midlands newspaper, but had in his opinion been 'one of the best games he had ever controlled'. The referee, Mr. J R Strawson of Lincoln, wrote:

> Not once was any decision that I gave questioned, the play of both sides was a credit to their clubs and a credit to the game.

In March the following year, after a season of football that saw Newton Heath still fighting for survival, the Manchester Civil Court judge, Mr Justice Day, granted Newton Heath one farthing damages, and ordered both parties to pay their own costs. This was a body blow indeed for the club.

The first club to be relegated

From that game with West Bromwich, early in the season, until the last game of the 1893–94 campaign, only three League victories came Newton Heath's way, so it was no surprise to anyone when they found themselves involved in the play-off Test Match again.

Liverpool had topped the Second Division, eight points clear of Small Heath, and when Blackburn's ground at Ewood Park was chosen as the venue for the deciding game, Newton Heath felt that the odds were stacked against them. The game ended in a 2–0 defeat, Liverpool were promoted from the Second Division, and Newton Heath became the first club ever to be relegated. They stayed in the Second Division for the next twelve seasons, but during that time the club was transformed, and perhaps that court case and its crippling outcome was fate playing a hand in the growth of Manchester United.

Newton Heath ended their first season in the Second Division in third place, again qualifying for the play-offs, but this time losing to Stoke, whose season had ended with them third from bottom in the First Division. Ironically, Liverpool were the only club to be relegated after losing their Test Match to Bury.

The play-off system was changed the following season to a mini-league among the qualifying clubs, among whom were again Newton Heath, who finished in second place in the regular season. They first played Burnley, who were the bottom club of the First Division, then after winning and losing to them, faced Sunderland. They drew at Bank Street, then lost in the north-east and stayed down.

A season later the play-offs were abandoned in favour of automatic promotion and relegation of the top two and bottom two clubs. Burnley and Newcastle United moved up to replace Stoke and Blackburn, leaving the two Manchester clubs, City and Newton Heath in third and fourth places in the Second Division. By the turn of the century Newton Heath had missed promotion by two places for two successive seasons, and seen their financial position worsen. Players' demands were not high, but they did have the backing of the Players' Union, predecessor of the Professional Footballers Association, formed in 1898 in Manchester, at the Spread Eagle Hotel in Corporation Street.

Saved by a St Bernard

Fate was to to take a hand again. Newton Heath had ended the 1901 season in tenth place. Attendances for their Second Division games had dropped off, and the club needed cash. It was decided to organise a grand bazaar, in St James' Hall in Oxford Street, and here one man and his dog stepped into the creation of a legend. In his official history of 1948 Alf Clarke wrote:

Below: The pocket version of the club's history written by Alf Clarke of the *Manchester Evening Chronicle* and published in 1948. The booklet told some of the stories included in this history and was printed to coincide with the club's FA Cup achievements of that year. Alf Clarke was one of the journalists who died at Munich

> A St Bernard dog, with a barrel fastened to its collar, was one of the attractions at the show. One night, after the place had closed (it was the third night of the four days of the bazaar) the dog apparently knocked over a part of a stall in the centre of the room. A hurried search revealed that the dog had broken loose and a fireman on duty in the hall saw two eyes staring at him in the darkness. He had no idea it was the dog and rushed out of the side entrance to the building. The St Bernard went out the same way.

Above: Perhaps one of the most important events in the history of Manchester United was the fund-raising bazaar of 1901. The efforts of Newton Heath to stay afloat in football's formative years led to the event being staged. It was from St James's Hall that Harry Stafford's dog strayed to find its way to J H Davies

John Henry Davies, first chairman of Manchester United and the man whose wealth created the club from the failing Newton Heath. Davies was managing director of Manchester Breweries and not only rescued the club from extinction when he became involved in 1901, but put up the £60,000 to build Old Trafford. The chance meeting of Davies and Harry Stafford was indeed a stroke of good fortune

What happened next has, over the years, become distorted somewhat, with parts added to give the story greater impact perhaps, but the *Manchester Evening News* of September 1906 (five years after the event, and 42 before Alf Clarke's recollections were published) told the story thus:

> The animal was found by a friend of Mr James Taylor, and was seen by Mr J H Davies, who fancied it. The making of the bargain led to the meeting of Mr Davies and Stafford, and the latter, knowing the low water in which his club was in, asked Mr Davies for a contribution to its funds. This led to the club changing hands.

Harry Stafford was the club right-back and captain, and he and Taylor and Davies, a brewer, were to play a part in saving the club from extinction, so the role of the St Bernard can hardly be exaggerated.

Early in 1902 Newton Heath's creditors could wait no longer. The club had debts of £2,670 and was on the verge of bankruptcy, a fate which had already seen Bootle FC forced to quit the League and be replaced by Liverpool. Would Newton Heath also slip out of existence?

A creditors' meeting was held at New Islington Hall, but although secretary James West reported that there were no new tradesmen's debts outstanding since the date of the winding-up order, the club still needed £2,000 to make it solvent again. Harry Stafford then got to his feet and told the meeting that he knew where he could get hold of the money, massive amount though it was.

Stafford said he had met four businessmen who were each willing to invest £500, but who in turn would require a direct interest in running the club. The Newton Heath directors agreed, or were forced into agreement by the creditors, and the four men, J Brown of Denton, W Deakin of Manchester, together with James Taylor and John Henry Davies, eventually came forward with their proposals.

Manchester United is born

On 28 April 1902 Newton Heath FC was no more. It was replaced by Manchester United Football Club.

The selection of the new title was not straightforward, though. While the 'uniting' of Davies's group and Stafford's club might have seemed an obvious inspiration for the name, others were tabled. Manchester Central was one suggestion, but this was rejected because it sounded too much like a railway station. There was in fact a Central Station in Manchester (now the site of the G-MEX Exhibition Centre) which later served the Old Trafford area, and with Newton Heath's railway connections perhaps the name was not as ridiculous as it seems. Manchester Celtic was also put forward but turned down on the grounds that it might be felt that there was some link with Celtic organisations.

Eventually Louis Rocca, a man who would play a leading role on the club's scouting staff for the next 48 years, came forward with the name Manchester United and it was unanimously adopted. A new president was elected, Mr John Henry Davies, and Harry Stafford teamed up with James West to organise the day-to-day running of the club. Stafford was given the licence for one of Davies's public houses, and the St Bernard settled into its new home with the brewer's daughter! The curtain came down on Newton Heath as the club finished just four places from the foot of the Second Division.

The following season, as Manchester United, new spirit and new players took them to fifth from the top, but they were forced to look on with some envy as their rivals Manchester City were promoted.

Ernest Mangnall

The 1903–04 season began with a home draw against Bristol City, and defeats at the hands of Burnley and Port Vale, a start which led to a call for action from the supporters. Then in late September 1903 there arrived on the scene a man who was to play as important a part in the building of the Manchester United of today as any other . . . Ernest Mangnall.

Mangnall was the club's first *real* manager and a man who knew how to use the media to promote football, and to a certain extent himself. He was a well-known sportsman with a love of cycling. So strong in fact was his affection for life in the saddle, that he rode from his home town of Bolton to Land's End, then to John O'Groats and back, before his career took him into football.

Ernest Mangnall's cycling activities saw him heavily involved with the National Cyclists Union, and Bolton Cycling Club and Bolton Harriers Athletic Club. He was involved at the turn of the century with the opening of Burnden Park, which was used for cycling and athletics as well as football, and eventually he was elected to Bolton Wanderers board of directors. In March 1900 he moved into management, taking over at Burnley from Harry Bradshaw, who moved south to manage Woolwich Arsenal. A football manager in the early years of the game was referred to as the club 'secretary' but he was responsible for selecting the team, deciding on the tactics to use, and conducting training sessions.

Mangnall was later to go on record as saying that he felt players should not use a ball too much during practice sessions, but should build up their physical fitness. 'A ball should only be used one day a week', he said, a true sign of the times.

In a series of articles for the *Manchester Evening News* he wrote:

> A great, intricate, almost delicate, and to the vast majority of the public an incomprehensible piece of machinery is the modern, up to date, football club. It is a creation peculiarly by itself. There is nothing like it and it is only when one takes an active and practical part in the manipulation of the strings that work such an organisation that one realises in the fullest sense what it all means.
>
> The veriest layman need not be told that the greatest and first essential to success is the selection of a capable team, but it requires a deep rooted and special knowledge to know and to obtain the right stamp of men. How many clubs have lamentably failed and steered perilously near the rocks of irretrievable adversity by starting out with men with reputations; 'stars' as they are popularly called?
>
> They are fickle, difficult to manage, and most times too supremely conscious of their own importance. 'Balloon headedness' is a disease which has ruined more promising players and brought greater disaster to clubs than anything else I know of.
>
> There must be a judicious blending of the young and old. A team may carry three or four men of small stature, but too many wee men, no matter how clever and artistic, will not do, for the reason that the strain of First Division football becomes more severe every season.
>
> As they say in the world of fisticuffs, 'Nothing beats a good little'un like a good big'un!'

Ernest Mangnall's approach to football was the direct route, he knew where he was going and woe betide anyone who stood in his path. Manchester United was to be a successful club and he would see to that. At the end of his first season as manager United were third in the Second Division table, two places ahead of his old club Burnley. Manchester City were runners-up in the First Division. No fewer than 28 players had appeared in first team games that season as Mangnall searched for the right blend.

The 1904–05 season began well, in fact it took on record-breaking proportions, when after drawing with Port Vale in the opening fixture, then beating Bristol City a week later, United lost to Bolton on 17 September 1904, and then went on a run of games which saw them not lose another game until February 1905. Eighteen games without defeat, 16 of them wins.

The season had started with a set-back for the club, or at least for Harry Stafford, now a director, and former secretary James West. Stafford as a publican had held the licence to sell alcohol at Bank Street for several years. As he was leaving his public house, and as James West was a licensee, West made an official application to Manchester City Magistrates to take over the sale of alcohol at the ground, and was turned down.

Not being able to sell drink inside the ground meant a loss of revenue to United, but taken in the light of modern developments it is remarkable to read the report of the court case in September 1904:

> Mr Fred Brocklehurst, appearing for the club, said that the decision would govern some 33 to 34 Saturdays during the season. The application was solely on the grounds of public requirement. It was only during the quarter of an hour's interval in the game that it became of serious moment to the spectators to have facilities for refreshments. Probably from 25,000 to 30,000 spectators were there every Saturday and they included a large number of visitors.
>
> There were three ways in which they might obtain refreshments. They might bring bottles containing drink into the ground, and he believed a great many would do so. Such a practice could not conduce to temperance. Whereas previously people had perhaps one small glass of whisky during the interval, they would probably take more upon the ground and consume it there. He believed that last Saturday, after a licence had been refused, there had been more drunkenness after the match than for the whole of the previous twelve months.
>
> There was a danger too that this taking bottles into the ground could be dangerous. People might use them as missiles if they did not agree with the decision of the referee (laughter).
>
> The Chairman: 'The spectators don't carry shooters with them like the Americans do?'
>
> Mr Brocklehurst: 'They don't, if they did we might have to put up notices saying "Don't

The club's influential captain Charlie Roberts, who appeared on the scene in 1904 and played until the outbreak of the First World War in 1914. Roberts played three times for England in 1905 and skippered United to all their major successes in the early 1900s. Roberts caused a minor sensation by insisting on playing in shorts which were above knee length

shoot the referee he's doing his best!" ' (renewed laughter).

Continuing, Mr Brocklehurst said it was suggested that pass-out checks could be issued but with so many people in the ground this would be impossible. The third alternative was to obtain an occasional licence. That there had been proper supervision and control in the past was shown by the fact that there had, in the past, been no complaint at all. Every Saturday fifteen policemen and fifteen other attendants were present to maintain order. There had recently been alterations to the ground and the bar was situated such as there was no temptation for people who did not want to drink to go to it. Mr Brocklehurst said it would really be in the interests of temperance to grant the licence.

Mr Johnston: 'Do you seriously suggest that more people went to public houses after the match?'

Mr Brocklehurst: 'Yes, they went to show that if they could not get one drink on the ground they could get three drinks off it!'

Mr J E Mangnall, secretary of the United Football Club, said a large number of empty bottles were found on the ground after the match on Saturday.

Mr Johnston: 'Did you see any bottles that had contained lemonade or milk?'

Mr Mangnall: 'No, I didn't see any of that kind.' (laughter)

The application was refused.

There was worse to come for secretary West and Harry Stafford. West had resigned to make way for Ernest Mangnall, but they were both later suspended from football by the FA for making illegal payments to players, something which was commonplace in the early years of the game.

Stafford later said: 'I have been the Lord High Everything for the club since it came under its present proprietorship. Everything I have done has been done under the best interests of the club.'

Stafford claimed he had been questioned and found guilty of only one misdemeanour and that was that after obtaining a player from Scotland, he had paid him his wages in advance before he had been registered as a 'fully accredited member' of the club.

Under Ernest Mangnall, United finished their second season in third place, missing promotion for the second year by one position. But the backbone of United's first successful side was being created by the manager. Jack Picken was signed from Plymouth Argyle, Harry Moger, the goalkeeper, from Southampton and Charlie Roberts from Grimsby Town. His fee of £400 was considered a bargain the year before Alf Common became the first ever £1,000 player when he left Sunderland to join neighbouring Middlesbrough. Roberts was to captain the side from his position at centre-half and was a revolutionary in that he wore shorts at a time when players were encouraged to keep their knees covered.

In 1905–06, Ernest Mangnall's third full season in charge, United won promotion, finishing second, four points behind Bristol City, the pair changing places with Nottingham Forest and Wolves. Manchester United were a First Division team.

That year, too, they reached the quarter-finals of the FA Cup, stepping into unknown territory after victories over Staple Hill, Norwich City and Aston Villa. They were then beaten by

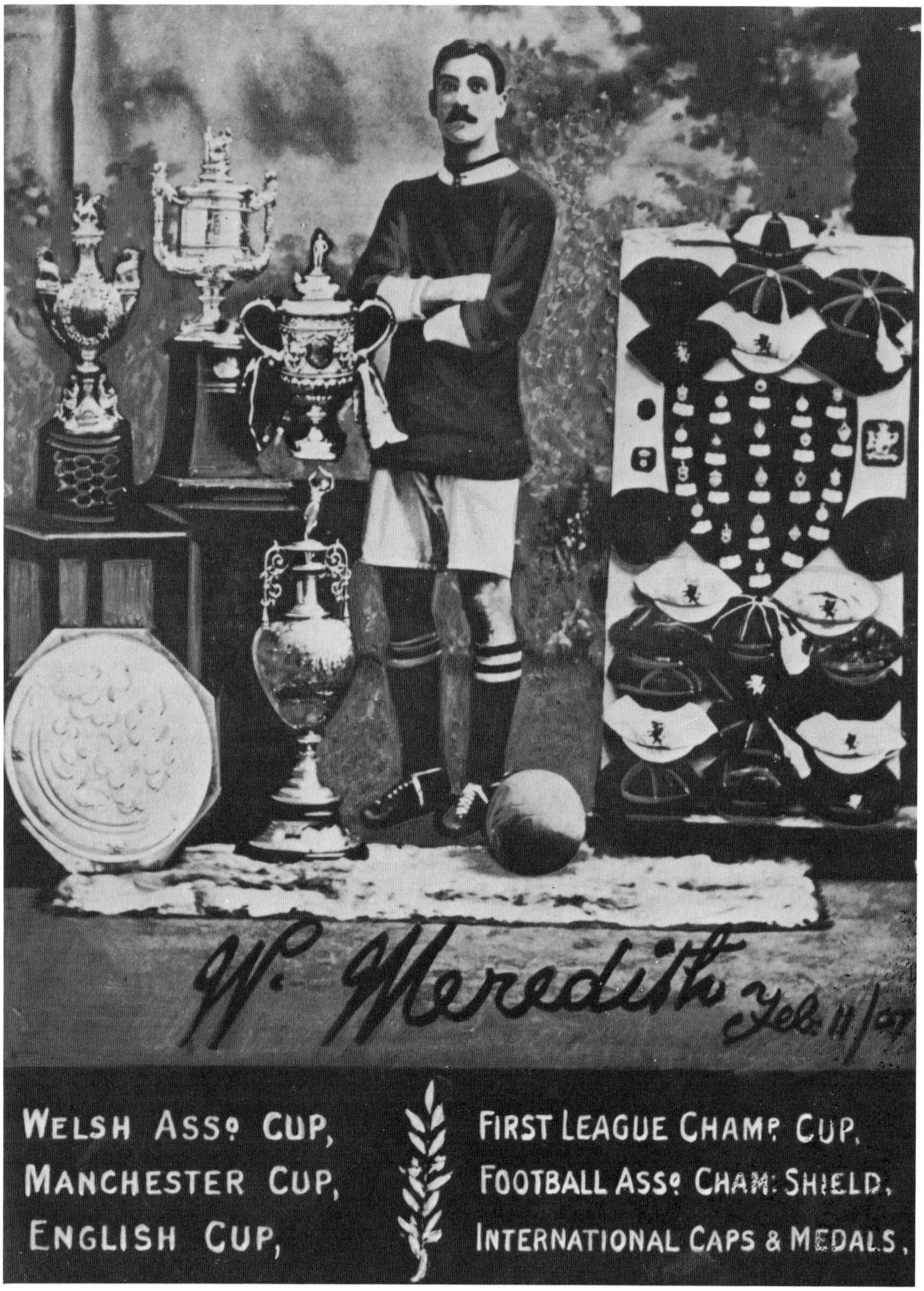

A man and his footballing achievements. Billy Meredith's playing career spanned almost 30 years in which he played for Chirk, where he helped them win the Welsh FA Cup; Northwich Victoria; Manchester City, with whom he won his first English FA Cup winners' medal in 1904 and United. After joining United he helped to win that trophy once again in 1909 and collected championship medals in 1908 and 1911. Meredith played 48 times for Wales, and eventually rejoined City in 1921

Woolwich Arsenal 3–2. It was obvious to the thousands following the team that real success was sure to come soon.

In 1904, when Manchester City had finished runners-up to Sheffield Wednesday in the First Division, they had thrilled the people of Manchester (or at least half of them) by reaching the FA Cup final. In 1900 Bury had shown the way for local football by bringing the Cup to the area for the first time, beating Southampton 4–0, and three years later they did it again, this time thrashing Derby County by the final's biggest winning margin to date, 6–0. The 1904 final saw City winning 1–0 at Crystal Palace in a local 'derby' final against Bolton Wanderers.

It was the backbone of that City side which was to turn United into a footballing power after a shrewd piece of negotiation by Ernest Mangnall.

A year after that great victory one of City's star players, the legendary winger Billy Meredith, was suspended from the game for three years, firstly for trying to bribe an Aston Villa player to throw a game, and then for illegally trying to obtain payment from City while under suspension – when his punishment included a ban on even going to the ground. Even though the suspension prevented Meredith from playing until April 1908, in May 1906 Mangnall signed him for £500. It would turn out to be money well spent.

United started their first term in the First Division well enough, winning at Bristol City, drawing with Derby and Notts County, then beating Sheffield United at Bramall Lane, but Mangnall was constantly on the look-out for new players in an effort to compete with their rivals from across Manchester.

Mangnall buys City players

Then a bombshell, which proved disaster to City and boom-time for United, hit the game. A Football Association inquiry, which had been investigating the activities of many clubs, discovered that Manchester City had been making illegal payments to their players. There was an uproar and five City directors were forced to resign. That was perhaps the lesser of the two 'sentences' heaped upon the club by the FA for in the other, 17 players – the backbone of the Cup-winning side – were banned from playing for City for life. In a move unheard of before or since, City had to sell most of their playing staff or the club would not be allowed to continue in the Football League.

The news was greeted with disguised delight by other clubs. The vultures would swoop to pick the bones of the successful City side and improve their own chances.

With Meredith having already been signed by United, the spotlight turned on Herbert Burgess, thought to be the best full-back in the game. Everton, Newcastle United, Bolton, Celtic and Chelsea all wanted him but it was Ernest Mangnall who beat them to the punch.

The FA's sentence on the City players also suspended them from playing football at all until January 1907, and two months before the punishment was due to end, City announced a meeting at the Queens Hotel, in Manchester's Piccadilly. Clubs interested in their players were invited to attend . . . it was an auction of footballers!

Ernest Mangnall had no intentions of competing against rival clubs, many much richer than United, so he made arrangements to approach the players he wanted before the meeting started. The other clubs did not like it at all, and Everton made an official complaint to the FA about their loss of Burgess to United – who also signed inside-forward Alec 'Sandy' Turnbull and Jimmy Bannister, another striker.

Everton claimed that on 8 November 1906 they had agreed to exchange Percy Hill with City for Burgess, placing a valuation of £600 on their player. City had given them a transfer form which was completed in every way except for Burgess's signature, but they had not been able to find the player to get him to sign. The reason for this was obvious. He was with Ernest Mangnall, who was persuading him to join United, and as a Manchester man he didn't need much persuasion!

The *Manchester Evening Chronicle* of December 1906 told how Burgess had sent a telegram to City, saying he would not sign for Everton, and they had allowed United officially to approach him. The story also told of the distribution of the City players:

> On inquiry at the Football Association offices in High Holborn today, our London correspondent learned that the following transfers of the suspended Manchester City players have been officially sanctioned and the registrations formally made.
>
> A Turnbull to Manchester United; T Hynds to Woolwich Arsenal; F Booth to Bury; J McMahon to Bury; James Bannister to Manchester United; J H Edmonson to Bolton Wanderers; G T Livingstone to Glasgow Rangers; H Burgess to Manchester United.
>
> So far as the Football Association is concerned with the transfer of Burgess, he is a Manchester United player.

Meredith's suspension was adjusted to end along with his former City colleagues and on 1 January 1907 a crowd of over 40,000 turned up at Bank Street to see United's new quartet in action against Aston Villa. They weren't disappointed. Sandy Turnbull got the only goal of the game, and United went on to end the season in eighth place in the First Division.

Champions . . . and bother abroad

There were greater things on the horizon. The following season, 1907–08, Manchester United won the League Championship for the first time, a feat even the great City team had failed to achieve. They won in fine style, nine points ahead of Aston Villa and City, winning 23 of their 38 games and only letting their form slip away after the title had been secured.

That summer Manchester United played in Europe. The club decided to take its players on a summer tour to Hungary and Austria and were one of the first northern sides to play abroad. As English champions they were a great attraction, but even in 1908 there were signs of a disease which would spread into the game in later years. Earlier that season United's players had been pelted with mud and stones after they left Bradford City's ground, and there had been reports of similar outbreaks of hooliganism at Sheffield Wednesday. In Hungary their 'friendly' was anything but amicable.

The *Manchester Evening News* report of the game tells how:

> It was by no means football weather when Manchester United arrived in Budapest from Vienna, for the sun had left its bronze impress even upon the face of Charlie Roberts.

Having seen their side score twice against United, even though losing 6–2, the Hungarians came to the second match hoping to see at least a draw, for the Ferenczvaros Torna Club are the leaders of the local league, and only one goal has been scored against them all season.

Alas, such are the vagaries of the game, that before the local lads knew where they were, little Jimmy Bannister had opened the account, and Meredith added a second. A moment from the second kick-off Meredith caught the ball on his toe and running fully half the length of the field at top speed, scored another brilliant goal. There were now fully 11,000 spectators and the applause was deafening.

From this point the attitude of the crowd changed. The weakness of the local lads was apparent at every point, and, what was more painful, all could see it. Then followed a series of incidents which augmented the chagrin all Hungarians felt. Up to this point the referee had been passable, then the hostility of the crowd led to a series of adverse and pitiable decisions against the United. One cause of discontent was the removal of men who were stationed beside each goal as additional referees to inform the referee proper what happened on the line. These men shouted 'offside', 'touch' or 'goal' repeatedly, until play near goal became impossible. Finally they were removed.

On renewing the game, Wall broke away on the left and scored with a great shot. Five minutes later he was badly fouled by one of the opposing half-backs and after a lengthy appeal, awarded a penalty. This was taken by Moger (the United goalkeeper) who easily beat the Hungarian. By this act of one goalkeeper shooting at the other, the feelings of the crowd were again intensified and trouble brewed all round the ground.

Soon after the change of ends Picken got away and put in a beautiful ground shot which swerved into the net out of the reach of the custodian, 6–0. It was not long after this that a regrettable incident occurred.

Thomson was pulled up for fouling and he protested loudly against the decision. The game was stopped. Thompson thereupon – unable to speak the language – caught hold of the referee's hand to direct him to the spot to demonstrate how and what really had happened. This act was misunderstood by Gabrilovitch, the referee, and his hand rose threateningly. The referee being a very tall man, Duckworth rushed up to aid the centre-half. Nobody understood each other and were ordered off. Both refused to go, and rightly so. For fully fifteen minutes arguments and gesticulation prevailed. Interpreters were requisitioned and eventually after an apology, the game was renewed, and Wall added another goal, the end coming in partial darkness with the score 7–0.

It was what happened next that made Ernest Mangnall vow: 'We will never go to Budapest again'. As the team left the field they were attacked by the crowd. Harry Renshaw, the *Manchester Evening News* reporter, wrote:

> Everybody made for the gateway through which the players must pass on their way to the dressing room . . . Harry Moger was struck across the shoulders by one of these [rioters] with a stick. Stacey was spat upon, Picken and Charlie Roberts struck, in fact nearly all the team were given a reminder. Then the police charged the rioters, and fully twenty were arrested and dragged into one of the club rooms which was utilised as a police station. Even in the dressing room the team were not safe and a shower of heavy stones let in more air and daylight.

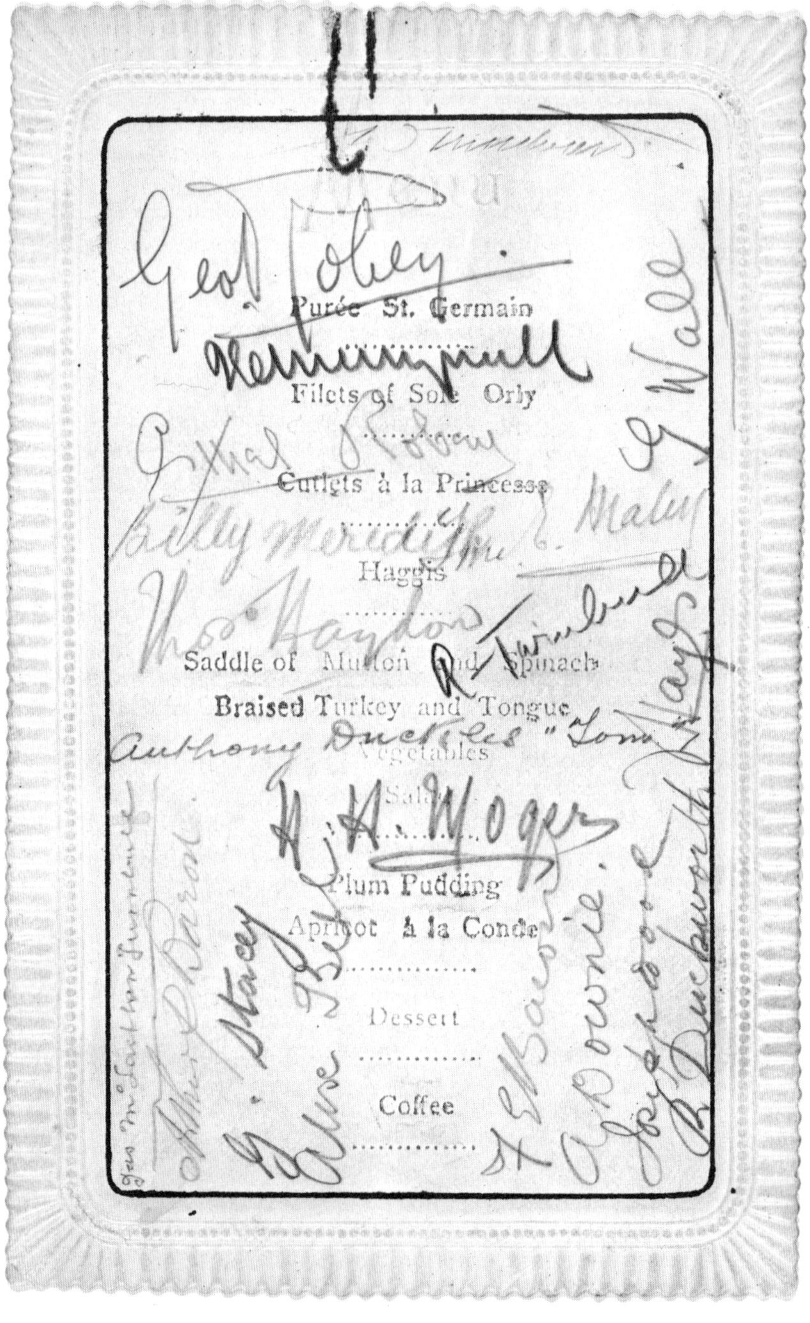

The menu from a celebration dinner signed by some of the guests. The signatures include those of entertainer George Robey, a close friend of Ernest Mangnall (whose autograph is below Robey's), and players Alex Bell, Dick Duckworth, Harry Moger, and Billy Meredith together with others who took part in the successful campaigns between 1908 and 1911

The players left the ground under police escort and were on their way back to their hotel in a row of coaches when the rioters attacked again:

> Particular attention was paid to the last carriage and a huge stone knocked me down and cut my head. Then Alec Bell was hit behind the ear, and Picken received another. I was then hit on the head again. It was so sudden that the players had no time to raise the hoods of the carriages. Mr Mangnall was hit and Thomson caught it badly in the neck, with Wall and several others. Many arrests were made and the police were compelled to draw their swords.

United were glad to get back to England again and although the Hungarian incident made headline news for several weeks, it was quickly forgotten as rumour strengthened that the club was about to move from Bank Street to a new ground. As early as August 1907 'Wanderer' had written in the *Manchester Evening Chronicle*:

> The club is sure to remain at Clayton another season, but the intention is to move to a new ground as soon as possible, and it is just about a thousand to one that the home chosen will be at Old Trafford and that when erected it will compare with any ground in the kingdom.
>
> There can be no better site than Old Trafford where the City and Salford cars [trams] meet, the Sale and Altrincham service is tapped, and the cricket ground station would be available. The air would be purer for both the crowd and the players, and everything seems in favour of such a change and choice.

'Wanderer' also tipped United to do well that season, and, as noted, they obliged with the First Division title. The following 1908–09 season was not quite so successful in the League, but the FA Cup was a different story.

Part one of a photographic mystery. The players of 1908-09 pose with the English Cup after their victory at Crystal Palace. However a virtually identical picture appears on page 110 showing the same players with the League Championship trophy of 1911. Both photographs have been published as authentic records of each event since 1909 but only one can have been taken at the exact time of the successes

Manchester United, 1908-9

(Reserve) (Reserve) MOGER HAYES BELL
MEREDITH DUCKWORTH ROBERTS J. TURNBULL A. TURNBULL STACEY
(Reserve) (Reserve) HALSE WALL

United up for the Cup

The Cup campaign began at Bank Street with a game against Brighton and Hove Albion who had little consolation for their long journey north. Facing a team determined to restore the faith of their supporters after a disappointing lapse of four defeats in their eight games before the first round of the Cup, Brighton had to defend in depth and United won by the only goal of the game.

The second round was played on 6 February, when Everton, who were to finish second in the League, came to Clayton, and again it was a one-goal victory. In the third round Blackburn Rovers, who ended the season in fourth place in the League, were thrashed 6–1 when the third successive tie was played at Bank Street.

Then came the decisive game of the victorious run, when fate played a hand. United were drawn away to Burnley and were losing one-nil when the game was abandoned because of a blinding snowstorm, casually described in the *Weekly Dispatch* as 'conditions of a most rigorous character'. Four days later, on 10 March 1909, United won the replayed game 3–2 and Ernest Mangnall was able to leave the ground of his former club with a feeling of satisfaction.

The semi-final was played at Bramall Lane with Newcastle United as the opposition. The Geordies were on their way to the League Championship, and many felt that they would win both competitions. But it was the year of United – Manchester United – and they reached the final for the first time, thanks to another one-goal success.

So to the final at Crystal Palace: Manchester United versus Bristol City, and United taking their first step into the last stage of the competition which had captured the imagination of the football following public, more so even than the Championship. Here, for one day, London belonged to the people of the north and the west. Trains carried supporters to the capital and a huge crowd gathered at the ground.

Before the final Ernest Mangnall had taken his players away from the distractions of Manchester, where supporters had caught 'Cup fever' for the first time. The Royal Forest Hotel at Chingford housed the players before their trip to the stadium, and they prepared for the game with training sessions, strolls in the nearby woodlands and games of golf.

With both United and Bristol being teams who played in red jerseys and white shorts, the Football Association made them select neutral colours. Bristol chose blue and white, while United proudly announced that they would play in 'an all white costume relieved with a thin red line at the neck and wrists, and with the red rose of Lancashire on the breast'. In order to obtain the best possible publicity for their Cup final build-up Ernest Mangnall arranged for music hall star George Robey to present the kit to the players – with the press on hand.

In the smart all-white strip, with its red V dropping from the shoulders to the centre of the chest United no doubt had the same effect on both spectators and opposition as did the first glimpse of Real Madrid almost 50 years later, when they earned themselves the title of 'the

Action from the 1909 English Cup Final as United put pressure on the Bristol City goal. Sandy Turnbull scored the only goal of the game to thrill the Manchester fans who travelled to London for the Crystal Palace final. The shirts worn by Turnbull and Meredith are on permanent display in the club's museum

Louis Rocca suggested the name Manchester United as Newton Heath was wound up, and there is no doubting his loyalty to the club. In 1909 he rode in style to Manchester Central Station to join the official welcoming party for the first United cup homecoming. His decorated carriage was the centre of attraction. Twenty years later Rocca was appointed assistant manager as the club again struggled to survive

Spanish ghosts'. The spectres of Manchester certainly haunted Bristol City on the afternoon of Saturday, 24 April 1909.

The almost annual visit of northerners to the capital was something the London press appeared to enjoy. They wrote of the Lancashire supporter with his voice which seemed deeper than that of his southern counterpart as supplying a 'pulsating drone note in the fantasia of enthusiasm'. One paragraph ran:

> The northern contingent pay great attention to the matter of commissariat. They bring stone jars of strong ale and sandwiches an inch thick, packed in little wicker baskets which are also used for conveying carrier pigeons.

Yes, Manchester was once again 'Up f' t' Cup' but this time it was the red and white of United taking over from the sky blue of City.

Like so many finals since, and probably some before, the game did not live up to its pre-match expectations. Sandy Turnbull scored the only goal and man of the match was Billy Meredith, adding another Cup winners' medal to the one he won with City in 1904.

Meredith was indeed an outstanding player noted for his casual approach to the game and his insistence on playing with a toothpick in his mouth. When play was in an area of the field away from him, Meredith would talk to the crowd, or put the toothpick to work, and he drew this description from Don Davies, the *Manchester Guardian* columnist 'Old International':

> Meredith was the Lloyd George of Welsh football. The parallel is by no means perfect, but it was curious how many points of resemblance could be traced. Both men had a following not far short of the entire Welsh nation; both were hailed by friends as the highest product of Welsh genius and by opponents as the lowest form of Welsh cunning. Both found it necessary to leave Wales to find adequate scope for their talents, yet both returned repeatedly in their hey-day to pay off debts in their heart-felt gratitude.
>
> Round 1894 when Meredith was a youth, the newly formed Manchester City Football Club sent a deputation to Chirk, North Wales, with orders to bring him back. This mission was fulfilled but not without some hair-raising experiences. The angry townsfolk, roused by the thought of a local genius being sold for alien gold, seized one of the deputation and threw him into a nearby horse-trough. It is safe to assume that the sight of the stripling for whom he had

suffered, did little to warm this gentleman's damp spirits on the journey home in the train! The Manchester United team in the final was: Moger, Stacey, Hayes, Duckworth, Roberts, Bell, Meredith, Halse, J Turnbull, A Turnbull, Wall.

The triumphant team returned home with the English Cup. Ernest Mangnall was the proudest man in the city as he strode from Central Station carrying the trophy in his right hand, grey jacket unbuttoned to reveal his waistcoat and watch-chain. His bowler hat was cocked slightly but his face was expressionless as he watched his players board a horse-drawn open-topped bus for the journey through the streets, three days after that memorable game.

Manchester turned out in its masses. Cloth caps filled the streets in a woollen ocean stretching as far as the players were able to see . . .

The *Manchester Evening News* of Tuesday, 27 April 1909 described the 'wild scenes greeting United's homecoming':

> An hour before the time the train was due to arrive at Central Station large crowds of people assembled outside the station and behind the barricades of the approach leading to the platform at which the London train usually comes in. The great majority wore the United colours, and an ice cream merchant attracted considerable attention with his huge red and white umbrella and his similarly coloured barrow. Gutter merchants who did a good business with 'memory cards' of Bristol City came in for a good deal of good humoured badinage, while the United favours attached to a cardboard representation of the English Cup sold like hot cakes.
>
> Five waggonettes, gaily decorated with red and white bannerettes and ribbon, were waiting, two containing members of the St Joseph's Industrial School Band. The arrival of Rocca's Brigade, gaudily dressed in the colours of the United Club, was the signal for an outburst of cheering.
>
> The London train hove in sight, and amid a scene of wild enthusiasm Mr Mangnall emerged carrying the cup on high, followed by the players, their wives, and other people who had travelled from the Metropolis.
>
> The band struck up 'See the Conquering Hero Comes' and there was a great scramble by the crowd, which had been permitted to enter the platform, to reach the players.
>
> Some were carried shoulder high, and ultimately were comfortably seated in the third waggonette. Sticks were waved and hats were thrown in the air and the enthusiasm was unbounded when Roberts, carrying the trophy, came into view.

So the conquering heroes made their journey to Manchester Town Hall in Albert Square, scene of so many homecomings in recent years, but this was United's first.

United had ended the 1908-09 season 13th in the League, but the Cup win meant success for Mangnall's men for the second time. Before the start of the next season football went through a major change, and the men of Manchester were largely responsible for it.

Charlie Roberts proudly holds the English Cup, predecessor of the FA Cup, as he stands with the United party on their arrival back in Manchester from the 1909 Cup Final. Chairman J H Davies is on his right, and next to him Ernest Mangnall, the club's secretary-manager. The players rode in carriages from Central Station to the town hall for a civic reception

The team become outcasts

Although the Union of Professional Footballers had been formed in 1898 at that meeting in the Spread Eagle Hotel, ten years later players were still having difficulty in getting their employers to recognise their rights as trade unionists. There were constant battles for wage increases in smaller clubs, and with amateur and part-time players available, the role of the full-time professional was not as secure or as rewarding as it might later, in some cases, become.

In 1908 United had played a game against Newcastle United to raise funds for their union, and they did it against the wishes of both the League and the Football Association. For the next twelve months the Players' Union sought affiliation to the Federation of Trades Unions and just before the 1909–10 season was due to start matters reached crisis point. The football authorities feared that, as Federation members, footballers might be drawn into arguments which were far removed from the game. If miners, cotton workers or railwaymen demanded a change in working conditions, would they ask for the support of other trade unionists? If they did, could they force the players to strike?

On 27 August 1909, five days before the start of the new season, representatives of the League clubs met in Birmingham and decided that any player admitting to being a member of the union should be suspended, have his wages stopped, and be banned from taking part in any game.

The move by the League and the Football Association was to try to prevent a strike. It almost caused one. Instead of persuading players that being part of a union would not be of any help to them, it convinced footballers all over the country that the only way for them to achieve their aims of better pay and conditions was to be part of such a body.

The next day Ernest Mangnall and the United board called the players to a mass meeting. Twenty-seven turned up, the exceptions being Harry Moger, who was attending a family funeral, and Jimmy Turnbull.

The players were told about the League directive, and under a headline 'Manchester United's Grave Position', the *Manchester Evening News* reported:

> The various speakers pointed out to the men the very serious position the club was in, having three matches to play in the opening six days of the season.
>
> Some discussion followed and the players said they would like it to be thoroughly understood that they had no grievance whatever with the club, but they were fighting for what they believed to be a just principle, and therefore they intended to retain their membership of the Players' Union.
>
> After the players left the room the committee held a meeting and it was decided to wire the Bradford City club immediately, so as to cause no inconvenience, to the effect that, owing to the Manchester United players having determined to remain members of the Players' Union, the club had no players, and consequently the League fixture which should be played with Bradford City, at Clayton, on

The United squad and Coleman of Everton form the 'Outcasts' line-up after being suspended for standing firm for their union rights. Only 24 hours before the 1909–10 season was about to start, the threatened strike by members of the Players' Union was called off

H. Moger, J. Picken, W. Corbett, R. Holden, H. Burgess, J. Clough, W. Meredith, G. Boswell
G. Wall, A. Turnbull, C. Roberts (Captain), T. Coleman, R. Duckworth.

Wednesday next, could not be proceeded with.

The decision of the United players will certainly cause a sensation in the football world, and looked at from any point of view the men cannot but be admired for the fight they have made. In the history of trade unionism there has never been a situation like the present one. By their loyalty to a cause which they believe to be a just one, twelve of the players have already forfeited £28 each, and by their attitude today they have incurred even further risks. Every player in the League who remains a member of the trade union will at once be suspended.

Two days before the new season, most clubs were claiming to have signed enough amateurs to get fixtures under way, but not United. The players joked about being the 'Outcasts' posing for a now famous photograph, but they stood firmly by their beliefs.

On 31 August, the eve of the new season, the authorities had a change of heart, and gave in. The Players' Union was recognised, the suspensions were removed, and the arrears of pay were allowed. In the eyes of many, this was one of Manchester United's most important victories. Had they not stayed together their cause would have been lost.

It would have been a tragedy if the strike had gone ahead because United were on the verge of moving to their new ground. Immediately after the Cup final success John Henry Davies had once again shown that his heart, and his wealth, were deeply embedded in the club he had taken over by chance. He pledged to lend the massive sum of £60,000, which even from the head of a company like Manchester Breweries Ltd was a gigantic amount, worth millions by today's standards. The move to Old Trafford was finalised.

The strike threat over, work was able to continue, and the days at Bank Street were numbered. A large crowd turned up to see the game against Bradford City and gave the 'Outcasts' a warm reception. They replied with a 1–0 win.

The season went reasonably well, and always there was the move to the new ground to look forward to. On 22 January 1910, United played their last game at Bank Street in front of a modest 7,000 or so loyal supporters. They won 5–0, a fine way to say goodbye to a ground which held many memories for the players and the club's followers. Charlie Roberts scored twice, Connor and Hooper added two more, and Billy Meredith brought down the curtain. A week before that last League game at Bank Street, Burnley had taken revenge for the Cup defeat the previous season by knocking United out of the competition in the first round. United buckled down to a Championship attempt.

The move to Old Trafford

The move to Old Trafford took place in midseason, and preparations were made for the opening game against Liverpool, on 19 February 1910. A week before the event invitations were sent out to local dignitaries:

> The President (Mr J H Davies) and Directors of the Manchester United Football Club ask your acceptance of enclosed, and extend a cordial invitation to attend the opening match on Saturday next.
>
> The ground is situated at Old Trafford near the County Cricket Ground, and can be reached by three tram routes: Deansgate, Piccadilly and St Peter's Square.
>
> The ground when completed will hold over 100,000 people. The present Stand will accommodate 12,000 people seated.

The formal opening of the ground took place during the week before the first match, after equipment had been moved into the new offices from the old ground at Clayton. And just in time. Two days before the Liverpool game fierce gales struck the Manchester area and the old wooden grandstand at Bank Street was blown down, wreckage spilling across into the roadway and badly damaging houses opposited. Had this happened during a game it would have been a terrible disaster. As it was no-one was injured.

So Old Trafford became the home of Manchester United and for the first game thousands walked the road in from Salford, others packed tramcars and carriages. The crowd inside looked in awe at the huge grandstand as it filled with well-known local faces, and tried to catch a glimpse of the celebrities present, including Ernest Mangnall's friend George Robey.

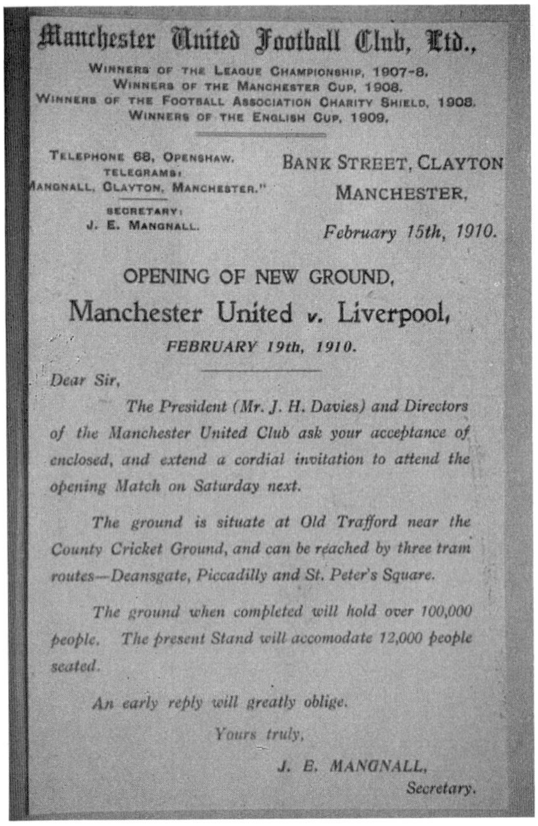

Manchester United Football Club, Ltd.,

WINNERS OF THE LEAGUE CHAMPIONSHIP, 1907-8.
WINNERS OF THE MANCHESTER CUP, 1908.
WINNERS OF THE FOOTBALL ASSOCIATION CHARITY SHIELD, 1908.
WINNERS OF THE ENGLISH CUP, 1909.

TELEPHONE 68, OPENSHAW.
TELEGRAMS:
"MANGNALL, CLAYTON, MANCHESTER."
SECRETARY:
J. E. MANGNALL.

BANK STREET, CLAYTON
MANCHESTER,
February 15th, 1910.

OPENING OF NEW GROUND,

Manchester United *v.* Liverpool,

FEBRUARY 19th, 1910.

Dear Sir,

The President (Mr. J. H. Davies) and Directors of the Manchester United Club ask your acceptance of enclosed, and extend a cordial invitation to attend the opening Match on Saturday next.

The ground is situate at Old Trafford near the County Cricket Ground, and can be reached by three tram routes—Deansgate, Piccadilly and St. Peter's Square.

The ground when completed will hold over 100,000 people. The present Stand will accomodate 12,000 people seated.

An early reply will greatly oblige.

Yours truly,

J. E. MANGNALL,
Secretary.

Left: Guests of the club received this invitation to the official opening of Old Trafford and were thrilled by what they saw. The ground never reached its predicted capacity of 100,000 but has a record of 76,962 achieved at the 1939 FA Cup semi-final. Today 25,500 seats form just under 50 per cent of the stadium's safety limit

Right: The Manchester County Football Asociation Cup, the first trophy to be won by Newton Heath. It was success in this competition which persuaded the club to reach for more distant horizons and which eventually led to League status. The trophy was unearthed in recent times and now stands in the club museum after many years in a bank vault

Below: The English Cup winners medal presented to Dick Duckworth in 1909 as United continued the successful run started a season earlier with their first Championship

United had injury problems. Alan Bell was missing at left-half, Blott taking his place alongside Charlie Roberts, with Dick Duckworth in his familiar position at right-half. George Stacey and Vince Hayes were the full-backs in front of Harry Moger in goal, and the forward line was Meredith, Harold Halse, Homer, Sandy Turnbull and George Wall.

Sandy Turnbull scored the first of United's three goals, latching on to a centre from Meredith, but Liverpool were always in contention, closing the score to 2–1 before George Wall got United's third, then levelling at 3–3 through Goddard and Stewart, before the latter got his second of the afternoon. So the Merseysiders spoiled the celebrations by winning 4–3.

But United were now able to compete in the status league as well as on the football field and Old Trafford became a showpiece ground, eventually staging the 1915 FA Cup final. In 1911 the replay between Bradford and Newcastle was played there, then in 1915 Sheffield United beat Chelsea 3–0 in Manchester.

The 1909–10 season ended with United in fifth place but a year later they were champions once more. Under Ernest Mangnall's direction they had won the League Championship of 1907–08; became the first winners of the FA

Manchester United F.C. 1st League Champions 1910-11.
Team for Season 1911-12.

At the start of the 1911–12 season the Manchester United players, secretary-manager Ernest Mangnall (left) and chairman John H Davies (centre), gathered at Old Trafford for a photo-session. The outcome of this has since puzzled many football historians. This picture shows the team with the League Championship trophy they won in 1910–11, but an identical picture of the same men in the same positions with the officials wearing the same clothes was also taken with the English FA Cup, which the club won in 1909 (see page 103). On this second photograph Charlie Roberts (seated third from left) is holding the ball, the only difference apart from the trophy. So did United borrow the Cup from holders Bradford City, or was this the work of a clever photo-artist in later years?

Charity Shield which was introduced in 1908, and the Manchester Cup the same year; then won the FA Cup in 1909. The Championship of 1910–11 would be their final peak under the man whose role in Manchester football is one of unquestionable importance.

New players came, familiar faces left Old Trafford, and the team that took the title by just one point from Aston Villa was quite different from the one which earned the title three years earlier.

Enoch 'Knocker' West had been bought from Nottingham Forest. He was a centre-forward with a reputation for goal-scoring and lived up to it by netting 19 in the League campaign. Other new faces were goalkeeper Edmonds, who played for the latter half of the season when Moger was out, Arthur Donnelly, who filled in both full-back positions, and Hoften, a right-back.

The season reached an exciting climax on the last Saturday, 29 April 1911, when Aston Villa, leading the table by one point, were away to Liverpool, and United were at home to Sunderland.

So fickle is the football supporter that, with the Championship a possibility, only 10,000 made the journey to Old Trafford for what turned out to be a decisive game. A week earlier United had lost 4–2 at Villa Park and that, it seemed, was that. But on that last day of the season Liverpool, lying in the lower half of the table, pulled off a remarkable victory, beating Villa 3–1, while United thrashed Sunderland 5–1, two goals from Harold Halse and one each from Turnbull and West, plus an own goal, giving them the title.

It would be 41 years before the League Championship would return to the club, and United's victory once again in the FA Charity Shield of 1911, when they beat Southern League Swindon Town 8–4, marked the end of a great era for the club.

In August 1912, after a season in which United had finished 13th in the First Division, and lost to Blackburn in the fourth round of the FA Cup, they also lost Ernest Mangnall. The manager who had been at their helm throughout their successful years left to join Manchester City.

The *Manchester Evening Chronicle* of 21 August 1912 reported under a single column headline that the United maestro had moved to Hyde Road, home of the Old Trafford club's biggest rivals:

> The City directors did not come to a decision without long and anxious consideration, and among the names before them were those of Mr J J Bentley and Mr H C Broomfield. At the last moment there seemed a possibility of the negotiations breaking down, but late last night the directors interviewed Mr Mangnall after a three hours' discussion, and an hour later the announcement was made that he had been appointed.
>
> Mr W H Wilkinson (chairman) welcomed the new manager and wished him every success. Mr Mangnall, in reply, said he hoped to see the Hyde Road club soon take the position which Manchester City ought to take. Nothing that he could do to attain that end should be left undone.

Ernest Mangnall's place as secretary-manager was taken by J J Bentley, and under his guidance United reached fourth place in the League in the 1912–13 season. But the great names were drifting out of the game, and those

who had been part of those championship-winning sides were now reaching the end of their playing days. Had Ernest Mangnall seen what the future held for the club when he decided to leave?

By the end of the 1913–14 season only Stacey, Duckworth, Meredith, Turnbull, West and Wall were left, and by the end of the following season crowds had dropped to below an average of 15,000, and United escaped relegation by just one point.

To make matters worse Mangnall's Manchester City ended the last season before the First World War, 1914–15, in fifth place, their highest since his departure from Old Trafford. The United side which began the season was almost unrecognisable:

Beale, Hodge, Stacey, Hunter, O'Connell, Knowles, Meredith, Anderson, Travers, West, Wall.

Although Ernest Mangnall had often been referred to in newspaper reports as United's 'manager', his actual title was secretary, and it wasn't until 1914 that the first official football manager of the club was appointed. John Robson, who arrived from Brighton and Hove Albion in December 1914, worked under secretary Bentley and took charge of playing arrangements. He stayed in the post until 1921.

The First World War brought football to a standstill and had a crippling effect on United, who were faced with massive overheads for the running of Old Trafford.

The club also lost a lot of its charisma with the departure of Mangnall, who was a great publicist and who took his gift to City.

The war also robbed United of one of its stars. Sandy Turnbull was killed in France, and when life returned to normal in 1919 and football resumed there was a very different line-up for the first game against Derby County:

Mew, Moore, Silcock, Montgomery, Hilditch, Whalley, Hodge, Woodcock, Spence, Potts, Hopkin.

Attendances rose following the turmoil of war, and by the end of the 1919–20 season crowds of over 40,000 were commonplace, but the League position of 12th place did little to inspire. A season later John Chapman replaced John Robson as manager, and also filled the secretarial role, but once more Ernest Mangnall stole the Manchester spotlight when his club

Football began again after the First World War, with United finishing in 12th place in Division One. This line-up includes goalkeeper George Mew who played in all 42 games that season, full-backs Charlie Moore (left) and John Silcock on either side of him, and in the centre of the front row Billy Meredith bridging the gap between the early 1900s and the twenties

opened its new ground at Maine Road. Mangnall was clearly leaving his mark on Manchester football.

Relegation and promotion

Then, in 1922, came the final blow for United. They were relegated, after winning just eight of their 42 games (the First Division had been increased to 22 clubs immediately after the war, when plans were also being made for the introduction of a Third Division).

Billy Meredith had left United in 1921 to re-sign for Ernest Mangnall, and by the time United played their first game in the Second Division for 16 years, none of the great stars of the successful pre-war years remained. They finished fourth in the table, having had hopes of winning promotion until defeats at Blackpool in late March and at home to Leicester in April had seen them slip out of contention.

A season later, 1923–24, they were 14th in the Second Division, but then came a breath of fresh air in the 1924–25 season. It began with a showpiece game at Maine Road, where a combined City and United side played Everton and Liverpool as a testimonial for Ernest Mangnall, now ready to retire from football management and take up a career in journalism. It ended with United winning promotion, finishing second to Leicester City, and a season later in 1925–26 the improvement was maintained with a respectable ninth place in the top flight.

Fate this year twisted the tail of Manchester City. The two Manchester clubs met in the semi-final of the FA Cup with City winning 3–0 at Bramall Lane, but then the Sky-blues not only lost the final 1–0 to Bolton Wanderers, but were relegated to the Second Division.

New stars had begun to emerge for United: Joe Spence, an outside-right who played a record 510 League and Cup games in his 14 years' service; Frank Barson, a towering centre-half who had been a blacksmith before turning to football; and Clarrie Hilditch, a wing-half who became player-manager in 1926–27 as the club looked for a new man to succeed John Chapman.

In 1927 John Henry Davies died. The man who had saved the club from slipping out of existence in 1902, and who had played such an important part in the creation of Manchester United, could no longer be turned to at difficult times. He was replaced by G H Lawton, who bridged the gap between two major benefactors.

A new manager was appointed. Herbert Bamlett's pedigree for football management was strange and somewhat unorthodox. Bamlett was a former referee – in fact he had gone down in the record books as the youngest to take charge of an FA Cup final when he officiated in 1914 when only 32. He had then moved into management and had been in charge at Oldham Athletic, the now defunct Wigan Borough and Middlesbrough.

Souvenir Programme. - Price 2d.
COMPLIMENTARY
Testimonial Inter-City Match
TO
Mr. J. E. MANGNALL,
Late Secretary-Manager, Manchester City Football Club.
EVERTON AND LIVERPOOL v. MANCHESTER CITY AND MANCHESTER UNITED
Maine Road, Moss Side,
Wednesday, September 10th.
KICK OFF 6.20 P.M.

In 1924 Manchester showed its appreciation of Ernest Mangnall's contribution to football with a testimonial game at Maine Road. Under Mangnall's leadership United won the championship in 1908 and 1911 and the Cup in 1909. He was not only influential in the building of Old Trafford, but of Maine Road too after moving to City as their secretary-manager

One of Bamlett's most unusual connections with United was that it was he who had been in charge of the controversial FA Cup quarter-final at Turf Moor in 1909 when the game was stopped by a blizzard. So bad was the weather that afternoon that young Mr Bamlett had been too cold to blow his whistle when he decided to abandon the match and had handed it to United's captain Charlie Roberts to call a halt to proceedings, much to the amusement of the Manchester supporters and the dismay of the locals.

Under Bamlett, whose assistant was Louis Rocca, the man who had been general 'dogsbody' at Newton Heath, and who had acted as a scout for the club during its successful years, United slipped slowly down the First Division: 15th in 1926–27; 18th in 1927–28; 12th in 1928–29; 17th in 1929–30; and then, in 1931, relegation as bottom club.

What a terrible season that was. As Tommy Docherty might have described it: 'They started off badly, then deteriorated.'

They lost their first game of the season, at home to Aston, and followed this with eleven more successive defeats, so that by October 1930 their record read:

P	W	D	L	F	A	Pts
12	0	0	12	14	49	0

Something had to be done, but what? United had massive debts and could not afford new players, but even so they plunged recklessly into the transfer market, only adding to their own downfall. By the end of that season they had scored 53 goals in their 42 games, and conceded a massive 115, winning only six times at Old Trafford. No wonder they went down.

Another financial rescue

So began the 1931–32 season, which was to have a lasting effect on the club, or at least, events which occurred during the period were. In the Second Division United again found themselves fighting for their lives. They lost their first two games, to Bradford City in Yorkshire and to Southampton at Old Trafford, before low attendances. Only 3,507 loyal souls turned up to watch the opening game of the season. The United supporters were voting with their feet, and the board of directors got the message.

Herbert Bamlett had lost his job in April 1931, and the manager's role was filled temporarily by Walter Crickmer, the club's secretary since 1926. His assistant was Louis Rocca, still dedicated to the club he had followed since the Newton Heath days. But times were getting harder. By December 1931 Manchester United was on the rocks. Deeply in debt, unable to pay off instalments on the loan made to the club to build Old Trafford, with no chance of paying for players they had obtained from other clubs, they faced bankruptcy. Another saviour was needed, but could Manchester produce another John Henry Davies?

Crisis came in Christmas week when the players went to pick up their wages and were told there was no money available. Stacey Lintott, a sportswriter, picked up the story, but before he wrote it he went to see a contact of his, James W Gibson, whose company was a major garment producer, specialising in army uniforms.

Gibson had a love of sport, and was persuaded to help the club. He met United's directors, laid down his terms and agreed to help out on the understanding that he would become chairman and be able to elect his own colleagues on the board. The directors had no choice – they either went to the wall with their club, or agreed to Gibson's proposals. So the club was once again saved from extinction.

James Gibson invested over £30,000 of his own money in the club – half the original cost of Old Trafford – paid the players' wages, settled outstanding accounts and began to put the ship back on an even keel again.

A new manager was found: Scott Duncan, who had risen to fame as a footballer with Glasgow Rangers and Newcastle United. This time United had an ex-player at the helm, an idea that had worked with other clubs, a former professional knowing how to approach the game in a professional manner. Scott Duncan spent money on new players as he tried to build a strong side, but whether he spent wisely is debatable.

In the season in which they had almost faded to obscurity United finished 12th in the Second Division, a year later they were sixth, and then in 1933–34 not even Gibson's money could prevent them from sliding to the lowest ebb in the club's history, just one point away from the Third Division.

In fact the future of the club in the Second Division hung by a slender thread as late as the final day of the season. The date, 5 May 1934 is significant in the club's history for on that day, and for the previous week since drawing with Swansea, the club was last but one in the table. Never since the days those railway workers started their team had the club been in such a lowly position.

Lincoln were bottom, and nothing could stop them from being relegated. United were above them, seven points better off, and one point behind Millwall, who filled the 20th position. On 5 May United were away to Millwall, and knew that they had their own fate in their hands.

New signing Hacking was in goal, playing his tenth game since his transfer from Oldham, and in front of him were full-backs Griffiths and Jones. The half-back line of Robertson, Vose and McKay supported a forward line which read: Cape, McLenahan, Ball, Hine and Manley. The last-named normally played wing-half but was brought in to play outside-left so that he would add his defensive qualities if things got tough.

United played their hearts out. Manley scored first, Cape added a second and United won 2–0 . . . but what might have happened to this great club had that result been reversed and Manchester United had begun 1934–35 as a Third Division side? Incidentally, the week that United spent in that lowest point in their history, began the day that Manchester City, with Matt Busby in the side, won the FA Cup.

The new season began with Scott Duncan's new players in the line-up and ended with United fifth from the top, a much improved performance and one which brought the crowds back to Old Trafford, especially those who had been embarrassed by the failure of the Red Devils while Manchester City had lifted the Cup. A season later and United had something to celebrate. Not since Ernest Mangnall's team had won the Championship and the FA Charity Shield in 1911, had Old Trafford's trophy room been blessed with a major piece of silverware. The club had got used to playing second fiddle to Manchester City, but times at last were beginning to change. In 1935–36 they won the Second Division title, not perhaps the most coveted award the game has to offer, but certainly better than facing relegation, and a big improvement on their achievements over the previous quarter of a century.

The players who won the Second Division Championship of 1935–36 gather at Old Trafford before the start of the following season, when they were relegated once again! On the extreme right is James Gibson, the chairman whose generosity saved the club from extinction. Standing second from the left is Tom Curry, and on the ground (front right) Bert Whalley, who remained with the club until both were killed in the Munich air disaster 22 years later

Scott Duncan's team had achieved this with a tremendous run-in to the end of the season, stringing together 19 games without defeat and clinching promotion with a 3–2 win over Bury at Gigg Lane, where two goals from Tom Manley and another from George Mutch brought the 31,562 fans spilling onto the pitch. It is interesting to note that in 1987, when United were drawn against Bury in the Littlewoods Cup, the game was switched from Gigg Lane to Old Trafford because the ground safety limit at Bury is now restricted to 8,000.

United's only defeat after the beginning of the year, apart from a 2–0 exit from the FA Cup at Stoke, had been to lose by the only goal of the game at Bradford City on 4 January, and even though Charlton Athletic tried to close the gap United won promotion by a single point after both clubs had each won 22 of their 42 games.

They had started the 1935–36 season with Hall pushing Breedon out of the goalkeeper's spot after just one game and they had the good fortune to have several players who were virtually ever-presents throughout the season. Tom Curry was responsible for the fitness of the players, and he must have been proud of their response. Of the full-backs, Griffiths and Porter, only John Griffiths missed a single game of the 42, right-half Jim Brown missed just two, one of them a defeat at Blackpool, and centre-half George Vose was absent only for the 4–0 win at home to Burnley. Of the others, George Mutch was an ever-present, playing either at inside-right or centre-forward and scoring 21 goals in the League, and Henry Rowley scored just two fewer despite missing five matches.

Constantly being able to field a virtually unchanged side, Scott Duncan knew that he had a chance of success, and the players he had brought into the club from a variety of backgrounds took United back into the First Division for the first time since the start of the decade. Their stay, however was short. If ever the expression 'after the Lord Mayor's Show comes the dustcart' could be applied to football, here surely was the perfect example as 1936–37 followed the celebrations of 1935–36.

There were changes in the line-up at the start of the season: John, Redwood, Porter, Brown, Vose, McKay, Bryant, Mutch, Bamford, Rowley and Manley starting the campaign. A young man named Walter Winterbottom made his League debut for the club at Elland Road, Leeds, as they slipped to their ninth defeat in 16 games, with only three victories to their name. Winterbottom was never renowned as a player, but became manager of England from 1946 to 1963.

By the end of the season United had won only ten games, eight of them at Old Trafford, and a season after celebrating their return from the Second Division, they were back there.

Scott Duncan resigned and went to manage non-league Ipswich Town, and top-scorer

George Mutch took the road to Preston and a place in the game's Hall of Fame. Mutch had scored 46 goals in his 112 League games for United and three more in his eight FA Cup appearances, but it was for one goal he scored for the club which bought him from United for £5,000 that he is remembered. It was in the 1938 FA Cup final at Wembley, when Preston met Huddersfield and the scores were level 0–0 in the dying minutes of extra-time. George Mutch ran into the penalty area with the ball and was tripped. A penalty, and the last kick of the game. Mutch took it and hit the ball with a powerful shot, which struck the underside of the square crossbar, bounced down over the line and spun into the back of the net. George Mutch had made footballing history, but it is worth noting that had Mutch not taken the kick himself, the man who would have gone into the record books in his place was Preston's second-string penalty taker, Bill Shankly.

Back for 36 years at the top

United were not too disappointed at the success of their ex-player, for as the FA Cup came back to the north-west, United also had something to celebrate. Their big-dipper ride through football was back at the top, after plunging to the depths a season earlier. They ended the 1937–38 season as runners-up in the Second division to Aston Villa.

United won promotion by the skin of their teeth. Hot on their heels were Sheffield United, who in their 42 games scored 73 goals against 56, giving them a goal average of 1.738. United, with exactly the same record, 22 wins and nine draws, netted 82 goals against 50, an average of 1.952 – they went up, Sheffield stayed down. Coventry were only a point behind.

The season had seen new players once again take their places in the line-up. Walter Crickmer had been given the reins for another spell as temporary manager, and with Tom Curry and Louis Rocca remaining in the backroom, United tried out a blend of youth and experience.

Rocca, on one of his visits to Ireland, had spotted a young forward, Johnny Carey, and after bringing him to Manchester was delighted with his progress into the first team. Carey made his debut on 25 September 1937, against Southampton, and played just one more game before a ten-match break. He returned in Christmas week to score in the 3–2 win over Nottingham Forest, the club he would later manage after a career with United which saw him recognised as one of the best full-backs the game had produced.

A month before Duncan had resigned he had bought Jack Rowley from Bournemouth. Rowley was a prolific goal-scorer, making his debut as an outside-left in a home win over Sheffield Wednesday on 23 October 1937. He arrived on the scene at the right time. United had started the season badly, and as it followed their year of relegation, crowds fell off. To make matters worse Manchester City had won the League Championship in 1936–37 and had been the major crowd pullers in the city as the Red fans stayed silent and at home.

Another new player to win his way into the side was Stan Pearson, a Salford-born lad who made his debut in a game which was the turning point of the season. From August until 6 November, three days before Scott Duncan resigned, United had won only five of their 14 matches. The side which started the season was Breen, Griffiths, Roughton, Gladwin, Vose, McKay, Bryant, Murray, Bamford, Baird and Manley. On 13 November, after Duncan had gone, the line-up looked different to say the least. Jack Breedon was in goal, Bert Redwood at right-back, Roughton at left. Right-half was Jim Brown, Vose remained at centre-half, and Bert Whalley played left-half. Bill Bryant stayed at outside-right with Baird inside him and Tommy Bamford centre-forward. Young Stan Pearson played inside-left, with Tom Manley outside him, a team of experience blending with young enthusiasm, and Chesterfield, the opposition, never knew what hit them.

Bamford scored four times, and Baird, Bryant and Manley scored to make it a 7–1 win. United lost just five more matches in the remainder of the season and were promoted. If some seasons have been of more importance to the history of Manchester United than others, that 1937–38 season must rank highly, even though the club failed to win any major trophies. Promotion to the First Division at such a time, with war impending, can only be looked upon as an act of good fortune. In that same season Manchester City were relegated along with West Bromwich Albion, and both failed to return a season later. United ended the 1938–39 campaign in 14th place in the First Division, but it was events outside football which would have a long-lasting effect on the club.

At the outbreak of the Second World War football was suspended. From 1939 until 1946–47 there was to be no League competition, and while United played no serious football during the period of the war, when the game began again after years of friendlies and make-shift matches, they would start again in the First Divison.

A major historical event had once again played an important role in the Manchester United story. Because of the Second World War the club found itself bracketed with the elite and was to remain in the upper section for 36 years. In that time United would achieve successes never dreamt of by Harry Stafford, reach peaks beyond the far-seeing imagination of Ernest Mangnall, and develop its stadium beyond the riches of men like John Henry Davies and James Gibson. It would also find itself a manager to reign longer than any who had gone before him, and that man would step into the breach after the war. His name . . . Matt Busby.

Manchester United at the start of the 1968–69 season proudly displaying the European Cup they had won the previous May. Back row: Bill Foulkes, John Aston, Jimmy Rimmer, Alex Stepney, Alan Gowling, David Herd, Middle: David Sadler, Tony Dunne, Shay Brennan, Pat Crerand, George Best, Francis Burns, Jack Crompton (trainer). Front: Jimmy Ryan, Nobby Stiles, Denis Law, Matt Busby (manager), Bobby Charlton, Brian Kidd, John Fitzpatrick. But despite the European triumph, the team had peaked. It was a side growing old gracefully and lacking the edge to keep them competing for fresh honours. Matt Busby was preparing to retire and a few of his stars were of like mind. They finished 11th that season and they never finished higher than eighth before relegation arrived six years after winning the European Cup

Beyond Busby: Search for a successor

So we come to the point where we started our story . . . the Matt Busby era, the most successful in the history of Manchester United and, of course, the most tragic.

We broke into history and make no apology for opening our book with the Busby Babes, the drama of European competition and the Munich catastrophe. It was a renaissance period for the whole of football as folk flocked back to the game after the grim days of the Second World War.

Under the guidance of Busby, Manchester United emerged a giant, surviving the most terrible of blows to conquer Europe. But even Sir Matt Busby couldn't go on for ever, nor could his great team of 1968, and so we pick up our tale again as the great man looks for a new commander to take his beloved club into the 1970s.

Even as they were winning the European Cup in 1968 and finishing runners-up for the Championship it was clear that some of the players were no longer in their prime and that changes would have to be made. Some of the decisions were going to be difficult, both in terms of judgement and feeling, and Busby thought long and hard about whether he wanted to be the manager to close one book and open yet another.

Busby tried to bolster the team by buying winger Willie Morgan, a Scottish international, for £110,000 from Burnley, but in September, October and November they managed to win just three games. Disappointingly, the most frequent result was only a draw.

Denis Law and George Best manfully shouldered the burden, but by the end of the season their goal figures were down on previous seasons. Law scored 19 and Best 14, and Bobby Charlton was reduced to five. Morgan managed six, and the slump was eventually reflected in a League placing of 11th. Three defeats in succession around Christmas gave Sir Matt food for thought and by January he had reached a decision . . . he would 'go upstairs' to become general manager and leave a new man to run the team. The club issued a statement which read:

> Sir Matt has informed the board that he wishes to relinquish the position of team manager at the end of the present season.
>
> The chairman and directors have tried to persuade him to carry on and it was only with great reluctance that his request has been accepted. The board fully appreciates the reason for his decision and it was unanimously agreed that Sir Matt be appointed general manager of the club which he is very happy to accept.

The chairman added:

> Of course we knew that it had to come but this does not mean that Sir Matt will be any less involved with Manchester United. In fact the post of general manager carries even wider responsibilities and my board are well content to think that in future they can call upon Sir Matt's unique football experience in both home and international fields.

Behind the scenes the chairman and directors had tried hard to persuade Busby to carry on, but his mind was made up. The clue to his thinking lay in a few words he had uttered spontaneously during the glow of European victory. 'Let us hope this is not the end, just the beginning,' he had said after making United the champions of Europe.

No doubt as he pondered that instinctive feeling, he explored how the task was to be accomplished and whether he really wanted to start all over again. He knew that it was the end of another era and that after 23 years at the helm it was a job for a younger man. He had built three great teams and now a fourth was required. His mind must have gone back to the time he had started out, young and ambitious and that that was what was required all over again.

The press had a field day searching out likely candidates. The names of Don Revie, Johnny Carey, Ron Greenwood, Jimmy Adamson and Brian Clough were freely mentioned, but few questioned whether such experienced managers would be willing to work under Sir Matt Busby.

Wilf McGuinness

The club solved the problem by looking within and deciding to promote one of their junior staff to take charge of the players with a title of chief coach. Wilf McGuinness, the 31-year-old trainer

with the reserves, was the man chosen to follow in the great man's footsteps.

The appointment of McGuinness came with the announcement in April 1969, saying:

> The board has given further consideration to the changes which will occur at the end of the season and has decided to appoint a chief coach who will be responsible for team selection, coaching, training and tactics.
>
> Mr Wilf McGuinness has been selected for this position and will take up his duties as from 1 June and in these circumstances it is not necessary to advertise for applications as was first intended.
>
> Sir Matt will be responsible for all other matters affecting the club and players and will continue as club spokesman.

Busby revealed his relief when he said:

> My trouble is that it is almost impossible to forget football for a minute of my waking life. I have it for breakfast, dinner and supper. Driving the car I'm thinking of it. If I go out socially, everybody wants to talk football. The only time I get a break is on the golf course. I'd like to read but I don't get the time. Really it's football all the way, other people's football, too. Sometimes I go to another match and they start speculating who I have come to see. But I haven't come to see anybody. I've just come to look and listen and enjoy a match and know what's going on.

If he needed any reminders of the pressures, his experience between the announcement of his semi-retirement in the January and the end of the season provided ample evidence of the wisdom of his decision. The team ran riot with an 8–1 win against Queen's Park Rangers at Old Trafford, including a hat-trick from Willie Morgan, but worryingly, there were other far less convincing performances that season.

Wilf McGuinness was Busby's recommendation and the appointment had the advantage of keeping the management within the family of Old Trafford; it did however beg the question of total control, and was in marked contrast to the conditions insisted upon by Busby when he was brought to the club as a young man.

McGuinness had the additional problem of being asked to take charge of players who were his contemporaries, but these thoughts were only clouds on a distant horizon when the enthusiastic Wilf assembled his players for pre-season training in the summer of 1969. Wilf was certainly steeped in the tradition of the club and had always possessed qualities of leadership. As a schoolboy he captained not only Manchester Boys, but Lancashire and England as well. In fact he quite enjoys pointing out that a certain Bobby Charlton played under his command at schoolboy level!

As a junior, McGuinness was one of the Busby Babes and played in three of the FA Youth Cup winning teams in the 1950s. He made his League debut against Wolves in October 1955, and remembers it vividly:

> I can still hear Jimmy Murphy winding me up for the game and urging me to remember everything I had been taught. He said we hate Wolves and everything in black and gold, and I kept dutifully saying yes Jimmy. He told me I would be up against Peter Broadbent and that he would be doing his best to take my win bonus out of my pocket and then I wouldn't have any money to take my mother a box of chocolates after the match. He had me so wound up that when we went out for the kick-off and Peter Broadbent came across like the gentleman he is to wish me as a youngster good luck on my debut, I just shouted at him: 'Shove off, you thieving beggar.'

His problem was that he was a left-half, and the great Duncan Edwards played in that position. His best season didn't come until after Munich. Then in 1958–59 he made 39 League appearances. Sadly, in the middle of the following season, he broke his leg playing for the reserves against Stoke. It was a bad break, and though he attempted a come-back it was impossible to continue playing and he was forced to retire at the age of 22. But at least he had his qualities of leadership and United had no hesitation recruiting him as assistant trainer to Jack Crompton in charge of the reserve team.

Before long the Football Association made him the England youth team coach and in 1968 he was appointed their manager after helping Sir Alf Ramsey as a training assistant during preparations for the 1966 World Cup.

So the youthful McGuinness was not without management experience when he was handed command of the Busby empire. Yet, looking back, was there a veiled doubt in the minds of the board from the start?

There was a definite probationary ring about the title they gave him. Chief coach was not even team manager, the phrase used originally when it

Left: Wilf McGuiness had the unenviable task of taking over from Sir Matt Busby as manager of Manchester United. United had the idea of keeping the appointment in the club family with the result that they called him up from his job as reserve team trainer to make him first-team coach. Later he was promoted to team manager, but though he did well enough by ordinary standards, it wasn't quite good enough for Old Trafford. He was in charge for 20 months, starting in April 1969, before being offered his old job back in December 1970

Below: Wilf McGuinness coaching the England youth side for the international tournament in Leipzig in 1969. He was made the England youth coach in 1968. A broken leg finished his playing career at the age of 22, but he had already made his mark as a leader of men and Manchester United did not hesitate to take him on to their staff following unsuccessful attempts to play again. The Football Association were also impressed by him and he was called by Sir Alf Ramsey to help as a junior coach to prepare the England team for the World Cup in 1966

was announced that Sir Matt would become general manager. Sir Matt explained:

> This is a sort of preliminary. All the great names in the game started this way. He has a bit of experience to pick up yet in management and it's a question of starting this way. I think he will have enough to bite on with responsibility for the team without taking on other things which could come later. The question of team manager could come probably in a year or so. We hope it will.

Obviously everyone hoped that, but did the qualified authority communicate to the players that here was a new boss who had yet to convince the club that he could do the job? Bobby Charlton, senior player, captain, distinguished international and a pal, wrote, perhaps significantly, in a foreword to a club book:

> No-one can be sure just how this change-over will work out. After all Sir Matt has been at the helm of Manchester United for 23 years. He has been the boss in every sense of the word . . . manager, tactician, coach, adviser, disciplinarian, simply everything. Even though he will be there in the background still, we are bound to miss him.

On the pitch at least the difficulties soon manifested themselves. The opening game of the 1969–70 season, away to Crystal Palace, was drawn 2–2, a fair start in the circumstances, but then came three successive defeats, including losing 2–0 to Everton at Old Trafford and then going down at home again 4–1 to Southampton. This was followed by a 3–0 defeat at Everton and the fans were starting to worry.

United bought a new centre-half to replace the veteran Bill Foulkes, who had been given quite a chasing by centre-forward Ron Davies in the Southampton game. They bought Ian Ure from Arsenal for £80,000. It later transpired that Ure was not McGuinness's choice but Busby's, underlining at a very early stage the difficulties of dividing responsibility for running a team.

The team continued to hold their own, but in terms of winning the Championship it was becoming clear that new blood was required. The goal scoring was shared mainly by George Best again with 15, a welcome increase to 12 by Bobby Charlton and a useful 12 from Brian Kidd. Willie Morgan scored seven. There were lapses like a 4–0 beating at Manchester City and a 5–1 crash at Newcastle, immediately avenged by a 7–0 win against West Bromwich at Old Trafford in the next match.

For the third season in succession, more than a million spectators had packed Old Trafford, but behind the scenes there were rumblings. No-one knew better than McGuinness that, despite two semi-finals, changes were needed, and at the end of the season came reorganisation and a clear-out of players.

Bill Foulkes retired after a glorious career spanning 18 seasons of First Division football. Denis Law was put up for sale at £60,000, Don Givens was listed at £15,000 and nine other players were given free transfers, including Shay Brennan, who had joined the club with Wilf McGuinness 16 years previously. The two of them were great pals. Each was best man at the other's wedding and it must have been difficult when Wilf had to break the news to his friend.

The club were looking ahead, promoting McGuinness from chief coach to team manager.

But there was still the feeling that the youthful McGuinness was heading for a crisis out on the pitch as season 1970–71 began. Another slow start posed questions.

The defence was built round Ian Ure with Nobby Stiles and Tony Dunne battling gamely. Paul Edwards, later to play at centre-half, had come in at right-back and John Fitzpatrick was a regular in midfield, wearing Pat Crerand's number four shirt. Bobby Charlton, Denis Law, George Best, Brian Kidd and David Sadler were all in the side with the likes of Willie Morgan, John Aston, Alan Gowling and Carlo Sartori challenging for regular places in the attack.

One of the problems was that while individually the older players still had a lot of football left in them, collectively as a team they were a bit long in the tooth. On their day they were still capable of producing winning performances, as they showed once again by reaching the semi-final of the League Cup.

But they struggled in the first leg against Aston Villa at Old Trafford. Perhaps demoralised by a 4–1 home defeat against Manchester City four days earlier, they found they just could not master their opponents.

The flaws of the first half of the season were mirrored as they slid to a 2–1 defeat in the second leg and exit from the competition. To lose yet again just one step short of Wembley, and this time to a Third Division team, was a bitter blow to the fans who thought they had a good Cup-fighting team, even if it was a side with problems sustaining an effort in the League. Certainly the defeat was the death warrant for the management career of Wilf McGuinness at Old Trafford, and after a 4–4 draw at Derby County three days later on Boxing Day, he was relieved of his first-team duties. Sir Matt announced in a statement:

> The directors had a special meeting last night to discuss the performances of the team and decided to release Wilf McGuinness from his duties as team manager. As he did not wish to leave the club, and as the club felt he still had a part to play, he was offered his former position as trainer of the Central League side, which he has accepted. The board have asked me to take over team matters for the time being and until a new appointment is made in the close season.

Sir Matt, grim-faced and upset, explained:

> I did not want to take charge of the team again, but my directors asked me to. At my age, I feel I have had enough of managerial worries at team level. It means becoming involved with players again. I shall be at their training sessions again. It's something I think

I am capable of doing for a while, though I would have preferred we were not in this situation. It is unfortunate that things have not worked out. I feel very sorry for Wilf, who was appointed on my recommendation. He might have been a wee bit raw.

Later Sir Matt told his protegé' where he thought he had gone wrong. 'You failed to get the players with you,' he said.

This was an apt summing up – whether the fault lay in McGuinness or the players is a moot point. Certainly at least two of the senior men had been to see Sir Matt behind the manager's back, perhaps in a genuine concern for the club's plight, though hardly a move calculated to help the manager's authority.

One player was reported anonymously in the *Sunday Times* as saying:

The problem for Wilf McGuinness was he had no personality. He did not understand that the team he was controlling needed handling in a special way. I am not saying we were special, but after all, we had won the European Cup and we were being told what to do by a man who had never been anywhere. People go on about us buying our way out of trouble, but I believe we would have been screwed even if Wilf had had a million quid to spend.

Sir Matt himself could still control them. The team clawed their way back up the table to finish eighth again, while McGuinness went back to running the reserves. Not for long though. After two months he decided to quit the club he loved, saying:

I thought I had time. I was on a contract which still had 18 months to run, but the simple truth is that the results went badly for me. We have been in three Cup semi-finals, something that cannot be claimed by any other club, and yet each time we fell short of reaching the final. If we had made it in any one of those competitions, things might have been so different.

The extent of the turmoil within McGuinness can be judged by the fact that soon afterwards, as he attempted to rebuild his career in Greece, his hair fell out almost overnight and what little grew again was white.

With hindsight it seems the board were more concerned with persuading Matt Busby to stay on as manager than in properly preparing a successor.

Below: Alex Stepney makes a brave save at the feet of Joe Royle the Everton centre forward. Stepney, who joined United from Chelsea after starting his career with Millwall, is one of the few Londoners to have settled at Old Trafford. In fact he took to life in the North so well that after leaving United to play in the United States he returned to make the Manchester area his home again. He played more than 500 League and Cup games for the Reds

Above: Ian Ure, left in the dark shirt, jumps high with team-mate John Aston during a troubled season. Ure was Wilf McGuinness's first signing as the new manager rushed to plug a leak early in season 1969–70. The Scot was bought from Arsenal after three heavy defeats in the four opening fixtures

Perhaps Wilf McGuinness would have made it if he had been brought on to the first-team scene a year earlier, so that he could have flexed his managerial muscles as a senior trainer instead of being thrust right into the spotlight from working in a backstage capacity.

The experience certainly did nothing for the image of Manchester United who were right back to square one with few, if any, of their problems solved. It had been the worst playing record since the Second World War, for although the club had finished lower in the League on occasions there had invariably been a good FA Cup run.

So there were still enormous difficulties waiting to be resolved. The fans were demanding new blood. United hadn't bought anyone for two years, with Ian Ure their last signing. In fact they had bought only three players in six years – Ure, Willie Morgan and Alex Stepney.

The behaviour of George Best did not help much either. Although he was top scorer with 18 League goals, he was becoming increasingly difficult to manage. Apart from periodic petulance on the field, usually involving referees, the first outward sign that all was not well came on Christmas Day. He simply failed to turn up for training, the only player to shirk an obviously unpopular chore. McGuinness was considerably annoyed because the player had no real excuse, beyond perhaps a sore head after Christmas Eve celebrations. It was agreed that he should be sent home when he reported the next day for the match at Derby County. Then came second thoughts. They fined him £50 instead and played him. Of course he scored to help achieve a 4–4 draw. But should expediency have come before discipline?

United received a poor reward for their leniency. Less than a fortnight later the player was due to meet Busby at Piccadilly Station to catch a train to London for a personal appearance in front of the FA disciplinary committee to answer for three bookings. He failed to turn up, and Sir Matt had to travel down on his own and then use all his eloquence to placate the commission whose members were in no mood to indulge a young man who could not even arrive on time for his disciplinary hearing. The hearing was put back until later in the day so that Best, who had pleaded feeling unwell when his housekeeper had arrived at his home in Bramhall first thing in the morning, could catch a later train. When he eventually arrived at Euston Station he was mobbed by photographers, reporters, television cameras and girls. George Best was a show on his own. It took him 10 minutes to fight his way through in his smart blue suit, pink shirt and white tie.

Above: Denis Law was the king as far as United fans were concerned. They liked the streak of villainy which ran through his play as well as his excellence as a goal scorer. Not a big man by any means, but as quick as lightning in front of goal, he spent 11 seasons at Old Trafford, scoring a remarkable 236 goals in 393 appearances in League, domestic cup and European competition. Born in Aberdeen, he came into English football with Huddersfield Town, moved to Manchester City and then went abroad to play for Torino in Italy. Matt Busby brought him back to England, paying a then record £115,000. He rejoined Manchester City and scored his final League goal with a back-flick which sent United into the Second Division

Left: Bobby Charlton's 100th international cap. In honour of the occasion he was made captain. Bobby Moore (left) follows as the skipper walks out with Northern Ireland captain Terry Neill for the match at Wembley in April 1970. Charlton made a record 106 appearances and scored a record 49 goals

He was given a suspended six-week suspension, but just five days later he missed another train. This time he failed to report for morning training before the team set off for London in readiness for a match at Chelsea the following day. Sir Matt expected him at the station, but he was still missing. John Aston was sent for as a replacement and Busby announced that Best need not bother coming at all. The player travelled to London anyway and went to ground hiding in the flat of his latest girlfriend. Busby expected him to report to the ground on Monday, but he was still in London besieged by the media. He was suspended by the club for a fortnight and it took the combined efforts of his agent, Ken Stanley, and business partner, Malcolm Mooney, to bring him back to face the music.

It emerged later that it wasn't just his playboy streak that turned him into the runaway soccer star. He had also grown somewhat disillusioned with the decline of the team, and he felt, probably rightly too, that too much was being expected of him. He once remarked: 'Everyone makes mistakes – mine just seem to get more publicity than other people's.'

That was certainly true, just as it was true that he had presented Wilf McGuinness with a stack of problems which even the experienced Busby found difficult enough. For a young man in his first big job it must have seemed like a nightmare. What should he have done for instance when he caught a girl in the player's room a few hours before a semi-final? Drop his best player in the interests of discipline, or let him get away with it and let the rest of the team rumble about one rule for George Best and another for the others?

The season also brought an end to the career of Nobby Stiles at Old Trafford. He had fought a losing battle with a knee injury and in February the club let it be known that they were willing to listen to offers. Three months later he was transferred to Middlesbrough for a modest £20,000, still only 29, but with a total of 363 League and Cup appearances to his credit, not to mention a reputation as one of the club's most enduringly popular players.

Nobby's first-team career at Old Trafford was brought to a close with the development of David Sadler in his role as cover alongside the centre-half, the position to become known as centre-back. Paul Edwards and Steve James competed for the centre-half berth, which dumped Ian Ure in the reserves for a long spell.

It all added up to a most difficult period of change which had proved too much for the youthful Wilf McGuinness, and though Sir Matt had galloped to the rescue to secure relief, the problems were still there as the board looked for someone to follow the legendary manager.

Frank O'Farrell takes over

The club were looking for an experienced manager this time after gambling unsuccessfully with their own youngster, and they finally settled on Frank O'Farrell, who had a good, solid record of achievement. He was to bring with him from Leicester City his partner at Filbert Street, Malcolm Musgrove, a coach who like his boss had grown up as a player in the think-tank era of West Ham with the likes of Malcolm Allison, Dave Sexton, Noel Cantwell, John Bond and Ken Brown.

The parallels with Sir Matt were strong, even down to strong convictions as Roman Catholics. They had both started from modest family backgrounds. Frank's first ambition was to follow in his father's footsteps and drive the express trains from Cork to Dublin. He did indeed start his working life shovelling coal on the Irish Railways.

O'Farrell started on the ground floor of management as player-coach with Weymouth and made club history by taking the Southern League team to the fourth round of the FA Cup. This brought him an invitation to manage Torquay and in his first season he brought them up from the Fourth Division to the Third. He followed Matt Gillies as manager of Leicester in December 1968, and failed to save them from dropping into the Second Division, but he did enjoy a run to Wembley in the FA Cup, where they lost to Manchester City. After two seasons he brought Leicester back to the First Division as Champions and it was his steady progress in management through all levels which attracted United.

O'Farrell looked an eminently sound choice and he accepted the invitation to come to Old Trafford proffered in the chairman's car parked on a lonely side road at Mackworth just outside Derby, and he said about his contract: 'It's long enough to achieve what I hope to achieve.'

Stung by criticism that his presence as general manager had not given McGuinness a fair chance, Sir Matt voluntarily gave up his paid post and joined the board as a director. He said:

> The idea seemed to build up that if I stayed as general manager I would want to interfere. It was a wrong impression, but it was splashed about and I admit the talk influenced me. Frank O'Farrell did not make an issue of it, in fact he said he hoped his coming was not the reason and he didn't mind whether I stayed on as general manager or director.

So O'Farrell had a clear field and he voiced firm ideas for the future, in keeping with the Busby traditions:

> I have no preconceived ideas. I don't prejudge any situation or individual. I just want to see for myself and make up my own mind. The entertaining image must be maintained, but at the same time if modifications in style are necessary to make the team a more efficient unit, then they must be made. In principle a team needs a sound defence. That is the basis, but it doesn't mean that I have to be defensive minded.

Malcolm Musgrove, who followed Jimmy Hill as chairman of the Professional Footballers' Association, believed United had made the right appointment. He said:

'Frank O'Farrell is one of the few people who could have come to Old Trafford. The job is so big it's hardly true. Yet Frank will measure up. He is the ideal choice. His greatest quality is his honesty, yet you don't pull the wool over his eyes. I think we make a good partnership and I hope it will show for Manchester United.'

That partnership was going to be sorely tried and tested in the next 18 months, both on and off the pitch, but there were no such fears as the new management team got off to a brilliant start. Although they drew 2–2 at Derby on the opening day, they won the next three and only lost one of their first 14 games. By early October they were at the top of the First Division, and as Christmas approached they were into a five-point lead, with only one other defeat.

The team had also taken in their stride the closure of Old Trafford for a fortnight at the start of the season because of a knife thrown on to the pitch the previous winter. This had meant playing the home game against Arsenal at Liverpool and meeting West Bromwich at Stoke. Both games had been won 3–1 and it seemed the Reds had found their form and could do nothing wrong as far as their results were concerned.

The first signs of cracking came in the League Cup in November with a fourth-round defeat against Stoke in a second replay. Then, after three successive draws in December, came seven successive defeats. United worryingly skidded down the table just about as fast as they had gone up it earlier in the season.

The inspiration of a new manager and the fresh coaching techniques of Malcolm Musgrove had fired some of the old skill and enthusiasm in the first half of the season, but it all vanished in the seven-match burn-out. O'Farrell knew it was time to turn to the transfer market, and he made two excellent signings in the space of a fortnight. First he moved to Aberdeen with £125,000 for Martin Buchan and then paid £200,000 for Ian Storey-Moore from Nottingham Forest.

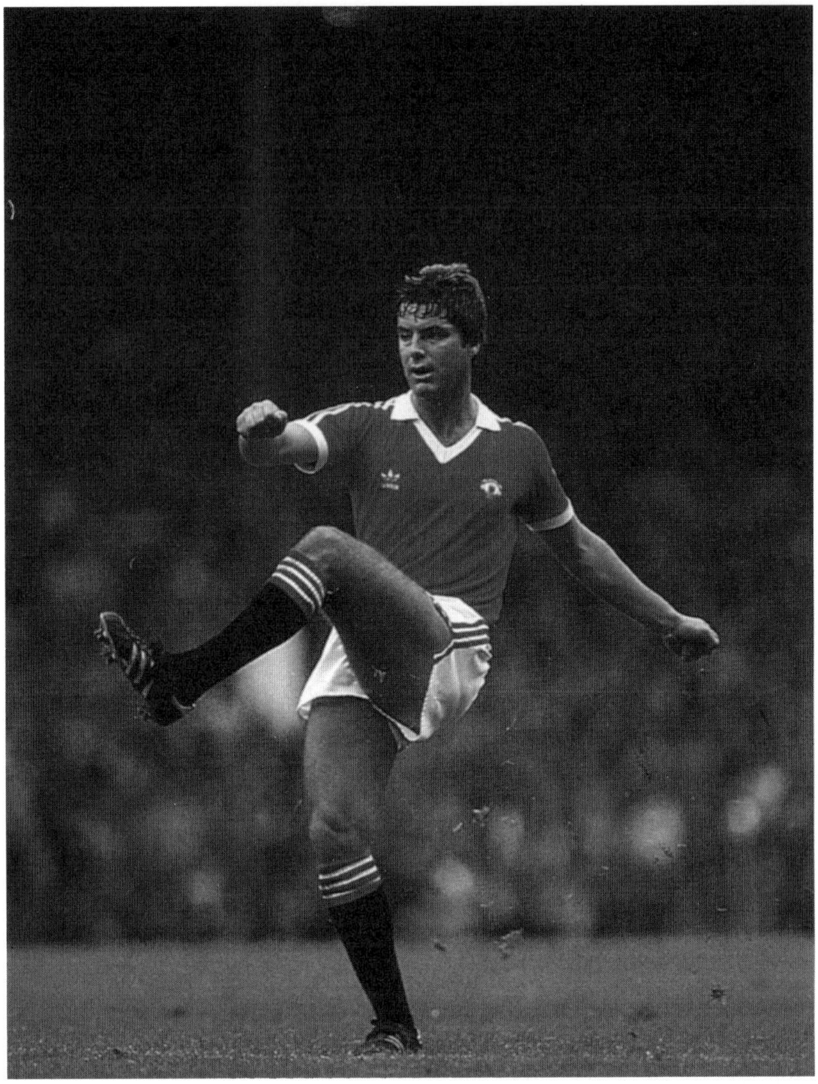

Above: Martin Buchan was the most valuable legacy of Frank O'Farrell's management. The United manager signed the Scot from Aberdeen for £125,000 in March 1972, and he played at Old Trafford for 12 seasons. He was a remarkable defender, a man who knew his own mind and an obvious captain. In 1977 he captained United to victory in the FA Cup against Liverpool to become the first player to skipper both English and Scottish Cup-winning teams. He subsequently played for Oldham and was briefly a manager at Burnley before returning to his native Aberdeen

Martin Buchan

Buchan at 23 was a super signing, who went on to play 455 League and Cup games for United, becoming their captain and a remarkable character. Already a Scottish international, he was the exception from Scotland who proved the rule, adjusting immediately to the pace of English football. His debut was marked by a 2–0 defeat at Spurs, but his influence on those around him was very evident and he quickly slowed the rate of descent down the League table. United lost only four of their last 12 games with Buchan playing.

Signing Buchan in February 1972 was Frank O'Farrell's best day's work and a handsome legacy long after he had departed. O'Farrell's second signing, a week later, was also a good buy, but Ian Moore eventually ran into bad luck with a series of injuries.

United thought at one point after agreeing terms with Forest that they had lost the player to Derby County. O'Farrell broke off discussing terms with the player so that Moore could fulfil a promise and speak to Brian Clough the Derby manager. Clough swept Moore away and actually got the player's signature on a transfer form. On the strength of that he paraded him round the Baseball Ground as Derby's new signing. Happily for Old Trafford the document didn't carry Forest's signature, so that it was meaningless, and United were able to complete the transfer for the player to make his debut against Huddersfield and score in a 2–0 win. Moore played the last 11 games and scored five goals, a splendid start, and with Buchan steadying the ship with strong defensive organisation, United recovered to finish eighth in the League again.

Moore was 27 and in 250 League games for Forest he had scored 120 goals, a good return for a winger and a welcome boost for United's scoring potential. For although Best finished as top scorer with 18 League goals he had got most of them in the first half of the season, and Law was down to 13 and Kidd 10.

Right: There was never any doubt about the ability of George Best to score as spectacularly off the field as he did on it. Actress Susan George certainly seems pleased with life with George when she was 19 and on holiday in Palma Nova

Best's disappearing act

The question marks against Best were mounting. During the summer the player went missing again, this time failing to report for duty with Northern Ireland, and the episode ended with him threatening to retire from football. He had been a source of worry for the new manager right from the start of the season. In only the second League game he was sent off against Chelsea at Stamford Bridge by Norman Burtenshaw for abusive language. An FA disciplinary commission cleared him after accepting his plea that his swearing had been directed at team-mate Willie Morgan and not at the referee.

Morgan backed up the player, who was well represented by Cliff Lloyd, the secretary of the Professional Footballers' Association who outshone Perry Mason on the day. United were very worried because if Best had been found guilty a six-week suspended ban would have come in to operation as well as any other further punishment. A lot of people thought Best lucky to escape, and O'Farrell privately indicated which version he believed.

Below: George Best in action for United against Colin Harvey of Everton

At least Best behaved for a while and in fact enjoyed fabulous form again, but in January he failed to turn up for training, and just when the team needed him. O'Farrell immediately dropped him, fined him two weeks' pay, ordered him to train in the afternoons as well as the mornings and cancelled his days off for five weeks to make up for the week's training he had skipped.

Then at the end of the season, after signing off with a goal in a 3–0 win against Stoke, the team which had knocked United out of the FA Cup in the sixth round, Best disappeared on the eve of the British Championships. The day after he should have joined the Northern Ireland squad he turned up at a luxury hotel in Marbella on the Spanish coast. Against a background of jet-set living and champagne by the side of a sun-soaked swimming pool, he announced that he had had his fill of football, Manchester United and the Irish international team. The day after announcing his retirement he celebrated his 26th birthday. Frank O'Farrell said:

I know he has been drinking a lot and has been going out with a lot of girl friends and keeping late hours. These things and pressures from outside the game have wrecked him.

He is, like all other geniuses, difficult to understand. I don't think he can cope with his own problems. And there is nobody he can really lean on for help. He is like a boy lost. He needs someone to help him. We at Old Trafford have done everything possible to help him. He acknowledges this, but the plain fact is he finds it extremely difficult to communicate his problems to other people and I feel we have not really reached him.

Best was expected to link up with his club in Tel Aviv for the final game of their summer tour, but he didn't make that either and was posted absent without leave. A few days later he crept back into Manchester and at a secret meeting with O'Farrell said it was all a big mistake and that he wanted to play again after all.

On the brighter side another boy from Belfast made a significant entrance on to the Old Trafford

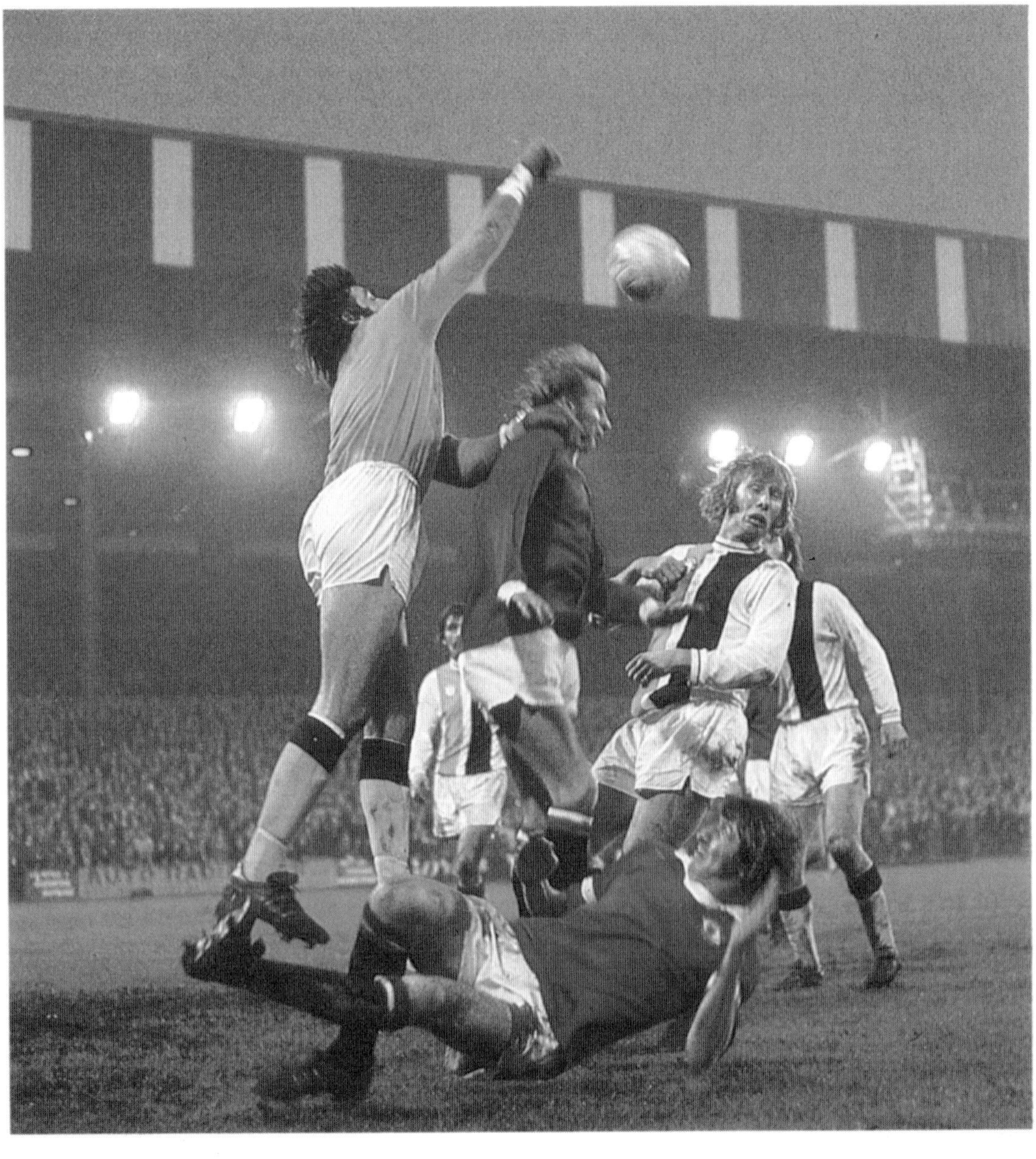

Left: United were sinking fast and had won only five League games when they crashed 5–0 at Crystal Palace on 16 December in 1972. Denis Law is in the thick of the action with Wyn Davies on the floor as the Reds struggle vainly for a goal. This was the game which hammered the final nail into the managerial coffin of Frank O'Farrell. The heavy defeat was the last straw as far as Sir Matt Busby and his directors were concerned. One of the spectators at Selhurst Park was Tommy Docherty, the manager of Scotland, and United moved quickly to ask him if he was interested in taking over at Old Trafford. The Doc needed asking only once!

Above: Ian Storey-Moore was a brilliant signing for United, a fast flying winger with an eye for scoring goals. He got five in 11 appearances after signing for Frank O'Farrell in March 1972, from Nottingham Forest. Unfortunately for both player and manager he seriously injured his ankle midway through the following season and it was virtually the end of his career. He also complained later about the dissension and cliques at Old Trafford which made things so difficult for O'Farrell

stage. Sammy McIlroy, sent over from Ireland by Bob Bishop, the scout who had nurtured Best as a boy, was given his League debut at the age of 17 against Manchester City at Maine Road. He scored an exciting goal in a 3–3 draw to win a bottle of champagne from Best, and in fact scored in each of his first four League games. He made such an impact that he played for Northern Ireland within three months of his League debut, still only 17. The team towards the end of Frank's first season read:

> Stepney, O'Neill, Dunne, Buchan, James, Sadler, Best, Kidd or McIlroy, Charlton, Law, Moore.

Pat Crerand hadn't played, though still retained as a player, and he had been put in charge of the youth team while Bill Foulkes looked after the reserves.

There was a lot still to accomplish, as Frank O'Farrell readily admitted, but few could have anticipated the disasters lying in wait as season 1972–73 got under way.

The team opened with a terrible string of results. They lost the first three games, drew the next four and then lost two more. Those first nine games saw them score only three goals. The alarm bells were ringing for Frank and he turned urgently to the transfer market.

He bought Wyn Davies from Manchester City for £60,000, and the Welshman scored on his debut against Derby at Old Trafford to help notch the first win of the season. But by now the Reds had gone to the bottom like a lead weight. A week later Frank swooped again to land Ted MacDougall from Third Division Bournemouth for £200,000. MacDougall scored on his second appearance for a 1–0 win against Birmingham, but pressure was building up. Losing 4–1 at home to Spurs didn't help; nor did a morale-sapping derby defeat at Maine Road.

The departures of O'Farrell and Best

Ironically United won their next two games, but the board were already making plans for a new manager. The Manchester Evening News carried a story with the headline 'Be Fair to Frank', urging the club to give the manager time, but that only succeeded in getting the joint author of this history, David Meek, banned from travelling on the team coach.

The final blow for O'Farrell came on 16 December at Crystal Palace where his team crashed 5–0. Significantly, Tommy Docherty, then manager of Scotland, was watching the match from the stands.

After the game Sir Matt Busby seized the opportunity to ask him if he was interested in coming to Old Trafford. The Doc indicated that he was; he could do little else since it had been his burning ambition to manage Manchester United for 25 years!

First had to come the night of the long knives, an evening of wining, dining and dancing to celebrate the finale of Bobby Charlton's testimonial. Frank O'Farrell, Malcolm Musgrove and John Aston were all at the banquet and ball which went on into the early hours. There could have been little sleep for the directors before they met at the offices of chairman Louis Edwards and the decision was taken to sack the management team. The statement issued on Tuesday, 19 December 1972, read:

> In view of the poor position in the League, it was unanimously decided that Mr O'Farrell, Malcolm Musgrove and John Aston be relieved of their duties forthwith.

Side by side with the sacking of the manager almost inevitably ran another chapter in the saga of George Best. Once again the Irishman was in crisis and gave notice that he was quitting in a letter to the board. He wrote:

> . . . therefore I have decided not to play football again, and this time no-one will change my mind. I would like to wish the club the best of luck for the remainder of the season and for the future. Because even though I personally have tarnished the club's name in recent times, to me and thousands of others, Manchester United still means something special.

The club were at some pains at the end to make it clear that they had in fact 'sacked' George Best as well as the manager before the player's letter of resignation had reached them. The statement announcing the sacking of Frank O'Farrell also said:

> Furthermore, George Best will remain on the transfer list and will not be selected again for Manchester United as it is felt it is in the best interest of the club and the player that he leaves Old Trafford.

So it turned out the board had beaten the player to the punch by a few hours, though it is difficult to see how it mattered, except perhaps to Frank O'Farrell, who might well have wished for that kind of backing from the directors a little earlier in the whole protracted drama with the player. Frank left the club with great bitterness, a feeling which persisted for many years, and perhaps will for the rest of his life. His departure certainly ended his career in football as a top manager, though he did return in an advisory capacity with Torquay for a while.

The senior players, from their point of view, saw Frank O'Farrell as someone distant and remote. Denis Law, for instance, once quipped: 'Frank O'Farrell – who's he?' He later summed up: 'Mr O'Farrell came as a stranger and went as a stranger.'

From where Frank stood, other teams had left United behind in terms of effort and team-work. He considered that players who had enjoyed success under the old regime resented his new methods. He likened Old Trafford to Sleepy Valley. The old stars were going out. Even that most dedicated and conscientious of players, Bobby Charlton, was on the brink of retirement. And all the time there had been the divisive problem of the wandering Best. Willie Morgan didn't pull any punches when he said:

> George thought he was the James Bond of soccer. He had everything he wanted and he pleased himself. He had money, girls and tremendous publicity. He lived from day to day. Until right at the end, he got away with it when he missed training or ran away. So he

Left: He broke all records and won everything possible, but remained completely unspoiled ... so wrote Sir Matt Busby in a tribute to the long-serving Bobby Charlton

didn't care. People always made excuses for him; he didn't even have to bother to make them himself.

The Irishman's letter of resignation was not quite the end of his association with Manchester United. He continued to flirt with the game, but with Slack Alice, the night club and disco he opened, claiming most of his attention it was not long before the aptly named Alice finally trapped her man.

Certainly there was need for a dynamic personality and bold leadership when the United directors looked round for Frank O'Farrell's successor, and of course in Tommy Docherty they found just the man.

But though things were bad on the field, there was still a lot going for the club. The ground itself, for instance, was looking better than ever, and the club was very healthy from the financial point of view. The enthusiasm for the club was boundless, as was shown on the night Glasgow Celtic came to Old Trafford to play a testimonial in honour of Bobby Charlton.

Tribute to Charlton

The date was 18 September 1972. The team had yet to win a League game that season, but the fans put that behind them to pay tribute to one of their favourites who had graced the game for 20 years. There were 60,538 people packed into Old Trafford probably feeling a little like Sir Matt Busby when he wrote in the testimonial programme:

> He has broken all records and won everything possible that there is to win. Yet he has remained completely unspoiled, still prepared to do more than his fair share for the cause of Manchester United. The shy boy has blossomed now into a man with a great sense of assurance, confidence and responsibility.

It was a night of nostalgia, which to a certain extent had been the problem for Frank O'Farrell. United had become a club living on its past. The giant was slumbering again . . . but not for long as Manchester braced itself for the arrival of Tommy Docherty, who reckoned he had the right prescription for an ailing club.

Below: Bobby Charlton made his debut for Manchester United in October 1956, scoring twice in a 4–2 win against Charlton Athletic at Old Trafford. He retired at the end of the season 1972–73 after a club record 604 League appearances. This is his farewell appearance at Old Trafford in the last but one match of the season with a guard of honour from the players of Manchester United and Sheffield United as he goes out for a presentation

The 1970s: Docherty and Sexton

Left: George Graham, the first player bought by Docherty as he added experience to the squad he had inherited from Frank O'Farrell. When his playing days had ended Graham himself moved into management. After four successful years at Millwall he returned to Arsenal, the club which sold him to United and quickly brought the championship trophy to Highbury

Docherty's 'wind of change' was a hurricane. It swept through Old Trafford, whipping up clouds of dust which for years had hidden the harsh truth from not only those in charge, but from the thousands who followed the team. Docherty could look at the situation from the position of the outsider, he had no axe to grind, neither had he any reason to feel that his actions would offend. It was no time to be sentimental, his target was success, and if it meant that his decisions might upset the normal pattern, he would make them anyway.

The re-building had to start quickly, and having been in charge of the Scottish side it was obvious where the new manager would turn. George Graham, from Arsenal's recent double-winning side, was bought for £120,000, a considerable increase on the £6,000 Docherty had paid for him when he signed him from Aston Villa in 1964 while manager of Chelsea. The story had hardly made the sports pages when another Scot was bought. Alex Forsyth, a sturdy full-back from Partick Thistle, signed for £100,000. Two days later Docherty added to his backroom staff by bringing Tommy Cavanagh from Hull City, where he left Terry Neill's coaching team.

Cavanagh's explosive approach was designed to bring discipline into the squad, and the Liverpudlian was keen to make a success of his new post. His and Docherty's paths had crossed briefly at Preston North End when Cavanagh had been signed as a young player while Docherty was already playing for the first team. While Tommy Docherty continued in the First Division, his friend went on to play for Stockport County, Huddersfield Town, Doncaster Rovers, Bristol City and Carlisle United before going into coaching. They had never played in the same League side but knew each other's methods.

Docherty's threat that he would not allow players to 'perform on their reputations' became apparent early in his reign as manager. 'There are players here who are not up to Manchester United standard,' he had said.

On 30 December United were due to play Everton at Old Trafford but the game was called off because of bad weather. It gave Tommy Docherty a little more breathing space. He needed time to get new players and to assess those already in his squad. As he said:

> I had other players in mind, but it was getting hold of them. I had already drawn up a list of who I would like to get and the chairman was fantastic, he just let me get on with it, he didn't want to see United in trouble and neither did I.

The first game under Docherty's direct influence was against Arsenal and the side was a mixture of the remnants of the Busby side of the 1960s, players brought in by O'Farrell and the Doc's new boys:

> Stepney, Young, Forsyth, Graham, Sadler, Buchan, Morgan, Kidd, Charlton, Law, Storey-Moore.

The changes did little to stop United slipping into further trouble and they lost 3–1. United had gone in the direction Docherty feared – instead of moving up the table they were now bottom.

The Scottish take-over

The rebuilding had to continue and the sports pages that weekend gave a clue as to who might be next on the Docherty shopping list. From Scotland came the news that Lou Macari had asked Glasgow Celtic for a transfer.

With United knocked out of the FA Cup 1–0 by Wolves, it was time to buy again, and Jim Holton a big, solid centre-half, was bought from Shrewsbury to increase the Docherty clan of Scots. Five days after the Cup defeat the club paid £200,000 for Macari, a record to a Scottish club at the time, and snatched him away from the grasp of Bill Shankly at Anfield.

Mick Martin, a Republic of Ireland midfield player, was bought from the Irish League club Bohemians, and was waiting in the wings as United played West Ham at Old Trafford, and the Stretford End became the tartan army.

There were 50,878 in Old Trafford to see goals from Bobby Charlton and Lou Macari, but still United could not take maximum points, and had to settle for a draw.

The crowd hoped for success for United and were perhaps disappointed that they had not seen a victory, but they certainly were not totally disheartened, because four days later just under 59,000 turned up for the re-arranged game with Everton, hoping that United could avenge the 2–0 defeat they had suffered at Goodison in the third game (and the third defeat) of the season. Everton were in mid-table, United bottom, and even though the game ended goalless it gave the United fans hope that the revival had started.

Since the sacking of Frank O'Farrell and the appointment of Tommy Docherty, United had hardly been out of the headlines and the Everton game produced another as Ted MacDougall stormed away from Old Trafford before the game ended, after being brought off and replaced by Brian Kidd.

Docherty's first win was on 10 February 1973, when once again a crowd of over 50,000 packed the stadium for the visit of Wolves.

The Wolverhampton players must have noticed a difference to the United side they had beaten a month earlier, not just from the new faces in the side, but from its vigorous approach. Bobby Charlton scored both goals in a victory which brought relief, and as it came the week after Jim Holton had earned a point by scoring in a 1–1 draw with Coventry, United rose to 18th position, almost as high in the table as they had been at any time that season.

Joy was short-lived. A week later at Ipswich they lost 4–1 to Bobby Robson's side, and again the threat of relegation loomed large.

The game at Ipswich turned out to be Ted MacDougall's last for the club. A week later he was sold to West Ham for £150,000.

Charlton retires and Law is transferred

Against all odds, United now had their best run of the season, and wins over Newcastle and Southampton sandwiching a draw at Tottenham kept three clubs below them in the table – West Brom, Norwich and Crystal Palace. They played Norwich next, and won 1–0 thanks to a Mick Martin goal. Four days later they beat Crystal Palace, and then they drew 2–2 at Stoke to ease themselves up into 16th place. Surely they were safe now.

Bobby Charlton took the opportunity to tell Tommy Docherty that he was retiring. The player who had been Britain's best ambassador for football had decided that he would go out at the top: 'I have had a wonderful life in the greatest game in the world, and I always said that only I would know when I would want to retire. That time has come, and I'll leave the game with some marvellous memories.'

Eighteenth place was the reward for United's run, and Crystal Palace and West Bromwich Albion were relegated. But although the campaign was over United were still in the news. Denis Law and Tony Dunne were given free transfers as Tommy Docherty prepared his squad for the following season, and the move was not seen as a compliment by Law.

Docherty promised the supporters that the future was bright: 'We have some good young players coming through. Boys like Sammy McIlroy, Brian Greenhoff and Gerry Daly are all going to make it to the top. All they need is time.'

But did Docherty have time? His critics were swift to point out that Denis Law, who had signed for Manchester City during the close season, still had his golden touch, and had scored twice on his debut against Birmingham City. Could Law still have offered United something had he been allowed to stay?

Ironically, no sooner had Law and Charlton left Old Trafford than the third member of the trinity which had achieved greatness, George Best, decided to return. George left behind the sunshine of Spain and told his club that he would like to play again. The prodigal son was allowed the opportunity.

Then nobody realised the extent of Best's drink problem, and it was only later that it became apparent that it was one reason for George's waywardness. He reappeared on 20 October 1973, not fully match fit, yet capable of demonstrating that his skills had not deserted him in a 1–0 win over Birmingham City. Mick Martin replaced him when his tiredness showed.

The only goal of that game was scored not by Best, but by Alex Stepney, the goalkeeper. It was his second goal of the season, the first being against Leicester at Old Trafford, when United were awarded a penalty. He had filled the role in pre-season friendlies, and Docherty had handed him the task when the new campaign began.

With Alex Forsyth still out of the side, Tommy Docherty signed another full-back, this time a recognised left-sided player, Stewart Houston, from Frank Blunstone's former club, Brentford. Docherty had come across the player briefly during

his last months as manager of Chelsea, and the tall, strong Scot held his place in the side for the remainder of the season.

Fracas at Maine Road

By early March, when United travelled to Bramall Lane to face Sheffield United, only one side had a worse record than them in the First Division and that was Norwich City, who added a twist to the story by signing none other than Ted MacDougall from West Ham in an effort to stay in the top flight. United won at Sheffield thanks to a Lou Macari goal. Then, eleven days later came a remarkable game, the clash with Manchester City.

The tension was higher than that of a normal derby and it reached boiling point when suddenly the diminutive Macari and City's rugged defender Mike Doyle began throwing punches at one another, close to the touchline in front of the main grandstand. The boxing mismatch was quickly over as players from both sides intervened, but referee Clive Thomas had his hands full to prevent a battle as the staff from both benches ran on to the field. The linesmen raced to help, and the Welsh referee ordered Macari and Doyle off.

They refused to go.

With the crowd howling, and outbreaks of fighting amongst supporters, Thomas marched both sets of players off the field, and it seemed at first as if he had abandoned the game, only for both teams to return minutes later without the two offenders.

The game had ended in a 0–0 draw and the point taken from City did little to help the plight of United. By the end of March they still stared relegation in the face and it seemed impossible for them to survive, especially as the change in the system meant that they had to reach the haven of 19th, and not 20th place.

Another Scot was bought, Jim McCalliog from Wolves, and another member of the European Cup-winning side played his final game for the club: Brian Kidd's last game was the 3–1 win at Chelsea which once more gave hope that Docherty could again play Houdini.

United were living from day to day, hanging on to the First Division by the tips of their fingers. Then they won three successive games – at Norwich then at home to Newcastle and Everton – with McCalliog scoring three times.

City and Law send United down

United had two games remaining and their rivals in relegation were ending the season that afternoon. Norwich City were bottom with 29 points, United above them with 32. Occupying the new relegation position of 20th place were Southampton on 34 points, one behind the club above them, Birmingham City. United's lifeline was thin but it was still there. If Birmingham were to lose and United could win their two remaining fixtures, the Midlands club would be relegated and United would survive. Southampton were away to Everton, and United at home to City!

The 57,000 crowd was hushed at half-time when the electronic scoreboard at Old Trafford printed out the scores from the other games . . . Everton 0 Southampton 2, Birmingham 2 Norwich 1. The derby game was goalless, but still there was hope. If United could win, and Norwich fight back.

Then, with eight minutes remaining, the death blow was struck. Through a ruck of players the ball bobbled and rebounded. The scrambling Alex Stepney was helpless as it passed out of his reach. A City player had his back to the goal, only feet away from the line. He back-heeled the ball over the line, and turned slowly upfield as his supporters and team-mates leapt in celebration. Denis Law had relegated the club that rejected him, but he felt only a bitter sadness.

As it happened, Birmingham won their game, so no matter what the outcome of the derby United could not have stayed in the top Division that they had occupied since before the Second World War. Docherty wept in the dressing room, but bravely faced the media only minutes after the game was called off. He said: 'Words can't describe how sick I feel at the moment. I can't believe that this has happened, but I know it has. All I can say is that we have gone down with the makings of a good side, and that hopefully that side will bring us back again as quickly as possible.'

Manchester United were in the Second Division: after the glory years of the 1960s, the brilliance of the 1950s and the building of the 1940s, the unbelievable had become a reality.

Tommy Docherty's team had been improving but he knew that there were areas which needed to be strengthened, and he was quick to move. In cloak and dagger style Stuart Pearson was signed from Cavanagh's former club Hull City. The transfer – £200,000 cash plus the lanky Peter Fletcher – went through on the eve of the Liverpool–Newcastle FA Cup final, and was lost in the publicity previewing the Wembley game.

United bounce straight back

United stepped into the unknown the following season, 1974–75, at London's Brisbane Road, Orient's ground having the claim to stage the first Manchester United Second Division game since 7 May 1938. United won 2–0 with goals from Stewart Houston and Willie Morgan.

Attendances at all games had risen, and at Old Trafford huge audiences witnessed the revival. When Sunderland, lying second, came to Manchester the biggest Second Division crowd in United's history turned out to watch the game: 60,585. The home supporters were stunned when Sunderland took a 2–1 lead through two goals from Billy Hughes, but such was the confidence of United that they fought back and goals from Morgan and McIlroy pushed them to a 3–2 win. Pearson had scored the first. It was a victory

Left: The sixth of September 1973 and George Best is back at Old Trafford. The bearded wanderer agreed to play again after retiring from football but his stay with United was both turbulent and short and after 12 appearances and two goals Best had gone again. 'It is one of the tragedies of life that we never saw the full potential of George,' said Tommy Docherty

in the style the long-serving supporters had come to associate with United.

A week later, however, there was major upset in another thrilling game. Jim Holton, by now well established as a Scottish international, broke his leg in a 4–4 draw at Sheffield Wednesday's Hillsborough. It turned out to be Holton's last senior game for the club.

The cricketing Arnie Sidebottom and Steve James filled the gap left by the big man and took United into the New Year still ahead of the pack, but Docherty was not yet satisfied. He sold McCalliog to Southampton and used the £40,000 he received to buy university graduate Steve Coppell from Tranmere Rovers. Coppell had played for the Wirral club while completing his studies at Liverpool University, and came on as substitute for United in the 4–0 victory over Cardiff City at Old Trafford, as a replacement for Willie Morgan.

Coppell's arrival signalled the end for Morgan, who played just four more games before leaving to join his former club Burnley during the summer of 1975. Morgan's departure was not amicable. He left after a series of much publicised incidents, and then a television condemnation of Tommy Docherty led to him being sued by his former manager for libel. The case was heard in 1978 and this in turn led to Docherty being charged with perjury after withdrawing from the first battle. Docherty appeared at the Old Bailey in 1981 and was found not guilty.

With Coppell firmly established in the side, nothing could stop United from winning promotion, and a Macari goal at the Dell put United back in the First Division on 5 April 1975. A fortnight later they were confirmed as Second Division Champions after drawing 2–2 with Notts County.

United's start to the 1975–76 season was remarkable. They won five of their first six games, three of them away from home. By mid-September they had been top of the First Division for five weeks. Tommy Jackson, an experienced midfield player with Everton and Nottingham Forest, had been added to the side, and by November, after a loss of form had seen the side slump to fifth place, Docherty paid out £70,000 for another bright young player, Millwall winger Gordon Hill.

Cup Final disappointment

While League form had slipped, United had a great run in the FA Cup, reaching the final. Home wins over Oxford and Peterborough, and a 2–1 away victory at Leicester, had seen them tipped to do well in the competition. Having reached the quarter-finals it looked as if their hopes had been dashed when they could only manage a draw with Wolves at Old Trafford on 6 March. But three days later they pulled off a remarkable victory at Molineux, taking the game 3–2 in extra time.

Their opponents in the semi-final were Derby County, one of the challengers for the League Championship, but neither side, each at one time chasing the 'double', were to win any honours. Gordon Hill's two goals took United to Wembley where they were to lose to Southampton.

By the time the 1976–77 season started only Alex Stepney and Martin Buchan were left of the players brought to the club by managers before Tommy Docherty. The Doc had built his team, and young hopefuls were emerging from Blunstone's efforts with the youth teams. Jimmy Nicholl was able to force the right full-back's role away from Alex Forsyth, Arthur Albiston proved himself to be a player of promise, and David McCreery was on the edge of the team being used regularly as substitute.

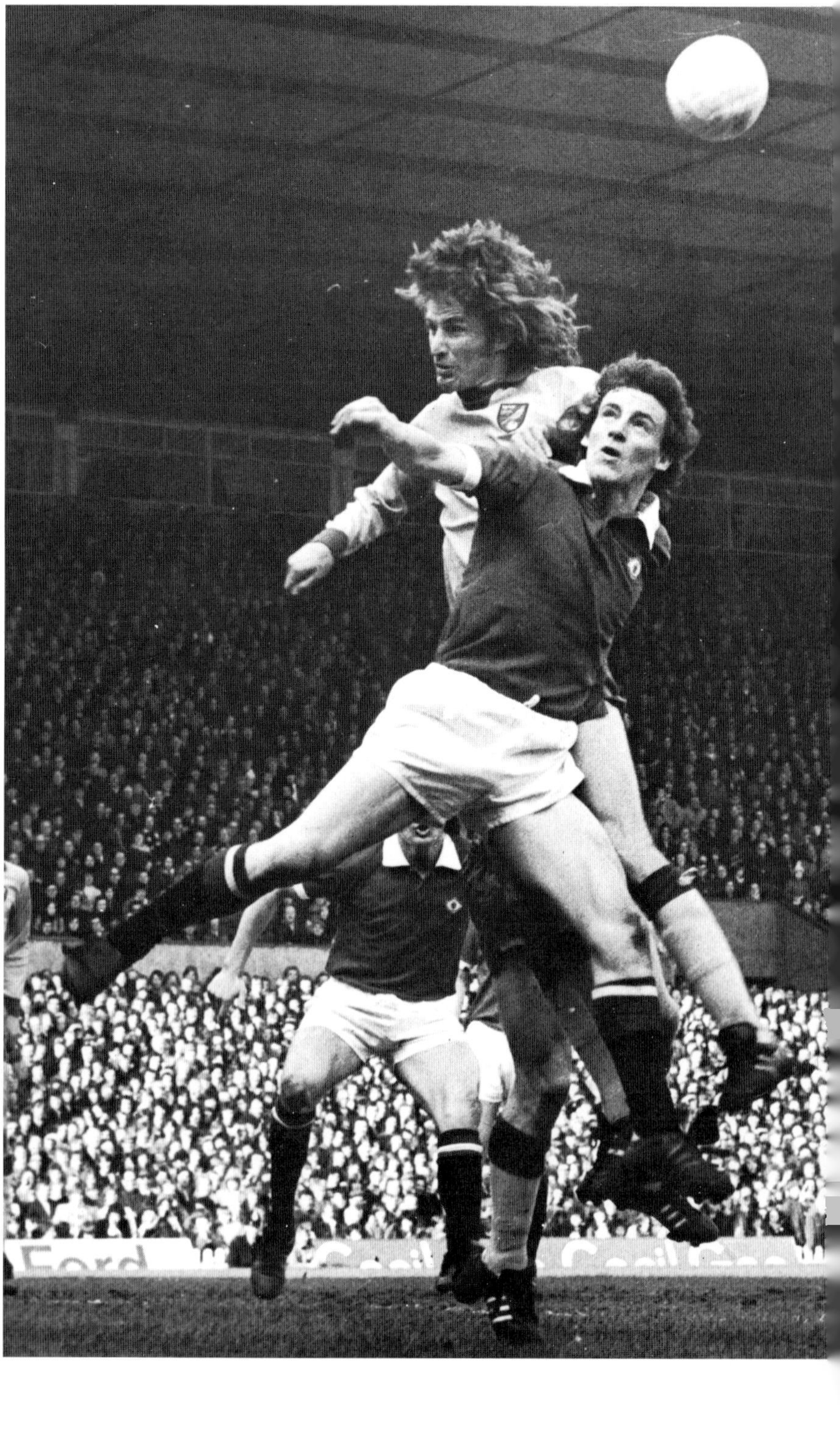

Right: The curtain comes down on the 1974–75 season and United are champions of the Second Division. Martin Buchan holds the trophy as manager Docherty and the rest of the team acknowledge the cheers of 58,769 supporters before the game with Blackpool. United were in buoyant mood winning 4–0 with goals from Stuart Pearson (2), Brian Greenhoff and Lou Macari

Yet another link with the European Cup side of 1968 had left the club. Pat Crerand, who had been appointed Docherty's assistant, left to move into full management. There were rumours of clashes between the two Scots and Docherty was later to reveal his feelings in his book:

> I dislike Pat Crerand, but my reasons for appointing him my number two were twofold. I did it because at the time I thought that he could do a good job, and I also thought that it was what Sir Matt Busby wanted.

The United manager claimed that Crerand left the club bearing a grudge against Docherty because he had not recommended him for the post of assistant manager at Glasgow Celtic:

> He must have been very disappointed to have left United at his own request, only to see us reach two successive Cup finals.

United reached that second final after a slump in League form of alarming proportions. At one stage they led the First Division, then went eight games without a victory and slumped to 17th. Out came the Docherty cheque book again and Jimmy Greenhoff, older brother of Brian, was bought from Stoke City. Luck had taken United through to round five and the draw for that part of the competition made the headlines: 'United to meet Saints – play it again Reds'.

Southampton versus Manchester United, a repeat of the 1976 final, and at the Dell. Had United's luck run out? No home advantage, and facing a side that had already beaten them, they had to be second favourites.

It ended in a 2–2 draw.

Two Jimmy Greenhoff goals saw United into the sixth round with a 2–1 win, David Peach again scoring for Southampton to nurse the unhappy memory of having netted three times and ending on the losing side.

The quarter-final draw gave United home advantage against Aston Villa, and Houston and Macari scored in a 2–1 win in front of the fourth successive crowd of over 57,000 in games at Old Trafford. The biggest of those attendances had been for the League game with Leeds United, when 60,612 filled the ground . . . and it was Leeds who provided the semi-final opposition.

In the other semi-final Liverpool and Everton met at Maine Road, while United travelled into Yorkshire to face Leeds at Hillsborough.

Wembley again

Within a quarter of an hour United had booked their ticket to Wembley. They played with confidence as Leeds seemed to be overcome by the occasion. First Jimmy Greenhoff scored, then Steve Coppell, and United's lively forward line continued to cause problems for the Leeds defence all through the match.

Left: Steve Coppell's graduation into the Second Division was swift. During his university days he played with Tranmere Rovers, but even though he was on the doorsteps of Liverpool and Everton he slipped through the Merseyside net and was bought for a bargain £40,000 in April 1975. He made his debut as substitute against Cardiff City and was a regular in the side until injury forced his retirement eight years and three managers later

All hopes of the Championship vanished in the days after the semi-final, as the team picked up only one point in four games. Then 18 days before Wembley, United lost to Liverpool at Anfield and Tommy Docherty amazed everyone by saying: 'We have learned something tonight. We can beat Liverpool at Wembley.'

Had they discovered the Achilles heel of Paisley's side? There were many who watched the 1–0 defeat who felt that United had been the better team, but had given away an unlucky goal to the side which was aiming for an incredible treble of League, FA Cup and European Cup. Kevin Keegan had scored in what, amazingly, was to be Liverpool's last win of the League campaign. They drew three out of their last four fixtures and lost the last, yet still won the Championship.

As for United's run-in to Wembley, they were hit by a devastating blow in a rough-house of a game at Bristol City when Stewart Houston was stretchered off with a broken ankle. Wembley was just a fortnight away when Arthur Albiston, a 19-year-old Scot, was called into the side. He played three full games before the final.

United and Docherty win the Cup

Liverpool were favourites to win. As League Champions and European Cup finalists their pedigree far outweighed Docherty's Dynamos, but it was United who rose to the occasion. The final was played at a hectic pace, Liverpool pressurising young Albiston, who showed that he had a bright future ahead of him as he handled the foraging of McDermott, and the speed of Heighway who switched wings to cause confusion.

United held out till half-time, and realised as the second half started that they were not playing an invincible side. With five minutes gone Jimmy Greenhoff broke downfield and found Pearson with a precision pass. The striker ran forward, brushing aside a challenge and fired a low shot towards the right-hand post. Clemence in the Liverpool goal seemed late to move to cover it and the ball passed his outstretched left arm before he could fully dive. United were ahead!

Back came Liverpool and a Joey Jones cross from the left was hit firmly by Case into the roof of Alex Stepney's net – two goals within three minutes and the cheers of the United fans choked by the sudden upsurge from Liverpool.

Another three minutes and United were ahead again thanks to a remarkable goal, and a strike which had a certain amount of luck attached to it. Tommy Smith and Jimmy Greenhoff tangled, Smith blocking a scoring chance from the United forward. The ball ran off to Macari who fired at goal, but the shot was well off target, and Clemence moved to his left to cover. The shot hit Greenhoff who was still between Macari and Smith, and deflected from his chest, over his right shoulder and into the net well beyond Clemence, for the winning goal.

The celebrations went on into the night. An official banquet at the Royal Lancaster Hotel was followed by a private party for the players and officials, their wives and friends at the Royal Garden Hotel where they were staying.

Martin Buchan ordered a trolley full of champagne and the joy of winning the cup was apparent . . . but Tommy Docherty had left the group to walk in Hyde Park, alone with his

Left: Stuart Pearson and Gordon Hill hold the FA Cup aloft after their 1977 2–1 win over Liverpool, but before the next visit to Wembley both had ended their playing days at Old Trafford. Hill was bought by Docherty after he was appointed manager of Derby County later in 1978 and Pearson stayed on before injury led to him being left out of the side and his announcement on the morning of the 1979 Cup final that he wouldn't play for United again

Above: United are back. Lou Macari scores his 16th goal of the 1974–75 season to clinch promotion one year and 21 days after the sadness of relegation. The 1–0 win at Southampton was followed by victory over Fulham at Old Trafford and a draw at Notts County secured the Second Division championship by three points from rivals Aston Villa

thoughts. He spent most of the night strolling in the silence of the park, making what for him was an important personal decision. Docherty was deciding how to break the news, before the media discovered it and splashed it, that he was leaving his wife to set up permanent home with another woman. That the woman was Mary Brown, wife of the club physiotherapist Laurie, made the situation more difficult than if she had no connections with United.

Docherty forced to go

News of the love affair became public. Accusing fingers were pointed at the club, and at the couple who had been forced to make the heartbreaking decision of ending two marriages in order that they could share their lives together. 'The Mary Brown Affair' was headline news for weeks and eventually, even though he claimed that he was given an assurance that his private life would not affect his position as manager, Tommy Docherty was called before the board.

The meeting was held in Louis Edwards' home in Alderley Edge. The directors met the man who had taken their club to Wembley 44 days earlier and asked for his resignation. He refused, and was dismissed.

Ten years after their private lives had become public, Tommy Docherty and Mary Brown were free to marry and did so.

Dave Sexton arrives

Just ten days after Docherty's dismissal, Dave Sexton was appointed manager, following in the Scot's footsteps for the third time in his career. Sexton succeeded Docherty at Chelsea, and Docherty had briefly been manager of Queen's Park Rangers before Sexton.

Having left Loftus Road Sexton realised the size of the task which lay ahead of him at Old Trafford. He was following the most successful manager the club had seen since Busby, and a man who was extremely popular with the supporters. The extrovert Docherty was a complete contrast to the introvert Sexton and Sexton would find him a hard act to follow.

The 1977–78 season could have had no better start for Sexton, Lou Macari scoring a hat-trick in a 4–1 home victory over Birmingham City – but this was the team Docherty had built and the supporters were quick to remind the new manager of this fact, chanting the Doc's name regularly.

It was these same supporters who involved the club in one of the most embarrassing moments in its history when the first season under Sexton was just a month old. Crowd trouble in St Etienne resulted in United at first being banned from the Cup Winners' Cup, then reinstated and ordered to play the second leg of their tie with the French club at around 300 kilometres from Manchester. They chose Home Park, Plymouth.

Sexton made his first major move in the transfer market on 6 January 1978 when he signed Joe Jordan from Leeds United for £350,000, but the big striker did not play for almost a month because he was 'Cup-tied' and under suspension. During his enforced absence United were knocked out of the FA Cup by West Brom after scraping through the third round with a replay victory over Carlisle.

On 9 February, Sexton bought again, bringing centre-half Gordon McQueen from Leeds for £495,000 to join his best friend Joe Jordan. Jordan had made his debut on 8 February, and McQueen made his first appearance at Anfield 17 days later. Even so, it was 8 April before United won a game with both their signings in the side.

A series of draws during March kept United in mid-table, and then in April the supporters were stunned when Gordon Hill, one of the most popular players in the side, was sold for £250,000. The buyer? Tommy Docherty, now managing Derby County.

Four victories, against QPR, Norwich, West Ham and Bristol, gave United the chance to end the season on a high note, but tenth in the table was not looked on as a sign of success by the fans and it was obvious that Dave Sexton would have to bring them trophies if his popularity was to match Docherty's.

The following season, 1978–79, saw the visit of Real Madrid for the club's centenary game with Dave Sexton proud to be in charge:

> No club has captured the imagination like Manchester United, and it is a great thrill for me to be here. But rather than looking back over what has happened before, I'd like to look ahead.

I feel that in the next ten years there will be changes. Football is a family game and I would like to see stadiums providing areas for family seating.

Sponsorship is another aspect of the game which can be developed and I wouldn't be surprised to see players wearing shirts bearing a sponsor's name before long.

We must also get ready to accept foreign players into our game, as well as some of our players going abroad. The only snag in this area, as far as I can see it, is our taxation system does not make a move to this country as attractive as one abroad.

United had opened the new season with Roche in goal and, despite winning only five games by November, were in the top six. They had been knocked out of the League Cup in a surprising game, Third Division Watford scoring twice through Luther Blissett, a self-confessed United supporter. This brought a comment from his chairman Elton John, which would no doubt be outweighed by other games in the future:

This has been the greatest moment of my time in football. To come to a place like Old Trafford and beat Manchester United is an incredible feeling – now I'd like to see us use all this enthusiasm to get into the Second Division.

On 11 October 1978 United were away to Birmingham City and lost 5–1. Immediately Sexton moved for the chequebook and agreed to buy Coventry City goalkeeper Jim Blyth. He said that Roche's confidence had been shattered, not just by the Birmingham scoreline, but by the lack of support he was getting from the fans, who felt that Stepney was being wasted in the Central League side. Blyth arrived at Old Trafford to face the bright lights of television crews who had been told of the signing. The media gathered for interviews and photographs, but then the extraordinary news came through that the deal was off. Blyth had not passed the insurance medical, and was not eligible to play.

Sexton was in a difficult position. Stepney had not played any first team games, Roche had already been told by the move to sign Blyth that he was no longer being considered as first choice goalkeeper, and United were 48 hours away from their next game. So on 18 November the name of Gary Bailey was written on the team sheet for the first time, and the tall young blond faced Ipswich Town, the side from his Suffolk birthplace.

Bailey had arrived at Old Trafford after playing university football in South Africa, where he had lived since his family emigrated there when he was four years old. Goalkeeping was in Bailey's blood, as his father Roy had kept goal for Ipswich Town from 1955 to 1964, and had been a member of the 1962 League Championship-winning side.

Young Gary Bailey had a steady debut in a 2–0 victory, and his form kept him in the side for the rest of the season.

The possibility of a Wembley return ended all rumblings about poor League form, but luck was again against the team when the sixth-round draw paired them with Tottenham at White Hart Lane. When a solid, professional performance earned them a replay at Old Trafford, the scent of Wembley was really in their nostrils. In the second game goals from McIlroy and Jordan powered United through to their third FA Cup semi-final in four years, but once more it was Liverpool who stood in their way.

The semi-final was at Maine Road and it was Liverpool who struck the first blow, Kenny Dalglish putting them ahead, but Jordan restored the balance. There was a moment of panic when Liverpool were awarded a hotly disputed penalty, but when McDermott missed United rallied, and Brian Greenhoff followed his brother's example by scoring a vital Cup goal to put them ahead. Six minutes from the end Hansen equalised, forcing United into their eighth game of the Cup campaign.

Four nights later, at Goodison Park, the elder Greenhoff scored yet another crucial goal, and

Below: Gordon McQueen lost a large percentage of his playing career through injury, but still became a popular figure at Old Trafford. The tall centre-half scored 26 goals in his 228 appearances, many of them spectacular headers from corner kicks and his determination won the hearts of the supporters. A cruel stroke of bad luck robbed him of a place in Scotland's World Cup side of 1978, when he slid into a goal-post, damaging his knee, during an international in Scotland

although Liverpool at times laid siege in the United half of the field, they were beaten. United were back at Wembley, and Dave Sexton had the chance of emulating Docherty and finally erasing all the disadvantageous comparisons.

The 'five-minute' final

In the build-up to Wembley Brian Greenhoff was injured, but felt he would be fit for the final. There was competition for places even as the side relaxed at Selsdon Park again, their 'lucky' hotel. Would Grimes edge out the nervous Thomas? Would young Ritchie's strength earn him a place? Sexton named his side. The eleven who had beaten Liverpool would start the final against Arsenal:

Bailey, Nicholl, Albiston, McIlroy, McQueen, Buchan, Coppell, Jimmy Greenhoff, Jordan, Macari, Thomas.

For the massive United contingent amongst the supporters the final was a dull affair. The yellow and blue banners of Arsenal were held high as first Talbot, and then Frank Stapleton scored before half-time. Sexton's side seemed to offer little resistance and all United had won was the toss of the coin to decide who would wear their normal red on the big day.

Then, with five minutes remaining United found hope. Gordon McQueen, lunging forward, scored. The United chants at last were louder than those of the Londoners. Suddenly supporters who had been preparing to make an unhappy exit from the stadium stopped gathering their belongings to turn their attention to the game again. Journalists who had already written the story of United's defeat began to scribble new words on their notepads, and when Sammy McIlroy danced through the tiring Arsenal defence and slid the ball into the net for a second goal, the game took on a whole new life.

The scores were level with seconds rather than minutes left. United had earned extra time and, looking the fresher team, were looking forward to the whistle and the extra half-hour.

Instead, Liam Brady ran forward for Arsenal, crossing into the United half unchallenged. Macari went after him, but Brady's pass out to the left found Graham Rix. He ran forward again evading his opponents and sent over a high cross. Bailey appeared to hesitate, expecting his defence to cover, and Alan Sunderland forced the ball home. Arsenal had won what became known as 'the five-minute final', 3–2.

Seven days later Dave Sexton continued the building of a side which he could call his own, and bought Ray Wilkins from Chelsea for a massive £777,777, as two more of Docherty's players were sold. The first of these was David McCreery, bought by the new Queen's Park Rangers manager Tommy Docherty. He had joined the relegated London club on the eve of United's Cup final. The next player sold was Brian Greenhoff, reversing his brother's move by joining Leeds for £350,000. The side which began the 1979–80 season contained five players introduced by Sexton.

The start to the new campaign was one of the best for several years, four wins and two draws taking United to the top of the table by mid-September, and there was optimism that the 13-year gap since the last Championship win might be bridged. By the turn of the year the lowest position United had filled was third, and this followed their first defeat away to Wolves. At home they were unbeaten, but they were out of the League Cup, having lost at Norwich.

Criticism of fans and chairman

However, it was events away from the field which made the headlines. First, two Middlesbrough fans were killed when a wall collapsed on spectators as they left Ayrsome Park, and accusing fingers were pointed at United's rowdy supporters. Then a television programme accused the club of operating outside the rules.

Granada Television's 'World in Action' produced by Geoffrey Seed, a United supporter, accused chairman Louis Edwards of instigating payments to young players as a method of persuading them to join the club. It claimed that United operated a secret cash fund to use for matters such as this, and also accused the chairman of irregular share dealings. Louis Edwards strongly denied the accusations, which became the subject of a joint inquiry by the Football League and the Football Association, and said: 'I have never done anything at Manchester United that I am ashamed of. I have always been proud to be chairman of this great club, and anything I have done has been in its best interests.'

A month after the allegations Louis Edwards died of a heart attack, to be succeeded by his son Martin as chairman of the club.

The battle for the Championship continued between Liverpool and United but an amazing scoreline on 1 March caused concern: Ipswich Town 6 United 0. And that match included two penalties saved by Bailey!

Since his arrival, Ray Wilkins had missed only two games. The first was the home defeat by Wolves, the second the trouncing at Ipswich in a game which Sir Matt Busby, the club's president-elect, described thus:

> It was not the sort of result to make you feel confident of winning the Championship, but I remember that one player was outstanding. Arnold Muhren, the Dutch mid-fielder was brilliant – his part in the victory for his side was one of great importance, and he linked up well with his fellow countryman Frans Thijssen.

Was Sexton's premonition about the influx of foreign players coming true? Perhaps it was, because United's substitute that afternoon was Nikola Jovanovic, the Yugoslav defender, signed from Red Star Belgrade.

From the Ipswich disgrace to the end of the season only three more games were lost, the final result deciding the destiny of the title. The first of

Left: The 'five-minute final' and United celebrate as Sammy McIlroy (rising on one knee, right) scores an incredible equaliser. United trailed 2–0 with five minutes to go, then Gordon McQueen put them back in the game before McIlroy's goal. Joy was short-lived as straight from the kick-off Arsenal scored another to win the 1979 FA Cup

these upsets came at Nottingham's City Ground, where in an ill-tempered game Sammy McIlroy was ordered off by Clive Thomas after disputing a penalty from which John Robertson put the home side in front. Forest won 2–0, with Garry Birtles scoring the second.

Three days later United and Liverpool began their run-in to the end of the season when they met at Old Trafford, and a 2–1 win for United narrowed the gap to four points with six games remaining. The game also saw Jimmy Greenhoff playing his first full match of the season – and scoring the winner.

During what turned out to be the club's most successful season since 1968, as far as League position was concerned, United were accused by the media of lacking warmth. Under a headline of 'Cold Trafford', Dave Sexton's weakness in handling day-to-day press inquiries was exposed. The article alleged that Sexton was so unlike his predecessor that journalists who specialised in reporting the club's affairs were having difficulty in going about their work.

His approach was directly opposite to that of Docherty, who was never out of the news, eager to talk about anything whether it involved his club or not. Yet, as the Championship battle reached its end, Sexton was willing to give his views: 'We are in with a definite chance. If we can do well in the last six fixtures then we can win the title, but we are also hoping for mistakes from Liverpool.'

Five successive wins following the Liverpool game was the players' response to the challenge, but it was to no avail. On the last afternoon of the season United lost 2–0 at Leeds, Liverpool won 4–1 at Anfield against Aston Villa, and the race was lost by two points.

Injuries sink Sexton

Injuries became a millstone around Dave Sexton's neck. Slowly they pulled him down, causing him to use 16 players in the first three fixtures. Nothing went right for United. In the first game Jordan limped off with a knee injury. Gary Bailey was able to disguise the fact that he had dislocated a finger making a save towards the end of the game, but he too was ruled out for the next two matches.

In the second game Grimes was hurt, and in the third Moran's bravery cost him dearly. He lunged at Birmingham's Keith Bertschin, and badly twisted his ankle, to be replaced by League debutant Mike Duxbury.

'We are in a desperate position as far as injuries go,' Sexton said after the game, 'but we aren't too worried. There's a long way to go in the season and I'm sure we'll get things right once we have our full squad back again.' And as for Moran's injury: 'This is the sort of thing we can expect from a player like Kevin, he is very brave and strong. He'd run through brick walls if you asked him, and he never thinks about personal safety.'

Moran, who had joined United from Pegasus, was missing for the next five League games and the two-legged League Cup clash with Coventry City. These League Cup-ties saw United out of the competition by early September, losing 1–0 at Old Trafford, and by the same scoreline at Highfield Road, with spurned goalkeeper Jim Blyth adding irony to the event by playing in both games for Coventry without conceding a goal.

Scoring goals was proving a problem and the club went six games with only one successful strike and that came from central defender Jovanovic in a 1–1 draw with Sunderland. By 13 September 1980 United had won just one game in the League, and drawn three of their four other First Division games. Sexton had tried Andy Ritchie at striker, alongside the rejuvenated Jimmy Greenhoff, who was fighting through the pain of a pelvic injury, and elsewhere gambled with young players. He was even forced to recall Chris McGrath from the reserve pool for his first game in three years. McGrath played one game, against Birmingham at St Andrews, and that was his last appearance for the club.

Right: Ray Wilkins was a fine ambassador for United both on and off the field. Injury led to him losing the captaincy of club and country to his friend Bryan Robson but it never affected his dedication to the game. Wilkins was bought by Dave Sexton in 1979 having been signed by the United manager when he was a 15-year-old starting his career with Chelsea. Ron Atkinson transferred him to AC Milan who paid a then record £1.5 million for the midfield player

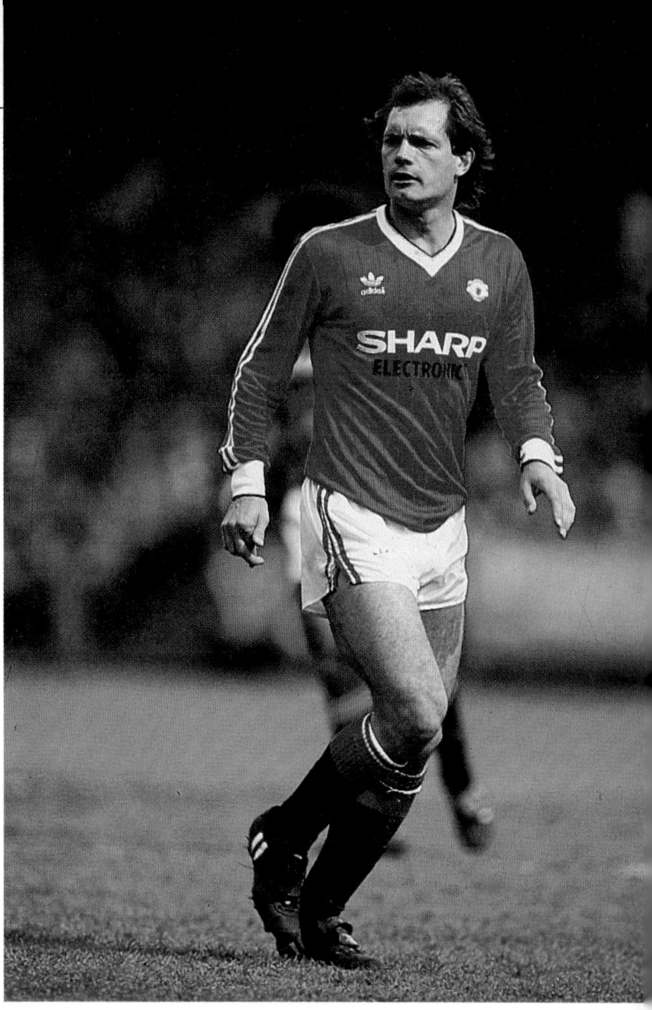

Ritchie also played his last game for United early that season in the 0–0 draw at Tottenham, which came four days after the League Cup exit. Injuries and the continuing poor results were increasing the pressure on Sexton to pull the club out of its misery.

By mid-October the murmurings of discontent were growing louder, as the injury list grew longer. Buchan had been added to the ever-growing numbers unfit to play, and McQueen aggravated his injury again when he tried a return in the derby game at Old Trafford which ended in another predictable draw. After 12 League games there had been one defeat, but only three wins and the eight drawn games were the subject of most contention.

The unhappy Ritchie was sold to Brighton, and the £500,000 paid for the teenager was used to balance the books when Sexton plunged for Garry Birtles of Nottingham Forest, a prolific scorer who had netted 32 times in his 87 League games under Brian Clough. This, it was felt, was a better pedigree than young Ritchie's 13 goals in 26 full appearances. Ritchie was, however, still a month away from his 20th birthday, and revealed after the move that he felt he had been the target of too much criticism from assistant manager Tommy Cavanagh, and this contributed to his eagerness to leave.

Birtles cost United a massive £1,250,000, the largest amount up to that time (October 1980) that the club had paid for any player. His inclusion in the side brought two successive victories, although Birtles himself failed to score.

After defeats at Arsenal and to West Brom, United stepped into 1981 with three games against Ritchie's club Brighton. Such is the irony of football that the clubs were paired against each other in the third round of the FA Cup a week before their League meeting at Old Trafford.

Ritchie was given a rapturous welcome by the Old Trafford crowd as Birtles returned for his first game in a month after he, too, had joined the ranks of the walking wounded with an ankle injury early in December. Those same supporters joined the travelling fans from Brighton to sing the praises of their former favourite as he headed his new club into a two-goal lead at half-time. The headlines were already being written when United staged a fightback to draw 2–2 and earn a replay at Brighton four days later.

United won 2–0 and Garry Birtles scored his first goal since his expensive move. Wilkins played in both matches although it was obvious that he was below full fitness.

Again fate played its part in the outcome of the season. Having beaten Brighton in the Cup, United were drawn at Nottingham Forest, meaning a return for Birtles. However, unlike Ritchie, Birtles was unable to score against his old club and Forest won 1–0. With 15 matches left there was only the Championship to aim for and there was speculation that Dave Sexton's future lay in the balance.

Would the selling of Ritchie, a player who had cost the club nothing, prove to be an expensive mistake by Sexton? Certainly Birtles had not shown anything like the goalscoring he had produced for Clough, and the result was a slump from the end of January until mid-March, when the club went without a win.

The solidarity given to the defence by the presence of McQueen had been a vital factor missing from the side. He had been out for all but four League games by the time that a revival began.

United were in mid-table and had lost four out of five games, one of these at home to Leeds United, when a lacklustre performance had the crowd shouting for Sexton's head. Was this the type of result to get a manager the sack? Sexton's response was a cold stare, and a reluctant reply: 'That's not the sort of question I can answer. We have had terrible injury problems this season, and everyone knows it.'

His players' response after the fourth of those defeats was to stage a late rally of nine games without losing, and after McQueen's return, seven successive victories, which was the best run by the team since the days of Busby in 1964. But it was too late and on 30 April 1980, five days after the closing victory over Norwich was watched by an Old Trafford crowd of 12,000 fewer than that of the previous season, Dave Sexton lost his job.

He was stunned by the news, but refused to criticise the club. He had taken United higher than anyone since Busby yet had failed, but he remained the gentleman to the end, saying only in private: 'There can be few managers who have lost their job after seven consecutive victories . . .'

The 1980s: Atkinson and Ferguson

Left: Republic of Ireland striker Frank Stapleton eludes Mark Lawrenson of Liverpool, one of his international colleagues. Only a decision to move to Anfield rather than Old Trafford prevented the two playing together at club level. Stapleton was bought by Atkinson in the summer of 1981 in a move which caused ill-feeling between United and the directors of Arsenal the club which reluctantly sold him

Below: The Dutch master, Arnold Muhren whose move to Old Trafford came when his contract at Ipswich Town ended. Muhren later returned to the Netherlands to continue his career with Ajax and in 1988 was in the Dutch side which won the European Championships in West Germany

Success, it would seem, is not the sole criteria by which the manager of Manchester United is judged. He can achieve success on the field yet still fail in the eyes of his employers, or the majority of supporters, or both. It is not the success but how it is achieved which matters most, and the narrowness of the line between pleasing board and fans or leaving them cold illustrates the fragility of the manager's position.

The man walking the tightrope may well be able to cross from end to end without a fall, but if he does so with no excitement for his audience, no hint that he might slip, then what is the point of him being up there in the first place?

Docherty walked the tightrope with a touch of flair and showmanship, yet still stumbled. Sexton was sure-footed but lost his balance when the audience failed to respond to his obvious talents. Whoever was to follow these two would need to be a combination of them both.

Such is the enormity of the managerial task it could be beyond the grasp of a man who simply knows how to select a winning side. He needs to be able to project the right image, mingle with both grass-root supporter and distinguished guest and not seem out of place with either, and have the gift of man management as well as a steady hand when dealing with large cash transactions. All this in one man?

Immediately after the decision to terminate the contracts of both Sexton and his assistant Tommy Cavanagh, United began the search for a replacement. As in the past, the name of Brian Clough was associated with United and reasons were given by the newspaper speculators as to why, and why not, the Nottingham Forest manager could be approached.

Lawrie McMenemy, who had taken Southampton from obscurity to success, was said to be the name at the top of the club's short list. McMenemy had the right public image to prove popular with the fans, had the obvious ability to manage, and if he could achieve such heights at a club as small as Southampton, then what would he do with a giant like United? McMenemy had been the man who had brought England's biggest star since George Best back to the Football League after he had earned his fortune in West Germany, and if he could persuade Kevin Keegan to play for him, could he get other world stars to respond in the same way?

McMenemy had his own views on management which seemed so close to the unwritten guidelines of the club: 'You don't have to win trophies to be successful. The biggest thing is getting the best out of what you have got, and giving the public what it wants.'

But, when given the chance, McMenemy turned down the opportunity to give Manchester United's public what it wanted.

Ron Atkinson gets the job

Bobby Robson's name was also linked with the vacancy, before eventually, in June 1981, the new man was chosen. He was a Liverpudlian, whose managerial rise had been swift. From the parochial surroundings of Kettering Town to the awe-inspiring heights of Old Trafford was the route for Ronald Frederick Atkinson.

Ron Atkinson had shown at West Bromwich Albion that he was capable of producing a first-class team with limited resources, and the step he took from the Hawthorns to Manchester United was perhaps for him not such a giant stride as had been his moving to West Bromwich from his first League club after Kettering, Cambridge United. His credentials were based on his previous successful managership. Ron Atkinson had been a hero of Oxford United in his playing days, taking part in their drive from Southern League to Second Division, but it was not his playing background which had seen him recognised as the right material to lead Manchester United back to greatness.

A larger-than-life character, his arrival at Old Trafford brought swift changes. In came Atkinson, and out went coaches Harry Gregg and Jack Crompton, youth coach Syd Owen, and physiotherapist Laurie Brown. The new broom was indeed making a clean sweep as Atkinson brought in his own backroom staff to replace those with links to the past. Crompton and Gregg had ties with the great sides of the three decades after the

Second World War, but Ron Atkinson wanted his own men in the backroom.

Mick Brown, his right-hand man at West Brom, was appointed assistant manager. Brian Whitehouse, another from the Hawthorns, became chief coach, and Eric Harrison took charge of the youth team after leaving Everton's staff. The man who replaced Laurie Brown was Jim Headridge, physiotherapist at Bolton Wanderers, but tragedy struck before the new season was under way when, during a training session, he collapsed and died at the Cliff Training Ground. The man described by Atkinson as 'the best physio in the business' was eventually replaced by Jim McGregor, a popular choice, who had been at Goodison Park with Harrison, and before that at Oldham Athletic.

The first gap Atkinson had to fill on the field was that left by Joe Jordan who, as soon as his contract allowed him, had signed for Italian giants AC Milan, adding more weight to the predictions of Sexton in 1978. The new manager bought Frank Stapleton from Arsenal, who unlike Brady, his fellow countryman, decided to seek his fortune in Manchester rather than follow him abroad when his contract also ended.

Atkinson signs Bryan Robson

In a deal worth more than £2 million West Brom agreed to sell Bryan Robson and Remi Moses to United. This fee, together with the £70,000 compensation for the loss of their manager certainly made the Midlands club richer financially, if poorer in the playing area. While the haggling over the total cost of both players went on, Moses was allowed to move north to his home town. He had been raised in Manchester's Moss Side, and he made his debut by coming on as substitute in the side's first win of the new season against Swansea City at Old Trafford.

That game also marked another milestone. Garry Birtles scored his first League goal, after 29 previous games without success. Was this to be the turning point Atkinson hoped for?

Robson was eventually signed too late to make his debut against Wolves on 3 October 1981, but he was paraded before a crowd of close on 47,000 and his presence, after the spectacle of an on-the-pitch signing, seemed to rub off on his new colleagues. The carnival atmosphere created by the event probably contributed to United running in their biggest win of the season, overwhelming struggling Wolves 5–0. Sammy McIlroy, sensing that his days in midfield might now be numbered, hit a hat-trick, and Birtles and Stapleton scored the other goals. Robson's fee had finally been settled at £1.5 million, making him the costliest player in Britain at that time, and he eventually made his league debut in the perfect setting of the derby game at Maine Road, in front of 52,037 supporters, who saw him give a solid performance in a 0–0 draw.

The extrovert Atkinson was also keen to encourage young players, giving Norman Whiteside, a strongly built boy who had joined straight

Left: It was a goal from Norman Whiteside which took United to Wembley for a second time in 1983. The youngster scored from long range as the Reds fought back from behind in the semi-final against Arsenal at Villa Park. Bryan Robson scored United's equaliser from a precise cross from Ashley Grimes and after the disappointment of the Milk Cup defeat, United booked their return ticket

Below: For Brighton's Manchester-born goalkeeper Graham Moseley the 1983 FA Cup final was an occasion to forget. He became the first 'keeper in post-war finals to concede a total of six goals, two in the original match and four in the replay. Here he grasps at fresh air as Ray Wilkins runs in to challenge, before Norman Whiteside grabs United's second

from school in Belfast, his League debut just a week after his 17th birthday. He took the team into third place in his first season and then the following year in 1982-83 had the Reds in the finals of both the Milk Cup and the FA Cup. The first trip to Wembley brought a 2-1 defeat against Liverpool but it was a different story in the FA Cup.

The other finalist, Brighton arrived at the stadium by helicopter, but it was a story of a different kind which made the headlines. After just two League games United had called up an unknown youngster, Alan Davies, a Manchester-born player who claimed a loyalty to Wales because his grandparents came from there. Davies wore the number 11 shirt vacated by Steve Coppell and soon got involved. 'I remember that I was quite nervous at the start and I wanted to make sure that I got into the game quickly. The other lads were great to me, Ray Wilkins and Arnold Muhren gave me plenty of encouragement and it was a tremendous moment for me.'

There were fears in the United camp that the game might go the same way as the 1976 final, when underdogs Southampton had beaten the favourites, and when Brighton scored first and still led at the interval Ron Atkinson had to lift his players. Ten minutes into the second period Mike Duxbury broke down the right, overlapping with Davies, and crossed the ball towards the edge of the penalty area. Whiteside flicked on across the face of the Brighton goal, and Frank Stapleton was there at the far post to force the ball home. Brighton's goalkeeper, Graham Moseley (a Manchester-born player) had no chance, and even less with United's second.

Ray Wilkins had scored few goals during his time at Old Trafford, but in the 74th minute he set Wembley alight with a bending long-range shot which curled around Moseley and into the net. Sixteen minutes remained and United led 2–1. It seemed as if the Cup was destined for Old Trafford until three minutes before the end of the game. Brighton's Gary Stevens then fired home a shot which beat Gary Bailey. The goal had started with a corner taken by Jimmy Case, scorer of Liverpool's equaliser against United in 1977. Was this to be his revenge for that previous defeat?

The game went into extra time and in one last desperate surge Brighton almost stole the Cup. Michael Robinson, whose career had seen him at one time playing in Manchester with City, pulled a cross over to the feet of Gordon Smith, scorer of the afternoon's first goal. Smith ran into the six-yard box, but Bailey, possibly remembering the last moments of his previous FA Cup final, threw himself bravely at the Brighton player, blocking the shot completely.

The game ended in deadlock, with a replay five days later. United fielded the same team:

Bailey, Duxbury, Albiston, Wilkins, Moran, McQueen, Robson, Muhren, Stapleton, Whiteside, Davies.

Cup winners again

Brighton had the suspended Foster back, but Moses' two-match suspension meant that he also missed the replay. However, he was there to celebrate as United ran Brighton into the ground.

Davies was magnificent and his performance caught the eye of the Welsh FA, who called him up for their summer internationals.

It was Davies who combined with Arthur Albiston to lay on the first of two first-half goals which destroyed the Brighton challenge. Robson scored from the final pass and then two minutes later Davies tipped on a corner from Arnie Muhren and Norman Whiteside scored to add another line to his pedigree. In a year when he had played his first full season, and with a World Cup behind him, he had scored in both Wembley finals of 1983.

Brighton hit back and Case came close to scoring, but Bailey made a good save as the ball seemed to be passing over his head. Then, almost on half time, Robson scored his second, running on to a Stapleton header. Three goals in front at the break, United were out of Brighton's reach. There was only one additional goal in the second half, scored from the penalty spot by Arnie Muhren after Robson had been pulled back by Gary Stevens, and the Cup was on its way back to the United trophy room.

United began the 1983–84 season with a 3–1 win over Queen's Park Rangers, but after leading 1–0 at half-time, lost to Nottingham Forest in the second successive home fixture.

The side began by playing attractive football, and eight wins and just two defeats in the eleven games to the end of October saw them sitting on

Above: The dreams of Brighton are shattered as Arnold Muhren scores United's fourth goal in the 1983 FA Cup final replay. Brighton had their moments of glory in the 2–2 draw five days earlier, but they found United in a ruthless mood for the second game and goals from Robson (2) and Whiteside paved the way for a memorable victory before Muhren hammered in the last nail

Left: The jubilant players celebrate victory in the replay of the 1983 FA Cup final. It was a case of third time lucky for United that season, having lost to Liverpool in the Milk Cup, then drawn with Brighton five days before the replay

top of the First Division, and there were signs that the future might be even brighter as a young striker emerged from the youth team.

Mark Hughes was beginning to cause a minor sensation in the lower teams. In a pre-season friendly against Port Vale he scored five times in a 10–0 win, and when United were paired with the Potteries club in the Milk Cup, Hughes came on as substitute in a 3–0 aggregate win.

Hughes eventually made his full debut at Oxford's Manor Ground in the fourth round of the Milk Cup, and scored in a 1–1 draw, but the tie proved to be the end of United in the competition that season. The replay at Old Trafford ended 1–1 after extra time and in the third game United were beaten 2–1 by an extra-time goal on a night when Gary Bailey was missing through injury, and Bryan Robson limped off before the final whistle.

The defence of the FA Cup was no luckier and Ron Atkinson's fury after his players were beaten 2–0 by Third Division Bournemouth was only matched by that of the supporters, who chanted 'Atkinson out!' And this to a manager whose team had won the FA Cup and Charity Shield the previous season and which was currently lying second in the table to Liverpool.

If Atkinson's turn on the Old Trafford tightrope was not providing the supporters with thrills, then they were hard to please, and by March, when Hughes was brought back into the side and played at Barcelona in the third round of the Cup-winners' Cup, the excitement reached fever pitch. This was the brilliant tie in which, after losing 2–0 at Nou Camp Stadium, United won 3–0 before 58,547 at Old Trafford, beating Barcelona and Maradona 3–2 on aggregate.

Once toppled from the top of the League table, United were constantly in the shadow of Liverpool, yet beat them at Old Trafford and drew at Anfield after leading for most of the game. Liverpool finished Champions, United fourth. During the season Graeme Hogg was introduced to the side, replacing McQueen, who was again injured at the start of 1984.

Wilkins goes to Italy

However, it was the transfer of a player away from the club which made the biggest impact. Ray Wilkins was sold to AC Milan for £1.4 million. Wilkins was a popular player, especially with the younger supporters, and had been a great ambassador for the club, always willing to talk to fans, in a patient, well-mannered and understanding way. Wilkins left sadly, despite the financial attractions of his new life abroad. He said later: 'I never wanted to leave, but it was obvious that there was no place for me in future plans, so when the deal was drawn up between Milan and United that was that.'

There was also a question mark over the future of Norman Whiteside. Although the young striker had proved himself at every level, he lost his place to Hughes at the close of the 1983–84 campaign, and during the summer Atkinson's efforts in the transfer market finalised the purchases of Strachan from Aberdeen, Jesper Olsen, the Danish winger who was playing for Dutch club Ajax, and Alan Brazil from Tottenham, a player Atkinson had pursued for over a year.

Mark Hughes makes his mark

United's chances of winning the League and Cup double in season 1984-85 were realistic, even though Everton were well ahead in the title race, and after beating Aston Villa 4–0 at Old Trafford, Atkinson was being tipped as the man to emulate Busby as a creator of champions. Hughes scored a hat-trick in this match and his performances in his first full season earned him the 'Young Foot-

Right: Distant horizons for Ray Wilkins brought an end to his days at Old Trafford. The player who lost both the England and United captaincy to his close friend Bryan Robson, reluctantly moved on to play in Italy with AC Milan. Wilkins began his career at Chelsea where his obvious flair for leadership led to him being appointed the youngest captain in the history of the London club

Far right: Quick talking, quick witted and quick off the mark Gordon Strachan found himself playing under Alex Ferguson for a second time when United replaced Ron Atkinson in 1986. Strachan, a creative midfield player with immense skill and control, was bought by Atkinson under the noses of German club FC Cologne to add width and penetration to the side

Left: The slightly built Jesper Olsen was brought to Old Trafford six months before he became a United player. The Dane was out of the game through injury when he agreed to move to English football from Dutch club Ajax. This gave Ron Atkinson the opportunity to introduce Olsen to his future colleagues before the transfer was finalised. Olsen was one of two United players to be included in the Danish squad for the 1986 World Cup, the other was full-back John Sivebaek

baller of the Year' award, given to him through the votes of his fellow professionals in the PFA.

When the club's hopes of European honours vanished in the Hungarian mud as Videoton won a UEFA Cup penalty 'shoot-out', it became clear where United's interests lay.

In the FA Cup they were drawn once more against Liverpool, and faced them at Anfield on 31 March 1985 in a League game, a fortnight before their semi-final date. United won 1–0 through a Frank Stapleton goal, and then went on to beat Leicester 2–1, and Stoke 5–0. Was this going to be the year of the Championship which had eluded the club since 1967?

Three days after the devastation of Stoke, Atkinson's hopes were dashed at Hillsborough when Lee Chapman pushed the ball over the line after Stephen Pears, playing his last senior game for United, failed to hold a Shirtliff shot from a Brian Marwood cross, and Wednesday won 1–0.

The gap between United and leaders Everton had been narrowed to just four points but this defeat, and Everton's victory in their next game, gave the Merseysiders a seven-point lead with seven games remaining. Everton seemed to be in an invincible position.

So it was the FA Cup which became the main target and supporters began to look forward to the possibility of a sixth Wembley final within a decade. United met Liverpool at Goodison Park, while Everton faced Luton Town in the other semi-final at Villa Park. The prospect of an all-Merseyside final had caught the imagination of the sporting press and the build-up to the games helped to create an amazing atmosphere, especially at the Everton ground.

United had no intention of sitting at home watching Liverpool play Everton in the final on television, and set about their task with great spirit. They forced a stream of corner kicks, held out when Rush broke through but shot over the bar, then took the lead.

The first goal came after a first half in which Hogg had been booked for a foul on Rush, Whiteside had been floored by Whelan and had clashed with Sammy Lee, and Gidman had created a scoring chance from a free-kick.

It was in the 69th minute when Hughes struck, ramming the ball home after a Robson shot had been blocked. The game seemed over until Ronnie Whelan tried a shot from outside the box four minutes from time and levelled the scores. Once more a Liverpool–United game went into extra time, and eight minutes into the first period Frank Stapleton's shot was deflected to make it 2–1 to United.

Surely this time United were through? But no, back came Liverpool, and in the final minute referee George Courtney ignored a linesman's flag and allowed a Paul Walsh goal to stand. It was a bitter blow for Atkinson: We had the game won, we did everything that we had to do this afternoon and still we haven't got to Wembley.'

The game was replayed at Maine Road four nights later and the own-goal jinx once again struck United. In the 39th minute Paul McGrath tried to head a cross over his own bar, and instead beat Bailey to put Liverpool in front. United were stunned, but having had the better of the play up to that time, were in confident mood and came back immediately the second half had started.

Bryan Robson ran at the Liverpool defence and unleashed a powerful shot which Grobbelaar could not reach and it was 1–1. Twelve minutes later the dynamic Hughes forced himself through

Left: Mark Hughes was the second influential player to emerge from the youth team of the 1980s, the first being Norman Whiteside. Hughes made his debut in a Milk Cup tie at Oxford and scored, an action he was to repeat when he played his first senior League game and his first international for Wales

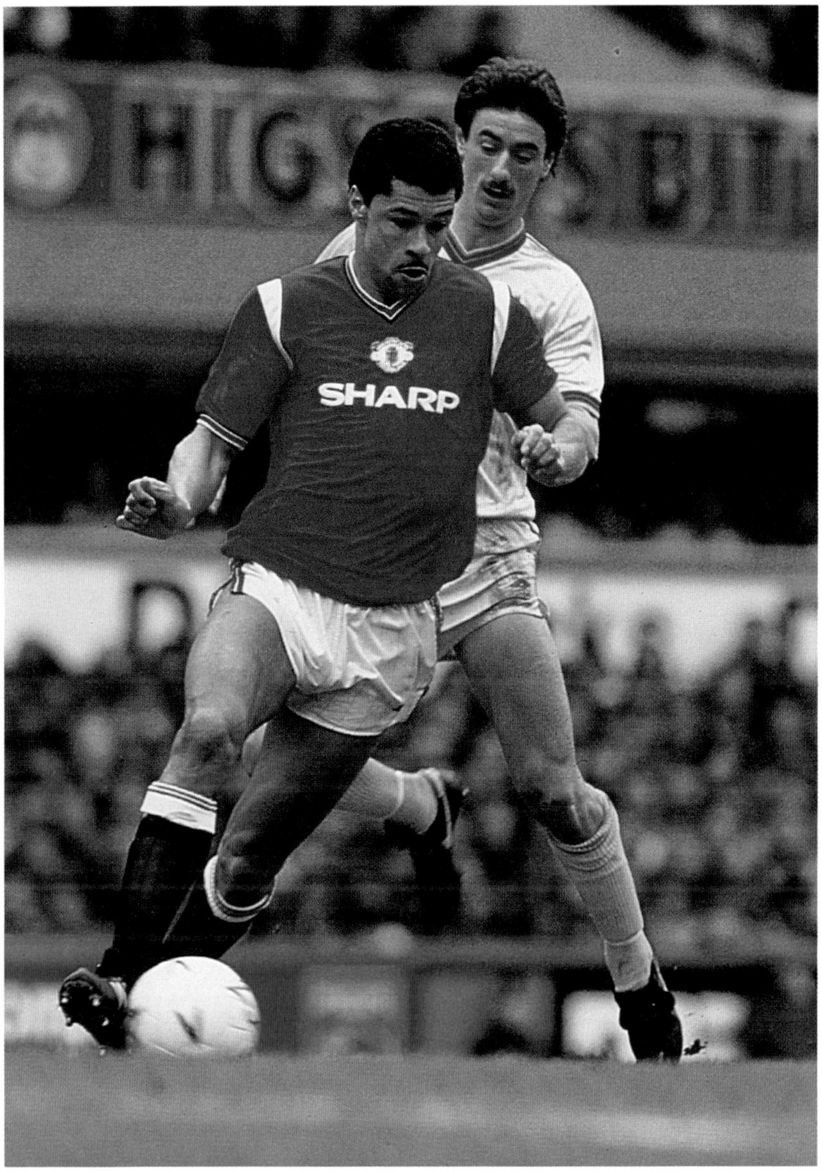

Above: Paul McGrath, an influential member of the Atkinson squad who was sold to Aston Villa in the summer of 1989 after a series of knee operations

the Liverpool back four as he chased a Strachan pass and hit the winner.

Everton, the League leaders, provided the opposition for the Wembley final on 18 May. Before that United saw their Championship hopes disappear completely as they drew with Southampton and Sunderland at Old Trafford, and even though they had victories at Luton and Norwich on each side of those games the four points lost were vital. A 3–1 win at QPR was followed by a debacle at Vicarage Road, Watford, where the Hornets beat United 5–1 in the last League game, but the players' minds by then were on the Cup final which was five days away.

Agony of Moran

The players spent that time in Windsor, at a Thames-side hideaway hotel far removed from the pressures of Wembley, and it was perfect preparation for the big game. They trained at nearby Bisham Abbey, and relaxed on the lawns of the hotel in tranquil surroundings as Ron Atkinson wrestled with a problem. He had to select the side he hoped would beat Everton at Wembley, but he had doubts about the fitness of certain key players.

Graeme Hogg had played regularly since the start of the year while Kevin Moran had been out for a 13-game spell, returning just before the season ended. Hogg had a pelvic problem and Atkinson knew this only too well, so he decided on the eve of the final to play Moran. It proved a crucial decision but not for obvious reasons.

Alan Brazil was the other unlucky player. He had taken over from the injured Hughes in the closing games, but even though he had scored 12 times in just 20 outings, he could not even win the substitute's shirt for the final. This went to Mike Duxbury. The United line up was:

Bailey, Gidman, Albiston, Whiteside, McGrath, Moran, Robson, Strachan, Hughes, Stapleton, Olsen. Sub: Duxbury.

Everton, by now champions, were favourites to win the final, but it was a game remembered not so much for its football as for a moment during the second half when Kevin Moran carved an unwanted niche in the history of the game.

It happened when Peter Reid, that dynamo of a midfielder, was running at full speed towards the United penalty area. The Everton player had picked up the ball from a moment of hesitation by McGrath and was clear of the Reds' defence. Moran threw himself feet first at Reid, his right foot pushing the ball away, his left catching the Everton player. Reid's momentum carried him into the air and he dramatically rolled over several times. Referee Peter Willis blew for a foul and called Moran to him.

The United player seemed angry that his challenge should be thought unfair by the referee, but said nothing, turning his back to the official so that Willis could note his number. Moran began to walk away after the caution and was then shocked to learn that he had been sent off. He was unhappily the first player ever to be dismissed in an FA Cup final.

Moran was stunned. He grabbed referee Willis in a vain attempt to plead his innocence. Willis stood firm, pointing to the touchline and growing angry at the player's attitude. Moran was incensed and had to be pulled away from the official by his team-mate at both club and international level, Frank Stapleton.

Bryan Robson pleaded with Willis and was ignored. The Everton players joined in, and Reid walked alongside Moran as he was led from the field by Jim McGregor, holding back tears and swaying as if about to faint.

Millions of television viewers were at that very moment being shown an action replay of the incident which clearly illustrated the intention of Moran's challenge. He had pushed the ball away from Reid with his right foot before making contact with the player, but the referee did not have the same opinion as the television commentary team, nor did he have the advantage of being able to see the incident from several different angles.

Moran had to sit on the United bench as the

game went into extra time. He said afterwards:

> It was the worst moment of my life. I couldn't believe what had happened to me, I honestly didn't think that I'd fouled Peter, but even if I did I didn't think it warranted a sending off. I went crazy, I didn't know what was happening, except that here was a man sending me off for something I thought I hadn't done. I asked for mercy and got none.

No goals had come in the first 90 minutes, but in extra time the ten men from Manchester found the inspiration to create just one vital opportunity, and it fell to Norman Whiteside.

Hughes, in his own half, pushed the ball forward beyond the Everton midfield. Whiteside ran after it, lengthening his stride as he found extra strength. Strachan raced alongside in support, and van den Hauwe, the Everton left-back, came to challenge. Whiteside turned inwards, the full-back stumbled and Whiteside hit a left-foot shot goalwards as van den Hauwe fell, obscuring the ball momentarily from the view of Southall in the Everton goal. The ball was level with the goalkeeper when he became aware of the danger, throwing himself outwards in an effort to block its path, but the ball was round him and into the net. United had won the FA Cup again.

The players went to collect their medals. Moran accompanied them and was told by an FA official that his was being withheld. A player sent off at Wembley does not qualify for a medal, winner or loser. However, such was the public outcry, backed by the television evidence, that several weeks later Moran was justly rewarded with his medal.

The sending-off had turned an ordinary final into one of major significance, and the interest created by Moran's misfortune transformed him into a folk hero.

When United returned with the Cup the following day there were wild scenes as the team travelled once more on their open-topped bus to Manchester town Hall, and, when Moran demonstrated his eloquence with political-style oratory, the tens of thousands gathered in Albert Square and listening on radio took him to their hearts. 'We won the Cup for the supporters of Manchester United, because they are the best. You are the greatest in the world', he said, emphasising each word with a punch of his fist, the rest of his speech being drowned in deafening cheers.

United had won another major trophy. They ended their First Division campaign by once again occupying fourth place.

The 1985–86 season began by United losing to Everton in the Charity Shield, Graeme Hogg replacing Moran who was suspended, and the new campaign proved to be one of great importance for Ron Atkinson.

Since his arrival his side had not ended a season outside the top four, had qualified for Europe and won the FA Cup twice, but he had still been unable totally to convince the majority of supporters that he was the right man for the managerial seat at Old Trafford. His record proved he was successful, but the supporters' comments, and their acceptance of Atkinson the man, showed that he was walking the tightrope without winning over his audience.

He was accepted by the media as a man who was easy to work with unless angered. He had dealt with a difficult personal problem in a way which caused not the slightest embarrassment to the club when he had called a 'press conference' to announce that he had left his wife to set up home with another woman, thus preventing any sensational exposures in the tabloid newspapers. He had a circle of close friends with whom he could confide, yet that vital relationship with the grass-roots supporter was missing, the same problem that had eventually spelled the end of the Old Trafford career of Dave Sexton.

Above: Drama in the 1985 FA Cup Final at Wembley as Kevin Moran becomes the first player to be sent off in football's showpiece. Referee Peter Willis points to the touchline and stands his ground as Moran pleads for leniency. Gordon Strachan tries to console Moran as Bryan Robson and Mark Hughes join their colleague. 'I almost hit the referee' Moran said afterwards

Brilliant start to 1985–86 league season

However, anyone with any doubts about his managerial capabilities had little evidence to use against him as United began their 1985–86 season by setting an impressive new club record for successive victories.

After the Charity Shield they beat Aston Villa, Ipswich, Arsenal, West Ham, Nottingham Forest, Newcastle, Oxford, Manchester City, West Brom and Southampton in the League. Ten games, ten wins, and naturally top of the First Division.

The victories had a price. John Gidman broke his leg in the second game at Ipswich, Jesper Olsen was hurt before the West Ham match, allowing Peter Barnes, signed during that summer, to make an impressive debut, and Gordon Strachan dislocated his shoulder scoring for United at West Brom.

United invested in a new goalkeeper, Chris Turner from Sunderland, who at £250,000 was the most costly number one the club had ever bought. But he was sidelined by the brilliant performances of Bailey in the record-breaking run.

United had qualified for Europe but there were no foreign competitions that season following the Heysel Stadium tragedy, when rioting at the Liverpool-Juventus European Cup final had led to the deaths of 39 Italian supporters. Instead a new competition was introduced, while at the same time the Football League decided to trim the First Division to 20 clubs by the 1988–89 season. The Super Cup became the target of those clubs prevented from playing in Europe by the UEFA ban; it was eventually won by Liverpool.

United's run of victories ended with a draw at Luton but it was November before they lost their first League game, going down 1–0 to Sheffield Wednesday at Hillsborough. Injuries had forced Atkinson to use no fewer than 18 players up to that fixture, only one of them, goalkeeper Turner, not having competed in the League.

Colin Gibson was bought from Aston Villa as Ron Atkinson decided that he wanted to strengthen his left full-back options and early in the new year a second Gibson, Terry from Coventry City, moved to Old Trafford in a player-plus-cash deal which took Alan Brazil to Highfield Road.

After the tremendous start things began to go wrong. After the Sheffield Wednesday defeat United were knocked out of the Milk Cup at Anfield, and got just two points from three further League games.

Injuries still plagued the club. Playing for England, Bryan Robson limped off at Wembley after chasing a ball behind the goal and tearing a hamstring. He returned for the game at Sheffield Wednesday and repeated the injury which kept him out until the New Year. Robson missed the remainder of the Milk Cup games after taking part in the two-legged second round against Crystal Palace – Steve Coppell's club – as goals from Peter Barnes and Norman Whiteside gave United a 1–0 win in each match.

In the third round there was controversy as United beat West Ham 1–0 at Old Trafford. Norman Whiteside scored what turned out to be the only goal of the game, converting an Olsen pass from the goal-line in the 76th minute, but it was a 'goal' that was not a goal which caused a stir. Mark Ward fired a 25-yard free-kick into Gary Bailey's net but as referee Frank Roberts had indicated that it was indirect there was no goal. Ward argued that Bailey had touched the ball in his efforts to make a save, which Bailey denied.

By December United were still top of the League, but their form slipped dramatically. Just one win in five games was followed by a 3 – I win at Villa Park. Then, when the first home defeat of the season occurred against Arsenal on 21 December a small section of the supporters demonstrated against the manager. 'What do they think they're talking about?' was Atkinson's retort. 'They seem to forget I've brought them the Cup twice – and would Bryan Robson be playing here if it wasn't for me? They have very short memories.'

Defeat at Goodison Park followed, and only bad weather prevented what might have been a tragic run of defeats as the long trip to Newcastle on 28 December was postponed.

Mark Hughes' form had also taken a significant slide. In his opening 13 games he had scored ten goals, then in the next 13 League fixtures, just two. The period bridged the start of the New Year and the start of the FA Cup campaign.

This opened with a tie against Rochdale, switched to Old Trafford because Spotland could not cater for the numbers who might attend, and United won 2–0. The tie saw the return to football of Mark Higgins, who had been forced to retire from the game after a bad injury. The former Everton captain had turned to Atkinson for a chance to try again and after training with United joined them, repaying the insurance claim he had received when he quit.

Robson returned for the next round of the Cup, against Sunderland at Roker Park. The game ended goalless, but the talking point was a clash between Robson and Barry Venison. Both players fell to the ground, Robson got up first and tried to step over the Sunderland player, catching him on the head with his boot. The linesman closest to the incident saw it as a deliberate kick, and Robson was sent off for the first time ever in his career.

United won the replay 3–0 with Robson in the side, but by the time his two-match suspension started he was injured again. Four days after the second Sunderland game the England captain limped off at Upton Park after twisting his ankle during a 2–1 League defeat, as United found themselves knocked off the top of the table.

Meanwhile the news had leaked out that Mark Hughes was set to join Barcelona for £1.8m at the end of the season. This angered United's supporters when they read of the speculation in the newspapers.

Left: FA Cup final 1985: Everton goalkeeper Neville Southall flings himself across goal in a vain attempt to stop Norman Whiteside's cup-winning shot from the far edge of the penalty area. The goal came in extra-time as United, reduced to ten men after having Kevin Moran sent off, staged a gallant fight against the odds

Atkinson is sacked

On Tuesday, 4 November 1986, United played their final game under Ron Atkinson. It was the replay against Southampton at the Dell, and a game which increased the injury burden which had weighed Atkinson down. Colin Gibson tore his hamstring again after just two partial outings at the start of the season, and Norman Whiteside limped off with a knee ligament injury before half-time. He was replaced by Nicky Wood, who had ended his studies at Manchester University to concentrate on his playing career. Moran was on instead of Gibson. A minute before half-time Southampton scored, and in the second half took control, winning 4–1.

The United manager was far from happy:

> Up to half-time I thought that we were the better team, I honestly believed that we would get into the game in the second half and make something of it, but George Lawrence ran riot. It's seldom that you can find any consolation in defeat, but we had problems with injurics again and I thought that the players battled terribly well considering those. Jimmy Case ran the show though, and there was nothing we could do about it.

Jimmy Case, tormentor of Manchester United, had contributed to the end of Ron Atkinson's spell on the Old Trafford tightrope.

The next day the club's directors met informally to discuss the situation, and 24 hours later at 10.30am on 6 November, Martin Edwards summoned Ron Atkinson and Mick Brown to his office at Old Trafford.

An hour later a statement was issued which said that the contracts of both men had been terminated. Atkinson was no longer manager.

The men and women of the media gathered outside the normally open gates of the Cliff training ground hoping for an opportunity to see the man who had been forced to stand down from his post, and shortly before noon were allowed into the courtyard where Atkinson held his final audience with the press:

> Obviously I'm disappointed. I'd go on record as saying that I have been at the club for five and a half years. Five of them have been very good years which I have enjoyed immensely, but this year things went against us and you have seen the outcome today. I actually had no indication of what was going to happen. I came down here today expecting to have a nice five-a-side and some training, but the chairman sent for me and told me reluctantly – I felt reluctantly – that they had decided to dispense with my services, because of the results over the last few months, and I accept that totally. I don't feel bitter about it, I don't hold any bitterness against the club.
>
> I honestly feel that we had just started to turn the corner with our recent run of results but I never expected this to happen. I don't think if you are a positive person you ever look

Left: Derby day in Manchester and Sammy McIlroy (left) in unfamiliar sky blue, urges his City colleagues on as the man who took his place at Old Trafford, Bryan Robson, battles for the ball

Right: Arthur Albiston made his debut for the club in 1977 and gave an impressive display in the FA Cup final that year as United beat Liverpool to win the cup. The Scottish left full-back won three FA Cup winning medals with United, the only player ever to achieve this feat. In 1988 Albiston was granted a testimonial and given a free transfer. 'In view of his fine record with the club it would not have been right for us to ask for a fee,' said Alex Ferguson

Left: Mark Higgins tussles with Frank McAvennie in the FA Cup fifth-round replay against West Ham at Old Trafford in March 1986. Mark seemed finished in football when he quit at Everton with a bad back injury, but Manchester United gave him a second life by repaying his insurance money to take him back into the Football League. He fought his way back into first-team football although he failed to win a regular place with United, his career was launched again and he moved on to play successfully for Bury

on the black side, you look on the positive side. I came here this morning knowing that we are playing Oxford on Saturday and to get a side capable of winning there. Now someone else has got that responsibility, and whoever it is I sincerely hope they do well.

I've no axe to grind at all. I've worked for a chairman who I consider to be as good as any chairman in the game, and I don't think that this job is any harder than being manager of any other club. True this is the biggest club in the country and the manager has his problems, but I don't think the manager of Rochdale would feel that his problems were any smaller than mine have been, or any bigger.

You are always aware that these things might happen but you must never look at it in that light. But I am sure that there are good times ahead for the club, once whoever takes over gets all the key players fit again.

Alex Ferguson is appointed

Atkinson bowed out and drowned his sorrows that night with a party at his Rochdale home, but by then he knew who would succeed him, for Martin Edwards was swift to appoint a new man. Three hours after sacking Ron Atkinson, the United chairman flew to Scotland where he had been given permission to talk to Aberdeen's manager, Alex Ferguson. The man who was to succeed Atkinson remembers the day clearly:

It was a beautiful sunny morning and I drove back to Pittodrie from a training session and I saw the chairman's car there. And I thought to myself 'the old yin's here early today' – it was about a quarter to twelve. I went into my office and he was sitting at my desk, and he had his hand on the telephone. I said hello to him and told him he was in early, and he threw me a piece of paper. 'I've been asked to phone this gentleman,' he said. On the paper was Martin Edwards' name and phone number.

He said 'Do you want me to 'phone him?' and I said that I did, and I went out of the room because I didn't want to be there. I just asked if he would tell me what had happened after the call.

I went back after going down to the dressing rooms and he said that he had spoken to Mr Edwards and that he was flying up straight away and would go to my house. He said that his son would collect the United chairman from the airport and take him there. I said it was quick, and he said 'If you want the job there's nothing we can do to stop you.'

There was nothing else I could do, so I went home and told my wife and sons, and right away they were against the idea. I think they were just shocked at the thought of leaving Aberdeen, because it's a lovely city and the boys were settled in at school. We had good players and a good club, but we sat down and my wife said that I was right, I had to take the job.

The following morning Alex Ferguson arrived at the Cliff, met his new players and immediately was impressed:

This is luxury for me, because at Aberdeen we didn't have our own training ground, we used school pitches. But I've got to put these things to good use and get down to picking a winning side. I know the club's had injury problems and my sympathy goes to Ron Atkinson in that sense. You need luck in football and he didn't have any.

The new manager was an optimist:

We aren't in a desperate position, the League can still be won. It's no use me coming here and not thinking that every game we play we can win, that's the only way that we can attack things. That's the attitude I had at Aberdeen – there's a game to be played and we must go out and win it. Tomorrow we have to win, simply that.

His new chairman, Martin Edwards said:

I am sure that we have made a wise choice. We had to move quickly – once we had decided to get rid of Ron we wanted to replace him as quickly as possible.

When we had the meeting to decide that we wanted to make the change we decided that Alex Ferguson was the man that we wanted to replace Ron Atkinson.

It was also evident that the United chairman knew what he expected from his new manager:

> We are looking to be the premier club in England and obviously to be that we have to win the First Division Championship. That was our aim throughout Ron Atkinson's reign and will continue to be our main priority. It would be very rash to call Ron Atkinson a failure because he didn't win the title. In the five full seasons he was here he never finished outside the top four, he won us the FA Cup twice and got us to the final of the Milk Cup, plus the semi-final of the European Cup Winners Cup, so I don't think under any circumstances you could class Ron Atkinson a failure. The only thing is that he didn't achieve the First Division Championship.

Ferguson brought Archie Knox, his assistant at Aberdeen, to be his right-hand man at Old Trafford, and the Scots injected new spirit into the club. Training became longer and harder and players responded to the new methods. Bryan Robson said after a few weeks:

> There's no doubt about it, things have changed, and the players seem to like the way things are being done. I've got to be honest and say that I've never felt stronger in my legs than I do now. I have had a lot of trouble with my hamstring, but the manager has got me doing different routines to strengthen my legs and they seem to be working.

On the pitch the new methods showed. United became a side which used fitness as well as skill to compete, and their willingness to run led to victory over Liverpool at Anfield – their only away win of the whole First Division campaign – as Ferguson tested his squad.

He used no fewer than 23 players during his first season, amongst them Terry Gibson, who had almost joined Watford in the week Atkinson was replaced, but who was eventually transferred to Wimbledon after waiting almost a year for his home debut. Gibson was given a chance by Ferguson, playing 12 First Division games and taking part in both FA Cup ties played during that season.

The first was against Manchester City at Old Trafford, when a crowd of 54,295 witnessed Norman Whiteside scoring the only goal of the afternoon in the 67th minute. But the state of the pitch was poor, and pointed the way to the trouble that was brewing and which would come to a head in the fourth round.

Media criticism and regular comments from supporters had led to the club installing an undersoil heating system, but, as if to back up comments previously made by chairman Edwards, it had proved unsatisfactory. Although costing over £80,000, sections of it had failed and consequently, when there was a hard frost, parts of the ground were frozen while others were perfect for play. Before the City tie, hot air machines were placed around the frozen sections pumping warmth under large blankets borrowed from the nearby cricket ground. The makeshift scheme worked and the pitch was perfect.

It was different for the next round, however, when United were again drawn at home, to Coventry City. Alex Ferguson took the players away to the Lake District to prepare for the game. Five wins and four draws had lifted them away from the relegation zone and the prospect of a good Cup run justified such preparations. On the morning of the game the manager was stunned when he arrived at Old Trafford. The pitch was bone hard, a sudden frost having caught out the groundstaff. The game was turned into a lottery, and United were the losers. Keith Houchen scored for Coventry with a 20th minute shot after the ball bobbled away from Turner on the slippery surface. Coventry went on to win the FA Cup and United replaced their undersoil heating during the summer of 1987.

After their Cup hopes ended, United spent the remainder of the season in mid-table, finishing the campaign in 11th place, their lowest position since the relegation season of 1973–74. But there were signs that the 1987–88 season would have more to offer.

During the months of Ferguson's management Gary Walsh, an 18-year-old goalkeeper, was drafted into the squad, and his presence led to Chris Turner asking for a transfer. Gary Bailey

Below: Gary Walsh, the young goalkeeper whose career was almost ended by injury. Walsh came into the game through the Government's YTS scheme and reached first team level at the end of 1986 and soon became first choice 'keeper. A year later an ankle problem forced him out and it was not until February 1991 that he returned

Above: Brian McClair signed for United at a joint signing ceremony with Viv Anderson in the club trophy room in 1987. Alex Ferguson obtained McClair for under £1 million, and in the next seven seasons the hard-working McClair made 330 appearances for the club.

Right: England right full-back Viv Anderson already had a string of honours to his name when he joined United. He was a member of Brian Clough's successful Nottingham Forest side before moving to Arsenal. However when his contract ended he was keen to join United, a club he had trained with as a schoolboy

came back from injury and played in five games before announcing that he was being forced into retirement by a knee problem identical to that which had led to the end of Steve Coppell's playing days.

Bailey returned to his parents' home in South Africa to continue the university studies he had abandoned to take up his footballing career, after a hastily arranged testimonial. He said:

> Obviously I am very sad to be giving up the game, when I could have another ten years or more at the top. But I am leaving with some tremendous memories and I feel honoured to have played for a club as great as Manchester United.

During the summer of 1987 Frank Stapleton was transferred to the Dutch team Ajax, where his former club-mate Arnie Muhren was extending his career, and John Sivebaek was sold to St Etienne of France.

Viv Anderson and Brian McClair arrive

In their places came Ferguson's first signings, England full-back Viv Anderson, and Scotland's Brian McClair.

Anderson had been a trialist with United as a boy, but had not been taken on and had eventually become a player with his home town club Nottingham Forest. He was then transferred to Arsenal after winning major honours with Forest, including the European Cup and the First Division Championship, and was a regular in the England side.

Anderson and McClair signed together on 1 July and both players had their transfer fees finalised by the Football League's independent tribunal. United paid £250,000 for Anderson, but McClair, scorer of 35 goals in his final season with Celtic, cost over three times as much. Celtic valued the player at £2 million, United offered well below that, and eventually a cheque was signed for £850,000.

For Ferguson it was the first step towards greater success and the drive towards a championship win:

> When I first arrived at this club I felt that I had to give myself time to look at the players I had taken over. I knew that I would eventually make changes, and I have gone on record as saying that I think I need to strengthen as many as five positions. It may be that I have the players for those positions already, it's up to them to show me that, but if not then I will find them elsewhere.

By the time the first full season under his management was about to commence Alex Ferguson had stamped out a clear message of intent to his players. He selected his strongest side from the squad and this shocked some.

Young Walsh was again in goal, although Turner had played in some pre-season matches, Anderson was at right-back, and Mike Duxbury on the left, in preference to the left-footed Albiston. Gibson was one of several players who had been informed that they might be made available for transfer should there be any enquiries, the others being Hogg and goalkeeper Turner. Peter Davenport was linked to other clubs, but began the season as one of the two substitutes allowed in all games after a change in the rules during the summer break.

For the opening game at Southampton McGrath and Moran formed the centre of the defence, Moses, Strachan, Robson and Olsen were in midfield and Whiteside returned to his role of attacker alongside McClair.

The Scot quickly began to repay his transfer fee, and by Christmas had scored 14 goals, more even than Hughes in his first full term, and Alex Ferguson added fuel to the flames of speculation by hinting that the prospect of McClair and the

Welsh striker playing together was not simply wishful thinking.

Hughes was finding that life with Barcelona was not what he had expected. He had flown home early in 1987 after being de-registered by the Spanish giants, which made him unable to play for them under the two-foreign-players rule, and he was immediately linked with his old club.

He played in the Gary Bailey Testimonial and scored four spectacular goals. Afterwards he said:

> I am still a Barcelona player and can do nothing unless my club wants me to do it. I have always said that if ever I came back to English football then there is only one club I would want to play for and that's United. I have a lot of friends here and get on well with the supporters.

Unofficially Hughes had hinted that he was ready to return, and this led to Alex Ferguson flying to Barcelona for talks with the player and his manager Terry Venables. After his trip he said:

> I want to bring Mark back to United, but at present the main problem is with the Inland Revenue. Mark has to stay abroad until after April 1988 otherwise he would be liable for taxation on the money he has earned since he left this country. We can do nothing until then, but I promise that I will do my best to get him playing for United again.

An injury to Paul McGrath forced Ferguson into the transfer market again in December 1987 and the target this time was Steve Bruce of Norwich City. The club was on the verge of paying £1 million to Glasgow Rangers for their England international centre-back Terry Butcher, but 24 hours before the deal would have become public knowledge, the player broke his leg. United had revealed their hand and when they turned to Norwich City for Bruce, after being rejected by Middlesbrough in a bid for Gary Pallister, they found the club difficult to deal with.

During the summer Alex Ferguson had failed to persuade Norwich to part with striker Kevin Drinkell, whom he saw as a likely partner for McClair, and when negotiations for Bruce opened he was told that the price was £1 million – the fee he had been ready to pay for Butcher. The clubs seemed to have reached agreement on a fee of £800,000 some 48 hours before United were due to play Oxford at Old Trafford on 12 December 1987. Nothing happened; the player had his bags packed ready to move north but was told that he was not being allowed to go. By 5 pm on Friday 11 December Bruce was still a Norwich player, and it took another six days before he was signed.

At first Norwich said they wanted to sign a replacement, then, after John O'Neill from QPR joined them, they said Bruce would not be released until a second player had been bought. Eventually Alex Ferguson called the deal off on 17 December, after Norwich chairman Robert Chase apparently attempted to increase the fee. Finally the Norfolk club had a change of heart and Bruce signed later that day.

Bruce made his debut in a game at Portsmouth which saw the almost rejected Turner playing in goal for his third successive game, all of them victories. Turner had won back his place after Walsh was concussed for the second time that season. The first injury was in the victory over Sheffield Wednesday at Hillsborough, the first time United had taken maximum points since the Yorkshire club's return to the First Division in 1984. The second came during a trip to Bermuda which caused a sensation for another reason, and also revealed Ferguson's strength as a man capable of dealing with a difficult situation.

The trip was arranged to coincide with United's 'blank Saturday', the fate befalling each First Division club during the 1987–88 season, when there were 21 teams competing. United played two games on the island, but it was not their football which made headline news.

Clayton Blackmore was arrested and held by police while investigations were carried out regarding a serious accusation being made against him by a young American woman. The police eventually released him after the Bermudan Attorney General ruled that there was no case to answer, but the woman told newspapers her version of the alleged incident.

News reporters besieged the airport as the team returned, but Blackmore had travelled back a day ahead of his colleagues with club solicitor Maurice Watkins. United found themselves the centre of media attention, but Alex Ferguson remained calm. He allowed sports journalists into the training ground, and as the team were about to leave for the game at QPR called Blackmore into his Friday press conference, where he answered questions from the same newspaper representatives who regularly gathered information from the club. By the weekend the spotlight had burnt itself out and the matter was closed.

Discipline was mentioned by Alex Ferguson when he faced shareholders at the club's annual meeting, and he told them that he had his own methods of dealing with such matters, but he added that these were not being discussed in such a public place as the packed Europa Suite, part of the club's lavish restaurant complex. As he looked out on the supporters gathered before him Alex Ferguson must have felt that he was amongst friends. He was the new man on the tightrope, but in his short time in charge he had shown that his heart was as much in the club as theirs. He was taking his first steps with caution, but with style. He had won over the staff under him, from the laundry ladies with whom he and Archie Knox share a daily cup of tea at 8.00 am to the chairman and his board of directors.

His natural gift for dealing with people from every walk of life was self-evident and he was filling the role of public relations officer as well as team manager. Small things mattered to Alex Ferguson. Requests for autographs became important and these were organised to coincide with Friday training sessions, when his players were faced with the week's demands for signed

Above: Steve Bruce joined United in December 1987 after a fortnight of negotiations with Norwich City. In the end he cost £800,000 and made his debut at Fratton Park, Portsmouth, on 19 December. Bruce's commitment made him a popular player immediately with the supporters and took him to the verge of full international honours in his first season at Old Trafford

Below: Paul McGrath was out of the side for five months because of injury

Below: A fee of £750,000 brought Scotland's goalkeeper Jim Leighton to Old Trafford

books, photographs and footballs, used to raise money for charity.

Pre-match preparation was re-organised. Instead of meeting at the ground and travelling to a city centre hotel for a Saturday morning meal the players were told to report to Old Trafford, where they would eat in the grill room, then relax in their lounge, or mingle with supporters.

Ferguson's influence led to the appointment of a new groundsman, the building of new dressing rooms, and a general awareness amongst his players and the administrative staff that all were responsible for the success of Manchester United.

The future for United

In 1987 the club introduced its own membership scheme to fall in line with government measures to curb football hooliganism. The United scheme was designed to give those who joined something in return for their entry fee. The club gave discount for all home games, and for goods bought at the souvenir shop. Members were sent badges and year books, and given free admission to all reserve games as well as a complimentary ticket for the club museum.

The scheme came in for some criticism in its early stages but by the end of 1987 over 40,000 supporters had joined. The idea had developed from suggestions put to the club by Bobby Charlton, and it was he, speaking at the 1987 annual meeting, who outlined his hopes for the future of Manchester United:

> I have been to Barcelona and seen the way that their membership scheme works. It enables them to raise huge amounts of capital at the start of every season, and that is one of the ways that they are able to compete with the best in Europe. It may take several years before this club can stand alongside them from a financial point of view, but we have started to take a step in that direction.
>
> Financial security is important, and in order to be successful on the field you have to be successful off it.
>
> As far as I, and my fellow directors are concerned, we have in Alex Ferguson the perfect man to lead us to success. Even in the short time he has been here he has shown us that he is doing things the right way. I can see no reason why Alex should not be here for the next 30 years, and I wish him every success for the future ... the future of Manchester United.

United entered 1988 with optimism. Victory over reigning champions Everton at Old Trafford had restored them to fourth place in the table, and although slim, the chance of Alex Ferguson taking the club to its first championship win for 21 years remained.

Liverpool stood in their way, leading the First Division and unbeaten in the League by the turn of the year. It seemed that nothing could prevent the First Division title from once more returning to Anfield, and when United drew with lowly Charlton Athletic on New Year's Day it became obvious that the fight was not only uphill, but virtually impossible.

Defeat in the Littlewoods Cup quarter-final at Oxford was soul-destroying: 'We were hoping for success in one of the domestic cup competitions,' Alex Ferguson said after losing 2–0 at the Manor Ground, 'now we have only the FA Cup to aim for.' He called for a positive response from his players, but unhelpful newspaper speculation that he would stage a wholesale clear-out at the end of the season did nothing to boost morale within the squad.

There was a glimmer of hope as the Oxford game was followed by a 2–1 televised win at Highbury, then victory over Chelsea before the biggest crowd of the season at Old Trafford as 50,700 witnessed a 2–0 win which took United through to the fifth round of the FA Cup and another visit to Arsenal's ground. This was a game which could have devastated the side for the rest of the season. After trailing 2–0 at half-time Brian McClair scored to put United back in the game. Confidence was restored and the pendulum swung United's way. After being totally dominated for the first 45 minutes they took the upper hand and pressurised Arsenal who were lucky to clear several chances away from their besieged goal, then Norman Whiteside was tripped with three minutes remaining and United were awarded a penalty, which McClair failed to convert.

It was an incident which would have left a lasting impression on many players, but McClair faced the media immediately after the game, claiming: 'When you score you are ready to take the bouquets, so you also have got to be prepared to stand up and take the criticism when you miss.' He also stepped forward to take the next penalty when the opportunity arose weeks later at Oxford. However, Alex Ferguson had removed this responsibility from his leading scorer who would have left Highbury with 21 goals to his name that season had his penalty been converted.

The media used the defeat to emphasise that United's season had ended even though February had not. Crowds began to fall and a League defeat at Norwich had Alex Ferguson demanding that his players 'show me that they want to play for Manchester United'. Many responded but Norman Whiteside and Paul McGrath reacted unexpectedly. Both said that they were unhappy at Old Trafford and asked for transfers in highly publicised moves which stunned United's followers. 'I have had some great years at Old Trafford,' said Whiteside, 'but I feel that the time has come for a change. I want to play abroad, I would not consider playing for another English club except United, but I would like to try my hand on the continent.'

McGrath's demand for a move came a short time after Whiteside's, although there had been newspaper speculation that all was not well between the player and the club following a much publicised motoring accident which led to

Left: Lee Sharpe was one of the first fruits of Alex Ferguson's revitalised Old Trafford youth policy. Signed from Torquay United as a 17-year old after only a handful of first team games, Sharpe matured from being one of 'Fergie's Fledglings' into a full England international. His early appearances in the United side indicated his attacking flair down the left flank, but injuries have curtailed his number of appearances

McGrath being injured and later fined and banned from driving on a drinks charge. 'I feel that I have gone stale,' he said, 'and I would like a new challenge.' The Republic of Ireland defender had been out of action for five months when Alex Ferguson decided that he was fit to play again but the supporters showed whose side they were on when McGrath was booed by the home fans during the game against Luton, and Whiteside was the target of chants of 'You only want the money!' as he sat on the substitute's bench during the same game.

Liverpool were champions elect, and the rivalry between the two clubs reached boiling point on Easter Monday – a week before the Luton game – when United held the Merseysiders to a 3–3 draw at Anfield in an inspired performance. United led as early as the second minute through a Bryan Robson goal, but Liverpool fought back and by the first minute of the second half were 3–1 ahead. To add to their problems United had Colin Gibson sent off for a second bookable offence but the ten men played inspired football, Robson got a second with a deflected shot and Gordon Strachan levelled the scores in the 77th minute.

A month later Liverpool were champions and United had secured second place just nine points behind them, cutting down a 17-point lead to just a three-game difference. Nottingham Forest were third, eight points adrift and Everton, who at one time had been favourites to finish runners-up to Liverpool, ended their season 11 points behind United and 20 points behind their Merseyside neighbours.

United collected 81 points, their biggest tally since the three-points-a-win system was introduced and there was much cause for optimism as the season ended: 'I know that we are not very far away from having a side which can take the championship. During the coming weeks I shall make every effort to strengthen areas of the team which I feel should be improved, and I know that we will challenge the best in our next campaign,' said Alex Ferguson at the end of his first full season as United's manager.

In May 1988 he bought Aberdeen's Scottish international goalkeeper Jim Leighton for a record £750,000 as his plans for rebuilding were put into action, but only one player was told that his services would no longer be required at the club. Arthur Albiston was given a free transfer as a career spanning 11 years of League football with the club came to a close with a testimonial game against Manchester City.

So Alex Ferguson was able to look towards the future with the words of his chairman echoing the thoughts of every United supporter: 'Time alone will tell but I am sure that Alex Ferguson will lead us to greater success than we have enjoyed in recent years. The fruits of his labours in rebuilding a vigorous youth policy, completely overhauling our scouting system and instilling a feeling of pride in everyone who wears a United shirt will I am positive be clear for all to see before very long . . . and I look forward to the future of Manchester United.'

The changes begin

The close season saw the return to Old Trafford of a player the fans had never wished to part with. Mark Hughes had left for Barcelona in 1986 but his stay there had not been a success. His return was greeted with great excitement and with Jim Leighton in goal United began the 1988–89 season confidently.

After seven games the new 'keeper had conceded just one goal – a Jan Molby penalty at Anfield – but Hughes and McClair had scored just one goal each and Ferguson's search for the right formula was constantly thwarted by injuries.

Davenport played alongside Hughes with McClair on the right side of midfield and Olsen the left.

Gordon Strachan found the going tough and after being substituted in four out of seven games began to doubt his future at the club.

Lee Martin played in the first game, a scoreless draw against Queens Park Rangers but two days later joined the queue of players in the treatment room and was out for three months.

McGrath and Whiteside were still at the club

Right: Debut delight for Neil Webb as he celebrates his goal for United against newly crowned champions Arsenal on the opening day of the 1989–90 season. The Reds won 4–1. Webb had been signed from Nottingham Forest during the summer with Mike Phelan of Norwich for a combined fee of £2 million. They were intended to fill the gap in midfield left by the departure of Gordon Strachan to Leeds United for £300,000. Less mobile than the diminutive Scot, Webb created many chances for his team-mates with his long passing. Unfortunately for Webb – and Alex Ferguson – his first season at Old Trafford was blighted by an injury he picked up while on international duty in Sweden in September 1989

though openly seeking pastures new and there was newspaper speculation that Ferguson was about to start a clear out.

The first player to leave was Peter Davenport who was bought by Middlesbrough. A month later Jesper Olsen was sold to Bordeaux, then Liam O'Brien began a new career with Newcastle United. Viv Anderson had surgery on his back, Mike Duxbury was hospitalised because of a hernia and not surprisingly the manager was forced to buy, with Northern Ireland skipper Mal Donaghy ending a long career at Luton Town.

Ferguson's revamped youth system was paying dividends and talent was coming through.

One such player was just 17 years old when he made his First Division debut in the home game against West Ham. He had been bought by United at the end of the 1987–88 season after some Ferguson cloak and dagger work in Torquay. At the time United were involved in a two day Festival of Football at Wembley, one of the events during the 100th anniversary year of the Football League. The manager went missing from the team hotel and the following day confessed that he and Archie Knox had driven to the south coast to get their man:

> I signed a young player last night who is the most expensive teenager I have ever bought but I'm sure he'll be worth every penny. His name is Lee Sharpe.

Sharpe himself recalls:

> It was late one night and I was told by my manager, the late Cyril Knowles, that Manchester United wanted to sign me. I don't remember too much about the details only that I agreed to come to Old Trafford.

Sharpe began his United career as a left full back as his new manager carefully guided him into top level football, but it was as a left sided attacking player that he made his name before injury slowed down his progress.

By the end of the 1988 season, Ferguson had used 23 players in 24 games.

Fergie's Fledglings

The arrival of Leighton eventually led to the departure of Chris Turner who moved to Wednesday in his native Sheffield, and the media was swift to emphasise signs that the Scottish 'keeper might be finding it difficult to adjust to the English game.

Leighton's confidence was dented in a much publicised incident when he dropped a harmless cross from Southampton's Graham Baker over his shoulder and into his own goal.

Statistics also showed a change of form and Leighton was under the microscope. In his first ten appearances he conceded just five goals, in the final ten matches of 1988 he was beaten on 11 occasions and had just three clean sheets.

But the goalkeeper alone was not to blame for United's slump in form. McClair and Hughes had not exactly struck gold up front.

In their first 25 games together Hughes scored 12 times but McClair had found himself restricted by his midfield role and had just eight goals to his credit. The previous season he had scored 16 in the same period.

United had been knocked out of the Littlewoods (League) Cup during a controversial game at Wimbledon's Plough Lane and many thought that a successful FA Cup run would be the season's only salvation. But the New Year's Day League clash with Liverpool gave some hope.

Martin was back in the side, and in his second League game for the club Russell Beardsmore, just out of his teens, gave a performance which overshadowed his more experienced colleagues. He scored one goal and helped McClair and Hughes to find the net as United won 3–1 to move to 6th in the League.

Within the next ten days more of "Fergie's Fledglings" emerged.

United were drawn at home to Queens Park Rangers in the Third Round of the FA Cup and at the last minute Ferguson found himself forced to make changes. Lee Sharpe had 'flu and Paul McGrath was withdrawn.

Mark Robins, a prolific goalscorer with the junior teams, was plunged into the side and two youngsters, Deiniol Graham and David Wilson found themselves on the substitutes' bench even though both had already played a game earlier on that morning.

The tie ended nil-nil.

For the replay four days later Sharpe had

recovered and joined Beardsmore, Martin and Tony Gill in the starting line-up with Graham and Wilson on the bench.

A pulsating game went into extra-time after Gill equalised, then United took the lead when Wilson crossed and Graham stabbed the ball home only for Rangers to force a second replay with a late goal.

Eventually United reached the quarter final stages of the competition but lost at home to Nottingham Forest.

Strachan goes to Leeds

More young players were given an opportunity to make the grade as Alex Ferguson realised that United had little chance of gaining any honours.

Guiliano Maiorana, a Cambridge boy with Italian parents, made his full debut in a televised game against Arsenal, Robins had his League debut against Derby County and Gill delighted the home supporters with an exciting goal against Millwall just seven days after that strike at QPR.

But injuries devastated the "Fledglings".

Deiniol Graham badly broke his arm and eventually left the club, Tony Gill broke a leg in March 1989, an injury which ended his career, and young Maiorana so badly damaged his knee it took two years to recover.

Gill's injury came in the week that the player he replaced had left the club.

Gordon Strachan was transferred to Leeds United for £300,000 moving to the Second Division club with the words:

> My one wish now is that I can return to Old Trafford in the not too distant future as Leeds celebrate promotion to the First Division and United are the champions.

Who would have thought that within the next three years and with Strachan as captain, Leeds would not only achieve their target of promotion but would beat United to the championship!

The season ended with murmurings of unrest on the terraces. Ferguson's critics used the tabloid press as well as radio and television to snipe at the manager.

Not surprisingly he hit back refusing access to certain journalists and making it clear to former players and managers that they, and their comments were not welcome.

The Michael Knighton affair

Then came a period in the club's history when its activities off the field received as much publicity as those on it.

There was understandable optimism when, during the summer of 1989 Ferguson spent £2 million on Neil Webb from Nottingham Forest and Michael Phelan the Norwich City captain.

But on the eve of the opening game of 1989–1990 news broke that businessman Michael Knighton was to buy the majority shareholding in the club. Chairman Martin Edwards called a press conference at Old Trafford and Knighton was introduced as a man who was ready to invest cash in the club. He eagerly outlined his plans, which included spending £10 million on the Stretford End.

Knighton promised great things for the future of his new club:

> Clearly this is a very big day in my life, but what I would like to say, and this is very important, Martin Edwards and myself have not just met, and it didn't just happen last night. We have reached a synergy together over the last six weeks, we've grown together as friends. I look forward to working with Alex Ferguson, he's got my 150 per cent support at the moment. I'm very anxious to make public from the outset that we intend completing this marvellous stadium we have at Old Trafford and making it literally one of the finest in the world . . . perhaps even the Mecca. Who knows? We've certainly got the legend to go with that. We will start immediately at the end of this season with the development of the Stretford End and certainly funds are in place to do that.

Knighton stole the headlines the following day

Left: While Ferguson was prepared to introduce unproven youngsters into his team, he was happy to part with a club record of £2.3 million for the experience of Middlesbrough's Gary Pallister. The 6ft 4in central defender soon linked up with Steve Bruce to form an awesome partnership. From his debut, an inauspicious 2–0 home defeat by Norwich on 30 August 1989, Pallister had an unbroken first team run well into the following season

Below: In mid-September 1989, Ferguson extended his purchasing programme by paying West Ham £2 million for midfielder Paul Ince and Southampton £1.5 million for lightning winger Danny Wallace. Ince's career at Old Trafford began encouragingly enough on 16 September with a 5–1 demolition of Millwall. The following Saturday, however, Ince and United were swept aside by derby rivals Manchester City at Maine Road. The final score – 5–1 to City

when Old Trafford gave him a rapturous welcome as he performed a ball juggling act in front of the 47,000 gathered for the game against Arsenal, making it difficult to imagine that this was a man who 24 hours earlier had claimed to be quiet and shy!

The showbiz start rubbed off on the players who slammed new champions Arsenal 4–1 with Neil Webb having a dream debut and scoring ten minutes from time. Mark Hughes and Brian McClair also got onto the scoresheet following a Steve Bruce goal in the second minute.

Ferguson had been criticised for his summer selling of Norman Whiteside to Everton and Paul McGrath to Aston Villa but the victory helped to silence those who spoke out against the manager.

With the season three games old he spent again, a record £2.3 million on Gary Pallister of Middlesbrough.

In mid-September he completed the £2 million purchase of Paul Ince of West Ham after a medical snag and bought Danny Wallace the speedy winger from Southampton for £1.5 million, but only after seeing the injury jinx hit another of his players.

Neil Webb was carried off during a Sweden-England game in Gothenburg after rupturing his Achilles tendon and was ruled out for the next seven months.

By the time Webb played again Michael Knighton no longer made the headlines but our story of United in the 1980's ends by looking at the spectacular series of events which followed the announcement that he was taking control of the club.

Robert Maxwell v Michael Knighton

So began a 55 day guessing game which saw media moguls using all their big guns to shoot down a man they claimed was insignificant.

The trouble started for Michael Knighton started when doubts were cast about his wealth. He had two months to come up with the capital to buy the Edwards shareholding and there were many who claimed he would fail.

The biggest campaign against him came from the *Daily Mirror*, the newspaper owned by Robert Maxwell whose efforts to take over United in January 1984 had themselves proved abortive.

A week after Knighton's arrival the *Manchester Evening News* printed a story naming two businessmen claiming to be providing Knighton's financial backing.

A relative of one of these men, Stanley Cohen, had allegedly told a neighbour that it was Cohen who was buying United and not Knighton, and from that tiny acorn . . .

The other alleged partner was Robert Thornton, chairman of Debenhams, who Knighton claimed was both his neighbour and friend.

By Friday 15 September the deal was said to be off because Cohen and Thornton had pulled out, but Knighton stunned his opponents by holding another Old Trafford press conference to announce that despite eveything that had been said, it was definitely on.

Aware of the Takeover Panel's rigid rules, newspaper publisher Eddie Shah claimed Knighton's representatives had approached him with documents which seemed to imply that control of the club was for sale. He had immediately contacted Martin Edwards and returned the dossier to him.

Edwards took out a high court injunction against Knighton to stop him approaching any other would-be buyers.

Within the United boardroom the directors were not happy with the situation and Amer Midani and Bobby Charlton openly said that they felt that the club should be floated on the Stock Market, with supporters investing.

Michael Edelson, Nigel Burrows, Maurice Watkins and Bobby Charlton held late night meetings at Old Trafford as newsmen waited outside. Then late on Tuesday, 10 October they streamed out of one such meeting and drove to the Midland Hotel (The Holiday Inn Crown Plaza) in the city centre.

In the hotel where Rolls met Royce the fate of Manchester United was decided.

On Wednesday, 11 October, 12 hours before the takeover deadline there was another press conference.

Rumour had it that Knighton had pulled out, unable to find the capital but he turned up, and faced the media flanked by Maurice Watkins, and Martin Edwards the man he had hoped to succeed.

The gathering was told that the contract under which M.K. Trafford Holdings (Knighton's company) was to buy the 50.6 per cent shareholding of Martin Edwards had been cancelled by mutual consent.

In return for withdrawing from the agreement Michael Knighton had been given a seat on the United board.

He firmly stood by his claim that he was ready to complete the takeover:

> There was no question in anyone's mind and certainly not in my mind that the funding was there to move ahead, and that the contract was legally watertight.
>
> Had I been the incredibly selfish and mercenary character that some people claim I might be, then I would not be here today, I would be going along to my bank and placing very large deposits of money.

The Knighton affair had amazed the fans who found it hard to believe. As for the players perhaps the final word on the matter should come from Bryan Robson:

> Obviously the players have been concerned about what has been happening during the take-over situation because it does affect us. But when people say to me that Manchester United has been dragged down into the gutter I can't agree. I think it all went on a long time and people made a lot of it because it was United.

SHA

The 1990s: Chasing the Championship

Left: The prodigious talent of Welsh-born Ryan Giggs was one of the reasons why Manchester United came so close to winning the coveted First Division title in 1991–92. Yet another product of the youth policy instigated by Alex Ferguson in his first years at Old Trafford, Giggs, made 51 League and Cup appearances, scored seven goals and thrilled fans up and down the country with his dazzling skills and pinpoint crossing. The quality of young players like Giggs married with the established reputations of some of the more expensive playing assets, make United a real force in the new Premier League

Alex Ferguson stepped into the 1990s wondering if he was in fact going to see much of them as manager of Manchester United. He was going backwards in the League and the ever eager media hawks were busy adding up the vast amounts of money he had spent only to find the elusive Championship looking further away than ever before.

But the turn of the decade also proved the turning point in the career of Ferguson at Old Trafford and for that he can thank the FA Cup. The road to Wembley had its anxious moments but it was a life-saver as far as his future with United was concerned, especially winning at Nottingham Forest in the third round as the storm clouds were gathering. United went to the City Ground against a background of a run of eight League games without a win, half of them defeats and the tabloid newspapers were seeking a vote of confidence from chairman Martin Edwards about the manager's future, invariably a kiss of death.

There was never any likelihood of the papers getting one because the chairman was well aware of the implications and as far as he was concerned the issue was simply not up for debate. Edwards and his fellow directors were well satisfied with the manager's work. Although naturally disappointed with the lack of progress in the League, they understood the reasons, such as the injuries to Bryan Robson and Neil Webb which had wrecked what Ferguson had hoped would be his midfield engine-room. The board were also impressed with the way their manager had completely restructured the scouting and coaching systems and they felt that given time things would start to come together.

Subsequent success has proved them absolutely right and it was good to see the club sticking by a few principles and avoiding the obvious knee-jerk reaction which so often accompanies a bad run. United in the past have been as guilty as the rest of football in this respect, but this time they stuck with their man, and a wise policy it proved to be. Nevertheless there was an unmistakable tension about the place as the Reds prepared for the Cup tie without the services of Robson, Webb, Wallace and Ince. Ferguson was forced to turn to his young ones like Mark Robins and Russell Beardsmore, and they didn't fail him. In fact Robins scored the goal in a 1–0 win which brought a great sigh of relief for those who felt that it was important Ferguson should be allowed to continue with his work at Old Trafford.

The youngster had pumped new life into the club the previous season at a crisis point and Robins went on to show that given a decent run in the team he could produce goals, whatever his other failings might be. That season he finished with a total of 10 goals in League and Cup, yet he started in only 13 games. He was brought on as a substitute in a further 10 matches, but it is still a remarkable scoring rate and one which has made a lot of people wonder why he hasn't been a more regular player in the first team.

The team continued to limp along in the League to finish 13th in the First Division. They could not have expected better when Mark Hughes was their top scorer in the League with 13 goals, Robins was next with seven while Brian McClair limped along with a mere five.

But the team had correctly sniffed Wembley and they somehow pulled themselves together for the FA Cup ties. The fourth round took them to Hereford and a very muddy pitch. It seemed tailor made for a Cup upset given United's erratic form in the League. It rained so hard that spectators who had parked early alongside the ground came out to find their cars marooned in a sea of water. Clayton Blackmore took the honours by scoring the only goal of the match with just four minutes to go.

The next round was at Newcastle where United won an exciting tussle 3–2 with goals from Danny Wallace, Brian McClair and Mark Robins again. United certainly did not get to Wembley the easy way, for the sixth round brought them yet another away tie, a tricky one against a hard-running Sheffield United side calculated to rattle the more sophisticated yet fragile Reds. McClair got them a 1–0 victory to line them up for a Lancashire derby semi-final against Oldham Athletic at Maine Road. At least United went into this match on the back of a couple of League wins,

though this hardly prepared them for a tremendous onslaught by their Second Division opponents who played out of their skins for a 3–3 draw after extra time. Robson and Webb scored the United goals with one from Wallace after coming on as a substitute. Robins proved the Cup hero again with the score locked at 1–1 at the end of normal time. He came on as an extra-time sub to score the winner and rescue Ferguson's season with an FA Cup final against Crystal Palace.

Palace manager Steve Coppell shocked his old club with the physical intensity of his team's approach, quite foreign to his own performances as a winger at Old Trafford in the 1970s. United still seemed to have the game sewn up after goals from Robson and Hughes had given them a 2–1 lead with half an hour to go. But Coppell had an ace up his sleeve and he brought on the dashing Ian Wright to score and send the tie into extra time. Wright, a couple of seasons later the First Division's top scorer with Arsenal, put Palace in front almost from the kick off in the extra period. It took another goal from Hughes to give the Reds a replay following the 3–3 see-saw match.

Jim Leighton had been worrying his manager for a few weeks and he was widely blamed for two of the goals. Ferguson, who had given the Scottish international his debut as a boy at Aberdeen agonised long and hard, and then finally dropped him for the replay. The United manager has since said that if he had his time over again he couldn't make the same decision, not because it was a wrong one for the team but because of the way it wrecked the career of a player who by now was virtually a friend, so long had they known each other. The decision made sense, though his replacement, Les Sealey, still represented a gamble. Sealey had been brought to Old Trafford on loan from Luton as emergency cover and because he had been frozen out at Kenilworth Road he had played only two first-team games in 18 months. Confidence is not lacking in the chirpy Cockney from Bethnal Green though and he took Wembley in his stride to steady the defence and present a more reliable front to Crystal Palace.

The Londoners again tried to rough the Reds up but underdogs rarely get a second chance and United won 1–0 with a goal after 60 minutes from a man who nearly didn't play. Lee Martin was within an ace of being left out of the replay because the manager was concerned about his ability to last through extra time without getting cramp. The full-back had been substituted in the three previous rounds after going down with leg muscle problems. But as Ferguson said later: 'It was touch and go whether I kept him in the side, but we decided that if we played our best defenders we could win in normal time. That's football for you, the one you nearly dropped wins the FA Cup for you.' It was only Martin's second goal for United in the first team and it crowned a splendid season for the Hyde-born youngster who had joined the club as a YTS boy. The team which won the Cup in the replay lined up:

Sealey, Ince, Martin, Bruce, Phelan, Pallister, Robson, Webb, McClair, Hughes, Wallace. Subs: (not used) Robins, Blackmore.

As a result of his part in the victory Sealey earned himself a permanent contract; Leighton retreated into the shadows and made only one more first-team appearance before going back home to Scotland two years later. Ferguson felt for him, but he was fighting for his own skin and winning the FA Cup silenced the doubters and gave him time to develop his team.

They immediately made a strong challenge in all three cup competitions the following season, reaching the sixth round of the FA Cup and the final of the Rumbelows Cup where they underestimated the opposition and lost 1-0 to Sheffield

Left: After Cup successes in 1990 and 1991, the fans' desire for a championship trophy to extend United's silverware collection was matched only by the manager's desire to deliver it. There was great interest, then, when Ferguson signed a relative unknown during the summer of 1991. Andrei Kanchelskis arrived from Donetsk of the Soviet Union for £650,000 and immediately caught the eye with his electrifying speed and intricate skills. During his first season he contributed eight goals in 48 appearances, which made him the club's third highest scorer behind McClair and Hughes

Above: Danish goalkeeper Peter Schmeichel and England international Paul Parker were two more astute signings at the commencement of the 1991–92 season

Wednesday. They were not helped by the preparations of a subdued Archie Knox leaving to become coach of Glasgow Rangers, though the promotion of Brian Kidd to fill the Knox role was to become a great success in subsequent seasons.

The board's faith in their manager was certainly rewarded, though, as the team charged through to win the European Cup Winner's Cup by beating Barcelona 2-1 in the final in Rotterdam. Mark Hughes scored both goals to give the club their first European trophy since 1968.

Off the field, the club was floated as a public company, raising £7m for the redevelopment of the Stretford End and along the way netting chairman Martin Edwards a similar amount as majority shareholder.

Season 1991-92 saw the team gathering even more momentum to finish brave runners-up to Leeds for the championship with the Rumbelows Cup their consolation after beating Nottingham Forest 1-0 in the final, the single goal coming from Brian McClair.

Then as United entered the newly formed Premiership League for season 1992-93 Alex Ferguson made a move in the transfer market which was to prove the turning point in the club's fortunes.

Right: Man of the match Brian McClair holds aloft the League Cup trophy that his goal secured for Manchester United in 1992. With Mark Hughes, McClair spearheaded the Reds' attack during the late 1980s and early 1990s and scored 25 goals in 1991–92. Remarkably, McClair had to wait until the 1992 European Championships before he found the net for his country, scoring one of Scotland's three goals against the Commonwealth of Independent States in his 25th international appearance

The arrival of Cantona

On Thursday 26 November chairman Edwards received a call from Bill Fotherby, the managing director of Leeds United. It was an inquiry about the possible purchase of Denis Irwin. Ferguson was with the chairman and refused, but asked, somewhat tongue-in-cheek, if Leeds were willing to part with Eric Cantona. Within days he was bought for £1 million.

The French international had arrived in England earlier in the year amid controversy. He was about to sign for Sheffield Wednesday when instead he opted for Leeds. His undeniable contribution to their Championship success had not gone unnoticed at Old Trafford.

That purchase would be seen by many as the moment when United took a major step towards the ending of the 26-year wait since the last Championship win. It led to Ferguson's comments as Cantona signed:

> I see Eric as a Manchester United player, the kind we want at this club. He has style, he has class and this club will suit him. His goal scoring was instrumental in the success of Leeds last year. I am happy to bring another striker to the club, one who has a good reputation and one who won't in any way be overawed at playing at Old Trafford.

He was right. Cantona was soon to be hailed 'Le Roi de Old Trafford', a new 'King' to succeed the last to carry that title, Denis Law.

Cantona was registered too late to play against Arsenal at Highbury but he saw his new colleagues win 1–0 thanks to a Mark Hughes goal. The Frenchman came on as substitute during the 2–1 derby win over Manchester City on 6 December, then made his full debut six days later in the victory over leaders Norwich. In that game Hughes scored again, his fourth strike in as many appearances. Cantona was providing the flair as well as the opportunities with a seemingly endless supply of passes to his colleagues. United moved into third place.

The unbeaten run continued into the New Year and included a sensational 3–3 draw at Hillsborough, where at one point United trailed 3–0. It was Cantona who scored the equaliser and in the last six frantic minutes just failed to get what would have been a sensational winner. Next, Coventry were beaten 5–0 at Old Trafford and Tottenham fell in similar style losing 4–1. United won 3–1 at Loftus Road against a Queens Park Rangers side which had been going well and Nottingham Forest were beaten 2–0 in a game which saw the return to Old Trafford of Neil Webb, sold back to his former club for £800,000 shortly before Cantona's arrival.

The season's fifth defeat came at Ipswich, then was followed by another surge, as with 11 games left the wheel turned full circle. United beat Liverpool 2–1 at Anfield to go top and avenge the disappointment of the previous year. They had been knocked out of the FA Cup at Bramall Lane by Sheffield United, the eventual semi-finalists, but Bryan Robson saw this as no disadvantage:

> Last season we did Leeds a big favour when we knocked them out of both cups. This year there won't be any fixture pile up for us as there was last time. We have one thing to concentrate on and I'm sure the lads can do it.

But would it be with or without Bryan Robson?

Injury to the long-serving skipper had restricted him to just six appearances by mid-March and there were fears he might not qualify for a winners award if United did take the title. It would have been a cruel irony, and Alex Ferguson quickly dispelled such talk:

Bryan has been a great servant to this club and if we are successful he will get his medal no matter what happens. The rules allow two discretionary awards to be made and he will get one of these if he doesn't play in the ten games he needs to qualify. But let us cross that bridge when we come to it – at present we have still to win the title.

Oldham Athletic decided that they would put an abrupt end to any Championship talk. Fighting for survival, they won 1–0 at Boundary Park. The newspapers loved it when it was revealed that Ron Atkinson had promised Oldham manager Joe Royle a bottle of champagne if Oldham did Villa a favour. After the game Royle demanded a whole case and the newspaper headlines asked:

Has Fergie got the bottle?

He was unmoved. His players would do the talking, but drawn games against Villa and Arsenal at Old Trafford, then City at Maine Road, saw them slip back to third. Villa led.

So began the most crucial period of the season and the club's most important run of results for 26 years. Norwich regained the leadership with a home win over Villa. Then came United's turn to go to Carrow Road and they would face the leaders without a key player. Mark Hughes was suspended, but manager Ferguson bravely named an attacking side which included Cantona, Kanchelskis, Giggs, Sharpe and McClair.

They hit Norwich with speed and skill and the home side had no answer. By the end of the night United were top of the League once more after a resounding 3–1 victory.

Giggs, Kanchelskis and Cantona each plundered goals in the first 21 minutes as they were inspired by the midfield efforts of Paul Ince. Before facing his former club an optimistic Steve Bruce had said:

Seven matches left and if we win all of them nobody can stop us!

Such optimism, but he was right and that is exactly what happened! That defeat at Oldham was the last of the season, and it was Bruce himself who played a crucial role in ensuring the first of those seven victories. It was against Sheffield Wednesday, who came to Old Trafford threatening to steal a game filled with incident as well as time-wasting tactics.

Wednesday played with a packed midfield. Tension was high and to add to the drama the crowd witnessed the unusual sight of a substitute referee. Michael Peck was replaced after pulling a muscle. Linesmen John Hilditch took over and almost immediately awarded Sheffield a penalty from which John Sheridan scored. With six minutes to go Bruce equalised and twelve minutes later headed the winner. The second half ended

Above: Andrei Kanchelskis adapted quickly to the United style and made a major contribution to both Championship campaigns of 1993 and 1994. He scored some important goals, perhaps none more so than against Leeds at Elland Road when United opened up a telling lead during the run-in to the 1994 title

53 minutes after it had commenced because of time added on.

A 1–0 win at Coventry was followed by a 3-0 home victory over Chelsea and then the night which in the eye of the United faithful decided the destiny of the Championship.

United were away to Crystal Palace as Aston Villa played Blackburn Rovers at Ewood Park. Before United had kicked off Villa were 2–0 down and went on to lose 3–0. Mark Hughes and Paul Ince scored at Selhurst Park and the United fans taunted their former manager:

Are you watching big fat Ron?
Is it true your bottle's gone?

As for Alex Ferguson, for the first time he spoke as though he felt the Championship could now be won:

We have got ourselves into a fantastic position: two games left and four points clear. We have a far superior goal difference. Now we need to finish the job properly. It would be lovely to win the Championship at Old Trafford in our last home game so that we can pay back a support that has waited so long.

Champions again at last

That game was against Blackburn on Monday, 3 May but United were Champions before that.

The previous day and against all odds Oldham beat Aston Villa 1–0 at Villa Park. There was no talk about champagne this time. The defeat ended Villa's aspirations and the Manchester fans celebrated.

The Blackburn game became a showpiece with United fighting from behind to win 3–1. Ryan Giggs, Paul Ince and Gary Pallister scored as the players were urged on by a fanatical crowd which chanted, sang and danced its way through a carnival 90 minutes.

The scenes bridged the 26-year gap as Steve Bruce, skipper for most of the season, and club captain Bryan Robson – who eventually appeared in 13 Premier League games – together collected the Championship trophy. Robson had reached that elusive milestone:

> People have talked about it being 26 years for Manchester United but I remember 17 years ago being top when I was at West Brom before we were overtaken by Liverpool. We finished fourth. I have wanted a Championship medal since that moment. At times I thought it would never happen.

One game remained, a return to Selhurst Park for a 2–1 victory over Wimbledon. Paul Ince got the opening goal, and fittingly it was Robson who scored his first of the season and the last of the season's campaign.

During the summer as Manchester continued its celebrations Alex Ferguson followed his now established pattern of making a major transfer move. It was the much speculated purchase of Nottingham Forest's Irish midfielder Roy Keane who cost close to £4 million. He made his debut at Wembley against Arsenal in the Charity Shield after going on the club's pre-season warm-up trip to South Africa where they had visited the townships and played in a tournament against their Wembley opponents.

Right: They ignored the rain and turned out in their thousands to cheer the Champions through the streets of Manchester on their open-topped bus. The players were soaked to the skin but like the supporters would not let a torrential downpour dampen their spirits. Manchester United were Champions, the first winners of the new FA Premier League. These scenes from 1993 were repeated a year later when United again paraded the trophy after retaining it . . . and this time the weather was kinder

The Wembley curtain-raiser ended 1–1 with Mark Hughes scoring for United and Ian Wright equalising before a penalty shoot-out decided that the shield should once again bear the name of Manchester United as its holders. It was a trophy collected before the season had even started but United wanted more.

Bryan Robson, who was about to commence his final year at Old Trafford, made their aim clear with this statement:

> We would dearly love to retain the Championship and there is no reason to believe that we cannot make a good challenge. Over the last two seasons we have the best record in the League. But we also have ambitions to do well in Europe. This club has never won two major trophies in the same season and I feel that would be a tremendous achievement.

United for the double? There was a long road ahead. They began their defence of their title at Carrow Road, scene of that important victory the previous season, and again came out winners. Ryan Giggs and the veteran Robson each scored with Norwich surprising their audience by facing the Champions with a defensive formation, fielding a sweeper to try to stem any of United's high speed breaks.

It was a sign of things to come for Ferguson and his players who would be subjected to the plotting of coaches, and the scrutiny of the media, especially television pundits and experts, for the rest of the season.

Sponsorship had led to the Premier League changing its title to the FA Carling Premiership, but little else was altered to the pattern of fixtures.

United began their season on Sunday, 15 August to meet the demands of television and three days later met Sheffield United in the midweek fixture at Old Trafford. It was Keane's home debut and his two goals in a 3–0 victory thrilled a large crowd.

United saw out August at the top of the table. They had played five games, winning four and drawing at Old Trafford against the revived Newcastle, who had been promoted at the end of the previous season. Then came their first defeat – and one which was to prove significant eight months later. They lost 1–0 at Stamford Bridge against a Chelsea side which was well organised but perhaps a little fortunate.

After a Cantona lob from close to the half-way line bounced onto the crossbar and was caught by Chelsea's retreating Russian goalkeeper Dmitri Kharine, the game's only goal came at the opposite end of the field. Kharine's clearance resulted in a shot on United's goal, Schmeichel failed to hold the ball and Gavin Peacock found himself on the scoresheet. A similar occurrence, while not in totally identical circumstances, would be reversed the following May when the sides met at Wembley in the FA Cup Final.

Before that though was a season filled with drama, joy and sadness for Manchester United. The first disappointment was the failure to get beyond the second round of the European Cup,

SHARP

Right: Sealed with a kiss. Alex Ferguson, the first manager since Sir Matt Busby to lead United to the Championship and, because of the changes in English football, first to hold the FA Premier League trophy. Since his arrival at Old Trafford Ferguson's record is remarkable. In 1990 he became the first manager to win the Scottish and English FA Cups, then, a year later, the first to have led two clubs to success in the European Cup Winners' Cup. In 1994, ten years after winning the League and Cup double with Aberdeen, he achieved a unique distinction by doing the same with United

with defeat under the away goals rule by Galatasaray, the little-known Turkish side, who fought back from two goals down to force a draw at Old Trafford in the first leg of the tie.

Before this United continued their domination of the Premiership with consecutive victories over Arsenal, Swindon, Sheffield Wednesday, Tottenham, Everton and QPR. After 13 games they were 11 points clear of the chasing Norwich, Arsenal, Blackburn and Aston Villa and 20 ahead of their rivals Manchester City, who provided the opposition immediately after the European upset.

It was another televised Sunday game, and the home supporters who had gathered at Maine Road could be forgiven for thinking that they were about to witness a shock. City led 2–0 at half time. Their season had been plagued with demonstrations against chairman Peter Swales and the demands for a change at the top which eventually led to the appointment of Francis Lee. The fact that United were dominating the League in such a fashion was hard to bear for the rival City fans.

Some consolation might come from victory against the 'old enemy' but United were not prepared to lie down. Eric Cantona scored twice during the second period and City fell apart well before Roy Keane scored the winning goal with three minutes to spare.

An unbeaten run – the scores against Galatasaray were 3–3 and 0–0 – had started on 22 September, after a side without Cantona, Giggs, Ince, Parker and Keane lost 2–1 in the first leg of a League Cup tie at Stoke. It continued for 34 League and Cup fixtures.

Blackburn staged a remarkable challenge and came closest to breaking the sequence on Boxing Day. They led 1–0 at Old Trafford, resisting all United could muster. There was relief for Ferguson and his players when with two minutes remaining Paul Ince scored an equaliser that was just reward for the effort of the afternoon.

After United had beaten Oldham 5–2 at Boundary Park, they began the New Year with a home draw against Leeds. This was followed by a sensational game at Anfield, where they led 3–0 at one stage thanks to goals from Bruce, Giggs and Irwin, only for Liverpool to fight back and draw 3–3. If United could give away such an advantage in a game, could they also be caught in the Championship they had dominated for so long?

Blackburn's efforts were paying off. They beat Everton then Villa, closing the gap. They also had two games in hand on United. Regardless of this the newspapers predicted that the race would end early with United clear winners. Alex Ferguson showed more caution:

> There is a long way to go and nobody at this club is taking anything for granted. We know what it is like to come close and miss out and we also know what it is like to go all the way. That experience will be to our advantage when the moment comes.

The draw for the Third Round of the FA Cup once again paired United with their namesakes in Sheffield with the tie attracting the attention of BBC television. In it United showed both sides of their character. They won easily but the petulance of Mark Hughes led to him being sent off close to the end after kicking an opponent in anger. He had already been cautioned and the second yellow card brought a one match suspension. The incident also provided TV with evidence it would hold against Ferguson and his players later.

Hughes then scored the only goal of the game as United took their League campaign to Tottenham, three days after drawing at home to

Right: United introduced a revolutionary new black strip at the start of the 1993–94 season, allowing supporters to follow the fashionable trend of wearing a variety of club colours. It also became fashionable for United to win away from home! Here Roy Keane and Denis Irwin (player's names and squad numbers on shirts were also introduced in the Premiership) celebrate the latter's goal at Southampton which sealed a 3–1 victory. United won twelve away games in retaining the Championship

Portsmouth in the Coca-Cola (League) Cup.

But before the next fixture, the club was plunged into mourning following the death of Sir Matt. The former manager passed away shortly before 5.30 pm on Thursday 20 January and his death struck everyone associated with United. Within minutes of the news being announced spectators began to gather outside Old Trafford to stand in silent homage. Floral tributes, scarves and banners were laid and many wept openly.

The following morning Alex Ferguson had the task of lifting his players as they trained. Each of them was aware of the significant role Sir Matt had played in the history of the club and Bryan Robson spoke on their behalf.

> Although none of us played under the great man we all knew him well. He was at the club every day and I will always remember him. He was a man who had time for everyone and anyone and I have never heard a bad word said about him. He will never be forgotten.

Sir Matt Busby

Old Trafford was turned into a shrine when Sir Matt Busby died on 20 January 1994, aged 84.

As the news spread supporters came from far and wide to gather at the ground in silent tribute to the man who made their theatre of dreams come alive. It was well before dawn when the first fan arrived to lay a single bunch of flowers on the concrete forecourt beneath the Munich clock memorial, the symbol of the tragic air disaster woven into the history of Manchester United and their distinguished manager who went on to become the President. Before that first day of mourning was over the roped off area below the clock had become a carpet of red and white, as grieving admirers of the grand old man of English football came with flowers and to lay their scarves and flags in his memory. One message summed up the feelings:

> You planted the seeds that have made Manchester United the greatest team in the world. Rest in peace Sir Matt, you have left us all in safe hands.

Later all the favours and personal mementoes were gathered up and compressed into bales, a concentration of loving tributes, which will be kept in the club museum.

But of course there were also appreciations of his work and contribution to football from around the world which were probably best summed up by Lennart Johansson, President of UEFA, who wrote from Berne to say:

> Sir Matt was a man of dignity, courage and warmth, who experienced both triumph and tragedy in the service of his club. He will be remembered for having built the wonderful Busby Babes team of the 1950s, and who knows what that team might have achieved in European football but for the Munich air disaster in 1958, which cost so many talented young footballers their lives. Sir Matt himself was seriously injured in the accident, but it was a mark of his great strength of character that he survived his injuries and returned to the game he loved despite the ordeal he had suffered.
>
> Within 10 years, Sir Matt had built a second great United team, which went on to win the Champion Clubs' Cup against Benfica on a night of high emotion at Wembley. This was perhaps Sir Matt's finest hour as a manager. His teams always embodied all that is best about football, style, panache and above all entertainment. These attributes made Manchester United loved by millions throughout the world.
>
> After his retirement as a manager, Sir Matt continued to give valuable service not only to United but also to the European Football Union as an advisor and expert. His opinions always deserved the greatest respect. He was, quite simply, a giant of a man. Those who follow European football will never forget his achievements, and European football will be the poorer with his passing. We shall all miss him.

Sir Matt's funeral procession stopped for a few moments beside Old Trafford, which Martin Edwards believes will be a permanent memorial to his achievements as the architect of today's Manchester United.

'To gauge the life and work of Sir Matt you have only to look at the magnificent stadium and think back to how it was at the end of the war, bombed and derelict,' he said.

A great many people felt that away from the football field Sir Matt became wedded to the city on the day in 1967 when he was made a Freeman of Manchester. It was a proud occasion, not just for the son of a Scottish miner, who had been killed in the First World War, and his family, but for the fans who had come to owe the great man so much. For Matthew Busby was Manchester's first Freeman from the world of sport, an honour recognising that his magic had radiated far beyond Old Trafford.

Below: Seven away games played and victory number six on its way as Andrei Kanchelskis leaves Manchester City skipper Keith Curie trailing in his slip-stream during the Maine Road derby. City led 2–0 at half time but a tremendous performance in the second period pulled United through to a sensational 3–2 victory which kept them firmly on top of the Premiership. There was added significance in the victory as it came immediately after the disappointment of the exit from the European Cup

Above: The incident which led to Eric Cantona's sending-off at Swindon as he stamps on John Moncur following a tussle for the ball. The Frenchman was in trouble again three days later when he was dismissed during the game at Arsenal and was suspended for five matches. That was his third red card of the season, although the first – shown after the final whistle in Istanbul – has been expunged from his record by UEFA

Right: An understandably angry Eric Cantona walks from the field at Highbury after being sent off for a second bookable offence. Television evidence proved that referee Vic Callow had been harsh in his treatment of the United striker. Six games remained after his ban; five ended in victory and one was drawn. Cantona scored five of his 25 goals during that period

That evening, the sombre stone walls of the Town Hall took on warmth as the city's adopted son accepted his honour and sketched his life from the day he was born in a pitman's cottage in a small village near Glasgow. He described his anxious days struggling to make his mark at Manchester City until a switch of position sparked the start of a success story, first as a player and then as manager of Manchester United and chose to reveal his deep love and feeling for football which made him such a man of substance behind all the honours and titles:

> I won't deny that it is pleasant to succeed in what you strive to do, but winning matches at all costs is not the test of true achievement.
>
> There is nothing wrong with trying to win, as long as you don't set the garland and the prize above the game. There is no dishonour in defeat, as long as you play to the limit of your strength and skill.
>
> There have been incidents which have brought no credit to the game. I think it is well, therefore, that I should say that what matters above all things is that the game should be played in the right spirit, with the utmost resource of skill and courage, with fair play and no favour, with every man playing as a member of a team, and the result accepted without bitterness or conceit.
>
> Football's great occasions are, for me at any rate, unequalled in the world of sport. I feel a sense of romance, wonder and mystery, a sense of beauty and poetry. The game becomes larger than life. It has something of the timeless, magical quality of legend.

Those words by the man who became a legend in his own lifetime summed up the philosophy which inspired his management and which has perhaps, set him apart from football's other leaders. There was invariably something special about his teams and people sensed that he was striving to make football better.

Football goes on

Life and football had to go on, and that Saturday, as the Championship pennant flew at half mast, Old Trafford stood in total silence before the League clash with Everton. There were unfortunate scenes however at Anfield and Ewood Park where Manchester City and Leeds supporters disrespectfully chanted during the one minute silence. Alex Ferguson said before facing the game with Everton:

> The result of today's game is irrelevant. I want my players to go out and play the way that Sir Matt would want them to. This game is for his memory and for what he did for football.

His words preceded a display of outstanding skill which remarkably produced only one goal but which had the crowd screaming for more.

Sir Matt's funeral came on the morning after United reached the semi-final of the Coca-Cola Cup by beating Portsmouth 1–0 in a replay they dominated, and three days later they were at Norwich in the FA Cup.

In that game Roy Keane and Eric Cantona scored in a 2–0 win, but Ferguson was angered by comments made on BBC television where slow motion replays were used to highlight an incident involving the Frenchman. He was seen to kick a Norwich player in the back as the two raced for a loose ball and the comments of pundit Jimmy Hill who accused Cantona of vicious play brought a sharp retaliation from the United manager:

> Jimmy Hill is a pratt!

Victories followed at QPR, in the first leg of the Coca-Cola Cup semi-final against Sheffield Wednesday, and in the FA Cup at Selhurst Park where Wimbledon were beaten 3–0. United were still top of the Premiership and one game away from the season's first cup final. Talk now was of the treble, a feat yet to be achieved in England.

They reached the Coca-Cola Cup Final following a display of all out attacking football at Hillsborough, where Sheffield Wednesday were beaten 4–1(5–1 on aggregate) but the lead in the League was cut to just four points on 5 March when Chelsea visited Old Trafford and won. They became the first side for two years to take six points from United in a season. Once again it was Peacock who scored.

After being drawn away from home for the opening three rounds of their FA Cup campaign United beat Charlton 3–0 at Old Trafford. They paid a hefty price for victory when Peter Schmeichel was sent off for a handling offence outside his area. He would unfortunately miss the Coca-Cola Cup Final.

So began the darkest part of the season when three players were dismissed, one of them on two occasions. Sheffield Wednesday were beaten 5–0 in the Premiership before two away fixtures full of controversy and talking points.

Swindon, the bottom club, bravely fought for a 2–2 draw. Eric Cantona was sent off for stamping on the chest of John Moncur and again this was highlighted by television. Three days later, in another 2–2 draw at Highbury, the Frenchman was again shown the red card after a second bookable offence. This time television came to Cantona's defence showing that the decision was harsh, with the United player the offended rather than the offender. Nevertheless Cantona was suspended for five games and became the target of vicious verbal attacks at away grounds for the remainder of the season.

Schmeichel's suspension meant Les Sealey took over in goal for the Wembley Final, which Aston Villa won 3–1 – and again there was a dismissal. Andrei Kanchelskis received his marching orders for deliberately handling the ball in the last minute and the resulting penalty at least gave Villa the chance to finish the match with what was in reality a flattering scoreline.

Cantona was present for the 1–0 League win over Liverpool at Old Trafford, then missed a 2–0 defeat at Blackburn (now just three points behind), a 3–2 victory over Oldham, and a 1–0 defeat at Wimbledon.

The Frenchman was also unfortunately absent for the FA Cup semi-final against Oldham and its eventual replay.

Against strong opposition from Old Trafford the Football Association decided that the semi-final should be played at Wembley. Oldham were in favour, but after two visits already that season United felt it was asking too much of their supporters to meet the heavy cost of travelling to another game in London.

The game was the turning point of United's season, although at one stage defeat stared them in the face. Goalless it went into extra time and in the 106th minute Oldham's Neil Pointon scored. United fought back throwing the teenage Nicky Butt into the fray to replace Paul Parker and the youngster found himself at the centre of things with only seconds left when he and Robson were part of a move which led to the ball finding its way to Mark Hughes. He scored a brilliant goal with 46 seconds of the 120 minutes to spare.

Hero Hughes was one of many who saw that single shot on goal as the decisive moment of the whole season:

> We were due to play Leeds three days later and they had been twelve days without a game. If we had lost we would have been on a low, but forcing a replay meant we had a second chance of reaching the final. We were not going to let that opportunity slip.

Oldham were despatched 4–1 at Maine Road

Below: One swallow may not make a summer but one goal can certainly influence the outcome of a season. Less than a minute of extra-time remained when the ball fell to Mark Hughes during the Wembley FA Cup semi-final against Oldham. He scored with a tremendous volley. The goal earned United a replay which they won, and with spirits lifted they went on to retain their Championship and become only the fourth side this century to win both major domestic honours

Above: Vive le Roi de Old Trafford! Eric Cantona's contribution to both Championship campaigns in 1993 and 1994 is undeniable, as is his claim to the 'crown', once the mantle of Denis Law. The chant of 'Cantona-King!' has been heard many times since his arrival from Leeds United and older supporters remembered this as the greeting reserved for the famous Scot of the 1960s team. Here King Eric takes the salute of his courtiers after scoring one of his two goals against City in the Manchester derby at Old Trafford

as Irwin, Kanchelskis, Robson and Giggs scored. It was to be Robson's last goal for the club and the key to another final. Poor Oldham's season collapsed into relegation.

Although United lost to Wimbledon three days after the win, Blackburn also fell at Southampton leaving the top of the table unchanged as goal difference separated the sides. United had played a game less than their rivals as Cantona returned to face neighbours City at Old Trafford and score twice in a 2–0 win.

The following day Blackburn drew at home to QPR, and when United played Leeds at Elland Road on Wednesday 27 April the 2–0 victory opened a two point lead. The scorers that night were Kanchelskis, whose performances were later rewarded with a new five-year contract, and Giggs. Once more the Championship was there for the taking.

United went to Portman Road and beat Ipswich 2–1. By the next evening, Monday, 2 May, the race was over. On the exact date when Aston Villa had lost at home to Oldham the previous year, Blackburn were beaten at Coventry.

United were beyond reach and for the first time since the days of the Babes had won back-to-back Championships. They beat Southampton 2–0 as Old Trafford was once again turned into a carnival of colour by 44,705 supporters.

But the Premiership trophy was not presented that night. Instead it was held back until Sunday, 8 May as television once again dictated proceedings. This was the date of the final home game against Coventry, which proved an anti-climax for many of the fans as Alex Ferguson fielded a side which was completely different to his normal line-up.

Peter Schmeichel had been injured at Ipswich and was replaced during that game, and for the final two Premiership fixtures, by Gary Walsh, who had made a remarkable comeback after being transfer listed at the start of the season. He so impressed that he won himself a new contract as the veteran Les Sealey was released.

As they played Coventry, Schmeichel was joined by Ince, Kanchelskis, Hughes, and Giggs on the injured list. With the FA Cup Final six days away, the team included two debutants in Colin Mckee and Gary Neville, plus Bryan Robson making his final appearance. The 0–0 draw saw United end the season eight points clear of the field – but ahead lay more glory.

United achieve the double

On Saturday 14 May it came. For the first time United won the elusive League and Cup double, joining Tottenham, Arsenal and Liverpool, the only clubs to achieve that feat this century.

It seemed fate would have a part to play as they faced Chelsea in the final. Remember how earlier

Right: Bryan Robson bids farewell to Old Trafford and goes out in style. This was the scene at the end of the final home game of the season as he and Steve Bruce collected the Premiership trophy for a second time. During the campaign the captaincy of the side was officially handed to Bruce who insisted that the long-serving Robson shared the honour of receiving the trophy with him. Bryan moved into management with Middlesbrough in the summer of 1994 planning also to continue playing for at least one more season. He rejected several playing offers from other Premiership clubs, saying he could not face the prospect of opposing United after 13 years at Old Trafford

Left: Spot the difference? Eric Cantona scores twice from the penalty spot during the 1994 FA Cup Final against Chelsea. Each goal came in identical fashion as on each occasion he sent Russian 'keeper Dmitri Kharine the wrong way as he placed the hall firmly into the opposite corner. It really was a case of double vision as United took a grip on their second trophy of the season. And the difference? The players in the background for goal number one have changed position for the second penalty

in the season Chelsea had beaten United twice? The scorer on each occasion was Gavin Peacock. Remember also how United lost at Stoke in the Coca-Cola Cup? The scorer of both Stoke's goals was Mark Stein. Both played at Wembley!

For the first half Chelsea dominated and, just as that season's result at Stamford Bridge might have hinged on Cantona's shot rebounding from the crossbar when a goal looked certain, Peacock was thwarted in similar style. He seemed destined to score once again but his shot went beyond the reach of Schmeichel, declared fit four days before Wembley, and rebounded to safety.

In the second half United began to play in a way many of their fans expected. Giggs slipped the ball through the legs of Newton and as Irwin ran at goal he was brought down heavily. Cantona's penalty opened the scoring and five minutes later he again struck from the spot after Kanchelskis was pushed over. It was a controversial decision, and Chelsea were finished. Two minutes later Sinclair failed to control the ball, Hughes pounced and made it three-nil as he claimed his fourth goal at Wembley that season.

Before the game Alex Ferguson had been forced into another heartbreaking decision. Just as in 1990 when Jim Leighton was left out of the replay against Crystal Palace, the manager had told Bryan Robson that he would not be involved against Chelsea. Robson could only look on reluctantly from the wings as substitutes Brian McClair and Lee Sharpe were brought into the game with five minutes remaining.

Ferguson named his side:

Schmeichel, Parker, Bruce, Pallister, Irwin, Kanchelskis, Keane, Ince, Giggs, Cantona, Hughes.

McClair was the player who would continue his career at Old Trafford as Robson moved into management and the Scot paid back his manager when he scored the final goal of a 4–0 win.

Manchester United had won the double. For Alex Ferguson it was the highlight of a remarkable career. He had won his sixth major trophy in five seasons, but he was still hungry.

So was Eric Cantona who after the final revealed that his grasp of English was far better than many had been led to believe:

> What we have achieved is fantastic, but I hope that we can go on and do even better. Not just the Championship but the European Cup, the FA Cup and perhaps even the Coca-Cola Cup as well. I want us to win everything there is to win.

Left: Manchester United have completed the elusive double for the first time in their history and there is none prouder than Steve Bruce. The central defender marks his first season as skipper in unique style after collecting the FA Cup from HRH The Duchess of Kent and turns to take the cheers of a packed Wembley. Including the FA Charity Shield, Bruce made a remarkable 62 appearances (one as substitute) during the 1993–94 season and scored seven goals

Right: Denis Irwin on international duty during USA 94 fends off Italy's Dino Baggio. Irwin, along with club team-mate Roy Keane, was part of a Republic of Ireland team which sensationally beat Italy, 1–0, in New York. Irwin showed his versatility in the finals, switching from right-back, where he had played most of his international career, to left-back. The Republic was the only team from the British Isles to qualify for the finals, eventually losing to Holland in the second round

The new season begins

There was no denying Cantona's contribution to United's success, and he had earned his place in the record books by collecting three successive Championship medals – his first with Leeds in 1992, the others with United in 1993 and 1994. But although his skill was unquestionable, rumbling below the surface was a fiery temperament which would seriously affect United's chances of more success in the season which followed that first-ever double.

No Manchester United manager had won three successive Championships, but Alex Ferguson realised he had a squad capable of achieving that goal. He made only one close-season signing, persuading David May to move from Blackburn for £1.2 million.

Even so, it was Rovers who proved to be his biggest rivals in the 1994–95 campaign.

They themselves had been strengthened by the record signing of striker Chris Sutton, who like Shearer two summers earlier was also linked with United before opting for Ewood Park.

Below: Andrei Kanchelskis evades a tackle from Newcastle's John Beresford. The Russian international delighted the United fans with his pace, skill and shooting ability. His 39 appearances for United yielded 15 goals in all competitions.

Above: Eric Cantona scores the only goal of the game with a superb header against championship rivals Blackburn on 22 January. It was the second time United had beaten Blackburn in four months, the first being a 4–2 thriller in October at Ewood Park, in which Cantona also scored

Both these players missed the curtain-raiser to the season when United easily won the Charity Shield, beating Blackburn at Wembley thanks to goals from Cantona and Ince, the Frenchman completing a unique hat-trick of three penalties in consecutive games at the stadium.

By this time Bryan Robson had ended his spell at Old Trafford and taken over as player-manager at Middlesbrough, whom he was to guide to the Premier League in his first season. During the summer others had moved too: Michael Phelan to West Brom, Les Sealey to Blackpool and youngsters Colin McKee and Neil Whitworth went to Kilmarnock.

Five players were booked in the Charity Shield and in the opening League game at Old Trafford, Clive Wilson of QPR was sent off after seven minutes, and Paul Parker played only four minutes after coming on as a substitute before he too was sent back to the dressing room.

As the season progressed, refereeing standards came under fire from every quarter. Television coverage intensified, putting players and officials under the microscope. Mistakes, foul play and bad behaviour were highlighted as much as spectacular moves.

Because of their popularity, United were constantly in the spotlight. While the club benefited from the extra income generated by television, there was a penalty to pay. If they stepped out of line, players were pilloried by commentators and after-match analysts. If they scored spectacular goals these would be shown time and time again, to the annoyance of those from other clubs who felt that they should be treated in the same way.

Newcastle set the pace in the Championship and by October United lay third, seven points adrift, with Blackburn second. Within five days United had to play both the clubs above them.

They won 4–2 at Blackburn in a sensational game which swung on an incident in the 44th minute when Lee Sharpe was barged off the ball as he was about to shoot. Henning Berg was sent off and United were awarded a penalty. Cantona stepped up and scored the equaliser as television played and replayed the incident.

Those pro-United saw it as a dangerous tackle, others as a harsh decision, perhaps a penalty but not a sending off. According to Kenny Dalglish after the defeat it was neither. Then came Newcastle and an outstanding performance by United, who thrilled an Old Trafford crowd of 43,755 with their best display of the season. Gary Pallister scored the first, Keith Gillespie replaced Giggs in the 66th minute and made it 2–0 ten minutes later in a move started by Cantona.

By this time 18 games had been played in the Premiership, which Blackburn led by one point. United had lost three, at Leeds, Ipswich and Sheffield Wednesday. They had also been knocked out of the Coca-Cola (League) Cup at Newcastle and been criticised for using most of their reserve side in the competition.

However they were in confident mood, despite being handicapped by injuries. Lee Sharpe fractured his ankle, Ryan Giggs was sidelined along with Roy Keane and Peter Schmeichel.

By the time the season reached the half-way stage United topped the table, but it was a short stay . . . just six hours! They won 3–2 at Chelsea on Boxing Day, but before many of the travelling supporters who had left at dawn for the 12 noon start were back in Manchester, Blackburn beat City at Maine Road to regain first place in the Premiership.

After United's win at Ewood Park, Blackburn strung together an undefeated run of eleven wins and one draw before the return fixture at Old Trafford. United themselves won seven of their Premiership games in the same period, one of them the 5–0 humiliation of Manchester City at Old Trafford. But they lost at home to Nottingham Forest when Collymore scored a spectacular opening goal.

After the game the player made his ambitions perfectly clear:

> Every schoolboy who is interested in football wants to play for the best and when you look around Old Trafford I defy anybody not to be impressed by it.

The arrival of Cole

Ten days into the New Year Alex Ferguson moved into the transfer market. Not for Collymore, but Andy Cole, the Newcastle United striker, whom he bought for a record £6 million, plus Keith Gillespie, the youngster who had helped knock the Tynesiders off the top of the table some weeks earlier.

Cole's debut was against Blackburn and it began as sensationally as his move south. In the opening seconds he was clean through on goal but missed the chance of making a remarkable start to his United career. He said:

> I have come to this club to win things and I know that is what is going to happen. I'm not bothered that I didn't score today, because we won. The goals will come later.

United did win, thanks to a superb goal from

Eric Cantona. Giggs created it on the left, first losing the ball to Berg then taking it back from him. He crossed from just beyond the edge of the penalty area, Cantona rose at the far post and it seemed the ball was out of reach, but he stretched his body to make perfect contact and head home.

Old Trafford erupted, but it was the final goal they would see from the Frenchman that season. On the night of 25 January 1995 United faced Crystal Palace at Selhurst Park.

Events at Selhurst Park

Football had never seen anything quite like Eric Cantona's kung-fu attack on Crystal Palace supporter Matthew Simmons that night. The 28-year-old French international had been sent off for retaliation five minutes after the interval by referee Alan Wilkie of Chester Le Street. Everyone seemed so stunned that only kit manager Norman Davies reacted, so that Cantona was on his own as he walked towards the dressing room.

The home crowd were naturally jeering and Simmons rushed down to the front of the main stand where he allegedly shouted abuse at Cantona, who clearly heard it, hesitated, moved on again but then obviously changed his mind. He ran towards Simmons and took everyone by surprise by leaping into the air to kick him in the chest. Cantona fell backwards and so did Simmons but they were quickly up to start swinging blows at each other.

A number of players rushed towards the trouble-spot. Paul Ince appeared to become involved in the incident and was later charged with assault, a case which was not heard until the end of the season when he was found not guilty. How much the affair affected his form is difficult to assess but it certainly couldn't have helped and it certainly cost him his place in the England team shortly after the incident.

Peter Schmeichel arrived on the chaotic scene and helped steer Cantona off the field. The player was allowed to travel home with the team that night as the media went into overdrive debating what should be done with him. Television showed the kung-fu kick time after time. The pictures were so unusual that they were transmitted round the world while the tabloid newspapers ran pages of stories and interviews examining the issues. Some said he should be booted out of the country and never allowed to play football in England again. Others wanted to see him given a life ban from the game.

The more balanced *Manchester Evening News* called the next day for an immediate suspension by his club to take the player out of the firing line and give everyone time to think. It was also clearly a police matter as well and eventually after lengthy inquiries and interviews Cantona was charged with common assault, appearing before Croydon magistrates to plead guilty to the offence on 23 March.

United were under pressure from the more hysterical sections of the media to sack the player but they kept their heads and just two days later they announced that he would be suspended until the end of the season and fined the maximum allowed of two weeks wages, amounting to some £20,000. It emerged later that United had been in close touch with the Football Association and had acted decisively in the belief that the FA would later endorse the punishment as appropriate and sufficient.

United knew he would still have to appear in front of an FA disciplinary commission which he duly did a month later when a three-man hearing confounded the club by extending his suspension until 30 September 1995. This meant he would be unable to make a fresh start at the beginning of the following season and that he would in fact be banned for about the first 10 games as well as being forced to miss the pre-season matches. They also fined him a further £10,000.

United decided not to appeal but felt betrayed. The FA pointed out that the men who sat on the commission were independent. United felt that they could have given the player a nominal suspension and then wait for the FA hearing to add to it, with the chance that the FA would merely have banned him until the end of the season.

But if United fans had been shocked by the FA it was nothing compared to the stunning verdict from Croydon magistrates, whose chairwoman Mrs Jean Pearch announced:

> You have pleaded guilty to common assault and the facts that we have heard show that this is a serious offence. We have heard from your counsel that you deeply regret your actions. We have taken this into account together with your previous good character and your guilty plea. We do feel however that you are a high profile public figure with undoubted gifts and as such you are looked up to by many young people. For this reason the only sentence that is appropriate for this offence is two week's imprisonment forthwith.

Below: Eric Cantona's extraordinary kung-fu attack on Crystal Palace supporter Matthew Simmons shocked the football world and undoubtedly affected United's title challenge. The Frenchman, sent off for a foul on Palace defender Richard Shaw, reacted violently to abuse apparently hurled at him by Simmons as he left the field. Paul Ince also got involved in the incident, and both were charged with assault. Cantona received 150 hours community service, but Ince was cleared

United immediately appealed and wiser counsel prevailed at Croydon Crown Court a week later when the judge said that Simmons had indulged in conduct that would 'provoke the most stoic'. The jail sentence was quashed and instead the court ordered Cantona to do 120 hours of community service instead of the lengthy prison term.

Eric, true to form, embarked on a flight of fancy at the Press conference which followed the court case, and said: 'When the seagulls follow the trawler it's because they think sardines will be thrown into the sea.'

The media mostly said they were mystified by this, possibly because they felt he was referring to them as vultures waiting for scraps from the great man. Anyway, Cantona duly completed his order working with 10-year-olds from Salford schools for four hours a day at the United training ground during April and May. He impressed everyone with the responsible and serious way he tackled his commitment and it was even said that the youngsters he coached were a key factor in persuading him to stay with Manchester United and sign a new contract.

This was the one big issue remaining. For a long time manager Alex Ferguson felt there would be too many difficulties for Cantona to continue his career in England, not least the hostility of rival fans at away games. Inter Milan hovered in the background confident that they would be able to offer him a new start and make United happy with a £4m fee.

The player, always full of surprises, delivered a major one on 28 April when he turned his back on Italy to sign a new three-year contract and say that he hoped to stay at Old Trafford for the rest of his career:

> It is a love story. It is something that is very strong for me. The love of the club is the most important weapon in the world. I just couldn't leave. It is something very strong for me.

In the meantime, Ferguson's plans to play Cole and Cantona together would have to be shelved until October.

Ironically Mark Hughes, seen by many to be surplus to requirements on Cole's arrival, was injured in the League game at Newcastle five days after Cole's transfer. Hughes was on crutches as Cantona was punished, and after rejecting a one-year contract before the incident, was granted his wish for a deal which would keep him at the club for a further two seasons.

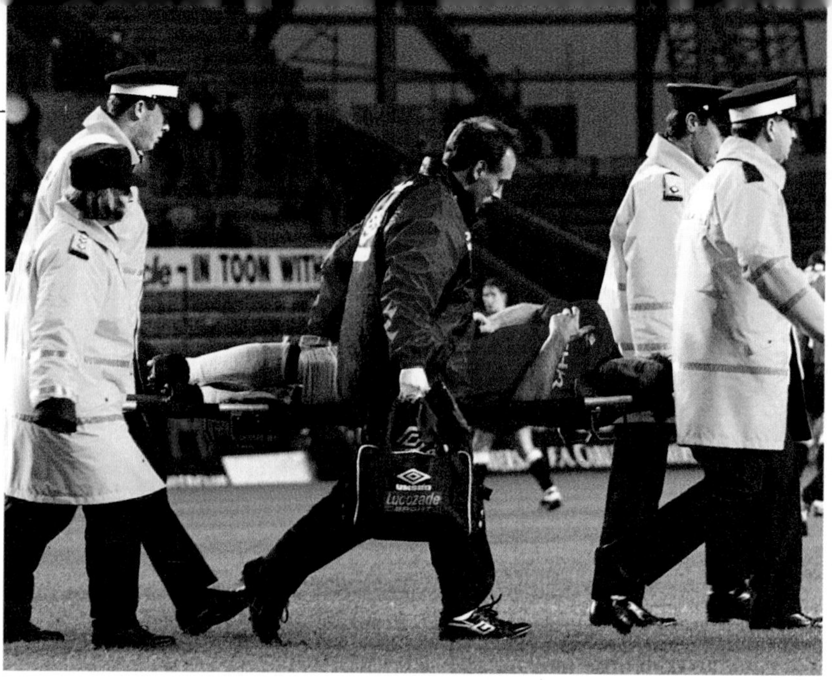

Above: Mark Hughes is stretchered off after a clash with Newcastle 'keeper Pavel Srnicek. Many thought that this would be Hughes' last game for United, but Cantona's flying exit from the season proved them wrong

Centre top: Andy Cole celebrates the first of five goals against Ipswich Town on 4 March. United went on to humiliate their opponents 9–0, by far the highest winning margin of the season

Centre middle: Paul Ince stretches Palace in the FA Cup semi-final. 'The guv'nor' proved to be the dynamo of the United midfield for another season, attracting the England manager's attention

Centre bottom: Tempers flare in the FA Cup semi-final replay against Crystal Palace at Villa Park. Roy Keane had stamped on Gareth Southgate in a moment of anger. Keane and Darren Patterson were sent off

Hughes missed five games, returning to score against Leeds as United progressed in the FA Cup. They had won at Sheffield United, and beaten Wrexham at Old Trafford before victory over Leeds took them to the quarter-finals.

In the League they beat Villa, where Cole got his first goal, then Manchester City 3–0 at Maine Road, and won 2–0 at Norwich before stumbling to a 1–0 defeat at Everton.

Then came another sensation: Ipswich were beaten 9–0 at Old Trafford. Cole scored five times, Hughes twice and Ince and Keane once each. Although they were still three points adrift of Blackburn at the top, they now had a superior goal difference.

In the FA Cup they beat QPR to go into the semi-finals where fate paired them with Crystal Palace. It took a replay to secure victory and in the second game Roy Keane was sent off after reacting violently to a fierce challenge by Gareth Southgate. Keane kicked out, stamping on Southgate's stomach as he lay on the turf.

Above: A disconsolate Ryan Giggs troops off after United's 1–0 defeat against Everton in the FA Cup final. Giggs came on as a substitute in the second half, but even he could not light up a scrappy match in which chances were few and far between

Players piled in, Keane and Palace's Darren Patterson were ordered off and the game turned sour. The two were later charged with bringing the game into disrepute.

There had been calls for calmness by the Football Association, who had ruled that the tie should go ahead against the wishes of Crystal Palace. One of their supporters had been killed in an incident outside a Walsall public house prior to the original game, and Palace asked their followers to boycott the replay.

Only 17,987 saw United win comfortably but many claimed it was the cost of tickets which kept some fans away rather than anything else.

Attendances were very much in United's thoughts and a month before the semi-finals, they announced plans for more rebuilding at Old Trafford to increase capacity to 55,300 with a giant grandstand replacing the cantilever building of 1965. Chairman Edwards revealed the plans for the £28 million development but added a footnote for his manager:

> Because of the amount of expenditure involved, £9 million to buy the land and £19 million in building costs, it means that we will be restricted in the transfer market for the next two seasons. That is why we invested £6 million in Andy Cole.

The climax to the season

Meanwhile big-spending Blackburn continued to lead the chase, but began to stumble as United applied the pressure. United won at Leicester, Rovers drew at Leeds. United drew with Chelsea, Rovers lost to Manchester City at Ewood Park. The nerves were beginning to show. Rovers lost to West Ham, United won at Coventry. It was neck and neck and by the time the final day of the season arrived and Blackburn were just within reach. Wins for United against Sheffield Wednesday and then Southampton closed the gap to just two points.

Then came one of the most disappointing weeks in the history of Manchester United.

Blackburn's closing game was at Anfield, while United were away to West Ham. Victory for United and anything less for Blackburn and the Championship would stay at Old Trafford.

Shearer scored for Blackburn, and West Ham went ahead through Michael Hughes. At halftime it seemed all over.

In Liverpool the home side fought back, while in London, United equalised through McClair. It was 1-1 in each game.

The West Ham goal was under siege. They pulled back every player and their goalkeeper Miklosko gave the performance of his life. Efforts from Cole, McClair, Hughes, Sharpe, and Bruce were thwarted and United could not get the second decisive goal. As the final whistle blew at Upton Park, Liverpool were scoring a last minute winner at Anfield.

Blackburn were Champions by a single point, taking the title for the first time in 81 years. So close was the contest that under the old rules of two points for a win and one for a draw United would have won on goal average!

Alex Ferguson congratulated Blackburn and Kenny Dalglish for a remarkable battle, but he also praised the efforts of his own players:

> I am really proud of my players, it has been a fantastic effort by them. To amass 88 points in second place is a marvellous performance. They are down on the floor at the moment but they have battled against adversity before and they will bounce back. If you look at our record over the last four years, we have only lost 22 games out of 168 and never finished lower than runners-up and that is remarkable. It takes a good team to beat us and having got to 89 points you cannot deny that Blackburn and Kenny Dalglish have done a great job taking the Championship off us. We at United accepted the spirit of the challenge and congratulate them on their performance.

Six days later the United manager was again gracious in defeat, this time after Everton won the FA Cup.

In an unattractive game in which chances were few and far between, Everton scored the only goal after breaking out of defence, Paul Rideout heading home a rebound from the underside of the crossbar after Graham Stuart thought he had wasted an easier opportunity.

United dominated the second half but were thwarted once again by a superb display of goalkeeping, this time from the veteran Neville Southall. Incredibly United were so close to repeating the double, yet had won nothing at senior level.

There was hope for the future with the youngsters winning the FA Youth Cup but there can be no doubting that Manchester United were glad to see the end of the 1994–95 season, a time when the club sailed through turbulent waters . . . with seagulls in their wake.

Right: Centre back Gary Pallister attacks the West Ham goal in the dramatic climax to the season, but loses out to Ludek Miklosko. Although Blackburn lost 2–1 at Anfield, United could only manage a 1–1 draw at West Ham. Blackburn took the title by a single point

Transfer surprises

The dust had hardly settled on the Cantona incident when suddenly clouds formed again over Old Trafford at the start of the 1995–96 season.

This time they were real as well as metaphoric. Workers moved in to demolish the North Stand and make way for a giant three-tier structure which would hold 26,500 seated spectators, and controversy filled the air as the transfers of both Paul Ince to Inter Milan, and Mark Hughes to Chelsea, were announced.

There had been speculation that Ince might go, but for Hughes to move was a sensation. Chairman Edwards quickly tried to pacify angered supporters, insisting the players were not being off-loaded to finance the £28 million building project:

> We have known for some time that Mark wanted to leave. He has been a great servant and we wish him all the best. As for Paul Ince, we had an offer for him at the end of the season and I put this to the manager. He is responsible for his squad, he is the one who decides who he wants next season. He decided that we have enough cover in midfield and accepted the offer.

Was this Alex Ferguson doing his own demolition, tearing apart his side as vigorously as the crews flattening the cantilever grandstand? The chairman continued:

> Only time will tell if it proves to be good business or bad. The manager of Manchester United decides on the squad he wants. All I would say to the fans is that after all the success he has had, we have to have some confidence in the manager's ability. If we were to lift a trophy next year people would say that it was not so bad after all. If however things turn sour they will point to this particular issue as being the start of it.

If Ferguson was reacting like the mad artist slashing his masterpiece he was taking a massive risk. He obviously felt his talented youngsters would succeed, and his decision to sell Ince gave credence to rumours that the player was causing problems in the dressing room. The manager was far from happy with Ince's attitude and the his purchase of a car number plate bearing the letters 'GUV' highlighted the problem.

No one knew what lay ahead but some observers felt Edwards was covering himself against disaster when he said it was the manager who would "stand or fall" by those transfer decisions. The buck stopped with Ferguson, but if the fans were unsettled after seeing two of their favourites depart, there was another shock to come. After weeks of speculation, Andrei Kanchelskis joined Everton. The Ukrainian claimed he could not work with Ferguson and the club was faced with a 'him or me' situation. There could only be one winner, and the player was sold.

It was a surprise. Ferguson had transferred Keith Gillespie, understudy to Kanchelskis, as part of the deal which brought Andy Cole to the club. That, and the fact that the Ukrainian still had four years of his contract to serve, was proof enough that United did not expect the Russian international to defect.

Ferguson made a bid for Tottenham and England winger Darren Anderton, but was rejected, so the supporters were uneasy as the new season began without a major signing. The media hawks were ready, their talons bared, as United faced Aston Villa on the opening day. By half-time they were circling ready for the kill as Villa led 3–0 and

Above: Ryan Giggs enjoyed a return to top form during 1995–96, attacking defences with his fast, penetrating runs. Cantona and Cole were the chief beneficiaries of the continual supply of crosses and through-balls, but he also scored 12 valuable goals himself. He added to his game during the season by getting more involved in midfield ball-winning and tackling

Left: Philip Neville figured in Alex Ferguson's plans for the whole season. The young full-back was a member of the 1992 youth squad who had come through to hold a regular place in the first team. Never afraid to push into attacking positions, Neville caught the eye of the England manager and was called up for international duty in the Euro 96 competition

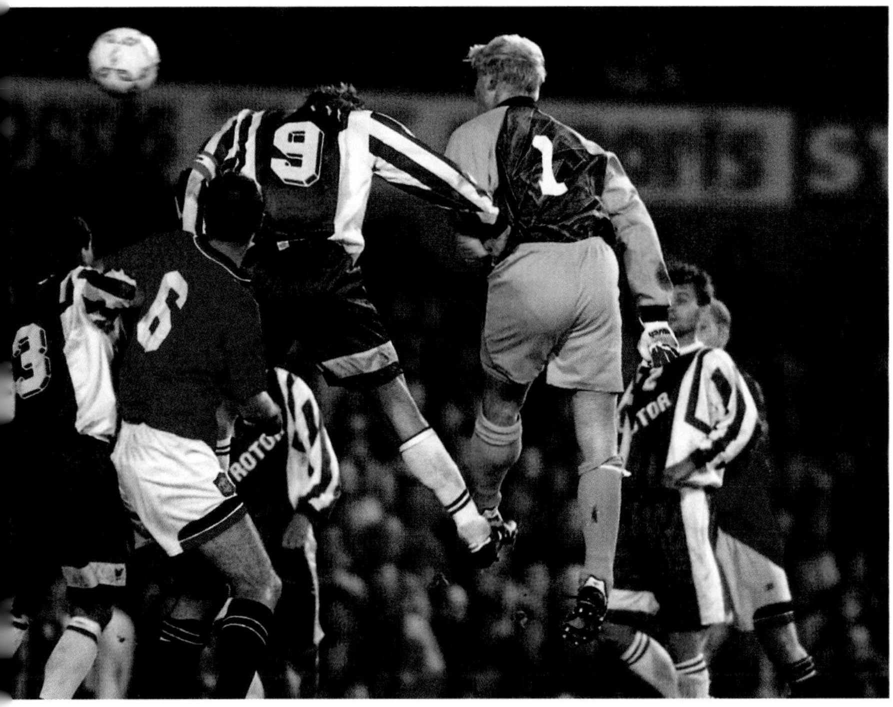

Above: Peter Schmeichel's outstanding ability has earned him the reputation as one of the best goalkeepers in the world. During the UEFA Cup game against Rotor Volgograd, he also proved himself to be the saviour of United's unbeaten home record in European competition, by scoring the most extraordinary goal of the season. With two minutes left and the Russian visitors leading 2–1, Schmeichel headed home a corner to equalise, but United went out on the away goals rule

after a 3–1 defeat they swooped on Ferguson with undisguised glee.

"Forget it!" said one headline. There would be no success for United this season.

"You will never win anything with kids" said television pundit Alan Hansen.

Ferguson felt he could, and replaced his stars with youngsters from his 1992 youth team.

Ince had made a tearful exit hinting that Ferguson was forcing him out. He said:

> The only thing I can say is it was a shock. The United fans know that I love them, there will always be a special place for those fans. It was hard for me to make the decision. I was shocked that the decision was made in the first place and here I am.

He may have seemed reluctant to leave, but insiders at Old Trafford claimed he made regular dressing room announcements that one day he would play in Italian football. Had Ferguson called his bluff, or simply had enough of 'The Guv'nor's' ways which could have been a disruptive influence on the younger players? Captain Ferguson wanted a tight ship.

Hughes appeared to have signed a new contract, but did not put pen to paper. His fear was that with Cole an expensive addition to the squad, and the summer announcement by Cantona that he would not be driven out by his ban, there would be little chance of playing many first team games when the Frenchman returned.

The departure of Kanchelskis was prolonged and soured feelings between United and Everton. When the sides met at Goodison in the fifth game of the season, Merseyside saw it as the day of reckoning.

United had recovered from that first defeat and chalked up victories over West Ham and Wimbledon at Old Trafford, followed by a 2-1 win at Blackburn. They were fourth in the table at kick-off and by the end of the game they were lying second.

United won 3-2 but Kanchelskis was put out of action for several weeks as controversy and irony came in one move. After a quarter of an hour the winger fell awkwardly and dislocated a shoulder following a challenge by Lee Sharpe. It was not malicious, but the Everton fans were angered as their new hero was helped from the pitch.

As the season progressed, David Beckham, Paul Scholes and the Neville brothers, Gary and Philip, were used on a regular basis. There were signs that United might be able to challenge for a trophy but Europe once again proved a stumbling block.

Later in the season there were celebrations following a ruling by the European Court, when UEFA were forced to change their foreign player restrictions, but the move came too late to help United in the 1995-96 campaign.

The court ruled that players from EEC countries had to be regarded equally. Scots, Welsh and Irish were no longer classed as foreigners in England as they had been by UEFA since 1991, nor were those from any other member country. Clubs were still restricted to three foreign players, but these were from outside Europe rather than beyond England's borders. The door was opening, but in the 1995-96 UEFA Cup it slammed in United's face, when they lost to the Russian club Rotor Volgograd.

There was little joy in the Coca-Cola (League) Cup where Ferguson followed his pattern of fielding a second string side in the early rounds and paid the penalty.

York City, a struggling side from the Third Division, were the opposition and the first leg at Old Trafford was a disaster. Reserve team goalkeeper Kevin Pilkington was beaten by a deflected shot, then came sensation as United were reduced to ten men when defender Pat McGibbon was sent off. To make matters worse the referee awarded York a penalty because McGibbon had pulled back an opponent in a "professional foul", but television later proved the infringement was outside the area. It mattered little, York scored from the spot kick and a minute later, with United in disarray, made it United 0 York 3. It was one for the record books! The line-up for the second leg was more recognisable, but a 3-1 win was not enough and United made a humiliating exit.

Cantona returns

Between those games, Eric Cantona returned. His exile ended on 30th September and the first side he faced was Liverpool at Old Trafford the following day.

The football world waited not knowing what to expect. Those who supported the Frenchman hoped he could pick up where he had left off, those who had screamed for his head wanted him to leap enraged into the crowd again.

Left: Nicky Butt was another player who successfully established himself in the first team after coming through the youth ranks, making 38 appearances for United during 1995-96. The midfielder proved himself to be a strong ball-winner and tough competitor, filling the gap left by Paul Ince with remarkable maturity

With that air of arrogance, Cantona stepped into the spotlight and was an immediate success.

In the months which followed he ignored endless provocation from rival spectators and attempts to rile him on the fields, as his influence helped transform the side once again.This was the new improved Cantona, a changed character who walked away from controversy and even played the role of the peacemaker when things became heated.

Cheers greeted the prodigal son on the perfect stage for his much publicised return. United scored in the opening minute. It was not Cantona, but Nicky Butt who grabbed the first goal but the crowd was stunned as they trailed in the second-half after two superb goals from Robbie Fowler. Then in the 70th minute Cantona marked his return in true style. Giggs was pulled down as he ran at goal, Cantona converted the penalty and Old Trafford exploded in noise. The Frenchman celebrated his goal by swinging from a net support and jumping into the crowd to embrace his worshippers. He was back.

Cantona had never been one to say much, his natural shyness and a reluctance to intentionally grab publicity meant that interviews with him were few and far between. There was also the language barrier, although Monsieur Cantona played down his real grasp of English.

After the Selhurst Park incident he had said little. Co-author Tom Tyrrell was possibly the only English journalist to speak on a one-to-one basis with him when he described his reason for staying at Old Trafford and his relationship with the supporters with the words:

It's a love story . . . a love story.

After this requests for an audience received a polite, "Sorry, but no thank you. I have nothing to say at the moment". In fact things remained that way until the end of the season. Cantona would do his talking on the field of play.

In the Premiership, the gap between United and leaders Newcastle widened as winter set in. Two points separated the sides after United beat Bryan Robson's Middlesbrough at Old Trafford but the difference grew to five following defeat at Arsenal. December was a disaster. It seemed there was little hope of winning the championship. Newcastle were in the driving seat, swept along by a run of victories and urged on by a tidal wave of support.

Roy Keane was sent off against Middlesbrough, his second dismissal of the season following a harsh red card at Blackburn. He served his suspension whilst recovering from a hernia operation; this too was his second of the year. Nicky Butt accumulated 21 disciplinary points and was given a three match ban, Gary Pallister was injured during a 1–1 draw at Nottingham Forest and goalkeeper Schmeichel had to have an operation on an elbow. Added to this, Steve Bruce picked up a hamstring injury, and it was no surprise when form slumped.

Three successive draws were followed by defeats at Leeds and Liverpool, three points from a possible fifteen. As Newcastle led by ten points Ferguson searched for a defender to bridge the gap left by Pallister's absence. Frenchman William Prunier, a friend of Cantona's and a free agent, came on trial and was in the 42,024 Old Trafford crowd as hopes were lifted and Newcastle defeated. Keane gave a superb performance in a 2–0 win and three days later Prunier made his debut against QPR. United won 2–1 and he did

Left: Paul Scholes proved himself an able understudy to Andy Cole, scoring 14 goals in 18 appearances during 1995–96. The young striker came on as a substitute in the 6–0 thrashing of Bolton at Burnden Park and scored twice

Right: Eric Cantona scores the only goal of the game with a superb solo effort to beat Spurs 1–0 at Old Trafford and continue United's 12 league game unbeaten run. The win was sweet revenge for the 4–1 defeat they had suffered at White Hart Lane, and was crucial in maintaining their title challenge

Above: Steve Bruce holds off the the challenge from Newcastle's David Ginola during the second clash of the Premiership contenders at St James' Park. United won the game 1–0, their second win over the Tyneside club in the league. Cantona scored the crucial goal in the second half after the United defence, in particular Peter Schmeichel, had performed brilliantly to absorb a relentless Newcastle attack

enough to be included in the side for the New Year's day game at Tottenham.

It was the last we saw of Prunier who made a swift return to his homeland following a 4–1 defeat, the heaviest United had endured since the Premiership was launched. Ferguson asked him to stay for another trial period, but English football was not for him.

So those early season predictions seemed to have a ring of truth about them; were United destined to fail for a second successive season? The defeat at Tottenham was not the end, however, but the beginning. The side went on an amazing run which started with a somewhat fortunate 2–2 home draw with Sunderland in the FA Cup third round when a Cantona equaliser in the 79th minute kept them in the competition. In the replay, Andy Cole scored a late winner and the show was on the road!

Ten consecutive wins followed as United clawed back Newcastle's lead and reached the quarter finals of the cup. Cantona was in explosive form scoring the only goal at West Ham, two on his media-hyped return to Selhurst Park, scene of his kung-fu attack, and cup goals against Reading in round four, plus a penalty against Manchester City in round five which levelled the scores before Lee Sharpe struck the winner.

Premiership dog-fight

In the league, a 6–0 win at Burnden Park pushed Bolton closer to eventual relegation but boosted United's goal difference as they prepared for the trip to Newcastle. The pressure was now on Kevin Keegan's side as Alex Ferguson predicted:

> There's a lot of important games to come up; you cannot place one in front of another. We have to win our games now and we are aware of that. If we win them then that might do the trick. Being there for the last four seasons must give us an advantage.

The confrontation at St James's Park was billed as the championship decider. Victory for Newcastle would keep them four points ahead with a game in hand, a win for United would close the gap to one point and increase United's psychological advantage.

Newcastle pounded United for the first 45 minutes but Schmeichel was invincible and the defence held out until half time when Ferguson could impart new instructions. In the 51st minute a touch of Cantona's brilliant finishing silenced the Newcastle support and Tyneside began to fear the worst. A home win over Southampton in the FA Cup earned a semi-final meeting with Chelsea and suddenly with nine league games remaining it became clear that Alex Ferguson's new look side could have another tilt at the double.

The double double? Surely not. To win the championship and the FA Cup in the same season

was difficult, to repeat it was virtually impossible. Could those fresh-faced youngsters reach greater heights than Chapman's Huddersfield and Arsenal, the Liverpool teams of Shankly and Paisley, or the United of Sir Matt ?

A 1–1 draw at QPR put them top but there was controversy as referee Robbie Hart added four minutes of stoppage time and Cantona scored half way through it. Rangers fans were furious and matters were not made any easier by the Loftus Road scoreboard clock breaking down after an hour. Its blank electronic screen normally signals that 90 minutes have elapsed but it stood that way for half an hour adding confusion to a tense game. One point was of value to United but the loss of two was disastrous to Rangers who were relegated a month later.

Within 48 hours Newcastle were top again, but wins over Arsenal and Tottenham put United in front once more. They reached the Cup final after beating Chelsea 2–1 at Villa Park, and emerged from the Easter games still at the top of the table with wins over Manchester City, another side destined for relegation, and Coventry, hours before Newcastle lost at Blackburn. At Christmas, United had trailed by ten points, after Easter Monday they were six points in front of the Tynesiders and now favourites to lift the championship for a third time in four seasons. The impossible now seemed possible.

Then they travelled to Southampton and caused a sensation when the players demanded a change of strip for the second half of the game as they trailed 0–3. They began in a grey outfit which had been launched as the new away kit at the start of the season. Fans took notice that the side had not won a game in these colours and dubbed them unlucky. Footballers are superstitious and few believed Alex Ferguson's claim after the 3–1 defeat that the change had been made because the players had difficulty seeing one another and merged with the crowd.

Defeat meant that the race was wide open again. United beat Leeds 1–0 at Old Trafford after a stirring fight by Howard Wilkinson's players who had been reduced to ten men when goalkeeper Mark Beeney was sent off for palming the ball away outside his penalty area. His replacement, full back Lucas Radebe, a former goalkeeper, played superbly but Ferguson's post-match remarks caused controversy:

> I am saying this in support of their manager, because he doesn't deserve that (result). What they have been doing for the rest of the season God knows. It will be interesting to see how they perform against Newcastle.

Psychological warfare ? Was this Alex Ferguson challenging Leeds to lift their game against Newcastle the following week, or was he winding up his rivals. For whatever reason Ferguson was genuinely angered.

Kevin Keegan was none too happy either. When they met a week later Newcastle beat Leeds 1–0 and Keegan appeared on television wide-eyed with rage, his voice cracking after the strain of yelling instructions for 90 minutes and lost many admirers as he bleated: "Oh, I hope we beat them, I hope we beat them!".

Above: Andy Cole is mobbed by his team-mates after scoring at Middlesbrough in the last league match of the season. The home team almost went ahead in the opening minutes, but David May put United in the lead. After the substitution of Paul Scholes, Cole came on and hit his 13th goal of the season with virtually his first touch. Ryan Giggs completed the 3–0 win, and the title belonged to United

Premier champions again

The final home game of the season had seen United in championship form and put added pressure on Newcastle as they hammered Nottingham Forest 5–0 at Old Trafford. In the closing six days Newcastle were away to Forest and at home to Tottenham.The ball was back in their court as they went to Nottingham for the game which proved decisive. Peter Beardsley put them ahead, Ian Woan struck a brilliant equaliser and with one game to go United were two points

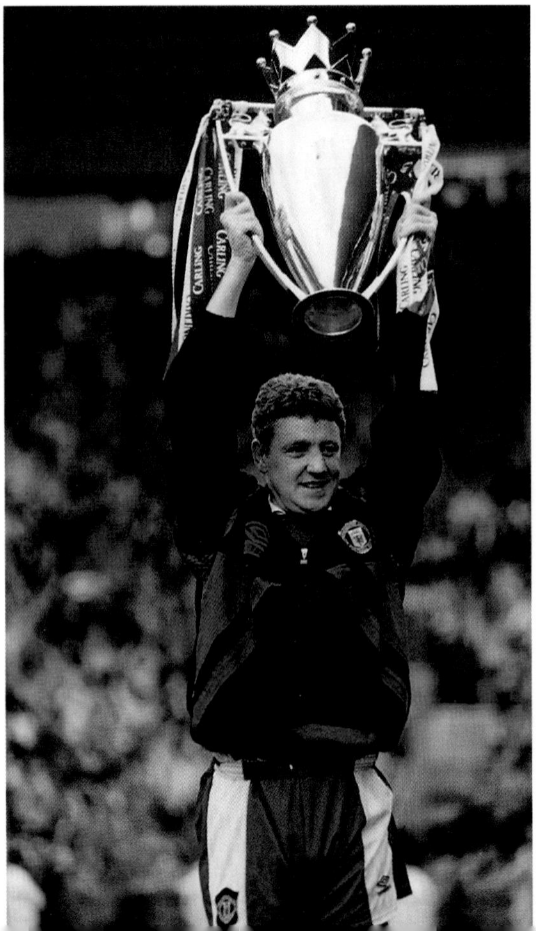

Left: Steve Bruce lifts the Premiership trophy for the third time in four years. Newcastle had to win at home to Spurs and United had to lose at Middlesbrough for the Tyneside club to lift the cup. In the end, Newcastle could only manage a draw and United won at the Riverside Stadium.
It had been a frustrating year for Bruce himself who was often injured. At the end of the season he announced that he would be leaving Old Trafford on a free transfer and joining Birmingham City

ahead and had a superior goal difference, 35 to 29, a difference of plus six. For Newcastle to win the title, United had to lose their last game, while they had to beat Tottenham at St James's Park.

United's closing fixture? Away to Bryan Robson's Middlesbrough! Football gossip was outrageous in its suggestion that Robson would make it easy for his former club, and in fact Middlesbrough fought like tigers to win the game. They almost scored three times before United took the lead through an unlikely hero. David May, brought into the side at the expense of skipper Steve Bruce, who was relegated to the bench, outjumped all others to head home a corner as the news came through that Newcastle were trailing to Tottenham.

Andy Cole was another left out of the starting line-up as Ferguson handed the striking role to Paul Scholes, as he had against Forest. After 53 minutes the manager made the switch, Cole on, Scholes off, and with his first touch, a clever flick over his shoulder, Cole scored the goal which virtually clinched the championship.

Newcastle pulled level just as Ryan Giggs rammed home a third superb goal after a weaving run. United were champions, their third success in four seasons and as the players danced in celebration after being handed the trophy, chairman Edwards summed up:

> It was a tense afternoon. Slightly different to last year where we went into the game knowing that if Blackburn won we couldn't win in. Today it was in our own hands. I was a bit nervous at half time, I knew it could still turn round, but once we got the second goal it became comfortable.

Was this the best championship of the three? He said:

> Clearly the first championship was important because we had waited so long. It was a tremendous relief but I think today was so good because we were under pressure. At the beginning of the season, having let three very experienced players go, everybody wondered how the youngsters would do. I think that is what is so pleasing about today. They told us we would win nothing with kids . . . I wonder what they are saying now?

The double double

So the stage was set for Manchester United to write a special page in the history of their club and go for a double double, a feat never before accomplished in English football. This was a golden opportunity for Alex Ferguson and his team.

Perhaps it was the enormity of the opportunity and prize which influenced the manager's tactics, dulled the player's minds and cramped their muscles because the performance never quite lived up to expectations and the display did not match the record book achievement. The purists quibbled afterwards, though that hardly spoiled the enjoyment of the United supporters or diminish the satisfaction of following a team which had broken new ground.

The football at Wembley lacked attacking flair, which came as something of a surprise because in the days leading up to the final everyone had predicted a match which would reveal all the best aspects of the game. Both teams had reputations for playing attractive, creative football and indeed it was a battle between two of the top three teams in the country. On the day itself, though, the defences dominated, and two powerful midfield forces cancelled each other out.

Liverpool, expected to stretch United every inch of the way, were particularly out of touch. The experienced John Barnes had a dismal day and Jamie Redknapp was overshadowed by the driving force of United's Irish dynamo, Roy Keane, voted the man of the match by the BBC. Steve McManaman tried hard with his long penetrating runs but he failed to reach Stan Collymore and Robbie Fowler up front. Peter Schmeichel in the United goal was rarely troubled, apart from pulling down high crosses.

United were not much better in terms of quality, with the exception perhaps of Ryan Giggs, who burst into action from time to time. Andy Cole was another player who looked a victim of of Cup final nerves and he was taken off in the second half to make way for the youngster, Paul Scholes. Eric Cantona also had a relatively quiet afternoon, except that once again he proved to be the complete match winner. He was lurking on

Right: David Beckham (no. 24) fires in a thunderous shot from the edge of the Liverpool penalty area in the FA Cup final, which David James can only push wide. United tore Liverpool apart during the first quarter of an hour, before the game settled and became unattractive as the two sides cancelled each other out. Roy Keane in particular again proved himself to be the driving force behind United's midfield strength and was voted man of the match

the edge of Liverpool's penalty box for a corner at a time when it looked as if the game would need extra time, and fittingly enough, after his marvellous season, he emerged the destroyer of Liverpool's dreams.

The decisive moment of the match came five minutes from the end when David Beckham's corner kick was punched out by David James. The goalkeeper appeared to have cleared the danger because he had got the ball out of the penalty area but he had not legislated for Cantona. The French genius arched his body and met the ball on the volley in the kind of situation which normally sees the shot sail over the goal and into the crowd. This time though there was power and poise behind the blast and the ball flew straight as an arrow past a startled James.

Alex Ferguson said later:

It was a quite magnificent goal. Eric showed great composure and such accuracy with the shot. It couldn't have come at a better time. Eric Cantona makes the difference. Even when he has a quiet day as he did in this match there is always something left in the tank. He doesn't sprint the games, he conserves energy so well. I don't know many players who could have hit the ball the way he did for the goal, away from the keeper. His contribution is often his mere presence. But what an impact. He won the Cup for us.

Completing the League and Cup double seemed to make everything worthwhile for Cantona after all the disciplinary troubles of the previous season. His role in United's championship success had seen him voted Player of the Year by the Footballer Writers Association and after scoring his 19th goal of the season he said:

Winning the final was important after last season. This is a great moment. I have the highest regard for Alex Ferguson as a man and as a manager. What can I say about the fans? I respect them and I love them and I try to give them the pleasure they need to receive. While I was banned they remembered me during every game even if it was just for 15 seconds. I will never forget that. I am settled in England and will certainly be staying here for the next two years of my contract, even longer than that, who knows?

As the well-travelled and controversial Frenchman led United up to the Royal box to receive the Cup as the team captain in the absence of the injured Steve Bruce, he seemed to have come a long way from the storm-tossed times of his Court case. To his great credit, he had tried to persuade Bruce to lead the team up the steps for the presentation, but the team captain would have none of it and in truth, Cantona had been the team's inspiration in both League and Cup.

Wembley also suggested that the player was more at peace with himself; when an angry Liverpool fan spat at him on the way up for the Cup he contented himself with only glaring at the offender. The moment seemed the symbol of his transformation, a remarkable rehabilitation which must surely represent one of Alex Ferguson's shrewdest moves in his management career.

It is impossible to exaggerate Cantona's role in the double double. Not only did he carry the team through March towards the championship, he also scored in nearly every round of the FA Cup and then of course it was his goal at Wembley which won the Cup. It used to be said that when

Above: Eric Cantona scores the only goal of the game in the FA Cup final. The Frenchman hit a superb volley after David James had punched the ball out towards the edge of the penalty area from a David Beckham corner. Alex Ferguson said later: 'It was a quite magnificent goal. Eric showed great composure and such accuracy with the shot. It couldn't have come at a better time. I don't know many players who could have hit the ball the way he did for the goal.'

Below: Eric Cantona lifts the FA Cup as United captain and winning goalscorer. United had won an incredible second double in three years, a record for an English club. It was the end of a remarkable year for the Reds and for Cantona himself. Many had written both off at the start of the season. United, it was claimed, would never win anything with 'kids' and Cantona would never return to his best form after serving his ban. The pundits were wrong

Bryan Robson was acting out his Captain Marvel role that Manchester United were a one-man team, but Cantona has taken over the mantle of the King of Old Trafford, an incredible man and a fantastic footballer.

The fans didn't need telling, of course. The French tricolour made a sea of colour at Wembley and again on the streets of Manchester for the homecoming on the traditional open top bus the following day. The only thing missing at the final was the Marseillaise, though the United fans had their own anthem and there was only one song on their lips. They made it clear that though Kevin Keegan was out of sight he was not forgotten. They filled the stadium with a non-stop refrain set to the Monkey's *Daydream Believer,* deriding the Newcastle manager's efforts.

It was a cruel jibe at the expense of one of their rivals, but fans are generous indeed to one of their own. Two days after the final there was a dinner to mark the retirement of their kit manager and quarter-master, Norman Davies, after 24 years with the club. There was warmth at the dinner also for the manager who had delivered ten trophies in as many years. Completing the double double must have given Alex Ferguson particular satisfaction after the way he had been treated by some of the fans at the start of the season; many thought that it was a time to strengthen the squad rather than strip it of three experienced and influential players. He later explained:

> We had our disappointments this season, like an early departure from the Coca-Cola Cup and a knockout in Europe, but for the most part I always felt we would achieve something. There were doubts in the early days following the departure of three experienced players but I always knew our youngsters would deliver. I didn't know exactly how they would cope with the big games but they had to be given their chance and I am delighted to say that they have shown themselves to be equipped with that final, important factor of temperament.

The only discordant note was struck when the manager made known his feelings on the subject of a new contract. He indicated that after what he had achieved, he wanted recognition financially as well as a six-year contract to take him up to the age of 60 and retirement in 2002.

Matters came to a head when the Manchester Evening News ran a story in the week following the Cup final with a front page banner headline declaring 'Fergie: I'll Quit in Pay Wrangle'. His threat to walk out unless the matter was settled before going on holiday at the weekend seemed to focus minds, for that night agreement was reached for a four-year deal reputed to double his salary to £600,000 a year which with bonuses could reach an annual £1m.

Ferguson said:

> It was important to me to get a contract which reflected what I had won and what I was worth. I am delighted with the terms and I can leave for my holiday happy that the issue has been resolved.

The United manager promised that he would be back for Euro 96 to study the cream of European football and hopefully sign two foreign players to strengthen his squad for the challenge of the European Champions League.

Manchester United match-by-match statistical record

Abbreviations

P:	games played	Pts: points
W:	wins	Appearances (goals) refer to League games only
D:	draws	Figures shown as 2 etc refer to goals scored by individual players
L:	defeats (losses)	Players' names in final column, from 1965–66 onwards, are substitutes
F:	goals scored	
A:	goals conceded	* own-goal

SEASON 1889–1890
FOOTBALL ALLIANCE

21 Sep	Sunderland A	H	W	4–1
23 Sep	Bootle	A	L	1–4
28 Sep	Crewe Alex	A	D	2–2
19 Oct	Walsall T Swifts	A	L	0–4
26 Oct	Birmingham St G	A	L	1–5
9 Nov	Long Eaton R	H	W	3–0
30 Nov	Sheffield Wed	A	L	1–3
7 Dec	Bootle	H	W	3–0
28 Dec	Darwen	A	L	1–4
25 Jan	Sunderland	A	L	0–2
8 Feb	Grimsby T	A	L	0–7
15 Feb	Nottingham F	A	W	3–1
1 Mar	Crewe Alex	H	L	1–2
15 Mar	Small Heath	A	D	1–1
22 Mar	Long Eaton R	A	W	3–1
29 Mar	Darwen	H	W	2–1
5 Apr	Nottingham F	H	L	0–1
7 Apr	Small Heath	H	W	9–1
14 Apr	Grimsby T	H	L	0–1
19 Apr	Birmingham St G	H	W	2–1
21 Apr	Walsall T Swifts	H	W	2–1
26 Apr	Sheffield Wed	H	L	1–2

FA Cup

18 Jan	Preston N E (1)	A	L	1–6

Football Alliance

	P	W	D	L	FA	Pts	
Newton Heath	22	9	2	11	40:45	20	8th

SEASON 1890–1891
FOOTBALL ALLIANCE

6 Sep	Darwen	H	W	4–2
13 Sep	Grimsby T	A	L	1–3
20 Sep	Nottingham F	H	D	1–1
27 Sep	Stoke C	A	L	1–2
11 Oct	Bootle	A	L	0–5
18 Oct	Grimsby T	H	W	3–1
1 Nov	Crewe Alex	H	W	6–3
8 Nov	Walsall T Swifts	A	L	1–2
22 Nov	Nottingham F	A	L	2–8
29 Nov	Sunderland	H	L	1–5
13 Dec	Small Heath	H	W	3–1
27 Dec	Bootle	H	W	2–1
5 Jan	Stoke C	H	L	0–1
10 Jan	Birmingham St G	A	L	1–6
17 Jan	Walsall T Swifts	H	D	3–3
24 Jan	Sheffield Wed	A	W	2–1
14 Feb	Crewe Alex	A	W	1–0
21 Feb	Sheffield Wed	H	D	1–1
7 Mar	Small Heath	A	L	1–2
14 Mar	Birmingham St G	H	L	1–3
28 Mar	Darwen	A	L	1–2
11 Apr	Sunderland	A	L	1–2

FA Cup

4 Oct	Higher Walton (Q1) (tie switched to Manchester)	H	W	2–0
25 Oct	Bootle Res (Q2)	A	L	0–1

Football Alliance

	P	W	D	L	F:A	Pts	
Newton Heath	22	7	3	12	37:55	17	9th

SEASON 1891–1892
FOOTBALL ALLIANCE

12 Sep	Burton Swifts	A	L	2–3
19 Sep	Bootle	H	W	4–0
26 Sep	Birmingham St G	A	W	3–1
10 Oct	Ardwick	H	W	3–1
17 Oct	Grimsby T	A	D	2–2
31 Oct	Burton Swifts	H	W	3–1
7 Nov	Crewe Alex	A	W	2–0
21 Nov	Lincoln C	H	W	10–1
28 Nov	Walsall T Swifts	A	W	4–1
12 Dec	Sheffield Wed	A	W	4–2
19 Dec	Ardwick	A	D	2–2
26 Dec	Small Heath	H	D	3–3
1 Jan	Nottingham F	H	D	1–1
9 Jan	Bootle	A	D	1–1
30 Jan	Crewe Alex	H	W	5–3
20 Feb	Sheffield Wed	H	D	1–1
27 Feb	Small Heath	A	L	2–3
5 Mar	Walsall T Swifts	H	W	5–0
19 Mar	Nottingham F	A	L	0–3
26 Mar	Grimsby T	H	D	3–3
2 Apr	Lincoln C	A	W	6–1
9 Apr	Birmingham St G	H	W	3–0

FA Cup

3 Oct	Ardwick (Q1)	H	W	5–1
24 Oct	Heywood (Q2) (scratched)	H	W	W–0
14 Nov	South Shore (Q3)	A	W	2–0
5 Dec	Blackpool (Q4)	H	L	3–4

Football Alliance

	P	W	D	L	F:A	Pts	
Newton Heath	22	12	7	3	69:33	31	2nd

SEASON 1892–1893
FOOTBALL LEAGUE (DIVISION 1)

3 Sep	Blackburn R	A	L	3–4
10 Sep	Burnley	H	D	1–1
17 Sep	Burnley	A	L	1–4
24 Sep	Everton	A	L	0–6
1 Oct	W B A	A	D	0–0
8 Oct	W B A	H	L	2–4
15 Oct	Wolverhampton W	H	W	10–1
19 Oct	Everton	H	L	3–4
22 Oct	Sheffield Wed	A	L	0–1
29 Oct	Nottingham F	A	D	1–1
5 Nov	Blackburn R	H	D	4–4
12 Nov	Notts Co	H	L	1–3
19 Nov	Aston Villa	H	W	2–0
26 Nov	Accrington S	A	D	2–2
3 Dec	Bolton W	A	L	1–4
10 Dec	Bolton W	H	W	1–0
17 Dec	Wolverhampton W	A	L	0–2
24 Dec	Sheffield Wed	H	L	1–5
26 Dec	Preston NE	A	L	1–2
31 Dec	Derby Co	H	W	7–1
7 Jan	Stoke C	A	L	1–7
14 Jan	Nottingham F	H	L	1–3
26 Jan	Notts Co	A	L	0–4
11 Feb	Derby Co	A	L	1–5
4 Mar	Sunderland	H	L	0–5
6 Mar	Aston Villa	A	L	0–2
31 Mar	Stoke C	H	W	1–0
1 Apr	Preston NE	H	W	2–1
4 Apr	Sunderland	A	L	0–6
8 Apr	Accrington S	H	D	3–3

Test Match

22 Apr	Small Heath (At Stoke)		D	1–1

Replay

27 Apr	Small Heath		W	5–2

Newton Heath kept First Division status

FA Cup

21 Jan	Blackburn R (1)	A	L	0–4

Football League

	P	W	D	L	F:A	Pts	
Newton Heath	30	6	6	18	50:85	18	16th

SEASON 1893–1894
FOOTBALL LEAGUE (DIVISION 1)

2 Sep	Burnley	H	W	3–2
9 Sep	W B A	A	L	1–3
16 Sep	Sheffield Wed	A	W	1–0
23 Sep	Nottingham F	H	D	1–1
30 Sep	Darwen	A	L	0–1
7 Oct	Derby Co	A	L	0–2
14 Oct	W B A	H	W	4–1
21 Oct	Burnley	A	L	1–4
28 Oct	Wolverhampton W	A	L	0–2
4 Nov	Darwen	H	L	0–1
11 Nov	Wolverhampton W	H	W	1–0
25 Nov	Sheffield U	A	L	1–3
2 Dec	Everton	H	L	0–3
6 Dec	Sunderland	A	L	1–4
9 Dec	Bolton W	A	L	0–2
16 Dec	Aston Villa	H	L	1–3
23 Dec	Preston NE	A	L	0–2
6 Jan	Everton	A	L	0–2
13 Jan	Sheffield Wed	H	L	1–2
3 Feb	Aston Villa	A	L	1–5
3 Mar	Sunderland	H	L	2–4
10 Mar	Sheffield U	H	L	0–2
12 Mar	Blackburn R	H	W	5–1
17 Mar	Derby Co	H	L	2–6
23 Mar	Stoke C	H	W	6–2
24 Mar	Bolton W	H	D	2–2
26 Mar	Blackburn R	A	L	0–4
31 Mar	Stoke C	A	L	1–3
7 Apr	Nottingham F	A	L	0–2
14 Apr	Preston NE	H	L	1–3

Test Match

28 Apr	Liverpool (At Ewood Park)		L	0–2

Newton Heath were relegated to Division Two

FA Cup

27 Jan	Middlesbrough (1)	H	W	4–0
10 Feb	Blackburn R (2)*	H	D	0–0
17 Feb	Blackburn R (2R)	A	L	1–5

* after extra time

Football League

	P	W	D	L	F:A	Pts	
Newton Heath	30	6	2	22	36:72	14	16th

SEASON 1894–1895
FOOTBALL LEAGUE (DIVISION 2)

8 Sep	Burton W	A	L	0–1
15 Sep	Crewe Alex	H	W	6–1
22 Sep	Leicester Fosse	A	W	3–2
6 Oct	Darwen	A	D	1–1
13 Oct	Arsenal	H	D	3–3
20 Oct	Burton Swifts	A	W	2–1
27 Oct	Leicester Fosse	H	D	2–2
3 Nov	Manchester C	A	W	5–2
10 Nov	Rotherham T	H	W	3–2
17 Nov	Grimsby T	A	L	1–2
24 Nov	Darwen	H	D	1–1
1 Dec	Crewe Alex	A	W	2–0
8 Dec	Burton Swifts	H	W	5–1
15 Dec	Notts Co	A	D	1–1
22 Dec	Lincoln C	H	W	3–0
24 Dec	Port Vale	A	W	5–2
26 Dec	Walsall	A	W	2–1
29 Dec	Lincoln C	A	L	0–3
1 Jan	Port Vale	H	W	3–0
5 Jan	Manchester C	H	W	4–1
12 Jan	Rotherham T	A	L	1–2
2 Mar	Burton W	H	D	1–1
23 Mar	Grimsby T	H	W	2–0
30 Mar	Arsenal	A	L	2–3
3 Apr	Walsall	H	W	9–0
6 Apr	Newcastle U	H	W	5–1
12 Apr	Bury	H	D	2–2
13 Apr	Newcastle U	A	L	0–3
15 Apr	Bury	A	L	1–2
20 Apr	Notts Co	H	D	3–3

Test Match

27 Apr	Stoke C (at Burslem)		L	0–3

Newton Heath stayed in Division 2

FA Cup

2 Feb	Stoke C (1)	H	L	2–3

Football League

	P	W	D	L	F:A	Pts	
Newton Heath	30	15	8	7	78:44	38	3rd

SEASON 1895–1896
FOOTBALL LEAGUE (DIVISION 2)

7 Sep	Crewe Alex	H	W	5–0
14 Sep	Loughborough T	A	D	3–3
21 Sep	Burton Swifts	H	W	5–0
28 Sep	Crewe Alex	A	W	2–0
5 Oct	Manchester C	H	D	1–1
12 Oct	Liverpool	A	L	1–7
19 Oct	Newcastle U	H	W	2–1
26 Oct	Newcastle U	A	L	1–2
2 Nov	Liverpool	H	W	5–2
9 Nov	Arsenal	A	L	1–2
16 Nov	Lincoln C	H	D	5–5
23 Nov	Notts Co	A	W	2–0
30 Nov	Arsenal	H	W	5–1
7 Dec	Manchester C	A	L	1–2
14 Dec	Notts Co	H	W	3–0
21 Dec	Darwen	A	L	0–3
1 Jan	Grimsby T	H	W	3–2
4 Jan	Leicester Fosse	A	L	0–3
11 Jan	Rotherham T	H	W	3–0
3 Feb	Leicester Fosse	H	W	2–0
8 Feb	Burton Swifts	A	L	1–4
29 Feb	Burton W	H	L	1–2
7 Mar	Rotherham T	A	W	3–2
14 Mar	Grimsby T	A	L	2–4
18 Mar	Burton T	A	L	1–5
23 Mar	Port Vale	A	L	0–3
3 Apr	Darwen	H	W	4–0
4 Apr	Loughborough T	H	W	2–0
6 Apr	Port Vale	H	W	2–1
11 Apr	Lincoln C	A	L	0–2

FA Cup

1 Feb	Kettering (1)	H	W	2–1
15 Feb	Derby Co (2)	H	D	1–1
19 Feb	Derby Co (2R)	A	L	1–5

Football League

	P	W	D	L	F:A	Pts	
Newton Heath	30	15	3	12	66:57	33	6th

SEASON 1896–1897
FOOTBALL LEAGUE (DIVISION 2)

1 Sep	Gainsborough T	H	W	2–0
5 Sep	Burton Swifts	A	W	5–3
7 Sep	Walsall	H	W	2–0
12 Sep	Lincoln C	H	W	3–1
19 Sep	Grimsby T	A	L	0–2
21 Sep	Walsall	A	W	3–2
26 Sep	Newcastle U	H	W	4–0
3 Oct	Manchester C	A	D	0–0
10 Oct	Small Heath	H	D	1–1
17 Oct	Blackpool	A	L	2–4
21 Oct	Gainsborough T	A	L	0–2
24 Oct	Burton W	H	W	3–0
7 Nov	Grimsby T	H	W	4–2
28 Nov	Small Heath	A	L	0–1
19 Dec	Notts Co	A	L	0–3
25 Dec	Manchester C	H	W	2–1
26 Dec	Blackpool	H	W	2–0
28 Dec	Leicester Fosse	A	L	0–1
1 Jan	Newcastle U	A	L	0–2
9 Jan	Burton Swifts	H	D	1–1
6 Feb	Loughborough T	H	W	6–0
20 Feb	Leicester Fosse	H	W	2–1
2 Mar	Darwen	H	W	3–1
13 Mar	Darwen	A	W	2–0
20 Mar	Burton W	A	W	2–1
22 Mar	Arsenal	H	D	1–1
27 Mar	Notts Co	H	D	1–1
1 Apr	Lincoln C	A	W	3–1
3 Apr	Arsenal	A	W	2–0
10 Apr	Loughborough T	A	L	0–2

Test Match

19 Apr	Burnley	A	L	0–2
21 Apr	Burnley	H	W	2–0
24 Apr	Sunderland	H	D	1–1
26 Apr	Sunderland	A	L	0–2

Newton Heath stayed in Division 2

FA Cup

12 Dec	West Manchester (Q1)	H	W	7–0
2 Jan	Nelson (Q2)	H	W	3–0
16 Jan	Blackpool (Q3)	H	D	2–2
20 Jan	Blackpool (Q3R)	A	W	2–1
30 Jan	Kettering (1)	H	W	5–1
13 Feb	Southampton (2)	A	D	1–1
17 Feb	Southampton (2R)	H	W	3–1
27 Feb	Derby Co (3)	A	L	0–2

Football League

	P	W	D	L	F:A	Pts	
Newton Heath	30	17	5	8	56:34	39	2nd

SEASON 1897–1898
FOOTBALL LEAGUE (DIVISION 2)

4 Sep	Lincoln C	H	W	5–0
11 Sep	Burton Swifts	A	W	4–0
18 Sep	Luton T	A	L	1–2
25 Sep	Blackpool	H	W	1–0
2 Oct	Leicester Fosse	H	W	2–0
9 Oct	Newcastle U	A	L	0–2
16 Oct	Manchester C	H	D	1–1
23 Oct	Small Heath	A	L	1–2
30 Oct	Walsall	H	W	6–0
6 Nov	Lincoln C	A	L	0–1
13 Nov	Newcastle U	H	L	0–1
20 Nov	Leicester Fosse	A	D	1–1
27 Nov	Grimsby T	H	W	2–1
11 Dec	Walsall	A	D	1–1
25 Dec	Manchester C	A	W	1–0
27 Dec	Gainsborough T	A	L	1–2
1 Jan	Burton Swifts	H	W	4–0
8 Jan	Arsenal	A	L	1–5
12 Jan	Burnley	H	D	0–0
15 Jan	Blackpool	H	W	4–0
26 Feb	Arsenal	H	W	5–1
7 Mar	Burnley	A	L	3–6
19 Mar	Darwen	A	W	3–2
21 Mar	Luton T	A	D	2–2
29 Mar	Loughborough T	H	W	5–1
2 Apr	Grimsby T	A	W	3–1
8 Apr	Gainsborough T	H	W	1–0
9 Apr	Small Heath	H	W	3–1
16 Apr	Loughborough T	A	D	0–0
23 Apr	Darwen	H	W	3–2

FA Cup

29 Jan	Walsall (1)	H	W	1–0
12 Feb	Liverpool (2)	H	D	0–0
16 Feb	Liverpool (2R)	A	L	1–2

Football League

	P	W	D	L	FA	Pts	
Newton Heath	30	16	6	8	64:35	38	5th

SEASON 1898–1899
FOOTBALL LEAGUE (DIVISION 2)

3 Sep	Gainsborough T	A	W	2–0
10 Sep	Manchester C	H	W	3–0
17 Sep	Glossop	A	W	2–1
24 Sep	Walsall	H	W	1–0
1 Oct	Burton Swifts	A	L	1–5
8 Oct	Port Vale	H	W	2–1
15 Oct	Small Heath	A	L	1–4
22 Oct	Loughborough T	H	W	6–1
5 Nov	Grimsby T	H	W	3–2
12 Nov	Barnsley	H	D	0–0
19 Nov	New Brighton	A	W	3–0
26 Nov	Lincoln C	H	W	1–0
3 Dec	Arsenal	A	L	1–5
10 Dec	Blackpool	H	W	3–1
17 Dec	Leicester Fosse	A	L	0–1
24 Dec	Darwen	H	W	9–0
26 Dec	Manchester C	A	L	0–4
31 Dec	Gainsborough T	H	W	6–1
2 Jan	Burton Swifts	H	D	2–2
14 Jan	Glossop	H	W	3–0
21 Jan	Walsall	A	L	0–2
4 Feb	Port Vale	A	L	0–1
18 Feb	Loughborough T	A	W	1–0
25 Feb	Small Heath	H	W	2–0
4 Mar	Grimsby T	A	L	0–3
18 Mar	New Brighton	H	L	1–2
25 Mar	Lincoln C	A	L	0–2
1 Apr	Arsenal	H	D	2–2
3 Apr	Blackpool	A	W	1–0
4 Apr	Barnsley	A	W	2–0
8 Apr	Luton T	A	W	1–0
12 Apr	Luton T	H	W	5–0
15 Apr	Leicester Fosse	H	D	2–2
22 Apr	Darwen	A	D	1–1

FA Cup

28 Jan	Tottenham H (1)	A	D	1–1
1 Feb	Tottenham H (1R)	H	L	3–5

Football League

	P	W	D	L	FA	Pts	
Newton Heath	34	19	5	10	67:43	43	4th

SEASON 1899–1900
FOOTBALL LEAGUE (DIVISION 2)

2 Sep	Gainsborough T	H	D	2–2
9 Sep	Bolton W	A	L	1–2
16 Sep	Loughborough T	H	W	4–0
23 Sep	Burton Swifts	A	D	0–0
30 Sep	Sheffield Wed	A	L	1–2
7 Oct	Lincoln C	H	W	1–0
14 Oct	Small Heath	A	L	0–1
21 Oct	New Brighton	H	W	2–1
4 Nov	Arsenal	H	W	2–0
11 Nov	Barnsley	A	D	0–0
25 Nov	Luton T	A	W	1–0
2 Dec	Port Vale	H	W	3–0
16 Dec	Middlesbrough	H	W	2–1
23 Dec	Chesterfield	A	L	1–2
26 Dec	Grimsby T	A	W	7–0
30 Dec	Gainsborough T	A	W	1–0
6 Jan	Bolton W	H	L	1–2
13 Jan	Loughborough T	A	W	2–0
20 Jan	Burton Swifts	H	W	4–0
3 Feb	Sheffield Wed	H	W	1–0
10 Feb	Lincoln C	A	L	0–1
17 Feb	Small Heath	H	W	3–2
24 Feb	New Brighton	A	W	4–1
3 Mar	Grimsby T	H	W	1–0
10 Mar	Arsenal	A	L	1–2
17 Mar	Barnsley	H	W	3–0
24 Mar	Leicester Fosse	A	L	0–2
31 Mar	Luton T	H	W	5–0
7 Apr	Port Vale	A	L	0–1
13 Apr	Leicester Fosse	H	W	3–2
14 Apr	Walsall	H	W	5–0
17 Apr	Walsall	A	D	0–0
21 Apr	Middlesbrough	A	L	0–2

28 Apr	Chesterfield	H	W	2–1

FA Cup

28 Oct	South Shore (Q1)	A	L	1–3

Football League

	P	W	D	L	F:A	Pts	
Newton Heath	34	20	4	10	63:27	44	4th

SEASON 1900–1901
FOOTBALL LEAGUE (DIVISION 2)

1 Sep	Glossop	A	L	0–1
8 Sep	Middlesbrough	H	W	4–0
15 Sep	Burnley	A	L	0–1
22 Sep	Port Vale	H	W	4–0
29 Sep	Leicester Fosse	A	L	0–1
6 Oct	New Brighton	H	W	1–0
13 Oct	Gainsborough T	A	W	1–0
20 Oct	Walsall	H	D	1–1
27 Oct	Burton Swifts	A	L	1–3
10 Nov	Arsenal	A	L	1–2
24 Nov	Stockport Co	A	L	0–1
1 Dec	Small Heath	H	L	0–1
8 Dec	Grimsby T	A	L	0–2
15 Dec	Lincoln C	H	W	4–1
22 Dec	Chesterfield	A	L	1–2
26 Dec	Blackpool	H	W	4–0
29 Dec	Glossop	H	W	3–0
1 Jan	Middlesbrough	A	W	1–2
12 Jan	Burnley	H	L	0–1
19 Jan	Port Vale	A	L	0–2
16 Feb	Gainsborough T	H	D	0–0
19 Feb	New Brighton	A	L	0–2
25 Feb	Walsall	A	D	1–1
2 Mar	Burton Swifts	H	D	1–1
13 Mar	Barnsley	H	W	1–0
16 Mar	Arsenal	H	W	1–0
20 Mar	Leicester Fosse	H	L	2–3
23 Mar	Blackpool	A	W	2–1
30 Mar	Stockport Co	H	W	3–1
5 Apr	Lincoln C	A	L	0–2
6 Apr	Small Heath	A	L	0–1
9 Apr	Barnsley	A	L	2–6
13 Apr	Grimsby T	H	W	1–0
27 Apr	Chesterfield	H	W	1–0

FA Cup

5 Jan	Portsmouth (S)	H	W	3–0
9 Feb	Burnley (1)	H	D	0–0
13 Feb	Burnley (1R)	A	L	1–7

Football League

	P	W	D	L	F:A	Pts	
Newton Heath	34	14	4	16	42:38	32	10th

SEASON 1901–1902
FOOTBALL LEAGUE (DIVISION 2)

7 Sep	Gainsborough T	H	W	3–0
14 Sep	Middlesbrough	A	L	0–5
21 Sep	Bristol C	H	W	1–0
28 Sep	Blackpool	A	W	4–2
5 Oct	Stockport Co	H	D	3–3
12 Oct	Burton U	A	D	0–0
19 Oct	Glossop	A	D	0–0
26 Oct	Doncaster R	H	W	6–0
9 Nov	W B A	H	L	1–2
16 Nov	Arsenal	A	L	0–2
23 Nov	Barnsley	H	W	1–0
30 Nov	Leicester Fosse	A	L	2–3
7 Dec	Preston NE	A	L	1–5
21 Dec	Port Vale	H	W	1–0
25 Dec	Lincoln C	A	L	0–2
1 Jan	Preston NE	H	L	0–2
4 Jan	Gainsborough T	A	D	1–1
18 Jan	Bristol C	A	L	0–4
25 Jan	Blackpool	H	L	0–1
1 Feb	Stockport Co	A	L	0–1
11 Feb	Burnley	H	W	2–0
15 Feb	Glossop	H	W	1–0
22 Feb	Doncaster R	A	L	0–4
1 Mar	Lincoln C	H	D	0–0
8 Mar	W B A	A	L	0–4
15 Mar	Arsenal	H	L	0–1
17 Mar	Chesterfield	A	L	0–3
22 Mar	Barnsley	A	L	2–3
28 Mar	Burnley	A	L	0–1
29 Mar	Leicester Fosse	H	W	2–0
7 Apr	Middlesbrough	H	L	1–2
19 Apr	Port Vale	A	D	1–1
21 Apr	Burton U	H	W	3–1
23 Apr	Chesterfield	H	W	2–0

FA Cup

14 Dec	Lincoln C (1R)	H	L	1–2

Football League

	P	W	D	L	F:A	Pts	
Newton Heath	34	11	6	17	38:53	28	15th

SEASON 1902–1903
FOOTBALL LEAGUE (DIVISION 2)

6 Sep	Gainsborough T	A	W	1–0
13 Sep	Burton U	H	W	1–0
20 Sep	Bristol C	A	L	1–3
27 Sep	Glossop	H	D	1–1
4 Oct	Chesterfield	H	W	2–1
11 Oct	Stockport Co	A	L	1–2
25 Oct	Arsenal	A	W	1–0
8 Nov	Lincoln C	A	W	3–1
15 Nov	Small Heath	H	L	0–1
22 Nov	Leicester F	A	D	1–1
6 Dec	Burnley	A	W	*2–0
20 Dec	Port Vale	A	D	1–1
25 Dec	Manchester C	H	D	1–1
26 Dec	Blackpool	H	D	2–2
27 Dec	Barnsley	H	W	2–1
3 Jan	Gainsborough T	H	W	3–1
10 Jan	Burton U	A	L	1–3
17 Jan	Bristol C	H	L	1–2
24 Jan	Glossop	A	W	3–1
31 Jan	Chesterfield	A	L	0–2
14 Feb	Blackpool	A	L	0–2
28 Feb	Doncaster R	A	D	2–2
7 Mar	Lincoln C	H	L	1–2
9 Mar	Arsenal	H	W	3–0
21 Mar	Leicester F	H	W	5–1
23 Mar	Stockport Co	H	D	0–0
30 Mar	Preston NE	H	L	0–1
4 Apr	Burnley	H	W	4–0
10 Apr	Manchester C	A	W	2–0
11 Apr	Preston NE	A	L	1–3
13 Apr	Doncaster R	H	W	4–0
18 Apr	Port Vale	H	W	2–1
20 Apr	Small Heath	A	L	1–2
25 Apr	Barnsley	A	D	0–0

FA Cup

1 Nov	Accrington S. (3Q)	H	W	7–0
13 Nov	Oswaldtwistle R (4Q)	H	W	3–2
29 Nov	Southport Cent. (5Q)	H	W	4–1
13 Dec	Burton U (Int)	H	D	1–1
17 Dec	Burton U (R)†	H	W	3–1
7 Feb	Liverpool (1)	H	W	2–1
21 Feb	Everton (2)	A	L	1–3

†away tie switched to Manchester (Bank Street)

Football League

	P	W	D	L	F:A	Pts	
Manchester U	34	15	8	11	53:38	38	5th

SEASON 1903–1904
FOOTBALL LEAGUE (DIVISION 2)

5 Sep	Bristol C	H	D	2–2
7 Sep	Burnley	A	L	0–2
12 Sep	Port Vale	A	L	0–1
19 Sep	Glossop	A	W	5–0
26 Sep	Bradford C	H	W	3–1
3 Oct	Arsenal	A	L	0–4
10 Oct	Barnsley	H	W	4–0
17 Oct	Lincoln C	A	D	0–0
24 Oct	Stockport Co	H	W	3–1
7 Nov	Bolton W	H	D	0–0
21 Nov	Preston NE	H	L	0–2
19 Dec	Gainsborough T	H	W	4–2
25 Dec	Chesterfield	H	W	3–1
26 Dec	Burton U	A	D	2–2
2 Jan	Bristol C	A	D	1–1
9 Jan	Port Vale	H	W	2–0
16 Jan	Glossop	H	W	3–1
23 Jan	Bradford C	A	D	3–3
30 Jan	Arsenal	H	W	1–0
13 Feb	Lincoln C	H	W	2–0
9 Mar	Blackpool	A	L	1–2
12 Mar	Burnley	H	W	3–1
19 Mar	Preston NE	A	D	1–1
26 Mar	Grimsby T	H	W	2–0
28 Mar	Stockport Co	A	W	3–0
1 Apr	Chesterfield	A	W	2–0
2 Apr	Leicester F	A	W	1–0
5 Apr	Barnsley	A	W	2–0
9 Apr	Blackpool	H	W	3–1
12 Apr	Grimsby T	A	L	1–3
16 Apr	Gainsborough T	A	W	1–0
23 Apr	Burton U	H	W	2–0
25 Apr	Bolton W	A	D	0–0
30 Apr	Leicester	H	W	5–2

FA Cup

12 Dec	Small Heath (Int)	H	D	1–1
16 Dec	Small Heath (IntR)†	A	D	1–1
21 Dec	Small Heath (IntR)† (at Bramall Lane)	N	D	1–1
11 Jan	Small Heath (IntR) (at Hyde Road, Manchester)	N	W	3–1
6 Feb	Notts Co (1)	A	D	3–3
10 Feb	Notts Co (1R)	H	W	2–1
20 Feb	Sheffield Wed (2)	A	L	0–6

†after extra time

Football League

	P	W	D	L	F:A	Pts	
Manchester U	34	20	8	6	65:33	48	3rd

SEASON 1904–1905
FOOTBALL LEAGUE (DIVISION 2)

3 Sep	Port Vale	A	D	2–2
10 Sep	Bristol C	H	W	4–1
17 Sep	Bolton W	H	L	1–2
24 Sep	Glossop	A	W	2–1
8 Oct	Bradford C	A	D	1–1
15 Oct	Lincoln C	H	W	2–0
22 Oct	Liecester F	A	W	3–0
29 Oct	Barnsley	H	W	4–0
5 Nov	W B A	A	W	2–0
12 Nov	Burnley	H	W	1–0
19 Nov	Grimsby T	A	W	1–0
3 Dec	Doncaster R	A	W	1–0
10 Dec	Gainsborough T	H	W	3–1
17 Dec	Burton U	A	W	3–2
24 Dec	Liverpool	H	W	3–1
26 Dec	Chesterfield	H	W	3–0
31 Dec	Port Vale	H	W	6–1
2 Jan	Bradford C	H	W	*7–0
3 Jan	Bolton W	A	W	4–2
7 Jan	Bristol C	A	D	1–1
21 Jan	Glossop	H	W	4–1
11 Feb	Lincoln C	A	L	0–3
18 Feb	Leicester F	H	W	4–1
25 Feb	Barnsley	A	D	0–0
4 Mar	W B A	H	W	2–0
11 Mar	Burnley	A	L	0–2
18 Mar	Grimsby T	H	W	2–1
25 Mar	Blackpool	H	W	1–0
1 Apr	Doncaster R	H	W	6–0
8 Apr	Gainsborough T	A	D	0–0
15 Apr	Burton U	H	W	5–0
21 Apr	Chesterfield	A	L	0–2
22 Apr	Liverpool	A	L	0–4
24 Apr	Blackpool	A	W	3–1

FA Cup

14 Jan	Fulham (Int)	H	D	2–2
18 Jan	Fulham (IntR†	A	D	0–0
23 Jan	Fulham (IntR) (at Villa Park)	N	L	0–1

†after extra time

Football League

	P	W	D	L	F:A	Pts	
Manchester U	34	24	5	5	81:30	53	3rd

SEASON 1905–1906
FOOTBALL LEAGUE (DIVISION 2)

2 Sep	Bristol C	H	W	5–1
4 Sep	Blackpool	H	W	2–1
9 Sep	Grimsby T	A	W	1–0
16 Sep	Glossop	A	W	2–1
23 Sep	Stockport C	H	W	3–1
30 Sep	Blackpool	A	W	1–0
7 Oct	Bradford C	H	D	0–0
14 Oct	W B A	A	L	0–1
21 Oct	Leicester	H	W	3–2
25 Oct	Gainsborough T	A	D	2–2
28 Oct	Hull C	A	W	1–0
4 Nov	Lincoln C	H	W	2–1
11 Nov	Chesterfield	A	L	0–1
18 Nov	Port Vale	H	W	*3–0
25 Nov	Barnsley	A	W	*3–0
2 Dec	Clapton O	H	W	4–0
9 Dec	Burnley	A	W	3–1
23 Dec	Burton U*	A	W	2–0
25 Dec	Chelsea	H	D	0–0
30 Dec	Bristol C	A	D	1–1
6 Jan	Grimsby T	H	W	5–0
15 Jan	Leeds C	H	L	0–3
20 Jan	Glossop	H	W	5–2
27 Jan	Stockport C	A	W	1–0
10 Feb	Bradford C	A	W	5–1
17 Feb	W B A	H	D	0–0
3 Mar	Hull C	H	W	5–1
17 Mar	Chesterfield	H	W	4–1
24 Mar	Port Vale	A	L	0–1
29 Mar	Leicester C	A	W	5–2
31 Mar	Barnsley	H	W	5–1
7 Apr	Clapton O	A	W	1–0
13 Apr	Chelsea	A	D	1–1
14 Apr	Bumley	H	W	1–0
16 Apr	Gainsborough T	H	W	2–0
21 Apr	Leeds C	A	W	3–1
25 Apr	Lincoln C	A	W	3–2
28 Apr	Burton U	H	W	6–0

FA Cup

13 Jan	Staple Hill (1)	H	W	7–2
3 Feb	Norwich (2)	H	W	3–0
24 Feb	Aston Villa (3)	H	W	5–1
10 Mar	Arsenal (4)	H	L	2–3

Football League

	P	W	D	L	F:A	Pts	
Manchester U	38	28	6	4	90:28	62	2nd

SEASON 1906–1907
FOOTBALL LEAGUE (DIVISION 1)

1 Sep	Bristol C	A	W	2–1
3 Sep	Derby Co	A	D	2–2
8 Sep	Notts Co	H	D	0–0
15 Sep	Sheffield U	A	W	2–0
22 Sep	Bolton W	H	L	1–2
29 Sep	Derby Co	H	D	1–1
6 Oct	Stoke C	A	W	2–1
13 Oct	Blackburn R	H	D	1–1
20 Oct	Sunderland	A	L	1–4
27 Oct	Birmingham	H	W	2–1
3 Nov	Everton	A	L	0–3
10 Nov	Arsenal	H	W	1–0
17 Nov	Sheffield Wed	A	L	2–5
24 Nov	Bury	H	L	2–4
1 Dec	Manchester C	A	L	0–3
8 Dec	Middlesbrough	H	W	3–1
15 Dec	Preston NE	A	L	0–2
22 Dec	Newcastle U	H	L	1–3
25 Dec	Liverpool	H	D	0–0
26 Dec	Aston Villa	A	L	0–2
29 Dec	Bristol C	H	D	0–0
1 Jan	Aston Villa	H	W	1–0
5 Jan	Notts Co	A	L	0–3
19 Jan	Sheffield U	H	W	2–0
26 Jan	Bolton W	A	W	1–0
2 Feb	Newcastle U	A	L	0–5
9 Feb	Stoke C	H	W	·4–1
16 Feb	Blackburn R	A	W	4–2
23 Feb	Preston NE	H	W	3–0
2 Mar	Birmingham	A	D	1–1
16 Mar	Arsenal	A	L	0–4
25 Mar	Sunderland	H	W	2–0
30 Mar	Bury	A	W	2–1
1 Apr	Liverpool	A	W	1–0
6 Apr	Manchester C	H	D	1–1
10 Apr	Sheffield Wed	H	W	5–0
13 Apr	Middlesbrough	A	L	0–2
22 Apr	Everton	H	W	3–0

FA Cup

12 Jan	Portsmouth(1)	A	D	2–2
16 Jan	Portsmouth (1R)	H	L	1–2

Football League

	P	W	D	L	F:A	Pts	
Manchester U	38	17	8	13	53:56	42	8th

SEASON 1907–1908
FOOTBALL LEAGUE (DIVISION 1)

2 Sep	Aston Villa	A	W	4–1
7 Sep	Liverpool	H	W	4–0
9 Sep	Middlesbrough	H	W	2–1
14 Sep	Middlesbrough	A	L	1–2
21 Sep	Sheffield U	H	W	2–1
28 Sep	Chelsea	A	W	4–1
5 Oct	Nottingham F	H	W	·4–0
12 Oct	Newcastle U	A	W	6–1
19 Oct	Blackburn R	A	W	5–1
26 Oct	Bolton W	H	W	2–1
2 Nov	Birmingham	A	W	4–3
9 Nov	Everton	H	W	4–3
16 Nov	Sunderland	A	W	2–1
23 Nov	Arsenal	H	W	4–2
30 Nov	Sheffield Wed	A	L	0–2
7 Dec	Bristol C	H	W	2–1
14 Dec	Notts Co	A	D	1–1
21 Dec	Manchester C	H	W	3–1
25 Dec	Bury	H	W	2–1
28 Dec	Preston NE	A	D	0–0
1 Jan	Bury	A	W	1–0
18 Jan	Sheffield U	A	L	0–2
25 Jan	Chelsea	H	W	1–0
8 Feb	Newcastle U	H	D	1–1
15 Feb	Blackburn R	H	L	1–2
29 Feb	Birmingham	H	W	1–0
14 Mar	Sunderland	H	W	3–0
21 Mar	Arsenal	A	L	0–1
25 Mar	Liverpool	A	L	4–7
28 Mar	Sheffield Wed	H	W	4–1
4 Apr	Bristol C	A	D	1–1
8 Apr	Everton	A	W	3–1
11 Apr	Notts Co	H	L	0–1
17 Apr	Nottingham F	A	L	0–2
18 Apr	Manchester C	A	D	0–0
20 Apr	Aston Villa	H	L	1–1
22 Apr	Bolton W	A	D	2–2
25 Apr	Preston NE	H	W	·2–1

FA Cup

11 Jan	Blackpool (1)	H	W	3–1
1 Feb	Chelsea (2)	H	W	1–0
22 Feb	Aston Villa (3)	A	W	2–0
7 Mar	Fulham (4)	A	L	1–2

Football League

	P	W	D	L	F:A	Pts	
Manchester U	38	23	6	9	81:48	52	1st

SEASON 1908–1909
FOOTBALL LEAGUE (DIVISION 1)

5 Sep	Preston NE	A	W	3–0
7 Sep	Bury	H	W	2–1
12 Sep	Middlesbrough	H	W	6–3
19 Sep	Manchester C	A	W	2–1
26 Sep	Liverpool	H	W	3–2
3 Oct	Bury	A	D	2–2
10 Oct	Sheffield U	H	W	2–1
17 Oct	Aston Villa	A	L	1–3
24 Oct	Nottingham F	H	D	2–2
31 Oct	Sunderland	A	L	1–6
7 Nov	Chelsea	H	L	0–1
14 Nov	Blackburn R	A	W	3–1
21 Nov	Bradford C	H	W	2–0
28 Nov	Sheffield Wed	H	W	3–1
5 Dec	Everton	A	L	2–3
12 Dec	Leicester F	H	W	4–2
19 Dec	Arsenal	A	W	1–0
25 Dec	Newcastle U	A	L	1–2
26 Dec	Newcastle U	H	W	1–0
1 Jan	Notts Co	H	W	4–3
2 Jan	Preston NE	H	L	0–2
9 Jan	Middlesbrough	A	L	0–5
23 Jan	Manchester C	H	W	3–1
30 Jan	Liverpool	A	L	1–3
13 Feb	Sheffield U	A	D	0–0
27 Feb	Nottingham F	A	L	0–2
13 Mar	Chelsea	A	D	1–1
15 Mar	Sunderland	H	D	2–2
20 Mar	Blackburn R	H	L	0–3
31 Mar	Aston Villa	H	L	0–2
3 Apr	Sheffield Wed	A	L	0–2
9 Apr	Bristol C	H	L	0–1
10 Apr	Everton	H	D	2–2
12 Apr	Bristol C	A	D	0–0
13 Apr	NottsC	A	W	1–0
17 Apr	Leicester F	A	L	2–3
27 Apr	Arsenal	H	L	1–4
29 Apr	Bradford C	A	L	0–1

FA Cup

16 Jan	Brighton (1)	H	W	1–0
6 Feb	Everton (2)	H	W	1–0
20 Feb	Blackburn R (3)	H	W	6–1
5 Mar	Burnley (4)	A	*	
10 Mar	Burnley (4)	A	W	3–2
27 Mar	Newcastle U (SF) (at Bramall Lane)	N	W	1–0
24 Apr	Bristol C (F) (at Crystal Palace)	N	W	1–0

*match abandoned after 72 minutes because of snow. Score Burnley 1 United 0

Football League

	P	W	D	L	F:A	Pts	
Manchester U	38	15	7	16	58:68	37	13th

SEASON 1909–1910
FOOTBALL LEAGUE (DIVISION 1)

1 Sep	Bradford C	H	W	1–0
4 Sep	Bury	H	W	2–0
6 Sep	Notts Co	H	W	2–1
11 Sep	Tottenham H	A	D	2–2
18 Sep	Preston NE	H	D	1–1
25 Sep	Notts Co	A	L	2–3
2 Oct	Newcastle U	H	D	1–1
9 Oct	Liverpool	A	L	2–3
16 Oct	Aston Villa	H	W	2–0
23 Oct	Sheffield U	A	W	1–0
30 Oct	Arsenal	H	W	1–0
6 Nov	Bolton W	A	W	3–2
13 Nov	Chelsea	H	W	2–0
20 Nov	Blackburn R	A	L	2–3
27 Nov	Nottingham F	H	L	2–6
4 Dec	Sunderland	A	L	0–3
18 Dec	Middlesbrough	A	W	2–1
25 Dec	Sheffield Wed	H	L	0–3
27 Dec	Sheffield Wed	A	L	1–4
1 Jan	Bradford C	A	W	2–0
8 Jan	Bury	A	D	1–1
22 Jan	Tottenham H	H	W	5–0
5 Feb	Preston NE	A	L	0–1
12 Feb	Newcastle U	A	W	4–3
19 Feb	Liverpool	H	L	3–4
26 Feb	Aston Villa	A	L	1–7
5 Mar	Sheffield U	H	W	1–0
12 Mar	Arsenal	A	D	0–0
19 Mar	Bolton W	H	W	5–0
25 Mar	Bristol C	H	W	2–1
26 Mar	Chelsea	A	D	1–1
28 Mar	Bristol C	A	L	1–2
2 Apr	Blackburn R	H	W	2–0
6 Apr	Everton	H	W	3–2
9 Apr	Nottingham F	A	L	0–2
16 Apr	Sunderland	H	W	2–0
23 Apr	Everton	A	D	3–3
30 Apr	Middlesbrough	H	W	4–1

FA Cup

15 Jan	Burnley (1)	A	L	0–2

Football League

	P	W	D	L	F:A	Pts	
Manchester U	38	19	7	12	69:61	45	5th

SEASON 1910–1911
FOOTBALL LEAGUE (DIVISION 1)

1 Sep	Arsenal	A	W	2–1
3 Sep	Blackburn R	H	W	3–2

10 Sep	Nottingham F	A	L	1–2
17 Sep	Manchester C	H	W	2–1
24 Sep	Everton	A	W	1–0
1 Oct	Sheffield Wed	H	W	3–2
8 Oct	Bristol C	A	W	1–0
15 Oct	Newcastle U	H	W	2–0
22 Oct	Tottenham H	A	D	2–2
29 Oct	Middlesbrough	H	L	1–2
5 Nov	Preston NE	A	W	2–0
12 Nov	Notts Co	H	D	0–0
19 Nov	Oldham	A	W	3–1
26 Nov	Liverpool	A	L	2–3
3 Dec	Bury	H	W	3–2
10 Dec	Sheffield U	A	L	0–2
17 Dec	Aston Villa	H	W	2–0
24 Dec	Sunderland	A	W	2–1
26 Dec	Arsenal	H	W	5–0
27 Dec	Bradford C	A	L	0–1
31 Dec	Blackburn R	A	L	0–1
2 Jan	Bradford C	H	W	*1–0
7 Jan	Nottingham F	H	W	4–2
21 Jan	Manchester C	A	D	1–1
28 Jan	Everton	H	D	2–2
11 Feb	Bristol C	H	W	3–1
18 Feb	Newcastle U	A	W	1–0
4 Mar	Middlesbrough	A	D	2–2
11 Mar	Preston NE	H	W	5–0
15 Mar	Tottenham H	H	W	3–2
18 Mar	Notts Co	A	L	0–1
25 Mar	Oldham	H	D	0–0
1 Apr	Liverpool	H	W	2–0
8 Apr	Bury	A	W	3–0
15 Apr	Sheffield U	H	D	1–1
17 Apr	Sheffield Wed	A	D	0–0
22 Apr	Aston Villa	A	L	2–4
29 Apr	Sunderland	H	W	*5–1

FA Cup

14 Jan	Blackpool (1)	A	W	2–1
4 Feb	Aston Villa (2)	H	W	2–1
25 Feb	West Ham (3)	A	L	1–2

Football League

	P	W	D	L	F:A	Pts	
Manchester U	38	22	8	8	72:40	52	1st

SEASON 1911–1912
FOOTBALL LEAGUE (DIVISION 1)

2 Sep	Manchester C	A	D	0–0
9 Sep	Everton	H	W	2–1
16 Sep	W B A	A	L	0–1
23 Sep	Sunderland	H	D	2–2
30 Sep	Blackburn R	A	D	2–2
7 Oct	Sheffield Wed	H	W	3–1
14 Oct	Bury	A	W	1–0
21 Oct	Middlesbrough	H	L	3–4
28 Oct	Notts C	A	W	1–0
4 Nov	Tottenham H	H	L	1–2
11 Nov	Preston NE	H	D	0–0
18 Nov	Liverpool	A	L	2–3
25 Nov	Aston Villa	H	W	3–1
2 Dec	Newcastle U	A	W	3–2
9 Dec	Sheffield U	H	W	1–0
16 Dec	Oldham	A	D	2–2
23 Dec	Bolton W	H	W	2–0
25 Dec	Bradford C	H	L	0–1
26 Dec	Bradford C	A	W	1–0
30 Dec	Manchester C	H	D	0–0
1 Jan	Arsenal	H	W	2–0
6 Jan	Everton	A	L	0–4
20 Jan	W B A	H	L	1–2
27 Jan	Sunderland	A	L	0–5
10 Feb	Sheffield Wed	A	L	0–3
17 Feb	Bury	H	D	0–0
2 Mar	Notts C	H	W	2–0
16 Mar	Preston NE	A	D	0–0
23 Mar	Liverpool	H	D	1–1
30 Mar	Aston Villa	A	L	0–6
5 Apr	Arsenal	A	L	1–2
6 Apr	Newcastle	H	L	0–2
9 Apr	Tottenham H	A	D	1–1
13 Apr	Sheffield U	A	L	1–6
17 Apr	Middlesbrough	A	L	0–3
20 Apr	Oldham	H	W	3–1
27 Apr	Bolton W	A	D	1–1
29 Apr	Blackburn R	H	W	3–1

FA Cup

13 Jan	Huddersfield T(1)	H	W	3–1
3 Feb	Coventry C (2)	A	W	5–1
24 Feb	Reading (3)	A	D	1–1
29 Feb	Reading (3R)	H	W	3–0
9 Mar	Blackburn R (4)	H	D	*1–1
14 Mar	Blackburn R (4R)†	A	L	2–4

†after extra time

Football League

	P	W	D	L	F:A	Pts	
Manchester U	38	13	11	14	45:60	37	13th

SEASON 1912–1913
FOOTBALL LEAGUE (DIVISION 1)

2 Sep	Arsenal	A	D	0–0
7 Sep	Manchester C	H	L	0–1
14 Sep	W B A	A	W	2–1
21 Sep	Everton	H	W	2–0
28 Sep	Sheffield Wed	A	D	3–3
5 Oct	Blackburn R	H	D	1–1
12 Oct	Derby C	A	L	1–2
19 Oct	Tottenham H	H	W	2–0
26 Oct	Middlesbrough	A	L	2–3
2 Nov	Notts Co	H	W	2–1
9 Nov	Sunderland	A	L	1–3
16 Nov	Aston Villa	A	L	2–4
23 Nov	Liverpool	H	W	3–1
30 Nov	Bolton W	A	L	1–2
7 Dec	Sheffield U	H	W	4–0
14 Dec	Newcastle U	A	W	3–1
21 Dec	Oldham	H	D	0–0
25 Dec	Chelsea	A	W	4–1
26 Dec	Chelsea	H	W	4–2
28 Dec	Manchester C	A	W	2–0
1 Jan	Bradford C	H	W	2–0
4 Jan	W B A	H	D	1–1
18 Jan	Everton	A	L	1–4
25 Jan	Sheffield Wed	H	W	2–0
8 Feb	Blackburn R	A	D	0–0
15 Feb	Derby C	H	W	4–0
1 Mar	Middlesbrough	H	L	2–3
8 Mar	Notts Co	A	W	2–1
15 Mar	Sunderland	H	L	1–3
21 Mar	Arsenal	H	W	2–0
22 Mar	Aston Villa	H	W	4–0
25 Mar	Bradford C	A	L	0–1
29 Mar	Liverpool	A	W	2–0
31 Mar	Tottenham H	A	D	1–1
5 Apr	Bolton W	H	W	2–1
12 Apr	Sheffield U	A	L	1–2
19 Apr	Newcastle U	H	W	3–0
26 Apr	Oldham	A	D	0–0

FA Cup

11 Jan	Coventry (1)	H	D	1–1
16 Jan	Coventry (1R)	A	W	2–1
1 Feb	Plymouth A (2)	A	W	2–0
22 Feb	Oldham (3)	A	D	0–0
26 Feb	Oldham (3R)	H	L	1–2

Football League

	P	W	D	L	F:A	Pts	
Manchester U	38	19	8	11	69:43	46	4th

SEASON 1913–1914
FOOTBALL LEAGUE (DIVISION 1)

6 Sep	Sheffield Wed	A	W	3–1
8 Sep	Sunderland	H	W	3–1
13 Sep	Bolton W	H	L	0–1
20 Sep	Chelsea	A	W	2–0
27 Sep	Oldham	H	W	4–1
4 Oct	Tottenham H	H	W	3–1
11 Oct	Burnley	A	W	2–1
18 Oct	Preston NE	H	W	3–0
25 Oct	Newcastle U	A	W	1–0
1 Nov	Liverpool	H	W	3–0
8 Nov	Aston Villa	A	L	1–3
15 Nov	Middlesbrough	H	L	0–1
22 Nov	Sheffield U	A	L	0–2
29 Nov	Derby Co	H	D	3–3
6 Dec	Manchester C	A	W	2–0
13 Dec	Bradford C	H	D	1–1
20 Dec	Blackburn R	A	W	1–0
25 Dec	Everton	H	L	0–1
26 Dec	Everton	A	L	0–5
27 Dec	Sheffield Wed	H	W	2–1
1 Jan	W B A	H	W	1–0
3 Jan	Bolton W	A	L	1–6
17 Jan	Chelsea	H	L	0–1
24 Jan	Oldham	A	D	2–2
7 Feb	Tottenham H	A	L	1–2
14 Feb	Burnley	H	L	0–1
21 Feb	Middlesbrough	A	L	1–3
28 Feb	Newcastle U	H	D	2–2
5 Mar	Preston NE	A	L	2–4
14 Mar	Aston Villa	H	L	0–6
4 Apr	Derby Co	A	L	2–4
10 Apr	Sunderland	A	L	0–2
11 Apr	Manchester C	H	L	0–1
13 Apr	W B A	A	L	1–2
15 Apr	Liverpool	A	W	2–1
18 Apr	Bradford C	A	D	1–1
22 Apr	Sheffield U	H	W	2–1
25 Apr	Blackburn R	H	D	0–0

FA Cup

10 Jan	Swindon T (1)	A	L	0–1

Football League

	P	W	D	L	F:A	Pts	
Manchester U	38	15	6	17	52:62	36	14th

SEASON 1914–1915
FOOTBALL LEAGUE (DIVISION 1)

2 Sep	Oldham	H	L	1–3
5 Sep	Manchester C	H	D	0–0
12 Sep	Bolton W	A	L	0–3
19 Sep	Blackburn R	H	W	2–0
26 Sep	Notts Co	A	L	2–4
3 Oct	Sunderland	H	W	3–0
10 Oct	Sheffield Wed	A	L	0–1
17 Oct	W B A	H	D	0–0
24 Oct	Everton	A	L	2–4
31 Oct	Chelsea	H	D	2–2
7 Nov	Bradford C	A	L	2–4
14 Nov	Burnley	H	L	0–2
21 Nov	Tottenham H	A	L	0–2
28 Nov	Newcastle U	H	W	1–0
5 Dec	Middlesbrough	A	D	1–1
12 Dec	Sheffield U	H	L	1–2
19 Dec	Aston Villa	A	D	3–3
26 Dec	Liverpool	A	D	1–1
1 Jan	Bradford	H	L	1–2
2 Jan	Manchester C	A	D	1–1
16 Jan	Bolton W	H	W	4–1
23 Jan	Blackburn R	A	D	3–3
30 Jan	Notts Co	H	D	2–2
6 Feb	Sunderland	A	L	0–1
13 Feb	Sheffield Wed	H	W	2–0
20 Feb	W B A	A	D	0–0
27 Feb	Everton	H	L	1–2
13 Mar	Bradford C	H	W	1–0
20 Mar	Burnley	A	L	0–3
27 Mar	Tottenham H	H	D	1–1
2 Apr	Liverpool	H	W	2–0
3 Apr	Newcastle	A	L	0–2
5 Apr	Bradford	A	L	0–5
6 Apr	Oldham	A	L	0–1
10 Apr	Middlesbrough	H	D	2–2
17 Apr	Sheffield U	A	L	1–3
19 Apr	Chelsea	A	W	3–1
26 Apr	Aston Villa	H	W	1–0

FA Cup

9 Jan	Sheffield Wed (1)	A	L	0–1

Football League

	P	W	D	L	F:A	Pts	
Manchester U	38	9	12	17	46:62	30	18th

SEASON 1915–1916

Lancs Principal Tournament

4 Sep	Oldham A	A	L	2–3
11 Sep	Everton	H	L	2–4
18 Sep	Bolton W	A	W	5–3
25 Sep	Manchester C	H	D	1–1
2 Oct	Stoke C	A	D	0–0
9 Oct	Burnley	H	L	3–7
16 Oct	Preston NE	A	D	0–0
23 Oct	Stockport Co	H	W	3–0
30 Oct	Liverpool	A	W	2–0
6 Nov	Bury	H	D	1–1
13 Nov	Rochdale	H	W	2–0
20 Nov	Blackpool	A	L	1–5
27 Nov	Southport	H	D	0–0
4 Dec	Oldham	H	W	2–0
11 Dec	Everton	A	L	0–2
18 Dec	Bolton W	H	W	1–0
25 Dec	Manchester C	A	L	1–2
1 Jan	Stoke C	H	L	1–2
8 Jan	Burnley	A	L	4–7
15 Jan	Preston NE	H	W	4–0
22 Jan	Stockport Co	A	L	1–3
29 Jan	Liverpool	H	D	1–1
5 Feb	Bury	A	L	1–2
12 Feb	Rochdale	A	D	2–2
19 Feb	Blackpool	H	D	1–1
26 Feb	Southport	A	L	0–5

	P	W	D	L	F:A	Pts	
Manchester U	26	7	8	13	41:51	22	11th

Lancs Subsidiary Tournament

4 Mar	Everton	H	L	0–2
11 Mar	Oldham	A	L	0–1
18 Mar	Liverpool	H	D	0–0
25 Mar	Manchester C	H	L	0–2
1 Apr	Stockport Co	A	L	3–5
8 Apr	Everton	A	L	1–5
15 Apr	Oldham	H	W	3–0
21 Apr	Stockport Co	H	W	3–2
22 Apr	Liverpool	A	L	1–7
29 Apr	Manchester C	A	L	1–2

	P	W	D	L	F:A	Pts	
Manchester U	10	2	1	7	12:24	5	6th

SEASON 1916–1917

Lancs Principal Tournament

2 Sep	Port Vale	H	D	2–2
9 Sep	Oldham	A	W	2–0
16 Sep	Preston NE	H	W	2–1
23 Sep	Burnley	A	L	1–7
30 Sep	Blackpool	A	D	2–2
7 Oct	Liverpool	H	D	0–0
14 Oct	Stockport Co	A	L	0–1
21 Oct	Bury	H	W	3–1
28 Oct	Stoke C	A	L	0–3
4 Nov	Southport	H	W	1–0
11 Nov	Blackburn R	A	W	2–1
18 Nov	Manchester C	H	W	2–1
25 Nov	Everton	A	L	2–3
2 Dec	Rochdale	H	D	1–1
9 Dec	Bolton W	A	L	1–5
23 Dec	Oldham	H	W	3–2
30 Dec	Preston NE	A	L	2–3
6 Jan	Burnley	H	W	3–1
13 Jan	Blackpool	H	W	3–2
20 Jan	Liverpool	A	D	3–3
27 Jan	Stockport Co	H	L	0–1
3 Feb	Bury	A	D	1–1
10 Feb	Stoke C	H	W	4–2
17 Feb	Southport	A	W	1–0
24 Feb	Blackburn R	H	W	1–0
3 Mar	Manchester C	A	L	0–1
10 Mar	Everton	H	L	0–2
17 Mar	Rochdale	A	L	0–2
24 Mar	Bolton W	H	W	6–3
6 Apr	Port Vale	A	L	0–3

	P	W	D	L	F:A	Pts	
Manchester U	30	13	6	11	48:54	33	7th

Lancs Subsidiary Tournament

31 Mar	Stoke C	A	L	1–2
7 Apr	Manchester C	H	W	5–1
9 Apr	Port Vale	H	W	5–1
14 Apr	Stoke C	H	W	1–0
21 Apr	Manchester C	A	W	1–0
28 Apr	Port Vale	A	L	2–5

	P	W	D	L	F:A	Pts	
Manchester U	6	4	0	2	15:9	8	4th

SEASON 1917–1918

Lancs Principal Tournament

1 Sep	Blackburn R	A	W	5–0
8 Sep	Blackburn R	H	W	6–1
15 Sep	Rochdale	A	L	0–3
22 Sep	Rochdale	H	D	1–1
29 Sep	Manchester C	A	L	1–3
6 Oct	Manchester C	H	D	1–1
13 Oct	Everton	A	L	0–3
20 Oct	Everton	H	D	0–0
27 Oct	Port Vale	H	D	3–3
3 Nov	Port Vale	A	D	2–2
10 Nov	Bolton W	H	L	1–3
17 Nov	Bolton W	A	L	2–4
24 Nov	Preston NE	H	W	2–1
1 Dec	Preston NE	A	D	0–0
8 Dec	Blackpool	H	W	1–0
15 Dec	Blackpool	A	W	3–2
22 Dec	Burnley	A	W	5–0
29 Dec	Burnley	H	W	1–0
5 Jan	Southport	A	L	0–3
12 Jan	Southport	H	D	0–0
19 Jan	Liverpool	A	L	1–5
26 Jan	Liverpool	H	L	0–2
2 Feb	Stoke C	A	L	1–5
9 Feb	Stoke C	H	W	2–1
16 Feb	Bury	H	D	0–0
23 Feb	Bury	A	W	2–1
2 Mar	Oldham	H	W	2–1
9 Mar	Oldham	A	L	0–2
16 Mar	Stockport Co	H	W	2–0
23 Mar	Stockport Co	A	L	1–2

	P	W	D	L	F:A	Pts	
Manchester U	30	11	8	11	45:49	30	8th

Lancs Subsidiary Tournament

29 Mar	Manchester C	A	L	0–3
30 Mar	Stoke C	H	W	2–1
1 Apr	Manchester C	H	W	2–0
6 Apr	Stoke C	A	D	0–0
13 Apr	Port Vale	H	W	2–0
20 Apr	Port Vale	A	L	0–3

	P	W	D	L	F:A	Pts	
Manchester U	6	3	1	2	6:7	7	8th

SEASON 1918–1919

Lancs Principal Tournament

7 Sep	Oldham	H	L	1–4
14 Sep	Oldham	A	W	2–0
21 Sep	Blackburn R	H	W	1–0
28 Sep	Blackburn R	A	D	1–1
5 Oct	Manchester C	H	L	0–2
12 Oct	Manchester C	A	D	0–0
19 Oct	Everton	H	D	1–1
26 Oct	Everton	A	L	2–6
2 Nov	Rochdale	H	W	3–1
9 Nov	Rochdale	A	L	0–1
16 Nov	Preston NE	A	L	2–4
23 Nov	Preston NE	H	L	1–2
30 Nov	Bolton W	A	L	1–3
7 Dec	Bolton W	H	W	1–0
14 Dec	Port Vale	A	L	1–3
21 Dec	Port Vale	H	W	5–1
28 Dec	Blackpool	A	D	2–2
11 Jan	Stockport Co	A	L	1–2
18 Jan	Stockport Co	H	L	0–2
25 Jan	Liverpool	A	D	1–1
1 Feb	Liverpool	H	L	0–1
8 Feb	Southport V	A	L	1–2
15 Feb	Southport V	H	L	1–3
22 Feb	Burnley	A	L	2–4
1 Mar	Burnley	H	W	4–0
8 Mar	Stoke C	A	W	2–1
15 Mar	Stoke C	H	W	3–1
22 Mar	Bury	A	W	2–0
29 Mar	Bury	H	W	5–1

	P	W	D	L	F:A	Pts	
Manchester U	30	11	5	14	51:50	27	9th

Lancs Subsidiary Tournament (Sec 'C')

5 Apr	Port Vale	A	W	3–1
12 Apr	Port Vale	H	W	2–1
18 Apr	Manchester C	A	L	0–3
19 Apr	Stoke C	H	L	0–1
21 Apr	Manchester C	H	L	2–4
26 Apr	Stoke C	A	L	2–4
30 Apr	Blackpool	H	W	5–1

	P	W	D	L	F:A	Pts	
Manchester U	6	2	0	4	9:14	4	3rd

SEASON 1919–1920
FOOTBALL LEAGUE (DIVISION I)

30 Aug	Derby Co	A	D	1–1
1 Sep	Sheffield Wed	H	D	0–0
6 Sep	Derby Co	H	L	0–2
8 Sep	Sheffield Wed	A	W	3–1
13 Sep	Preston NE	A	W	3–2
20 Sep	Preston NE	H	W	5–1
27 Sep	Middlesbrough	A	D	1–1
4 Oct	Middlesbrough	H	D	1–1
11 Oct	Manchester C	A	D	3–3
18 Oct	Manchester C	H	W	1–0
25 Oct	Sheffield U	A	D	2–2
1 Nov	Sheffield U	H	W	3–0
8 Nov	Burnley	A	L	1–2
15 Nov	Burnley	H	L	0–1
22 Nov	Oldham	A	W	3–0
6 Dec	Aston Villa	A	L	0–2
13 Dec	Aston Villa	H	L	1–2
20 Dec	Newcastle U	H	W	2–1
26 Dec	Liverpool	H	D	0–0
27 Dec	Newcastle U	A	L	1–2
1 Jan	Liverpool	A	D	0–0
3 Jan	Chelsea	H	L	0–2
17 Jan	Chelsea	A	L	0–1
24 Jan	W B A	A	L	1–2
7 Feb	Sunderland	A	L	0–3
11 Feb	Oldham	H	D	1–1
14 Feb	Sunderland	H	W	2–0
21 Feb	Arsenal	A	W	3–0
25 Feb	W B A	H	L	1–2
28 Feb	Arsenal	H	L	0–1
6 Mar	Everton	H	W	1–0
13 Mar	Everton	A	D	0–0
20 Mar	Bradford C	H	D	0–0
27 Mar	Bradford C	A	L	1–2
2 Apr	Bradford P A	H	L	0–1
3 Apr	Bolton W	H	D	1–1
6 Apr	Bradford P A	A	W	4–1
10 Apr	Bolton W	A	W	5–3
17 Apr	Blackburn R	H	D	1–1
24 Apr	Blackburn R	A	L	0–5
26 Apr	Notts Co	H	D	0–0
1 May	Notts Co	A	W	2–0

FA Cup

10 Jan	Port Vale (1)	A	W	1–0
31 Jan	Aston Villa (2)	H	L	1–2

Football League

	P	W	D	L	F:A	Pts	
Manchester U	42	13	14	15	54:50	40	12th

SEASON 1920–1921
FOOTBALL LEAGUE (DIVISION 1)

28 Aug	Bolton W	H	L	2–3
30 Aug	Arsenal	A	L	0–2
4 Sep	Bolton W	A	D	1–1
6 Sep	Arsenal	H	D	1–1
11 Sep	Chelsea	H	W	3–1
18 Sep	Chelsea	A	W	2–1
25 Sep	Tottenham H	H	L	0–1
2 Oct	Tottenham H	A	L	1–4
9 Oct	Oldham	H	W	4–1
16 Oct	Oldham	A	D	*2–2
23 Oct	Preston NE	H	W	1–0
30 Oct	Preston NE	A	D	0–0
6 Nov	Sheffield U	H	W	2–1
13 Nov	Sheffield U	A	D	0–0
20 Nov	Manchester C	H	D	1–1
27 Nov	Manchester C	A	L	0–3
4 Dec	Bradford	H	W	5–1
11 Dec	Bradford	A	W	4–2
18 Dec	Newcastle	H	W	2–0
25 Dec	Aston Villa	A	W	4–3
27 Dec	Aston Villa	H	L	1–3
1 Jan	Newcastle U	A	L	3–6
15 Jan	W B A	H	L	1–4
22 Jan	W B A	A	W	2–0
5 Feb	Liverpool	H	D	1–1
9 Feb	Liverpool	A	L	0–2
12 Feb	Everton	H	L	1–2
20 Feb	Sunderland	H	W	3–0
5 Mar	Sunderland	A	W	3–2
9 Mar	Everton	A	L	0–2
12 Mar	Bradford C	H	D	1–1
19 Mar	Bradford C	A	D	1–1
25 Mar	Burnley	A	L	0–1
26 Mar	Huddersfield T	A	L	2–5

28 Mar	Burnley	H	L	0–3
2 Apr	Huddersfield T	H	W	2–0
9 Apr	Middlesbrough	A	W	4–2
16 Apr	Middlesbrough	H	L	0–1
23 Apr	Blackburn R	A	L	0–2
30 Apr	Blackburn R	H	L	0–1
2 May	Derby Co	A	D	1–1
7 May	Derby Co	H	W	3–0

FA Cup

8 Jan	Liverpool (1)	A	D	1–1
12 Jan	Liverpool (1R)	H	L	1–2

Football League

	P	W	D	L	F:A	Pts	
Manchester U	42	15	10	17	64:68	40	13th

SEASON 1921–1922
FOOTBALL LEAGUE (DIVISION 1)

27 Aug	Everton	A	L	0–5
29 Aug	W B A	H	L	2–3
3 Sep	Everton	H	W	2–1
7 Sep	W B A	A	D	0–0
10 Sep	Chelsea	A	D	0–0
17 Sep	Chelsea	H	D	0–0
24 Sep	Preston NE	A	L	2–3
1 Oct	Preston NE	H	D	1–1
8 Oct	Tottenham H	A	D	2–2
15 Oct	Tottenham H	H	W	2–1
22 Oct	Manchester C	A	L	1–4
29 Oct	Manchester C	H	W	3–1
5 Nov	Middlesbrough	H	L	3–5
12 Nov	Middlesbrough	A	L	0–2
19 Nov	Aston Villa	A	L	1–3
26 Nov	Aston Villa	H	W	1–0
3 Dec	Bradford C	A	L	1–2
10 Dec	Bradford C	H	D	1–1
17 Dec	Liverpool	A	L	1–2
24 Dec	Liverpool	H	D	0–0
26 Dec	Burnley	H	L	0–1
27 Dec	Burnley	A	L	2–4
31 Dec	Newcastle U	A	L	0–3
2 Jan	Sheffield U	A	L	0–3
14 Jan	Newcastle U	H	L	0–1
21 Jan	Sunderland	A	L	1–2
28 Jan	Sunderland	H	W	3–1
11 Feb	Huddersfield T	H	D	1–1
18 Feb	Birmingham	A	W	1–0
25 Feb	Birmingham	H	D	1–1
27 Feb	Huddersfield T	A	D	1–1
11 Mar	Arsenal	H	W	1–0
18 Mar	Blackburn R	H	L	0–1
25 Mar	Blackburn R	A	L	0–3
1 Apr	Bolton W	H	L	0–1
5 Apr	Arsenal	A	L	1–3
8 Apr	Bolton W	A	L	0–1
15 Apr	Oldham	H	L	0–3
17 Apr	Sheffield U	H	W	3–2
22 Apr	Oldham	A	D	1–1
29 Apr	Cardiff C	H	D	1–1
6 May	Cardiff C	A	L	1–3

FA Cup

7 Jan	Cardiff C(1)	H	L	1–4

Football League

	P	W	D	L	F:A	Pts	
Manchester U	42	8	12	2	41:73	28	22nd

SEASON 1922–1923
FOOTBALL LEAGUE (DIVISION 2)

26 Aug	Crystal Palace	H	W	2–1
28 Aug	Sheffield Wed	A	L	0–1
2 Sep	Crystal Palace	A	W	3–2
4 Sep	Sheffield Wed	H	W	1–0
9 Sep	Wolverhampton W	A	W	1–0
16 Sep	Wolverhampton W	H	W	1–0
23 Sep	Coventry C	A	L	0–2
30 Sep	Coventry C	H	W	2–1
7 Oct	Port Vale	H	L	1–2
14 Oct	Port Vale	A	L	0–1
21 Oct	Fulham	H	D	1–1
28 Oct	Fulham	A	D	0–0
4 Nov	Clapton O	H	D	0–0
11 Nov	Clapton O	A	D	1–1
18 Nov	Bury	A	D	2–2
25 Nov	Bury	H	L	0–1
2 Dec	Rotherham U	H	W	3–0
9 Dec	Rotherham U	A	D	1–1
16 Dec	Stockport Co	H	W	1–0
23 Dec	Stockport Co	A	L	0–1
25 Dec	West Ham U	H	L	1–2
26 Dec	West Ham U	A	W	2–0
30 Dec	Hull C	A	L	1–2
1 Jan	Barnsley	H	W	1–0
6 Jan	Hull C	H	W	*3–2
20 Jan	Leeds U	H	D	0–0
27 Jan	Leeds U	A	W	1–0
10 Feb	Notts Co	A	W	6–1
17 Feb	Derby Co	H	D	0–0
21 Feb	Notts Co	H	D	1–1
3 Mar	Southampton	H	L	1–2
14 Mar	Derby Co	A	D	1–1
17 Mar	Bradford C	A	D	1–1
21 Mar	Bradford C	H	D	1–1
30 Mar	South Shields	H	W	3–0
31 Mar	Blackpool	A	L	0–1
2 Apr	South Shields	A	W	3–0
7 Apr	Blackpool	H	W	2–1
11 Apr	Southampton	A	D	0–0
14 Apr	Leicester C	A	W	1–0
21 Apr	Leicester C	H	L	0–2
28 Apr	Barnsley	A	D	2–2

FA Cup

13 Jan	Bradford C (1)	A	D	1–1
17 Jan	Bradford C (1R)	H	W	2–0
3 Feb	Tottenham H (2)	A	L	0–4

Football League

	P	W	D	L	F:A	Pts	
Manchester U	42	17	14	11	51:36	48	4th

SEASON 1923–1924
FOOTBALL LEAGUE (DIVISION 2)

25 Aug	Bristol C	A	W	2–1
27 Aug	Southampton	H	W	1–0
1 Sep	Bristol C	H	W	2–1
3 Sep	Southampton	A	D	0–0
8 Sep	Bury	A	L	0–2
15 Sep	Bury	H	L	0–1
22 Sep	South Shields	A	L	0–1
29 Sep	South Shields	H	D	1–1
6 Oct	Oldham	A	L	*2–3
13 Oct	Oldham	H	W	2–0
20 Oct	Stockport Co	H	W	3–0
27 Oct	Stockport Co	A	L	2–3
3 Nov	Leicester C	A	D	2–2
10 Nov	Leicester C	H	W	3–0
17 Nov	Coventry C	A	D	*1–1
1 Dec	Leeds U	A	D	0–0
8 Dec	Leeds U	H	W	3–1
15 Dec	Port Vale	A	W	1–0
22 Dec	Port Vale	H	W	5–0
25 Dec	Barnsley	H	L	1–2
26 Dec	Barnsley	A	L	0–1
29 Dec	Bradford C	A	D	0–0
2 Jan	Coventry C	H	L	1–2
5 Jan	Bradford C	H	W	3–0
19 Jan	Fulham	A	L	1–3
26 Jan	Fulham	H	D	0–0
6 Feb	Blackpool	A	L	0–1
9 Feb	Blackpool	H	D	0–0
16 Feb	Derby Co	A	L	0–3
23 Feb	Derby Co	H	D	0–0
1 Mar	Nelson	A	W	2–0
8 Mar	Nelson	H	L	0–1
15 Mar	Hull C	H	D	1–1
22 Mar	Hull C	A	D	1–1
29 Mar	Stoke C	H	D	2–2
5 Apr	Stoke C	A	L	0–3
12 Apr	Crystal Palace	H	W	5–1
18 Apr	Clapton O	A	L	0–1
19 Apr	Crystal Palace	A	D	1–1
21 Apr	Clapton O	H	D	2–2
26 Apr	Sheffield Wed	H	W	2–0
3 May	Sheffield Wed	A	L	0–2

FA Cup

12 Jan	Plymouth A (1)	H	W	1–0
2 Feb	Huddersfield (2)	H	L	0–3

Football League

	P	W	D	L	F:A	Pts	
Manchester U	42	13	14	15	52:44	40	14th

SEASON 1924–1925
FOOTBALL LEAGUE (DIVISION 2)

30 Aug	Leicester C	H	W	1–0
1 Sep	Stockport Co	A	L	1–2
6 Sep	Stoke C	A	D	0–0
8 Sep	Barnsley	H	W	1–0
13 Sep	Coventry C	H	W	5–1
20 Sep	Oldham	A	W	3–0
27 Sep	Sheffield Wed	H	W	2–0
4 Oct	Clapton O	A	W	1–0
11 Oct	Crystal Palace	H	W	1–0
18 Oct	Southampton	A	W	2–0
25 Oct	Wolverhampton W	A	D	0–0
1 Nov	Fulham	H	W	2–0
8 Nov	Portsmouth	A	D	1–1
15 Nov	Hull C	H	W	2–0
22 Nov	Blackpool	A	D	1–1
29 Nov	Derby Co	H	D	1–1
6 Dec	South Shields	A	W	2–1
13 Dec	Bradford C	H	W	3–0
20 Dec	Port Vale	A	L	1–2
25 Dec	Middlesbrough	A	D	1–1
26 Dec	Middlesbrough	H	W	2–0
27 Dec	Leicester C	A	L	0–3
17 Jan	Chelsea	H	W	1–0
3 Jan	Stoke C	H	W	2–0
1 Jan	Coventry C	A	L	0–1
24 Jan	Oldham	H	L	0–1
7 Feb	Clapton O	H	W	4–2
14 Feb	Crystal Palace	A	L	1–2
23 Feb	Sheffield Wed	A	D	1–1
28 Feb	Wolverhampton W	H	W	3–0
7 Mar	Fulham	A	L	0–1
14 Mar	Portsmouth	H	W	2–0
21 Mar	Hull C	A	W	1–0
28 Mar	Blackpool	H	D	0–0
4 Apr	Derby Co	A	L	0–1
10 Apr	Stockport Co	H	W	2–0
11 Apr	South Shields	H	W	1–0
13 Apr	Chelsea	A	D	0–0
18 Apr	Bradford C	A	W	1–0
22 Apr	Southampton	H	D	1–1
25 Apr	Port Vale	H	W	4–0
2 May	Barnsley	A	D	0–0

FA Cup

10 Jan	Sheffield Wed (1)	A	L	0–2

Football League

	P	W	D	L	F:A	Pts	
Manchester U	42	23	11	8	57:23	57	2nd

SEASON 1925–1926
FOOTBALL LEAGUE (DIVISION 1)

29 Aug	West Ham U	A	L	0–1
2 Sep	Aston Villa	H	W	3–0
5 Sep	Arsenal	H	L	0–1
9 Sep	Aston Villa	A	D	2–2
12 Sep	Manchester C	A	D	1–1
16 Sep	Leicester C	H	W	3–2
19 Sep	Liverpool	A	L	0–5
26 Sep	Burnley	H	W	6–1
3 Oct	Leeds U	A	L	0–2
10 Oct	Newcastle U	H	W	2–1
17 Oct	Tottenham H	H	D	0–0
24 Oct	Cardiff C	A	W	2–0
31 Oct	Huddersfield T	H	D	1–1
7 Nov	Everton	A	W	3–1
14 Nov	Birmingham	H	W	3–1
21 Nov	Bury	A	W	3–1
28 Nov	Blackburn R	H	W	2–0
5 Dec	Sunderland	A	L	1–2
12 Dec	Sheffield U	H	L	1–2
19 Dec	W B A	A	L	1–5
25 Dec	Bolton W	H	W	2–1
28 Dec	Leicester C	A	W	3–1
2 Jan	West Ham U	H	W	2–1
16 Jan	Arsenal	A	L	2–3
23 Jan	Manchester C	H	L	1–6
6 Feb	Burnley	A	W	1–0
13 Feb	Leeds U	H	W	2–1
27 Feb	Tottenham H	A	W	1–0
10 Mar	Liverpool	H	D	3–3
13 Mar	Huddersfield T	A	L	0–5
17 Mar	Bolton W	A	L	1–3
20 Mar	Everton	H	D	0–0
2 Apr	Notts Co	A	W	3–0
3 Apr	Bury	H	L	0–1
5 Apr	Notts Co	H	L	0–1
10 Apr	Blackburn R	A	L	0–7
14 Apr	Newcastle U	A	L	1–4
19 Apr	Birmingham	A	L	1–2
21 Apr	Sunderland	H	W	5–1
24 Apr	Sheffield U	A	L	0–2
28 Apr	Cardiff C	H	W	1–0
1 May	W B A	H	W	3–2

FA Cup

9 Jan	Port Vale (3)	A	W	3–2
30 Jan	Tottenham (4)	A	D	2–2
3 Feb	Tottenham (4R)	H	W	2–0
20 Feb	Sunderland (5)	A	D	3–3
24 Feb	Sunderland (5R)	H	W	2–1
6 Mar	Fulham (6)	A	W	2–1
21 Mar	Manchester C (SF) (at Bramall Lane)	N	L	0–3

Football League

	P	W	D	L	F:A	Pts	
Manchester U	42	19	6	17	66:73	44	9th

SEASON 1926–1927
FOOTBALL LEAGUE (DIVISION 1)

28 Aug	Liverpool	A	L	2–4
30 Aug	Sheffield U	A	D	2–2
4 Sep	Leeds U	H	D	2–2
11 Sep	Newcastle U	A	L	2–4
15 Sep	Arsenal	H	D	2–2
18 Sep	Burnley	H	W	2–1
25 Sep	Cardiff C	A	W	2–0
2 Oct	Aston Villa	H	W	2–1
9 Oct	Bolton W	A	L	0–4
16 Oct	Bury	A	W	3–0
23 Oct	Birmingham	H	L	0–1
30 Oct	West Ham U	A	L	0–4
6 Nov	Sheffield Wed	H	D	0–0
13 Nov	Leicester C	A	W	3–2
20 Nov	Everton	H	W	2–1
27 Nov	Blackburn R	A	L	1–2
4 Dec	Huddersfield T	H	D	0–0
11 Dec	Sunderland	A	L	0–6
18 Dec	W B A	H	W	2–0
25 Dec	Tottenham H	A	D	1–1
27 Dec	Tottenham H	H	W	2–1
28 Dec	Arsenal	A	L	0–1
1 Jan	Sheffield U	H	W	5–0
15 Jan	Liverpool	H	L	0–1
22 Jan	Leeds U	A	W	3–2
5 Feb	Burnley	A	L	0–1
9 Feb	Newcastle U	H	W	3–1
12 Feb	Cardiff C	H	D	1–1
19 Feb	Aston Villa	A	L	0–2
26 Feb	Bolton W	H	D	0–0
5 Mar	Bury	H	L	1–2
12 Mar	Birmingham	A	L	0–4
19 Mar	West Ham U	H	L	0–3
26 Mar	Sheffield Wed	A	L	0–2
2 Apr	Leicester C	H	W	1–0
9 Apr	Everton	A	D	0–0
15 Apr	Derby Co	H	D	2–2
16 Apr	Blackburn R	H	W	2–0
18 Apr	Derby Co	A	D	2–2
23 Apr	Huddersfield T	A	D	0–0
30 Apr	Sunderland	H	D	0–0
7 May	W B A	A	D	2–2

FA Cup

8 Jan	Reading (3)	A	D	1–1
12 Jan	Reading (3R)†	H	D	2–2
17 Jan	Reading (3R) (at Villa Park)	N	L	1–2

!after extra time

Football League

	P	W	D	L	F:A	Pts	
Manchester U	42	13	14	15	52:64	40	15th

SEASON 1927–1928
FOOTBALL LEAGUE (DIVISION 1)

27 Aug	Middlesbrough	H	W	3–0
29 Aug	Sheffield Wed	A	W	2–0
3 Sep	Birmingham	A	D	0–0
7 Sep	Sheffield Wed	H	D	1–1
10 Sep	Newcastle U	H	L	1–7
17 Sep	Huddersfield T	A	L	2–4
19 Sep	Blackburn R	A	L	0–3
24 Sep	Tottenham H	H	W	3–0
1 Oct	Leicester C	A	L	0–1
8 Oct	Everton	A	L	2–5
15 Oct	Cardiff C	H	D	2–2
22 Oct	Derby Co	H	W	5–0
29 Oct	West Ham U	A	W	2–1
5 Nov	Portsmouth	H	W	2–0
12 Nov	Sunderland	A	L	1–4
19 Nov	Aston Villa	H	W	5–1
26 Nov	Burnley	A	L	0–4
3 Dec	Bury	H	L	0–1
10 Dec	Sheffield U	A	L	1–2
17 Dec	Arsenal	H	W	4–1
24 Dec	Liverpool	A	L	0–2
26 Dec	Blackburn R	H	D	1–1
31 Dec	Middlesbrough	A	W	2–1
7 Jan	Birmingham	H	D	1–1
21 Jan	Newcastle U	A	L	1–4
4 Feb	Tottenham H	A	L	1–4
11 Feb	Leicester C	H	W	5–2
25 Feb	Cardiff C	A	L	0–2
7 Mar	Huddersfield T	H	D	0–0
10 Mar	West Ham U	H	D	1–1
14 Mar	Everton	H	W	1–0
17 Mar	Portsmouth	A	L	0–1
28 Mar	Derby Co	A	L	0–5
31 Mar	Aston Villa	A	L	1–3
6 Apr	Bolton W	A	L	2–3
7 Apr	Burnley	H	W	4–3
9 Apr	Bolton W	H	W	2–1
14 Apr	Bury	A	L	3–4
21 Apr	Sheffield U	H	L	2–3
25 Apr	Sunderland	H	W	2–1
28 Apr	Arsenal	A	W	1–0
5 May	Liverpool	H	W	6–1

FA Cup

14 Jan	Brentford (3)	H	W	7–1
28 Jan	Bury (4)	A	D	1–1
1 Feb	Bury (4R)	H	W	1–0
18 Feb	Birmingham (5)	H	W	1–0
3 Mar	Blackburn (6)	A	L	0–2

Football League

	P	W	D	L	F:A	Pts	
Manchester U	42	16	7	19	72:80	39	18th

SEASON 1928–1929
FOOTBALL LEAGUE (DIVISION 1)

25 Aug	Leicester C	H	D	1–1
27 Aug	Aston Villa	A	D	0–0
1 Sep	Manchester C	A	D	2–2
8 Sep	Leeds U	A	L	2–3
15 Sep	Liverpool	H	D	2–2
22 Sep	West Ham U	A	L	1–3
29 Sep	Newcastle U	H	W	5–0
6 Oct	Burnley	A	W	4–3
13 Oct	Cardiff C	H	D	1–1
20 Oct	Birmingham	H	W	1–0
27 Oct	Huddersfield T	A	W	2–1
3 Nov	Bolton W	H	D	1–1
10 Nov	Sheffield Wed	A	L	1–2
17 Nov	Derby Co	H	L	0–1
24 Nov	Sunderland	A	L	1–5
1 Dec	Blackburn R	H	L	1–4
8 Dec	Arsenal	A	L	1–3
15 Dec	Everton	H	D	1–1
22 Dec	Portsmouth	A	L	0–3
25 Dec	Sheffield U	H	D	1–1
26 Dec	Sheffield U	A	L	1–6
29 Dec	Leicester C	A	L	1–2
1 Jan	Aston Villa	H	D	2–2
5 Jan	Manchester C	H	L	1–2
19 Jan	Leeds U	H	L	1–2
2 Feb	West Ham U	H	L	2–3
9 Feb	Newcastle U	A	L	0–5
13 Feb	Liverpool	A	W	3–2
16 Feb	Burnley	H	W	1–0
23 Feb	Cardiff C	A	D	2–2
2 Mar	Birmingham	A	D	1–1
9 Mar	Huddersfield T	H	W	1–0
16 Mar	Bolton W	A	D	1–1
23 Mar	Sheffield Wed	H	W	2–1
29 Mar	Bury	A	W	3–1
30 Mar	Derby Co	A	L	1–6
1 Apr	Bury	H	W	1–0
6 Apr	Sunderland	H	W	3–0
13 Apr	Blackburn R	A	W	3–0
20 Apr	Arsenal	H	W	4–1
27 Apr	Everton	A	W	4–2
4 May	Portsmouth	H	D	0–0

FA Cup

12 Jan	Port Vale (3)	A	W	3–0
26 Jan	Bury (4)	H	L	0–1

Football League

	P	W	D	L	F:A	Pts	
Manchester U	42	14	13	15	66:76	41	12th

SEASON 1929–1930
FOOTBALL LEAGUE (DIVISION 1)

31 Aug	Newcastle U	A	L	1–4
2 Sep	Leicester C	A	L	1–4
7 Sep	Blackburn R	H	W	1–0
11 Sep	Leicester C	H	W	2–1
14 Sep	Middlesbrough	A	W	3–2
21 Sep	Liverpool	H	L	1–2
28 Sep	West Ham U	A	L	1–2
5 Oct	Manchester C	H	L	1–3
7 Oct	Sheffield U	A	L	1–3
12 Oct	Grimsby T	H	L	2–5
19 Oct	Portsmouth	A	L	0–3
26 Oct	Arsenal	H	W	1–0
2 Nov	Aston Villa	A	L	0–1
9 Nov	Derby Co	H	W	3–2
16 Nov	Sheffield Wed	A	L	2–7
23 Nov	Burnley	H	W	1–0
30 Nov	Sunderland	A	W	4–2
7 Dec	Bolton W	H	D	1–1
14 Dec	Everton	A	D	0–0
21 Dec	Leeds U	H	W	3–1
25 Dec	Birmingham	H	D	0–0
26 Dec	Birmingham	A	W	1–0
28 Dec	Newcastle U	H	W	5–0
4 Jan	Blackburn R	A	L	4–5
18 Jan	Middlesbrough	H	L	0–3
25 Jan	Liverpool	A	L	0–1
1 Feb	West Ham U	H	W	4–2
8 Feb	Manchester C	A	W	1–0
15 Feb	Grimsby T	A	D	2–2
22 Feb	Portsmouth	H	W	3–0
1 Mar	BoltonW	A	L	1–4
8 Mar	Aston Villa	H	L	2–3
12 Mar	Arsenal	A	L	2–4
15 Mar	Derby Co	A	D	1–1
29 Mar	Burnley	A	L	0–4
5 Apr	Sunderland	H	W	2–1
14 Apr	Sheffield Wed	H	D	2–2
18 Apr	Huddersfield T	H	W	1–0
19 Apr	Everton	H	D	3–3
22 Apr	Huddersfield T	A	D	2–2
26 Apr	Leeds U	A	L	1–3
3 May	Sheffield U	H	L	1–5

FA Cup

11 Jan	Swindon (3)	H	L	0–2

Football League

	P	W	D	L	F:A	Pts	
Manchester U	42	15	8	19	67:88	38	17th

SEASON 1930–1931
FOOTBALL LEAGUE (DIVISION 1)

30 Aug	Aston Villa	H	L	3–4
3 Sep	Middlesbrough	A	L	1–3
6 Sep	Chelsea	A	L	2–6
10 Sep	Huddersfield T	H	L	0–6
13 Sep	Newcastle U	H	L	4–7
15 Sep	Huddersfield T	A	L	0–3
20 Sep	Sheffield Wed	A	L	0–3
27 Sep	Grimsby T	H	L	0–2
4 Oct	Manchester C	A	L	1–4
11 Oct	West Ham U	A	L	1–5
18 Oct	Arsenal	H	L	1–2
25 Oct	Portsmouth	A	L	1–4
1 Nov	Birmingham	H	W	2–0
8 Nov	Leicester C	A	L	4–5

15 Nov	Blackpool	H	D	0–0
22 Nov	Sheffield U	A	L	1–3
29 Nov	Sunderland	H	D	1–1
6 Dec	Blackburn R	A	L	1–4
13 Dec	Derby Co	H	W	2–1
20 Dec	Leeds U	A	L	0–5
25 Dec	Bolton W	A	L	1–3
26 Dec	Bolton W	H	D	1–1
27 Dec	Aston Villa	A	L	0–7
1 Jan	Leeds U	H	D	0–0
3 Jan	Chelsea	H	W	1–0
17 Jan	Newcastle U	A	L	3–4
28 Jan	Sheffield Wed	H	W	4–1
31 Jan	Grimsby T	A	L	1–2
7 Feb	Manchester C	H	L	1–3
14 Feb	West Ham U	H	W	1–0
21 Feb	Arsenal	A	L	1–4
7 Mar	Birmingham	A	D	0–0
16 Mar	Portsmouth	H	L	0–1
21 Mar	Blackpool	A	L	1–5
25 Mar	Leicester C	H	D	0–0
28 Mar	Sheffield U	H	L	1–2
3 Apr	Liverpool	A	D	1–1
4 Apr	Sunderland	A	W	2–1
6 Apr	Liverpool	H	W	4–1
11 Apr	Blackburn R	H	L	0–1
18 Apr	Derby Co	A	L	1–6
2 May	Middlesbrough	H	D	4–4

FA Cup

10 Jan	Stoke C (3)	A	D	3–3
14 Jan	Stoke C (3R)†	H	D	0–0
19 Jan	Stoke C (3R) (at Anfield)	N	W	4–2
24 Jan	Grimsby (4)	A	L	0–1

†after extra time

Football League

	P	W	D	L	F:A	Pts	
Manchester U	42	7	8	27	53:115	22	22nd

SEASON 1931–1932
FOOTBALL LEAGUE (DIVISION 2)

29 Aug	Bradford	A	L	1–3
2 Sep	Southampton	H	L	2–3
5 Sep	Swansea	H	W	2–1
7 Sep	Stoke C	A	L	0–3
12 Sep	Tottenham H	H	D	1–1
16 Sep	Stoke C	H	D	1–1
19 Sep	Nottingham F	A	L	1–2
26 Sep	Chesterfield	H	W	3–1
3 Oct	Burnley	A	L	0–2
10 Oct	Preston NE	H	W	3–2
17 Oct	Barnsley	A	D	0–0
24 Oct	Notts Co	H	D	3–3
31 Oct	Plymouth A	A	L	1–3
7 Nov	Leeds U	H	L	2–5
14 Nov	Oldham	A	W	5–1
21 Nov	Bury	H	L	1–2
28 Nov	Port Vale	A	W	2–1
5 Dec	Millwall	H	W	2–0
12 Dec	Bradford C	A	L	3–4
19 Dec	Bristol C	H	L	0–1
25 Dec	Wolverhampton W	H	W	3–2
26 Dec	Wolverhampton W	A	L	0–7
2 Jan	Bradford	H	L	0–2
16 Jan	Swansea	A	L	1–3
23 Jan	Tottenham H	A	L	1–4
30 Jan	Nottingham F	H	W	3–2
6 Feb	Chesterfield	A	W	3–1
17 Feb	Burnley	H	W	5–1
20 Feb	Preston NE	A	D	0–0
27 Feb	Barnsley	H	W	3–0
5 Mar	Notts Co	A	W	2–1
12 Mar	Plymouth A	H	W	2–1
19 Mar	Leeds U	A	W	4–1
25 Mar	Charlton A	H	L	0–2
26 Mar	Oldham	H	W	5–1
28 Mar	Charlton A	A	L	0–1
2 Apr	Bury	A	D	0–0
9 Apr	Port Vale	H	W	2–0
16 Apr	Millwall	A	D	1–1
23 Apr	Bradford C	H	W	1–0
30 Apr	Bristol C	A	L	1–2
7 May	Southampton	A	D	1–1

FA Cup

9 Jan	Plymouth A (3)	A	L	1–4

Football League

	P	W	D	L	F:A	Pts	
Manchester U	42	17	8	17	71:72	42	12th

SEASON 1932–1933
FOOTBALL LEAGUE (DIVISION 2)

27 Aug	Stoke C	H	L	0–2
29 Aug	Charlton A	A	W	1–0
3 Sep	Southampton	A	L	*2–4
7 Sep	Charlton A	H	D	1–1
10 Sep	Tottenham H	A	L	1–6
17 Sep	Grimsby T	H	D	1–1
24 Sep	Oldham	A	D	1–1
1 Oct	Preston NE	H	D	0–0
8 Oct	Burnley	A	W	3–2
15 Oct	Bradford	H	W	2–1
22 Oct	Millwall	H	W	7–1
29 Oct	Port Vale	A	D	3–3
5 Nov	Notts Co	H	W	2–0
12 Nov	Bury	A	D	2–2
19 Nov	Fulham	H	W	4–3
26 Nov	Chesterfield	A	D	1–1
3 Dec	Bradford C	H	L	0–1
10 Dec	West Ham U	A	L	1–3
17 Dec	Lincoln C	H	W	*4–1
24 Dec	Swansea	A	L	1–2
26 Dec	Plymouth A	A	W	3–2
31 Dec	Stoke C	A	D	0–0
2 Jan	Plymouth A	H	W	4–0
7 Jan	Southampton	H	L	1–2
21 Jan	Tottenham H	H	W	2–1
31 Jan	Grimsby T	A	D	1–1
4 Feb	Oldham	H	W	2–0
11 Feb	Preston NE	A	D	3–3
22 Feb	Burnley	H	W	2–1
4 Mar	Millwall	A	L	0–2
11 Mar	Port Vale	H	D	1–1
18 Mar	Notts Co	A	L	0–1
25 Mar	Bury	H	L	1–3
1 Apr	Fulham	A	L	1–3
5 Apr	Bradford	A	D	1–1
8 Apr	Chesterfield	H	W	2–1
14 Apr	Nottingham F	A	L	2–3
15 Apr	Bradford C	A	W	2–1
17 Apr	Nottingham F	H	W	2–1
22 Apr	West Ham U	H	L	1–2
29 Apr	Lincoln C	A	L	2–3
6 May	Swansea	H	D	1–1

FA Cup

14 Jan	Middlesbrough (3)	H	L	1–4

Football League

	P	W	D	L	F:A	Pts	
Manchester U	42	15	13	14	71:68	43	6th

SEASON 1933–1934
FOOTBALL LEAGUE (DIVISION 2)

26 Aug	Plymouth A	A	L	0–4
30 Aug	Nottingham F	H	L	0–1
2 Sep	Lincoln C	H	D	1–1
6 Sep	Nottingham F	A	D	1–1
9 Sep	Bolton W	H	L	1–5
16 Sep	Brentford	A	W	4–3
23 Sep	Burnley	H	W	5–2
30 Sep	Oldham	A	L	0–2
7 Oct	Preston NE	H	W	1–0
14 Oct	Bradford	A	L	1–6
21 Oct	Bury	A	L	1–2
28 Oct	Hull C	H	W	4–1
4 Nov	Fulham	A	W	2–0
11 Nov	Southampton	H	W	*1–0
18 Nov	Blackpool	A	L	1–3
25 Nov	Bradford C	H	W	2–1
2 Dec	Port Vale	A	W	*3–2
9 Dec	Notts Co	H	L	1–2
16 Dec	Swansea	A	L	1–2
23 Dec	Millwall	H	D	1–1
25 Dec	Grimsby T	H	L	1–3
26 Dec	Grimsby T	A	L	3–7
30 Dec	Plymouth A	H	L	0–3
6 Jan	Lincoln C	A	L	1–5
20 Jan	Bolton W	A	L	1–3
27 Jan	Brentford	H	L	1–3
3 Feb	Burnley	A	W	4–1
10 Feb	Oldham	H	L	2–3
21 Feb	Preston NE	A	L	2–3
24 Feb	Bradford	H	L	0–4
3 Mar	Bury	H	W	2–1
10 Mar	Hull C	A	L	1–4
17 Mar	Fulham	H	W	1–0
24 Mar	Southampton	A	L	0–1
30 Mar	West Ham U	H	L	0–1
31 Mar	Blackpool	H	W	2–0
2 Apr	West Ham U	A	L	1–2
7 Apr	Bradford C	A	D	1–1
14 Apr	Port Vale	H	W	2–0
21 Apr	Notts Co	A	D	0–0
28 Apr	Swansea	H	D	1–1
5 May	Millwall	A	W	2–0

FA Cup

13 Jan	Portsmouth (3)	H	D	1–1
17 Jan	Portsmouth (3R)	A	L	1–4

Football League

	P	W	D	L	F:A	Pts	
Manchester U	42	14	6	22	59:85	34	20th

SEASON 1934–1935
FOOTBALL LEAGUE (DIVISION 2)

25 Aug	Bradford C	H	W	2–0
1 Sep	Sheffield U	A	L	2–3
3 Sep	Bolton W	A	L	*1–3
8 Sep	Barnsley	H	W	4–1
12 Sep	Bolton W	H	L	0–3
15 Sep	Port Vale	A	L	2–3
22 Sep	Norwich C	H	W	5–0
29 Sep	Swansea	H	W	3–1
6 Oct	Burnley	A	W	2–1
13 Oct	Oldham	H	W	4–0
20 Oct	Newcastle U	A	W	1–0
27 Oct	West Ham U	H	W	3–1
3 Nov	Blackpool	A	W	2–1
10 Nov	Bury	H	W	1–0
17 Nov	Hull C	A	L	2–3
24 Nov	Nottingham F	H	W	3–2
1 Dec	Brentford	A	L	1–3
8 Dec	Fulham	H	W	1–0
15 Dec	Bradford	A	W	2–1
22 Dec	Plymouth A	H	W	3–1
25 Dec	Notts Co	H	W	2–1
26 Dec	Notts Co	A	L	0–1
29 Dec	Bradford C	A	L	0–2
1 Jan	Southampton	H	W	3–0
5 Jan	Sheffield U	H	D	3–3
19 Jan	Barnsley	A	W	2–0
2 Feb	Norwich C	A	L	2–3
6 Feb	Port Vale	H	W	2–1
9 Feb	Swansea	A	L	0–1
23 Feb	Oldham	A	W	1–3
2 Mar	Newcastle U	H	L	0–1
9 Mar	West Ham U	A	D	0–0
16 Mar	Blackpool	H	W	3–2
23 Mar	Bury	A	W	1–0
27 Mar	Burnley	H	L	3–4
30 Mar	Hull C	H	W	3–0
6 Apr	Nottingham F	A	D	2–2
13 Apr	Brentford	H	D	0–0
20 Apr	Fulham	A	L	1–3
22 Apr	Southampton	A	L	0–1
27 Apr	Bradford	H	W	2–0
4 May	Plymouth A	A	W	2–0

FA Cup

12 Jan	Bristol R (3)	A	W	3–1
26 Jan	Nottingham F (4)	A	D	0–0
30 Jan	Nottingham F (4R)	H	L	0–3

Football League

	P	W	D	L	F:A	Pts	
Manchester U	42	23	4	15	76:55	50	5th

SEASON 1935–1936
FOOTBALL LEAGUE (DIVISION 2)

31 Aug	Plymouth A	A	L	1–3
4 Sep	Charlton A	H	W	3–0
9 Sep	Bradford C	H	W	3–1
11 Sep	Charlton A	A	D	0–0
14 Sep	Newcastle U	A	W	2–0
18 Sep	Hull C	H	W	2–0
21 Sep	Tottenham H	H	D	0–0
28 Sep	Southampton	A	L	1–2
5 Oct	Port Vale	A	W	3–0
12 Oct	Fulham	H	W	1–0
19 Oct	Sheffield U	H	W	3–1
26 Oct	Bradford	A	L	0–1
2 Nov	Leicester C	H	L	0–1
9 Nov	Swansea	A	L	1–2
16 Nov	West Ham U	H	L	2–3
23 Nov	Norwich C	A	W	5–3
30 Nov	Doncaster R	H	D	0–0
7 Dec	Blackpool	A	L	1–4
14 Dec	Nottingham F	H	W	5–0
26 Dec	Barnsley	H	D	1–1
28 Dec	Plymouth A	H	W	3–2
1 Jan	Barnsley	A	W	3–0
4 Jan	Bradford C	A	L	0–1
18 Jan	Newcastle U	H	W	3–1
1 Feb	Southampton	H	W	*4–0
5 Feb	Tottenham H	A	D	0–0
8 Feb	Port Vale	H	W	7–2
22 Feb	Sheffield U	A	D	1–1
29 Feb	Blackpool	H	W	3–2
7 Mar	West Ham U	A	W	2–1
14 Mar	Swansea	H	W	3–0
21 Mar	Leicester C	A	D	1–1
28 Mar	Norwich C	H	W	2–1
1 Apr	Fulham	A	D	2–2
4 Apr	Doncaster R	A	D	0–0
10 Apr	Burnley	A	D	2–2
11 Apr	Bradford	H	W	4–0
13 Apr	Burnley	H	W	4–0
18 Apr	Nottingham F	A	D	1–1
25 Apr	Bury	H	W	2–1
29 Apr	Bury	A	W	3–2
2 May	Hull C	A	D	1–1

FA Cup

11 Jan	Reading (3)	A	W	3–1
25 Jan	Stoke C (4)	A	D	0–0
29 Jan	Stoke C (4R)	H	L	0–2

Football League

	P	W	D	L	F:A	Pts	
Manchester U	42	22	12	8	85:43	56	1st

SEASON 1936–1937
FOOTBALL LEAGUE (DIVISION 1)

29 Aug	Wolverhampton W	H	D	1–1
2 Sep	Huddersfield T	A	L	1–3
5 Sep	Derby Co	A	L	4–5
9 Sep	Huddersfield T	H	W	3–1
12 Sep	Manchester C	H	W	3–2
19 Sep	Sheffield Wed	H	D	1–1
26 Sep	Preston NE	A	L	1–3
3 Oct	Arsenal	H	W	2–0
10 Oct	Brentford	A	L	0–4
17 Oct	Portsmouth	A	L	1–2
24 Oct	Chelsea	H	D	0–0
31 Oct	Stoke C	A	L	0–3
7 Nov	Charlton A	H	D	0–0
14 Nov	Grimsby T	A	L	2–6
21 Nov	Liverpool	H	L	2–5
28 Nov	Leeds U	A	L	1–2
5 Dec	Birmingham	H	L	1–2
12 Dec	Middlesbrough	A	L	2–3
19 Dec	West Brom A	H	D	2–2
25 Dec	Bolton W	H	W	1–0
26 Dec	Wolverhampton W	A	L	1–3
28 Dec	Bolton W	A	W	4–0
1 Jan	Sunderland	H	W	2–1
2 Jan	Derby Co	H	D	2–2
9 Jan	Manchester C	A	L	0–1
23 Jan	Sheffield Wed	A	L	0–1
3 Feb	Preston NE	H	D	1–1
6 Feb	Arsenal	A	D	1–1
13 Feb	Brentford	H	L	1–3
20 Feb	Portsmouth	H	L	0–1
27 Feb	Chelsea	A	L	2–4
6 Mar	Stoke C	H	W	2–1
13 Mar	Charlton A	A	L	0–3
20 Mar	Grimsby T	H	D	1–1
26 Mar	Everton	H	W	2–1
27 Mar	Liverpool	A	L	0–2
29 Mar	Everton	A	W	3–2
3 Apr	Leeds U	H	D	0–0
10 Apr	Birmingham	A	D	2–2
17 Apr	Middlesbrough	H	W	2–1
21 Apr	Sunderland	A	D	1–1
24 Apr	W B A	A	L	0–1

FA Cup

16 Jan	Reading (3)	H	W	1–0
30 Jan	Arsenal (4)	A	L	0–5

Football League

	P	W	D	L	F:A	Pts	
Manchester U	42	10	12	20	55:78	32	21st

SEASON 1937–1938
FOOTBALL LEAGUE (DIVISION 2)

28 Aug	Newcastle U	H	W	3–0
30 Aug	Coventry C	A	L	0–1
4 Sep	Luton T	A	L	0–1
8 Sep	Coventry C	H	D	2–2
11 Sep	Barnsley	H	W	4–1
13 Sep	Bury	A	W	2–1
18 Sep	Stockport Co	A	L	0–1
25 Sep	Southampton	H	L	1–2
2 Oct	Sheffield U	H	L	0–1
9 Oct	Tottenham H	A	W	1–0
16 Oct	Blackburn R	A	D	1–1
23 Oct	Sheffield Wed	H	W	1–0
30 Oct	Fulham	A	L	0–1
6 Nov	Plymouth A	H	D	0–0
13 Nov	Chesterfield	A	W	7–1
20 Nov	Aston Villa	H	W	3–1
27 Nov	Norwich C	A	W	3–2
4 Dec	Swansea	H	W	5–1
11 Dec	Bradford	A	L	0–4
27 Dec	Nottingham F	H	W	4–3
28 Dec	Nottingham F	A	W	3–2
1 Jan	Newcastle U	A	D	2–2
15 Jan	Luton T	H	W	4–2
29 Jan	Stockport Co	H	W	3–1
2 Feb	Barnsley	A	D	2–2
5 Feb	Southampton	A	D	3–3
17 Feb	Sheffield U	A	W	2–1
19 Feb	Tottenham H	H	L	0–1
23 Feb	West Ham U	H	W	4–0
26 Feb	Blackburn R	H	W	2–1
5 Mar	Sheffield Wed	A	W	3–1
12 Mar	Fulham	H	W	1–0
19 Mar	Plymouth A	A	D	1–1
26 Mar	Chesterfield	H	W	4–1
2 Apr	Aston Villa	A	L	0–3
9 Apr	Norwich C	H	D	0–0
15 Apr	Burnley	A	L	0–1
16 Apr	Swansea	A	D	2–2
18 Apr	Burnley	H	W	4–0
23 Apr	Bradford	H	W	3–1
30 Apr	West Ham U	A	L	0–1
7 May	Bury	H	W	2–0

FA Cup

8 Jan	Yeovil (3)	H	W	3–0
22 Jan	Barnsley (4)	A	D	2–2
26 Jan	Barnsley (4R)	H	W	1–0
12 Feb	Brentford (5)	A	L	0–2

Football League

	P	W	D	L	F:A	Pts	
Manchester U	42	22	9	11	82:50	53	2nd

SEASON 1938–1939
FOOTBALL LEAGUE (DIVISION 1)

27 Aug	Middlesbrough	A	L	1–3
31 Aug	Bolton W	H	D	*2–2
3 Sep	Birmingham	H	W	4–1
7 Sep	Liverpool	A	L	0–1
10 Sep	Grimsby T	A	L	0–1
17 Sep	Stoke C	A	D	1–1
24 Sep	Chelsea	H	W	5–1
1 Oct	Preston NE	A	D	1–1
8 Oct	Charlton A	H	L	0–2
15 Oct	Blackpool	H	D	0–0
22 Oct	Derby Co	A	L	1–5
29 Oct	Sunderland	H	L	0–1
5 Nov	Aston Villa	A	W	2–0
12 Nov	Wolverhampton W	H	L	1–3
19 Nov	Everton	A	L	0–3
26 Nov	Huddersfield T	H	D	1–1
3 Dec	Portsmouth	A	D	0–0
10 Dec	Arsenal	H	W	1–0
17 Dec	Brentford	A	W	5–2
24 Dec	Middlesbrough	H	D	1–1
26 Dec	Leicester C	H	W	3–0
27 Dec	Leicester C	A	D	1–1
31 Dec	Birmingham	A	D	3–3
14 Jan	Grimsby T	H	W	3–1
21 Jan	Stoke C	H	L	0–1
28 Jan	Chelsea	A	W	1–0
4 Feb	Preston NE	H	D	1–1
11 Feb	Charlton A	A	L	1–7
18 Feb	Blackpool	A	W	5–3
25 Feb	Derby Co	H	D	1–1
4 Mar	Sunderland	A	L	2–5
11 Mar	Aston Villa	H	D	1–1
18 Mar	Wolverhampton W	A	L	0–3
29 Mar	Everton	H	L	0–2
1 Apr	Huddersfield T	A	D	1–1
7 Apr	Leeds U	H	D	0–0
8 Apr	Portsmouth	H	D	1–1
10 Apr	Leeds U	A	L	1–3
15 Apr	Arsenal	A	L	1–2
22 Apr	Brentford	H	W	3–0
29 Apr	Bolton W	A	D	0–0
6 May	Liverpool	H	W	2–0

FA Cup

7 Jan	W B A (3)	A	D	0–0
11 Jan	W B A (3R)	H	L	1–5

Football League

	P	W	D	L	F:A	Pts	
Manchester U	42	11	16	15	57:65	38	14th

SEASON 1939–1940
ALL MATCHES

Western Division Wartime Regional League

21 Oct	Manchester C	H	L	0–4
28 Oct	Chester	A	W	4–0
11 Nov	Crewe Alex	H	W	5–1
18 Nov	Liverpool	A	L	0–1
25 Nov	Port Vale	H	W	8–1
2 Dec	Tranmere R	A	W	4–2
9 Dec	Stockport Co	A	W	7–4
23 Dec	Wrexham	H	W	5–1
6 Jan	Everton	A	L	2–3
20 Jan	Stoke C	H	W	4–3
10 Feb	Manchester C	A	L	0–1
24 Feb	Chester	H	W	5–1
9 Mar	Crewe Alex	A	W	4–1
16 Mar	Liverpool	H	W	1–0
23 Mar	Port Vale	A	W	3–1
30 Mar	Tranmere R	H	W	6–1
6 Apr	Stockport Co	H	W	6–1
6 May	New Brighton	H	W	6–0
13 May	Wrexham	A	L	2–3
18 May	New Brighton	H	L	0–6
25 May	Stoke C	A	L	2–3
1 Jun	Everton	H	L	0–3

	P	W	D	L	F:A	Pts	
Manchester U	22	14	0	8	74:41	28	14th

Football League War Cup

20 Apr	Manchester C (1st leg)	H	L	0–1
27 Apr	Manchester C (2nd leg)	A	W	2–0
4 May	Blackburn R (1st leg)	A	W	2–1
11 May	Blackburn R (2nd leg)	A	L	1–3

SEASON 1940–1941

North Regional League

31 Aug	Rochdale	A	W	3–1
7 Sep	Bury	H	D	0–0
14 Sep	Oldham	A	L	1–2
21 Sep	Oldham	H	L	2–3
28 Sep	Manchester C	A	L	1–4
5 Oct	Manchester C	H	L	0–1
12 Oct	Burnley	A	W	1–0
19 Oct	Preston NE	H	W	4–1
26 Oct	Preston NE	A	L	1–3
2 Nov	Burnley	H	W	4–1
9 Nov	Everton	A	L	2–5
16 Nov	Everton	H	D	0–0
23 Nov	Liverpool	A	D	2–2
30 Nov	Liverpool	H	W	2–0
7 Dec	Blackburn R	A	D	5–5
14 Dec	Rochdale	H	L	3–4

21 Dec	Bury	A	L	1–4
25 Dec	Stockport Co	A	W	3–1
28 Dec	Blackburn R	H	W	9–0
4 Jan	Blackburn R	A	W	2–0
11 Jan	Blackburn R	H	D	0–0
18 Jan	Bolton W	A	L	2–3
25 Jan	Bolton W	H	W	4–1
1 Mar	Chesterfield	A	D	1–1
8 Mar	Bury	H	W	7–3
22 Mar	Oldham	A	W	1–0
29 Mar	Blackpool	A	L	0–2
5 Apr	Blackpool	H	L	2–3
12 Apr	Everton	A	W	2–1
14 Apr	Manchester C	A	W	7–1
19 Apr	Chester	A	W	6–4
26 Apr	Liverpool	A	L	1–2
3 May	Liverpool	H	D	1–1
10 May	Bury	A	L	1–5
17 May	Burnley	H	W	1–0

	P	W	D	L	F:A	Pts	
Manchester U	35	15	7	13	82:65	37	7th*

*Positions according to goal average not points

Football League War Cup

15 Feb	Everton (1st leg)	H	D	2–2
22 Feb	Everton (2nd leg)	A	L	1–2

SEASON 1941–1942
ALL MATCHES

30 Aug	New Brighton	H	W	13–1
6 Sep	New Brighton	A	D	3–3
13 Sep	Stockport Co	A	W	5–1
20 Sep	Stockport Co	H	W	7–1
27 Sep	Everton	H	L	2–3
4 Oct	Everton	A	W	3–1
11 Oct	Chester	A	W	7–0
18 Oct	Chester	H	W	8–1
25 Oct	Stoke C	A	D	1–1
1 Nov	Stoke C	H	W	3–0
8 Nov	Tranmere R	H	W	6–1
15 Nov	Tranmere R	A	D	1–1
22 Nov	Liverpool	A	D	1–1
29 Nov	Liverpool	H	D	2–2
6 Dec	Wrexham	H	W	10–3
13 Dec	Wrexham	A	W	4–3
20 Dec	Manchester C	A	L	1–2
25 Dec	Manchester C	H	D	2–2

Football League North Region: First Championship

	P	W	D	L	F:A	Pts	
Manchester U	18	10	6	2	79:27	26	4th

27 Dec	Bolton W (Cup Q)	H	W	3–1
3 Jan	Bolton W (Cup Q)	A	D	2–2
10 Jan	Oldham (Cup Q)	H	D	1–1
17 Jan	Oldham (Cup Q)	A	W	3–1
31 Jan	Southport (Cup Q)	A	W	3–1
14 Feb	Sheffield U (Cup Q)	A	W	2–0
21 Feb	Preston NE (Cup Q)	H	L	0–2
28 Feb	Preston NE (Cup Q)	A	W	3–1
21 Mar	Sheffield U (Cup Q)	H	D	2–2
28 Mar	Southport (Cup Q)	H	W	4–2
4 Apr	Blackburn R (Cup KO)	A	W	2–1
6 Apr	Blackburn R (Cup KO)	H	W	3–1
11 Apr	Wolverhampton W (Cup KO)	H	W	5–4
18 Apr	Wolverhampton W (Cup KO)!	A	L	0–2
25 Apr	Oldham A (Lancs Cup)	H	W	5–1
2 May	Oldham A (Lancs Cup)	A	W	2–1
9 May	Blackburn R (Lancs Cup)	A	D	1–1
16 May	Blackburn R (Lancs Cup)	H	L	0–1
23 May	Manchester C	A	W	3–1

†after extra time

League & Cup games were played as part of the **North Region Second Championship** (Results counted for each competition)

Football League North Region: Second Championship

	P	W	D	L	F:A	Pts	
Manchester U	19	12	4	3	44:25	28	1st

SEASON 1942–1943
ALL MATCHES

29 Aug	Everton	A	D	2–2
5 Sep	Everton	H	W	2–1
12 Sep	Chester	H	L	0–2
19 Sep	Chester	A	D	2–2
26 Sep	Blackburn R	A	L	2–4
3 Oct	Blackburn R	H	W	5–2
10 Oct	Liverpool	H	L	3–4
17 Oct	Liverpool	A	L	1–2
24 Oct	Stockport Co	A	W	4–1
31 Oct	Stockport Co	H	W	3–1
7 Nov	Manchester C	H	W	2–1
14 Nov	Manchester C	A	W	5–0
21 Nov	Tranmere R	A	W	5–0
28 Nov	Tranmere R	H	W	5–1
5 Dec	Wrexham	H	W	6–1
12 Dec	Wrexham	A	W	5–2
19 Dec	Bolton W	A	W	2–0
25 Dec	Bolton W	H	W	4–0

Football League North Region: First Championship

	P	W	D	L	F:A	Pts	
Manchester U	18	12	2	4	58:26	26	4th

26 Dec	Chester (Cup Q)	H	W	3–0
2 Jan	Chester (Cup Q)	A	L	1–4
9 Jan	Blackpool (Cup Q)	A	D	1–1
16 Jan	Blackpool (Cup Q)	H	W	5–3
23 Jan	Everton (Cup Q)	H	L	1–4
30 Jan	Everton (Cup Q)	A	W	5–0
6 Feb	Manchester C (Cup Q)	A	D	0–0
13 Feb	Manchester C (Cup Q)	H	D	1–1
20 Feb	Crewe A (Cup Q)	H	W	7–0
27 Feb	Crewe A (Cup Q)	A	W	3–2
6 Mar	Manchester C (Cup KO)	H	L	0–1
13 Mar	Manchester C (Cup KO)	A	L	0–2
20 Mar	Bury (Lancs Cup)	H	W	4–1
27 Mar	Bury (Lancs Cup)	A	W	5–3
3 Apr	Crewe A (Lancs Cup)	H	W	4–1
10 Apr	Crewe A (Lancs Cup)	A	W	6–0
17 Apr	Oldham (Lancs Cup)	H	W	3–0
24 Apr	Oldham (Lancs Cup)	A	L	1–3
1 May	Sheffield U	H	W	2–0
8 May	Liverpool (Lancs Cup F)	A	W	3–1
15 May	Liverpool (Lancs Cup F)	H	D	3–3

Games played between 26 Dec and 1 May (inc) formed the **North Region Second Championship**

Football League North Region: Second Championship

	P	W	D	L	F:A	Pts	
Manchester U	19	11	3	5	52:26	25	6th

SEASON 1943–1944
ALL MATCHES

28 Aug	Stockport Co	H	W	6–0
4 Sep	Stockport Co	A	D	3–3
11 Sep	Everton	H	W	4–1
18 Sep	Everton	A	L	1–6
25 Sep	Blackburn R	H	W	2–1
2 Oct	Blackburn R	A	L	1–2
9 Oct	Chester	H	W	3–1
16 Oct	Chester	A	L	4–5
23 Oct	Liverpool	A	W	4–3
30 Oct	Liverpool	H	W	1–0
6 Nov	Manchester C	A	D	2–2
13 Nov	Manchester C	H	W	3–0
20 Nov	Tranmere R	H	W	6–3
27 Nov	Tranmere R	A	W	1–0
4 Dec	Wrexham	A	W	4–1
11 Dec	Wrexham	H	W	5–0
18 Dec	Bolton W	H	W	3–1
25 Dec	Bolton W	A	W	3–1

Football League North Region: First Championship

	P	W	D	L	F:A	Pts	
Manchester U	18	13	2	3	56:30	28	2nd

27 Dec	Halifax T (Cup Q)	H	W	6–2
1 Jan	Halifax T (Cup Q)	A	D	1–1
8 Jan	Stockport Co (Cup Q)	A	W	3–2
15 Jan	Stockport Co (Cup Q)	H	W	4–2
22 Jan	Manchester C (Cup Q)	H	L	1–3
29 Jan	Manchester C (Cup Q)	A	W	3–2
5 Feb	Bury (Cup Q)	A	W	3–0
12 Feb	Bury (Cup Q)	H	D	3–3
19 Feb	Oldham (Cup Q)	H	W	3–2
26 Feb	Oldham (Cup Q)	A	D	1–1
4 Mar	Wrexham (Cup KO)	A	W	4–1
11 Mar	Wrexham (Cup KO)	H	D	2–2
18 Mar	Birmingham (Cup KO)	A	L	1–3
25 Mar	Birmingham (Cup KO)	H	D	1–1
1 Apr	Bolton W	A	L	0–3
8 Apr	Bolton W	H	W	3–2
10 Apr	Manchester C	A	L	1–4
15 Apr	Burnley	H	W	9–0
22 Apr	Burnley	A	D	3–3
29 Apr	Oldham	H	D	0–0
6 May	Oldham	A	W	3–1

Football League North Region: Second Championship

	P	W	D	L	F:A	Pts	
Manchester U	21	10	7	4	55:38	27	9th

SEASON 1944–1945
ALL MATCHES

26 Aug	Everton	A	W	2–1
2 Sep	Everton	H	L	1–3
9 Sep	Stockport Co	H	L	3–4
16 Sep	Stockport Co	A	D	4–4
23 Sep	Bury	H	D	2–2
30 Sep	Bury	A	L	2–4
7 Oct	Chester	A	L	0–2
14 Oct	Chester	H	W	1–0
21 Oct	Tranmere R	H	W	6–1
28 Oct	Tranmere R	A	W	4–2
4 Nov	Liverpool	A	L	2–3
11 Nov	Liverpool	H	L	2–5
18 Nov	Manchester C	H	W	3–2
25 Nov	Manchester C	A	L	0–4
2 Dec	Crewe A	A	W	4–1
9 Dec	Crewe A	H	W	2–0
16 Dec	Wrexham	H	W	1–0
23 Dec	Wrexham	A	L	1–2

Football League North Region: First Championship

	P	W	D	L	F:A	Pts	
Manchester U	18	8	2	8	40:40	18	30th

26 Dec	Sheffield U	A	W	4–3
30 Dec	Oldham (Cup Q)	A	W	4–3
6 Jan	Huddersfield T (Cup Q)	H	W	1–0
13 Jan	Huddersfield T (Cup Q)	A	D	2–2
3 Feb	Manchester C (Cup Q)	H	L	1–3
10 Feb	Manchester C (Cup Q)	A	L	0–2
17 Feb	Bury (Cup Q)	H	W	2–0
24 Feb	Bury (Cup Q)	A	L	1–3
3 Mar	Oldham (Cup Q)	H	W	3–2
10 Mar	Halifax T (Cup Q)	A	L	0–1
17 Mar	Halifax T (Cup Q)	H	W	2–0
24 Mar	Burnley (Cup KO)	H	W	3–2
31 Mar	Burnley (Cup KO)	H	W	4–0
2 Apr	Blackpool	A	L	1–4
7 Apr	Stoke C (Cup KO)	H	W	6–1
14 Apr	Stoke C (Cup KO)	A	W	4–1
21 Apr	Doncaster R (Cup KO)	A	W	2–1
28 Apr	Doncaster R (Cup KO)	H	W	3–1
5 May	Chesterfield (Cup SF)	H	D	1–1
12 May	Chesterfield (Cup SF)	H	W	1–0
19 May	Bolton W (Cup F)	A	L	0–1
26 May	Bolton W (Cup F)	H	D	2–2

Football League North Region: Second Championship

	P	W	D	L	F:A	Pts	
Manchester U	22	13	3	6	47:33	29	9th

SEASON 1945–1946
ALL MATCHES

25 Aug	Huddersfield T	A	L	2–3
1 Sep	Huddersfield T	H	L	2–3
8 Sep	Chesterfield	H	L	0–2
12 Sep	Middlesbrough	A	L	1–2
15 Sep	Chesterfield	A	D	1–1
20 Sep	Stoke C	A	W	2–1
22 Sep	Barnsley	A	D	2–2
29 Sep	Barnsley	H	D	1–1
6 Oct	Everton	H	D	0–0
13 Oct	Everton	A	L	0–3
20 Oct	Bolton W	A	D	1–1
27 Oct	Bolton W	H	W	2–1
3 Nov	Preston NE	H	W	6–1
10 Nov	Preston NE	A	D	2–2
17 Nov	Leeds U	A	D	3–3
24 Nov	Leeds U	H	W	6–1
1 Dec	Burnley	H	D	3–3
8 Dec	Burnley	A	D	2–2
15 Dec	Sunderland	H	W	2–1
22 Dec	Sunderland	A	L	2–4
25 Dec	Sheffield U	A	L	0–1
26 Dec	Sheffield U	H	L	2–3
29 Dec	Middlesbrough	H	W	4–1
12 Jan	Grimsby T	H	W	5–0
19 Jan	Grimsby T	A	L	0–1
2 Feb	Blackpool	H	W	4–2
9 Feb	Liverpool	H	W	2–1
16 Feb	Liverpool	A	W	5–0
23 Feb	Bury	A	D	1–1
2 Mar	Bury	H	D	1–1
9 Mar	Blackburn R	H	W	6–2
16 Mar	Blackburn R	A	W	3–1
23 Mar	Bradford	A	L	1–2
27 Mar	Blackpool	A	W	5–1
30 Mar	Bradford	H	W	4–0
6 Apr	Manchester C	H	L	1–4
13 Apr	Manchester C	A	W	3–1
19 Apr	Newcastle U	H	W	1–0
20 Apr	Sheffield Wed	A	W	4–0
22 Apr	Newcastle U	A	W	4–1
27 Apr	Sheffield Wed	A	L	0–1
4 May	Stoke C	H	W	2–1

Football League North

	P	W	D	L	F:A	Pts	
Manchester U	42	19	11	12	98:62	49	4th

SEASON 1946-1947
FOOTBALL LEAGUE (Division 1)

31 Aug	Grimsby T	H	W	2-1
4 Sep	Chelsea	A	W	3-0
7 Sep	Charlton A	A	W	*3-1
11 Sep	Liverpool	H	W	5-0
14 Sep	Middlesbrough	H	W	1-0
18 Sep	Chelsea	H	D	1-1
21 Sep	Stoke C	A	L	2-3
28 Sep	Arsenal	H	W	5-2
5 Oct	Preston NE	H	D	1-1
12 Oct	Sheffield U	A	D	2-2
19 Oct	Blackpool	A	L	1-3
26 Oct	Sunderland	H	L	0-3
2 Nov	Aston Villa	A	D	0-0
9 Nov	Derby Co	H	W	4-1
16 Nov	Everton	A	D	2-2
23 Nov	Huddersfield T	H	W	5-2
30 Nov	Wolverhampton W	A	L	2-3
7 Dec	Brentford	H	W	4-1
14 Dec	Blackburn R	A	L	1-2
25 Dec	Bolton W	A	D	2-2
26 Dec	Bolton W	H	W	1-0
28 Dec	Grimsby T	A	D	0-0
4 Jan	Charlton A	H	W	4-1
18 Jan	Middlesbrough	A	W	4-2
1 Feb	Arsenal	A	L	2-6
5 Feb	Stoke C	H	D	1-1
22 Feb	Blackpool	H	W	3-0
1 Mar	Sunderland	A	D	1-1
8 Mar	Aston Villa	H	W	2-1
15 Mar	Derby Co	A	L	3-4
22 Mar	Everton	H	W	3-0
29 Mar	Huddersfield T	A	D	2-2
5 Apr	Wolverhampton W	H	W	3-1
7 Apr	Leeds U	H	W	3-1
8 Apr	Leeds U	A	W	2-0
12 Apr	Brentford	A	D	0-0
19 Apr	Blackburn R	H	W	*4-0
26 Apr	Portsmouth	A	W	1-0
3 May	Liverpool	A	L	0-1
10 May	Preston NE	A	D	1-1
17 May	Portsmouth	H	W	3-0
26 May	Sheffield U	H	W	6-2

FA Cup

11 Jan	Bradford (3)	A	W	3-0
25 Jan	Nottingham F (4)	H	L	0-2

Football League

	P	W	D	L	F:A	Pts	
Manchester U	42	22	12	8	95:54	56	2nd

SEASON 1947-1948
FOOTBALL LEAGUE (Division 1)

23 Aug	Middlesbrough	A	D	2-2
27 Aug	Liverpool	H	W	2-0
30 Aug	Charlton A	H	W	6-2
3 Sep	Liverpool	A	D	2-2
6 Sep	Arsenal	A	L	1-2
8 Sep	Burnley	A	D	0-0
13 Sep	Sheffield U	H	L	0-1
20 Sep	Manchester C	A	D	0-0
27 Sep	Preston NE	A	L	1-2
4 Oct	Stoke C	H	D	1-1
11 Oct	Grimsby T	H	L	3-4
18 Oct	Sunderland	A	L	0-1
25 Oct	Aston Villa	H	W	2-0
1 Nov	Wolverhampton W	A	W	6-2
8 Nov	Huddersfield T	H	D	4-4
15 Nov	Derby Co	A	D	1-1
22 Nov	Everton	H	D	2-2
29 Nov	Chelsea	A	W	4-0
6 Dec	Blackpool	H	D	1-1
13 Dec	Blackburn R	A	D	1-1
20 Dec	Middlesbrough	H	W	2-1
25 Dec	Portsmouth	H	W	3-2
27 Dec	Portsmouth	A	W	3-1
1 Jan	Burnley	H	W	5-0
3 Jan	Charlton A	A	W	2-1
17 Jan	Arsenal	H	D	1-1
31 Jan	Sheffield U	A	L	1-2
14 Feb	Preston NE	H	D	1-1
21 Feb	Stoke C	A	W	2-0
6 Mar	Sunderland	H	W	3-1
17 Mar	Grimsby T	A	D	1-1
20 Mar	Wolverhampton W	H	W	3-2
22 Mar	Aston Villa	A	W	1-0
26 Mar	Bolton W	H	L	0-2
27 Mar	Huddersfield T	A	W	2-0
29 Mar	Bolton W	A	W	1-0
3 Apr	Derby Co	H	W	1-0
7 Apr	Manchester C	H	D	1-1
10 Apr	Everton	A	L	0-2
17 Apr	Chelsea	H	W	5-0
28 Apr	Blackpool	A	L	0-1
1 May	Blackburn	H	W	4-1

FA Cup

10 Jan	Aston Villa (3)	A	W	6-4
24 Jan	Liverpool (4) (at Goodison Park)	H	W	3-0
7 Feb	Charlton A (5) (at Huddersfield)	H	W	2-0
28 Feb	Preston NE (6) (at Maine Road)	H	W	4-1
13 Mar	Derby Co (SF) (at Hillsborough)	N	W	3-1
24 Apr	Blackpool (F) (at Wembley)	N	W	4-2

Football League

	P	W	D	L	F:A	Pts	
Manchester U	42	19	14	9	81:48	52	2nd

SEASON 1948-1949
FOOTBALL LEAGUE (Division 1)

21 Aug	Derby Co	H	L	1-2
23 Aug	Blackpool	A	W	3-0
28 Aug	Arsenal	A	W	1-0
1 Sep	Blackpool	H	L	3-4
4 Sep	Huddersfield T	H	W	4-1
8 Sep	Wolverhampton W	A	L	2-3
11 Sep	Manchester C	A	D	0-0
15 Sep	Wolverhampton W	H	W	2-0
18 Sep	Sheffield U	A	D	2-2
25 Sep	Aston Villa	H	W	3-1
2 Oct	Sunderland	A	L	1-2
9 Oct	Charlton A	H	D	1-1
16 Oct	Stoke C	A	L	1-2
23 Oct	Burnley	H	D	1-1
30 Oct	Preston NE	A	W	6-1
6 Nov	Everton	H	W	2-0
13 Nov	Chelsea	A	D	1-1
20 Nov	Birmingham C	H	W	3-0
27 Nov	Middlesbrough	A	W	4-1
4 Dec	Newcastle U	H	D	1-1
11 Dec	Portsmouth	A	D	2-2
18 Dec	Derby Co	A	W	3-1
25 Dec	Liverpool	H	D	0-0
26 Dec	Liverpool	A	W	2-0
1 Jan	Arsenal	H	W	2-0
22 Jan	Manchester C	H	D	0-0
19 Feb	Aston Villa	A	L	1-2
5 Mar	Charlton A	A	W	3-2
12 Mar	Stoke C	H	W	3-0
19 Mar	Birmingham C	A	L	0-1
6 Apr	Huddersfield T	A	L	1-2
9 Apr	Chelsea	H	D	1-1
15 Apr	Bolton W	A	W	1-0
16 Apr	Burnley	A	W	2-0
18 Apr	Bolton W	H	W	3-0
21 Apr	Sunderland	H	L	1-2
23 Apr	Preston NE	H	D	2-2
27 Apr	Everton	A	L	0-2
30 Apr	Newcastle U	A	W	1-0
2 May	Middlesbrough	H	W	1-0
4 May	Sheffield U	H	W	3-2
7 May	Portsmouth	H	W	3-2

FA Cup

8 Jan	Bournemouth (3)	H	W	6-0
29 Jan	Bradford (4)	H	D	1-1
5 Feb	Bradford (4R)	A	D	1-1
7 Feb	Bradford (4R)	H	W	5-0
12 Feb	Yeovil (5)	H	W	8-0
26 Feb	Hull C (6)	A	W	1-0
26 Mar	Wolverhampton W (SF) (at Hillsborough)	N	D	1-1
2 Apr	Wolverhampton W (SFR) (at Goodison)	N	L	0-1

Football League

	P	W	D	L	F:A	Pts	
Manchester U	42	21	11	10	77:44	53	2nd

SEASON 1949-1950
FOOTBALL LEAGUE (Division 1)

20 Aug	Derby Co	A	W	1-0
24 Aug	Bolton W	H	W	3-0
27 Aug	W B A	H	D	1-2
31 Aug	Bolton W	A	W	2-1
3 Sep	Manchester C	H	W	2-1
7 Sep	Liverpool	A	D	1-1
10 Sep	Chelsea	A	D	1-1
17 Sep	Stoke C	H	D	2-2
24 Sep	Burnley	A	L	0-1
1 Oct	Sunderland	H	L	1-3
8 Oct	Charlton A	H	W	3-2
15 Oct	Aston Villa	A	W	4-0
22 Oct	Wolverhampton W	H	W	3-0
29 Oct	Portsmouth	A	D	0-0
5 Nov	Huddersfield T	H	W	6-0
12 Nov	Everton	A	D	0-0
19 Nov	Middlesbrough	H	W	2-0
26 Nov	Blackpool	A	D	3-3
3 Dec	Newcastle U	H	D	1-1
10 Dec	Fulham	A	L	0-1
17 Dec	Derby Co	H	L	0-1
24 Dec	W B A	A	W	2-1
26 Dec	Arsenal	H	W	2-0
27 Dec	Arsenal	A	D	0-0
31 Dec	Manchester C	A	W	2-1
14 Jan	Chelsea	H	W	1-0
21 Jan	Stoke C	A	L	1-3
4 Feb	Burnley	H	W	3-2
18 Feb	Sunderland	A	D	2-2
25 Feb	Charlton A	A	W	2-1
8 Mar	Aston Villa	H	W	7-0
11 Mar	Middlesbrough	A	W	3-2
15 Mar	Liverpool	H	D	0-0
18 Mar	Blackpool	H	L	1-2
25 Mar	Huddersfield T	A	L	1-3
1 Apr	Everton	H	D	1-1
7 Apr	Birmingham C	H	L	0-2
8 Apr	Wolverhampton W	A	D	1-1
10 Apr	Birmingham C	A	D	0-0
15 Apr	Portsmouth	H	L	0-2
22 Apr	Newcastle U	A	L	1-2
29 Apr	Fulham	H	W	3-0

	FA Cup			
7 Jan	Weymouth (3)	H	W	4-0
28 Jan	Watford (4)	A	W	1-0
11 Feb	Portsmouth (5)	H	D	3-3
15 Feb	Portsmouth (5R)	A	W	3-1
4 Mar	Chelsea (6)	A	L	0-2

Football League

	P	W	D	L	F:A	Pts	
Manchester U	42	18	14	10	69:44	50	4th

SEASON 1950-1951 FOOTBALL LEAGUE (Division 1)

19 Aug	Fulham	H	W	1–0
23 Aug	Liverpool	A	L	1–2
26 Aug	Bolton W	A	L	0–1
30 Aug	Liverpool	H	W	1–0
2 Sep	Blackpool	H	W	1–0
4 Sep	Aston Villa	A	W	3–1
9 Sep	Tottenham H	A	L	0–1
13 Sep	Aston Villa	H	D	0–0
16 Sep	Charlton A	H	W	3–0
23 Sep	Middlesbrough	A	W	2–1
30 Sep	Wolverhampton W	A	D	0–0
7 Oct	Sheffield Wed	H	W	3–1
14 Oct	Arsenal	A	L	0–3
21 Oct	Portsmouth	H	D	0–0
28 Oct	Everton	A	W	4–1
4 Nov	Burnley	H	D	1–1
11 Nov	Chelsea	A	L	0–1
18 Nov	Stoke C	H	D	0–0
25 Nov	W B A	A	W	1–0
2 Dec	Newcastle U	H	L	1–2
9 Dec	Huddersfield T	A	W	3–2
16 Dec	Fulham	A	D	2–2
23 Dec	Bolton W	H	L	2–3
25 Dec	Sunderland	A	L	1–2
26 Dec	Sunderland	H	L	3–5
13 Jan	Tottenham H	H	W	2–1
20 Jan	Charlton A	A	W	2–1
3 Feb	Middlesbrough	H	W	1–0
17 Feb	Wolverhampton W	H	W	2–1
26 Feb	Sheffield Wed	A	W	4–0
3 Mar	Arsenal	H	W	3–1
10 Mar	Portsmouth	A	D	0–0
17 Mar	Everton	H	W	3–0
23 Mar	Derby Co	H	W	2–0
24 Mar	Burnley	A	W	2–1
26 Mar	Derby Co	A	W	4–2
31 Mar	Chelsea	H	W	4–1
7 Apr	Stoke C	A	L	0–2
14 Apr	W B A	H	W	3–0
21 Apr	Newcastle U	A	W	2–0
28 Apr	Huddersfield T	H	W	6–0
5 May	Blackpool	A	D	1–1

FA Cup

6 Jan	Oldham (3)	H	W	*4–1
27 Jan	Leeds U (4)	H	W	4–0
10 Feb	Arsenal (5)	H	W	1–0
24 Feb	Birmingham C (6)	A	L	0–1

Football League

	P	W	D	L	F:A	Pts	
Tottenham H	42	25	10	7	82:44	60	1st
Manchester U	42	24	8	10	74:40	56	2nd

SEASON 1951–1952 FOOTBALL LEAGUE (DIVISION 1)

18 Aug	W B A	A	D	3–3	Allen	Carey	Redman	Cockburn	Chilton	McGlen	McShane	Pearson	Rowley3	Downie	Bond
22 Aug	Middlesbrough	H	W	4–2	..	..	..	Gibson	..	Cockburn	..	..1	..3	..	..
25 Aug	Newcastle U	H	W	2–1	..	..	..	..	..	..	..	..	..1	..1	..
29 Aug	Middlesbrough	A	W	4–1	..	..	..	..	..	..	..	..	..	..	..
1 Sep	Bolton W	A	L	0–1	..	..	..	..	..	..	Berry	..	..	..	..
5 Sep	Charlton A	H	W	3–2	..	..	..	..	..	..	..	..	..2	..1	..
8 Sep	Stoke C	H	W	4–0	..	..	..	..	..	..	..	..1	..3	..	McShane
12 Sep	Charlton A	A	D	2–2	..	..	..	..	..	..	..	..	..	..2	..
15 Sep	Manchester C	A	W	2–1	..	..	..	..	..	..	..1	..	Cassidy	..	..1
22 Sep	Tottenham H	A	L	0–2	..	..	..	..	..	..	..	..	Rowley	..	..
29 Sep	Preston NE	H	L	1–2	..	..	..	..	..	..	..	Walton	Aston1	Pearson	Rowley
6 Oct	Derby Co	H	W	2–1	..	..	..	..	..	..	..1	..	Rowley	..1	McShane
13 Oct	Aston Villa	A	W	5–2	..	McNulty	..	..	..	..	..	Pearson2	..2	Downie	Bond1
20 Oct	Sunderland	H	L	0–1	..	Carey	..	..	..	McGlen	..	Downie	..	Pearson	McShane
27 Oct	Wolverhampton W	A	W	2–0	..	..	..	..	..	Cockburn	McShane	Pearson1	..1	Birch	Bond
3 Nov	Huddersfield T	H	D	1–1	..	..	..	..	..	..	..	..1	..	..	..
10 Nov	Chelsea	A	L	2–4	..	..	..	..	..	..	Berry	..1	Aston	Downie	Rowley1
17 Nov	Portsmouth	H	L	1–3	..	..	..	..	..	..	..	..	..	..1	..
24 Nov	Liverpool	A	D	0–0	Crompton	..	Byrne	Blanchflower	..	..	..	..	Rowley	..	Bond
1 Dec	Blackpool	H	W	3–1	..	McNulty	..	Carey	..	..	..	..	..1	..2	..
8 Dec	Arsenal	A	W	*3–1	..	..	..	..	..	..	..	..1	..1	..	..
15 Dec	W B A	H	W	5–1	Allen	..	..	..	..	..	..1	..2	..	..2	..
22 Dec	Newcastle U	A	D	2–2	..	..	..	..	..	..1	..	..	..	..	..1
25 Dec	Fulham	H	W	3–2	..	..	..	Chilton	Jones M	..	..1	..	..1	..	..1
26 Dec	Fulham	A	D	3–3	..	..	..	..	..	..	..	..1	..1	..	..1
29 Dec	Bolton W	H	W	1–0	..	..	..	..	..	..	..	..1	..	..	..
5 Jan	Stoke C	A	D	0–0	..	..	..	Carey	Chilton	..	..	..	..	..	..
19 Jan	Manchester C	H	D	1–1	..	..	..	..1	..	..	..	..	Aston	..	Rowley
26 Jan	Tottenham H	H	W	*2–0	..	..	..	..	..	..	..	Clempson	..	Pearson1	..
9 Feb	Preston NE	A	W	2–1	..	..	..	..	..	..	..1	..	..1	..	..
16 Feb	Derby Co	A	W	3–0	Crompton	..	..	..	..	..	..	..	..1	..1	..1
1 Mar	Aston Villa	H	D	1–1	..	..	..	..	..	..	..1	..	..	..	..
8 Mar	Sunderland	A	W	2–1	..	..	..	..	..	..1	..	..	..	..	..1
15 Mar	Wolverhampton W	H	W	2–0	..	..	..	..	..	..	..	..1	..1	..	..
22 Mar	Huddersfield T	A	L	2–3	..	..	..	..	..	..	..	..1	..	..1	..
5 Apr	Portsmouth	A	L	0–1	..	..	..	..	..	Whitefoot	..	..	..	Downie	Bond
11 Apr	Burnley	A	D	1–1	Allen	..	Aston	..	..	Cockburn	..	Downie	Rowley	Pearson	Byrne1
12 Apr	Liverpool	H	W	4–0	..	..	..	..	..	Whitefoot	..	..1	..1	..	..2
14 Apr	Burnley	H	W	6–1	..	..	..	..1	..	..	..	..1	..1	..1	..2
19 Apr	Blackpool	A	D	2–2	..	..	..	..	..	Cockburn	..	..	..1	..	..1
21 Apr	Chelsea	H	W	*3–0	..	..	..	..	..	..	..	..	..	..	..
26 Apr	Arsenal	H	W	6–1	..	..	..	..	..	..	..	..	..3	..2	..1
	FA Cup														
12 Jan	Hull City (3)	H	L	0–2	Allen	McNulty	Byrne	Carey	Chilton	Cockburn	Berry	Pearson	Rowley	Downie	Bond

1951–1952

Appearances (goals)

Allen	33	
Aston	18	4
Berry	36	6
Birch	2	
Blanchflower	1	
Bond	19	4
Byrne	24	7
Carey	38	3
Cassidy	1	
Chilton	42	
Clempson	8	2
Cockburn	38	2
Crompton	9	
Downie	31	11
Gibson	17	
Jones M	3	
McGlen	2	
McNulty	24	
McShane	12	1
Pearson	41	22
Redman	18	
Rowley	40	30
Walton	2	
Whitefoot	3	
Own goals		3
Total 24 players		95

Football League

	P	W	D	L	F:A	Pts	
Manchester U	42	23	11	8	95:52	57	1st

SEASON 1952–1953 FOOTBALL LEAGUE (DIVISION 1)

23 Aug	Chelsea	H	W	2–0	Wood	McNulty	Aston	Carey	Chilton	Gibson	Berry1	Downie1	Rowley	Pearson	Byrne
27 Aug	Arsenal	A	L	1–2	Crompton	..	..	..	..	Cockburn	..	..	..1	..	
30 Aug	Manchester C	A	L	1–2	..	..	..	..	..	..	..	..1	..	..	..
3 Sep	Arsenal	H	D	0–0	..	Carey	Byrne	Gibson	..	..	..	Clempson	Aston	..	Bond
6 Sep	Portsmouth	A	L	0–2	..	McNulty	..	..	..	..	..	..	..	..	Rowley
10 Sep	Derby Co	A	W	3–2	..	..	Aston	Carey	..	Gibson	..	Downie	Rowley	..3	Byrne
13 Sep	Bolton W	H	W	1–0	Allen	..	..	..	..	..	..1	..	..	..	..
20 Sep	Aston Villa	A	D	3–3	Wood	..	..	..	..	..	..	..1	..2	..	..
27 Sep	Sunderland	H	L	0–1	..	..	..	Jones M	..	..	..	..	Clempson	..	..
4 Oct	Wolverhampton W	A	L	2–6	Allen	..	..	Carey	..	..	..	..	Rowley2	..	Scott
11 Oct	Stoke C	H	L	0–2	Wood	..	..	..	..	..	..	Clempson	..	Downie	..
18 Oct	Preston NE	A	W	5–0	Crompton	Carey	Byrne	Whitefoot	..	..	..	Downie	Aston2	Pearson2	Rowley1
25 Oct	Burnley	H	L	1–3	..	..	..	..	..	..	..	..	..1	..	..
1 Nov	Tottenham H	A	W	2–1	..	McNulty	..	..	..	..	..2	..	..	..	McShane
8 Nov	Sheffield Wed	H	D	1–1	..	..	..	..	..	..	..	..	..	..1	..
15 Nov	Cardiff C	A	W	2–1	..	..	..	Cockburn	..	..	..	..	..1	..1	..
22 Nov	Newcastle U	H	D	2–2	..	..	..	..	..	..	..	..	..1	..1	..
29 Nov	W B A	A	L	1–3	..	..	..	..	..	..	..	..	Lewis1	..	..
6 Dec	Middlesbrough	H	W	3–2	..	..	..	Carey	..	Cockburn	..	Doherty	Aston1	..2	Pegg
13 Dec	Liverpool	A	W	2–1	..	Foulkes	..	..	..	..	..	..	..2	..1	..
20 Dec	Chelsea	A	W	3–2	..	..	..	..	..	..	..	..2	..1	..	..
25 Dec	Blackpool	A	D	0–0	Wood	McNulty	..	..	..	..	..	..	..	..	..
26 Dec	Blackpool	H	W	2–1	..	..	..	..1	..	..	..	Lewis1	..	..	..
1 Jan	Derby Co	H	W	1–0	..	Redman	..	..	..	..	..	Aston	Lewis1	..	..
3 Jan	Manchester C	H	D	1–1	..	Aston	..	..	..	Whitefoot	..	Doherty	..	..1	..
17 Jan	Portsmouth	H	W	1–0	..	..	..	..	..	Cockburn	..	Rowley	..1	..	..
24 Jan	Bolton W	A	L	1–2	..	..	..	..	..	..	..	..	..1	..	..
7 Feb	Aston Villa	H	W	3–1	..	..	..	..	..	..	..	Lewis1	Rowley2	..	..
18 Feb	Sunderland	A	D	2–2	Carey	..	..	Gibson	..	..	..	..1	..	..	..1
21 Feb	Wolverhampton W	H	L	0–3	Wood	..	..	Carey	..	..	..	..	..	..	..
28 Feb	Stoke C	A	L	1–3	Crompton	McNulty	..	Chilton	Jones M	Gibson	..1	Aston	..	Downie	..
7 Mar	Preston NE	H	W	5–2	..	Aston	..	Carey	Chilton	Cockburn	..	Rowley1	Taylor T2	Pearson	..2
14 Mar	Burnley	A	L	1–2	..	..	..1	..	..	..	..	..	..	..	..
25 Mar	Tottenham H	H	W	3–2	..	..	..	Gibson	..	..	..	..	..	..2	..1
28 Mar	Sheffield Wed	A	D	0–0	..	..	..	Carey	..	..	..	..	..	..	..
3 Apr	Charlton A	A	D	2–2	..	..	..	..	..	Blanchflower	..2	..	..1	..	..
4 Apr	Cardiff C	H	L	1–4	..	..	..1	Gibson	..	Edwards	..	..	..	..	..
6 Apr	Charlton A	H	W	3–2	..	McNulty	..	Carey	..	Whitefoot	..	Lewis	..2	..	Rowley1
11 Apr	Newcastle U	A	W	2–1	Olive	..	..	..	..	..	Viollet	Pearson	Aston	Taylor T2	..
18 Apr	W B A	H	D	2–2	..	..	..	..	..	..	..1	..1	..	..	..
20 Apr	Liverpool	H	W	3–1	Crompton	Aston	..	..	..	..	Berry1	Downie	Taylor T	Pearson1	..1
25 Apr	Middlesbrough	A	L	0–5	..	McNulty	..	..	..	..	..	Viollet	Aston	Taylor T	..

1952–1953

Appearances (goals)

Allen	2	
Aston	40	8
Berry	40	7
Blanchflower	1	
Bond	1	
Byrne	40	2
Carey	32	1
Chilton	42	
Clempson	4	
Cockburn	22	
Crompton	25	
Doherty	5	2
Downie	20	3
Edwards	1	
Foulkes	2	
Gibson	20	
Jones M	2	
Lewis	10	7
McNulty	23	
McShane	5	
Olive	2	
Pearson	39	16
Pegg	19	4
Redman	1	
Rowley	26	11
Scott	2	
Taylor T	11	7
Viollet	3	1
Whitefoot	10	
Wood	12	
Total 30 players		69

Football League

	P	W	D	L	F:A	Pts	
Arsenal	42	21	12	9	97:64	54	1st
Manchester U	42	18	10	14	69:72	46	8th

	FA Cup														
10 Jan	Millwall (3)	A	W	1–0	Wood	Aston	Byrne	Carey	Chilton	Cockburn	Berry	Downie	Lewis	Pearson1	Rowley
31 Jan	Walthamstow A (4)	H	D	1–1	..	..	..	..	..	..	..	..	..1	..	..
5 Feb	Walthamstow A (4R)	A	W	5–2	..	..	..1	..	..	..	..	Lewis1	Rowley2	..1	Pegg
	(at Highbury)														
14 Feb	Everton (5)	A	L	1–2	..	..	..	..	..	..	..	..	..1	..	..

1953–1954

Appearances (goals)

Aston	12	2
Berry	37	5
Blanchflower	27	13
Byrne	41	3
Chilton	42	1
Cockburn	18	
Crompton	15	
Edwards	24	
Foulkes	32	1
Gibson	7	
Lewis	6	1
McFarlane	1	
McNulty	4	
McShane	9	
Pearson	11	2
Pegg	9	
Redman	1	
Rowley	36	12
Taylor T	35	22
Viollet	29	11
Webster	1	
Whitefoot	38	
Wood	27	
Total 23 players	73	

Football League

	P	W	D	L	F:A	Pts	
Wolves	42	25	7	10	96:56	57	1st
Manchester U	42	18	12	12	73:58	48	4th

SEASON 1953–1954 FOOTBALL LEAGUE (DIVISION 1)

19 Aug	Chelsea	H	D	1–1	Crompton	Aston	Byrne	Gibson	Chilton	Cockburn	Berry	Rowley	Taylor T	Pearson1	Pegg
22 Aug	Liverpool	A	D	4–4	..	..	..1	..	..	..	..	..1	..1	Lewis1	..
26 Aug	W B A	H	L	1–3	..	..	..	..	..	..	..	..	..1	..	..
29 Aug	Newcastle U	H	D	1–1	Wood	McNulty	Aston	Whitefoot	..1	..	..	Byrne	..	..	Rowley
2 Sep	W B A	A	L	0–2	..	Aston	Byrne	..	..	..	..	Lewis	..	Viollet	..
5 Sep	Manchester C	A	L	0–2	..	..	..	..	..	..	..	Viollet	..	Pearson	..
9 Sep	Middlesbrough	H	D	2–2	..	McNulty	..	..	..	..	..	Lewis	Rowley2	..	McShane
12 Sep	Bolton W	A	D	0–0	..	..	..	..	..	..	..	Taylor T	..	..	..
16 Sep	Middlesbrough	A	W	4–1	..	..	..1	..	..	..	..	..2	..1	..	..
19 Sep	Preston NE	H	W	1–0	..	Foulkes	..1	..	..	..	..	..	..	..	..
26 Sep	Tottenham H	A	D	1–1	..	..	..	..	..	..	..	..	..1	..	..
3 Oct	Burnley	H	L	1–2	..	..	..	..	..	..	..	..	..	..1	..
10 Oct	Sunderland	H	W	1–0	..	Aston	..	..	..	..	..	..	..1	..	..
17 Oct	Wolverhampton W	A	L	1–3	..	Foulkes	..	..	..	..	..	Pearson	Taylor T1	Rowley	..
24 Oct	Aston Villa	H	W	1–0	..	..	..	..	..	..	..1	..	..	..	..
31 Oct	Huddersfield	A	D	0–0	..	..	..	..	..	Edwards	..	Blanchflower	..	Viollet	Rowley
7 Nov	Arsenal	H	D	2–2	..	..	..	..	..	..	..	..1	..	..	..1
14 Nov	Cardiff C	A	W	6–1	..	..	..	..	..	..	..1	..1	..1	..2	..1
21 Nov	Blackpool	H	W	4–1	..	..	..	..	..	..	..	..	..3	..1	..
28 Nov	Portsmouth	A	D	1–1	..	..	..	..	..	..	Webster	..	..1	..	..
5 Dec	Sheffield U	H	D	2–2	..	..	..	..	..	..	Berry	..2	..	..	..
12 Dec	Chelsea	A	L	1–3	..	..	..	..	..	..	..1	..	..	..	..
19 Dec	Liverpool	H	W	5–1	..	..	..	..	..	..	..	..2	..2	..1	..
25 Dec	Sheffield Wed	H	W	5–2	..	..	..	..	..	..	..	..1	..3	..1	..
26 Dec	Sheffield Wed	A	W	1–0	..	..	..	..	..	..	..	..	..	..1	..
2 Jan	Newcastle U	A	W	2–1	..	..1	..	..	..	..	..	..1	..	..	..
16 Jan	Manchester C	H	D	1–1	..	..	..	..	..	..	..1	..	..	..	Pegg
23 Jan	Bolton W	H	L	1–5	..	..	..	..	..	..	..	..	..1	..	..
6 Feb	Preston NE	A	W	3–1	Crompton	..	..	..	..	..	..	..	..1	..	Rowley1
13 Feb	Tottenham H	H	W	2–0	..	..	..	..	..	..	McFarlane	..1	..1	..	..1
20 Feb	Burnley	A	L	0–2	..	..	..	..	..	..	Berry	..	..	..	Pegg
27 Feb	Sunderland	A	W	2–0	Wood	..	..	..	..	..	..	..1	..1	..	Rowley
6 Mar	Wolverhampton W	H	W	1–0	..	..	..	..	..	..	..1	..	..	..	..
13 Mar	Aston Villa	A	D	2–2	Crompton	..	..	..	..	Cockburn	..	..	..2	..	..
20 Mar	Huddersfield T	H	W	3–1	..	..	..	..	..	Edwards	..	..1	..	..1	..1
27 Mar	Arsenal	A	L	1–3	..	..	..	Gibson	..	..	..	..	..1	..	..
3 Apr	Cardiff C	H	L	2–3	..	..	Redman	Whitefoot	..	..	..	..	Lewis	..1	..1
10 Apr	Blackpool	A	L	0–2	..	..	Byrne	..	..	..	..	..	Aston	..	..
16 Apr	Charlton A	H	W	2–0	..	..	..	..	..	..	Gibson	..	..1	..1	Pegg
17 Apr	Portsmouth	H	W	2–0	..	..	..	..	..	..	..	..1	..	..1	..
19 Apr	Charlton A	A	L	0–1	..	..	..	..	..	Cockburn	..	..	..	..	..
24 Apr	Sheffield U	A	W	3–1	..	..	..	..	..	..	Berry	..1	..1	..1	Rowley
	FA Cup														
9 Jan	Burnley (3)	A	L	3–5	Wood	Foulkes	Burne	Whitefoot	Chilton	Edwards	Berry	Blanchflower1	Taylor T1	Viollet1	Rowley

1954–1955

Appearances (goals)

Bent	2	
Berry	40	3
Blanchflower	29	10
Byrne	39	2
Chilton	29	
Cockburn	1	
Crompton	5	
Edwards	33	6
Foulkes	41	
Gibson	32	
Goodwin	5	
Greaves	1	
Jones	13	
Kennedy	1	
Pegg	6	1
Rowley	22	7
Scanlon	14	4
Taylor	30	20
Viollet	34	20
Webster	17	8
Whelan	7	1
Whitefoot	24	
Wood	37	
Own goals		2
Total 23 players	84	

Football League

	P	W	D	L	F:A	Pts	
Chelsea	42	20	12	10	81:57	52	1st
Manchester U	42	20	7	15	84:74	47	5th

SEASON 1954–1955 FOOTBALL LEAGUE (DIVISION 1)

21 Aug	Portsmouth	H	L	1–3	Wood	Foulkes	Byrne	Whitefoot	Chilton	Edwards	Berry	Blanchflower	Webster	Viollet	Rowley
23 Aug	Sheffield Wed	A	W	4–2	..	..	..	..	..	..	..	..2	..	..2	..1
28 Aug	Blackpool	A	W	4–2	..	..	..	..	..	..	..	..1	..1	..1	..
1 Sep	Sheffield Wed	H	W	2–0	..	..	..	..	..	..	..	..	..	..2	..
4 Sep	Charlton A	H	W	3–1	..	..	..	..	..	..	..	..	Taylor1	..	..2
8 Sep	Tottenham H	A	W	2–0	..	..	..	..	..	..	..1	..	Webster1	..	..
11 Sep	Bolton W	A	D	1–1	..	..	..	..	..	..	..	..	..1	..	..
15 Sep	Tottenham H	H	W	2–1	..	..	..	..	..	..	..	..	Taylor	..1	..1
18 Sep	Huddersfield T	H	D	1–1	..	..	..	..	..	..	..	..	..	..1	..
25 Sep	Manchester C	A	L	2–3	..	..	..	Gibson	..	..	..	..1	..1	..	..
2 Oct	Wolverhampton W	A	L	2–4	Crompton	Greaves	Kennedy	..	..	Cockburn	..	Edwards	..	..1	..1
9 Oct	Cardiff C	H	W	5–2	Wood	Foulkes	Byrne	..	..	Edwards	..	Blanchflower	..4	..1	..
16 Oct	Chelsea	A	W	6–5	..	..	..	..	..	..	..	..1	..2	..3	..
23 Oct	Newcastle U	H	D	*2–2	..	..	..	..	..	..	..	..	..1	..	..
30 Oct	Everton	A	L	2–4	..	..	..	..	..	..	..	..	..1	..	..1
6 Nov	Preston NE	H	W	2–1	..	..	..	..	..	..	..	..	..	..2	..
13 Nov	Sheffield U	A	L	0–3	..	..	..	..	..	..	..	..	..	..	..
20 Nov	Arsenal	H	W	2–1	..	..	..	..	..	Goodwin	..	..1	..1	..	Scanlon
27 Nov	W B A	A	L	0–2	..	..	..	..	..	Edwards	..	..	..	..	..
4 Dec	Leicester C	H	W	3–1	..	..	..	..	..	Whitefoot	..	..	Webster1	..1	Rowley1
11 Dec	Burnley	A	W	4–2	..	..	Bent	..	..	..	..	..	..3	..1	..
18 Dec	Portsmouth	A	D	0–0	..	..	Byrne	..	..	Edwards	..	..	..	..	..
27 Dec	Aston Villa	H	L	0–1	..	..	..	..	..	..	..	..	..	..	..
28 Dec	Aston Villa	A	L	1–2	..	..	..	..	..	..	..	Webster	Taylor1	..	Pegg
1 Jan	Blackpool	H	W	4–1	..	..	..	..	..	..1	..	Blanchflower2	..	..1	..
22 Jan	Bolton W	H	D	1–1	..	..	..	..	..	..	..	..	..1	..	Rowley
5 Feb	Huddersfield T	A	W	3–1	..	..	..	..	..	Whitefoot	..1	..	Webster	Edwards1	Pegg1
12 Feb	Manchester C	H	L	0–5	..	..	..	..	..	..	..	..	..	..	..
23 Feb	Wolverhampton W	H	L	2–4	..	..	..	..	..	..	Webster	Viollet	Taylor1	..1	..
26 Feb	Cardiff C	A	L	0–3	..	..	..	..	Jones	..	..	..	..	..	..
5 Mar	Burnley	H	W	1–0	..	..	..	..	..	..	Berry	Taylor	Webster	..1	Scanlon
19 Mar	Everton	H	L	1–2	..	..	..	..	..	..	..	..	..	..	..1
26 Mar	Preston NE	A	W	2–0	..	..	..1	..	..	..	..	Whelan	Taylor	..	..1
2 Apr	Sheffield U	H	W	5–0	..	..	Bent	..	..	..	..1	..1	..2	Viollet1	..
8 Apr	Sunderland	A	L	3–4	..	..	Byrne	..	..	..	..	..	..	Edwards2	..1
9 Apr	Leicester C	A	L	0–1	Crompton	..	..	..	..	..	..	..	..	..	..
11 Apr	Sunderland	H	D	2–2	..	..	..1	..	..	..	..	..	..1	..	..
16 Apr	W B A	H	W	3–0	..	..	..	Goodwin	..	..	..	..	..2	Viollet1	..
18 Apr	Newcastle U	A	L	0–2	..	..	..	Gibson	..	..	..	..	..	..	..
23 Apr	Arsenal	A	W	*3–2	Wood	..	..	..	..	Goodwin	..	Blanchflower2	..	..	..
26 Apr	Charlton A	A	D	1–1	..	..	..	..	..	..	..	..	..	..1	..
30 Apr	Chelsea	H	W	2–1	..	..	..	..	..	..	..	..	..1	..	..1
	FA Cup														
8 Jan	Reading (3)	A	D	1–1	Wood	Foulkes	Byrne	Gibson	Chilton	Edwards	Berry	Blanchflower	Webster1	Viollet	Rowley
12 Jan	Reading (3R)	H	W	4–1	..	..	..	..	..	..	..	..	..2	..1	..1
29 Feb	Manchester C (4)	A	L	0–2	..	..	..	..	..	..	..	..	Taylor	..	..

SEASON 1955–1956 FOOTBALL LEAGUE (DIVISION 1)

20 Aug	Birmingham C	A	D	2–2	Wood	Foulkes	Byrne	Whitefoot	Jones	Edwards	Webster	Blanchflower	Taylor	Viollet2	Scanlon
24 Aug	Tottenham H	H	D	2–2	..	..	..	..	..	..	Berry1	..	Webster1	..	..
27 Aug	W B A	H	W	3–1	..	..	..	..	..	..	Webster	..	Lewis1	..1	..1

31 Aug	Tottenham H	A	W	2–1	..	..	..	..	..	..2	..	..	..	..	..
3 Sep	Manchester C	A	L	0–1	..	..	..	..	..	Goodwin	..	..	..	Edwards	..
7 Sep	Everton	H	W	2–1	..	..	..	..	..	..	..	..1	..	..1	..
10 Sep	Sheffield U	A	L	0–1	..	..	..	..	..	..	Berry	Whelan	Webster	Blanchflower	Pegg
14 Sep	Everton	A	L	2–4	..	..	..	Whitehurst	..	..	Webster1	..	Blanchflower1	Doherty	Berry
17 Sep	Preston NE	H	W	3–2	..	..	..	Whitefoot	..	..	..	Blanchflower	Taylor1	Viollet1	Pegg1
24 Sep	Burnley	A	D	0–0	..	..	..	..	..	..	Berry	..	..	..	..
1 Oct	Luton T	H	W	3–1	..	..	Bent	..	..	..	..	..	..2	Webster1	..
8 Oct	Wolverhampton W	H	W	4–3	..	Byrne	..	..	..	McGuinness	..	Doherty1	..2	..	..1
15 Oct	Aston Villa	A	D	4–4	..	Foulkes	Byrne	..	..	..	..1	Blanchflower1	..	..1	..2
22 Oct	Huddersfield T	H	W	3–0	Crompton	..	Bent	..	..	Edwards	..	..	..1	Viollet	..1
29 Oct	Cardiff C	A	W	1–0	Wood	..	Byrne	..	..	..	..	..	..1	..	..
5 Nov	Arsenal	H	D	1–1	..	..	..	..	..	..	..	..	..1	..	..
12 Nov	Bolton W	A	L	1–3	..	..	..	Colman	..	..	..	..	..1	Webster	..
19 Nov	Chelsea	H	W	3–0	..	..	..1	..	..	..	..	Doherty	..2	Viollet	..
26 Nov	Blackpool	A	D	0–0	..	Greaves	..	..	..	..	..	..	..	..	..
3 Dec	Sunderland	H	W	2–1	..	Foulkes	..	..	..	..	..	..1	..	..1	..
10 Dec	Portsmouth	A	L	2–3	..	..	..	..	..	..	..	..	..1	..	..
17 Dec	Birmingham C	H	W	2–1	..	..	..	..	..1	..	..	..	..	..1	..1
24 Dec	W B A	A	W	4–1	..	..	..	..	..	..	..	..	..1	..3	..
26 Dec	Charlton A	H	W	5–1	..	..	..1	..	..	..	..	..1	..1	..2	..
27 Dec	Charlton A	A	L	0–3	..	..	..	..	..	..	..	..	..	..	..
31 Dec	Manchester C	H	W	2–1	..	..	..	..	..	..	..	..	..1	..1	..
14 Jan	Sheffield U	H	W	3–1	..	..	..	..	..	..	..1	Whelan	..1	..	..
21 Jan	Preston NE	A	L	1–3	..	..	..	..	..	..	Scott	..1	Webster	..	..1
4 Feb	Burnley	H	W	2–0	..	Greaves	..	..	..	..	Berry	..	Taylor1	..1	..
11 Feb	Luton T	A	W	2–0	..	..	..	Goodwin	..	Blanchflower	..	..1	..	..1	..
18 Feb	Wolverhampton W	A	W	2–0	..	..	..	Colman	..	Edwards	..	..	..2	..	..
25 Feb	Aston Villa	H	W	1–0	..	..	..	..	..	..	..	..1	..	..	..
3 Mar	Chelsea	A	W	4–2	..	..	..	..	..	..	..	..	..1	..2	..
10 Mar	Cardiff C	H	D	1–1	..	..	..1	..	..	..	..	..	..	..	..1
17 Mar	Arsenal	A	D	1–1	..	..	..	..	..	..	..	..	..	..1	..
24 Mar	Bolton W	H	W	1–0	..	..	..	..	..	..	..	..	..1	..	..
30 Mar	Newcastle U	H	W	5–2	..	..	..	..	..	..	..	Doherty1	..1	..2	..1
31 Mar	Huddersfield T	A	W	2–0	..	..	..	..	..	..	..	..	..2	..	..
2 Apr	Newcastle U	A	D	0–0	..	..	..	..	..	..	..	..	..	..	..
7 Apr	Blackpool	H	W	2–1	..	..	..	..	..	..	..1	..	..1	..	..
14 Apr	Sunderland	A	D	2–2	..	..	Bent	..	..	McGuinness1	..	Whelan1	Blanchflower	..	..
21 Apr	Portsmouth	H	W	1–0	..	..	Byrne	..	..	Doherty	..	Doherty	Taylor	..1	..
	FA Cup														
7 Jan	Bristol R (3)	A	L	0–4	Wood	Foulkes	Byrne	Colman	Jones	Whitefoot	Berry	Doherty	Taylor	Viollet	Pegg

1955–1956

Appearances (goals)

Bent	4	
Berry	34	4
Blanchflower	18	3
Byrne	39	3
Colman	25	
Crompton	1	
Doherty	16	4
Edwards	33	3
Foulkes	26	
Goodwin	8	
Greaves	15	
Jones	42	1
Lewis	4	1
McGuinness	3	1
Pegg	35	9
Scanlon	6	1
Scott	1	
Taylor	33	25
Viollet	34	20
Webster	15	4
Whelan	13	4
Whitefoot	15	
Whitehurst	1	
Wood	41	
Total 24 players	83	

Football League

	P	W	D	L	F:A	Pts	
Manchester U	42	25	10	7	83:51	60	1st

SEASON 1956–1957 FOOTBALL LEAGUE (DIVISION 1)

18 Aug	Birmingham C	H	D	2–2	Wood	Foulkes	Byrne	Colman	Jones M	Edwards	Berry	Whelan	Taylor T	Viollet2	Pegg
20 Aug	Preston NE	A	W	3–1	..	..	..	..	..	..	..	..1	..2	..	..
25 Aug	W B A	A	W	3–2	..	..	..	..	..	..	..	..1	..1	..1	..
29 Aug	Preston NE	H	W	3–2	..	..	..	..	..	..	..	..	..	..3	..
1 Sep	Portsmouth	H	W	3–0	..	..	..	..	..	..	..1	..	..	..1	..1
5 Sep	Chelsea	A	W	2–1	..	..	..	..	..	..	..	..1	..1	..	..
8 Sep	Newcastle U	A	D	1–1	..	..	..	..	..	..	..	..1	..	..	..
15 Sep	Sheffield Wed	H	W	4–1	..	..	..	..	..	..	..1	..1	..1	..1	..
22 Sep	Manchester C	H	W	2–0	..	..	..	..	..	..	..	..1	..	..1	..
29 Sep	Arsenal	A	W	2–1	..	..	..	..	Cope	..	..1	..1	..	..	..
6 Oct	Charlton A	H	W	4–2	..	..	Bent	..	Jones M	McGuinness	..1	..1	Charlton2	..	..
13 Oct	Sunderland	A	W	*3–1	..	..	Byrne	..	..	Edwards	..	..1	Taylor T	..1	..
20 Oct	Everton	H	L	2–5	..	..	..	..	..	..	..	..1	..	Charlton1	..
27 Oct	Blackpool	A	D	2–2	Hawksworth	..	..	..	..	..	..	..	..2	Viollet	..
3 Nov	Wolverhampton W	H	W	3–0	Wood	..	..	..	..	..	..	..1	..1	Charlton	..
10 Nov	Bolton W	A	L	0–2	..	..	..	..	..	..	..	..	..	..	..1
17 Nov	Leeds U	H	W	3–2	..	..	..	..	..	McGuinness	..	..2	..	..1	..
24 Nov	Tottenham H	A	D	2–2	..	..	..	..1	Blanchflower	..	..1	..	..	Edwards	..
1 Dec	Luton T	H	W	3–1	..	..	..	..	Jones M	..	..	..	..1	..1	..
8 Dec	Aston Villa	A	W	3–1	..	..	Bent	..	..	Edwards	..	..	..2	Viollet1	..1
15 Dec	Birmingham C	A	L	1–3	..	..	..	..	..	..	..	..1	..	..	..
26 Dec	Cardiff C	H	W	3–1	..	..	Byrne	..	..	..	..	..1	..1	..1	..
29 Dec	Portsmouth	A	W	3–1	..	..	..	..	..	McGuinness	..	..	Edwards1	..1	..
1 Jan	Chelsea	H	W	3–0	..	..	..	..	..	Edwards	..	..1	Taylor T2	..	..1
12 Jan	Newcastle U	H	W	6–1	..	..	..	..	..	..	..	..2	..	..2	..
19 Jan	Sheffield Wed	A	L	1–2	..	..	..	..	..	..	..	..	..1	..	..2
2 Feb	Manchester C	A	W	4–2	..	..	..	..	..	..1	..	..1	..1	..1	..
9 Feb	Arsenal	H	W	6–2	..	..	..	..	..	..1	..2	..2	..1	..	..
18 Feb	Charlton A	A	W	5–1	..	Byrne	Bent	..	..	McGuinness	..	..	..2	Charlton3	..
23 Feb	Blackpool	H	L	0–2	..	Foulkes	Byrne	..	..	Edwards	..	..	..	..	..
6 Mar	Everton	A	W	2–1	..	Byrne	Bent	Goodwin	Blanchflower	McGuinness	..	..	Webster2	Doherty	..
9 Mar	Aston Villa	H	D	1–1	..	Foulkes	Byrne	..	..	..	..	..	Edwards	Charlton1	..
16 Mar	Wolverhampton W	A	D	1–1	Clayton	..	..	Colman	..	Edwards	..	..	Webster	..	..
25 Mar	Bolton W	H	L	0–2	Wood	..	..	..	..	McGuinness	..	..	Edwards	..	..
30 Mar	Leeds U	A	W	2–1	..	..	..	..	..	Edwards	..1	..	Webster	..1	..
6 Apr	Tottenham H	H	D	0–0	..	..	Bent	..	..	McGuinness	..	..	Taylor T	Viollet	Scanlon
13 Apr	Luton T	A	W	2–0	..	..	Byrne	Goodwin	..	Edwards	..	Viollet	..2	Charlton	..
19 Apr	Burnley	A	W	3–1	..	..	..	..	..	..	..	Whelan3	..		Pegg
20 Apr	Sunderland	H	W	4–0	..	..	..	Colman	..	..1	..	..2	..1	..	..
22 Apr	Burnley	H	W	2–0	..	..	Greaves	Goodwin	Cope	McGuinness	Webster1	Doherty	Dawson1	Viollet	Scanlon
27 Apr	Cardiff C	A	W	3–2	..	..	..	Colman	Blanchflower	..	..	Whelan	..1	..	..2
29 Apr	W B A	H	D	1–1	Clayton	Greaves	Byrne	Goodwin	Jones M	..	Berry	Doherty	..1	..	..
	FA Cup														
5 Jan	Hartlepool U (3)	A	W	4–3	Wood	Foulkes	Byrne	Colman	Jones M	Edwards	Berry1	Whelan2	Viollet	Pegg	..
26 Jan	Wrexham (4)	A	W	5–0	..	..	..1	..	..	..	..	Webster	..2	..	..
16 Feb	Everton (5)	H	W	1–0	..	..	..	..	..	..1	Berry	..	..	..	..
2 Mar	Bournemouth (6)	A	W	2–1	..	..	..	..	..	McGuinness	..2	Edwards	..	..	..
23 Mar	Birmingham C (SF) (at Hillsborough)	N	W	2–0	..	..	..	..	Blanchflower	Edwards	..1	Charlton1	..	..	..
4 May	Aston Villa (F) (at Wembley)	N	L	1–2	..	..	..	..	..	..	..	Taylor T1	Charlton	..	..
	European Cup														
12 Sep	RSC Anderlecht (P)	A	W	2–1	Wood	Foulkes	Byrne	Colman	Jones M	Blanchflower	Berry	Whelan	Taylor T1	Viollet1	Pegg
26 Sep	RSC Anderiecht (P)	†H	W	10–0	..	..	..	..	..	Edwards	..1	..2	..3	..4	..
17 Oct	Borussia D'mund (1)	†H	W	3–2	..	..	..	..	..	..	..	..	..	..2	..1
21 Nov	Borussia D'mund (1)	A	D	0–0	..	..	..	..	..	McGuinness	..	..	..	Edwards	
16 Jan	Athletico Bilbao(2)	A	L	3–5	..	..	..	..	..	Edwards	..	..1	..1	Viollet1	..
6 Feb	Athletico Bilbao (2)	†H	W	3–0	..	..	..	..	..	..	..	..1	..1	..1	..
11 Apr	Real Madrid (SF)	A	L	1–3	..	..	..	..	Blanchflower	..	..	..	..1	..	..
25 Apr	Real Madrid (SF)	†H	D	2–2	..	..	..	..	..	..	..	..	..1	Charlton 1	..
	†at Maine Road														

1956–1957

Appearances (goals)

Bent	6	
Berry	40	8
Blanchflower	11	
Byrne	36	
Charlton	14	10
Clayton	2	
Colman	36	1
Cope	2	
Dawson	3	3
Doherty	3	
Edwards	34	5
Foulkes	39	
Goodwin	6	
Greaves	3	
Hawksworth	1	
Jones M	29	
McGuinness	13	
Pegg	37	6
Scanlon	5	2
Taylor T	32	22
Viollet	27	16
Webster	5	3
Whelan	39	26
Wood	39	
Own goals		1
Total 24 players	103	

Football League

	P	W	D	L	F:A	Pts	
Manchester U	42	28	8	6	103:54	64	1st

SEASON 1957–1958 FOOTBALL LEAGUE (DIVISION 1)

24 Aug	Leicester C	A	W	3–0	Wood	Foulkes	Byrne	Colman	Blanchflower	Edwards	Berry	Whelan3	Taylor T	Viollet	Pegg

1957–1958

Appearances (goals)

Berry	20	4
Blanchflower	18	
Brennan	5	
Byrne	26	
Charlton	21	8
Colman	24	
Cope	13	
Crowther	11	
Dawson	12	5
Doherty	1	1
Edwards	26	6
Foulkes	42	
Gaskell	3	
Goodwin	16	
Greaves	12	
Gregg	19	
Harrop	5	
Heron	1	
Jones M	10	
Jones P	1	
McGuinness	7	
Morgans	13	
Pearson	8	
Pegg	21	4
Scanlon	9	3
Taylor E	11	2
Taylor T	25	16
Viollet	22	16
Webster	20	6
Whelan	20	12
Wood R	20	
Own goals		2
Total 31 players	85	

Football League

	P	W	D	L	F:A	Pts	
Wolverhampton W	42	28	8	6	103:47	64	1st
Manchester U	42	16	11	15	85:75	43	9th

28 Aug	Everton	H	W	*3–0	..	..	..	..	..	..	..	..1	..1	..	..
31 Aug	Manchester C	H	W	4–1	..	..	..	..	..	..1	..1	..	..1	..1	..
4 Sep	Everton	A	D	3–3	..	..	..	..	..	..	..1	..1	..	..1	..
7 Sep	Leeds U	H	W	5–0	..	..	..	..	..	..	..2	..	..2	..1	..
9 Sep	Blackpool	A	W	4–1	..	..	..	..	..	..	..	..2	..	..2	..
14 Sep	Bolton W	A	L	0–4	..	..	..	..	..	..	..	..	..	..	..
18 Sep	Blackpool	H	L	1–2	..	..	..	..	..	..1	..	..	..	..	..
21 Sep	Arsenal	H	W	4–2	..	..	..	..	..	..	..	..2	..1	..	..1
28 Sep	Wolverhampton W	A	L	1–3	..	..	McGuinness	Goodwin	..	..	..	Doherty1	..	Charlton	..
5 Oct	Aston Villa	H	W	*4–1	..	..	Byrne	Colman	Jones M	McGuinness	..	Whelan	..2	..	..1
12 Oct	Nottingham F	A	W	2–1	..	..	..	..	Blanchflower	Edwards	..	..1	..	Viollet1	..
19 Oct	Portsmouth	H	L	0–3	..	..	Jones MP	..	..	McGuinness	..	..	Dawson	..	..
26 Oct	W B A	A	L	3–4	..	..	Byrne	Goodwin	..	Edwards	..	..1	Taylor T2	Charlton	..
2 Nov	Burnley	H	W	1–0	..	..	..	..	..	..	..	..	..1	Webster	..
9 Nov	Preston NE	A	D	1–1	..	..	..	..	..	..	..	..1	..	..	..
16 Nov	Sheffield Wed	H	W	2–1	..	..	..	Colman	..	..	..	..	..	..2	..
23 Nov	Newcastle U	A	W	2–1	..	..	..	..	..	..1	Scanlon	..	..1	..	..
30 Nov	Tottenham H	H	L	3–4	Gaskell	..	..	..	..	..	..	..1	Webster	Charlton	..2
7 Dec	Birmingham C	A	D	3–3	Wood	..	..	..	Jones M	..	Berry	..	Taylor T1	Viollet2	..
14 Dec	Chelsea	H	L	0–1	..	..	..	..	..	..	..	..	..	..	..
21 Dec	Leicester C	H	W	4–0	Gregg	..	..	..	..	..	Morgans	Charlton1	..	..2	Scanlon1
25 Dec	Luton T	H	W	3–0	..	..	..	..	..	..1	..	..1	..1	..	..
26 Dec	Luton T	A	D	2–2	..	..	..	..	..	..	Berry	..	..1	..	..1
28 Dec	Manchester C	A	D	2–2	..	..	..	..	..	..	Morgans	..1	Dawson	..1	..
11 Jan	Leeds U	A	D	1–1	..	..	..	..	..	..	..	..	Taylor T	..1	..
18 Jan	Bolton W	H	W	7–2	..	..	..	..	..	..1	..	..3	..	..2	..1
1 Feb	Arsenal	A	W	5–4	..	..	..	..	..	..1	..	..1	..2	..1	..
22 Feb	Nottingham F	H	D	1–1	..	..	Greaves	Goodwin	Cope	Crowther	Webster	Taylor E	Dawson	Pearson	Brennan
8 Mar	W B A	H	L	0–4	..	..	..	..	..	Harrop	..	..	..	..	Charlton
15 Mar	Burnley	A	L	0–3	..	..	..	..	..	Crowther	..	Harrop	..	..	..
29 Mar	Sheffield Wed	A	L	0–1	..	..	Cope	..	Greaves	..	..	Taylor E	..	Charlton	Brennan
31 Mar	Aston Villa	A	L	2–3	..	..	..	..	..	..	..1	Pearson	..1	..	..
4 Apr	Sunderland	H	D	2–2	..	..	Greaves	..	Cope	..	..	Taylor E	..1	..1	..
5 Apr	Preston NE	H	D	0–0	..	..	..	..	..	..	Morgans	..	Webster	..	Heron
7 Apr	Sunderland	A	W	2–1	..	..	..	..	Harrop	McGuinness	..	..	..2	..	Pearson
12 Apr	Tottenham H	A	L	0–1	..	..	..	..	Cope	Crowther	..	..	..	..	..
16 Apr	Portsmouth	A	D	3–3	..	..	..	Crowther	..	McGuinness	Dawson1	..1	..1	Pearson	Morgans
19 Apr	Birmingham C	H	L	0–2	..	..	..	Goodwin	..	Crowther	..	..	..	..	..
21 Apr	Wolverhampton W	H	L	0–4	..	..	..	..	..	McGuinness	..	Brennan	..	Viollet	..
23 Apr	Newcastle U	H	D	1–1	..	..	..	Crowther	..	..	..1	Taylor E	..	Charlton	..
26 Apr	Chelsea	A	L	1–2	..	..	..	Goodwin	..	Crowther	..	..1	Charlton	Viollet	Webster
	FA Cup														
4 Jan	Workington T (3)	A	W	3–1	Gregg	Foulkes	Byrne	Colman	Jones M	Edwards	Morgans	Charlton	Taylor T	Viollet3	Scanlon
25 Jan	Ipswich T (4)	H	W	2–0	..	..	..	..	..	..	..	..2	..	..	..
19 Feb	Sheffield Wed (5)	H	W	3–0	..	..	Greaves	Goodwin	Cope	Crowther	Webster	Taylor E	Dawson1	Pearson	Brennan2
1 Mar	W B A (6)	A	D	2–2	..	..	..	..	..	..	..	..1	..1	..	Charlton
5 Mar	W B A (6R)	H	W	1–0	..	..	..	..	..	Harrop	..1	..	..	..	..
22 Mar	Fulham (SF)	N	D	2–2	..	..	..	..	..	Crowther	..	..	..	Chartton2	Pearson
	(at Villa Park)														
26 Mar	Fulham (SFR)	N	W	5–3	..	..	..	..	..	..	..	..	..3	..1	Brennan1
	(at Highbury)														
3 May	Bolton W (F)	N	L	0–2	..	..	..	..	..	..	Dawson	..	Charlton	Viollet	Webster
	(at Wembley)														
	European Cup														
25 Sep	Shamrock R (P)	A	W	6–0	Wood	Foulkes	Byrne	Goodwin	Blanchflower	Edwards	Berry1	Whelan2	Taylor T2	Viollet	Pegg1
2 Oct	Shamrock R (P)	H	W	3–2	..	..	..	Colman	Jones M	McGuinness	..	Webster	..	..2	..1
21 Nov	Dukla Prague (1)	H	W	3–0	..	..	..	..	Blanchflower	Edwards	..	Whelan	..1	Webster1	..1
4 Dec	Dukla Prague (1)	A	L	0–1	..	..	..	..	Jones M	..	Scanlon	..	..	..	..
14 Jan	Red Star Belgrade (2)	H	W	2–1	Gregg	..	..	..1	..	..	Morgans	Charlton1	..	Viollet	Scanlon
5 Feb	Red Star Belgrade (2)	A	D	3–3	..	..	..	..	..	..	..	..2	..	..1	..
8 May	A C Milan (SF)	H	W	2–1	..	..	Greaves	Goodwin	Cope	Crowther	..	Taylor E1	Webster	..1	Pearson
14 May	A C Milan (SF)	A	L	0–4	..	..	..	..	..	..	..	..	..	..	..

1958–1959

Appearances (goals)

Bradley	24	12
Brennan	1	
Carolan	23	
Charlton	38	29
Cope	32	2
Crowther	2	
Dawson	11	4
Foulkes	32	
Goodwin	42	6
Greaves	34	
Gregg	41	
Harrop	5	
Hunter	1	
McGuinness	39	1
Morgans	2	
Pearson	4	1
Quixall	33	4
Scanlon	42	16
Taylor E	11	
Viollet	37	21
Webster	7	5
Wood	1	
Own goals		2
Total 22 players	103	

Football League

	P	W	D	L	F:A	Pts	
Wolves	42	28	5	9	110:49	61	1st
Manchester U	42	24	7	11	103:66	55	2nd

SEASON 1958–1959 FOOTBALL LEAGUE (DIVISION 1)

23 Aug	Chelsea	H	W	5–2	Gregg	Foulkes	Greaves	Goodwin	Cope	McGuinness	Dawson	Taylor E	Viollet	Charlton3	Scanlon
27 Aug	Nottingham F	A	W	3–0	..	..	..	..	..	..	..	..	..	..2	..1
30 Aug	Blackpool	A	L	1–2	..	..	..	..	..	..	..	..	..1	..	..
3 Sep	Nottingham F	H	D	1–1	..	..	..	..	..	..	..	..	..	..1	..
6 Sep	Blackburn R	H	W	6–1	..	..	..	..	..	..	Webster1	..	..2	..2	..1
8 Sep	West Ham U	A	L	2–3	..	..	..	..	..	..1	..1	..	..	..	..
13 Sep	Newcastle U	A	D	1–1	..	..	..	..	..	Crowther	..	..	..	..1	..
17 Sep	West Ham U	H	W	4–1	..	..	..	..	..	McGuinness	..1	..	Dawson	..	..3
20 Sep	Tottenham H	H	D	2–2	..	..	..	..	..	..	..2	Quixall	..	..	..
27 Sep	Manchester C	A	D	1–1	..	..	..	..	..	..	Viollet	..	Webster	..1	..
4 Oct	Wolverhampton W	A	L	0–4	Wood	..	..	..	Harrop	Crowther	..	..	..	Pearson	..
8 Oct	Preston NE	H	L	0–2	Gregg	..	..	..	Cope	McGuinness	..	Taylor E	Dawson	Charlton	..
11 Oct	Arsenal	H	D	1–1	..	..	..	..	..	..	..1	Quixall	Charlton	Taylor E	
18 Oct	Everton	A	L	2–3	..	..	..	..	..2	..	..	..	..	..	..
25 Oct	W B A	H	L	1–2	..	..	..	..1	Harrop	..	..	..	Dawson	Charlton	
1 Nov	Leeds U	A	W	2–1	..	..	..	..1	..	..	Morgans	..	..	..	..
8 Nov	Burnley	H	L	1–3	..	..	..	..	..	..	..	..1	..	..	..1
15 Nov	Bolton W	A	L	3–6	..	..	..	..	Cope	..	Bradley	..	..2	..1	..
22 Nov	Luton T	H	W	2–1	..	..	Carolan	..	..	..	..	..	Viollet1	..2	..
29 Nov	Birminghan C	A	W	4–0	..	..	..	..	..	..	..1	..	..	..1	..
6 Dec	Leicester C	H	W	4–1	..	..	..	..	..	..	..1	..	..1	..1	..1
13 Dec	Preston NE	A	W	4–3	..	..	..	..	..	..	..1	..	..1	..1	..1
20 Dec	Chelsea	A	W	*3–2	..	..	..	..1	..	..	..	..	..	Pearson	..1
26 Dec	Aston Villa	H	W	2–1	..	..	..	..	..	..	..	..1	..1	..1	..
27 Dec	Aston Villa	A	W	2–0	..	..	Greaves	..	..	..	Hunter	..	..1	Charlton2	..
3 Jan	Blackpool	H	W	3–1	..	..	Carolan	..	..	..	Bradley	..	..1	..1	..
31 Jan	Newcastle U	H	D	4–4	..	..	..	Harrop	Goodwin	..	..	..1	..	..2	..1
7 Feb	Tottenham H	A	W	3–1	..	Greaves	..	Goodwin	Cope	..	..	..	..	..	..1
16 Feb	Manchester C	H	W	4–1	..	..	..	..1	..	..	..2	..	..1	..1	..1
21 Feb	Wolverhampton W	H	W	2–1	..	..	..	..	..	..	..	..	..1	..	..
28 Feb	Arsenal	A	L	2–3	..	..	..	..	..	..	..1	..	..	..	..
2 Mar	Blackburn R	A	W	3–1	..	..	..	..	..	..	..2	..	..	..	..1
7 Mar	Everton	H	W	2–1	..	..	..	..1	..	..	..	..	..	..	..1
14 Mar	W B A	A	W	3–1	..	..	..	..	..	..	..1	..	..3	..	..1
21 Mar	Leeds U	H	W	4–0	..	..	..	..	..	..	..	..	..2	..1	..
27 Mar	Portsmouth	H	W	*6–1	..	..	..	..	..	..	..1	..	..1	..2	..
28 Mar	Burnley	A	L	2–4	..	..	..	..1	..	..	..	..	..	..	..
30 Mar	Portsmouth	A	W	3–1	..	..	..	..	Foulkes	..	..1	..	..1	..2	..
4 Apr	Bolton W	H	W	3–0	..	..	..	..	..	..	..	..	..	..1	..1
11 Apr	Luton T	A	D	0–0	..	..	..	..	..	..	..	..	..	Pearson	..
18 Apr	Birmingham C	H	W	1–0	..	..	..	..	..	..	..	..1	..	Charlton	..
25 Apr	Leicester C	A	L	1–2	..	..	..	..	..	Brennan	..1	..	..	..	..
	FA Cup														
10 Jan	Norwich C (3)	A	L	0–3	Gregg	Foulkes	Carolan	Goodwin	Cope	McGuinness	Bradley	Quixall	Viollet	Charlton	Scanlon

SEASON 1959–1960 FOOTBALL LEAGUE (DIVISION 1)

22 Aug	W B A	A	L	2–3	Gregg	Greaves	Carolan	Goodwin	Foulkes	McGuinness	Bradley	Quixall	Viollet2	Charlton	Scanlon
26 Aug	Chelsea	H	L	0–1	..	..	..	..	..	..	..	..	Dawson	Viollet	Charlton
29 Aug	Newcastle U	H	W	3–2	..	Cope	..	Brennan	..	..	..	.. 2	Viollet2	Charlton1	Scanlon
2 Sep	Chelsea	A	W	6–3	..	..	..	..	..	..	..2	..1	..2	..1	..1
5 Sep	Birmingham C	A	D	1–1	..	..	..	..	..	..	..	..2	..	..	..1
9 Sep	Leeds U	H	W	6–0	..	..	..	..	..	..	..2	..	..1	..2	..1
12 Sep	Tottenham H	H	L	1–5	..	..	..	Goodwin	..	..	..	Giles	..1	..	..
16 Sep	Leeds U	A	D	*2–2	..	Foulkes	..	Brennan	Cope	..	..	Quixall	..	..1	..
19 Sep	Manchester C	A	L	0–3	..	..	..	..	..	..	..	..	..	..	..
26 Sep	Preston NE	A	L	0–4	..	..	..	Viollet	..	..	..	..	Dawson	..	..
3 Oct	Leicester C	H	W	4–1	Gaskell	..	..	Goodwin	..	..	..	..1	Viollet2	..1	..
10 Oct	Arsenal	H	W	*4–2	Gregg	..	..	..	..	..	..	..1	..1	..1	..
17 Oct	Wolverhampton W	A	L	*2–3	..	..	..	..	..	..	..	Giles	..1	Pearson	..
24 Oct	Sheffield Wed	H	W	3–1	..	..	..	..	..	..	..1	Quixall	..2	Charlton	..
31 Oct	Blackburn R	A	D	1–1	..	..	..	..	..	..	..	..1	..	..	..
7 Nov	Fulham	H	D	3–3	..	..	..	..	..	..	..	..	..1	..1	..1
14 Nov	Bolton W	A	D	1–1	..	..	..	..	..	..	..	..	..	..	Dawson1
21 Nov	Luton T	H	W	4–1	..	..	..	..1	..	..	..	..1	..2	..	Scanlon
28 Nov	Everton	A	L	1–2	..	..	..	..	..	..	..	..	..1	..	..
5 Dec	Blackpool	H	W	3–1	Gaskell	..	..	..	..	Brennan	Dawson	..	..2	Pearson1	..
12 Dec	Nottingham F	A	W	5–1	..	..	..	..	..	..	..1	..	..3	..	..1
19 Dec	W B A	H	L	2–3	..	..	..	..	..	..	..1	..1	..	..	..
26 Dec	Burnley	H	L	1–2	..	..	..	..	..	..	..	..1	..	Charlton	..
28 Dec	Burnley	A	W	4–1	..	..	..	..	..	..	..	..	..2	..	..2
2 Jan	Newcastle U	A	L	3–7	..	..	..	..	..	..	..	..2	..	..	..
16 Jan	Birmingham C	H	W	2–1	Gregg	..	..	Setters	..	..	Bradley	..1	..1		..
23 Jan	Tottenham H	A	L	1–2	..	..	..	..	..	..	..1	..	..		..
6 Feb	Manchester C	H	D	0–0	..	..	..	..	..	..	..	..	..	..	..
13 Feb	Preston NE	H	D	1–1	..	..	..	..	..	..	..	..	..1	..	..
24 Feb	Leicester C	A	L	1–3	..	..	..	..	..	..	Viollet	..	Dawson	..	..1
27 Feb	Blackpool	A	W	6–0	..	..	..	..	..	..	..2	..	..	..3	..1
5 Mar	Wolverhampton W	H	L	0–2	..	..	..	..	..	..	..	..	..	..	..
19 Mar	Nottingham F	H	W	3–1	..	..	..	..	..	..	Giles	Viollet	..1	Pearson	Charlton2
26 Mar	Fulham	A	W	5–0	..	..	..	..	..	..	..1	..2	..1	..1	..
30 Mar	Sheffield Wed	A	L	2–4	Gaskell	..	Heron	..	..	..	Bradley	..1	..	..	..1
7 Apr	Bolton W	H	W	2–0	..	..	Carolan	..	..	..	..	Giles	..	..	..2
9 Apr	Luton T	A	W	3–2	Gregg	..	..	..	..	..	..1	..	..2	Lawton	Scanlon
15 Apr	West Ham U	A	L	1–2	..	..	..	..	..	..	..	..	..1	..	Charlton
16 Apr	Blackburn R	H	W	1–0	..	..	..	..	..	....	..	.	..1	..	..
18 Apr	West Ham U	H	W	5–3	..	..	..	..	..	..	Giles	Quixall1	..2	Viollet	..2
23 Apr	Arsenal	A	L	2–5	..	..	..	..	..	..	..1	..	..	Pearson1	..
30 Apr	Everton	H	W	5–0	..	..	..	..	..	..	Bradley1	..1	..3	..	..
	FA Cup														
9 Jan	Derby Co (3)	A	W	*4–2	Gregg	Foulkes	Carolan	Goodwin1	Cope	Brennan	Dawson	Quixall	Viollet	Charlton1	Scanlon1
30 Jan	Liverpool (4)	H	W	3–1	..	..	..	Setters	..	..	Bradley1	..	..	..2	..
20 Feb	Sheffield Wed (5)	A	L	0–1	..	..	..	..	..	..	..	..	..	..	..

1959–1960

Appearances (goals)

Bradley	29	8
Brennan	29	
Carolan	41	
Charlton	37	18
Cope	40	
Dawson	22	15
Foulkes	42	
Gaskell	9	
Giles	10	2
Goodwin	18	1
Greaves	2	
Gregg	33	
Heron	1	
Lawton	3	
McGuinness	19	
Pearson	10	3
Quixall	33	13
Scanlon	31	7
Setters	17	
Viollet	36	32
Own goals		3
Total 20 players	102	

Football League

	P	W	D	L	F:A	Pts	
Burnley	42	24	7	11	85:61	55	1st
Manchester U	42	19	7	16	102:80	45	7th

SEASON 1960–1961 FOOTBALL LEAGUE (DIVISION 1)

20 Aug	Blackburn R	H	L	1–3	Gregg	Cope	Carolan	Setters	Haydock	Brennan	Giles	Quixall	Viollet	Charlton1	Scanlon
24 Aug	Everton	A	L	0–4	..	Brennan	..	..	..	Nicholson	..	..	..	..	..
31 Aug	Everton	H	W	4–0	..	Foulkes	Brennan	..	..	..1	Quixall	Giles	Dawson2	Viollet	Chartlon1
3 Sep	Tottenham H	A	L	1–4	..	..	..	..	..	..	..	..	..	..1	..
5 Sep	West Ham U	A	L	1–2	..	..	..	..	Cope	..	..1	..	..	..	..
10 Sep	Leicester C	H	D	1–1	..	..	..	..	..	..	..	..1	..	..	..
14 Sep	West Ham U	H	W	6–1	..	..	..	..	..	..	..1	..	Viollet2	Charlton2	Scanlon1
17 Sep	Aston Villa	A	L	1–3	..	..	..	..	..	..	Giles	Quixall	..1	..	..
24 Sep	Wolverhampton W	H	L	1–3	..	..	..	..	..	..	..	..	..	..1	..
1 Oct	Bolton W	A	D	1–1	..	Setters	..	Stiles	Foulkes	..	Moir	Giles1	Dawson	..	..
15 Oct	Burnley	A	L	3–5	..	..	Dunne A	..	..	..	Quixall	..	Viollet3	Pearson	Charlton
22 Oct	Newcastle U	H	W	3–2	..	..1	Brennan	..	..	..	Dawson1	..	..	Charlton	Scanlon
24 Oct	Nottingham F	H	W	2–1	..	Dunne A	..	..	..	..	..	..	..2	Pearson	..
29 Oct	Arsenal	A	L	1–2	..	Brennan	Heron	..	..	..	..	..	..	Quixall1	Charlton
5 Nov	Sheffield Wed	H	D	0–0	..	Setters	Brennan	..	..	..	..	..	..	..	
12 Nov	Birmingham C	A	L	1–3	..	..	..	..	..	..	..	..	..	Pearson	..1
19 Nov	W B A	H	W	3–0	..	..	..	..	..	..	Bradley	Quixall1	Dawson1	Viollet1	..
26 Nov	Cardiff C	A	L	0–3	..	Brennan	Cantwell	Setters	..	..	..	..	..	..	..
3 Dec	Preston NE	H	W	1–0	..	..	..	..	..	..	..	..	..1	Pearson..	
10 Dec	Fulham	A	D	4–4	..	..	..	..	..	..	..	..2	..	1	..1
17 Dec	Blackburn R	A	W	2–1	..	..	..	..	..	..	Quixall	Stiles	..	2	..
24 Dec	Chelsea	A	W	2–1	..	..	..	..	..	..	..	..	..1	..	..1
26 Dec	Chelsea	H	W	6–0	..	..	..	..	..	..2	..	..	..3	..	..1
31 Dec	Manchester C	H	W	5–1	..	..	..	..	..	..	..	..	3	..	..2
14 Jan	Tottenham H	H	W	2–0	..	..	..	..	..	..	..	..1	..	..1	..
21 Jan	Leicester C	A	L	0–6	Briggs	..	..	..	..	..	..	..	..	..	..
4 Feb	Aston Villa	H	D	1–1	Pinner	..	..	..	..	..	..	..	..	..	1
11 Feb	Wolverhampton W	A	L	1–2	..	..	..	..	..	..1	..	..	..	..	..
18 Feb	Bolton W	H	W	3–1	..	..	..	Stiles	..	Setters	Morgans	Quixall1	..2	..	..
25 Feb	Nottingham F	A	L	2–3	Gregg	..	..	Setters	..	Nicholson	..	..1	..	1	
4 Mar	Manchester C	A	W	3–1	..	..	..	..	..	Stiles	Moir	..	..1	..1	..1
11 Mar	Newcastle U	A	D	1–1	Pinner	..	..	..	..	..	..	..	Lawton	..	..1
18 Mar	Arsenal	H	W	1–1	Gaskell	..	..	..	..	..	..1	..	..	Dawson	..
25 Mar	Sheffield Wed	A	L	1–5	..	..	..	..	..	..	..	..	..	..	..1
31 Mar	Blackpool	A	L	0–2	..	..	..	..	..	..	..	..	..	..	..
1 Apr	Fulham	H	W	3–1	..	..	..	..	..	Nicholson	Giles	..1	Viollet1	..	..1
3 Apr	Blackpool	H	W	*2–0	..	..	..	..	..	..1	..	..	..	..	..
8 Apr	W B A	A	D	1–1	..	..	..	..	..	..	..	..	..	..1	..
12 Apr	Burnley	H	W	6–0	..	..	..	..	..	Stiles	..	..3	..3	..	Moir
15 Apr	Birmingham C	H	W	4–1	..	..	..	..	..	..	..	..1	..1	..2	..
22 Apr	Preston NE	A	W	4–2	..	Dunne A	Brennan	..2	..	..	..	..	..	..	Charlton2
29 Apr	Cardiff C	H	D	3–3	..	Brennan	Cantwell	..1	..	..	..	..	..	..	..2
	FA Cup														
7 Jan	Middlesbrough (3)	H	W	3–0	Gregg	Brennan	Cantwell1	Setters	Foulkes	Nicholson	Quixall	Stiles	Dawson2	Pearson	Charlton
28 Jan	Sheffield Wed (4)	A	D	1–1	Briggs	..	..1	..	..	..	Viollet	..	..	..	..
1 Feb	Sheffield Wed (4)R	H	L	2–7	..	..	..	..	..	..	Quixall	..	..1	..1	..
	Football League Cup														
19 Oct	Exeter C (1)	A	D	1–1	Gregg	Setters	Brennan	Stiles	Foulkes	Nicholson	Dawson1	Lawton	Viollet	Pearson	Scanlon
26 Oct	Exeter C (1R)	H	W	4–1	Gaskell	Dunne A	Carolan	..	Cope	..	..	Giles1	Quixall2	..1	..
2 Nov	Bradford C (2)	A	L	1–2	Gregg	Setters	Brennan	Bratt	Foulkes	..	..	..	Viollet1	..	..

1960–1961

Appearances (goals)

Bradley	4	
Brennan	41	
Briggs	1	
Cantwell	24	
Carolan	2	
Charlton	39	21
Cope	6	
Dawson	28	16
Dunne A	3	
Foulkes	40	
Gaskell	10	
Giles	23	2
Gregg	27	
Haydock	4	
Heron	1	
Lawton	1	
Moir	8	1
Morgans	2	
Nicholson	31	5
Pearson	27	7
Pinner	4	
Quixall	38	13
Scanlon	8	1
Setters	40	4
Stiles	26	2
Viollet	24	15
Own goals		1
Total 26 players	88	

Football League

	P	W	D	L	F:A	Pts	
Tottenham H	42	31	4	7	115:55	66	1st
Manchester U	42	18	9	15	88:76	45	7th

SEASON 1961–1962 FOOTBALL LEAGUE (DIVISION 1)

19 Aug	West Ham U	A	D	1–1	Gregg	Brennan	Cantwell	Stiles1	Foulkes	Setters	Quixall	Viollet	Herd	Pearson	Charlton
23 Aug	Chelsea	H	W	3–2	..	..	..	..	..	..	..	..	..1	..1	..1
26 Aug	Blackburn R	H	W	6–1	..	..	..	..	..	..1	..2	..	..2	..	1
30 Aug	Chelsea	A	L	0–2	..	..	..	..	..	..	..	..	..	..	..

1961–1962

Appearances (goals)

Bradley	6	
Brennan	41	2
Briggs	8	
Cantwell	17	2
Charlton	37	8
Chisnall	9	1
Dawson	4	2
Dunne A	28	
Foulkes	40	
Gaskell	21	
Giles	30	2
Gregg	13	
Haydock	1	
Herd	27	14
Lawton	20	6
McMillan	11	6
Moir	9	
Nicholson	17	
Pearson	17	1
Quixall	21	10
Setters	38	3
Stiles	34	7
Viollet	13	7
Own goals		1
Total 23 players	72	

Football League

	P	W	D	L	F:A	Pts	
Ipswich	42	24	8	10	93:67	56	1st
Manchester U	42	15	9	18	72:75	39	15th

2 Sep	Blackpool	A	W	3–2	..	..	..	..	..	..	Bradley	..2	..	..	..1
9 Sep	Tottenham H	H	W	1–0	..	..	..	..	..	..	Quixall1	..	..	..	..
16 Sep	Cardiff C	A	W	2–1	..	..	..	..	..	..	..1	..	Dawson1	..	..
18 Sep	Aston Villa	A	D	1–1	Gaskell	..	Dunne A	..1	..	..	..	..	Herd	..	..
23 Sep	Manchester C	H	W	*3–2	Gregg	..	..	..1	..	..	..	..1	..	..	..
30 Sep	Wolverhampton W	H	L	0–2	..	..	Cantwell	..	..	Lawton	..	Giles	Dawson	..	..
7 Oct	W B A	A	D	1–1	Gaskell	..	..	..	..	..	Moir	Quixall	1	Giles	..
14 Oct	Birmingham C	H	L	0–2	Gregg	..	..	..	Haydock	..	Bradley	Giles	..	Herd	Moir
21 Oct	Arsenal	A	L	1–5	..	..	..	Nicholson	Foulkes	..	Moir	..	Herd	Viollet1	Charlton
28 Oct	Bolton W	H	L	0–3	..	..	Dunne A	..	..	Setters	..	Quixall	..	..	..
4 Nov	Sheffield Wed	A	L	1–3	..	..	Cantwell	Stiles	..	..	Bradley	Giles	Viollet1	Charlton	McMillan
11 Nov	Leicester C	H	D	2–2	Gaskell	..	..	..	..	..	..	..1	..1	..	..
18 Nov	Ipswich T	A	L	1–4	..	..	Dunne A	..	..	..	..	..	Herd	..	
25 Nov	Burnley	H	L	1–4	..	..	..	..	..	..	..	..	..1	Quixall	Charlton
2 Dec	Everton	A	L	1–5	..	..	..	Nicholson	..	..	Chisnall	..	1	Lawton	..
9 Dec	Fulham	H	W	3–0	..	..	..	..	..	..	..	..	..2	..1	..
16 Dec	West Ham U	H	L	1–2	..	..	..	..	..	..	..	..	..1	..	..
26 Dec	Nottingham F	H	W	6–3	..	..1	..	..	..	..	..	..	1	..3	..1
13 Jan	Blackpool	H	L	0–1	..	..	..	..	..	..	..	..	..	..	..
15 Jan	Aston Villa	H	W	2–0	..	..	..	..	..	..	..	..	Quixall1	..	..1
20 Jan	Tottenham H	A	D	2–2	..	..	..	..	..	..	..	Stiles1	Lawton	Giles	..1
3 Feb	Cardiff C	H	W	3–0	..	..	..	..	..	..	..	1..	..1	1	..
10 Feb	Manchester C	A	W	2–0	..	..	..	Stiles	Setters	Nicholson	..1	Giles	Herd1	Lawton	..
24 Feb	W B A	H	W	4–1	Briggs	..	..	..	Foulkes	Setters1	Quixall1	..	..	..	..2
28 Feb	Wolverhampton W	A	D	2–2	..	..	..	Setters	..	Nicholson	..	Stiles	..1	..1	..
3 Mar	Birmingham C	A	D	1–1	..	..	..	Stiles	..	Setters	..	Giles	1	..	..
17 Mar	Bolton W	A	L	0–1	..	..	..	Nicholson	..	..	..	..	Lawton	Stiles	..
20 Mar	Nottingham F	A	L	0–1	..	..	..	..	..	..	..	..	..	..	Moir
24 Mar	Sheffield Wed	H	D	1–1	Gaskell	..	..	Stiles	..	..	Moir	..	Viollet	Lawton	Charlton1
4 Apr	Leicester C	A	L	3–4	..	Setters	..	..	..	Nicholson	..	Quixall1	Herd	..	McMillan2
7 Apr	Ipswich T	H	W	5–0	Briggs	Brennan	..	..1	..	Setters1	..	Giles	Quixall3	McMillan	Charlton
10 Apr	Blackburn R	A	L	0–3	Gaskell	..	..	..	..	..	..	..	Cantwell	Pearson	McMillan
14 Apr	Burnley	A	W	3–1	Briggs	..1	..	..	..	..	Giles	Pearson	..1	Herd1	..
16 Apr	Arsenal	H	L	2–3	..	..	Cantwell1	..	..	..	..	..	Herd	McMillan1	Charlton
21 Apr	Everton	H	D	1–1	Gaskell	..	Dunne A	..	..	..	..	..	Cantwell	Herd1	..
23 Apr	Sheffield U	H	L	0–1	..	..	..	..	..	..	..	..	Herd	McMillan	..
24 Apr	Sheffield U	A	W	3–2	..	..	..	Nicholson	..	..	..	..	McMillan2	Stiles1	..
28 Apr	Fulham	A	L	0–2	..	..	..	Setters	..	Nicholson	..	..	..	..	..
	FA Cup														
6 Jan	Bolton W (3)	H	W	2–1	Gaskell	Brennan	Dunne A	Nicholson1	Foulkes	Setters	Chisnall	Giles	Herd1	Lawton	Charlton
31 Jan	Arsenal (4)	H	W	1–0	..	..	..	..	..	..1	..	..	Stiles	Lawton	..
17 Feb	Sheffield Wed (5)	H	D	0–0	..	..	..	Setters	..	Nicholson	..		Herd	Lawton	..
21 Feb	Sheffield Wed (5R)	A	W	2–0	..	..	..	Stiles	..	Setters	Quixall	..1	..	..	..1
10 Mar	Preston NE (6)	A	D	0–0	..	..	..	Nicholson	..	..	Chisnall	..	Cantwell	..	..
14 Mar	Preston NE (6R)	H	W	2–1	..	..	..	Stiles	..	..	Quixall	..	Herd1	..	..1
31 Mar	Tottenham H (SF) (at Hillsborough)	N	L	1–3	..	Dunne A	Cantwell	..	..	..	..	..	..1	..	..

1962–1963

Appearances (goals)

Brennan	37	
Cantwell	25	1
Charlton	28	7
Chisnall	6	1
Crerand	19	
Dunne A	25	
Foulkes	41	
Gaskell	18	
Giles	36	4
Gregg	24	
Haydock	1	
Herd	37	19
Law	38	23
Lawton	12	
McMillan	4	
Moir	9	1
Nicholson	10	
Pearson	2	
Quixall	31	7
Setters	27	1
Stiles	31	2
Walker	1	
Own goals		1
Total 22 players	67	

Football League

	P	W	D	L	F:A	Pts	
Everton	42	25	11	6	84:42	61	1st
Manchester U	42	12	10	20	67:81	34	19th

SEASON 1962–1963 FOOTBALL LEAGUE (DIVISION 1)

18 Aug	W B A	H	D	2–2	Gaskell	Brennan	Dunne A	Stiles	Foulkes	Setters	Giles	Quixall	Herd1	Law1	Moir
22 Aug	Everton	A	L	1–3	..	..	..	..	..	..	..	Pearson	..	..	1
25 Aug	Arsenal	A	W	3–1	..	..	..	Nicholson	..	Lawton	..	Chisnall1	..2	..	..
29 Aug	Everton	H	L	0–1	..	..	..	..	..	..	..	..	..	..	..
1 Sep	Birmingham C	H	W	2–0	..	..	..	..	..	..	..1	..	..1	..	..
5 Sep	Bolton W	A	L	0–3	..	..	..	..	..	..	..	Quixall	..	..	..
8 Sep	Leyton O	A	L	0–1	..	..	..	..	..	..	Moir	Setters	..	..	McMillan
12 Sep	Bolton W	H	W	3–0	..	..	..	Stiles	..	Setters	Giles	Lawton	..2	..	Cantwell1
15 Sep	Manchester C	H	L	2–3	..	..	..	..	..	Nicholson	..	..	..	..2	..
22 Sep	Burnley	H	L	2–5	..	..	..	..		Lawton	..	Law 2	..	Pearson	Moir
29 Sep	Sheffield Wed	A	L	0–1	Gregg	..	..	..	..	..	..	..	Quixall	Chisnall	McMillan
6 Oct	Blackpool	A	D	2–2	..	..	..	..	..	Nicholson	..	..	Herd2	Lawton	..
13 Oct	Blackburn R	H	L	0–3	..	..	..	..	..	..	..	..	..	..	Charlton
20 Oct	Tottenham H	A	L	2–6	..	..	Cantwell	..	..	Setters	..	Quixall1	..1	Law	Charlton
27 Oct	West Ham U	H	W	3–1	..	..	..	..	..	..	..	..2	..	..1	..
3 Nov	Ipswich T	A	W	5–3	..	..	..	..	..	..	..	..1	..4	..	
10 Nov	Liverpool	H	D	3–3	..	..	..	..	..	..	..1	..	..	..4	..
17 Nov	Wolverhampton W	A	W	3–2	..	..	..	..	..	..	..	..	..1	..2	..
24 Nov	Aston Villa	H	D	2–2	..	..	..	..	..	..	..	..2	..	..	..
1 Dec	Sheffield U	A	D	1–1	..	..	..	..	..	..	..	..	..	Lawton	..1
8 Dec	Nottingham F	H	W	5–1	..	..	..	Nicholson	..	Lawton	..1	..	..2	Law1	..1
15 Dec	W B A	A	L	0–3	..	..	..	Stiles	..	Nicholson	..	..	..	..	Moir
26 Dec	Fulham	A	W	1–0	..	..	..	..	..	Setters	..	..	..	..	Charlton1
23 Feb	Blackpool	H	D	1–1	..	..	..	Crerand	..	..	..	..	..1	Chisnall	..
2 Mar	Blackburn R	A	D	2–2	..	..	..	..	..	..	..	..	..	Law1	..1
9 Mar	Tottenham H	H	L	0–2	..	..	..	..	..	Stiles	..	..	..	..	..
18 Mar	West Ham U	A	L	1–3	..	..	..	..	..	Setters	..	Stiles	..1	..	..
23 Mar	Ipswich T	H	L	0–1	..	..	..	..	..	..	..	Quixall	..	..	..
1 Apr	Fulham	H	L	0–2	..	..	Dunne A	..	..	..	..	Chisnall	Quixall	..	..
9 Apr	Aston Villa	A	W	2–1	..	..	Cantwell	..	..	..	..	Stiles1	Herd	Quixall	..1
13 Apr	Liverpool	A	L	0–1	..	..	Dunne A	..	..	..	..	..	Quixall	Law	..
15 Apr	Leicester C	H	D	2–2	..	..	..	..	..	..	Quixall	..	Herd1	..	..1
16 Apr	Leicester C	A	L	3–4	..	..	..	..	..	..	..	..	..	..3	..
20 Apr	Sheffield U	H	D	1–1	..	..	..	..	..	..	..	..	..	..1	..
22 Apr	Wolverhampton W	H	W	2–1	Gaskell	..	..	..	..	..	..	..	..1	..1	..
1 May	Sheffield Wed	H	L	1–3	..	..	Cantwell	..	..	..1	..	..	..	..	..
4 May	Burnley	A	W	1–0	..	Dunne A	..	..	..	..	Giles	..	Quixall	..1	..
6 May	Arsenal	H	L	2–3	..	..	..	..	..	..	..	..	..	..2	..
10 May	Birmingham C	A	L	1–2	..	..	..	..	..	Stiles	Quixall	Giles	Herd	..1	..
15 May	Manchester C	A	D	1–1	..	..	..	..	..	..	..1	..	..	..	..
18 May	Leyton O	H	W	*3–1	..	..	..	..	..	Setters	..	..	..	..1	..1
20 May	Nottingham F	A	L	2–3	..	..	..	..	Haydock	Brennan	..	Stiles	..	Giles	Walker
	FA Cup														
4 Mar	Huddersfield T (3)	H	W	5–0	Gregg	Brennan	Cantwell	Stiles	Foulkes	Setters	Giles1	Quixall1	Herd	Law3	Charlton
11 Mar	Aston Villa (4)	H	W	1–0	..	..	..	..	..	..	..	..1	..	..	..
16 Mar	Chelsea (5)	H	W	2–1	..	..	..	..	..	..	..	..1	..	..1	..
30 Mar	Coventry C (6)	A	W	3–1	..	..	Dunne A	Crerand	..	..	..	..1	..	..	..2
27 Apr	Southampton (SF) (at Villa Park)	N	W	1–0	Gaskell	Dunne A	Cantwell	..	..	..	..	Stiles	..	..1	..
25 May	Leicester C (F) (at Wembley)	N	W	3–1	..	..	..	..	..	..	..	Quixall	..2	..1	..

SEASON 1963–1964 FOOTBALL LEAGUE (DIVISION 1)

24 Aug	Sheffield Wed	A	D	3–3	Gregg	Dunne A	Cantwell	Crerand	Foulkes	Setters	Moir1	Chisnall	Sadler	Law	Charlton2
28 Aug	Ipswich T	H	W	2–0	..	..	..	..	..	..	..	..	..	..2	..
31 Aug	Everton	H	W	5–1	..	..	..	..	..	Stiles	..	..2	..1	..2	..
3 Sep	Ipswich T	A	W	7–2	..	..	..	..	..	Setters1	..1	..1	..1	..3	..
7 Sep	Birmingham C	A	D	1–1	..	..	..	..	..	..	..	..1	..	..	..

11 Sep	Blackpool	H	W	3–0	..	..	..	..	..	..	..	..	..	..1	..2
14 Sep	W B A	H	W	1–0	..	..	..	..	..	..	Best	Stiles	..1	Chisnall	..
16 Sep	Blackpool	A	L	0–1	..	..	..	..	..	..	Moir	..	..	..	..
21 Sep	Arsenal	A	L	1–2	..	..	..	..	..	..	Herd1	Chisnall	..	Law	..
28 Sep	Leicester C	H	W	3–1	..	..	..	..	..	..1	Moir	..	..	Herd2	..
2 Oct	Chelsea	A	D	1–1	..	..	..	..	..	..1	..	..	..	..	..
5 Oct	Bolton W	A	W	1–0	..	..	..	..	..	..	Herd1	..	..	Stiles	..
19 Oct	Nottingham F	A	W	2–1	..	..	..	..	..	..	Quixall1	..1	Herd	Law	..
26 Oct	West Ham U	H	L	0–1	..	..	..	..	..	..	Moir	..	..	..	..
28 Oct	Blackburn R	H	D	2–2	..	..	..	..	..	Stiles	..	..	Quixall2	..	..
2 Nov	Wolverhampton W	A	L	0–2	..	..	..	..	..	Setters	..	..	..	..	..
9 Nov	Tottenham H	H	W	4–1	..	..	..	..	..	..	Quixall	Moore	Herd1	..3	..
16 Nov	Aston Villa	A	L	0–4	..	..	..	..	..	..	..	..	..	..	..
23 Nov	Liverpool	H	L	0–1	..	..	..	..	..	..	..	..	..	..	..
30 Nov	Sheffield U	A	W	2–1	Gaskell	..	..	..	..	..	..	..	..	..2	..
7 Dec	Stoke C	H	W	5–2	..	..	..	..	..	..	..	..	..1	..4	..
14 Dec	Sheffield Wed	H	W	3–1	..	Brennan	Dunne A	..	..	..	Chisnall	..	Sadler	Herd3	..
21 Dec	Everton	A	L	0–4	..	Dunne A	Cantwell	..	..	..	Moir	..	..	..	..
26 Dec	Burnley	A	L	1–6	..	..	..	..	..	..	Quixall	..	Charlton	..1	Brennan
28 Dec	Burnley	H	W	5–1	..	..	..	..	..	..	Anderson	..2	..	..2	Best1
11 Jan	Birmingham C	H	L	1–2	..	..	..	..	..	..	Herd	..	Sadler1	Law	..
18 Jan	W B A	A	W	4–1	..	..	..	..	..	..	..	..	Charlton1	..2	..1
1 Feb	Arsenal	H	W	3–1	..	Brennan	Dunne A	Stiles	..	..1	..1	..	..	..1	..
8 Feb	Leicester C	A	L	2–3	..	..	..	Crerand	..	..	..1	..	..	..1	..
19 Feb	Bolton W	H	W	5–0	..	..	..	..	..	..	..2	Stiles	..1	..	..2
22 Feb	Blackburn R	A	W	3–1	..	..	..	..	..	..	..	Chisnall1	..	..2	..
7 Mar	West Ham U	A	W	2–0	..	..	..	..	Tranter	Stiles	Anderson	..	Sadler1	Herd1	Moir
21 Mar	Tottenham H	A	W	3–2	..	..	..	..	Foulkes	..	Best	Moore1	..	Law1	Charlton1
23 Mar	Chelsea	H	D	1–1	..	..	..	..	..	..	..	..	..	..1	..
27 Mar	Fulham	A	D	2–2	..	..	..	..	..	..	..	..	Herd1	..1	..
28 Mar	Wolverhampton W	H	D	2–2	Gregg	..	Cantwell	..	..	..	..	Chisnall	..1	Setters	..1
30 Mar	Fulham	H	W	3–0	..	..	Dunne A	..1	..1	..	Moir	Moore	..1	Law	..
4 Apr	Liverpool	A	L	0–3	..	..	..	..	..	Setters	Best	Stiles	..	..	..
6 Apr	Aston Villa	H	W	1–0	..	..	..	..	..	Stiles	..	Charlton	..	..1	Moir1
13 Apr	Sheffield U	H	W	2–1	..	..	Cantwell	..	..	..	..	..	..	..1	..1
18 Apr	Stoke C	A	L	1–3	..	..	Dunne A	..	..	..	..	..1	Sadler	Herd	..
25 Apr	Nottingham F	H	W	3–1	Gaskell	..	..	..	..	Setters	..	Moore1	Herd	Law2	Charlton
	FA Cup														
4 Jan	Southampton (3)	A	W	3–2	Gaskell	Dunne A	Cantwell	Crerand1	Foulkes	Setters	Anderson	Moore1	Charlton	Herd1	Best
25 Jan	Bristol R (4)	H	W	4–1	..	..	..	..	..	..	Herd1	Chisnall	..	Law3	..
15 Feb	Barnsley (5)	A	W	4–0	..	Brennan	Dunne A	..	..	..	..1	Stiles	..	..2	..1
29 Feb	Sunderland (6)	H	D	3–3	..	..	..	..	..	..	..	..	..1	..	..1
4 Mar	Sunderland (6R)	A	D	2–2	..	..	..	..	..	..	..	Chisnall	..1	..1	..
9 Mar	Sunderland (6R)	N	W	5–1	..	..	..	..	..	..	..1	..1	..	..3	..
	(at Huddersfield)														
14 Mar	West Ham U (SF)	N	L	1–3	..	..	..	..	..	..	..	..	..	..1	..
	(at Hillsborough)														
	European Cup Winners' Cup														
25 Sep	Willem II (1)	A	D	1–1	Gregg	Dunne A	Cantwell	Crerand	Foulkes	Setters	Herd1	Chisnall	Sadler	Law	Charlton
15 Oct	Willem II (1R)	H	W	6–1	..	..	..	..	..	..1	Quixall	..1	Herd	..3	..1
3 Dec	Tottenham H (2)	A	L	0–2	Gaskell	..	..	..	..	..	..	Stiles	..	..	..
10 Dec	Tottenham H (2)	H	W	4–1	..	..	..	..	..	..	..	Chisnall	Sadler	Herd2	..2
26 Feb	Sporting Lisbon (3)	H	W	4–1	..	Brennan	Dunne A	..	..	..	Herd	Stiles	Charlton1	Law3	Best
18 Mar	Sporting Lisbon (3)	A	L	0–5	..	..	..	..	..	..	..	Chisnall	..	..	..

1963–1964

Appearances (goals)

Anderson	2	
Best	17	4
Brennan	17	
Cantwell	28	
Charlton	40	9
Chisnall	20	6
Crerand	41	1
Dunne A	40	
Foulkes	41	1
Gaskell	17	
Gregg	25	
Herd	30	20
Law	30	30
Moir	18	3
Moore	18	4
Quixall	9	3
Sadler	19	5
Setters	32	4
Stiles	17	
Tranter	1	
Total 20 players	90	

Football League

	P	W	D	L	F:A	Pts	
Liverpool	42	26	5	11	92:45	57	1st
Manchester U	42	23	7	12	90:62	53	2nd

SEASON 1964–1965 FOOTBALL LEAGUE (DIVISION 1)

22 Aug	W B A	H	D	2–2	Gaskell	Brennan	Dunne A	Setters	Foulkes	Stiles	Connelly	Charlton1	Herd	Law1	Best
24 Aug	West Ham U	A	L	1–3	..	..	..	..	..	..	..	..	..	..1	..
29 Aug	Leicester C	A	D	2–2	..	..	..	Crerand	..	..	..	..	Sadler1	..1	..1
2 Sep	West Ham U	H	W	3–1	..	..	..	..	..	..	..1	..	..	..1	..
5 Sep	Fulham	A	L	1–2	..	..	..	..	..	..	..1	..	..	..	..
8 Sep	Everton	A	D	3–3	Dunne P	..	..	..	..	..	..1	..	Herd1	..1	..
12 Sep	Nottingham F	H	W	3–0	..	..	..	..	..	Setters	..1	..	..2	Stiles	..
16 Sep	Everton	H	W	2–1	..	..	..	..	..	Stiles	..	..	..	Law	..
19 Sep	Stoke C	A	W	2–1	..	..	..	..	..	Setters	..1	..	..1	Stiles	..
26 Sep	Tottenham H	H	W	4–1	..	..	..	..2	..	Stiles	..	..	..	Law2	..
30 Sep	Chelsea	A	W	2–0	..	..	..	..	..	..	..	..	..	..1	..1
6 Oct	Burnley	A	D	0–0	..	..	..	..	..	..	..	..	..	..	..
10 Oct	Sunderland	H	W	1–0	..	..	..	..	..	..	..	..	..1	..	..
17 Oct	Wolverhampton W	A	W	*4–2	..	..	..	..	..	..	..	..	..1	..2	..
24 Oct	Aston Villa	H	W	7–0	..	..	..	..	..	Setters	..1	Stiles	..2	..4	..
31 Oct	Liverpool	A	W	2–0	..	..	..	..1	..	Stiles	..	Charlton	..1	..	..
7 Nov	Sheffield Wed	H	W	1–0	..	..	..	..	..	..	..	..	..1	..	..
14 Nov	Blackpool	A	W	2–1	..	..	..	..	..	..	..1	..	..1	..	Moir
21 Nov	Blackburn R	H	W	3–0	..	..	..	..	..	..	..1	..	..1	..	Best1
28 Nov	Arsenal	A	W	3–2	..	..	..	..	..	..	..1	..	..	..2	..
5 Dec	Leeds U	H	L	0–1	..	..	..	..	..	..	..	..	..	..	..
12 Dec	W B A	A	D	1–1	..	..	..	..	..	..	..	..	..	..1	..
16 Dec	Birmingham C	H	D	1–1	..	..	..	..	..	..	..	..1	Sadler	Herd	..
26 Dec	Sheffield U	A	W	1–0	..	..	..	..	..	..	..	..	..	..	..1
28 Dec	Sheffield U	H	D	1–1	..	..	..	..	..	..	..	..	..	..1	..
16 Jan	Nottingham F	A	D	2–2	..	..	..	..	..	..	..	..	Herd	Law2	..
23 Jan	Stoke C	H	D	1–1	..	..	..	..	..	..	..	..	..	..1	..
6 Feb	Tottenham H	A	L	0–1	..	..	..	..	..	..	..	..	..	..	..
13 Feb	Burnley	H	W	3–2	..	..	..	..	..	..	..	..1	..1	..	..1
24 Feb	Sunderland	A	L	0–1	..	..	..	..	..	Fitzpatrick	..	..	..	..	..
27 Feb	Wolverhampton W	H	W	3–0	..	..	..	..	..	Stiles	..1	..2	..	..	..
13 Mar	Chelsea	H	W	4–0	..	..	..	..	..	..	..	..	..2	..1	..1
15 Mar	Fulham	H	W	4–1	..	..	..	..	..	..	..2	..	..2	..	..
20 Mar	Sheffield Wed	A	L	0–1	..	..	..	..	..	..	..	..	..	..	..
22 Mar	Blackpool	H	W	2–0	..	..	..	..	..	..	..	..	..	..2	..
3 Apr	Blackburn R	A	W	5–0	..	..	..	..	..	..	..1	..3	..1	..	..
12 Apr	Leicester C	H	W	1–0	..	..	..	..	..	..	..	..	..1	Best	Aston
17 Apr	Leeds U	A	W	1–0	..	..	..	..	..	..	..1	..	..	Law	Best
19 Apr	Birmingham C	A	W	4–2	..	..	..	..	..	..	..	..1	Cantwell1	..	..2
24 Apr	Liverpool	H	W	3–0	..	..	..	..	..	..	..1	..	..	..2	..
26 Apr	Arsenal	H	W	3–1	..	..	..	..	..	..	..	..	Herd	..2	..1
28 Apr	Aston Villa	A	L	1–2	..	..	..	Fitzpatrick	..	..	..	..1	..	..	..
	FA Cup														
9 Jan	Chester (3)	H	W	2–1	Dunne P	Brennan	Dunne A	Crerand	Foulkes	Stiles	Connelly	Charlton	Herd	Kinsey1	Best1
30 Jan	Stoke C (4)	A	D	0–0	..	..	..	..	..	..	..	..	..	Law	..
3 Feb	Stoke C (4R)	H	W	1–0	..	..	..	..	..	..	..	..	..1	..	..
20 Feb	Burnley (5)	H	W	2–1	..	..	..	..1	..	..	..	..	..	..1	..
10 Mar	Wolverhampton W (6)	A	W	5–3	..	..	..	..1	..	..	..	..	..1	..2	..1
27 Mar	Leeds U (SF)	N	D	0–0	..	..	..	..	..	..	..	..	..	..	..
	(at Hillsborough)														
31 Mar	Leeds U (SFR)	N	L	0–1	..	..	..	..	..	..	..	..	..	..	..
	(at City Ground)														

1964–1965

Appearances (goals)

Aston	1	
Best	41	10
Brennan	42	
Cantwell	2	1
Charlton	41	10
Connelly	42	15
Crerand	39	3
Dunne A	42	
Dunne P	37	
Fitzpatrick	2	
Foulkes	42	
Gaskell	5	
Herd	37	20
Law	36	28
Moir	1	
Sadler	6	1
Setters	5	
Stiles	41	
Own goals		1
Total 18 players	89	

Football League

	P	W	D	L	F:A	Pts	
Manchester U	42	26	9	7	89:39	61	1st

	Inter–Cities Fairs Cup															
23 Sep	Djurgaarden (1)	A	D	1–1	Dunne P	Brennan	Dunne A	Crerand	Foulkes	Stiles	Connelly	Charlton	Herd1	Setters	Best	
27 Oct	Djurgaarden (1)	H	W	6–1	..	..	..	..	..	..	..	..2	..	Law3	..1	
11 Nov	Borussia Dortmund (2)	A	W	6–1	..	..	..	..	..	..	..	..3	..1	..1	..1	
2 Dec	Borussia Dortmund (2)	H	W	4–1	..	..	..	..	..	..	..1	..2	..	..1	..	
20 Jan	Everton	H	D	1–1	..	..	..	..	..	..	..1	..	..	..	..	
9 Feb	Everton	A	W	2–1	..	..	..	..	..	..	..1	..	..1	..	..	
12 Mar	Racing Strasbourg (4)	A	W	5–0	..	..	..	..	..	..	..1	..1	..1	..2	..	
19 May	Racing Strasbourg (4)	H	D	0–0	..	..	..	..	..	..	..	..	..	..	..	
31 May	Ferencvaros (5)	H	W	3–2	..	..	..	..	..	..	..	..	..2	..1	..	
6 Jun	Ferencvaros (5)	A	L	0–1	..	..	..	..	..	..	..	..	..	..	..	
16 Jun	Ferencvaros (5)	A	L	1–2	..	..	..	..	..	..	..1	..	..	..	..	

1965–1966

Appearances (goals)

Anderson	23	4
Aston	22	4
Best	31	9
Brennan	28	
Cantwell	23	2
Charlton	38	16
Connelly	31	5
Crerand	41	
Dunne A	40	1
Dunne P	8	
Fitzpatrick	3	
Foulkes	33	
Gaskell	8	
Gregg	26	
Herd	36	24
Law	33	15
Noble	2	
Ryan	4	1
Sadler	10	4
Stiles	39	2
Own goals		1
Total 20 players	84	

Football League

	P	W	D	L	F:A	Pts	
Liverpool	42	26	9	7	79:34	61	1st
Manchester U	42	18	15	9	84:59	51	4th

SEASON 1965–1966 FOOTBALL LEAGUE (DIVISION 1)

21 Aug	Sheffield Wed	H	W	1–0	Dunne P	Brennan	Dunne A	Crerand	Foulkes	Stiles	Anderson	Charlton	Herd1	Best	Aston	
24 Aug	Nottingham F	A	L	2–4	..	..	..	..	..	..	Connelly	..	..	..1	..1	
28 Aug	Northampton T	A	D	1–1	Gaskell	Dunne A	Cantwell	..	..	..	..1	..	..	Law	Best	
1 Sep	Nottingham F	H	D	0–0	..	Brennan	Dunne A	..	..	..	..	..	..	..	..	
4 Sep	Stoke C	H	D	1–1	..	..	..	..	..	..	..	..	..1	..	..	
8 Sep	Newcastle U	A	W	2–1	..	..	..	..	..	..	..	..	..1	..1	..	
11 Sep	Burnley	A	L	0–3	..	..	..	..	..	..	..	..	..	..	..	
15 Sep	Newcastle U	H	D	1–1	..	..	..	..	..	..1	..	..	..	..	..	
18 Sep	Chelsea	H	W	4–1	..	..	..	..	..	..	..	..1	..	..3	Aston	
25 Sep	Arsenal	A	L	2–4	Dunne P	..	..	..	..	..	..	..1	..	..	..1	
9 Oct	Liverpool	H	W	2–0	..	..	..	..	..	..	..	Best1	Charlton	..1	..	
16 Oct	Tottenham H	A	L	1–5	..	..	..	..	..	..	..	..	..1	..	..	Fitzpatrick for Law
23 Oct	Fulham	H	W	4–1	..	..	..	..	..	..	..	..	..1	Herd3	..	
30 Oct	Blackpool	A	W	2–1	Gregg	..	..	..	..	..	..	..	..	..2	..	
6 Nov	Blackburn R	H	D	2–2	..	..	..	..	..	..	Best	Law1	..1	..	..	Connelly for Aston
13 Nov	Leicester C	A	W	5–0	..	Dunne A	Cantwell	..	..	..	..1	..	..1	..2	Connelly1	
20 Nov	Sheffield U	H	W	3–1	..	..	..	..	Sadler	..	..2	..1	..	..	..	
4 Dec	West Ham U	H	D	0–0	Dunne P	..	..	..	Foulkes	..	..	..	..	..	..	
11 Dec	Sunderland	A	W	3–2	..	..	..	..	..	..	..2	..	..	..1	..	
15 Dec	Everton	H	W	3–0	Gregg	..	..	..	..	..1	..	..	..1	..1	..	
18 Dec	Tottenham H	H	W	*5–1	..	..	..	..	..	..	..	..2	..1	..	..	
27 Dec	W B A	H	D	1–1	..	..	..	..	..	..	..	..1	..	..	..	
1 Jan	Liverpool	A	L	1–2	..	..	..	..	..	..	..	..1	..	..	..	
8 Jan	Sunderland	H	D	1–1	..	..	..	..	..	..	..1	..	..	..	Aston	
12 Jan	Leeds U	A	D	1–1	..	..	..	..	..	..	..	..	..	..1	..	
15 Jan	Fulham	A	W	1–0	..	..	..	..	..	..	..	..	..1	..	..	
29 Jan	Sheffield Wed	A	D	0–0	..	..	..	..	..	..	..	..	..	..	..	
5 Feb	Northampton T	H	W	6–2	..	..	..	..	..	..	..	..2	..3	..	Connelly1	
19 Feb	Stoke C	A	D	2–2	..	Brennan	Dunne A	..	..	..	Connelly1	Best	..	..1	Aston	
26 Feb	Burnley	H	W	4–2	..	..	..	..	..	..	Best	Law	..1	..3	Connelly	
12 Mar	Chelsea	A	L	0–2	..	..	..	..	..	..	..	..	..	..	..	
19 Mar	Arsenal	H	W	2–1	..	..	..	..	..	..1	..	..1	..	..	..	
6 Apr	Aston Villa	A	D	1–1	Gaskell	..	..	..	..	Fitzpatrick	Connelly	..	Anderson	Cantwell1	..	
9 Apr	Leicester C	H	L	1–2	Gregg	..	Noble	..	Sadler	Stiles	Best	Anderson	Charlton	Herd	..1	
16 Apr	Sheffield U	A	L	1–3	..	..	Cantwell	Fitzpatrick	Foulkes	..	Connelly	Sadler1	..	Aston		
25 Apr	Everton	A	D	0–0	..	..	Dunne A	Crerand	Cantwell	..	Anderson	Law	..	Charlton	..	
27 Apr	Blackpool	H	W	2–1	..	..	..	..	..	..	Connelly	..1	..	..1	..	
30 Apr	West Ham U	A	L	2–3	..	..	..	..	..1	..	..	..	..	..	..1	Herd for Dunne A
4 May	W B A	A	D	3–3	..	..	..1	..	..	Fitzpatrick	Ryan	..	..	Herd1	..1	Anderson for Fitzpatrick
7 May	Blackburn R	A	W	4–1	..	..	..	..	..	Stiles	..	Charlton1	..1	..2	..	
9 May	Aston Villa	H	W	6–1	..	..	..	..	..	..	..1	Herd2	..2	Charlton1	..	
19 May	Leeds U	H	D	1–1	..	..	Noble	..	..	Dunne A	..	..1	..	Law	..	
	FA Cup															
22 Jan	Derby Co	A	W	5–2	Gregg	Dunne A	Cantwell	Crerand	Foulkes	Stiles	Best2	Law2	Charlton	Herd1	Aston	
12 Feb	Rotherham U (4)	H	D	0–0	..	..	..	..	..	..	..	..	..	..	Connelly	
15 Feb	Rotherham U (4R)	A	W	1–0	..	Brennan	Dunne A	..	..	..	..	..	..	..	..1	
5 Mar	Wolverhampton W (5)	A	W	4–2	..	..	..	..	..	..	..1	..2	..	..1	..	
26 Mar	Preston NE (6)	A	D	1–1	..	..	..	..	..	..	..	..	..	..1	..	
30 Mar	Preston NE (6R)	H	W	3–1	..	..	..	..	..	..	Connelly1	..2	..	..	Aston	
23 Apr	Everton (SF) (at Burnden Park)	N	L	0–1	..	..	..	..	..	..	Anderson	..	..	..	Connelly	
	European Cup															
22 Sep	HJK Helsinki (P)	A	W	3–2	Gaskell	Brennan	Dunne A	Fitzpatrick	Foulkes	Stiles	Connelly1	Charlton	Herd1	Law1	Aston	
6 Oct	HJK Helsinki (P)	H	W	6–0	Dunne P	..	..	Crerand	..	..	..3	Best2	Charlton1	..	..	
17 Nov	ASK Vorwaerts (1)	A	W	2–0	Gregg	Dunne A	Cantwell	..	..	..	Best	Law1	..	Herd	Connelly	
1 Dec	ASK Vorwaerts (1)	H	W	3–1	Dunne P	..	..	..	..	..	..	..	..	..3	..	
2 Feb	Benfica (2)	H	W	3–2	Gregg	..	..	..	..1	..	..	..1	..	..1	..	
9 Mar	Benfica (2)	A	W	5–1	..	Brennan	Dunne A	..1	..	..	..2	..	..1	..	..1	
13 Apr	FK Partizan Belgrade (SF)	A	L	0–2	..	..	..	..	..	..	Anderson	..	..	..	..	
20 Apr	FK Partizan Belgrade (SF)	H	W	1–0	..	..	..	..	..	..1	..	..	..	..	..	

1966–1967

Appearances (goals)

Aston	26	5
Best	42	10
Brennan	16	
Cantwell	4	
Charlton	42	12
Connelly	6	2
Crerand	39	3
Dunne A	40	
Fitzpatrick	3	
Foulkes	33	4
Gaskell	5	
Gregg	2	
Herd	28	16
Law	36	23
Noble	29	
Ryan	4	
Sadler	35	5
Stepney	35	
Stiles	37	3
Own goals		1
Total 19 players	84	

Football League

	P	W	D	L	F:A	Pts	
Manchester U	42	24	12	6	84:45	60	1st

SEASON 1966–1967 FOOTBALL LEAGUE (DIVISION 1)

20 Aug	W B A	H	W	5–3	Gaskell	Brennan	Dunne A	Fitzpatrick	Foulkes	Stiles1	Best1	Law2	Charlton	Herd1	Connelly	
23 Aug	Everton	A	W	2–1	..	..	..	..	..	..	..	..2	..		..	
27 Aug	Leeds U	A	L	1–3	..	..	..	..	..	..	..1	..	..	..	..	
31 Aug	Everton	H	W	3–0	..	..	..	Crerand	..1	..	Connelly1	..1	..	..	Best	
3 Sep	Newcastle U	H	W	3–2	Gregg	..	..	..	..	..	..1	..1	..	..1	..	
7 Sep	Stoke C	A	L	0–3	..	..	..	..	..	..	..	..	..	..	..	
10 Sep	Tottenham H	A	L	1–2	Gaskell	..	..	..	..	..	Best	..1	Sadler	..	Charlton	Aston for Sadler
17 Sep	Manchester C	H	W	1–0	Stepney	..	..	..	..	..	..	..1	..	Charlton	Aston	
24 Sep	Burnley	H	W	4–1	..	..	..	..1	..	..	Herd1	..1	..1	..	Best	Aston for Law
1 Oct	Nottingham F	A	L	1–4	..	..	..	..	..	..	Best	Charlton1	..	Herd	Aston	
8 Oct	Blackpool	A	W	2–1	..	Dunne A	Noble	..	Cantwell	..	Herd	Law2	..	Charlton	Best	
15 Oct	Chelsea	H	D	1–1	..	..	..	..	..	..	..	..1	..	..	..	
29 Oct	Arsenal	H	W	1–0	..	..	..	..	..	..	..	..	..1	..	..	
5 Nov	Chelsea	A	W	3–1	..	Brennan	..	..	Foulkes	..	..	Aston2	..	..	..1	
12 Nov	Sheffield Wed	H	W	2–0	..	Dunne A	..	..	..	..	..1	Law	..	..1	..	Aston for Foulkes
19 Nov	Southampton	A	W	2–1	..	..	..	..	Cantwell	..	..	..	..2	..	..	Aston for Cantwell
26 Nov	Sunderland	H	W	5–0	..	..	..	..	Sadler	..	Best	..1	Charlton	Herd4	Aston	
30 Nov	Leicester C	A	W	2–1	..	..	..	..	..	..	..1	..1	..	..	..	
3 Dec	Aston Villa	A	L	1–2	..	..	..	..	..	..	..	..	..	..1	..	
10 Dec	Liverpool	H	D	2–2	..	Brennan	..	..	..	Dunne A	..2	Ryan	..	..	..	Anderson for Dunne A
17 Dec	W B A	A	W	4–3	..	..	..	..	..	Stiles	..	Law1	..	..3	..	
26 Dec	Sheffield U	A	L	1–2	..	Dunne A	..	..	Foulkes	Sadler	..	..	..	..1	..	
27 Dec	Sheffield U	H	W	2–0	..	..	..	..1	..	..	..	..	..	..1	..	
31 Dec	Leeds U	H	D	0–0	..	..	..	..	..	..	..	..	..	..	..	
14 Jan	Tottenham H	H	W	1–0	..	..	..	..	..	..	..	Ryan	..	..1	..	
21 Jan	Manchester C	A	D	1–1	..	..	..	..	..1	Stiles	Ryan	Charlton	Sadler	..	Best	
4 Feb	Burnley	A	D	1–1	..	..	..	..	..	..	Best	Law	..1	..	Charlton	
11 Feb	Nottingham F	H	W	1–0	..	..	..	..	..	..	..	..1	..	..	..	Ryan for Foulkes
25 Feb	Blackpool	H	W	*4–0	..	..	..	..	..	..	..	..1	..	Charlton2	Aston	

3 Mar	Arsenal	A	D	1–1	..	..	..	..	..	..	..	..	..	..	..1	
11 Mar	Newcastle U	A	D	0–0	..	..	..	..	..	..	..	..	..	..	..	
18 Mar	Leicester C	H	W	5–2	..	..	..	..	..	..	..	..1	Charlton1	Herd1	..1	Sadler1 for Herd
25 Mar	Liverpool	A	D	0–0	..	..	..	..	..	..	..	..	Sadler	Charlton	..	
27 Mar	Fulham	A	D	2–2	..	..	..	..	..	..1	..1	..	..	..	..	
28 Mar	Fulham	H	W	2–1	..	..	..	..	..1	..1	..	..	..	..	..	
1 Apr	West Ham U	H	W	3–0	..	..	..	..	..	..	..1	..1	..	..1	..	
10 Apr	Sheffield Wed	A	D	2–2	..	..	..	..	..	..	..	..	..	..2	..	
18 Apr	Southampton	H	W	3–0	..	..	..	..	..	..	..	..1	..1	..1	..	
22 Apr	Sunderland	A	D	0–0	..	..	..	..	..	..	..	..	..	..	..	
29 Apr	Aston Villa	H	W	3–1	..	Brennan	Dunne A	..	..	..	..1	..1	..	..	..1	
6 May	West Ham U	A	W	6–1	..	..	..	..1	..1	..	..1	..2	..	..1	..	
13 May	Stoke C	H	D	0–0	..	..	..	..	..	..	..	Ryan	..	..	..	
	FA Cup															
28 Jan	Stoke C (3)	H	W	2–0	Stepney	Dunne A	Noble	Crerand	Foulkes	Stiles	Best	Law1	Sadler	Herd1	Charlton	
18 Feb	Norwich C (4)	H	L	1–2	..	..	..	..	Sadler	..	Ryan	..1	Charlton	..	Best	
	Football League Cup															
14 Sep	Blackpool (2)	A	L	1–5	Dunne P	Brennan	Dunne A	Crerand	Foulkes	Stiles	Connelly	Best	Sadler	Herd1	Aston	

SEASON 1967–1968 FOOTBALL LEAGUE (DIVISION 1)

19 Aug	Everton	A	L	1–3	Stepney	Brennan	Dunne A	Crerand	Foulkes	Stiles	Best	Law	Charlton1	Kidd	Aston	Sadler for Crerand
23 Aug	Leeds U	H	W	1–0	..	..	..	..	..	..	Ryan	..	..1	..	..	
26 Aug	Leicester C	H	D	1–1	..	..	..	Sadler	..1	..	Best	..	..	..	..	
2 Sep	West Ham U	A	W	3–1	..	Dunne A	Burns	Crerand	..	..	Ryan1	Sadler1	..	..1	Best	
6 Sep	Sunderland	A	D	1–1	..	..	..	..	..	..	..	..	..	..1	..	Fitzpatrick for Stiles
9 Sep	Burnley	H	D	2–2	..	..	..1	..1	..	Fitzpatrick	..	..	..	..	..	Kopel for Fitzpatrick
16 Sep	Sheffield Wed	A	D	1–1	..	..	..	..	..	Stiles	Best1	..	..	Law	Kidd	
23 Sep	Tottenham H	H	W	3–1	..	..	..	..	..	..	..2	..	..	..1	..	
30 Sep	Manchester C	A	W	2–1	..	..	..	..	..	..	..	..	..2	..	..	Aston for Foulkes
7 Oct	Arsenal	H	W	1–0	..	..	..	..	Sadler	..	..	Kidd	..	..	Aston1	
14 Oct	Sheffield U	A	W	3–0	..	..	..	..	..	..	..	..1	..	..1	..1	Fitzpatrick for Stiles
25 Oct	Coventry C	H	W	4–0	..	..	..	..	..	Fitzpatrick	..1	..	..1	..	..2	
28 Oct	Nottingham F	A	L	1–3	..	Kopel	..	..	..	..	..1	..	..	..	..	
4 Nov	Stoke C	H	W	1–0	..	Dunne A	..	..	Foulkes	Sadler	Ryan	..	..1	Best	..	
8 Nov	Leeds U	A	L	0–1	..	..	..	..	..	..	..	..	..	..	..	Fitzpatrick for Ryan
11 Nov	Liverpool	A	W	2–1	..	..	..	..	..	..	Fitzpatrick	..	..	..2	..	
18 Nov	Southampton	H	W	3–2	..	..	..	..	..	..	..	..1	..1	..	..1	
25 Nov	Chelsea	A	D	1–1	..	Brennan	Dunne A	..	..	..	Burns	..1	..	..	..	
2 Dec	W B A	H	W	2–1	..	..	..	..	..	..	..	..	..	..2	..	
9 Dec	Newcastle U	A	D	2–2	..	..	..1	..	..	..	..	..1	..	..	..	
16 Dec	Everton	H	W	3–1	..	Dunne A	Burns	..	..	..1	Best	..	..	Law1	..1	
23 Dec	Leicester C	A	D	2–2	..	..	..	..	..	..	..	..	..1	..1	..	
26 Dec	Wolverhampton W	H	W	4–0	..	..	..	..	..	..	..2	..1	..1	..	..	
30 Dec	Wolverhampton W	A	W	3–2	..	..	..	..	..	..	..	..1	..1	..	..1	
6 Jan	West Ham U	H	W	3–1	..	..	..	..	Sadler	Fitzpatrick	..1	..	..1	..	..1	
20 Jan	Sheffield Wed	H	W	4–2	..	..	..	..	..	..	..2	..1	..1	..	..	
3 Feb	Tottenham H	A	W	2–1	..	..	..	..	..	..	..1	..	..1	Herd	..	
17 Feb	Burnley	A	L	1–2	..	..	..	..	..	Stiles	..1	..	..	Law	..	
24 Feb	Arsenal	A	W	*2–0	..	..	..	..	..	..	..1	..	Fitzpatrick	..	..	
2 Mar	Chelsea	H	L	1–3	..	..	..	..	..	..	..	..1	Charlton	Ryan	..	
16 Mar	Coventry C	A	L	0–2	..	Brennan	..	..	..	..	..	..	..	Fitzpatrick	Herd	Aston for Kidd
23 Mar	Nottingham F	H	W	3–0	..	..1	..1	..	..	..	Fitzpatrick	Herd1	..	Best	Aston	
27 Mar	Manchester C	H	L	1–3	..	..	..	..	..	..	..	Law	..	..1	Herd	Aston for Herd
30 Mar	Stoke C	A	W	4–2	..	..	..	..	..	Fitzpatrick	Best1	Gowling1	..	Herd	Aston1	Ryan1 for Gowling
6 Apr	Liverpool	H	L	1–2	..	Dunne A	..	..	..	..	..1	..	..	..	..	
12 Apr	Fulham	A	W	4–0	..	..	..	..	..	Stiles	..2	Kidd1	..	Law1	..	
13 Apr	Southampton	A	D	2–2	..	..	..	..	Foulkes	Sadler	..1	..	..1	Gowling	..	
15 Apr	Fulham	H	W	3–0	Rimmer	..	..	..	..	..	..1	..	..1	Law	..1	
20 Apr	Sheffield U	H	W	1–0	Stepney	Brennan	Dunne A	..	Sadler	Stiles	..	..	..	..1	..	
27 Apr	W B A	A	L	3–6	..	Dunne A	Burns	..	..	..	..	..2	..	..1	..	
4 May	Newcastle U	H	W	6–0	..	Brennan	Dunne A	..	Foulkes	Sadler1	..3	..2	..	Gowling	..	
11 May	Sunderland	H	L	1–2	..	..	..	..	..	Stiles	..1	..	..	Sadler	..	Gowling for Foulkes
	FA Cup															
27 Jan	Tottenham H (3)	H	D	2–2	Stepney	Dunne A	Burns	Crerand	Sadler	Fitzpatrick	Best1	Kidd	Charlton1	Law	Aston	
31 Jan	Tottenham H (3R)	A	L	0–1	..	..	..	..	..	..	..	..	..	Herd	..	
	European Cup															
20 Sep	Hibernians (Malta) (1)	H	W	4–0	Stepney	Dunne A	Burns	Crerand	Foulkes	Stiles	Best	Sadler2	Charlton	Law2	Kidd	
27 Sep	Hibernians (1)	A	D	0–0	..	..	..	..	..	..	..	..	..	..	..	
15 Nov	FK Sarajevo (2)	A	D	0–0	..	..	..	..	..	Sadler	Fitzpatrick	Kidd	..	Best	Aston	
29 Nov	FK Sarajevo (2)	H	W	2–1	..	Brennan	Dunne A	..	..	..	Burns	..	..	..1	..1	
28 Feb	Gornik Zabrze (3)	H	W	*2–0	..	Dunne A	Burns	..	Sadler	Stiles	Best	..1	..	Ryan	..	
13 Mar	Gornik Zabrze (3)	A	L	0–1	..	..	..	..	..	..	Fitzpatrick	Charlton	Herd	Kidd	Best	
24 Apr	Real Madrid (SF)	H	W	1–0	..	..	..	..	..	..	Best1	Kidd	Charlton	Law	Aston	
15 May	Real Madrid (SF)	A	D	*3–3	..	Brennan	Dunne A	..	Foulkes1	..	..	..	..	Sadler1	..	
29 May	Benfica (F) (at Wembley)	N	W	4–1	..	..	..	..	..	..	..1	..1	..2	..	..	

1967–1968

Appearances (goals)

Aston	34	10
Best	41	28
Brennan	13	1
Burns	36	2
Charlton	41	15
Crerand	41	1
Dunne A	37	1
Fitzpatrick	14	
Foulkes	24	1
Gowling	4	1
Herd	6	1
Kidd	34	15
Kopel	1	
Law	23	7
Rimmer	1	
Ryan	7	2
Sadler	40	3
Stepney	41	
Stiles	20	
Own goals		1
Total 19 players	89	

Football League

	P	W	D	L	F:A	Pts	
Manchester C	42	26	6	10	86:43	58	1st
Manchester U	42	24	8	10	89:55	55	2nd

SEASON 1968–1969 FOOTBALL LEAGUE (DIVISION 1)

10 Aug	Everton	H	W	2–1	Stepney	Brennan	Dunne A	Crerand	Foulkes	Stiles	Best1	Kidd	Charlton1	Law	Aston	
14 Aug	W B A	A	L	1–3	..	..	..	..	..	..	..	..	..1	..	..	Sadler for Foulkes
17 Aug	Manchester C	A	D	0–0	..	Kopel	..	Fitzpatrick	Sadler	..	..	Gowling	..	Kidd	..	Burns for Aston
21 Aug	Coventry C	H	W	1–0	..	..	..	..	..	..	Ryan1	Kidd	..	Burns	Best	
24 Aug	Chelsea	H	L	0–4	..	..	..	Crerand	..	..	..	..	..	..	..	
28 Aug	Tottenham H	H	W	3–1	..	Brennan	..	Fitzpatrick2	..	..	Morgan	..	..	Law	..	
31 Aug	Sheffield Wed	A	L	4–5	..	..	..	..	..	..	..	..	..1	..2	..1	Burns for Dunne A
7 Sep	West Ham U	H	D	1–1	..	Dunne A	Burns	..	Foulkes	..	..	Sadler	..	..1	..	
14 Sep	Burnley	A	L	0–1	..	..	..	..	..	..	..	..	..	..	..	
21 Sep	Newcastle U	H	W	3–1	..	..	..	Crerand	Sadler	..	..	Fitzpatrick	..	..1	..2	Kidd for Crerand
5 Oct	Arsenal	H	D	0–0	..	..	..	..	Foulkes	..	..	..	..	..	..	
9 Oct	Tottenham H	A	D	2–2	..	..	..	..1	..	..	..	..	..	..1	..	Sartori for Burns
12 Oct	Liverpool	A	L	0–2	..	Brennan	Kopel	..	James	..	Ryan	..	..	Gowling	Sartori	
19 Oct	Southampton	H	L	1–2	..	Kopel	Dunne A	..	Foulkes	..	Morgan	Sadler	..	Sartori	Best1	Fitzpatrick for Foulkes
26 Oct	Q P R	A	W	3–2	..	Brennan	..	..	Sadler	..	..	Kidd	..	Law1	..2	
2 Nov	Leeds U	H	D	0–0	..	..	..	..	..	..	..	..	..	..	..	
9 Nov	Sunderland	A	D	1–1	..	..	..	..	..	..	..	..	..	Sartori	..	
16 Nov	Ipswich T	H	D	0–0	..	..	..	..	James	..	..	..	..	..	..	Kopel for Kidd
23 Nov	Stoke C	A	D	0–0	..	Kopel	..	..	..	..	..	Best	..	Fitzpatrick	Sartori	
30 Nov	Wolverhampton W	H	W	2–0	..	..	..	..	Sadler	..	..	Sartori	..	Law1	Best1	Fitzpatrick for Stiles
7 Dec	Leicester C	A	L	1–2	..	Dunne A	Burns	..	..	..	..	..	..	..1	..	
14 Dec	Liverpool	H	W	1–0	..	..	..	..	James	..	Best	Sadler	..	..1	Sartori	
21 Dec	Southampton	A	L	0–2	..	..	..	..	..	..	..	..	..	..	..	
26 Dec	Arsenal	A	L	0–3	..	..	..	..	..	..	..	..	..	..	Kidd	Sartori for Crerand
11 Jan	Leeds U	A	L	1–2	..	..	..	..	..	..	..	Fitzpatrick	..1	..	Sartori	
18 Jan	Sunderland	H	W	4–1	Rimmer	..	..	Fitzpatrick	..	..	Morgan	Sartori	..	..3	Best1	
1 Feb	Ipswich T	A	L	0–1	Stepney	Fitzpatrick	Dunne A	Crerand	..	..	..	Kidd	..	..	..	
15 Feb	Wolverhampton W	A	D	2–2	..	..	..	..	..	Sadler	..	..	..1	Sartori	..1	Foulkes for Sartori
8 Mar	Manchester C	H	L	0–1	..	Brennan	Fitzpatrick	..	Foulkes	Stiles	..	..	..	Sadler	..	

1968–1969

Appearances (goals)

Aston	13	2
Best	41	19
Brennan	13	
Burns	14	
Charlton	32	5
Crerand	35	1
Dunne A	33	
Fitzpatrick	28	3
Foulkes	10	
Gowling	2	
James	21	1
Kidd	28	1
Kopel	7	
Law	30	14
Morgan	29	6
Rimmer	4	
Ryan	6	1
Sadler	26	
Sartori	11	
Stepney	38	
Stiles	41	1
Own goals		3
Total 21 players	57	

Football League

	P	W	D	L	F:A	Pts	
Leeds U	42	27	13	2	66:26	67	1st
Manchester U	42	15	12	15	57:53	42	11th

10 Mar	Everton	A	D	0–0	..	..	Dunne A	..	James	..	Best	..	Fitzpatrick	..	Aston	Foulkes for Brennan
15 Mar	Chelsea	A	L	2–3	..	Fitzpatrick	..	..	..1	..	Morgan	..	Sadler	Law1	Best	
19 Mar	Q P R	H	W	8–1	..	..	..	..	..	..1	..3	..1	Aston1	..	..2	
22 Mar	Sheffield Wed	H	W	1–0	..	..	..	..	..	..	..	..	Best1	..	Aston	
24 Mar	Stoke C	H	D	1–1	..	..	..	..	..	..	..	..	Aston1	..	Best	Sadler for Morgan
29 Mar	West Ham U	A	D	0–0	..	..	..	..	..	..	Ryan	..	..	..	..	Sadler for Dunne A
31 Mar	Nottingham F	A	W	1–0	..	..	Stiles	..	..	Sadler	..	..	..	..	..1	
2 Apr	W B A	H	W	2–1	..	..	..	..	..	..	Morgan	Ryan	..	Kidd	..2	Foulkes for Ryan
5 Apr	Nottingham F	H	W	3–1	..	..	..	..	..	..	..2	Kidd	..	Law	..1	
8 Apr	Coventry C	A	L	1–2	..	..1	..	..	..	..	..	..	..	Charlton	..	
12 Apr	Newcastle U	A	L	0–2	Rimmer	..	..	..	..	..	..	..	Charlton	Law	..	
19 Apr	Burnley	H	W	*2–0	..	Brennan	Fitzpatrick	..	Foulkes	Stiles	..	..	Aston	..	..1	
17 May	Leicester C	H	W	3–2	..	..	Burns	..	..	..	..1	..	Charlton	..1	..1	
	FA Cup															
4 Jan	Exeter C (3)	A	W	*3–1	Stepney	Dunne A	Burns	Fitzpatrick1	James	Stiles	Best	Kidd1	Charlton	Law	Sartori	Sadler for Best
25 Jan	Watford (4)	H	D	1–1	Rimmer	Kopel	Dunne A	..	..	..	Morgan	Best	..	..1	..	
3 Feb	Watford (4R)	A	W	2–0	Stepney	Fitzpatrick	..	Crerand	..	..	..	Kidd	..	..2	Best	
8 Feb	Birmingham C (5)	A	D	2–2	..	..	..	..	..	..	..	..	..	..1	..1	
24 Feb	Birmingham C (5R)	H	W	6–2	..	..	..	..1	..	..	..1	..1	..	..3	..	
1 Mar	Everton (6)	H	L	0–1	..	..	..	..	..	..	..	..	..	..	..	
	European Cup															
18 Sep	Waterford (1)	A	W	3–1	Stepney	Dunne A	Burns	Crerand	Foulkes	Stiles	Best	Law3	Charlton	Sadler	Kidd	Rimmer for Stepney
2 Oct	Waterford (1)	H	W	7–1	..	..	..1	..	..	..1	..	..4	..1	..	..	
13 Nov	RSC Anderlecht (2)	H	W	3–0	..	Brennan	Dunne A	..	Sadler	..	Ryan	Kidd1	..	Law2	Sartori	
27 Nov	RSC Anderlecht (2)	A	L	1–3	..	Kopel	..	..	Foulkes	..	Fitzpatrick	Law	..	Sadler	..1	
26 Feb	Rapid Vienna (3)	H	W	3–0	..	Fitzpatrick	..	..	James	..	Morgan1	Kidd	..	Law	Best2	
5 Mar	Rapid Vienna (3)	A	D	0–0	..	..	..	..	..	..	..	..	..	Sadler	..	
23 Nov	AC Milan (SF)	A	L	0–2	Rimmer	Brennan	Fitzpatrick	..	Foulkes	..	..	..	..	Law	..	Burns for Stiles
15 May	AC Milan (SF)	H	W	1–0	..	..	Burns	..	..	..	..	..	..1	..	..	
	World Club Championship															
25 Sep	Estudiantes	A	L	0–1	Stepney	Dunne A	Burns	Crerand	Foulkes	Stiles	Morgan	Sadler	Charlton	Law	Best	
16 Oct	Estudiantes	H	D	1–1	..	Brennan	Dunne A	..	..	Sadler	..1	Kidd	..	..	..	Sartori for Law

1969–1970

Appearances (goals)

Aston	21	1
Best	37	15
Brennan	8	
Burns	30	3
Charlton	40	12
Crerand	25	1
Dunne A	33	
Edwards	18	
Fitzpatrick	20	3
Foulkes	3	
Givens	4	1
Gowling	6	3
James	2	
Kidd	33	12
Law	10	2
Morgan	35	7
Rimmer	5	
Sadler	40	2
Sartori	13	2
Stepney	37	
Stiles	8	
Ure	34	1
Own goals		1
Total 22 players	66	

Football League

	P	W	D	L	F:A	Pts	
Everton	42	29	8	5	72:34	66	1st
Manchester U	42	14	17	11	66:61	45	8th

SEASON 1969–1970 FOOTBALL LEAGUE (DIVISION 1)

9 Aug	Crystal Palace	A	D	2–2	Rimmer	Dunne A	Burns	Crerand	Foulkes	Sadler	Morgan1	Kidd	Charlton1	Law	Best	Givens for Dunne A
13 Aug	Everton	H	L	0–2	..	Brennan	..	..	..	..	..	..	..	..	..	Givens for Foulkes
16 Aug	Southampton	H	L	1–4	..	..	..	..	..	..	..1	..	..	..	..	
19 Aug	Everton	A	L	0–3	Stepney	Fitzpatrick	..	..	Edwards	..	..	..	Givens	Best	Aston	
23 Aug	Wolverhampton W	A	D	0–0	..	..	..	..	Ure	..	..	..	Charlton	Law	Best	Givens for Law
27 Aug	Newcastle U	H	D	0–0	..	..	Dunne A	..	..	..	..	..	..	Givens	..	
30 Aug	Sunderland	H	W	3–1	..	..	..	..	..	..	..	..1	..	..1	..1	
6 Sep	Leeds U	A	D	2–2	..	..	..	Burns	..	..	..	Givens	..	Gowling	..2	
13 Sep	Liverpool	H	W	1–0	..	..	..	..	..	..	..1	Kidd	..	..	..	
17 Sep	Sheffield Wed	A	W	3–1	..	..	..	..	..	..	..	..1	..	..	..2	Aston for Gowling
20 Sep	Arsenal	A	D	2–2	..	..	..	..	..	..1	..	..	..	Aston	..1	
27 Sep	West Ham U	H	W	5–2	..	..	..	..1	..	..	..	..1	..1	..	..2	
4 Oct	Derby Co	A	L	0–2	..	..	..	..	..	..	..	..	..	..	..	Sartori for Aston
8 Oct	Southampton	A	W	3–0	..	..	..	..1	..	..	..	..1	..	..	..1	
11 Oct	Ipswich T	H	W	2–1	..	..	..	..	..	..	..	..1	..	..	..1	Brennan for Best
18 Oct	Nottingham F	H	D	1–1	..	..	..	..	..	..	..	..	..	..	..1	
25 Oct	W B A	A	L	1–2	..	Brennan	..	..	..	..	Sartori	..1	..	..	..	Givens for Aston
1 Nov	Stoke C	H	D	1–1	..	..	..	..	..	..	Law	..	..1	..	..	
8 Nov	Coventry C	A	W	2–1	..	..	..	..	..	..	Sartori	Best	..	Law1	Aston1	
15 Nov	Manchester C	A	L	0–4	..	..	..	..	..	..	..	..	..	..	..	Kidd for Sartori
22 Nov	Tottenham H	H	W	3–1	..	Fitzpatrick	..	..1	..	..	..	Kidd	..2	Best	..	Edwards for Fitzpatrick
29 Nov	Burnley	A	D	1–1	..	Edwards	..	..	..	..	Best1	..	..	Stiles	..	
6 Dec	Chelsea	H	L	0–2	..	..	..	..	..	..	..	..	..	..	..	Ryan for Kidd
13 Dec	Liverpool	A	W	*4–1	..	Brennan	..	..	..1	..	Morgan1	Best	..1	Crerand	..	Sartori for Aston
26 Dec	Wolverhampton W	H	D	0–0	..	Edwards	..	..	..	..	..	Crerand	..	Kidd	Best	
27 Dec	Sunderland	A	D	1–1	..	..	Brennan	..	..	..	..	..	..	..1	..	
10 Jan	Arsenal	H	W	2–1	..	..	Dunne A	..	..	..	..1	..	..	..	Aston	Sartori1 for Dunne A
17 Jan	West Ham U	A	D	0–0	Rimmer	..	Burns	Crerand	..	..	..	Sartori	..	..	..	
26 Jan	Leeds U	H	D	2–2	Stepney	..	..	..	..	..1	..	..	..	..1	..	
31 Jan	Derby C	H	W	1–0	..	..	..	..	..	..	..	..	..1	..	..	..
10 Feb	Ipswich T	A	W	1–0	..	..	Dunne A	..	..	..	..	..	..	..1	Best	
14 Feb	Crystal Palace	H	D	1–1	..	..	..	..	..	..	..	..	..	..1	..	
28 Feb	Stoke C	A	D	2–2	..	..	..	..	..	..	..1	..1	..	..	..	Burns for Sadler
17 Mar	Burnley	H	D	3–3	Rimmer	..	..	..1	..	..	..	..	..	Law1	..1	
21 Mar	Chelsea	A	L	1–2	Stepney	..	Burns	..	..	Stiles	..1	..	..	..	..	
28 Mar	Manchester C	H	L	1–2	..	..	Dunne A	..	Sadler	Burns	..	..	..	Kidd1	..	Law for Sartori
30 Mar	Coventry C	H	D	1–1	..	..	..	Fitzpatrick	Ure	Sadler	..	Best	Law	..1	Aston	Burns for Kidd
31 Mar	Nottingham F	A	W	2–1	..	Stiles	..	Crerand	James	..	..	Fitzpatrick	Charlton1	Gowling	Best	
4 Apr	Newcastle U	A	L	1–5	..	Fitzpatrick	..	..	..	..	..	Gowling	..1	Stiles	Aston	Sartori for Aston
8 Apr	W B A	H	W	7–0	..	Stiles	..	..	Ure	..	..	Fitzpatrick2	..2	Gowling2	Best1	
13 Apr	Tottenham H	A	L	1–2	..	Edwards	..	..	..	Stiles	..	..1	..	Kidd	..	Gowling for Morgan
15 Apr	Sheffield Wed	H	D	2–2	..	..	..	..	Sadler	..	..	..	..1	..	..1	
	FA Cup															
3 Jan	Ipswich T (3)	A	W	*1–0	Stepney	Edwards	Brennan	Burns	Ure	Sadler	Morgan	Crerand	Charlton	Kidd	Best	Aston for Morgan
24 Jan	Manchester C (4)	H	W	3–0	..	..	Burns	Crerand	..	..	..1	Sartori	..	..2	Aston	
7 Feb	Northampton T (5)	A	W	8–2	..	..	Dunne A	..	..	..	..	..	..	..2	Best6	Burns for Charlton
21 Feb	Middlesbrough (6)	A	D	1–1	..	..	..	..	..	..	..	..1	..	..	..	
25 Feb	Middlesbrough (6R)	H	W	2–1	..	Dunne A	Burns	..	..	..	..1	..	..1	..	..	
14 Mar	Leeds U (SF) (at Hillsborough)	N	D	0–0	..	Edwards	Dunne A	..	..	..	..	..	..	..	..	
23 Mar	Leeds U (SFR) (at Villa Park)	N	D	0–0	..	..	..	..	Sadler	Stiles	..	..	..	..	..	Law for Sartori
26 Mar	Leeds U (SFR) (at Burnden Park)	N	L	0–1	..	..	..	..	..	..	..	..	..	..	..	Law for Sartori
10 Apr	Watford (playoff) (at Highbury)	N	W	2–0	..	Stiles	..	..	Ure	Sadler	..	Fitzpatrick	..	..2	..	
	League Cup															
3 Sep	Middlesbrough (2)	H	W	1–0	Stepney	Fitzpatrick	Dunne A	Crerand	James	Sadler1	Morgan	Kidd	Charlton	Givens	Best	Gowling for Kidd
23 Sep	Wrexham (3)	H	W	2–0	..	..	..	Burns	Ure	..	..	..1	..	Aston	..1	
14 Oct	Burnley (4)	A	D	0–0	..	..	..	..	..	..	..	..	..	..	..	
20 Oct	Burnley (4R)	H	W	1–0	..	..	..	..	..	..	..	..	..	..	..1	Sartori for Fitzpatrick
12 Nov	Derby Co (5)	A	D	0–0	..	Brennan	..	..	..	..	Sartori	Best	..	Law	Aston	
19 Nov	Derby Co (5R)	H	W	1–0	..	Fitzpatrick	..	..	..	..	Best	Kidd1	..	..	..	Sartori for Law
3 Dec	Manchester C (SF)	A	L	1–2	..	Edwards	..	..	..	..	..	..	..1	Stiles	..	
17 Dec	Manchester C (SF)	H	D	2–2	..	..1	..	Stiles	..	..	Morgan	Crerand	..	Law1	Best	

SEASON 1970–1971 FOOTBALL LEAGUE (DIVISION 1)

15 Aug	Leeds U	H	L	0–1	Stepney	Edwards	Dunne A	Crerand	Ure	Sadler	Fitzpatrick	Stiles	Charlton	Kidd	Best	Gowling for Stiles
19 Aug	Chelsea	H	D	0–0	..	..	..	..	..	..	Morgan	Fitzpatrick	..	Stiles	..	
22 Aug	Arsenal	A	L	0–4	..	Stiles	..	..	..	..	..	..	..	Law	..	Edwards for Stepney
25 Aug	Burnley	A	W	2–0	Rimmer	Edwards	..	Fitzpatrick	..	..	..	Law2	..	Stiles	..	
29 Aug	West Ham U	H	D	1–1	..	..	..	..1	..	..	..	..	..	..	..	Gowling for Stiles
2 Sep	Everton	H	W	2–0	..	..	..	..	..	..	Stiles	..	..1	Kidd	..1	

5 Sep	Liverpool	A	D	1–1	..	..	..	..	..	..	..	..	..	..1	..	
12 Sep	Coventry C	H	W	2–0	..	..	..	..	..	..	..	..	..1	..	..1	
19 Sep	Ipswich T	A	L	0–4	..	..	..	..	..	..	..	..	..	Gowling	..	Young for Dunne A
26 Sep	Blackpool	H	D	1–1	..	Watson	Burns	..	James	..	Morgan	Gowling	..	Kidd	..1	
3 Oct	Wolverhampton W	A	L	2–3	..	..	..	..	..	..	..	..1	..	..1	..	Sartori for James
10 Oct	Crystal Palace	H	L	0–1	..	Edwards	Dunne A	..	Ure	Stiles	..	Best	..	..	Aston	
17 Oct	Leeds U	A	D	2–2	..	..	..	..1	..	..	Burns	..	..1	..	..	Sartori for Stiles
24 Oct	W B A	H	W	2–1	..	..	..	..	..	Burns	Law1	..	..	..1	..	
31 Oct	Newcastle U	A	L	0–1	..	..	..	..	James	Sadler	Burns	..	..	..	..	
7 Nov	Stoke C	H	D	2–2	..	..	Burns	..	..	..1	Law1	..	..	..	..	
14 Nov	Nottingham F	A	W	2–1	..	Watson	Dunne A	..	..	..	..	..	..	Gowling1	Sartori1	
21 Nov	Southampton	A	L	0–1	..	..	..	..	..	..	..	..	..	Kidd	Aston	Sartori for Fitzpatrick
28 Nov	Huddersfield T	H	D	1–1	..	..	..	..	..	..	..	..1	..	..	..	
5 Dec	Tottenham H	A	D	2–2	..	..	..	..	..	..	..1	..1	..	..	..	
12 Dec	Manchester C	H	L	1–4	..	..	..	..	..	Stiles	..	..	..	..1	..	Sartori for Law
19 Dec	Arsenal	H	L	1–3	..	..	..	Crerand	..	Fitzpatrick	Morgan	..	..	..	Sartori1	
26 Dec	Derby Co	A	D	4–4	..	Fitzpatrick	..	..	Ure	Sadler	..	..1	..	..1	Law2	
9 Jan	Chelsea	A	W	2–1	Stepney	..	..	..	Edwards	Stiles	..1	Law	..	Gowling1	Aston	
16 Jan	Burnley	H	D	1–1	..	..	..	..	..	..	..	..	..	..	..1	
30 Jan	Huddersfield	A	W	2–1	..	..	Burns	..	..	Sadler	..	..1	..	..	Best	Aston1 for Law
6 Feb	Tottenham H	H	W	2–1	..	..	..	..	..	..	..1	Kidd	..	..	..1	
20 Feb	Southampton	H	W	5–1	..	..	..	..	..	..	..1	Best	..	..4	Aston	
23 Feb	Everton	A	L	0–1	..	..	Dunne A	..	..	..	..	..	..	..	..	Burns for Gowling
27 Feb	Newcastle U	H	W	1–0	..	..	..	..	..	..	..	..	..	Kidd	..	
6 Mar	W B A	A	L	3–4	..	..	..	..	..	..	..	..1	..	..1	..1	
13 Mar	Nottingham F	H	W	2–0	..	..	..	..	..	..	..	..1	..	Law1	..	Burns for Aston
20 Mar	Stoke C	A	W	2–1	..	..	..	..	..	..	..	..2	..	..	..	
3 Apr	West Ham U	A	L	1–2	..	..	..	..	..	..	..	..1	..	..	..	Burns for Sadler
10 Apr	Derby Co	H	L	1–2	..	Dunne A	Burns	..	..	Stiles	..	..	..	..1	..	Gowling for Aston
12 Apr	Wolverhampton W	H	W	1–0	..	..	..	..	..	..	Best	Gowling1	..	..	Morgan	Kidd for Law
13 Apr	Coventry C	A	L	1–2	..	..	..	..	..	..	..1	..	..	Kidd	..	
17 Apr	Crystal Palace	A	W	5–3	..	Fitzpatrick	Dunne A	..	..	Sadler	..2	..	..	Law3	..	Burns for Crerand
19 Apr	Liverpool	H	L	0–2	..	Dunne A	Burns	..	..	..	..	..	..	..	..	
24 Apr	Ipswich T	H	W	3–2	..	..	..	..	James	..	Law	..	..1	Kidd1	Best1	Sartori for Sadler
1 May	Blackpool	A	D	1–1	..	..	..	..	..	..	..	..	..	..	..	
5 May	Manchester C	A	W	4–3	..	O'Neil	..	..	..	..	..1	..	..1	..	..2	
	FA Cup															
2 Jan	Middlesbrough (3)	H	D	0–0	Rimmer	Fitzpatrick	Dunne A	Crerand	Ure	Sadler	Morgan	Best	Charlton	Kidd	Law	
5 Jan	Middlesbrough (3R)	A	L	1–2	..	..	..	..	Edwards	..	..	..1	..	..	..	Gowling for Kidd
	League Cup															
9 Sep	Aldershot (2)	A	W	3–1	Rimmer	Edwards	Dunne A	Fitzpatrick	Ure	Sadler	Stiles	Law1	Charlton	Kidd1	Best1	James for Dunne A
7 Oct	Portsmouth (3)	H	W	1–0	..	Donald	Burns	..	..	..	Morgan	Gowling	..1	..	..	Aston for Sadler
28 Oct	Chelsea (4)	H	W	2–1	..	Edwards	Dunne A	..	James	..	Law	Best1	..1	..	Aston	Burns for Law
18 Nov	Crystal Palace (5)	H	W	4–2	..	Watson	..	..1	..	..	..	..	..1	..2	..	
16 Dec	Aston Villa (SF)	H	D	1–1	..	..	..	..	..	Stiles	Sartori	..	..	..1	..	
23 Dec	Aston Villa (SF)	A	L	1–2	..	Fitzpatrick	..	Crerand	Ure	Sadler	Morgan	..	..	..1	Law	

1970–1971

Appearances (goals)

Aston	19	3
Best	40	18
Burns	16	
Charlton	42	5
Crerand	24	
Dunne A	35	
Edwards	29	
Fitzpatrick	35	2
Gowling	17	8
James	13	
Kidd	24	8
Law	28	15
Morgan	25	3
O'Neil	1	
Rimmer	20	
Sadler	32	1
Sartori	2	2
Stepney	22	
Stiles	17	
Ure	13	
Watson	8	
Total 21 players	65	

Football League

	P	W	D	L	F:A	Pts	
Arsenal	42	29	7	6	71:29	65	1st
Manchester U	42	16	11	15	65:66	43	8th

SEASON 1971–1972 FOOTBALL LEAGUE (DIVISION 1)

14 Aug	Derby Co	A	D	2–2	Stepney	O'Neil	Dunne A	Gowling1	James	Sadler	Morgan	Kidd	Charlton	Law1	Best	
18 Aug	Chelsea	A	W	3–2	..	Fitzpatrick	..	..	..	..	..1	..1	..1	..	..	
20 Aug	Arsenal (Anfield)	H	W	3–1	..	O'Neil	..	..1	..	..	..	..1	..1	..	..	Aston for Best
23 Aug	W B A (Stoke)	H	W	3–1	..	..	..	..1	..	..	..	..	..	Best2	Aston	Burns for Charlton
28 Aug	Wolverhampton W	A	D	1–1	..	..	..	..	..	..	..	..	..	Law	Best	
31 Aug	Everton	A	L	0–1	..	..	..	..	..	..	..	..	..	..	..	
4 Sep	Ipswich T	H	W	1–0	..	..	..	..	..	..	..	..	..	..	..1	Aston for Law
11 Sep	Crystal Palace	A	W	3–1	..	..	..	..	..	..	..	..1	..	..2	..	Aston for Gowling
18 Sep	West Ham U	H	W	4–2	..	..	..	..	..	..	..	..	..1	..	..3	
25 Sep	Liverpool	A	D	2–2	..	..	Burns	..	..	..	..	..	..1	..1	..	
2 Oct	Sheffield U	H	W	2–0	..	..	Dunne A	..1	..	..	..	..	..	Best1	Aston	Burns for Dunne A
9 Oct	Huddersfield T	A	W	3–0	..	..	..	..	..	..	..	..	..1	Law1	Best1	
16 Oct	Derby Co	H	W	1–0	..	..	..	..	..	..	..	..	..	..	..1	
23 Oct	Newcastle U	A	W	1–0	..	..	..	..	..	..	..	..	..	..	..1	Aston for Gowling
30 Oct	Leeds U	H	L	0–1	..	..	..	..	..	..	..	..	..	..	..	Sartori for Kidd
6 Nov	Manchester C	A	D	3–3	..	..	..	..1	..	..	..	..	..	McIlroy1	..	Aston for Dunne A
13 Nov	Tottenham H	H	W	3–1	..	..	Burns	..	..	..	..	..1	..	Law2	..	
20 Nov	Leicester C	H	W	3–2	..	..	..	..	..	Edward	..	McIlroy1	..	..2	..	McIlroy for Law
27 Nov	Southampton	A	W	5–2	..	..	..	..	..	Sadler	..	Kidd1	..	McIlroy1	..3	Aston for Best
4 Dec	Nottingham F	H	W	3–2	..	..	..	..	..	..	..	..1	..	Law1	..	
11 Dec	Stoke C	A	D	1–1	..	..	..	..	..	..	..	..2	..	..1	..	McIlroy for Kidd
18 Dec	Ipswich T	A	D	0–0	..	Dunne A	..	..	..	..	..	..	..	..	..	
27 Dec	Coventry C	H	D	2–2	..	..	..	..	..1	..	..	..	..	..1	..	
1 Jan	West Ham U	A	L	0–3	..	..	..	..	Edwards	..	..	..	..	..	..	
8 Jan	Wolverhampton W	H	L	1–3	..	..	..	..	..	..	..	..	..	..	McIlroy1	Sartori for Gowling
22 Jan	Chelsea	H	L	0–1	..	O'Neil	..	..	..	..	..	McIlroy	..	..	Best	Aston for McIlroy
29 Jan	W B A	A	L	1–2	..	..	Dunne A	Burns	James	..	..	Kidd1	..	..	..	
12 Feb	Newcastle U	H	L	0–2	..	..	Burns	Gowling	..	..	..	..	..	..	..	
19 Feb	Leeds U	A	L	1–5	..	..	Dunne A	Burns1	..	..	..	..	..	Gowling	..	McIlroy for Kidd
4 Mar	Tottenham H	A	L	0–2	..	..	..	Buchan	..	..	..	Gowling	..	Law	..	
8 Mar	Everton	H	D	0–0	..	..	..	..	..	..	Burns	..	..	..	..	McIlroy for Gowling
11 Mar	Huddersfield T	H	W	2–0	..	..	..	..	..	..	Morgan	Kidd	Kidd	Best1	Storey–Moore1	
25 Mar	Crystal Palace	H	W	4–0	..	..	..	..	..	Gowling1	Best	..	Charlton1	Law1	..1	McIlroy for Kidd
1 Apr	Coventry C	A	W	3–2	..	..	..	..	..	..	Morgan	Best1	..1	..	..1	
3 Apr	Liverpool	H	L	0–3	..	..	..	..	..	..	..	..	..	..	..	Young for Law
4 Apr	Sheffield U	A	D	1–1	Connaughton		..	..	..	Sadler1	Best	McIlroy	..	Young	..	
8 Apr	Leicester C	A	L	0–2	..	..	..	..	Sadler	Morgan	..	..	..	..	..	Gowling for McIlroy
12 Apr	Manchester C	H	L	1–3	..	..	..	..1	James	Sadler	..	Gowling	..	Kidd	..	Law for Gowling
15 Apr	Southampton	H	W	3–2	Stepney	..	..	..	..	..	..1	Young	..	Law	..1	
22 Apr	Nottingham F	A	D	0–0	..	..	..	..	..	..	Morgan	Kidd	Kidd1	..	..	Young for James
25 Apr	Arsenal	A	L	0–3	..	..	..	..	Sadler	Gowling	Best	Young	Charlton	Kidd	..	McIlroy for Young
29 Apr	Stoke C	H	W	3–0	..	..	..	..	James	Young	..1	McIlroy	..1	Law	..1	Gowling for Charlton
	FA Cup															
15 Jan	Southampton (3)	A	D	1–1	Stepney	O'Neil	Burns	Gowling	Edwards	Sadler	Morgan	Kidd	Charlton1	Law	Best	McIlroy for Kidd
19 Jan	Southampton (3R)	H	W	4–1	..	..	..	..	..	..1	..	McIlroy	..	..	..2	Aston1 for McIlroy
5 Feb	Preston NE (4)	A	W	2–0	..	Dunne A	..	..2	James	..	..	Kidd	..	..	..	
26 Feb	Middlesbrough (5)	H	D	0–0	..	O'Neil	Dunne A	Burns	..	..	..	Gowling	..	..	..	
29 Feb	Middlesbrough (5R)	A	W	3–0	..	..	..	..	..	..	..1	..	..1	..	..1	
18 Mar	Stoke C (6)	H	D	1–1	..	..	..	Buchan	..	..	..	Kidd	..	..	..1	Gowling for Sadler
22 Mar	Stoke C (6R)	A	L	1–2	..	..	..	Gowling	..	Buchan	..	..	..	..	..1	McIlroy for Morgan
	League Cup															
7 Sep	Ipswich T (2)	A	W	3–1	Stepney	O'Neil	Dunne A	Gowling	James	Sadler	Morgan1	Kidd	Charlton	Best2	Aston	
6 Oct	Burnley (3)	H	D	1–1	..	..	..	..	..	..	..	..	..1	..	..	
18 Oct	Burnley (3R)	A	W	1–0	..	..	..	..	..	..	..	..	..1	Law	Best	
27 Oct	Stoke C (4)	H	D	1–1	..	..	Burns	..1	..	..	..	..	..	..	..	Aston for Kidd
8 Nov	Stoke C (4R)	A	D	0–0	..	..	..	..	..	..	..	..	..	McIlroy	..	Aston for Kidd
15 Nov	Stoke C (4R)	A	L	1–2	..	..	..	..	..	..	..	McIlroy	..	Sartori	..1	

1971–1972

Appearances (goals)

Aston	2	
Best	40	18
Buchan	13	1
Burns	15	1
Charlton	40	8
Connaughton	3	
Dunne A	34	
Edwards	4	
Fitzpatrick	1	
Gowling	35	6
James	37	1
Kidd	34	10
Law	32	13
McIlroy	8	4
Morgan	35	1
O'Neil	37	
Sadler	37	1
Stepney	39	
Storey–Moore	11	5
Young	5	
Total 20 players	69	

Football League

	P	W	D	L	F:A	Pts	
Derby Co	42	24	10	8	69:33	58	1st
Manchester U	42	19	10	13	69:61	48	8th

1972–1973

Appearances (goals)

Anderson	2	1
Best	19	4
Buchan	42	
Charlton	34	6
Davies	15	4
Donald	4	
Dunne A	24	
Edwards	1	
Fitzpatrick	5	
Forsyth	8	
Graham	18	1
Holton	15	3
James	22	
Kidd	17	4
Law	9	1
Macari L	16	5
Macdougall	18	5
McIlroy	4	
Martin	14	2
Morgan	39	2
O'Neil	16	
Rimmer	4	
Sadler	19	
Sidebottom	2	
Stepney	38	
Storey–Moore	26	5
Watson	3	
Young	28	
Own goals		1
Total 28 players	44	

Football League

	P	W	D	L	F:A	Pts
Liverpool	42	25	10	7	72:42	60 1st
Manchester U	42	12	13	17	44:60	37 18th

SEASON 1972–1973 FOOTBALL LEAGUE (DIVISION 1)

12 Aug	Ipswich T	H	L	1–2	Stepney	O'Neil	Dunne A	Morgan	James	Buchan	Best	Kidd	Charlton	Law1	Storey–Moore	McIlroy for Charlton
15 Aug	Liverpool	A	L	0–2	..	..	..	Young	..	..	Morgan	..	..	Best	..	McIlroy for Kidd
19 Aug	Everton	A	L	0–2	..	..	..	Buchan	..	Sadler	..	Fitzpatrick	Kidd	..	..	McIlroy for James
23 Aug	Leicester C	H	D	1–1	..	..	..	..	..	..	..		McIlroy	..1	..	Kidd for McIlroy
26 Aug	Arsenal	H	D	0–0	..	..	..	..	..	..	..	Young	..	..	..	
30 Aug	Chelsea	H	D	0–0	..	..	..	..	..	..	..	Fitzpatrick	Law	..	..	Charlton for Storey–Moore
2 Sep	West Ham U	A	D	2–2	..	..	..	..	..	..	..	Law	Charlton	..1	..1	McIlroy for Law
9 Sep	Coventry C	H	L	0–1	..	..	Buchan	Fitzpatrick	..	..	McIlroy	..	..	..	..	Young for Charlton
16 Sep	Wolverhampton W	A	L	0–2	..	Buchan	Dunne A	..	..	..	Young	McIlroy	..	..	..	Kidd for Sadler
23 Sep	Derby Co	H	W	3–0	..	Donald	..	Young		Buchan	Morgan1	Davies1	..	..	..1	
30 Sep	Sheffield U	A	L	0–1	..	..	..	..	..	..	..	..	..	..		McIlroy for Storey–Moore
7 Oct	W B A	A	D	2–2	..	..	..	..	..	..	..	Macdougall1	Davies	..1	..	
14 Oct	Birmingham C	H	W	1–0	..	Watson	..	..	Sadler	..	..	..1	..	..	..	
21 Oct	Newcastle U	A	L	1–2	..	..	..	..	..	..	..	..	..	..	..1	Charlton for Storey–Moore
28 Oct	Tottenham H	H	L	1–4	..	..	..	Law	..	..	..	..	..	..	Charlton1	
4 Nov	Leicester C	A	D	2–2	..	Donald	..	Morgan	..	..	Best1	..	..1	Charlton	Storey–Moore	
11 Nov	Liverpool	H	W	2–0	..	O'Neil	..	..	..	..	..	..1	Charlton	Davies1	..	McIlroy for Dunne A
18 Nov	Manchester C	A	L	0–3	..	..	..	..	..	..	..	..	..	..	..	Kidd for Morgan
25 Nov	Southampton	H	W	2–1	..	..	..	..	Edwards	..	..	..1	..	..1	..	
2 Dec	Norwich C	A	W	2–0	..	..	..	..	Sadler	..	Young	..1	..	..	..1	
9 Dec	Stoke C	H	L	0–2	..	..	..	Young	..	..	Morgan	..	..	..	..	Law for Young
16 Dec	Crystal Palace	A	L	0–5	..	..	..	..	..	..	..	..	Kidd	..	..	Law for Dunne A
23 Dec	Leeds U	H	D	1–1	..	..	..	Law	..	..	..	..1	Charlton	..	..	Kidd for Law
26 Dec	Derby Co	A	L	1–3	..	..	..	Kidd	..	..	..	..	..	..	..1	Young for Dunne A
6 Jan	Arsenal	A	L	1–3	..	Young	Forsyth	Graham	..	..	..	Kidd1	..	Law	..	
20 Jan	West Ham U	H	D	2–2	..	..	..	Law	Holton	..	..	Macdougall	..1	Macari1	Graham	Davies for Law
24 Jan	Everton	H	D	0–0	..	..	..	Martin	..	..	..	..	..	..	..	Kidd for Macdougall
27 Jan	Coventry C	A	D	1–1	..	..	..	Graham	..1	..	..	..	..	..	Martin	
10 Feb	Wolverhampton W	H	W	2–1	..	..	..	..	..	..	..	..	..2	..	..	
17 Feb	Ipswich T	A	L	1–4	..	Forsyth	Dunne A	..	..	..	Martin	..	..	..1	Kidd	
3 Mar	W B A	H	W	2–1	..	Young	Forsyth	..	James	..	Morgan	Kidd1	..	..1	Storey–Moore	Martin for Storey–Moore
10 Mar	Birmingham C	A	L	1–3	Rimmer	..	..	..	..	..	..	..	..	..1	..	Martin for Storey–Moore
17 Mar	Newcastle U	H	W	2–1	..	..	James	..	Holton1	..	..	..	..	..	Martin1	
24 Mar	Tottenham H	A	D	1–1	..	..	..	..1	..	..	..	..	..	..	..	
31 Mar	Southampton	A	W	2–0	..	..	..	..	..1	..	..	..	..1	..	..	Anderson for Kidd
7 Apr	Norwich C	H	W	1–0	Stepney	..	..	..	..	..	..	..	..	Law	..1	Anderson for Kidd
11 Apr	Crystal Palace	H	W	2–0	..	..	..	..	..	..	..1	..1	..	Macari	..	Anderson for Kidd
14 Apr	Stoke C	A	D	*2–2	..	..	..	..	..	..	..	Anderson	..	..1	..	Fletcher for Anderson
18 Apr	Leeds U	A	W	1–0	..	..	..	..	..	..	..	..1	..	..	..	Fletcher for Anderson
21 Apr	Manchester C	H	D	0–0	..	..	..	..	..	..	..	Kidd	..	..	..	Anderson for James
23 Apr	Sheffield U	H	L	1–2	..	..	Sidebottom		..	..	..	..1	..	..	..	
28 Apr	Chelsea	A	L	0–1	..	..	..	..	..	..	..	..	..	..	..	Anderson for Kidd
	FA Cup															
13 Jan	Wolverhampton W (3)	A	L	0–1	Stepney	Young	Forsyth	Law	Sadler	Buchan	Morgan	Davies	Charlton	Kidd	Graham	Dunne A for Kidd
	League Cup															
6 Sep	Oxford U (2)	A	D	2–2	Stepney	O'Neil	Dunne A	Buchan	James	Sadler	Morgan	Charlton1	Law1	Best	Storey–Moore	McIlroy for Dunne A
12 Sep	Oxford U (2R)	H	W	3–1	..	Fitzpatrick	Buchan	Young	..	..	..	Law	Charlton	..2	..1	McIlroy for Law
3 Oct	Bristol R (3)	A	D	1–1	..	Donald	Dunne A	..	..	Buchan	..1	Kidd	..	..	..	
11 Oct	Bristol R (3R)	H	L	1–2	..	Watson	..	..	..	..	..	..	..	..	..	McIlroy1 for Kidd

1973–1974

Appearances (goals)

Anderson	11	1
Best	12	2
Bielby	2	
Buchan M	42	
Daly	14	1
Fletcher	2	
Forsyth	18	1
Graham	23	1
Greenhoff	36	3
Griffiths C	7	
Holton	34	2
Houston	20	2
James	21	2
Kidd B	21	2
Macari	34	5
McCalliog	11	4
McIlroy	24	6
Martin	12	
Morgan	41	2
Sadler	2	
Sidebottom	2	
Stepney	42	2
Storey–Moore	2	1
Young	29	1
Total 24 players	38	

Football League

	P	W	D	L	F:A	Pts
Leeds U	42	24	14	4	66:31	62 1st
Manchester U	42	10	12	20	38:48	32 21st

SEASON 1973–1974 FOOTBALL LEAGUE (DIVISION 1)

25 Aug	Arsenal	A	L	0–3	Stepney	Young	Buchan M	Daly	Holton	James	Morgan	Anderson	Macari	Graham	Martin	McIlroy for Daly
29 Aug	Stoke C	H	W	1–0	..	..	..	Martin	..	..1	..	..	..	..	Micllroy	Fletcher for James
1 Sep	Q P R	H	W	2–1	..	..	..	..	..1	Sidebottom	..	..	..	..	..1	Fletcher for Martin
5 Sep	Leicester C	A	L	0–1	..	..	..	Daly	..	Sadler	..	..	Kidd	..	..	Martin for Daly
8 Sep	Ipswich T	A	L	1–2	..	..	..	..	Sadler	Greenhoff	..	..1	..	..	..	Macari for Kidd
12 Sep	Leicester C	H	L	1–2	..1	Buchan M	Young	Martin	Holton	James	..	..	Macari	..	Storey–Moore	
15 Sep	West Ham U	H	W	3–1	..	..	..	..	..	..	..	Kidd1	Anderson	..	..1	Buchan G for Holton
22 Sep	Leeds U	A	D	0–0	..	..	..	Greenhoff	..	..	..	Anderson	Macari	Kidd	Graham	Buchan G for Macari
29 Sep	Liverpool	H	D	0–0	..	..	..	..	..	..	..	..	..	..	..	Buchan G for Graham
6 Oct	Wolverhampton W	A	L	1–2	..	..	..	..	..	..	..	..	..	..	..	McIlroy1 for Anderson
13 Oct	Derby Co	H	L	0–1	..	..	Forsyth	..	..	..	..	Young	Kidd	Anderson	..	
20 Oct	Birmingham C	H	W	1–0	..1	..	Young	..	..	..	..	Kidd	Macari	Graham	Best	Martin for Best
27 Oct	Burnley	A	D	0–0	..	..	..	..	James	Griffiths	..	..	..	..	..	Sadler for Kidd
3 Nov	Chelsea	H	D	2–2	..	..	..1	..1	..	..	..	Macari	Kidd	..1		
10 Nov	Tottenham H	A	L	1–2	..	..	..	..	Holton	James	..	..	..	..	..1	
17 Nov	Newcastle U	A	L	2–3	..	..	..	..	..	..	..	..1	..	..1	..	
24 Nov	Norwich C	H	D	0–0	..	..	..	..	..	..	..	..	..	..	..	Fletcher for Morgan
8 Dec	Southampton	H	D	0–0	..	..	Forsyth	..	James	Griffiths	..	Young	..	McIlroy	..	Anderson for Kidd
15 Dec	Coventry C	H	L	2–3	..	..	..	..	..	..	..1	Macari	McIlroy	Young	..1	Martin for James
22 Dec	Liverpool	A	L	0–2	..	..	Young	..	Sidebottom		..	..	Kidd	Graham	..	McIlroy for Kidd
26 Dec	Sheffield U	H	L	1–2	..	Young	Griffiths	..	Holton	Buchan M	..	..1	McIlroy	..	..	
29 Dec	Ipswich T	H	W	2–0	..	..	..	..	..	..	..	..1	..1	..	..	
1 Jan	Q P R	A	L	0–3	..	..	Houston	..	..	..	..	..	..	..	..	
12 Jan	West Ham U	A	L	1–2	..	Forsyth	..	..	..	..	..	..	Kidd	Young	Graham	McIlroy1 for Kidd
19 Jan	Arsenal	H	D	1–1	..	Buchan M	..	..	..	James1	..	..	McIlroy	..	Martin	
2 Feb	Coventry C	A	L	0–1	..	..	..	..	..	..	..	..	..	Kidd	Young	Forsyth for McIlroy
9 Feb	Leeds U	H	L	0–2	..	..	..	..	..	..	..	..	Kidd	Young	Forsyth	McIlroy for Forsyth
16 Feb	Derby Co	A	D	2–2	..	Forsyth	..1	..1	..	Buchan M	..	Fletcher	..	Macari	McIlroy	Daly for Morgan
23 Feb	Wolverhampton W	H	D	0–0	..	..	..	..	..	..	..	..	..	..	..	Daly for McIlroy
2 Mar	Sheffield U	A	W	1–0	..	..	..	..	..	..	..	Macari1	McIlroy	Daly	Martin	
13 Mar	Manchester C	A	D	0–0	..	..	..	Martin	..	..	..	..	Greenhoff	..	Bielby	Graham for Martin
16 Mar	Birmingham C	A	L	0–1	..	..	..	..	..	..	McCalliog	..	..	Graham	..	
23 Mar	Tottenham H	H	L	0–1	..	..	..	Greenhoff	James	..	Morgan	McIlroy	Kidd	McCalliog	Daly	Bielby for Kidd
30 Mar	Chelsea	A	W	3–1	..	..	..	Daly1	..	..	..1	..1	Greenhoff	..	Martin	Bielby for James
3 Apr	Burnley	H	D	3–3	..	..1	..	..	Holton1	..	..	..1	..	..	..	
6 Apr	Norwich C	A	W	2–0	..	..	..	Greenhoff1	..	..	..	Macari1	McIlroy	..	Daly	
13 Apr	Newcastle U	H	W	1–0	..	..	..	..	..	..	..	Daly	McCalliog1	Macari	McIlroy	
15 Apr	Everton	H	W	3–0	..	Young	..1	..	..	..	..	Macari	McIlroy	McCalliog2	Daly	Martin for McIlroy
20 Apr	Southampton	A	D	1–1	..	..	..	..	..	..	..	..	..	..1	..	
23 Apr	Everton	A	L	0–1	..	Forsyth	..	..	..	..	..	..	..	..	..	
27 Apr	Manchester C	H	L	0–1	..	..	..	..	..	..	..	..	..	..	..	
29 Apr	Stoke C	A	L	0–1	..	..	..	..	..	..	..	..	..	..	Martin	
	FA Cup															
5 Jan	Plymouth A (3)	H	W	1–0	Stepney	Young	Forsyth	Greenhoff	Holton	Buchan M	Morgan	Macari1	Kidd	Graham	Martin	McIlroy for Martin
26 Jan	Ipswich T (4)	H	L	0–1	..	Buchan M	..	..	..	James	..	..	McIlroy	Young	..	Kidd for Macari
	League Cup															
8 Oct	Middlesbrough (2)	H	L	0–1	Stepney	Buchan M	Young	Greenhoff	Holton	James	Morgan	Daly	Macari	Kidd	Graham	Buchan G for Macari

SEASON 1974–1975 FOOTBALL LEAGUE (DIVISION 2) **1974–1975**

17 Aug	Orient	A	W	2–0	Stepney	Forsyth	Houston1	Greenhoff	BHolton	Buchan M	Morgan1	Macari	Pearson	McCalliog	Daly	McIlroy for Macari
24 Aug	Millwall	H	W	4–0	..	..	..	..	..	..	..	McIlroy	..1	Martin	..3	
28 Aug	Portsmouth	H	W	2–1	..	..	..	..	..	..	..	..1	..	..	..1	
31 Aug	Cardiff C	A	W	1–0	..	..	..	..	..	..	..	..	..	..	..1	Young for Pearson
7 Sep	Nottingham F	H	D	2–2	..	..	..	..	..	..	..	..	Martin	McCalliog	..	Macari for Greenhoff B
14 Sep	W B A	A	D	1–1	..	..	..	Martin	..	..	..	..	Pearson1	..	..	Greenhoff B for Martin
16 Sep	Millwall	A	W	1–0	..	..	..	Greenhoff B	Sidebottom	..	..	..	Macari	..	..1	Young for Daly
21 Sep	Bristol R	H	W	2–0	..	..	..	..1	Holton	..	..	..	..	..	..	Young for McCalliog
25 Sep	Bolton W	H	W	*3–0	..	..	..1	..	Sidebottom	..	..	..1	..	..		
28 Sep	Norwich C	A	L	0–2	..	..	..	..	..	..	..	..	..	..	..	Young for Morgan
5 Oct	Fulham	A	W	2–1	..	..	..	..	Holton	..	..	..	Pearson2	..	..	Macari for Daly
12 Oct	Notts Co	H	W	1–0	..	..	..	..	..	..	..	..1	Macari	..	..	Young for McCalliog
15 Oct	Portsmouth	A	D	0–0	..	..	Albiston	..	..	..	..	..	..	..	..	McCreery for Morgan
19 Oct	Blackpool	A	W	3–0	..	..1	Houston	..	..	..	..	..	..1	..1	..	McCreery for Daly
26 Oct	Southampton	H	W	1–0	..	..	..	..	..	..	..	..	..	..	..	Pearson1 for Morgan
2 Nov	Oxford U	H	W	4–0	..	..	..	..	Sidebottom	..	Macari1	..	Pearson3	..	..	Morgan for Greenhoff B
9 Nov	Bristol C	A	L	0–1	..	..	..	..	..	..	..	..	..	..	..	Graham for Daly
16 Nov	Aston Villa	H	W	2–1	..	..	..	Macari	..	..	Morgan	..	..	..	..2	Greenhoff B for Pearson
23 Nov	Hull C	A	L	0–2	..	..	..	..	..	..	..	..	Greenhoff B	..		
30 Nov	Sunderland	H	W	3–2	..	..	..	Greenhoff B	Holton	..	..1	..1	Pearson1	Macari	..	Davies for Greenhoff B
7 Dec	Sheffield Wed	A	D	4–4	..	..	..1	..	..	..	..	..	..1	..2	McCalliog	Davies for Holton
14 Dec	Orient	H	D	0–0	..	..	..	..	Sidebottom	..	..	..	..	..	Daly	Davies for Greenhoff B
21 Dec	York C	A	W	1–0	..	Young	..	..	..	..	..	..	..1	..	..	Davies for Sidebottom
26 Dec	W B A	H	W	2–1	..	..	..	..	..	..	..	..1	..1	..	..1	
28 Dec	Oldham	A	L	0–1	..	..	Albiston	..	..	..	..	..	..	..	..	Davies for Greenhoff B
11 Jan	Sheffield Wed	H	W	2–0	..	Forsyth	Houston	..	James	..	..	..	..	..	McCalliog2	Daly for Morgan
18 Jan	Sunderland	A	D	0–0	..	..	..	..	..	..	..	..	Baldwin	..	..	
1 Feb	Bristol C	H	L	0–1	..	..	..	Daly	..	..	..	..	..	..	..	Young for Daly
8 Feb	Oxford U	A	L	0–1	Roche	..	..	Greenhoff B	..	..	..	..	Pearson	..	Young	Davies for Morgan
15 Feb	Hull C	H	W	2–0	..	..	..1	..	..	..	Young	..	..1	..	Martin	Davies for James
22 Feb	Aston Villa	A	L	0–2	Stepney	..	..	..	Sidebottom	..	..	..	..	..	..	Davies for Martin
1 Mar	Cardiff C	H	W	4–0	..	..	..1	..	James	..	Morgan	..1	..1	..1	Daly	Coppell for Morgan
8 Mar	Bolton W	A	W	1–0	..	..	..	..	..	..	Coppell	..	..1	..	..	Young for Houston
15 Mar	Norwich C	H	D	1–1	..	..	..	..	..	..	..	..	..1	..	..	Young for Coppell
22 Mar	Nottingham F	A	W	1–0	..	..	..	..	..	..	..	..	..	..	..1	
28 Mar	Bristol R	A	D	1–1	..	..	..	..	..	..	..	..	..	..1	..	Morgan for James
29 Mar	York C	H	W	2–1	..	..	..	Morgan	Greenhoff B	..	..1	..	..1	..		
31 Mar	Oldham	H	W	3–2	..	..	..	..	..	..	..1	..1	..	..1	..	Martin for Daly
5 Apr	Southampton	A	W	1–0	..	..	..	Young	..	..	Morgan	..	..	..1	..	Nicholl for Buchan M
12 Apr	Fulham	H	W	1–0	..	..	..	Greenhoff B	James	Morgan	Coppell	..	..	..	..1	
19 Apr	Notts Co	A	D	2–2	..	..	..1	..1	..	..	..	..	..	..	..	
26 Apr	Blackpool	H	W	4–0	..	..	..	..1	..	..	..	..	..2	..1	..	
	FA Cup															
4 Jan	Walsall (3)	H	D	0–0	Stepney	Young	Houston	Greenhoff B	Sidebottom	Buchan M	Morgan	McIlroy	Pearson	Macari	Daly	Davies for Morgan
7 Jan	Walsall (3R)	A	L	2–3	..	..	..	..	..	..	McCalliog	..1	..	..	..1	Davies for Daly
	League Cup															
11 Sep	Charlton A (2)	H	W	*5–1	Stepney	Forsyth	Houston1	Martin	Holton	Buchan M	Morgan	McIlroy1	Macari2	McCalliog	Daly	Young for Forsyth
9 Oct	Manchester C (3)	H	W	1–0	..	..	Albiston	Greenhoff B	..	..	..	..	Pearson	..	..1	Macari for Pearson
13 Nov	Burnley (4)	H	W	3–2	..	..	Houston	..	Sidebottom	..	Macari2	..	..	..	..	Morgan1 for Greenhoff B
4 Dec	Middlesbrough (5)	A	D	0–0	..	..	..	..	Holton	..	Morgan	..	..	Macari	..	Young for Morgan
18 Dec	Middlesbrough (5R)	H	W	3–0	..	Young	..	..	Sidebottom	..	..	..1	..1	..1	..	McCalliog for Greenhoff B
15 Jan	Norwich C (SF)	H	D	2–2	..	Forsyth	..	..	James	..	..	..	Daly	..	McCalliog	Young for Daly
22 Jan	Norwich C (SF)	A	L	0–1	..	..	..	..	..	..	..	..	..	..	..	Young for James

Appearances (goals)

Albiston 2– Baldwin 2 – Buchan M 41 – Connell 9(1) – Daly 36 (11) – Forsyth 39 (1)– Greenhoff B 39 (4) – Holton 14 – Houston 40 (6) – James 13 – Macari 36 (11) – McCalliog –20 (3) – McIlroy 41 (7) – Martin 7 – Morgan 32 (3) – Pearson 30 (17) –Roche 2 – Sidebottom 12 – Stepney 40 – Young 7– Own goals 2 – Total 20 players 66

Football League

	P	W	D	L	F:A	Pts
Manchester U	42	26	9	7	66:30	61 1st

SEASON 1975–1976 FOOTBALL LEAGUE (DIVISION 1) **1975–1976**

16 Aug	Wolverhampton W	A	W	2–0	Stepney	Forsyth	Houston	Jackson	Greenhoff B	Buchan M	Coppell	McIlroy	Pearson	Macari2	Daly	Nicholl for Pearson
19 Aug	Birmingham C	A	W	2–0	..	..	..	..	..	..	..	..2	McCreery	..	..	Nicholl for Stepney
23 Aug	Sheffield U	H	W	5–1	..	..	..	..	..	..	..	..1	Pearson2	..1	..1	Nicholl for Forsyth
27 Aug	Coventry C	H	D	1–1	..	..	..	..	..	..	..	..	..1	..	..	
30 Aug	Stoke C	A	W	*1–0	..	..	..	..	..	..	..	..	..	..	..	
6 Sep	Tottenham H	H	W	*3–2	..	Nicholl	..	..	..	..	..	..	..	..	..2	
13 Sep	Q P R	A	L	0–1	..	..	Albiston	..	Houston	..	..	..	..	..	..	Young for Jackson
20 Sep	Ipswich T	H	W	1–0	..	..	Houston1	McCreery	Greenhoff B	..	..	..	..	..	..	
24 Sep	Derby Co	A	L	1–2	..	..	..	..	..	..	..	..	..	..	..1	
27 Sep	Manchester C	A	D	2–2	..	..	..1	..	..	..	..	..	..	..1	..	
4 Oct	Leicester C	H	D	0–0	..	..	..	Jackson	..	..	..	..	..	..	..	
11 Oct	Leeds U	A	W	2–1	..	..	..	..	..	..	..	..2	..	..	..	Grimshaw for Houston
18 Oct	Arsenal	H	W	3–1	..	..	..	..	..	..	..2	..	..1	..	..	
25 Oct	West Ham U	A	L	1–2	..	..	..	..	..	..	..	..	..	..1	..	McCreery for Daly
1 Nov	Norwich C	H	W	1–0	Roche	..	..	..	..	..	..	..	..1	..	..	
8 Nov	Liverpool	A	L	1–3	..	..	..	..	..	..	..1	..	..	..	..	McCreery for Jackson
15 Nov	Aston Villa	H	W	2–0	..	..	..	Daly	..	..	..1	..1	..	..	..Hill	
22 Nov	Arsenal	A	L	1–3	..	..	..	..	..	..	..	..	..1	..	..	McCreery for McIlroy
29 Nov	Newcastle U	H	W	1–0	Stepney	..	..	..1	..	..	..	..	..	..	..	McCreery for Pearson
6 Dec	Middlesbrough	A	D	0–0	..	Forsyth	..	..	..	..	..	..	..	..		Nicholl for Forsyth
13 Dec	Sheffield U	A	W	4–1	..	..	..	..	..	..	..	..	..2	..1	..1	McCreery for McIlroy
20 Dec	Wolverhampton W	H	W	1–0	..	..	..	..	..	..	..	..	..	..	..1	Kelly for Greenhoff B
23 Dec	Everton	A	D	1–1	..	..	..	..	..	..	..	..	..	..1	..	
27 Dec	Burnley	H	W	2–1	..	..	..	..	..	..	..	..1	..	..1	..	McCreery for Pearson
10 Jan	Q P R	H	W	2–1	..	..	..	..	..	..	..	..1	..	..	..1	
17 Jan	Tottenham H	A	D	1–1	..	..	..	..	..	..	..	..	..	..	..1	McCreery for McIlroy
31 Jan	Birmingham C	H	W	3–1	..	..1	..	..	..	..	..	..1	..	..1		McCreery for Pearson
7 Feb	Coventry C	A	D	1–1	..	..	..	..	..	..	..	..	..	..1	..	McCreery for Pearson
18 Feb	Liverpool	H	D	0–0	..	..	..	..	..	..	..	..	..	..	..	McCreery for McIlroy
21 Feb	Aston Villa	A	L	1–2	..	..	..	..	..	..	..	..	..	..1	..	Coyne for Macari
25 Feb	Derby Co	H	D	1–1	..	..	..	..	..	..	..	..	..1	..	..	McCreery for Hill
28 Feb	West Ham U	H	W	4–0	..	..1	..	..	..	..	..	..	..1	..1	..	McCreery1 for McIlroy
13 Mar	Leeds U	H	W	3–2	..	..	..1	..1	..	..	..	..	..1	McCreery	..	
16 Mar	Norwich C	A	D	1–1	..	..	..	..	..	..	..	..	..	..	..1	
20 Mar	Newcastle U	A	W	*4–3	..	..	..	..	..	..	..	..	..2	..	..	
27 Mar	Middlesbrough	H	W	3–0	..	..	..	..1	..	..	..	..	..	..1	..1	
10 Apr	Ipswich T	A	L	0–3	..	..	..	..	..	..	..	..	..	..	..	
17 Apr	Everton	H	W	*2–1	..	..	..	..	..	..	..	..	..	Macari	..	McCreery1 for Coppell
19 Apr	Burnley	A	W	1–0	..	..	..	..	..	..	McCreery	..	..	..1	..	Jackson for Pearson
21 Apr	Stoke C	H	L	0–1	..	..	..	..	..	..	Jackson	..	McCreery	..	..	Nicholl for Jackson
24 Apr	Leicester C	A	L	1–2	..	..	..	Nicholl	..	..	..	McCreery	Coyne1	..	..	Albiston for Houston
4 May	Manchester C	H	W	2–0	..	..	..	Daly	Albiston	..	Coppell	McIlroy1	Pearson	Jackson	..1	McCreery for Pearson
	FA Cup															
3 Jan	Oxford U (3)	H	W	2–1	Stepney	Forsyth	Houston	Daly2	Greenhoff B	Buchan M	Coppell	McIlroy	Pearson	Macari	Hill	Nicholl for Forsyth
24 Jan	Peterborough (4)	H	W	3–1	..	..1	..	..	..	..	..	..1	..	..	..1	
14 Feb	Leicester C (5)	A	W	2–1	..	..	..	..1	..	..	..	..	..	..1	..	McCreery for Hill

6 Mar	Wolverhampton W (6)	H	D	1–1	..	..	..	..	..1	..	..	..	..	..	..	
9 Mar	Wolverhampton W (6R)	A	W	3–2	..	..	..	..	..	..1	..	..	..1	..	..	Nicholl for Macari
3 Apr	Derby Co (SF)	N	W	2–0	..	..	..	..	..	..	..	..	..	McCreery	..2	
	(at Hillsborough)															
1 May	Southampton (F)	N	L	0–1	..	..	..	..	..	..	..	..	..	Macari	..	McCreery for Hill
	(at Wembley)															
	League Cup															
10 Sep	Brentford (2)	H	W	2–1	Stepney	Nicholl	Houston	Jackson	Greenhoff B	Buchan M	Coppell	McIlroy1	Pearson	Macari1	Daly	Grimshaw for Jackson
8 Oct	Aston Villa (3)	A	W	2–1	..	..	..	..	..	..	..1	..	..1	..	..	
12 Nov	Manchester C (4)	A	L	0–4	Roche	..	..	..	..	..	..	..	..	..	..	

Appearances (goals)

Albiston 2 – Buchan M 42 – Coppell 39 (4) – Coyne 1 1 – Daly 41 (7) – Forsyth 28(2) – Greenhoff B 40 – Hill 26(7) – Houston 42 2 – Jackson 16 – Macari 36 (13) – McCreery 12 (4)– McIlroy 41 (10) – Nicholl 15 – Pearson 39 (13) – Roche 4 – Stepney 38 – Own goals 5 – Total 17 players (68)

Football League

	P	W	D	L	F:A	Pts
Liverpool	42	23	14	5	66:31	60 1st
Manchester U	42	23	10	9	68:42	56 3rd

SEASON 1976–1977 FOOTBALL LEAGUE (DIVISION 1) — 1976–1977

21 Aug	Birmingham C	H	D	2–2	Stepney	Nicholl	Houston	Daly	Greenhoff B	Buchan M	Coppell1	McIlroy	Pearson1	Macari	Hill	Foggon for Daly
24 Aug	Coventry C	A	W	2–0	..	..	..	..	..	..	..	..	..	..1	..1.	
28 Aug	Derby Co	A	D	0–0	..	..	..	..	..	..	..	..	..	..	..	
4 Sep	Tottenham H	H	L	2–3	..	..	..	..	..	..	..1	..	..1	..	..	McCreery for McIlroy
11 Sep	Newcastle U	A	D	2–2	..	..	..	..	..1	..	..	..	..1	..	..	Foggon for Hill
18 Sep	Middlesbrough	H	W	*2–0	..	..	..	..	..	..	..	..	..1	..	..	Foggon for Daly
25 Sep	Manchester C	A	W	3–1	..	..	..	..1	..	..	..1	..	..	..	..	McCreery1 for Pearson
2 Oct	Leeds U	A	W	2–0	..	..	..	..1	..	..	..1	..	..	..	..	McCreery for Pearson
16 Oct	W B A	A	L	0–4	..	..	..	..	..	Waldron	..	..	..	..	..	McCreery for Macari
23 Oct	Norwich C	H	D	2–2	..	..	..	..1	..	..	..	..	..	..	..1	McGrath for McIlroy
30 Oct	Ipswich T	H	L	0–1	..	..	Albiston	..	..	Houston	..	..	..	..	..	McCreery for Macari
6 Nov	Aston Villa	A	L	2–3	..	..	..	..	..	..	McGrath	..	..1	..	Coppell..1	
10 Nov	Sunderland	H	D	3–3	Roche	Albiston	Houston	..	Paterson	Waldron	Coppell	Greenhoff B1	..1	Macari	..1	Clark for Waldron
20 Nov	Leicester C	A	D	1–1	Stepney	Nicholl	Albiston	..1	Greenhoff B	Paterson	..	McIlroy	..	Greenhoff J	..	
27 Nov	West Ham U	H	L	0–2	..	Forsyth	..	..	..	Houston	..	..	..	..	..	
18 Dec	Arsenal	A	L	1–3	..	..	Houston	McIlroy1	..	Buchan M	McCreery	Greenhoff J	..	Macari	..	McGrath for Greenhoff B
27 Dec	Everton	H	W	4–0	..	Nicholl	..	..	..	..	Coppell	..1	..1	..1	..1	McCreery for Coppell
1 Jan	Aston Villa	H	W	2–0	..	..	..	..	..	..	..	..	..2	..	..	McCreery for Pearson
3 Jan	Ipswich T	A	L	1–2	..	..	Albiston	..	..	..	McCreery	..	..1	..	..	McGrath for Pearson
15 Jan	Coventry C	H	W	2–0	..	..	Houston	..	..	..	Coppell	..	..	..1	..	McCreery for Hill
19 Jan	Bristol C	H	W	2–1	..	..	..	..	..	..1	..	..	..1	..	..	
22 Jan	Birmingham C	A	W	3–2	..	..	..1	..	..	..	..	..1	..1	..	..	
5 Feb	Derby Co	H	W	3–1	..	..	..1	..	..	..	..	..	..	..1	Daly	
12 Feb	Tottenham H	A	W	3–1	..	..	..	..1	..	..	..	..	..	..1	Hill1	
16 Feb	Liverpool	H	D	0–0	..	..	..	..	..	..	..	..	..	..	..	
19 Feb	Newcastle U	H	W	3–1	..	..	..	..	..	..	..	..3	..	..	..	Albiston for Hill
5 Mar	Manchester C	H	W	3–1	..	..	..	..	..	..	..1	..	..1	..	..1	McCreery for Hill
12 Mar	Leeds U	H	W	1–0	..	..	..	..	..	..	..	..	..	..	..	McCreery for Hill
23 Mar	W B A	H	D	2–2	..	..	Albiston	..	Houston	..	..1	..	..	..	..1	McCreery for McIlroy
2 Apr	Norwich C	A	L	1–2	..	..	Houston	..	Greenhoff B	..	..	..	McCreery	..	..	McGrath for Hill
5 Apr	Everton	A	W	2–1	..	..	Albiston	..	..	..	..	..	Pearson	McCreery	..2	McGrath for Hill
9 Apr	Stoke C	H	W	3–0	..	..	Houston1	..	..	..	..	..	..1	Macari1	..	McCreery for Greenhoff J
11 Apr	Sunderland	A	L	1–2	..	..	..	..	..	..	..	McCreery	..	..	..1	Albiston for Macari
16 Apr	Leicester C	H	D	1–1	..	..	Albiston	..	..	..	..	Greenhoff J1	..	..	McCreery	Hill for McCreery
19 Apr	QPR	A	L	0–4	..	..	..	..	..	Houston	..	..	..	..	..	Forsyth for Greenhoff B
26 Apr	Middlesbrough	A	L	0–3	..	..	Houston	..	..	Buchan M	..	..	..	..	Hill	
30 Apr	QPR	H	W	1–0	..	..	..	..	..	..	..	..	..	..1	..	McCreery for Hill
3 May	Liverpool	A	L	0–1	..	..	..	..	Forsyth	Albiston	..	..	..	..	..	McCreery for Greenhoff J
7 May	Bristol C	A	D	1–1	..	..	..	Jackson	Greenhoff B	Buchan M	..	..1	McCreery	..	Albiston	McIlroy for Houston
11 May	Stoke C	A	D	3–3	..	..	Albiston	..	..	..	..	McCreery1	McGrath	..	Hill2	
14 May	Arsenal	H	W	3–2	..	..	..	McIlroy	..	..	..	Greenhoff J1	Pearson	..1	..1	McCreery for Pearson
16 May	West Ham U	A	L	2–4	Roche	..	..	..	..	..	..	..	..1	..	..1	McCreery for Greenhoff J
	FA Cup															
8 Jan	Walsall (3)	H	W	1–0	Stepney	Nicholl	Houston	McIlroy	Greenhoff B	Buchan M	Coppell	Greenhoff J	Pearson	Macari	Hill1	McCreery for Hill
29 Jan	Q P R (4)	H	W	1–0	..	..	..	..	..	..	..	..	..	..1	..	
26 Feb	Southampton (5)	A	D	2–2	..	..	..	..	..	..	..	..	..	..1	..1	McCreery for Greenhoff J
8 Mar	Southampton (5R)	H	W	2–1	..	..	..	..	..	..	..	..	..	..	..	
19 Mar	Aston Villa (6)	H	W	2–1	..	..	..1	..	..	..	..1	..	..	..1	..	McCreery for Greenhoff B
23 Apr	Leeds U(SF)	N	W	2–1	..	..	..	..	..	..	..1	..1	..	..		
	(at Hillsborough)															
21 May	Liverpool (F)	N	W	2–1	..	..	Albiston	..	..	..	..	..1	..1	..	..	McCreery for Hill
	(at Wembley)															
	League Cup															
1 Sep	Tranmere R (2)	H	W	5–0	Stepney	Nicholl	Houston	Daly2	Greenhoff B	Buchan M	Coppell	McIlroy	Pearson1	Macari1	Hill1	McCreery for McIlroy
22 Sep	Sunderland (3)	H	D	*2–2	..	..	..	..	..	..	McCreery	..	..1	..	..	
4 Oct	Sunderland (3R)	A	D	2–2	..	..	..	..1	Waldron	..	Coppell	..	McCreery	Greenhoff B1	..	Albiston for Greenhoff B
6 Oct	Sunderland (3R)	H	W	1–0	..	..	..	..	Greenhoff B1	..	..	..	Macari	..	..	Albiston for Hill
27 Oct	Newcastle U (4)	H	W	7–2	..	..1	Albiston	..	..	Houston1	..1	..	Pearson1	..	..3	McGrath for Pearson
1 Dec	Everton (5)	H	L	0–3	..	Forsyth	..	..	Paterson	Greenhoff B	..	..	..	Jackson	..	McCreery for Daly
	UEFA Cup															
15 Sep	Ajax (1)	A	L	0–1	Stepney	Nicholl	Houston	Daly	Greenhoff B	Buchan M	Coppell	McIlroy	Pearson	Macari	Hill	McCreery for Daly
29 Sep	Ajax (1)	H	W	2–0	..	..	..	..	..	..	..	..1	MacCreery	..1	..	Albiston for Daly, Paterson for Hill
20 Oct	Juventus (2)	H	W	1–0	..	..	Albiston	..	..	Houston	..	..	Pearson	..	..1	McCreery for Daly
3 Nov	Juventus (2)	A	L	0–3	..	..	..	..	..	..	..	..	..	..	..	McCreery for McIlroy, Paterson for Macari

Appearances (goals)

Albiston 14 – Buchan M 33 – Coppell 40 (7) – Daly 16 (4) – Forsyth 3 – Greenhoff B 40 (3) – Greenhoff J 27 (8) – Hill 38 (15) – Houston 3 7 (3) – Jackson (2) – Macari 3 (89) – McCreery 9 (2) – McGrath 2 – McIlroy 39 (2) – Nicholl 39 – Paterson 1 – Pearson 39 (15) – Roche 2 – Stepney 40 – Waldron 3 – Own goals 3 – Total 20 players (71)

Football League

	P	W	D	L	F:A	Pts
Liverpool	42	23	11	8	62:33	57 1st
Manchester U	42	18	11	13	71:62	47 6th

SEASON 1977–1978 FOOTBALL LEAGUE (DIVISION 1) — 1977–1978

20 Aug	Birmingham C	A	W	4–1	Stepney	Nicholl	Albiston	McIlroy	Greenhoff B	Buchan M	Coppell	McCreery	Pearson	Macari2	Hill1	Grimes for Pearson
24 Aug	Coventry C	H	W	2–1	..	..	..	..	..	..	..	..1	..	..	..1	
27 Aug	Ipswich T	H	D	0–0	..	..	..	..	..	..	McGrath	..	Coppell	..	..	Grimes for McIlroy
3 Sep	Derby Co	A	W	1–0	..	Forsyth	..	..	Nicholl	..	Coppell	..	Pearson	..1	..	
10 Sep	Manchester C	A	L	1–3	..	..	..	..	..1	..	..	..	..	..	..	McGrath for Macarl
17 Sep	Chelsea	H	L	0–1	..	Nicholl	..	..	Greenhoff B	..	..	..	..	..	..	McGrath for Buchan M
24 Sep	Leeds U	A	D	1–1	..	..	..	..	..	Houston	McGrath	Coppell	..	..	..1	
1 Oct	Liverpool	H	W	2–0	..	..	..	..1	..	Buchan M	..	..	Greenhoff J	..1	..	
8 Oct	Middlesbrough	A	L	1–2	..	..	..	McCreery	..	..	..	Greenhoff J	Coppell1	..	..	
15 Oct	Newcastle U	H	W	3–2	..	..	..	McIlroy	Houston	..	..	..1	..1	..1	..	
22 Oct	W B A	A	L	0–4	..	Forsyth	Rogers	..	Nicholl	..	Coppell	McCreery	Pearson	..	..	McGrath for McCreery
29 Oct	Aston Villa	A	L	1–2	..	Nicholl1	Albiston	..	Houston	..	McGrath	Coppell	..	McCreery	..	Grimes for Hill
5 Nov	Arsenal	H	L	1–2	..	..	..	..	..	..	..	..	..	..	..1	Grimes for McGrath

12 Nov	Nottingham F	A	L	1–2	Roche	..	Houston	..	Greenhoff B	..	..	..	..1	..	..	
19 Nov	Norwich C	H	W	1–0	..	..	..	..	..	..	Coppell	Greenhoff J	..1	Macari	..	McCreery for McIlroy
26 Nov	Q P R	A	D	2–2	..	..	..	Grimes	..	..	..	..	..	..	..2	McGrath for Macari
3 Dec	Wolverhampton W	H	W	3–1	..	..	Albiston	McIlroy1	..	Houston	..	..1	..1	Grimes	..	McGrath for Grimes
10 Dec	West Ham U	A	L	1–2	..	..	..	Coppell	..	..	McGrath1	..	..	..	..	
17 Dec	Nottingham F	H	L	0–4	..	..	Houston	McIlroy	..	Buchan M	Coppell	..	..	Macari	..	Grimes for Pearson
26 Dec	Everton	A	W	6–2	..	..	..	..1	..	..	..1	..1	Ritchie	..2	..1	
27 Dec	Leicester C	H	W	3–1	..	..	Albiston	..	Houston	..	..1	..1	..	..	..1	
31 Dec	Coventry C	A	L	0–3	..	..	Houston	..	Greenhoff B	..	..	..	..	..	..	McGrath for Buchan M
2 Jan	Birmingham C	H	L	1–2	..	..	..	..	..	..	..	..1	..	..	..	
14 Jan	Ipswich T	A	W	2–1	..	..	Albiston	..1	Houston	..	..	..	Pearson1	..	..	
21 Jan	Derby Co	H	W	4–0	..	..	..	..	..	..1	..	..	..1	..	..2	
8 Feb	Bristol C	H	D	1–1	..	..	..	..	..	..	..	Jordan	..	..	..1	Greenhoff for Buchan M
11 Feb	Chelsea	A	D	2–2	..	..	..	..1	..	Greenhoff B	..	..	..	..	..	
25 Feb	Liverpool	A	L	1–3	..	..	..	..1	McQueen	Houston	..	..	..	..	..	
1 Mar	Leeds U	H	L	0–1	..	..	..	..	Greenhoff B	..	..	Greenhoff J	Jordan	..	..	McGrath for Hill
4 Mar	Middlesbrough	H	D	0–0	..	..	Houston	..	McQueen	Greenhoff B	..	..	..	..	..	
11 Mar	Newcastle U	A	D	2–2	..	..	..	..	..	..	..	..	..1	..	..1	
15 Mar	Manchester C	H	D	2–2	Stepney	..	..	..	..	..	..	..	..	..	..2	Albiston for Jordan
18 Mar	W B A	H	D	1–1	..	..	..	..	..1	..	..	..	Pearson	..	..1	
25 Mar	Leicester C	A	W	3–2	..	..	..	..	..	..	..	..1	..1	..	..1	
27 Mar	Everton	H	L	1–2	..	..	Albiston	..	..	..	..	..	..	..	..	
29 Mar	Aston Villa	H	D	1–1	..	Greenhoff B	Houston	..1	..	Buchan M	..	..	..	..1	Jordan	
1 Apr	Arsenal	A	L	1–3	..	..	..	..	..	..	..	Jordan1	..	..	Hill	
8 Apr	Q P R	H	W	3–1	..	..	..	..	..	..	..1	..	..2	Grimes1	McCreery	
15 Apr	Norwich C	A	W	3–1	..	Albiston	..	..1	..	..	..	..1	..	Greenhoff B	..	
22 Apr	West Ham U	H	W	3–0	..	..	..	Greenhoff B..	..	..	..	..1	Grimes1	McIlroy1		
25 Apr	Bristol City	A	W	1–0	Roche	..	..	McIlroy	..	Nicholl	..	..	..1	..	Greenhoff B	
29 Apr	Wolverhampton W	A	L	1–2	Stepney	..	..	..	..	..	..	..	..	Greenhoff B1	Grimes	McCreery for Greenhoff B
	FA Cup															
7 Jan	Carlisle U (3)	A	D	1–1	Roche	Nicholl	Albiston	McIlroy	Greenhoff B	Buchan M	Coppell	Greenhoff J	Pearson	Macari1	Grimes	McCreery for Grimes
10 Jan	Carlisle U (3R)	H	W	4–2	..	..	..	..	Houston	..	..	..	..2	..2	Hill	
28 Jan	W B A (4)	H	D	1–1	..	..	..	..	..	..	..1	Jordan	..	..	..	
1 Feb	W B A (4R)	A	L	2–3	..	..	..	..	..	..	..	..	..1	..	..1	Greenhoff for Albiston
	League Cup															
30 Aug	Arsenal (2)	A	L	2–3	Stepney	Nicholl	Albiston	Grimes	Greenhoff B	Buchan M	Coppell	McCreery1	Pearson1	Macari	Hill	McGrath for Greenhoff B
	European Cup–Winners' Cup															
14 Sep	St Etienne (1)	A	D	1–1	Stepney	Nicholl	Albiston	McIlroy	Greenhoff B	Buchan M	McGrath	McCreery	Pearson	Coppell	Hill1	
5 Oct	St Etienne (1) (at Plymouth)	N	W	2–0	..	..	..	..	..	..	Coppell1	Greenhoff J	..1	Macari	..	McGrath for Pearson
19 Oct	F C Porto (2)	A	L	0–4	..	..	..	..	Houston	..	McGrath	McCreery	Coppell	..	..	Forsyth for Houston, Grimes for Coppell
2 Nov	F C Porto (2)	H	W	*5–2	..	..1	..	..	..	..	..	Coppell2	Pearson	McCreery	..	

Appearances (goals)

Albiston 27 – Buchan M 28 (1) – Coppell 42 (5) – Greenhoff B 31 (1) – Greenhoff J 22 (6) – Grimes 7 (2) – Hill 37 (17) – Houston 30 – Jordan 14 (3) – Macari 32 (8) – McCreery 13 (1) – McGrath 9 (1) – McIlroy 39 (9) – McQueen 14 (1) – Nicholl 37 (2) – Pearson 30 (10) – Ritchie 4 – Roche 19 – Rogers 1 – Stepney 23 – Total 20 players (67)

Football League

	P	W	D	L	F:A	Pts	
Nottingham F	42	25	14	3	69:24	64	1st
Manchester U	42	16	10	16	67:63	42	10th

SEASON 1978–1979 FOOTBALL LEAGUE (DIVISION 1) — 1978–1979

19 Aug	Birmingham C	H	W	1–0	Roche	Greenhoff B	Albiston	McIlroy	McQueen	Buchan M	Coppell	Greenhoff J	Jordan1	Macari	McCreery	
23 Aug	Leeds United	A	W	3–2	..	..	..	..1	..1	..	..	..	..	..1	..	
26 Aug	Ipswich T	A	L	0–3	..	..	..	..	..	..	..	..	..	..	..	McGrath for McCreery
2 Sep	Everton	H	D	1–1	..	Nicholl	..	..	Greenhoff B	..1	..	..	..	..	..	Grimes for McCreery
9 Sep	Q P R	A	D	1–1	..	Greenhoff B	..	..	McQueen	..	..	..1	..	..	..	
16 Sep	Nottingham F	H	D	1–1	..	..	..	..	..	..	..	..1	..	..	..	Grimes for McCreery
23 Sep	Arsenal	A	D	1–1	..	Albiston	Houston	Greenhoff B	..	..	..1	..	..	..	McIlroy	
30 Sep	Manchester C	H	W	1–0	..	..	..	..	..	..	..	..	..1	..	..	
7 Oct	Middlesbrough	H	W	3–2	..	..	..	McCreery	..	..	..	..	..1	..2	..	Grimes for Greenhoff J
14 Oct	Aston Villa	A	D	2–2	..	..	..	McIlroy1	..	..	..	..	..	..1	Grimes	
21 Oct	Bristol C	H	L	1–3	..	..	..	..	..	..	..	..1	..	..	..	Greenhoff B for McIlroy
28 Oct	Wolverhampton W	A	W	4–2	..	Nicholl	..	Greenhoff B1	..	..	..	..2	..1	..	McIlroy	Grimes for McQueen
4 Nov	Southampton	H	D	1–1	..	..	..	McIlroy	Greenhoff B	..	..	..1	..	..	Grimes	
11 Nov	Birmingham C	A	L	1–5	..	..	..	McCreery	..	..	..	..	..1	..	McIlroy	Albiston for Nicholl
18 Nov	Ipswich T	H	W	2–0	Bailey	Albiston	..	Greenhoff B	McQueen	..	..1	..1	..	Sloan	..	McGrath for Sloan
21 Nov	Everton	A	L	0–3	..	..	..	..	..	..	..	..	..	..	..	Macari for Sloan
25 Nov	Chelsea	A	W	1–0	..	Greenhoff B	..	McIlroy	..	..	..	..1	..	Macari	Thomas	
9 Dec	Derby Co	A	W	3–1	..	..	..	..1	..	..	..	..1	Ritchie1	..	..	
16 Dec	Tottenham H	H	W	2–0	..	..	..	..1	..	..	..	..	..1	..	..	Paterson for Houston
22 Dec	Bolton W	A	L	0–3	..	..	Connell	..	..	..	..	..	..	..	..	Nicholl for Greenhoff J
26 Dec	Liverpool	H	L	0–3	..	..	..	..	..	..	..	..	..	..	..	
30 Dec	W B A	H	L	3–5	..	..1	Houston	..1	..1	..	..	..	..	McCreery	..	Sloan for Greenhoff J
3 Feb	Arsenal	H	L	0–2	..	..	..	Nicholl	..	..	..	..	Macari	McIlroy	..	Ritchie for Greenhoff J
10 Feb	Manchester C	A	W	3–0	..	..	Albiston	McIlroy	..	..	..2	..	Ritchie1	Macari	..	
24 Feb	Aston Villa	H	D	1–1	..	..	..	..	..	..	..	..1	..	..	..	Nicholl for Macari
28 Feb	Q P R	H	W	2–0	..	..	..	..	..	..	..1	..1	..	Nicholl	..	
3 Mar	Bristol C	A	W	2–1	..	Nicholl	..	..	..1	..	..	..	..1	Grimes	..	
20 Mar	Coventry C	A	L	3–4	..	..	..	..1	..	..	..2	..	Greenhoff B	..	Jordan	
24 Mar	Leeds U	H	W	4–1	..	..	..	..	..	..	..	..	Ritchie3	..	..1	Paterson for Greenhoff J
27 Mar	Middlesbrough	A	D	2–2	..	..	..	..	..1	..	..1	..	Jordan	..	..	
7 Apr	Norwich C	A	D	2–2	..	Albiston	Houston	..	..1	..	..	..	..	Macari1	..	
11 Apr	Bolton W	H	L	1–2	..	Nicholl	Albiston	..	..	..1	..	Ritchie	..	..	..	
14 Apr	Liverpool	A	L	0–2	..	..	..	..	Greenhoff B	..	..	..	..	..	..	Houston for Ritchie
16 Apr	Coventry C	H	D	0–0	..	..	..	..	McQueen	..	..	..	..	Greenhoff B	..	McCreery for Ritchie
18 Apr	Nottingham F	A	D	1–1	..	..	..	..	..	..	..	McCreery	..1	..	..	Grimes for Buchan M
21 Apr	Tottenham H	A	D	1–1	..	..	..	..	..1	Greenhoff B	..	..	..	Macari	..	Grimes for Thomas
25 Apr	Norwich C	H	W	1–0	..	..	..	..	..	Buchan M	..	..	..	..1	..	Grimes for Buchan M
28 Apr	Derby Co	H	D	0–0	..	McCreery	..	..	Houston	Nicholl	..	Ritchie	..	..	..	Grimes for Ritchie
30 Apr	Southampton	A	D	1–1	..	Albiston	Houston	Sloan	McQueen	Moran	..	Paterson	Ritchie1	..	Grimes	
5 May	W B A	A	L	0–1	..	..	..	McIlroy	..	Greenhoff B	..	Greenhoff J	Jordan	..	Thomas	Grimes for Thomas
7 May	Wolverhampton W	A	W	3–2	..	Nicholl	Albiston	Greenhoff B	Houston	Buchan M	..1	Ritchie1	..1	..	..	Grimes for Greenhoff B
16 May	Chelsea	H	D	1–1	..	Albiston	Houston	McIlroy	McQueen	Nicholl	..1	Greenhoff J	..	McCreery	..	Grimes for Greenhoff J
	FA Cup															
15 Jan	Chelsea (3)	H	W	3–0	Bailey	Greenhoff B	Houston	McIlroy	McQueen	Buchan M	Coppell1	Greenhoff J1	Pearson	Nicholl	Grimes1	
31 Jan	Fulham (4)	A	D	1–1	..	..	..	..	..	..	..	..	..	Macari	Thomas	Nicholl for Pearson
12 Feb	Fulham (4R)	H	W	1–0	..	..	Albiston	..	..	..	..	..1	Ritchie	..	..	
20 Feb	Colchester (5)	A	W	1–0	..	..	..	..	..	..	..	..1	..	..	..	Nicholl for Greenhoff B
10 Mar	Tottenham H (6)	A	D	1–1	..	Nicholl	..	..	..	..	..	..	..	Grimes	..1	Jordan for Titchie
14 Mar	Tottenham H (6R)	H	W	2–0	..	..	..	..	..	..	..	..	Jordan1	..	..	
31 Mar	Liverpool (SF) (at Maine Road)	N	D	2–2	..	..	..	..	..	..	..	..	..1	Greenhoff B1	..	
4 Apr	Liverpool (SFR) (at Goodison Park)	N	W	1–0	..	..	..	..	..	..	..	..1	..	Macari	..	Ritchie for Macari
12 May	Arsenal (F) (at Wembley)	N	L	2–3	..	..	..	..1	..1	..	..	..	..	..	..	
	League Cup															
30 Aug	Stockport Co (2)	H	W	3–2	Roche	Greenhoff B	Albiston	McIlroy1	McQueen	Buchan M	Coppell	Greenhoff J1	Jordan1	Macari	Grimes	
4 Oct	Watford (3)	H	L	1–2	..	Albiston	Houston	Greenhoff B	..	..	..	..	..1	McIlroy	..	McCreery for Greenhoff B

Appearances (goals)

Albiston 32 – Bailey 28 – Buchan M 37 (2) – Connell 2 – Coppell 42 (11) – Greenhoff B 32 (2)– Greenhoff J 33 (11) – Grimes 5 – Houston 21 – Jordan 30 (6) – Macari 31 (6) – McCreery 14 – McIlroy 40 (6) – McQueen 36 (6) – Moran 1 – Nicholl 19 – Paterson 1 – Ritchie 16 (9) – Roche 14 – Sloan 3 – Thomas 25 (1) – Total 21 players (60)

Football League

	P	W	D	L	F:A	Pts
Liverpool	42	30	8	4	85:16	68 1st
Manchester U	42	15	15	12	60:63	45 9th

SEASON 1979–1980 FOOTBALL LEAGUE (DIVISION 1) **1979–1980**

18 Aug	Southampton	A	D	1–1	Bailey	Nicholl	Albiston	McIlroy	McQueen1	Buchan M	Coppell	Wilkins	Jordan	Macari	Thomas	
22 Aug	W B A	H	W	2–0	..	..	..	..	..1	..	..1	..	..	..	..	Ritchie for McIlroy
25 Aug	Arsenal	A	D	0–0	..	..	..	..	..	..	..	..	..	..	..	Paterson for Coppell
1 Sep	Middlesbrough	H	W	2–1	..	..	..	..	..	..	..	..	..	..2	..	
8 Sep	Aston Villa	A	W	3–0	..	..	..	..	..	..	..1	..	..	..	..1	Grimes1 for Jordan
15 Sep	Derby Co	H	W	*1–0	..	..	..	..	..	..	..	..	Ritchie	..	Grimes	
22 Sep	Wolverhampton W	A	L	1–3	..	..	..	..	..	..	Grimes	..	Coppell	..1	Thomas	
29 Sep	Stoke C	H	W	4–0	..	..	..	..1	..2	..	..	..1	..	..	..	Sloan for Macari
6 Oct	Brighton	H	W	2–0	..	..	..	..	..	..	..	..	..1	..1	..	
10 Oct	W B A	A	L	0–2	..	..	..	..	..	..	..	..	..	..	..	
13 Oct	Bristol C	A	D	1–1	..	..	..	..	..	..	..	..	..	..1	..	
20 Oct	Ipswich T	H	W	1–0	..	..	..	..	..	..	..1	..	..	..	..	
27 Oct	Everton	A	D	0–0	..	..	..	..	..	..	..	..	..	..	..	Sloan for Albiston
3 Nov	Southampton	H	W	1–0	..	..	Houston	..	Moran	..	..	..	..	..1	..	
10 Nov	Manchester C	A	L	0–2	..	..	..	..	..	..	..	..	..	..	..	
17 Nov	Crystal Palace	H	D	1–1	..	..	..	..	..	..	Coppell	..	Jordan1	..	..	Grimes for Thomas
24 Nov	Norwich C	H	W	5–0	..	..	Grimes	..	..1	..	..1	..	..2	..1	..	
1 Dec	Tottenham H	A	W	2–1	..	..	..	..	..	..	..1	..	..	..1	..	
8 Dec	Leeds U	H	D	1–1	..	..	..	..	..	..	..	..	..	..	..1	
15 Dec	Coventry C	A	W	2–1	..	..	Houston	..	McQueen1	..	..	..	..	..1	..	
22 Dec	Nottingham F	H	W	3–0	..	..	..	..	..1	..	..	..	..2	..	..	
26 Dec	Liverpool	A	L	0–2	..	..	..	..	..	..	..	..	..	..	..	Grimes for Thomas
29 Dec	Arsenal	H	W	3–0	..	..	..	..1	..1	..	..	..	..1	..	..	
12 Jan	Middlesbrough	A	D	1–1	..	..	..	..	..	..	..	..	..	..	..1	McGrath for Thomas
2 Feb	Derby Co	A	W	*3–1	..	..	..	..1	..	..	..	Jovanovic	..	..	..1	Grimes for Jovanovic
9 Feb	Wolverhampton W	H	L	0–1	..	..	..	..	..	..	..	Wilkins	..	..	..	Grimes for Wilkins
16 Feb	Stoke C	A	D	1–1	..	..	..	..	..	..	..1	..	..	..	Grimes	Ritchie for Macari
23 Feb	Bristol C	H	W	*4–0	..	..	..	..1	..	..	..	..	..2	..	..	Ritchie for McQueen
27 Feb	Bolton W	H	W	2–0	..	..	..	..	..1	..	..1	..	..	..	..	Sloan for Wilkins
1 Mar	Ipswich T	A	L	0–6	..	..	..	..	..	..	..	Sloan	..	..	..	Jovanovic for Nicholl
12 Mar	Everton	H	D	0–0	..	..	Albiston	..	..	..	..	Wilkins	..	..	..	Greenhoff for Macari
15 Mar	Brighton	A	D	0–0	..	..	..	..	..	..	..	..	..	..	..	
22 Mar	Manchester C	H	W	1–0	..	..	..	..	..	..	..	..	..	..	Thomas1	Grimes for Thomas
29 Mar	Crystal Palace	A	W	2–0	..	..	..	..	..	..	..	..	..1	..	..1	
2 Apr	Nottingham F	A	L	0–2	..	..	..	..	..	..	..	..	..	..	..	
5 Apr	Liverpool	H	W	2–1	..	..	..	Greenhoff1	..	..	..	..	..	..	..1	
7 Apr	Bolton W	A	W	3–1	..	..	..	McIlroy	..1	..	..1	..	..	Grimes	..1	Ritchie for Wilkins
12 Apr	Tottenham H	H	W	4–1	..	..	..	..	..	..	..	..1	..	Ritchie2	..	
19 Apr	Norwich C	A	W	2–0	..	..	..	..	Moran	..	..	..	..2	..	..	
23 Apr	Aston Villa	H	W	2–1	..	..	..	..	..	..	..	Greenhoff	..2	Macari	..	
26 Apr	Coventry C	H	W	2–1	..	..	..	..2	..	..	..	..	..	..	..	Sloan for Greenhoff
3 May	Leeds U	A	L	0–2	..	..	..	..	McQueen	..	..	..	..	..	..	Ritchie for Buchan M
	FA Cup															
5 Jan	Tottenham H (3)	A	D	1–1	Bailey	Nicholl	Houston	McIlroy1	McQueen	Buchan M	Coppell	Wilkins	Jordan	Macari	Thomas	
9 Jan	Tottenham H (3R)	H	L	0–1	..	..	..	..	..	..	..	..	..	..	..	
	League Cup															
29 Aug	Tottenham H (2)	A	L	1–2	Bailey	Nicholl	Albiston	Paterson	McQueen	Buchan M	Ritchie	Wilkins	Jordan	Macari	Thomas1	
5 Sep	Tottenham H (2)	H	W	*3–1	..	..	..	McIlroy	Houston	..	Coppell1	..	..	..	..1	Ritchie for Houston
26 Sep	Norwich C (3)	A	L	1–4	..	..	..	..1	McQueen	..	Grimes	..	Coppell	..	..	Ritchie for McIlroy

Appearances (goals)

Albiston 25 – Bailey 42 – Buchan M 42 – Coppell 42 (8) – Greenhoff J 4 1 – Grimes 20 (2) – Houston 14 – Jordan 32 (13) – Jovanovic 1 – Macari 39 (9) – McIlroy 41 (6) – McQueen 33 (9) – Moran 9 1 – Nicholl 42 – Ritchie 3 3 – Sloan 1 – Thomas 35 8 – Wilkins 37 2 – Own goals 3 – Total 18 players 65

Football League

	P	W	D	L	F:A	Pts
Liverpool	42	25	10	7	81:30	60 1st
Manchester U	42	24	10	8	65:35	58 2nd

SEASON 1980–1981 FOOTBALL LEAGUE (DIVISION 1) **1980–1981**

16 Aug	Middlesbrough	H	W	3–0	Bailey	Nicholl	Albiston	McIlroy	Moran	Buchan M	Coppell	Greenhoff J	Jordan	Macari1	Thomas1	Grimes1 for Jordan
19 Aug	Wolverhampton W	A	L	0–1	Roche	..	..	..	..	..	Grimes	..	Coppell	..	..	Ritchie for Grimes
23 Aug	Birmingham C	A	D	0–0	..	..	..	..	..	..	McGrath	Coppell	Ritchie	..	..	Duxbury for Moran
30 Aug	Sunderland	H	D	1–1	Bailey	..	..	..	Jovanovic1	..	Coppell	Greenhoff J	..	..	..	
6 Sep	Tottenham H	A	D	0–0	..	..	..	..	..	..	..	..	..	..	..	Duxbury for Ritchie
13 Sep	Leicester C	H	W	5–0	..	..	..	..	..2	..	Grimes1	..	Coppell1	..1	..	McGarvey for Macari
20 Sep	Leeds U	A	D	0–0	..	..	..	..	..	..	..	..	..	..	..	Duxbury for Macari
27 Sep	Manchester C	H	D	2–2	..	..	..1	..	McQueen	..	..	..	..1	Duxbury	..	Sloan for Duxbury
4 Oct	Nottingham F	A	W	2–1	..	..	..	..	Jovanovic	Moran	Duxbury	Coppell1	Jordan	Macari 1	..	
8 Oct	Aston Villa	H	D	3–3	..	..	..	..2	..	..	..	..1	..	..	..	Greenhoff J for Macari
11 Oct	Arsenal	H	D	0–0	..	..	..	..	..	..	Grimes	..	..	Duxbury	..	
18 Oct	Ipswich T	A	D	1–1	..	..	..	..1	..	..	Coppell	Duxbury	..	Macari	..	
22 Oct	Stoke C	A	W	2–1	..	..	..	..	..	..	..	Birtles	..1	..1	..	Duxbury for Jovanovic
25 Oct	Everton	H	W	2–0	..	..	..	..	Moran	Duxbury	..1	..	..1	..	..	
1 Nov	Crystal Palace	A	L	0–1	..	..	..	..	Jovanovic	Moran	..	..	..	..	..	
8 Nov	Coventry C	H	D	0–0	..	..	..	..	..	..	..	..	..	..	..	Sloan for Jovanovic
12 Nov	Wolverhampton W	H	D	0–0	..	..	..	..	Moran	Duxbury	..	..	..	..	..	
15 Nov	Middlesbrough	A	D	1–1	..	..	..	..	..	..	..	..	..1	..	..	
22 Nov	Brighton	A	W	4–1	..	..	..	..1	Jovanovic	Moran	..	..	..2	Duxbury1	..	Grimes for Birtles
29 Nov	Southampton	H	D	1–1	..	Jovanovic	..	..	Moran	Duxbury	..	..	..1	Macari	Grimes	Whelan for Birtles
6 Dec	Norwich C	A	D	*2–2	..	Nicholl	..	..	Jovanovic	Buchan M	..1	Greenhoff J	..	..	Duxbury	
13 Dec	Stoke C	H	D	2–2	..	..	..	..	..	Moran	..	Duxbury	..1	..1	Thomas	
20 Dec	Arsenal	A	L	1–2	..	..	..	..	..	..	..	..	..	..1	..	
26 Dec	Liverpool	H	D	0–0	..	..	..	..	..	..	..	..	..	..	..	
27 Dec	W B A	A	L	1–3	..	..	..	..	..1	..	..	..	..	..	..	
10 Jan	Brighton	H	W	2–1	..	..	..	Wilkins	McQueen1	Buchan M	..	Birtles	..	..1	..	Duxbury for Wilkins
28 Jan	Sunderland	A	L	0–2	..	..	..	Duxbury	..	..	..	..	..	..	..	
31 Jan	Birmingham C	H	W	2–0	..	..	..	..	..	..	..	..	..1	..1	..	McIlroy for Thomas
7 Feb	Leicester C	A	L	0–1	..	..	..	..	Jovanovic	..	..	..	..	..	..	Wilkins for Jovanovic
17 Feb	Tottenham H	H	D	0–0	..	..	..	..	Moran	..	..	Wilkins	Birtles	..	McIlroy	
21 Feb	Manchester C	A	L	0–1	..	..	..	..	..	..	..	..	..	..	..	McGarvey for Duxbury
28 Feb	Leeds U	H	L	0–1	..	..	..	Wilkins	..	..	..	Birtles	Jordan	..	..	
7 Mar	Southampton	A	L	0–1	..	..	..	..	..	..	..	..	..	..	..	
14 Mar	Aston Villa	A	D	3–3	..	..	..	..	..	..	..	..	..2	..	..1	
18 Mar	Nottingham F	H	D	*1–1	..	..	..	..	..	..	..	..	..	..	..	Duxbury for McIlroy
21 Mar	Ipswich T	H	W	2–1	..	..1	..	Moran	McQueen	..	..	..	..	Duxbury	Thomas1	
28 Mar	Everton	A	W	1–0	..	..	..	..	..	..	..	..	..1	..	..	Macari for Nicholl
4 Apr	Crystal Palace	H	W	1–0	..	Duxbury1	..	..	..	..	..	..	..	Macari	..	Wilkins for Thomas
11 Apr	Coventry C	A	W	2–0	..	..	..	..	..	..	..	..	..2	..	Wilkins	
14 Apr	Liverpool	A	W	1–0	..	..	..	..	..1	..	..	..	..	..	..	

18 Apr	W B A	H	W	2–1	..	..	..	..	..	..	..	..	..1	..1	..	
25 Apr	Norwich C	H	W	1–0	..	..	..	..	..	..	..	..	..1	..	..	
	FA Cup															
3 Jan	Brighton (3)	H	D	2–2	Bailey	Nicholl	Albiston	McIlroy	Jovanovic	Moran	Coppell	Birtles	Jordan	Macari	Thomas1	Duxbury1 for McIlroy
7 Jan	Brighton (3R)	A	W	2–0	..	..1	..	Wilkins	McQueen	Buchan M	..	..1	..	..	..	Duxbury for Wilkins
24 Jan	Nottingham F (4)	A	L	0–1	..	..	..	..	..	..	..	..	..	..	..	
	League Cup															
27 Aug	Coventry C (2)	H	L	0–1	Bailey	Nicholl	Albiston	McIlroy	Jovanovic	Buchan M	Coppell	Greenhoff J	Ritchie	Macari	Thomas	Sloan for Greenhoff J
2 Sep	Coventry C (2)	A	L	0–1	..	..	..	..	..	..	..	..	..	..	..	
	UEFA Cup															
17 Sep	Widzew Lodz (1)	H	D	1–1	Bailey	Nicholl	Albiston	McIlroy1	Jovanovic	Buchan M	Grimes	Greenhoff J	Coppell	Macari	Thomas	Duxbury for Nicholl
1 Oct	Widzew Lodz (1)	A	D	0–0	..	..	..	..	..	..	..	Coppell	Jordan	Duxbury	..	Moran for Buchan M

Appearances (goals)

Albiston 42 (1) – Bailey 40 – Birtles 25 – Buchan M 26 – Coppell 42 (6) – Duxbury 27 (2) – Greenhoff J 8 – Grimes 6 (2) – Jordan 33 (15) – Jovanovic 19 (4) – Macari 37 (9) – McGrath 1 – McIlroy 31 (5) – McQueen 11 (2) – Moran 32 – Nicholl 36 (1) – Ritchie 3 – Roche 2 – Thomas 30 (2) – Wilkins 11 – Own goals 2 – Total 20 players (51)

Football League

	P	W	D	L	F:A	Pts
Aston Villa	42	26	8	8	72:40	60 1st
Manchester U	42	15	18	9	51:36	48 8th

SEASON 1981–1982 FOOTBALL LEAGUE (DIVISION 1)

1981–1982

29 Aug	Coventry C	A	L	1–2	Bailey	Gidman	Albiston	Wilkins	McQueen	Buchan M	Coppell	Birtles	Stapleton	Macari1	McIlroy	
31 Aug	Nottingham F	H	D	0–0	..	..	..	..	..	..	..	..	..	..	..	
5 Sep	Ipswich T	H	L	1–2	..	..	..	..	..	..	..	..	..1	..	..	Duxbury for McIlory
12 Sep	Aston Villa	A	D	1–1	..	..	..	..	..	..	..	..	..1	..	..	
19 Sep	Swansea	H	W	1–0	..	..	..	..	..	..	..	..1	..	..	..	Moses for McIlroy
22 Sep	Middlesbrough	A	W	2–0	..	..	..	..	..	..	..	..1	..1	..	Moses	Duxbury for Buchan M
26 Sep	Arsenal	A	D	0–0	..	..	..	..	..	..	..	..	..	..	..	
30 Sep	Leeds U	H	W	1–0	..	..	..	..	..	..	..	..	..1	McIlroy	..	Duxbury for McQueen
3 Oct	Wolverhampton W	H	W	5–0	..	..	..	..	Moran	..	..	..1	..1	..3	..	
10 Oct	Manchester C	A	D	0–0	..	..	..	..	..	..	Robson	..	..	..	..	Coppell for Birtles
17 Oct	Birmingham C	H	D	1–1	..	..	..	..	..	..	..	..	..	Moses	Coppell1	
21 Oct	Middlesbrough	H	W	1–0	..	..	..	..	Duxbury	..	..	..	..	..1	..	
24 Oct	Liverpool	A	W	2–1	..	..	..1	..	Moran1	..	..	..	..	..	..	
31 Oct	Notts Co	H	W	2–1	..	..	..	..	Duxbury	..	..	..1	..	..1	..	
7 Nov	Sunderland	A	W	5–1	..	..	..	..	Moran1	..	..1	..1	..2	..	..	Macari for Robson
21 Nov	Tottenham H	A	L	1–3	Roche	Duxbury	..	..	..	..	..	..1	..	..	McIlroy	Duxbury for Gidman
28 Nov	Brighton	H	W	2–0	..	Gidman	..	..	..	McQueen	..	..1	..1	..	..	Nicholl for Buchan M
5 Dec	Southampton	A	L	2–3	..	..	..	..	..	..	..1	..	..1	..	..	
6 Jan	Everton	H	D	1–1	Bailey	..	..	..	..	Buchan M	..	McGarvey	..1	McIlroy	Coppell	
23 Jan	Stoke C	A	W	3–0	..	Duxbury	..	..	..	McQueen	..	Birtles1	..1	Macari	..1	
27 Jan	West Ham U	H	W	1–0	..	..	..	..	..	..	..	..	..	..1	..	
30 Jan	Swansea	A	L	0–2	..	..	..	..	..	..	..	..	..	..	..	
6 Feb	Aston Villa	H	W	4–1	..	Gidman	..	..	..2	Buchan M	..1	..	..	Duxbury	..1	Gidman for McQueen
13 Feb	Wolverhampton W	A	W	1–0	..	..	..	..	..	..	..	..1	..	..	..	McGarvey for Birtles
20 Feb	Arsenal	H	D	0–0	..	..	..	..	..	..	..	..	..	..	..	
27 Feb	Manchester C	H	D	1–1	..	..	..	..	..1	..	..	..	..	..	..	
6 Mar	Birmingham C	A	W	1–0	..	..	..	..	..	..	..	..1	..	..	..	
17 Mar	Coventry C	H	L	0–1	..	..	..	..	..	..	..	..	..	Moses	..	McGarvey for Moran
20 Mar	Notts Co	A	W	3–1	..	..	..	..	..	..	..	..	..1	..	..2	Duxbury for Robson
27 Mar	Sunderland	H	D	0–0	..	..	..	..	McQueen	..	..	..	..	..	..	McGarvey for Moran
3 Apr	Leeds U	A	D	0–0	..	Duxbury	..	..	Moran	..	..	McGarvey	..	..	..	McGarvey for Birtles
7 Apr	Liverpool	H	L	0–1	..	..	..	..	..	..	..	..	..	..	..	
10 Apr	Everton	A	D	3–3	..	Gidman	..	..	..	Duxbury	..	..	..	..	..2	Grimes for Buchan M
12 Apr	W B A	H	W	1–0	..	..	..	..	..1	McQueen	..	..	..	Grimes	..	Grimes 1 for Moses
17 Apr	Tottenham H	H	W	2–0	..	..	..	..	..	..	..	..1	..	..	..1	
20 Apr	Ipswich T	A	L	1–2	..	..1	..	..	..	..	..	..	..	..	Duxbury	
24 Apr	Brighton	A	W	1–0	..	..	..	..1	..	..	..	..	..	..	..	Birtles for Wilkins
1 May	Southampton	H	W	1–0	..	..	..	..	Duxbury	..	..	..1	..	..	Davies	Whiteside for Duxbury
5 May	Nottingham F	A	W	1–0	..	..	..	..	Moran	Duxbury	..	..	..1	..	Coppell	
8 May	West Ham U	A	D	1–1	..	..	..	..	..1	..	Moses	Birties	..	..	..	McGarvey for Birtles
12 May	W B A	A	W	3–0	..	..	..	..	..	McQueen	Robson1	..1	..	..	..1	
15 May	Stoke C	H	W	2–0	..	..	..	..	..	..	..1	..	Whiteside1	..	..	McGarvey for Birtles
	FA Cup															
2 Jan	Watford (3)	A	L	0–1	Bailey	Gidman	Albiston	Wilkins	Moran	Buchan M	Robson	Birtles	Stapleton	Moses	McIlroy	Macari for Moses
	Milk Cup															
7 Oct	Tottenham H (2)	A	L	0–1	Bailey	Gidman	Albiston	Wilkins	Moran	Buchan M	Coppell	Birties	Stapleton	McIlroy	Robson	Duxbury for Birtles
28 Oct	Tottenham H (2)	H	L	0–1	..	..	..	..	..	..	Robson	..	..	Moses	Coppell	

Appearances (goals)

Albiston 42 (1) – Bailey 39 – Birtles 32 (11) – Buchan M 27 – Coppell 35 (9) – Davies 1 – Duxbury 19 – Gidman 36 (1) – Grimes 9 (1) – Macari 10 (2) – McGarvey 10 (2) – McIlroy 12 (3) – McQueen 21 – Moran 30 (7) – Moses 20 (2) – Robson 32 (5) – Roche 3 – Stapleton 41 (13) – Whiteside 1 1 – Wilkins 42 (1) – Total 20 players 59

Football League

	P	W	D	L	F:A	Pts
Liverpool	42	26	9	7	80:32	87 1st
Manchester U	42	22	12	8	59:29	78 3rd

SEASON 1982–1983 FOOTBALL LEAGUE (DIVISION 1)

1982–1983

28 Aug	Birmingham C	H	W	3–0	Bailey	Duxbury	Albiston	Wilkins	Moran1	McQueen	Robson	Muhren	Stapleton1	Whiteside	Coppell1	
1 Sep	Nottingham F	A	W	3–0	..	..	..	..1	..	..	..1	..	..	..1	..	
4 Sep	W B A	A	L	1–3	..	..	..	..	..	..	..1	..	..	..	..	
8 Sep	Everton	H	W	2–1	..	..	..	..	..	..	..1	..	..	..1	..	
11 Sep	Ipswich T	H	W	3–1	..	..	..	..	..	..	..	..	..	..2	..1	
18 Sep	Southampton	A	W	1–0	..	..	..	..	Buchan M	..	..	Grimes	..	..	..	Macari 1 for Coppell
25 Sep	Arsenal	H	D	0–0	..	..	..	..	Moran	..	..	..	..	..	Macari	
2 Oct	Luton T	A	D	1–1	..	..	..	..	..	..	..	..1	..	..	Moses	
9 Oct	Stoke C	H	W	1–0	..	..	..	..	..	..	..1	..	..	..	..	
16 Oct	Liverpool	A	D	0–0	..	..	..	..	..	..	..	..	..	..	Coppell	
23 Oct	Manchester C	H	D	2–2	..	..	..	..	..	..	..	Muhren	..2	..	..	Macari for Muhren
30 Oct	West Ham U	A	L	1–3	..	..	..	Grimes	..1	Buchan M	..	..	..	..	..	
6 Nov	Brighton	A	L	0–1	..	..	..	Moses	..	McQueen	..	..	..	..	..	Macari for Moran
13 Nov	Tottenham H	H	W	1–0	..	..	..	..	McGrath	..	..	..1	..	..	..	
20 Nov	Aston Villa	A	L	1–2	..	..	..	..	Moran	..	..	..	..1	..	..	McGarvey for Whiteside
27 Nov	Norwich C	H	W	3–0	..	..	..	..	..	..	..2	..1	..	..	..	
4 Dec	Watford	A	W	1–0	..	..	..	..	Buchan M	..	..	..	..	..1	..	
11 Dec	Notts Co	H	W	4–0	..	..1	..	..	Moran	..	..1	..	..1	..1	..	Grimes for Robson
18 Dec	Swansea	A	D	0–0	..	..	..	..	..	..	..	..	..	..	..	
27 Dec	Sunderland	H	D	0–0	..	..	..	..	..	..	..	..	..	..	..	
28 Dec	Coventry C	A	L	0–3	..	..	..	..	..	..	..	Wilkins	..	McGarvey	Grimes	
1 Jan	Aston Villa	H	W	3–1	..	..	..	..	..	..	..	Muhren	..2	Whiteside	Coppell1	
3 Jan	W B A	H	D	0–0	..	..	..	..	..	..	..	..	..	..	..	
15 Jan	Birmingham C	A	W	2–1	..	..	..	..	..	..	..1	..	..	..	..1	
22 Jan	Nottingham F	H	W	2–0	..	..	..	..	..	..	..	..1	..	..	..1	
5 Feb	Ipswich T	A	D	1–1	..	..	..	..	..	..	..	..	..1	..	..	
26 Feb	Liverpool	H	D	1–1	..	..	..	..	..	..	Wilkins	..1	..	..	..	Macari for Moran
2 Mar	Stoke C	A	L	0–1	..	..	..	..	McGrath	..	..	..	..	..	..	

5 Mar	Manchester C	A	W	2–1	..	..	..	..	..	..	..	..	..2	..	..	
19 Mar	Brighton	H	D	1–1	..	Gidman	..1	Grimes	..	Duxbury	..	..	..	..	..	Macari for Wilkins
22 Mar	West Ham U	H	W	2–1	..	..	..	Moses	..	..	..	..	..1	McGarvey1	..	Macari for Stapleton
2 Apr	Coventry C	H	W	*3–0	Wealands	Duxbury	..	..	..	McQueen	..	..	..1	Whiteside	..	Macari 1 for Whiteside
4 Apr	Sunderland	A	D	0–0	..	..	..	..	..	..	..	..	..	Macari	..	McGarvey for Macari
9 Apr	Southampton	H	D	1–1	Bailey	..	..	..	..	..	Robson1	..	..	Whiteside	Wilkins	
19 Apr	Everton	A	L	0–2	Wealands	..	..	..	..	..	..	Wilkins	..	..	Grimes1	Cunningham for Whiteside
23 Apr	Watford	H	W	2–0	Wealands	..	..	..	..	..	..	..	..	..	..	Cunningham1 for Albiston
30 Apr	Norwich C	A	D	1–1	Bailey	..	Grimes	..	Moran	..	..	..	..	..1	Cunningham	
2 May	Arsenal	A	L	0–3	..	..	..	..	..	..	McGrath	..	McGarvey	..	..	
7 May	Swansea	H	W	2–1	..	..	..	Wilkins	..	..	Robson1	Muhren	Stapleton1	..	..	Davies for Muhren
9 May	Luton T	H	W	3–0	..	..	..	McGrath2	..	..	..	..	..1	..	Davies	McGarvey for Whiteside
11 May	Tottenham H	A	L	0–2	..	..	Albiston	Moses	..	McGrath	..	..	..	..	Grimes	McGarvey for Robson
14 May	Notts Co	A	L	2–3	Wealands	Gidman	..	..	McGrath1	Duxbury	Wilkins	..1	..	..	Davies	
	FA Cup															
8 Jan	West Ham U (3)	H	W	2–0	Bailey	Duxbury	Albiston	Moses	Moran	McQueen	Robson	Muhren	Stapleton1	Whiteside	Coppell1	
29 Jan	Luton T (4)	A	W	2–0	..	..	..	..1	..1	..	..	..	..	..	..	
19 Feb	Derby Co (5)	A	W	1–0	..	..	..	..	..	..	..	..	..	..1	..	
12 Mar	Everton (6)	H	W	1–0	..	..	..	..	..	..	Wilkins	..	..1	..	..	Macari for Duxbury
16 Apr	Arsenal (SF)	N	W	2–1	..	..	..	..	..	..	Robson1	Wilkins	..	..1	Grimes	McGrath for Moran
	(at Villa Park)															
21 May	Brighton (F)	N	D	2–2	..	..	..	Wilkins1	..	..	..	Muhren	..1	..	Davies	
	(at Wembley)															
26 May	Brighton (FR)	N	W	4–0	..	..	..	..	..	..	..2	..1	..	..1	..	
	(at Wembley)															
	Milk Cup															
6 Oct	Bournemouth (2)	H	W	*2–0	Bailey	Duxbury	Albiston	Wilkins	Moran	McQueen	Robson	Grimes	Stapleton1	Beardsley	Moses	Whiteside for Beardsley
26 Oct	Bournemouth(2)	A	D	2–2	..	..	..	..	Grimes	Buchan M	..	Muhren1	..	Whiteside	Coppell1	Macari for Wilkins
10 Nov	Bradford C (3)	A	D	0–0	..	..	..	Moses	McGrath	McQueen	..	..	..	..	..	
24 Nov	Bradford C (3R)	H	W	4–1	..	..	..1	..1	Moran1	..	..	..	..	Macari	..1	Whiteside for Coppell
1 Dec	Southampton (4)	H	W	2–0	..	..	..	..	..	..1	..	..	..	Whiteside1	..	
19 Jan	Nottingham F (5)	H	W	4–0	..	..	..	..	..	..2	..1	..	..	..	..1	
15 Feb	Arsenal (SF)	A	W	4–2	..	..	..	..	..	..	..	..	..1	..1	..2	
23 Feb	Arsenal (SF)	H	W	2–1	..	..	..	..	..1	..	..	..	..	..	..1	Wilkins for Robson
26 Mar	Liverpool (F)	N	L	1–2	..	..	..	..	..	..	Wilkins	..	..	..1	..	
	(at Wembley)															
	UEFA Cup															
15 Sep	Valencia (1)	H	D	0–0	Bailey	Duxbury	Albiston	Wilkins	Buchan M	McQueen	Robson	Grimes	Stapleton	Whiteside	Coppell	
29 Oct	Valencia (1)	A	L	1–2	..	..	..	..	Moran	Buchan M	..1	..	..	..	Moses	Coppell for Moses, Macari for Buchan M

Appearances (goals)

Albiston 38 (1) – Bailey 37 – Buchan M 3 – Coppell 29 (4) – Cunningham 3 (1) – Davies 2 – Duxbury 42 (1) – Gidman 3 – Grimes 15 (2) – Macari 2 (2) – McGarvey 3 (1) – McGrath 14 (3) – McQueen 37 – Moran 29 2 – Moses 29 – Muhren 32 (5) – Robson 33 (10) – Stapleton 41 (14) – Wealands 5 – Whiteside 39 (8) – Wilkins 26 (1) – Own goals 1 – Total 21 players (56)

Football League

	P	W	D	L	F:A	Pts
Liverpool	42	24	10	8	87:37	82 1st
Manchester U	42	19	13	10	56:38	70 3rd

SEASON 1983–1984 FOOTBALL LEAGUE (DIVISION 1) — 1983–1984

27 Aug	Q P R	H	W	3–1	Bailey	Duxbury	Albiston	Wilkins	Moran	McQueen	Robson	Muhren2	Stapleton1	Whiteside	Graham	Macari for Whiteside
29 Aug	Nottingham F	H	L	1–2	..	..	..	..	..1	..1	..	..	..	..	..	Macari for Duxbury
3 Sep	Stoke C	A	W	1–0	..	Gidman	..	..	..	..	..	..1	..	..	..	
6 Sep	Arsenal	A	W	3–2	..	..	..	..	..1	..	..1	..	..1	..	..	Moses for Graham
10 Sep	Luton T	H	W	2–0	..	..	..1	..	..	..	..	..1	..	..	..	Moses for Robson
17 Sep	Southampton	A	L	0–3	..	Duxbury	..	..	..	..	Moses	..	..	..	..	
24 Sep	Liverpool	H	W	1–0	..	..	..	..	..	..	Robson	..	..1	..	..	
1 Oct	Norwich C	A	D	3–3	..	..	..	..	..	McGrath	..	..	..1	..2	..	Moses for Muhren
15 Oct	W B A	H	W	3–0	..	..	..1	..	..	McQueen	..	..	..	..1	..1	
22 Oct	Sunderland	A	W	1–0	..	..	..	..1	..	..	..	Moses	..	..	..	Macari for McQueen
29 Oct	Wolverhampton W	H	W	3–0	..	Gidman	..	..	Duxbury	..	..1	Muhren	..2	..	..	Moses for Gidman
5 Nov	Aston Villa	H	L	1–2	..	Duxbury	..	..	Moran	..	..1	Moses	..	..	..	Macari for Whiteside
12 Nov	Leicester C	A	D	1–1	..	..	..	..	..	..	..1	..	..	..	..	
19 Nov	Watford	H	W	4–1	..	Moses	..	..	Duxbury	..	..1	Muhren	..	..3	Crooks	
27 Nov	West Ham U	A	D	1–1	..	..	..	..1	..	..	..	..	..	..	..	Whiteside for Muhren
3 Dec	Everton	H	L	0–1	..	Duxbury	..	..	Moran	..	..	Moses	..	..	Whiteside	
10 Dec	Ipswich T	A	W	2–0	..	..	..	..	..	..	..	..	..	..1	Graham1	
16 Dec	Tottenham H	H	W	4–2	..	Moses	..	..	..2	Duxbury	..	Muhren	..	Whiteside	..2	Macari for Stapleton
26 Dec	Coventry C	A	D	1–1	..	Duxbury	..	..	..	McQueen	Moses	..1	..	Crooks	..	
27 Dec	Notts Co	H	D	3–3	Wealands	..	..	..	..1	..1	..	..	..	..1	..	Whiteside for Crooks
31 Dec	Stoke City	H	W	1–0	..	..	..	..	..	..	..	..	..	Whiteside	..1	
2 Jan	Liverpool	A	D	1–1	Bailey	..	..	..	..	..	..	..	..	..1	..	Crooks for McQueen
13 Jan	Q P R	A	D	1–1	..	..	Moses	..	..	Hogg	Robson1	..	..	..	..	
21 Jan	Southampton	H	W	3–2	..	..	..	..	..	..	..1	..1	..1	..	..	Hughes for Whiteside
4 Feb	Norwich C	H	D	0–0	..	Moses	Albiston	..	..	Duxbury	..	..	..	..	..	
7 Feb	Birmingham C	A	D	2–2	..	Duxbury	..	..	..	Hogg1	..	Moses	..	..1	..	
12 Feb	Luton T	A	W	5–0	..	..	..	..	..	..	..2	Muhren	..1	..2	Moses	Graham for Robson
18 Feb	Wolverhampton W	A	D	1–1	..	..	..	..	..	..	..	..	..	..1	..	Graham for Wilkins
25 Feb	Sunderland	H	W	2–1	..	..	..	..	..2	..	..	..	..	..	..	Graham for Moran
3 Mar	Aston Villa	A	W	3–0	..	..	..	..	McGrath	..	..1	..	..	..1	..1	Graham for Whiteside
10 Mar	Leicester C	H	W	2–0	..	..	..	..	Moran	..	..	..	..	Hughes1	..1	
17 Mar	Arsenal	H	W	4–0	..	..	..	..	..	..	..1	..2	..1	Whiteside	..	Hughes for Whiteside
31 Mar	W B A	A	L	0–2	..	..	..	..	..	..	..	Graham	..	..	..	
7 Apr	Birmingham C	H	W	1–0	..	..	..	..	..	..	..1	..	..	..	..	Hughes for Whiteside
14 Apr	Notts Co	A	L	0–1	..	..	..	..	..	..	McGrath	Moses	..	..	Davies	Hughes for Davies
17 Apr	Watford	A	D	0–0	..	..	..	..	..	..	Davies	McGrath	..	..	Graham	
21 Apr	Coventry C	H	W	4–1	..	..	..	..1	..	..	McGrath1	Moses	..	Hughes2	..	Whiteside for Wilkins
28 Apr	West Ham U	H	D	0–0	..	..	..	..	..	..	..	..	..	..	..	Whiteside for McGrath
5 May	Everton	A	D	1–1	..	..	..	..	..	..	Robson	..	..1	..	Davies	Whiteside for Davies
7 May	Ipswich T	H	L	1–2	..	..	..	..	..	McGrath	..	..	..	..1	Graham	Whiteside1 for Stapleton
12 May	Tottenham H	A	D	1–1	..	..	..	..	..	..	..	..	..	..	..	Whiteside for Graham
16 May	Nottingham F	A	L	0–2	..	..	..	..	..	..	..	Blackmore	..	..	..	
	FA Cup															
7 Jan	Bournemouth (3)	A	L	0–2	Bailey	Moses	Albiston	Wilkins	Hogg	Duxbury	Robson	Muhren	Stapleton	Whiteside	Graham	Macari for Albiston
	Milk Cup															
3 Oct	Port Vale (2)	A	W	1–0	Bailey	Duxbury	Albiston	Wilkins	Moran	McGrath	Robson	Muhren	Stapleton1	Whiteside	Graham	Moses for Duxbury
26 Oct	Port Vale (2)	H	W	2–0	..	Gidman	..	..1	Duxbury	McQueen	..	Moses	..	..1	..	Hughes for Whiteside
8 Nov	Colchester U (3)	A	W	2–0	..	Duxbury	..	..	Moran	..1	..	..1	..	..	..	Macari for Whiteside
30 Nov	Oxford U (4)	A	D	1–1	..	..	..	..	..	..	..	..	..	..	Hughes1	
7 Dec	Oxford U (4R)	H	D	1–1	..	..	..	..	..	..	..	..	..1	..	Graham	
19 Dec	Oxford U (4R)	A	L	1–2	Wealands	Moses	..	..	..	Duxbury	..	Muhren	..	..	..1	Macari for Robson
	European Cup–Winners' Cup															
14 Sep	Dukla Prague (1)	H	D	1–1	Bailey	Duxbury	Albiston	Wilkins1	Moran	McQueen	Robson	Muhren	Stapleton	Macari	Graham	Moses for Muhren, Gidman for Robson
27 Sep	Dukla Prague (1)	A	D	2–2	..	..	..	..	..	..	..1	..	..1	Whiteside	..	
19 Oct	Spartak Varna (2)	A	W	2–1	..	..	..	..	..	..	..1	..	..	..	..1	
2 Nov	Spartak Varna (2)	H	W	2–0	..	..	..	Moses	..	..	..	Macari	..2	..	..	Dempsey for Moran, Hughes for Whiteside
7 Mar	Barcelona (3)	A	L	0–2	..	..	..	Wilkins	..	Hogg	..	Muhren	..	Hughes	Moses	
21 Mar	Barcelona (3)	H	W	3–0	..	..	..	..	..	..	..2	..	..1	Whiteside	..	Hughes for Whiteside
11 Apr	Juventus (SF)	H	D	1–1	..	..	..	McGrath	..	..	Graham	Moses	..	..	Gidman	Davies1 for Gidman
25 Apr	Juventus (SF)	A	L	1–2	..	..	..	Wilkins	..	..	McGrath	..	..	Hughes	Graham	Whiteside1 for Stapleton

Appearances (goals)

Albiston 40 (2) – Bailey 40 – Blackmore 1 – Crooks 6 (2) – Davies 3 – Duxbury 39 – Gidman 4 – Graham 33 (5) – Hogg 16 (1) – Hughes 7 (4) – McGrath 9 (1) – McQueen 20 (1) – Moran 38 (7) – Moses 31 (2) – Muhren 26 – Robson 33 (12) – Stapleton 42 (13) – Wealands 2 – Whiteside 30 (10) – Wilkins 42 (3) – Total 20 players (71)

Football League

	P	W	D	L	F:A	Pts	
Liverpool	42	22	14	6	73:32	80	1st
Manchester U	42	20	14	8	71:41	74	4th

SEASON 1984–1985 FOOTBALL LEAGUE (DIVISION 1) — 1984–1985

25 Aug	Wattord	H	D	1–1	Bailey	Duxbury	Albiston	Moses	Moran	Hogg	Robson	Strachan1	Hughes	Brazil	Olsen	Whiteside for Brazil
28 Aug	Southampton	A	D	0–0	..	..	..	..	..	..	..	..	..	..	..	
1 Sep	Ipswich T	A	D	1–1	..	..	..	..	..	..	..	..	..1	..	..	Whiteside for Brazil
5 Sep	Chelsea	H	D	1–1	..	..	..	..	..	..	..	..	..	Whiteside	..1	
8 Sep	Newcastle U	H	W	5–0	..	..	..	..1	..	..	..	..2	..1	..	..1	
15 Sep	Coventry C	A	W	3–0	..	..	..	..	..	..	..1	..	..	..2	..	
22 Sep	Liverpool	H	D	1–1	..	..	..	..	..	..	..	..1	..	..	..	Muhren for Moran
29 Sep	W B A	A	W	2–1	..	..	..	..	..	..	..1	..1	..	Brazil	..	
6 Oct	Aston Villa	A	L	0–3	..	..	..	..	..	..	Strachan	Muhren	..	..	..	
13 Oct	West Ham U	H	W	5–1	..	..	..	..1	McQueen1	..	Robson	Strachan	..1	..1	..	
20 Oct	Tottenham H	H	W	1–0	..	Gidman	..	..	Moran	..	..	..	..1	..	..	
27 Oct	Everton	A	L	0–5	..	Moran	..	..	McQueen	..	..	..	..	..	..	Stapleton for Moran
2 Nov	Arsenal	H	W	4–2	..	Gidman	..	..	Moran	..	..1	..2	..1	Stapleton	..	
10 Nov	Leicester C	A	W	3–2	..	..	..	..	Garton	..	..	..1	..1	Brazil1	..	Whiteside for Olsen
17 Nov	Luton T	H	W	2–0	..	..	..	..	McQueen	Duxbury	..	..	..	Whiteside2	..	Stapleton for Robson
24 Nov	Sunderland	A	L	2–3	..	..	Duxbury	..	..	Garton	..1	..	..1	..	..	Muhren for Olsen
1 Dec	Norwich C	H	W	2–0	..	..	..	..	..	McGrath	..1	..	..1	..	..	
8 Dec	Nottingham F	A	L	2–3	..	Duxbury	Blackmore	..	..	..	..	..2	Stapleton	Brazil	Muhren	
15 Dec	Q P R	H	W	3–0	..	Gidman1	Albiston	..	..	Duxbury1	..	..	..	..1	Olsen	
22 Dec	Ipswich T	H	W	3–0	..	..1	..	..	..	..	..1	..1	Hughes	Stapleton	..	
26 Dec	Stoke C	A	L	1–2	..	..	..	..	..	..	..	..	..	..1	Muhren	Brazil for Strachan
29 Dec	Chelsea	A	W	3–1	..	Duxbury	..	..1	..	McGrath	..	..	Stapleton1	Hughes1	..	
1 Jan	Sheffield Wed	H	L	1–2	..	..	..	..	..	..	..	..	Hughes1	Brazil	..	
12 Jan	Coventry C	H	L	0–1	Pears	..	..	..	..	..	..	..	Stapleton	Hughes	..	Brazil for Robson
2 Feb	W B A	H	W	2–0	..	Gidman	..	..	Moran	Hogg	McGrath	..2	Hughes	Whiteside	Olsen	
9 Feb	Newcastle U	A	D	1–1	..	..	..	..	..1	..	..	..	..	..	..	Stapleton for Olsen
23 Feb	Arsenal	A	W	1–0	Bailey	..	..	Duxbury	..	..	..	..	..	Stapleton	..	Whiteside1 for Moran
2 Mar	Everton	H	D	1–1	..	..	..	..	McGrath	..	Strachan	Brazil	..	Whiteside	..1	
12 Mar	Tottenham H	A	W	2–1	..	..	..	..	..	..	..	Whiteside1	..1	Stapleton	..	
15 Mar	West Ham U	A	D	2–2	..	..	..	..	..	..	..	..	..	..1	..	Robson1 for Whiteside
23 Mar	Aston Villa	H	W	4–0	..	..	..	Whiteside1	..	..	Robson	Strachan	..3	..	..	
31 Mar	Liverpool	A	W	1–0	..	..	..	..	..	..	..	..	..	..1	..	
3 Apr	Leicester C	H	W	2–1	..	..	..	..	..	..	..1	..	..	..1	..	
6 Apr	Stoke C	H	W	5–0	..	..	..	..1	..	..	..	..	..2	..	..2	Duxbury for Robson
9 Apr	Sheffield Wed	A	L	0–1	Pears	..	..	Duxbury	..	..	..	..	..	..	..	Brazil for Duxbury
21 Apr	Luton T	A	L	1–2	Bailey	..	..	Whiteside1	..	..	..	Muhren	..	..	..	
24 Apr	Southampton	H	D	0–0	..	..	..	..	..	..	..	Strachan	..	..	..	Duxbury for Stapleton
27 Apr	Sunderland	H	D	2–2	..	..	..	..	..	Moran1	..1	..	..	Brazil	..	Duxbury for Gidman
4 May	Norwich C	A	W	1–0	..	..	..	..	..	..1	..	..	..	Stapleton	..	
6 May	Nottingham F	H	W	2–0	..	..1	..	..	Moran	Hogg	McGrath	..	Stapleton1	Brazil	..	Muhren for Moran
11 May	Q P R	A	W	3–1	..	..	..	..	McGrath	..	Duxbury	..1	..	..2	..	Muhren for Hogg
13 May	Watford	A	L	1–5	..	..	..	..	..	Moran1	..	..	Hughes	Stapleton	Brazil	Muhren for Whiteside
	FA Cup															
5 Jan	Bournemouth (3)	H	W	3–0	Bailey	Duxbury	Albiston	Moses	McQueen1	McGrath	Robson	Strachan1	Stapleton1	Hughes	Muhren	
26 Jan	Coventry C (4)	H	W	2–1	Pears	Gidman	..	..	Moran	Hogg	McGrath1	..	Whiteside	..1	Olsen	Brazil for Hughes
15 Feb	Blackburn R (5)	A	W	2–0	Bailey	..	..	..	..	..	..1	..1	Hughes	Whiteside	..	
9 Mar	West Ham U (6)	H	W	4–2	..	..	..	Duxbury	McGrath	..	Strachan	Whiteside3	..1	Stapleton	..	
13 Apr	Liverpool (SF)	N	D	2–2	..	..	..	Whiteside	..	..	Robson	Strachan	..1	..1	..	
	(at Goodison Park)															
17 Apr	Liverpool (SFR)	N	W	2–1	..	..	..	..	..	..	..1	..	..1	..	..	
	(at Maine Road)															
18 May	Everton (F)†	N	W	1–0	..	..	..	..1	..	Moran	..1	..	..	..	..	Duxbury for Albiston
	(at Wembley)															
	† after extra time															
	Milk Cup															
26 Sep	Burnley (2)	H	W	4–0	Bailey	Duxbury	Albiston	Moses	Garton	Hogg	Robson1	Graham	Hughes3	Whiteside	Muhren	Brazil for Whiteside
9 Oct	Burnley (2)	A	W	3–0	..	..	..	..	Moran	..	Strachan	Blackmore	Stapleton	Brazil2	Olsen1	
30 Oct	Everton (3)	H	L	1–2	..	Gidman	..	..	..	..	Robson	Strachan	Hughes	..1	..	Stapleton for Olsen
	UEFA Cup															
19 Sep	Raba Gyor (1)	H	W	3–0	Bailey	Duxbury	Albiston	Moses	Moran	Hogg	Robson1	Muhren1	Hughes1	Whiteside	Olsen	
3 Oct	Raba Gyor (1)	A	D	2–2	..	..	..	..	..	..	..	..1	..	Brazil1	..	Gidman for Robson
24 Oct	Eindhoven (2)	A	D	0–0	..	Gidman	..	..	..	..	..	Strachan	..	..	..	
7 Nov	Eindhoven (2)	H	W	1–0	..	..	..	..	..	..	..	..1	..	Stapleton	..	Garton for Moran, Whiteside for Stapleton
28 Nov	Dundee U (3)	H	D	2–2	..	..	..	..	McQueen	Duxbury	..1	..1	..	Whiteside	..	Stapleton for Whiteside
12 Dec	Dundee U (3)	A	W	*3–2	..	..	..	..	..	..	..	..	Stapleton	Hughes1	Muhren1	
6 Mar	Videoton (4)	H	W	1–0	..	..	..	Duxbury	McGrath	Hogg	Strachan	Whiteside	Hughes	Stapleton1	Olsen	
20 Mar	Videoton (4)	A	L	0–1	..	..	..	..	..	..	Robson	Strachan	..	..	Whiteside	Olsen for Robson
	(4–5 pens after extra time)															

Appearances (goals)

Albiston 39 – Bailey 38 – Blackmore 1 – Brazil 17 (5) – Duxbury 27 (1(– Garton 2 – Gidman 27 (3) – Hogg 29 – Hughes 38 (16) – McGrath P 23 – McQueen 12 (1) – Moran 19 (4) – Moses R 26 (3) – Muhren 7 Olsen 36 (5) – Pears 4 – Robson 32 (9) – Stapleton 21 (6) – Strachan 41 (15) – Whiteside 23 (9) – Total 20 players (77)

Football League

	P	W	D	L	F:A	Pts	
Everton	42	28	6	8	88:43	90	1st
Manchester U	42	22	10	10	77:47	76	4th

SEASON 1985–1986 FOOTBALL LEAGUE (DIVISION 1) — 1985–1986

17 Aug	Aston Villa	H	W	4–0	Bailey	Gidman	Albiston	Whiteside1	McGrath	Hogg	Robson	Moses	Hughes2	Stapleton	Olsen1	Duxbury for Moses
20 Aug	Ipswich T	A	W	1–0	..	..	..	..	..	..	..1	Strachan	..	..	..	Duxbury for Gidman
24 Aug	Arsenal	A	W	2–1	..	Duxbury	..	..	..1	..	..	..	..1	..	..	
26 Aug	West Ham U	H	W	2–0	..	..	..	..	..	..	..	..1	..1	..	..	
31 Aug	Nottingham F	A	W	3–1	..	..	..	..	..	..	..	..	..1	..1	Barnes1	Brazil for Strachan
4 Sep	Newcastle U	H	W	3–0	..	..	..	..	..	..	..	..	..1	..2	..	Brazil for Stapleton
7 Sep	Oxford U	H	W	3–0	..	..	..	..1	..	..	..1	..	..	..	..1	Brazil for Stapleton
14 Sep	Manchester C	A	W	3–0	..	..1	..1	..	..	..	..1	..	..	..	..	Brazil for Stapleton
21 Sep	W B A	A	W	5–1	..	..	..	..	..	..	..	..1	Brazil2	..1	Blackmore1	Moran for Strachan
28 Sep	Southampton	H	W	1–0	..	..	..	..	..	Moran	..	Moses	Hughes1	..	Barnes	Brazil for Whiteside
5 Oct	Luton T	A	D	1–1	..	..	..	..	..	..	..	..	..1	..	..	
12 Oct	Q P R	H	W	2–0	..	..	..	..	..	..	..	Olsen1	..1	..	..	
19 Oct	Liverpool	H	D	1–1	..	..	..	..	Moran	Hogg	McGrath1	Moses	..	..	Olsen	Barnes for Moses
26 Oct	Chelsea	A	W	2–1	..	..	..	..	..	..	..	Olsen1	..1	..	Barnes	
2 Nov	Coventry C	H	W	2–0	..	Garton	..	..	..	..	..	..2	..	..	..	
9 Nov	Sheffield Wed	A	L	0–1	..	Gidman	..	..	McGrath	Moran	Robson	..	..	..	..	Strachan for Robson
16 Nov	Tottenham H	H	D	0–0	..	..	..	..	..	..	Strachan	..	..	..	..	
23 Nov	Leicester C	A	L	0–3	..	..	..	..	Moran	Hogg	McGrath	Strachan	..	..	Olsen	Brazil for Albiston
30 Nov	Watford	H	D	1–1	..	..	Gibson C	..	..	..	..	..	..	..	..	Brazil1 for Moran
7 Dec	Ipswich T	H	W	1–0	..	..	..	..	McGrath	..	Dempsey	..	..	..1	..	Brazil for Hughes
14 Dec	Aston Villa	A	W	3–1	Turner	..	..	..	..	Garton	Blackmore1	..1	..1	..	..	Brazil for Stapleton

21 Dec	Arsenal	H	L	0–1	Bailey	..	..	..	..	..	..	..	..	..	..	
26 Dec	Everton	A	L	1–3	..	..	..	..	..	Hogg	..	..	..	..1	..	Wood for Olsen
1 Jan	Birmingham C	H	W	1–0	Turner	..	Albiston	..	..	Garton	..	..	..	..	Gibson C1	Brazil for McGrath
11 Jan	Oxford U	A	W	3–1	Bailey	..	..	..1	Moran	..	..	..	..1	..	..1	
18 Jan	Nottingham F	H	L	2–3	..	..	..	..	..	..	Olsen2	..	..	..	..	
2 Feb	West Ham U	A	L	1–2	..	..	..	..	McGrath	Moran	Robson1	Olsen	..	..	..	Gibson T for Robson
9 Feb	Liverpool	A	D	1–1	Turner	..	..	..	..	..	Sivebaek	Gibson T	..	Gibson C1	Olsen	Stapleton for Olsen
22 Feb	W B A	H	W	3–0	..	..	..	Blackmore	..	..	Strachan	Gibson C	..	Stapleton	..3	Gibson T for Gidman
1 Mar	Southampton	A	L	0–1	..	Duxbury	..	Gibson C	..	..	Robson	Strachan	..	..	..	Gibson T for Olsen
15 Mar	Q P R	A	L	0–1	..	..	..	Blackmore	..	..	Olsen	..	Davenport	..	Gibson C	Gibson T for Olsen
19 Mar	Luton T	H	W	2–0	..	..	..	Whiteside	..1	..	Gibson C	..	Hughes1	Davenport	Olsen	Stapleton for Moran
22 Mar	Manchester C	H	D	2–2	..	..	..	..	..	Higgins	..1	..1	..	..	Barnes	Stapleton for Barnes
29 Mar	Birmingham C	A	D	1–1	..	Gidman	..	..	..	..	Robson1	..	..	..	Gibson C	Stapleton for Gibson C
31 Mar	Everton	H	D	0–0	..	..	..	..	..	..	..	..	..	..	..	Stapleton for Davenport
5 Apr	Coventry C	A	W	3–1	..	..	..	..	..	..	..1	..1	..	..	..1	Stapleton for Gibson C
9 Apr	Chelsea	H	L	1–2	..	..	..	Duxbury	..	..	..	..	..	..	Olsen1	Stapleton for Strachan
13 Apr	Sheffield Wed	H	L	0–2	..	..	..	..	..	..	..	Sivebaek	..	..	..	Gibson T for Davenport
16 Apr	Newcastle U	A	W	4–2	..	..	..	Whiteside1	..	Garton	..1	Gibson T	..2	Stapleton	Blackmore	Sivebaek for Gibson T
19 Apr	Tottenham H	A	D	0–0	..	..	..	..	..	..	Duxbury	Davenport	..	..	..	Olsen for Davenport
26 Apr	Leicester C	H	W	4–0	..	..	..	..	..	..	..	..1	..1	..1	..1	Olsen for Whiteside
3 May	Watford	A	D	1–1	..	Garton	..	..	..	Hogg	..	..	..1	..	..	Olsen for Davenport
	FA Cup															
9 Jan	Rochdale (3)	H	W	2–0	Turner	Duxbury	Albiston	Whiteside	Higgins	Garton	Blackmore	Strachan	Hughes1	Stapleton1	Gibson C	Olsen for Hughes
25 Jan	Sunderland (4)	A	D	0–0	Bailey	Gidman	..	..	McGrath	Moran	Robson	..	Stapleton	Blackmore	Olsen	
29 Jan	Sunderland (4R)	H	W	3–0	..	..	..	..1	..	..	..	..	..	Olsen2	Gibson C	Blackmore for Strachan
5 Mar	West Ham U (5)	A	D	1–1	Turner	Duxbury	..	..	..	..	..	..	Hughes	Stapleton1	..	Olsen for Robson
9 Mar	West Ham U (5R)	H	L	0–2	..	..	..	..	..	Higgins	Olsen	..	..	..	..	Blackmore for Higgins
	Milk Cup															
24 Sep	Crystal Palace (2)	A	W	1–0	Bailey	Duxbury	Albiston	Whiteside	McGrath	Moran	Robson	Blackmore	Brazil	Stapleton	Barnes1	
9 Oct	Crystal Palace (2)	H	W	1–0	..	..	..	..1	..	..	..	Olsen	Hughes	..	..	Brazil for Hughes
29 Oct	West Ham U (3)	H	W	1–0	..	..	..	..1	Moran	Hogg	McGrath	..	..	..	..	Brazil for Duxbury
26 Nov	Liverpool (4)	A	L	1–2	..	Gidman	Blackmore	..	..	..	..1	Strachan	Stapleton	Brazil	Olsen	

Appearances (goals)

Albiston 37 (1) – Bailey 25 – Barnes 12 (2) – Blackmore 12 (3) – Brazil 1 (3) – Davenport 11 (1) – Dempsey 1 – Duxbury 21 (1) – Garton 10 – Gibson C 18 (5) – Gibson T 2 – Gidman 24 – Higgins 6 – Hughes 40 17 – Hogg 17 – McGrath 40 (3) – Moran 18 – Moses 4 – Olsen 25 (11) – Robson 21 (7) – Sivebaek 2 – Stapleton 34 (7) – Strachan 27 (5) – Turner 17 – Whiteside 37 (4) – Total 25 players (70)

Football League

	P	W	D	L	F:A	Pts
Liverpool	42	26	10	6	89:37	88 1st
Manchester U	42	22	10	10	70:36	76 4th

SEASON 1986–1987 FOOTBALL LEAGUE (DIVISION 1) — 1986–1987

23 Aug	Arsenal	A	L	0–1	Turner	Duxbury	Albiston	Whiteside	McGrath	Moran	Strachan	Blackmore	Stapleton	Davenport	Gibson C	Olsen for Gibson C
25 Aug	West Ham U	H	L	2–3	..	..	..	..	..	..	..	..	..1	..1	..	Olsen for Gibson C
30 Aug	Charlton A	H	L	0–1	..	..	..	..	..	..	..	..	..	..	Olsen	Gibson T for Whiteside
6 Sep	Leicester C	A	D	1–1	..	Sivebaek	..	..1	..	Hogg	..	Duxbury	..	Gibson T	..	Davenport for Gibson T
13 Sep	Southampton	H	W	5–1	..	..	..	..1	..	Moran	Robson	Strachan	..2	Davenport1	..1	Gibson T for Strachan
16 Sep	Watford	A	L	0–1	..	..	..	Moses	..	..	..	Blackmore	..	..	..	
21 Sep	Everton	A	L	1–3	..	..	..	Whiteside	..	..	..1	Strachan	..	..	Moses	Olsen for Whiteside
28 Sep	Chelsea	H	L	0–1	..	..	..	..	..	..	..	..	..	..	..	Olsen for Whiteside
4 Oct	Nottingham F	A	D	1–1	..	..	..	..	..	..	..1	..	..	..	Olsen	
11 Oct	Sheffield Wed	H	W	3–1	..	..	..	..1	..	Hogg	..	..	..	..2	Barnes	
18 Oct	Luton T	H	W	1–0	..	..	..	..	..	..	..	..	..1	..	..	Gibson T for Strachan
26 Oct	Manchester C	A	D	1–1	..	..	..	..	..	..	..	Moses	..1	..	..	
1 Nov	Coventry C	H	D	1–1	..	..	..	..	..	..	..	Strachan	..	..1	Olsen	Moses for Robson
8 Nov	Oxford U	A	L	0–2	..	Duxbury	..	Moran	..	..	Blackmore	Moses	..	..	Barnes	Olsen for McGrath
15 Nov	Norwich C	A	D	0–0	..	Sivebaek	Duxbury	Moses	..	..	Olsen	Blackmore	..	..	..	Moran for Sivebaek
22 Nov	Q P R	H	W	1–0	..	..1	..	..	..	..	..	..	..	..	..	Strachan for Barnes
29 Nov	Wimbledon	A	L	0–1	..	..	..	..	..	Moran	..	..	..	..	..	Robson for Barnes
7 Dec	Tottenham H	H	D	3–3	..	..	..	..	..	..	Robson	Strachan	Whiteside1	..2	Olsen	Stapleton for McGrath
13 Dec	Aston Villa	A	D	3–3	Walsh	..	..	..	Moran	Hogg	..	..	..1	..2	..	Stapleton for Davenport
20 Dec	Leicester C	H	W	2–0	..	..	Gibson C1	O'Brien	..	..	..	..	..	..	..	Stapleton1 for O'Brien
26 Dec	Liverpool	A	W	1–0	..	..	..	Whiteside1	..	Duxbury	..	..	Stapleton	..	..	
27 Dec	Norwich C	H	L	0–1	..	..	..	..	Garton	..	..	..	..	..	..	O'Brien for Robson
1 Jan	Newcastle U	H	W	*4–1	Turner	..	..	O'Brien	..	Moran	Duxbury	..	Whiteside1	..	..1	Stapleton1 for Whiteside
3 Jan	Southampton	A	D	1–1	..	Duxbury	..	..	..	..	Gill	..	Stapleton	Gibson T	..1	Davenport for Gill
24 Jan	Arsenal	H	W	2–0	..	Sivebaek	Duxbury	Whiteside	..	..	Blackmore	..1	..	..1	..	McGrath for Duxbury
7 Feb	Charlton A	A	D	0–0	..	..	Gibson C	Duxbury	..	..	Robson	..	..	..	..	Davenport for Gibson T
14 Feb	Watford	H	W	3–1	..	Garton	..	..	McGrath1	..	..	..1	Davenport1	..	..	Stapleton for Garton
21 Feb	Chelsea	A	D	1–1	Bailey	Duxbury	..	Whiteside	..	..	..	..	..1	..	..	Stapleton for Olsen
28 Feb	Everton	H	D	0–0	..	..	..	..	..	..	..	Hogg	..	..	Strachan	O'Brien for Davenport
7 Mar	Manchester C	H	W	*2–0	..	Sivebaek	..	Duxbury	..	..	..1	..	Whiteside	..	O'Brien	Davenport for Strachan
14 Mar	Luton T	A	L	1–2	..	..	..	..	..	..	..1	..	..	..	..	Davenport for Gibson C
21 Mar	Sheffield Wed	A	L	0–1	..	Garton	Duxbury	O'Brien	..	..	..	..	..	Davenport	Gibson C	Gibson T for Garton
28 Mar	Nottingham F	H	W	2–0	Walsh	Sivebaek	Gibson C	..	..1	Duxbury	..1	Moses	Stapleton	Whiteside	Wood	Albiston for Wood
4 Apr	Oxford U	H	W	3–2	..	..	..	..	..	..	..1	Moses	..	Wood	Davenport2	Albiston for Wood
14 Apr	West Ham U	A	D	0–0	..	Duxbury	..	Moses	..	Moran	..	Strachan	..	Gibson T	..	Albiston for Robson
18 Apr	Newcastle U	A	L	1–2	..	..	..	..	..	..	O'Brien	..1	Gibson T	Whiteside	..	Stapleton for Gibson T
20 Apr	Liverpool	H	W	1–0	..	Sivebaek	Albiston	..	..	..	Duxbury	..	Whiteside	Davenport1	Gibson C	Stapleton for Albiston
25 Apr	Q P R	A	D	1–1	..	Duxbury	..	..	..	..	Robson	..1	..	..	..	Sivebaek for Moses
2 May	Wimbledon	H	L	0–1	..	..	..	..	..	..	..	..	Davenport	Olsen	..	Stapleton for Moses
4 May	Tottenham H	A	L	0–4	..	Sivebaek	Gibson C	Duxbury	..	..	..	..	Gibson T	Whiteside	Olsen	Blackmore for Sivebaek
6 May	Coventry C	A	D	1–1	..	Garton	Albiston	..	..	..	..	..	Whiteside1	Davenport	Gibson C	Blackmore for Strachan
9 May	Aston Villa	H	W	3–1	..	..	..	..	..	..	..	Blackmore	..	..	..	Olsen for Whiteside
	FA Cup															
10 Jan	Manchester C (3)	H	W	1–0	Turner	Sivebaek	Gibson C	Whiteside1	Garton	Moran	Duxbury	Strachan	Stapleton	Davenport	Olsen	Gibson T for Davenport
31 Jan	Coventry C (4)	H	L	0–1	..	..	Duxbury	..	..	..	Blackmore	..	..	Gibson T	..	Davenport for Stapleton, McGrath for Blackmore
	Littlewoods Cup															
24 Sep	Port Vale (2)	H	W	2–0	Turner	Duxbury	Albiston	Whiteside1	McGrath	Moran	Robson	Strachan	Stapleton1	Davenport	Moses	Whiteside for Moran, Gibson T for Stapleton
7 Oct	Port Vale (2)	A	W	5–2	..	Sivebaek	..	Moses2	..	..	..	..	..1	..1	Barnes1	Olsen for Moses, Gibson T for Davenport
29 Oct	Southampton (3)	H	D	0–0	..	Duxbury	..	Whiteside	..	Hogg	..	Moses	..	..	..	Moran for Gibson C, Wood for Whiteside
4 Nov	Southampton (3R)	A	L	1–4	..	..	..	..	..	..	Moses	Olsen	..	..	Gibson C	

Appearances (goals)

Albiston 19 – Bailey 5 – Barnes 7 – Blackmore 10 (1) – Davenport 34 (14) – Duxbury 32 (1) – Garton 9 – Gibson C 24 (1) – Gibson T 12 (1) – Gill 1 – Hogg 11 – McGrath 34 (2) – Moran 32 – Moses 17 – O'Brien 9 – Olsen 22 (3) – Robson 29 (7) – Sivebaek 27 (1) – Stapleton 25 (7) – Strachan 33 (4) – Turner 23 – Walsh 14 – Whiteside 31 (8) – Wood 2 – Own goals 2 – Total 24 players (52)

Football League

	P	W	D	L	F:A	Pts
Everton	42	26	8	8	76:31	86 1st
Manchester U	42	14	14	14	52:45	56 11th

SEASON 1987–1988 FOOTBALL LEAGUE (DIVISION 1) — 1987–1988

15 Aug	Southampton	A	D	2–2	Walsh	Anderson	Duxbury	Moses	McGrath	Moran	Robson	Strachan	McClair	Whiteside2	Olsen	Albiston for Moses, Davenport for Olsen
19 Aug	Arsenal	H	D	0–0	..	..	..	..	..	..	..	..	..	..	..	
22 Aug	Watford	H	W	2–0	..	..	..	..	..1	..	..	..	..1	..	..	Albiston for Olsen, Davenport for Strachan
29 Aug	Charlton A	A	W	3–1	..	..	..	..	..1	..	..1	..	..1	..	..	Gibson C for Duxbury, Davenport for Olsen
31 Aug	Chelsea	H	W	3–1	..	..	Albiston	..	..	..	Duxbury	..1	..1	..1	..	Gibson C for Albiston

5 Sep	Coventry C	A	D	0–0	..	..	..	..	..	..	..	..	..	..	..	Gibson C for Albiston, Davenport for Olsen
12 Sep	Newcastle U	H	D	2–2	..	..	Duxbury	..	..	..	Robson	..	..1	..	..1	Davenport for Olsen
19 Sep	Everton	A	L	1–2	..	..	..	..	..	Hogg	..	..	..	..1	..	Garton for Hogg, Davenport for Strachan
26 Sep	Tottenham H	H	W	1–0	..	..	Gibson C	Garton	..	Duxbury	..	..	..1	..	..	Blackmore for Anderson, Davenport for Strachan
3 Oct	Luton T	A	D	1–1	..	Blackmore	..	..	..	..	..	..	..1	..	..	O'Brien for Blackmore
10 Oct	Sheffield W	A	W	4–2	..	Garton	..	Duxbury	..	Moran	..1	..	..2	..	..	Blackmore1 for Moran, Davenport for Strachan
17 Oct	Norwich C	H	W	2–1	..	..	..	..	..	Davenport1	..1	Blackmore	..	..	..	Moran for Gibson C, O'Brien for Blackmore
25 Oct	West Ham U	A	D	1–1	..	Anderson	..1	..	..	Moran	..	Strachan	..	Davenport	..	Blackmore for Strachan
31 Oct	Nottingham F	H	D	2–2	..	..	..	..	Garton	..	..1	Davenport	..	Whiteside1	..	Strachan for Whiteside
15 Nov	Liverpool	H	D	1–1	..	..	..	..	Blackmore	..	..	Strachan	..	..1	..	Davenport for Moran
21 Nov	Wimbledon	A	L	1–2	..	..	Duxbury	Moses	..1	..	..	Graham	..	..	..	Albiston for Duxbury, O'Brien for Graham
5 Dec	Q P R	A	W	2–0	Turner	Duxbury	Albiston	..	Moran	O'Brien	..1	Strachan	..	Davenport1..		
12 Dec	Oxford United	H	W	3–1	..	..	Gibson C	..	..	Davenport	..	..2	..	Whiteside	..1	Albiston for Robson
19 Dec	Portsmouth	A	W	2–1	..	..	..	Bruce	..	Moses	..1	..	..1	..	..	Davenport for Olsen
26 Dec	Newcastle U	A	L	0–1	..	..	..	..	..	..	..	..	..	..	Davenport	Anderson for Gibson C, Olsen for Moses
28 Dec	Everton	H	W	2–1	..	Anderson	..	..	..	Duxbury	..	..	..2	..	Olsen	Davenport for Whiteside, Moses for Strachan
1 Jan	Charlton A	H	D	0–0	..	..	..	..	Duxbury	Moses	..	..	..	Davenport	..	Blackmore for Olsen, O'Brien for Moses
2 Jan	Watford	A	W	1–0	..	..	Albiston	..	Moran	Duxbury	..	..	..1	Whiteside	Gibson C	Davenport for Albiston, O'Brien for Moran
16 Jan	Southampton	H	L	0–2	..	..	Gibson C	..	..	Moses	..	Duxbury	..	Davenport	Olsen	Strachan for Gibson C, O'Brien for Moran
24 Jan	Arsenal	A	W	2–1	..	..	Duxbury	..	Blackmore	Hogg	..	Strachan1	..1	Whiteside	..	O'Brien for Blackmore
6 Feb	Coventry C	H	W	1–0	..	..	..	..	O'Brien1	..	..	..	..	..	..	Albiston for O'Brien
10 Feb	Derby Co	A	W	2–1	..	..	..	..	..	..	..	..1	..	..1	..	Albiston for Duxbury, Davenport for Olsen
13 Feb	Chelsea	A	W	2–1	..	..	Albiston	..1	..1	..	..	Davenport	..	..	Gibson C	Blackmore for Gibson C
23 Feb	Tottenham H	A	D	1–1	..	..	Duxbury	..	..	..	Davenport	Blackmore	..1	..	..	Strachan for Hogg, Olsen for Anderson
5 Mar	Norwich C	A	L	0–1	..	Blackmore	..	..	..	Moran	Robson	Strachan	..	Davenport	..	Olsen for Duxbury
12 Mar	Sheffield W	H	W	4–1	..	..1	Gibson C	..	Duxbury	Hogg	..	..	..2	..1	Olsen	
19 Mar	Nottingham F	A	D	0–0	..	Anderson	Blackmore	..	..	..	Whiteside	Olsen	..	..	Gibson C	O'Brien for Gibson C, McGrath for Hogg
26 Mar	West Ham U	H	W	3–1	..	..1	..	..	McGrath	Duxbury	Robson1	Strachan1	..	..	..	Olsen for Strachan
2 Apr	Derby Co	H	W	4–1	..	..	..	Duxbury	..	Hogg	..	..	..3	..	..1	Olsen for Davenport, O'Brien for McGrath
4 Apr	Liverpool	A	D	3–3	..	..	..	Bruce	..	Duxbury	..2	..1	..	..	..	Olsen for Blackmore, Whiteside for McGrath
12 Apr	Luton T	H	W	3–0	..	..	..	..	..	..	..1	..	..1	..1	..	Olsen for Gibson C
30 Apr	Q P R	H	W	*2–1	..	..	..	..1	..	..	..	..	..	..	Olsen	O'Brien for Blackmore
2 May	Oxford U	A	W	2–0	..	..1	Gibson C	..	..	..	..	..1	..	..	..	Blackmore for Anderson
7 May	Portsmouth	H	W	4–1	..	..	..	..	..	..	..1	..	..2	..1	..	Blackmore for Anderson, Hogg for McGrath
9 May	Wimbledon	H	W	2–1	..	Duxbury	Blackmore	..	..	Moses	..	..	..2	..	Gibson C	Martin for Moses
	FA Cup															
10 Jan	Ipswich Town (3)	A	W	*2–1	Turner	Anderson1	Duxbury	Bruce	Moran	Moses	Robson	Strachan	McClair	Whiteside	Gibson C	Davenport for Moses, Olsen for Gibson C
30 Jan	Chelsea (4)	H	W	2–0	..	..	..	..	Blackmore	Hogg	..	..	..1	..1	Olsen	O'Brien for Blackmore
20 Feb	Arsenal (5)	A	L	1–2	..	..	Gibson C	..	Duxbury	..	Davenport	..	..1	..	..	O'Brien for Hogg, Blackmore for Olsen
	Littlewoods Cup															
23 Sep	Hull C (2)	H	W	5–0	Walsh	Anderson	Gibson C	Moses	McGrath1	Duxbury	Robson	Strachan1	McClair1	Whiteside1	Davenport1	Garton for Moses
7 Oct	Hull C (2)	A	W	1–0	Turner	Blackmore	..	Garton	..	..	..	..	..1	..	Olsen	O'Brien for Gibson C, Graham for Duxbury
28 Oct	Crystal Palace (3)	H	W	2–1	..	Anderson	..	Duxbury	Garton	Moran	..	..	..2	..	Davenport	Blackmore for Robson, Olsen for Davenport
18 Nov	Bury (4)	H	W	2–1	Walsh	..	..	..	Blackmore	Davenport	..	..	..1	..1	Olsen	O'Brien for Gibson C, Moses for Davenport
20 Jan	Oxford U (5)	A	L	0–2	Turner	..	..	Blackmore	Moran	Duxbury	..	..	..	..	..	Hogg for Moran, Davenport for Strachan

Appearances (goals)

Albiston 5 – Anderson 30 (2) – Blackmore 15 (3) – Bruce 21 (2) – Davenport 21 (5) – Duxbury 39 – Garton 5 – Gibson C 26 (2) – Graham 1 – Hogg 9 – McClair 40 (24) – McGrath 21 (2) – Moran 20 – Moses 16 – O'Brien 6 (2) – Olsen 31 (2) – Robson 36 (11) – Strachan 33 (8) – Turner 24 – Walsh 16 – Whiteside 25 (7) – Own goals 1 – Total 21 players (71)

Football League

	P	W	D	L	F:A	Pts
Liverpool	40	26	12	2	87:24	90 1st
Manchester U	40	23	12	5	71:38	81 2nd

SEASON 1988–1989 FOOTBALL LEAGUE (DIVISION 1)

1988–1989

27 Aug	Q P R	H	D	0–0	Leighton	Blackmore	Martin	Bruce	McGrath	McClair	Robson	Strachan	Davenport	Hughes	Olsen	O'Brien for Davenport
3 Sep	Liverpool	A	L	0–1	..	Anderson	Blackmore	..	..	Duxbury	..	..	McClair	..	..	Garton for McGrath, Davenport for Strachan
10 Sep	Middlesbrough	H	W	1–0	..	Garton	..	..	..	..	..1	Davenport	..	..	..	
17 Sep	Luton	A	W	2–0	..	..	..	..	..	..	..1	..1	..	..	..	
24 Sep	West Ham	H	W	2–0	..	Blackmore	Sharpe	..	Garton	..	..	Strachan	..	..1	Davenport1	Beardsmore for Garton, Olsen for Sharpe
1 Oct	Tottenham	A	D	2–2	..	Garton	..	..	McGrath	..	..	..	..1	..1	..	Anderson for Garton, Olsen for Davenport
22 Oct	Wimbledon	A	D	1–1	..	Blackmore	..	..	Garton	..	..	..	..	..1	..	Beardsmore for Strachan, Robins for Davenport
26 Oct	Norwich	H	L	1–2	..	..	..	..	..	..	..	..	..	..1	..	Olsen for Davenport
30 Oct	Everton	A	D	1–1	..	Garton	Blackmore	..	Duxbury	Donaghy	..	..	..	..1	Olsen	Gibson for Strachan, O'Brien for Duxbury
5 Nov	Aston V	H	D	1–1	..	Blackmore	Gibson	..1	O'Brien	..	..	..	..	..	..	Duxbury for Gibson
12 Nov	Derby C	A	D	2–2	..	Garton	Blackmore	..	Duxbury	..	..	..	..1	..1	Sharpe	Olsen for Duxbury
19 Nov	Southampton	H	D	2–2	..	..	Sharpe	..	Blackmore	..	..1	..	..	..1	Milne	Gill for Sharpe
23 Nov	Sheffield Wed	H	D	1–1	..	..	..	..	..	..	..	..	..	..1	..	Gill for Strachan, Wilson for Blackmore
27 Nov	Newcastle	A	D	0–0	..	..	Blackmore	..	Gill	..	..	Milne	..	..	Sharpe	Martin for Milne, Robins for Sharpe
3 Dec	Charlton	H	W	3–0	..	..	Martin	..	Blackmore	..	..	Strachan	..1	..1	Milne1	
10 Dec	Coventry	A	L	0–1	..	..	..	..	..	..	..	..	..	..	Sharpe	Gill for Garton, Milne for Gill
17 Dec	Arsenal	A	L	1–2	..	Martin	Sharpe	..	..	..	..	..	..	..1	Milne	Gill for Blackmore, Beardsmore for Martin
26 Dec	Nottingham F	H	W	2–0	..	..	..	..	Beardsmore	..	..	..	..	..1	..1	
1 Jan	Liverpool	H	W	3–1	..	..	..	..	..1	..	..	..	..1	..1	..	McGrath for Martin, Robins for Strachan
2 Jan	Middlesbrough	A	L	0–1	..	Gill	..	..	McGrath	..	..	Beardsmore	..	..	..	Robins for McClair, Wilson for Gill
14 Jan	Millwall	H	W	3–0	..	Martin	..	..	Beardsmore	..	Gill	Blackmore1	..	..1	..	Wilson for Beardsmore, Maiorana for Milne
21 Jan	West Ham	A	W	3–1	..	Gill	Martin1	..	Blackmore	..	Robson	Strachan1	..1	..	..	Sharpe for Strachan
5 Feb	Tottenham	H	W	1–0	..	Martin	Sharpe	..	..	..	..	..	..1	..	..	McGrath for Sharpe, Beardsmore for Strachan
11 Feb	Sheffield Wed	A	W	2–0	..	Blackmore	Martin	..	McGrath	..	..	..	..2	..	..	Beardsmore for McClair
25 Feb	Norwich	A	L	1–2	..	..	Sharpe	..	..	..	..	..	..	..	..	Martin for Milne, Beardsmore for Blackmore
12 Mar	Aston Villa	A	D	0–0	..	Beardsmore	Martin	..	..	..	..	..	..	..	Sharpe	Blackmore for Beardsmore, Milne for Martin
25 Mar	Luton	H	W	2–0	..	Martin	Blackmore	..	..	..	..	Beardsmore	..	..	Milne1	Maiorana for Beardsmore
27 Mar	Nottingham F	A	L	0–2	..	Anderson	..	..	..	..	..	..	..	..	..	Martin for McGrath, Gill for Milne
2 Apr	Arsenal	H	D	*1–1	..	..	Donaghy	..	..	Whiteside	..	..	..	..	Maiorana	Blackmore for Beardsmore, Martin for Maiorana
8 Apr	Millwall	A	D	0–0	..	..	..	..	..	..	..	..	..	..	Martin	Maiorana for McGrath
15 Apr	Derby	H	L	0–2	..	..	Martin	..	..	Donaghy	Robins	..	..	..	Maiorana	Duxbury for Robins, Wilson for Anderson
22 Apr	Charlton	A	L	0–1	..	Duxbury	Donaghy	..	..	Whiteside	Robson	..	..	..	Milne	Robins for Milne
29 Apr	Coventry	H	L	0–1	..	..	..	..	..	..	..	..	..	..	Martin	Robins for Martin
2 May	Wimbledon	H	W	1–0	..	..	..	..	..	..	..	..	..1	..	..	Maiorana for Whiteside
6 May	Southampton	A	L	1–2	..	..	..	..	..	..	..	..1	..	..	..	Sharpe for Martin, Milne for Robson
8 May	Q P R	A	L	*2–3	..	..	Sharpe	..1	Blackmore1	Donaghy	Milne	..	..	..	..	
10 May	Everton	H	L	1–2	..	..	..	..	..	..	..	..	..	..1	..	Robins for Blackmore, Brazil for Duxbury
13 May	Newcastle	H	W	2–0	..	..	Martin	..	..	..	Robson1	..	..1	..	Milne	Sharpe for Blackmore, Robins for Milne
	FA Cup															
7 Jan	Q P R (3)	H	D	0–0	Leighton	Gill	Martin	Bruce	Beardsmore	Donaghy	Robson	Robins	McClair	Hughes	Milne	
11 Jan	Q P R (3R)	A	D	2–2	..	Martin	Sharpe	..	..	..	Gill1	Blackmore	..	..	..	Wilson for Sharpe, Graham1 for Blackmore
23 Jan	Q P R (3R2)	H	W	3–0	..	..	..	..	Blackmore	..	Robson1	Strachan	..2	..	..	McGrath for Milne, Beardsmore for Blackmore
28 Jan	Oxford (4)	H	W	*4–0	..	Blackmore	..	..1	McGrath	..	..1	..	..	..1	..	Gill for McGrath, Beardsmore for Sharpe
18 Feb	B'mouth (5)	A	D	1–1	..	..	Martin	..	..	..	..	..	..	..1	..	Sharpe for Martin
22 Feb	B'mouth (5R)	H	W	1–0	..	..	Sharpe	..	..	..	..	..	..1	..	..	Gill for Milne
18 Mar	Nott For (6)	H	L	0–1	..	Beardsmore	..	..	..	..	..	..	..	..	..	Martin for Sharpe, Blackmore for Milne
*Includes own goal																
†After extra time																
	Littlewoods Cup															
28 Sep	Rth'ham (2)	A	W	1–0	Leighton	Blackmore	Sharpe	Bruce	McGrath	Duxbury	Robson	Strachan	McClair	Hughes	Davenport1	Beardsmore for Sharpe, Olsen for Strachan
12 Oct	Rth'ham (2)	H	W	5–0	..	Beardsmore	Blackmore	..1	Garton	..	..1	..	..3	..	..	Davenport for Robson, Robins for Duxbury
2 Nov	Wimbledon (3)	A	L	1–2	..	Blackmore	Gibson	..	..	..	..1	O'Brien	..	..	Olsen	Anderson for Olsen, Strachan for Duxbury
	F.A. Centenary Trophy															
29 Aug	Everton	H	W	1–0	Leighton	Anderson	Blackmore	Bruce	Garton	Duxbury	Robson	Strachan1	McClair	Hughes	Olsen	Davenport for Olsen
21 Sep	Newcastle	H	W	2–0†	..	Blackmore	Sharpe	..1	..	..	..	Davenport	..1	..	..	Beardsmore for Olsen, O'Brien for Davenport

9 Oct	Arsenal (F) (at Villa Park)	N	L	1–2	..	..1	..	..	..	..	..	..	..	..	..	Strachan for Olsen, Beardsmore for Davenport

Appearances (goals)

Anderson 8 – Beardsmore 33 (2) – Blackmore 40 (4) – Brazil 1 – Bruce 51 (5) – Davenport 13 (3) – Donaghy 37 – Duxbury 23 – Garton 19 – Gibson 3 – Gill 14 (2) – Graham 1 1 – Hughes 51 (16) – Leighton 5 Maiorana 6 – Martin 30 (1) – McClair 51 (17) – McGrath 26 (1) – Milne 29 (3) – O'Brien 7 – Olsen 15 – Robins 12 – Robson 46 (8) – Sharpe 32 – Strachan 31 (2) – Whiteside 6 – Wilson 5 – Own Goals 2 – Total 27 players (67)

Football League

	P	W	D	L	F:A	Pts
Arsenal	38	22	10	6	73:36	76 1st
Manchester U	38	13	12	13	45:45	51 11th

SEASON 1989–1990 FOOTBALL LEAGUE (DIVISION 1) — **1989–1990**

19 Aug	Arsenal	H	W	4–1	Leighton	Duxbury	Blackmore	Bruce1	Phelan	Donaghy	Robson	Webb1	McClair1	Hughes1	Sharpe	Martin for Sharpe
22 Aug	C Palace	A	D	1–1	..	..	..	..	..	..	..1	..	..	..	..	
26 Aug	Derby C	A	L	0–2	..	..	Martin	..	..	Blackmore	..	..	..	..	..	Graham for Martin
30 Aug	Norwich	H	L	0–2	..	..	Blackmore	..	..	Pallister	..	..	..	..	..	Martin for Robson, Robins for Blackmore
9 Sep	Everton	A	L	2–3	..	..	Martin	..	..	..	Donaghy	Blackmore	..1	..	..	Anderson for Duxbury, Beardsmore1 for Martin
16 Sep	Millwall	H	W	5–1	..	Anderson	Donaghy	..	..	..	Robson1	Ince	..	..3	Sharpe1	Duxbury for Ince, Beardsmore for Bruce
23 Sep	Man City	A	L	1–5	..	..	..	Duxbury	..	..	Beardsmore	..	..	..1	Wallace	Sharpe for Beardsmore
14 Oct	Sheffield Wed	H	D	0–0	..	..	..	..	..	..	Robson	..	..	..	..	Martin for Duxbury, Sharpe for Wallace
21 Oct	Coventry	A	W	4–1	..	Donaghy	Martin	Bruce1	..1	..	..	..	..	..2	Sharpe	Duxbury for Ince, Maiorana for Sharpe
28 Oct	Southampton	H	W	2–1	..	..	..	..	..	..	..	..	..2	..	..	Blackmore for Ince
4 Nov	Charlton	A	L	0–2	..	..	..	..	..	..	..	..	..	..	..	Blackmore for Donaghy, Wallace for Sharpe
12 Nov	Nottingham F	H	W	1–0	..	Blackmore	..	..	..	..1	..	..	..	..	Wallace	Sharpe for Wallace
18 Nov	Luton	A	W	3–1	..	..1	..	..	..	..	..	..	..	..1	..1	
25 Nov	Chelsea	H	D	0–0	..	..	..	..	..	..	..	..	..	..	..	Duxbury for Martin, Beardsmore for Wallace
3 Dec	Arsenal	A	L	0–1	..	..	..	..	..	..	..	..	..	..	..	Beardsmore for Blackmore
9 Dec	C Palace	H	L	1–2	..	Beardsmore1	..	..	..	..	..	..	..	Sharpe	..	Hughes for Sharpe, Blackmore for Phelan
16 Dec	Tottenham	H	L	0–1	..	..	Sharpe	..	..	..	..	..	..	Hughes	..	Anderson for Bruce, Blackmore for Beardsmore
23 Dec	Liverpool	A	D	0–0	..	Blackmore	Martin	..	..	..	..	..	..	..	..	Sharpe for Wallace
26 Dec	Aston V	A	L	0–3	..	Anderson	..	..	..	..	Blackmore	..	..	..	Sharpe	Duxbury for Martin, Robins for Blackmore
30 Dec	Wimbledon	A	D	2–2	..	..	..	..	..	..	..	..	..	..1	Robins1	Sharpe for Ince
1 Jan	Q P R	H	D	0–0	..	..	..	..	..	..	Sharpe	Blackmore	..	..	..	Duxbury for Sharpe, Beardsmore for Blackmore
13 Jan	Derby C	H	L	1–2	..	..	..	..	..	..1	Beardsmore	..	..	..	..	Duxbury for Anderson, Milne for Beardsmore
21 Jan	Norwich	A	L	0–2	..	..	..	..	..	..	Robins	Ince	..	..	Wallace	Blackmore for Phelan, Beardsmore for Ince
3 Feb	Man City	H	D	1–1	..	..	..	Donaghy	..	..	Blackmore1	Duxbury	..	..	..	Beardsmore for Donaghy, Robins for Wallace
10 Feb	Millwall	A	W	2–1	..	..	..	Beardsmore	..	..	..	..	..	..1	..1	Brazil for Anderson, Robins for Blackmore
24 Feb	Chelsea	A	L	0–1	..	..	..	Bruce	..	..	Duxbury	Ince	..	..	..	Donaghy for Anderson, Beardsmore for Duxbury
3 Mar	Luton	H	W	4–1	..	..	..	..	..	..	Robins1	Ince	..	..1	..1	Beardsmore for Wallace
14 Mar	Everton	H	D	0–0	..	Duxbury	..	..	..	..	..	..	..1	..	..	Blackmore for Robins, Beardsmore for Hughes
18 Mar	Liverpool	H	L	*1–2	..	Anderson	..	..	..	..	Blackmore	..	..	..	..	Duxbury for Anderson, Beardsmore for Wallace
21 Mar	Sheffield Wed	A	L	0–1	..	Donaghy	..	..	..	..	Beardsmore	Gibson	..	..	Blackmore	Ince for Blackmore, Wallace for Beardsmore
24 Mar	Southampton	A	W	2–0	..	..	..	..	..	..	Gibson1	Ince	..	..	Wallace	Webb for Gibson, Robins1 for Hughes
31 Mar	Coventry	H	W	3–0	..	..	Gibson	..	..	..	Webb	..	..	..2	..	Martin for Donaghy, Robins1 for Wallace
14 Apr	Q P R	A	W	2–1	Sealey	Ince	Martin	..	..	..	Robson	Webb1	..	..	..	Gibson for Bruce, Robins1 for Hughes
17 Apr	Aston V	H	W	2–0	..	Anderson	Gibson	Robins2	..	..	..	..	..	..	..	Blackmore for Gibson, Beardsmore for Anderson
21 Apr	Tottenham	A	L	1–2	Leighton	Robins	Martin	Bruce1	..	..	..	..	..	..	..	Blackmore for Webb, Beardsmore for Wallace
30 Apr	Wimbledon	H	D	0–0	Bosnich	Anderson	..	..	..	..	Beardsmore	Ince	..	..	Gibson	Wallace for Robins, Blackmore for Gibson
2 May	Nottingham F	A	L	0–4	Leighton	Duxbury	Blackmore	..	..	..	..	Webb	Robins	Robins	Wallace	
5 May	Charlton	H	W	1–0	..	Ince	Martin	..	..	..1	Robson	..	McClair	Hughes	..	
	FA Cup															
7 Jan	N Forest (3)	A	W	1–0	..	Anderson	..	..	..	..	Beardsmore	Blackmore	..	..	Robins1	Duxbury for Blackmore
28 Jan	Hereford (4)	A	W	1–0	..	..	..	Donaghy	Duxbury	..	Blackmore1	Ince	..	..	Wallace	Beardsmore for Ince
18 Feb	Newcastle (5)	A	W	3–2	..	..	..	Bruce	Phelan	..	Robins1	Duxbury	..1	..	..1	Ince for Duxbury, Beardsmore for Robins
11 Mar	Sheff Utd (6)	A	W	1–0	..	..	..	..	..	..	..	Ince	..1	..	..	Duxbury for Anderson
8 Apr	Oldham (SF) (at Maine Rd)	N	D	3–3†	..	Martin	Gibson	..	..	..	Robson1	..	..	..	Webb1	Wallace1 for Robins, Robins for Martin
11 Apr	Oldham (SFR) (at Maine Rd)	N	W	2–1	..	Ince	Martin	..	..	..	..	Webb	McClair1	..	Wallace	Gibson for Webb, Robins1 for Martin
12 May	C Palace (F) (at Wembley)	N	D	3–3†	..	..	..	..	..	..	..1	..	..	..2	..	Robins for Pallister, Blackmore for Martin
17 May	C Palace (FR) (at Wembley)	N	W	1–0	Sealey	..	..1	..	..	..	..	..	..	..	..	
†After extra time																
	Littlewoods Cup															
10 Sep	Portsm'th (2)	A	W	3–2	Leighton	Anderson	Donaghy	Beardsmore	..	..	..	Ince2	..	..	..1	Duxbury for Robson, Sharpe for McClair
3 Oct	Portsm'th (2)	H	D	0–0	..	Duxbury	..	Bruce	..	..	..	..	..	..	..	
25 Oct	Tottenham (3)	H	L	0–3	..	Donaghy	Martin	..	..	..	..	..	..	..	Sharpe	Maiorana for Martin

Appearances (goals)

Anderson 23 – Beardsmore 28 (2) – Blackmore 33 (3) – Bosnich 1 – Bruce 43 (3) – Brazil 1 – Donaghy 19 – Duxbury 24 – Gibson 8 (1) – Graham 1 – Hughes 48 (15) – Ince 36 2 – Leighton 45 – Maiorana 2 – Martin 40 (1) – Milne 1 – McClair 48 (8) – Pallister 46 (3) – Phelan 48 (1) – Robins 24 (10) – Robson 27 (4) – Sealey 3 – Sharpe 22 (1) – Wallace 34 (6) – Webb 15 (3) – Own goals 1 – Total 25 players (64)

Football League

	P	W	D	L	F:A	Pts
Liverpool	38	23	10	5	78:37	79 1st
Manchester U	38	13	9	16	46:47	48 13th

SEASON 1990–1991 FOOTBALL LEAGUE (DIVISION 1) — **1990–1991**

25 Aug	Coventry	H	W	2–0	Sealey	Irwin	Donaghy	Bruce1	Phelan	Pallister	Webb1	Ince	McClair	Hughes	Blackmore	Beardsmore for Ince
28 Aug	Leeds	A	D	0–0	..	..	..	..	..	..	..	..	..	..	..	Beardsmore for Donaghy, Robins for Hughes
1 Sep	Sunderland	A	L	1–2	..	..	..	..	..	..	..	..	..1	..	..	Hughes for Robins, Donaghy for Beardsmore
4 Sep	Luton Town	A	W	1–0	..	..	Blackmore	..	..	..	..	..	..	Robins1	Beardsmore	
8 Sep	Q P R	H	W	3–1	..	..	..	..	..	..	..	..	..1	..2	..	Beardsmore for Ince, Donaghy for Pallister
16 Sep	Liverpool	A	L	0–4	..	..	..	..	..	..	..	..	..	Hughes	Robins	Sharpe for Irwin, Beardsmore for Robins
22 Sep	Southampton	H	W	3–2	..	..	..	Donaghy	..	..	..	Robins	..1	..1	Blackmore1	Hughes for Robins, Martin for Beardsmore
29 Sep	Nottingham F	H	L	0–1	..	..	Blackmore	..	..	..	..	Ince	..	Robins	Beardsmore	Martin for Irwin, Robins for Sharpe
20 Oct	Arsenal	H	L	0–1	..	..	..	Bruce	..	..	..	..	..	..	Sharpe	Wallace for Sharpe
27 Oct	Man City	A	D	3–3	..	..	Martin	..	Blackmore	..	..	..1	..	Hughes1	..	Martin for Wallace
3 Nov	C Palace	H	W	2–0	..	..	Blackmore	..	Phelan	..	..	..1	..	Wallace1	..	Donaghy for Irwin, Wallace for Sharpe
10 Nov	Derby C	A	D	0–0	..	..	..	..	..	..	..	..	..	Hughes	..	Wallace for Irwin
17 Nov	Sheffield Utd	H	W	2–0	..	..	..	..1	..	..	..	..	..	..1	..	Martin for Blackmore, Sharpe for Phelan
25 Nov	Chelsea	H	L	2–3	..	..	..	..	..	..	..	..	..	..1	Wallace1	Martin for Sharpe, Webb for Ince
1 Dec	Everton	A	W	1–0	..	..	..	Donaghy	..	..	Sharpe1	..	..	..	..	Donaghy for Phelan, Robson for Irwin
8 Dec	Leeds	H	D	1–1	..	..	..	Bruce	..	..	..	Webb1	..	..	..	Irwin for Ince, Robson for Sharpe
15 Dec	Coventry	A	D	2–2	..	Blackmore	Sharpe	..	..	..	Webb	Ince	..	..1	..1	Wallace for Blackmore
22 Dec	Wimbledon	A	W	3–1	..	..	Donaghy	..2	..	..	Robson	..	..	..1	Webb	Donaghy for Sharpe, Phelan for Robson
26 Dec	Norwich	H	W	3–0	..	Irwin	Blackmore	..	Webb	..	..	..	..2	..1	Sharpe	Phelan for Robson
29 Dec	Aston V	H	D	1–1	..	..	..	..1	..	..	..	..	..	..	..	Martin for Irwin, Robins for Phelan
1 Jan	Tottenham	A	W	2–1	..	..	..	..1	Phelan	..	Webb	..	..1	..	..	Robins for Ince, Phelan for Webb
12 Jan	Sunderland	H	W	3–0	..	..	..	..	Webb	..	Robson	..	..1	..2	..	Sharpe for Martin, Robins for Beardsmore
19 Jan	Q P R	A	D	1–1	..	..	Martin	..	Phelan1	Donaghy	Beardsmore	Webb	..	..	Blackmore	Wallace for Webb, Martin for Phelan
3 Feb	Liverpool	H	D	1–1	..	..	Blackmore	..1	..	Pallister	Robson	..	..	..	Sharpe	Ferguson for Webb, Robins for Robson
26 Feb	Sheffield Utd	A	L	1–2	Walsh	..	Martin	Webb	Donaghy	..	..	Ince	..	Blackmore1	Wallace	Beardsmore for Martin, Giggs for Irwin
2 Mar	Everton	H	L	0–2	Sealey	..	..	Ferguson	..	..	Sharpe	..	..	..	..	Wallace for Blackmore
10 Mar	Chelsea	A	L	2–3	..	Blackmore	..	Donaghy	Phelan	..	Robson	..	..1	Hughes1	Sharpe	Ferguson for Whitworth, Robins for Beardsmore
13 Mar	Southampton	A	D	1–1	..	Whitworth	..	..	..	..	Beardsmore	..1	..	..	..	Donaghy for Martin
16 Mar	Nottingham F	A	D	1–1	..	Irwin	..	Bruce	..	..	Robson	..	Blackmore1	..	Wallace	Robins1 for Wallace
23 Mar	Luton Town	H	W	4–1	..	..	Blackmore	..2	..	..	..	Wallace	McClair1	..	Sharpe	Wratten for Sharpe, Robins for Bruce
2 Apr	Wimbledon	H	W	2–1	Walsh	..	Donaghy	..1	..	..	Webb	Ince	..1	Blackmore	..	Robins for Phelan

6 Apr	Aston V	A	D	1–1	Sealey	..	..	..	..	..	Robson	Webb	..	Hughes	Sharpe1	McClair1 for Webb
16 Apr	Derby C	H	W	3–1	Bosnich	..	..	..	Webb	..	..1	Ince	Blackmore1	..	Wallace	Donaghy for Giggs
4 May	Man City	H	W	1–0	Walsh	..	Blackmore	..	Phelan	..	Robson	Webb	McClair	..	Giggs1	Beardsmore for Hughes, Ferguson for Robson
6 May	Arsenal	A	L	1–3	..	Phelan	..	..1	Webb	Donaghy	..	Ince	..	..	Robins	Beardsmore for Pallister, Wratten for Robins
11 May	C Palace	A	L	0–3	..	Irwin	Donaghy	..	..	Pallister	Kanchelskis	..	Robins	Ferguson	Wallace	Donaghy for Irwin, Robins for Wallace
20 May	Tottenham	H	D	1–1	Bosnich	..	Blackmore	..	Phelan	..	Robson	..1	McClair	Hughes	..	
	FA Cup															
7 Jan	Q P R (3)	H	W	2–1	Sealey	Irwin	Blackmore	Bruce	Phelan	Pallister	Robson	Ince	McClair1	Hughes1	Sharpe	
26 Jan	Bolton (4)	H	W	1–0	..	..	..	..	..	..	..	Webb	..	..1	..	Robins for Phelan
18 Feb	Norwich (5)	A	L	1–2	..	..	Martin	..	Blackmore	..	..	Ince	..1	..	..	Wallace for Martin
	European Cupwinners Cup															
19 Sep	Pesci	H	W	2–0	Sealey	Irwin	Blackmore1	Bruce	Phelan	Pallister	Webb1	Ince	McClair	Robins	Beardsmore	Hughes for Robins, Sharpe for Ince
	Munkas (1)															
3 Oct	Pesci	A	W	1–0	..	Anderson	Donaghy	..	..	..	..	Blackmore	..1	Hughes	Martin	Sharpe for Martin
	Munkas (1)															
23 Oct	Wrexham (2)	H	W	3–0	..	Blackmore	Martin	..1	Sharpe	..1	..	Ince	..1	..	Wallace	Robins for Wallace, Beardsmore for Ince
7 Dec	Wrexham (2)	A	W	2–0	..	Irwin	Blackmore	..1	Phelan	..	..	..	..	Robins1	..	Donaghy for Ince, Martin for McClair
6 Mar	Montpellier (3)	H	D	1–1	..	Blackmore	Martin	Donaghy	..	..	Robson	..	..1	Hughes	Sharpe	Wallace for Martin
19 Mar	Montpellier (3)	A	W	2–0	..	Irwin	Blackmore1	Bruce1	..	..	..	..	..	..	..	Martin for Ince
10 Apr	Legia	A	W	3–1	..	..	..	..1	..		Webb	..	..1	..1	..	Donaghy for Phelan
	Warsaw (SF)															
24 Apr	Legia	H	D	1–1	Walsh	..	..	..	..	..	Robson	Webb	..	..	..1	Donaghy for Blackmore
	Warsaw (SF)															
15 May	Barcelona (F)	N	W	2–1	Sealey	..	..	..	..	..	..	Ince	..	..2	..	
(at Stadion Feijenoord Rotterdam)																
	Rumbelows Cup															
26 Sep	Halifax (2)	A	W	3–1	Leighton	Irwin	Blackmore1	Donaghy	Phelan	Pallister	Webb1	Ince	McClair1	Hughes	Beardsmore	Martin for Ince, Robins for Hughes
10 Oct	Halifax (2)	H	W	2–1	Sealey	Anderson	..	Bruce1	..	..	..	Irwin	..	..	Martin	Wallace for Blackmore, Robins for Irwin
31 Oct	Liverpool (3)	H	W	3–1	..	Irwin	..	..1	..	..	..	Ince	..	..1	Sharpe1	Donaghy for Phelan, Wallace for Hughes
28 Nov	Arsenal (4)	A	W	6–2	..	..	..1	..	..	..	Sharpe3	..	..	..1	Wallace1	Donaghy for Bruce
16 Jan	S`thampton (5)	A	D	1–1	..	Donaghy	..	..	..	..	Robson	Webb	..	..1	Sharpe	Irwin for Webb
23 Jan	S`thampton (5)	H	W	3–2	..	Irwin	..	..	..	..	..	..	..	..3	..	Donaghy for Irwin, Robins for Sharpe
10 Feb	Leeds (SF1)	H	W	2–1	..	..	Martin	..	Blackmore	..	..	Ince	..1	..	..1	Donaghy for Irwin, Wallace for Martin
24 Feb	Leeds (SF2)	A	W	1–0	..	Donaghy	Blackmore	Webb	Phelan	..	Robson	..	..	..	..1	Martin for Webb
21 Apr	Sheff Wed (F)	N	L	0–1	..	Irwin	..	Bruce	Webb	..	..	..	..	..	..	Phelan for Webb

Football League

	P	W	D	L	F:A	Pts
Arsenal*	38	24	13	1	74:18	83 1st
Manchester U**	38	16	12	10	58:45	59 6th

*Two points deducted **One point deducted

Appearances (goals)

Anderson 3 (1) – Beardsmore 16 – Blackmore 57 (9) – Bruce 50 (19) – Bosnich 2 – Donaghy 38 – Ferguson 5 – Giggs 2 (1) – Hughes 52 (21) – Ince 47(3) – Irwin 52 – Kanchelskis 1 – Leighton 1 – Martin 24 – McClair 58 (21) Pallistor 58 (1) – Phelan 51 (1) – Robins 27 (5) – Robson 29 (1) – Sealey 51 – Sharpe 40 (9) – Wallace 29 (4) – Walsh 6 – Webb 47 (5) – Whitworth 1 – Wratten 1 – Total 26 players (101)

SEASON 1991–1992 FOOTBALL LEAGUE (DIVISION 1) **1991–1992**

17 Aug	Notts City	H	W	2–0	Schmeichel	Irwin	Blackmore	Bruce	Ferguson	Parker	Robson1	Ince	McClair	Hughes	Kanchelskis	Pallister for Ince, Giggs for Ferguson
21 Aug	Aston V	A	W	1–0	..	..	..	..1	Donaghy	..	..	..	..	..	..	
24 Aug	Everton	A	D	0–0	..	..	..	..	..	..	..	..	..	..	Giggs	Pallister for Irwin, Webb for Blackmore
28 Aug	Oldham Ath	H	W	1–0	..	Parker	Irwin	..	Webb	Pallister	..	..	..1	..	..	Blackmore for Ince, Ferguson for Webb
31 Aug	Leeds	H	D	1–1	..	..	..	..	..	..	..1	..	..	..	Blackmore	Phelan for Bruce, Giggs for Ince
3 Sep	Wimbledon	A	W	2–1	..	..	Donaghy	..	Phelan	..1	..	Webb	..	..	..1	Irwin for Phelan
7 Sep	Norwich	H	W	3–0	..	..	Irwin1	..	Webb	..	..	Kanchelskis	..1	..	Giggs1	Blackmore for Kanchelskis, Phelan for Webb
14 Sep	Southampton	A	W	1–0	..	Phelan	..	..	..	..	..	Ince	..	..1	..	Ince for Kanchelskis
21 Sep	Luton Town	H	W	5–0	..	..	..	..1	..	..	..	..1	Blackmore	..1	..	McClair2 for Blackmore
28 Sep	Tottenham	A	W	2–1	..	..	..	..	Kanchelskis	..	..1	..	McClair	..1	..	Blackmore for Kanchelskis
6 Oct	Liverpool	H	D	0–0	..	..	..	..	Blackmore	..	..	..	..	..	..	Kanchelskis for Phelan, Donaghy for Ince
19 Oct	Arsenal	H	D	1–1	..	Blackmore	..	..1	Webb	..	..	..	..	..	..	Kanchelskis for Webb
26 Oct	Sheffield Wed	A	L	2–3	..	Parker	..	..	..	..	..	Kanchelskis	..2	Blackmore	..	Martin for Bruce
2 Nov	Sheffield Utd	H	W	*2–0	..	..	Blackmore	..	..	Donaghy	Kanchelskis1	Ince	..	Robins	..	Robson for Ince, Pallister for Giggs
16 Nov	Man City	A	D	0–0	..	..	Irwin	..	..	Pallister	Robson	Blackmore	..	Hughes	..	Ince for Webb
23 Nov	West Ham	H	W	2–1	..	..	..	..	..	..	..1	Kanchelskis	..1	..	..1	Blackmore for Parker
30 Nov	C Palace	A	W	3–1	..	..	..	..	..1	..	..	..1	..	..	..	Blackmore for Irwin
7 Dec	Coventry	H	W	4–0	..	..	..	..1	..1	..	..	Ince	..1	..1	..	Blackmore for Parker
15 Dec	Chelsea	A	W	3–1	..	..	..1	..1	..	..	Kanchelskis	..	..1	..	..	Blackmore for Giggs
26 Dec	Oldham Ath	A	W	6–3	..	..	..1	..	..	..	Robson	..	..2	..	..1	Giggs1 for Robson, Blackmore for Irwin
29 Dec	Leeds	A	D	1–1	..	..	..	..	..1	..	Kanchelskis	..	..	..	..	Donaghy for Kanchelskis, Sharpe for Blackmore
1 Jan	Q P R	H	L	1–4	..	..	Blackmore	..	..	..	Phelan	..	..1	..	Sharpe	Giggs for Sharpe
11 Jan	Everton	H	W	1–0	..	..	..	..	..	..	Kanchelskis	..	..	..	Giggs	Donaghy for Blackmore
18 Jan	Notts City	A	D	1–1	..	..	Irwin	..	..	..	..	..	..	..	..	Robins for Giggs, Blackmore1 for Bruce
22 Jan	Aston V	H	W	1–0	..	Donaghy	..	..	..	..	Robson	..	..	..1	Kanchelskis	
1 Feb	Arsenal	A	D	1–1	..	Parker	..	Donaghy	..	..	..	..	..	..	..	Giggs for Ince
8 Feb	Sheffield Wed	H	D	1–1	..	Giggs	..	..	..	..	..	..1	..1	..	..	Phelan for Webb, Sharpe for Giggs
22 Feb	C Palace	H	W	2–0	..	..	..	..	..	..	..	..	..	..2	..	Parker for Robson, Blackmore for Kanchelskis
26 Feb	Chelsea	H	D	1–1	Walsh	Donaghy	..	Giggs	..	..	..	..	..	..1	..	Blackmore for Kanchelskis
29 Feb	Coventry	A	D	0–0	..	Parker	..	Donaghy	..	..	Kanchelskis	..	..	..	Giggs	Blackmore for Bruce
14 Mar	Sheffield Utd	A	W	2–1	Schmeichel	..	..	Bruce	Phelan	..	Robson	..	..1	Sharpe	Kanchelkis	Kanchelskis for Hughes, Giggs for Webb
18 Mar	Nottingham F	A	L	0–1	..	Blackmore	..	..	Webb	..	Phelan	..	..	Hughes	Sharpe	Sharpe for Webb
21 Mar	Wimbledon	H	D	0–0	..	..	..	..	..	..	Kanchelskis	..	..	..	Giggs	Sharpe for Kanchelskis
28 Mar	Q P R	A	D	0–0	..	Donaghy	..	..	Phelan	..	Robson	Kanchelskis	..	..	..	Blackmore for Robson
31 Mar	Norwich	A	W	3–1	..	..	..	..	Giggs	..	..	Ince2	..1	..	Sharpe	Kanchelskis for Blackmore
7 Apr	Man City	H	D	1–1	..	..	..	..	Blackmore	..	Giggs1	..	..	..	..	Webb for Ince
16 Apr	Southampton	H	W	1–0	..	Parker	..	..	Phelan	..	Kanchelskis1	..	..	..	Giggs	Kanchelskis for Hughes, Blackmore for Parker
18 Apr	Luton Town	A	D	1–1	..	..	..	..	..	..	Giggs	Webb	..	..	Sharpe1	Hughes for Webb, Donaghy for Sharpe
20 Apr	Nottingham F	H	L	1–2	..	Blackmore	..	..	..	..	Kanchelskis	..	..1	Giggs	Sharpe	Ferguson for Donaghy, Kanchelskis for Blackmore
22 Apr	West Ham	A	L	0–1	..	Donaghy	..	..	..	..	Blackmore	Giggs	..	Hughes	..	Phelan for Pallister
26 Apr	Liverpool	A	L	0–2	..	..	..	..	Kanchelskis	..	Robson	Ince	..	..	Giggs	Sharpe for Ince
2 May	Tottenham	H	W	3–1	..	Ferguson	..	..	Phelan	Donaghy	Kanchelskis	..	..1	..2	..	
*Includes own goal																
	FA Cup															
15 Jan	Leeds (3)	A	W	1–0	Schmeichel	Parker	Irwin	Bruce	Webb	Pallister	Kanchelskis	Ince	McClair	Hughes1	Giggs	
27 Jan	S'thampton (4)	A	D	0–0	..	..	..	Donaghy	..	..	Robson	..	..	..	Blackmore	Giggs for Blackmore
5 Feb	S'thampton (4R)	H	D	2–2P	..	..	..	..	..	..	..	..	..1	Giggs	Kanchelskis	Hughes for Kanchelskis, Sharpe for Donaghy
	European Cupwinners Cup															
18 Sep	Athinaikos (1)	A	D	0–0	Schmeichel	Phelan	Irwin	Bruce	Webb	Pallister	Robins	Ince	McClair	Hughes	Beardsmore	Wallace for Beardsmore
2 Oct	Athinaikos (1)	H	W	2–0†	..	..	Martin	,.	Kanchelskis	..	Robson	..	..1	..1	Wallace	Robins for Wallace, Beardsmore for Martin
23 Oct	Ath Madrid (2)	A	L	0–3	..	Parker	Irwin	..	Webb	..	..	..	..	..	Phelan	Martin for McClair, Beardsmore for Phelan
6 Nov	Ath Madrid (2)	H	D	1–1	Walsh	..	Blackmore	..	..	Phelan	..	Robins	..	..1	Giggs	Pallister for Robins, Martin for Phelan
	European Super Cup Final															
19 Nov	Red Star	H	W	1–0	Schmeichel	Martin	Irwin	Bruce	Webb	Pallister	Kanchelskis	Ince	McClair1	Hughes	Blackmore	Giggs for Martin
	Belgrade															
(Final reduced to one game because of Civil War in Yugoslavia)																
	Rumbelows Cup															
25 Sep	Cambridge (2)	H	W	3–0	Walsh	Phelan	Irwin	Bruce1	Webb	Pallister	Robson	Ince	McClair1	Hughes	Blackmore	Giggs1 for Webb
9 Oct	Cambridge (2)	A	D	1–1	Wilkinson	Donaghy	..	..	Blackmore	..	..	..	..1	..	Martin	Giggs for Martin, Robins for Pallister
30 Oct	Portsmouth (3)	H	W	3–1	Schmeichel	Parker	..	..	Webb	..	Donaghy	Kanchelskis	..	Blackmore	Giggs	Robson1 for Webb, Robins2 for Irwin
4 Dec	Oldham Ath (4)	H	W	2–0	..	..	..	..	..	..	Robson	..1	..1	Hughes	..	Ince for Robson, Blackmore for Giggs
8 Jan	Leeds (5)	A	W	3–1	..	..	Blackmore1	..	..	..	Kanchelskis1	Ince	..	..	..1	Donaghy for Giggs, Sharpe for Kanchelskis
4 Mar	Mid'bro (SF1)	A	D	0–0	..	..	Irwin	Donaghy	..	..	Robson	..	..	..	..	Phelan for Donaghy, Sharpe for Ince

11 Mar	Mid'bro (SF2)	H	W	2–1†	..	..	..	Bruce	..	..	..	..	..	Sharpe1	..1	Robins for Sharpe
12 Apr	Nott F (F) (at Wembley)	N	W	1–0	..	..	..	..	Phelan	..	Kanchelskis	..	..1	Hughes	..	Sharpe for Kanchelskis

!After extra time

Appearances (goals)

Beardsmore 3 – Blackmore 42 (4)– Bruce 50 (6) – Donaghy 26 – Ferguson 4 – Giggs 51 (7) – Hughes 52 (14) – Ince 47 (3) – Irwin 51 (4) – Kanchelskis 42 (8) – Martin 6 – McClair 58 (25) – Pallister 56 (1) – Parker 37 – Phelan 24 – Robins 8 (2) – Robson 38 (5) – Schmeichel 53 – Sharpe 20 (2) – Wallace 2 – Walsh 4 – Webb 44 (3) – Wilkinson 1 – Own goals 1 – Total 23 players (85)

Football League

	P	W	D	L	F:A	Pts
Leeds U	42	22	16	4	74:37	82 1st
Manchester U	42	21	15	6	63:33	78 2nd

SEASON 1992–1993 FA PREMIER LEAGUE 1992–1993

15 Aug	Sheff Utd	A	L	1–2	Schmeichel	Irwin	Blackmore	Bruce	Ferguson	Pallister	Kanchelskis	Ince	McClair	Hughes1	Giggs	Phelan for Ince, Dublin for Kanchelskis
19 Aug	Everton	H	L	0–3	..	..	..	..	..	..	..	..	..	..	..	Phelan for Ince, Dublin for Giggs
22 Aug	Ipswich	H	D	1–1	..	..1	..	..	..	..	..	Phelan	..	..	..	Webb for Blackmore, Dublin for Kanchelskis
24 Aug	Southampton	A	W	1–0	..	Phelan	Irwin	..	..	..	Dublin1	Ince	..	..	..	
29 Aug	Nottm For	A	W	2–0	..	..	..	..	..	..	..	..	..	..1	..1	Blackmore for Phelan, Kanchelskis for Hughes
2 Sep	Crystal Pal	H	W	1–0	..	Blackmore	..	..	..	..	..	..	..	..1	..	Kanchelskis for Dublin
6 Sep	Leeds Utd	H	W	2–0	..	..	..	..1	..	..	Kanchelskis1	..	..	..	..	
12 Sep	Everton	A	W	2–0	..	Irwin	Blackmore	..1	..	..	..	..	..1	..	..	
19 Sep	Tottenham	A	D	1–1	..	..	..	..	..	..	..	..	..	..	..1	Wallace for Kanchelskis
26 Sep	Q P R	H	D	0–0	..	..	..	..	..	..	..	..	..	..	..	Wallace for Kanchelskis
3 Oct	Midds 'boro	A	D	1–1	..	..	Phelan	..1	..	..	Blackmore	..	..	..	..	Robson for Hughes, Kanchelskis for Phelan
18 Oct	Liverpool	H	D	2–2	..	Parker	Irwin	..	..	..	Kanchelskis	..	..	..2	..	Blackmore for Kanchelskis
24 Oct	Blackburn	A	D	0–0	..	..	..	..	..	..	Blackmore	..	..	..	..	Kanchelskis for Ferguson
31 Oct	Wimbledon	H	L	0–1	..	..	Blackmore	..	..	..	Kanchelskis	..	..	..	..	Robson for Kanchelskis
7 Nov	Aston Villa	A	L	0–1	..	..	..	..	..	..	Robson	..	Sharpe	..	..	McClair for Ferguson
21 Nov	Oldham Ath	H	W	3–0	..	..	Irwin	..	Sharpe	..	..	..	McClair2	..1	..	Phelan for Irwin, Butt for Ince
28 Nov	Arsenal	A	W	1–0	..	..	..	..	..	..	..	..	..	..1	..	
6 Dec	Man City	H	W	2–1	..	..	..	..	..	..	..	..1	..	..1	..	Cantona for Giggs
12 Dec	Norwich	H	W	1–0	..	..	..	..	..	..	Cantona	..	..	..1	..	
19 Dec	Chelsea	A	D	1–1	..	..	..	..	Phelan	..	..1	..	..	..	Sharpe	Kanchelskis for Phelan
26 Dec	Sheff Wed	A	D	3–3	..	..	..	..	Sharpe	..	..1	..	..2	..	Giggs	Kanchelskis for Giggs
28 Dec	Coventry	H	W	5–0	..	..	..1	..	..1	..	..1	..	..	..1	..1	Kanchelskis for Giggs, Phelan for Bruce
9 Jan	Tottenham	H	W	4–1	..	..1	..1	..	..	..	..1	..	..1	..	..	Kanchelskis for Giggs, Phelan for Ince
18 Jan	QPR	A	W	3–1	..	..	..	..	..	..	Kanchelskis1	..1	..	..	..1	Phelan for Hughes
27 Jan	Nottm For	H	W	2–0	..	..	..	..	..	..	Cantona	..1	..	..1	..	
30 Jan	Ipswich	A	L	1–2	..	..	..	..	..	..	..	..	..1	..	..	Kanchelskis for Sharpe
6 Feb	Sheff Utd	H	W	2–1	..	..	..	..	..	..	..1	..	..1	..	..	Kanchelskis for Giggs
8 Feb	Leeds	A	D	0–0	..	..	..	..	..	..	..	..	..	..	..	Kanchelskis for Giggs
20 Feb	Southampton	H	W	2–1	..	..	..	..	..	..	..	..	..	..	..2	
27 Feb	Middls'boro	H	W	3–0	..	..	..1	..	..	..	..1	..	..	..	..1	
6 Mar	Liverpool	A	W	2–1	..	..	..	..	..	..	Kanchelskis	..	..1	..1	..	
9 Mar	Oldham	A	L	0–1	..	..	..	..	..	..	..	..	..	..	..	Dublin for Kanchelskis
14 Mar	Aston Villa	H	D	1–1	..	..	..	..	..	..	Cantona	..	..	..1	..	
20 Mar	Man City	A	D	1–1	..	..	..	..	..	..	..1	..	..	..	..	
24 Mar	Arsenal	H	D	0–0	..	..	..	..	..	..	..	..	..	..	..	Robson for Hughes
5 Apr	Norwich	A	W	3–1	..	..	..	..	..	..	..1	..	..	Kanchelskis1	..1	Robson for Kanchelskis
10 Apr	Sheff Wed	H	W	2–1	..	..	..	..2	..	..	..	..	..	Hughes	..	Robson for Parker
12 Apr	Coventry	A	W	1–0	..	..	..1	..	..	..	..	..	..	..	..	Robson for Cantona
17 Apr	Chelsea	H	W	*3–0	..	..	..	..	..	..	..1	..	..	..1	..	Robson for McClair, Kanchelskis for Giggs
21 Apr	Crystal Pal	A	W	2–0	..	..	..	..	Kanchelskis	..	..	..1	..	..1	..	Robson for Kanchelskis
3 May	Blackburn	H	W	3–1	..	..	..	..	Sharpe	..1	..	..1	..	..	..1	Robson for Sharpe, Kanchelskis for McClair
9 May	Wimbledon	A	W	2–1	..	..	..	..	..	..	Robson1	..1	..	..	Cantona	Giggs for Irwin
*Includes own goal																
	FA Cup															
5 Jan	Bury (3)	H	W	2–0	Schmeichel	Parker	Irwin	Bruce	Sharpe	Pallister	Cantona	Phelan1	McClair	Hughes	Gillespie1	Robson for McClair, Blackmore for Irwin
23 Jan	Brighton (4)	H	W	1–0	..	..	..	..	..	..	Wallace	Ince	..	Phelan	Giggs1	Gillespie for Wallace
14 Feb	Sheff Utd (5)	A	L	1–2	..	..	..	..	..	..	Kanchelskis	..	..	Hughes	..1	
	UEFA Cup															
16 Sep	Torpedo Moscow (1)	H	D	0–0	Walsh	Irwin	Martin	Bruce	Blackmore	Pallister	Kanchelskis	Webb	McClair	Hughes	Wallace	Neville for Martin
29 Sep	Torpedo Moscow (1)	A	LP	0–0	Schmeichel	..	Phelan	..	Webb	..	Wallace	Ince	..	..	Giggs	Parker for Phelan, Robson for Wallace
(LP – Lost on penalties)																
	Coca Cola (League) Cup															
23 Sep	Brighton (2)	A	D	1–1	Walsh	Irwin	Martin	Bruce	Blackmore	Pallister	Kanchelskis	Ince	McClair	Hughes	Wallace1	Beckham for Kanchelskis
7 Oct	Brighton (2)	H	W	1–0	Schmeichel	Parker	Irwin	..	Kancheskis	..	Robson	..	..	..1	Giggs	
28 Oct	Aston Villa (3)	A	L	0–1	..	..	..	..	Ferguson	..	Blackmore	..	..	..	..	Kanchelskis for Irwin

Appearances (goals)

Beckham 1 – Blackmore 17 – Bruce 50 (5) – Butt 1 – Cantona 23 (9) – Dublin 7 (1) – Ferguson 16 – Giggs 46 (11) – Gillespie 2 (1) – Hughes 48 (16) – Ince 47 (6) – Irwin 48 (5) – Kanchelskis 30 (3) – McClair 50 (9) – Martin 2 – Neville 1 – Pallister 50 (1) – Parker 37 (1) – Phelan 14 (1) – Robson 17 (1) – Schmeichel 48 – Sharpe 30 (1) – Walsh 2 – Wallace 6 (1) – Webb 4 – Own goals 1 – Total 25 players (73)

FA Premier League

	P	W	D	L	F:A	Pts
Manchester U	42	24	12	6	67:31	84 1st

SEASON 1993–1994 FA PREMIER LEAGUE 1993–1994

15 Aug	Norwich	A	W	2–0	Schmeichel	Parker	Irwin	Bruce	Kanchelskis	Pallister	Robson1	Ince	Keane	Hughes	Giggs1	
18 Aug	Sheff Utd	H	W	3–0	..	..	..	..	..	..	..	..	..2	..1	..	McClair for Robson
21 Aug	Newcastle	H	D	1–1	..	..	..	..	..	..	..	..	..	..	..1	Sharpe for Parker, McClair for Kanchelskis
23 Aug	Aston Villa	A	W	2–1	..	..	..	..	Sharpe2	..	Kanchelskis	..	..	..	..	
28 Aug	Southampton	A	W	3–1	..	..	..1	..	..1	..	Cantona1	..	..	..	..	McClair for Giggs, Kanchelskis for Keane
1 Sep	West Ham	H	W	3–0	..	..	..	..1	..1	..	..1	..	..	Kanchelskis	..	McClair for Ince, Robson for Kanchelskis
11 Sep	Chelsea	A	L	0–1	..	..	..	..	..	..	..	..	..	Robson	..	McClair for Robson
19 Sep	Arsenal	H	W	1–0	..	..	..	..	..	..	..1	..	..	Hughes	..	McClair for Hughes
25 Sep	Swindon T	H	W	4–2	..	..	..	..	..	..	..1	..	..	..2	Kanchelskis1	McClair for Sharpe, Giggs for Kanchelskis
2 Oct	Sheff Wed	A	W	3–2	..	..	..	..	..	..	..	..	..	..2	Giggs1	Kanchelskis for Giggs
16 Oct	Tottenham	H	W	2–1	..	..	..	..	..1	..	..	Robson	..1	..	..	McClair for Robson, Butt for Giggs
23 Oct	Everton	A	W	1–0	..	Martin	..	..	..1	..	..	Ince	McClair	..	Keane	
30 Oct	Q P R	H	W	2–1	..	Parker	..	..	..	Phelan	..1	..	Keane	..1	Giggs	
7 Nov	Man City	A	W	3–2	..	..	..	..	..	Pallister	..2	..	..1	..	Kanchelskis	Giggs for Kanchelskis
20 Nov	Wimbledon	H	W	3–1	..	..	..	..	..	..1	..	..	Robson	..1	..1	Phelan for Robson
24 Nov	Ipswich	H	D	0–0	..	..	..	..	..	..	..	..	..	..	..	Giggs for Kanchelskis, Ferguson for Robson
27 Nov	Coventry	A	W	1–0	..	..	..	..	..	..	..1	..	Ferguson	..	Giggs	
4 Dec	Norwich	H	D	2–2	..	..	..	..	Kanchelskis	..	..	..	McClair1	..	..1	Sharpe for Kanchelskis
7 Dec	Sheff Utd	A	W	3–0	..	..	..	..	Sharpe1	..	..1	..	..	..1	..	Keane for McClair
11 Dec	Newcastle	A	D	1–1	..	..	..	..	..	..	..	..1	..	..	..	Kanchelskis for Hughes, Keane for McClair
19 Dec	Aston Villa	H	W	3–1	..	..	..	..	..	..	..2	..1	Keane	..	Kanchelskis	Giggs for Sharpe
26 Dec	Blackburn	H	D	1–1	..	..	..	..	..	..	..	..1	..	..	Giggs	McClair for Parker, Ferguson for Hughes
29 Dec	Oldham	A	W	5–2	..	..	..	..1	..	..	..1	..	..	Kanchelskis1	..1	McClair for Cantona, Robson for Ince
1 Jan	Leeds Utd	H	D	0–0	..	..	..	..	Robson	..	..	Keane	McClair	..	..	
4 Jan	Liverpool	A	D	3–3	..	..	..1	..1	Keane	..	..	Ince	..	..	..1	
15 Jan	Tottenham	A	W	1–0	..	..	..	..	Kanchelskis	..	..	..	Keane	Hughes1	..	McClair for Hughes
22 Jan	Everton	H	W	1–0	..	..	..	..	..	..	..	..	..	..	..	

5 Feb	Q P R	A	W	3–2	..	..	..	..	..1	..	..1	..	..	..	..1	
26 Feb	West Ham	A	D	2–2	..	..	..	..	..	..	..	..1	McClair	..1	Keane	Dublin for Kanchelskis, Thornley for Irwin
5 Mar	Chelsea	H	L	0–1	..	..	..	..	..	..	Keane	..	..	..	Giggs	Robson for McClair, Dublin for Parker
16 Mar	Sheff Wed	H	W	5–0	..	..	..	..	..	..	Cantona2	..1	Keane	..1	..1	McClair for Giggs, Robson for Kanchelskis
19 Mar	Swindon T	A	D	2–2	..	..	..	..	Keane1	..	..	..1	McClair	..	..	
22 Mar	Arsenal	A	D	2–2	..	..	..	..	Sharpe2	..	..	..	Keane	..	..	McClair for Sharpe
30 Mar	Liverpool	H	W	1–0	..	..	..	..	..	..	..	..1	..	..	Kanchelskis	Giggs for Sharpe, Robson for Cantona
2 Apr	Blackburn	A	L	0–2	..	..	..	..	..	..	Kanchelskis	..	..	..	Giggs	McClair for Parker
4 Apr	Oldham Ath	H	W	3–2	..	Irwin	Sharpe	..	Kanchelskis	..	Keane	..1	McClair	..	..1	Dublin1 for McClair
16 Apr	Wimbledon	A	L	0–1	..	Parker	Irwin	..	..	..	Robson	..	..	..	..	Sharpe for Robson, Dublin for Parker
23 Apr	Man City	H	W	2–0	..	..	..	..	Sharpe	..	Cantona2	..	Keane	..	Kanchelskis	Giggs for Sharpe
27 Apr	Leeds Utd	A	W	2–0	..	..	..	..	Kanchelskis1	..	..	..	..	..	Giggs1	
1 May	Ipswich	A	W	2–1	..	..	..	..	..	..	..1	..	..	..	..1	Sharpe for Giggs, Walsh for Schmeichel
4 May	Southampton	H	W	2–0	Walsh	..	..	Keane	Sharpe	..	..	..	Kanchelskis1	..1	..	
8 May	Coventry	H	D	0–0	..	G Neville	..	Bruce	..	..	..	Robson	McKee	Dublin	McClair	Parker for Bruce, Keane for McKee
	FA Cup															
9 Jan	Sheff Utd (3)	A	W	1–0	Schmeichel	Parker	Irwin	Bruce	Kanchelskis	Pallister	Cantona	Ince	Keane	Hughes1	Giggs	McClair for Hughes
30 Jan	Norwich (4)	A	W	2–0	..	..	..	..	..	..	..1	..	..1	..	..	
20 Feb	Wimbledon (5)	A	W	3–0	..	..	..1	..	..	..	..1	..1	..	..	..	McClair for Cantona, Dublin for Hughes
12 Mar	Charlton (6)	H	W	3–1	..	..	..	..	..2	..	..	..	..	..1	..	Sealey for Parker*
10 Apr	Oldham (SF)	N+	D	†1–1	..	..	..	..	Sharpe	..	Dublin	..	McClair	..1	..	Robson for Dublin, Butt for Parker
13 Apr	Oldham (SFR)	N–	W	4–1	..	..	..1	..	Kanchelskis1	..	Robson1	..	Keane	..	..1	Sharpe for Hughes, McClair for Keane
14 May	Chelsea (F)	N+	W	4–0	..	..	..	..	..	..	Cantona2	..	..	..1	..	Sharpe for Irwin, McClair1 for Kanchelskis

* Goalkeeper Schmeichel was sent off with Sealey taking over in goal after Parker was withdrawn.
N+ = Wembley
N– = Maine Road
† = Extra time

	Coca–Cola (League) Cup															
22 Sep	Stoke (2)	A	L	1–2	Schmeichel	Martin	Irwin	Phelan	Kanchelskis	Pallister	Robson	Ferguson	McClair	Hughes	Dublin1	Bruce for Phelan, Sharpe for Robson
6 Oct	Stoke (2)	H	W	2–0	..	..	..	Bruce	Sharpe1	..	..	Kanchelskis	..1	..	Keane	Giggs for Martin
27 Oct	Leicester (3)	H	W	5–1	..	Phelan	Martin	..2	..1	..	..	..	..1	..1	..	Irwin for Pallister, Giggs for Sharpe
30 Nov	Everton (4)	A	W	2–0	..	Parker	Irwin	..	Kanchelskis	..	Cantona	Ince	Robson	..1	Giggs1	Ferguson for Robson
12 Jan	Portsmouth (5)	H	D	2–2	..	..	..	..	..	..	..1	Robson	McClair	..	..1	Keane for Hughes, Dublin for McClair
26 Jan	Portsmouth (R)	A	W	1–0	..	..	..	..	..	..	..	Ince	Keane	McClair1	..	
13 Feb	Sheff Wed (SF1)	H	W	1–0	..	..	..	..	..	..	..	..	..	Hughes	..1	
2 Mar	Sheff Wed (SF2)	A	W	4–1	..	..	..	..	..1	..	Keane	..	McClair1	..2	..	
27 Mar	Aston V (F)	N	L	1–3	Sealey	..	..	..	..	..	Cantona	..	Keane	..1	..	Shape for Giggs, McClair for Bruce
	European Cup															
15 Sep	Honved (1)	A	W	3–2	Schmeichel	Parker	Irwin	Bruce	Sharpe	Pallister	Robson	Ince	Cantona1	Keane2	Giggs	Phelan for Giggs
29 Sep	Honved (1)	H	W	2–1	..	..	..	..2	..	..	..	..	..	Hughes	..	Martin for Irwin, Phelan for Ince
20 Oct	Galatasaray (2)	H	D	*3–3	..	Martin	Sharpe	..	Keane	..	..1	..	..1	..	..	Phelan for Robson
3 Nov	Galatasaray (2)	A	D	†0–0	..	Parker	Irwin	..	Sharpe	Phelan	..	..	..	Keane	..	Dublin for Keane, G Neville for Phelan

*Includes own goal
†Galatasaray won under away goals rule

	FA Charity Shield															
7 Aug	Arsenal	N	D	1–1P	Schmeichel	Parker	Irwin	Bruce	Kanchelskis	Pallister	Cantona	Ince	Keane	Hughes1	Giggs	Robson for Giggs

(at Wembley)
P – United won 5–4 on penalties

Appearances (goals)

Bruce 61 (7) – Butt 2 – Cantona 48 (25) – Dublin 11 (2) – Ferguson 5 – Giggs 57 (17) – Hughes 55 (21) – Ince 55 (9) – Irwin 61 (4) – Kanchelskis 46 (10) – Keane 53 (8) – Martin 6 – McClair 25 (6) – McKee 1 – G. Neville 1 – Pallister 60 (1) – Parker 57– Phelan 7 – Robson 25 (3) – Schmeichel 59 – Sealey 1 – Sharpe 41 (11) – Thornley 1 – Walsh 3 – Own goals 1 – Total 24 players (125)

FA Premier League

	P	W	D	L	F:A	Pts	
Manchester U	42	27	11	4	80:38	92	1st

SEASON 1994–1995 FA PREMIER LEAGUE **1994–1995**

20 Aug	QPR	H	W	2–0	Schmeichel	May	Irwin	Bruce	Sharpe	Pallister	Kanchelskis	Ince	McClair	Hughes	Giggs	Parker for May, Keane for Sharpe
22 Aug	Nottingham F	A	D	1–1	..	..	..	..	..	..	..	1	..	..	..	Keane for Giggs
27 Aug	Tottenham H	A	W	1–0	..	..	..	..	1	..	..	..	..	..	..	
31 Aug	Wimbledon	H	W	3–0	..	..	..	..	..	..	Cantona1	Kanchelskis	.. 1	..	.. 1	
11 Sep	Leeds Utd	A	L	1–2	..	..	..	..	Kanchelskis	..	.. 1	Ince	..	..	..	Sharpe for Giggs, Butt for McClair
17 Sep	Liverpool	H	W	2–0	..	..	..	..	Sharpe	..	..	..	Kanchelskis1	..	..	McClair for Hughes
24 Sep	Ipswich Town	A	L	2–3	Walsh	Keane	..	..	..	..	..1	..	McClair	Kanchelskis	..	Butt for McClair, Scholes1 for Sharpe
1 Oct	Everton	H	W	2–0	Schmeichel	May	..	..	.. 1	..	..	..	Keane	Hughes	Kanchelskis1	McClair for Hughes
8 Oct	Sheff Wed	A	L	0–1	..	Parker	..	..	..	..	Gillespie	..	McClair	..	Keane	May for Parker, Scholes for Gillespie
15 Oct	West Ham	H	W	1–0	..	May	..	..	..	..	Cantona1	..	Kanchelskis	..	Giggs	Butt for May
24 Oct	Blackburn R	A	W	4–2	..	Keane	..	..	..	..	..1	..	Butt	..1	Kanchelskis2	McClair for Butt
29 Oct	Newcastle	H	W	2–0	..	..	..	..	Kanchelskis	..1	..	..	McClair	..	..	Gillespie1 for Giggs
6 Nov	Aston Villa	A	W	2–1	Walsh	..	..	..	Butt	..	..	..1	Scholes	Kanchelskis1	Giggs	McClair for Butt, Gillespie for Scholes
10 Nov	Man City	H	W	5–0	Schmeichel	..	..	..	Kanchelskis3	..	..1	..	McClair	Hughes1	..	Scholes for Giggs
19 Nov	Crystal Pal	H	W	3–0	..	G.Neville	..1	May	..1	..	..1	..	..	..	Davies	Pilkington for Schmeichel, Gillespie for Kanchelskis, Scholes for Davies
26 Nov	Arsenal	A	D	0–0	Walsh	..	..	..	..	..	..	..	..	..	Gillespie	Davies for Gillespie, Butt for Kanchelskis
3 Dec	Norwich City	H	W	1–0	..	..	..	..	..	..	..1	..	..	..	Davies	Butt for Kanchelskis, Gillespie for Davies
10 Dec	QPR	A	W	3–2	..	..	..	Bruce	Keane1	..	Kanchelskis	..	..	Scholes2	..	Butt for Davies, Gillespie for Neville
17 Dec	Nottingham F	H	L	1–2	..	Keane	..	..	Kanchelkis	..	Cantona1	..	..	Hughes	Giggs	Butt for Giggs, G. Neville for Kanchelskis
26 Dec	Chelsea	A	W	3–2	..	..	..	..	Butt	..	..1	..	..1	..1	..	G. Neville for Ince, Kanchelskis for Butt
28 Dec	Leicester C	H	D	1–1	..	G. Neville	..	..	Kanchelskis1	..	..	Keane	..	..	..	Scholes for Hughes
31 Dec	Southampton	A	D	2–2	..	May	G. Neville	..	Butt1	..1	..	..	..	..	..	Gillespie for McClair
3 Jan	Coventry	H	W	2–0	..	G. Neville	Irwin	..	..	..	..1	..	Scholes1	Gillespie	..	McClair for Keane
15 Jan	Newcastle	A	D	1–1	Schmeichel	Butt	..	..	Sharpe	..	..	..	McClair	Hughes1	Giggs	Scholes for Hughes, May for Butt
22 Jan	Blackburn R	H	W	1–0	..	Keane	..	..	..	..	..1	Ince	..	Cole	..	Kanchelskis for Sharpe
25 Jan	Crystal Pal	A	D	1–1	..	..	..	May1	..	..	..	..	..	..	..	Kanchelskis for Sharpe
4 Feb	Aston Villa	H	W	1–0	..	G. Neville	..	Bruce	..	..	Scholes	..	..	..1	..	May for Neville, Kanchelskis for Giggs
11 Feb	Man City	A	W	3–0	..	P. Neville	..	..	..	..	Kanchelskis1	..1	..	..1	..	May for Kanchelskis, Scholes for Neville
22 Feb	Norwich City	A	W	2–0	..	Keane	Sharpe	..	Kanchelskis1	..	McClair	..1	Cole	Hughes	..	
25 Feb	Everton	A	L	0–1	..	..	Irwin	..	Sharpe	..	..	..	..			Kanchelskis for McClair
4 Mar	Ipswich	H	W	9–0	..	..1	..	..	Kanchelskis	..	..	..1	..5	..2	..	Sharpe for Keane, Butt for Bruce
7 Mar	Wimbledon	A	W	1–0	..	G. Neville	..	..1	Sharpe	..	..	..	..	..	..	
15 Mar	Tottenham H	H	D	0–0	..	Irwin	Sharpe	..	Kanchelskis	..	..	..	..	..	..	Butt for McClair
19 Mar	Liverpool	A	L	0–2	..	Keane	Irwin	..	Sharpe	..	Kanchelskis	..	McClair	..	..	Cole for Sharpe, Butt for Keane
22 Mar	Arsenal	H	W	3–0	..	..	..	..	..1	..	..1	..	Cole	..1	..	
2 Apr	Leeds Utd	H	D	0–0	..	G. Neville	..	Keane	Beckham	..	McClair	..	..	..	..	
15 Apr	Leicester C	A	W	4–0	..	..	..	Bruce	Sharpe1	..	..	..1	..2	..	Butt	Beckham for Sharpe, Scholes for Hughes
17 Apr	Chelsea	H	D	0–0	..	..	..	..	Beckham	..	..	..	..	..	..	Davies for Beckham, Scholes for Davies
1 May	Coventry	A	W	3–2	..	..	..	May	Sharpe	..	..	Scholes1	..2	..	..	Beckham for Scholes
7 May	Sheff Wed	H	W	1–0	..	..	..	..1	..	..	..	Ince	..	..	Scholes	P. Neville for May, Butt for Scholes
10 May	Southampton	H	W	2–1	..	..	..1	Bruce	..	..	..	..	..1	..	Butt	Scholes for Hughes
14 May	West Ham	A	D	1–1	..	..	..	..	..	..	Keane	..	..	McClair1	..	Hughes for Butt, Scholes for Keane
	FA Cup															
9 Jan	Sheff Utd (3)	A	W	2–0	Schmeichel	O'Kane	Irwin	Bruce	Butt	Pallister	Cantona1	Keane	McClair	Hughes1	Giggs	Sharpe for O'Kane, Scholes for McClair
28 Jan	Wrexham (4)	H	W	*5–2	..	P. Neville	..2	May	Sharpe	..	Keane	Ince	..1	Scholes	..1	Kanchelskis for Keane, Beckham for McClair
19 Feb	Leeds Utd (5)	H	W	3–1	..	Keane	..	Bruce1	..	..	Kanchelskis	..	..1	Hughes1	..	
12 Mar	QPR (6)	H	W	2–0	..	G. Neville	..1	..	..1	..	..	..	..	..	..	Keane for Giggs
9 Apr	Crystal Pal (SF)	N–	D	2–2E	..	..	..1	Keane	..	..1	Beckham	..	..	..	..	Butt for Beckham
12 Apr	Crystal Pal (SFR)	N–	W	2–0	..	..	..	Bruce1	..	..1	Keane	..	..	..	..	McClair for Giggs
20 May	Everton (F)	N+	L	0–1 ..	..	..	..	..	..	..	..	..	..	Butt	..	Giggs for Bruce, Scholes for Sharpe Giggs for Bruce, Scholes for Sharpe

N– = Villa Park
N+ = Wembley
* = Includes own goal
E = After extra time

Coca–Cola (League) Cup

Sep 21	Port Vale (2)	A	W	2–1	Walsh	G. Neville	Irwin	Butt	May	Keane	Gillespie	Beckham	McClair	Scholes2	Davies	Sharpe for Butt, O'Kane for Neville
Oct 5	Port Vale (2)	H	W	2–0	..	Casper	O'Kane	..	..1	Pallister	..	..	..1	..	..	Tomlinson for Gillespie, Neville for Davies
Oct 26	Newcastle (3)	A	L	0–2	..	G. Neville	Irwin	Bruce	Butt	..	..	..	..	..	..	Sharpe for Irwin, Tomlinson for Sharpe

European Cup (UEFA Champions' League)

Sep 14	Gothenburg	H	W	4–2	Schmeichel	May	Irwin	Bruce	Sharpe1	Pallister	Kanchelskis1	Ince	Butt	Hughes	Giggs2	
Sep 28	Galatasaray	A	D	0–0	..	..	Sharpe	..	Butt	..	..	..	Keane	..	..	Parker for Giggs
19 Oct	Barcelona	H	D	2–2	..	Parker	Irwin	May	..	..	..	..	..	..1	Sharpe1	Bruce for May, Scholes for Sharpe
2 Nov	Barcelona	A	L	0–4	Walsh	..	..	Bruce	..	..	..	..	..	..	Giggs	Scholes for Giggs
23 Nov	Gothenburg	A	L	1–3	..	May	..	..	Kanchelskis	..	Cantona	..	McClair	..1	Davies	G. Neville for May, Butt for Davies
7 Dec	Galatasaray	H	W	*4–0	..	G. Neville	..	..	Keane1	..	..	Butt	..	Beckham1	..1	

*Includes own goal

FA Charity Shield

14 Aug	Blackburn R	N	W	2–0	Schmeichel	May	Bruce	Pallister	Ince1	McClair	Kanchelskis	Cantona1 (p)	Hughes	Sharpe	Giggs

(at Wembley)

Appearances (goals)

Beckham 10 (1) – Bruce 47 (4) – Butt 35 (1) – Cantona 24 (14) – Casper 1 – Cole 18 (12) – Davies 10 1 – Gigs 39 (4) – Gillespie 10 (1) – Hughes 45 (12) – Ince 47 (6) – Irwin 54 (6) – Kanchelskis 39 (15) – Keane 36 (3) – May 27 (3) – McClair 51 (8) – G. Neville 27 – P. Neville 3 – OcKane 3 – Pallister 57 (4) – Parker 5 – Pilkington 1 – Scholes 24 (7) – Schmeichel 42 – Sharpe 40 (6) – Sharpe 40 (6) – Tomlinson 2 Walsh 16 – Own Goals 2 – Total 27 players 110

FA Premier League

	P	W	D	L	F:A	Pts
Blackburn	42	27	8	7	80:39	89 1st
Manchester U	42	26	10	6	77:28	88 2nd

SEASON 1995-1996 FA PREMIER LEAGUE 1995-1996

19	Aug	Aston Villa	A	L	1-3	Schmeichel	Parker	Irwin	G.Neville	Pallister	Sharpe	Butt	Keane	McClair	Scholes	P.Neville	Beckham1 for P. Neville, Kane for Pallister
23	Aug	West Ham	H	W	2-1	“	G.Neville	“	Bruce	“	“	“	“1	“	“1	Beckham	Cole for Scholes, Thornley for McClair
26	Aug	Wimbledon	H	W	3-1	“	“	“	“	“	“	“	“2	Cole1	“	“	Giggs for Cole, Davies for Scholes
28	Aug	Blackburn	A	W	2-1	“	“	“	“	“	“1	“	“	“	“	“1	Giggs for Beckham, Davies for Scholes
9	Sep	Everton	A	W	3-2	“	“	“	“	“	“2	“	“	“	“	“	Giggs1 fo rBeckham, Davies for Cole
16	Sep	Bolton	H	W	3-0	“	Parker	P.Neville	“	“	“	“	Cooke	Beckham	“2	Giggs 1	Davies for Cooke
23	Sep	Sheff. Wed.	A	D	0-0	“	“	Irwin	“	“	Davies	“	Beckham	McClair	“	“	Cooke for Davies
1	Oct	Liverpool	H	D	2-2	“	G.Neville	P.Neville	“	“	Sharpe	“1	Keane	Cole	Cantona1	“	Scholes for P.Neville, Beckham for Butt
14	Oct	Man. City	H	W	1-0	“	“	“	“	“	Beckham	“	“	“	Scholes1	”	Sharpe for Scholes, McClair for Keane
21	Oct	Chelsea	A	W	4-1	“	“	Irwin	”	“	Scholes2	“	“	“	Cantona	“1	McClair1 for Scholes
28	Oct	Middlesbro	H	W	2-0	“	“	“	“	“1	”	“	“	“1	“	”	McClair for Scholes
4	Nov	Arsenal	A	L	0-1	“	“	“	“	“	“	“	“	“	“	”	Sharpe for Butt, McClair for Irwin, Beckham for Scholes
18	Nov	Southpton	H	W	4-1	“	“	“	“	“	“1	“	Beckham	“1	“	”2	Sharpe fo rGiggs, McClair for Scholes, P. Neville for Irwin
22	Nov	Coventry	A	W	4-0	“	“	“1	“	“	McClair2	“	“1	“	“	”	Sharpe for Butt, May for Bruce, P. Neville for G. Neville
27	Nov	Nottm. For.	A	D	1-1	“	“	“	“	“	“	“	“	“	“1	“	Sharpe for Beckham, Scholes for McClair
2	Dec	Chelsea	H	D	1-1	Pilkington	“	“	“	May	Sharpe	McClair	“1	“	“	Scholes	Cooke for Cole
9	Dec	Sheff. Wed.	H	D	2-2	“	“	P.Neville	“	“	“	“	“	“	“2	“	Davies for Scholes, Cooke for Sharpe
17	Dec	Liverpool	A	L	0-2	Schmeichel	“	Irwin	”	“	“	“	“	“	“	“	Scholes for Cole
24	Dec	Leeds	A	L	1-3	“	Parker	“	“	G.Neville	McClair	Butt	Keane	“1	“	Beckham	May for Parker, Scholes for Beckham, P. Neville for Bruce
27	Dec	Newcastle	H	W	2-0	“	P.Neville	“	May	“	Beckham	“	“1	“1	“	Giggs	McClair for May
30	Dec	QPR	H	W	2-1	“	“	“	Prunier	“	“	“	“	“1	“	”1	Parker for P.Neville, Sharpe for Beckham, McClair for Cole
1	Jan	Tottenham	A	L	1-4	“	Parker	P.Neville	“	“	“	“	“	“1	“	”	Pilkington for Schmeichel, Sharpe for P.Neville, McClair for Keane
13	Jan	Aston Villa	H	D	0-0	“	P.Neville	Irwin	Bruce	G.Neville	Sharpe	“	“	“	“	“	Scholes for Sharpe
22	Jan	West Ham	A	W	1-0	“	“	“	“	“	“	“	“	“	“1	“	Beckham for Cole
3	Feb	Wimbledon	A	W	4-2*”	“	“	“	“	“	“	“	“	“1	“2	“	Beckham for Bruce
10	Feb	Blackburn	H	W	1-0	“	“	“	May	Pallister	“1	Beckham	“	“	“	”	
21	Feb	Everton	H	W	2-0	“	“	“	Bruce	“	“	Butt	“1	“	“	”1	Beckham for Sharpe
25	Feb	Bolton	A	W	6-0	“	“	“	“1	“	Beckham1	“1	“	“1	“	”	Scholes2 for Cantona, McClair for Giggs
4	Mar	Newcastle	A	W	1-0	“	“	“	“	G.Neville	Sharpe	“	“	“	“1	”	
16	Mar	QPR	A	D	1-1	“	G.Neville	“	“	May	Beckham	McClair	“	“	“1	”	Sharpe for Beckham, Butt for May, Scholes for McClair
20	Mar	Arsenal	H	W	1-0	“	“	P.Neville	“	“	Sharpe	Butt	“	“	“1	”	Scholes for Cole
24	Mar	Tottenham	H	W	1-0	“	“	“	“	“	“	“	“	“	“1	”	McClair for Cole, Beckham for P. Neville
6	Apr	Man. City	A	W	3-2	“	P.Neville	Irwin	”	G.Neville	Beckham	“	“	“1	“1	”1	Sharpe for Cole, May for Bruce
8	Apr	Coventry	H	W	1-0	“	Irwin	Sharpe	May	“	“	“	McClair	“	“1	”	
13	Apr	Southpton	A	L	1-3	“	“	“	Bruce	“	“	“	Keane	“	“	“1	Scholes for Butt, May for Sharpe
17	Apr	Leeds	H	W	1-0	“	“	P.Neville	“	Pallister	“	McClair	“1	“	“	“	May for Bruce, Scholes for McClair, Sharpe for Cole
28	Apr	Nottm. For	H	W	5-0	“	“	“	May	“	“2	Sharpe	“	Scholes1	“1	“1	G. Neville for P.Neville
5	May	Middlesbro	A	W	3-0	“	“	“	“1	“	“	Butt	“	“	“	“1	Cole1 for Scholes

*Includes own goal

FA Cup

6	Jan	Sunderland	(3)	H	D	2-2	Pilkington	G.Neville	Irwin	Bruce	Pallister	Beckham	Butt1	Keane	Cole	Cantona1	Giggs	Sharpe for Beckham, P. Neville for G.Neville
16	Jan	Sunderland	(3R)	A	W	2-1	Schmeichel	Parker	“	”	G.Neville	P. Neville	“	“	“1	“	“	Sharpe for Parker, Scholes1 for Butt
27	Jan	Reading	(4)	A	W	3-0	“	Irwin	P.Neville	“	“	Sharpe	“	“	“	“1	“1	Parker1 for P. Neville
18	Feb	Man.City	(5)	H	W	2-1	“	“	“	”	Pallister	“1	“	“	“	“1	“	
11	Mar	Southmton	(6)	H	W	2-0	“	“	“	”	G.Neville	“1	“	“	“	“1	“	
31	Mar	Chelsea	(SF)	N-	W	2-1	“	P.Neville	Sharpe	May	”	Beckham2	“	“	“1	“	“	
11	May	Liverpool	(F)	N+	W	1-0	“	Irwin	P.Neville	“	Pallister	“	“	“	“	“1	“	Scholes for Cole, G. Neville for Beckham

N- Villa Park
N+ Wembley

Coca-Cola (League) Cup

20	Sep	York City	(2)	H	L	0-3	Pilkington	Parker	Irwin	McGibbon	Pallister	Sharpe	Beckham	P.Neville	McClair	Davies	Giggs	Cooke for P. Neville, Bruce for Davies
3	Oct	York City	(2)	A	W	1-3	Schmeichel	G. Neville	Sharpe	Bruce	“	Beckham	Cooke1	Scholes2	Cole	Cantona	“	P. Neville for Sharpe, Keane for Cooke

UEFA Cup

12	Sep	Rotor Vol.	(1)	A	D	0-0	Schmeichel	G.Neville	Irwin	Bruce	Pallister	Sharpe	Butt	Beckham	Keane	Scholes	Giggs	Davies for Keane, Parker for Scholes
26	Sep	Rotor Vol.	(2)	H	D#	2-2	”1	O'Kane	P.Neville	“	“	“	“	“	“	Cole	”	Scholes1 for O'Kane, Cooke for Beckham

(# Lost on away goals)

Appearances

Beckham 33 (8): Bruce 38 (1): Butt 38 (3): Cantona 38 (19): Cooke 2 (1): Cole 41 (13): Davies 2 (0): Giggs 41 (12): Irwin 39 (1): Keane 36 (6): May 13 (1): McClair 13 (3): McGibbon 1 (0): G. Neville 37 (0): P. Neville 29 (0): O'Kane 1 (0): Pallister 28 (1): Parker 7 (1): Pilkington 4 (0): Prunier 2 (0): Schmeichel 45 (1): Scholes 18 (14): Sharpe 29 (6) Own goals 1 Total 23 players (92)

FA Premier League

	P	W	D	L	F	:	A	Pts	
Manchester U	38	25	7	6	73	:	35	82	1st

INDEX